F.

SOVIET POLITICS
and
GOVERNMENT
A Reader

SOVIET POLITICS

and

GOVERNMENT

➤ *A Reader* ◄

Edited with Introductory Notes by

RANDOLPH L. BRAHAM

The City College of the City University of New York

 Alfred · A · Knopf New York 1965

L. C. catalog card number: 65–17484

THIS IS A BORZOI BOOK,
PUBLISHED BY ALFRED A. KNOPF, INC.

Copyright © 1965 by Alfred A. Knopf, Inc.

FIRST EDITION

Preface

The emergence of the Soviet Union as one of the two super-powers of the world and the phenomenal spread of Communism during the post-World War II period have naturally widened interest in the theory and practice of Marxism–Leninism. While before the war only a handful of American institutions of higher learning offered any courses for the systematic study of Communism, the postwar period witnessed the establishment and development of scores of specialized institutes operating either independently or under the auspices of various types of educational institutions. Indeed, in many states the study of Communism is now required by law either as a special course or as part of existing courses.

The American people have become increasingly aware of the fact that a sound educational program on Communism can be both a potent defense weapon in the cold war and a preventive measure against Communist take-over. The demand for an adequate and effective program has grown in intensity in direct proportion to the advances made by world Communism during the postwar period. There is a growing realization that the struggle between Communism and democracy has become the overriding issue of our time. The challenge of Communist totalitarianism is being increasingly conceived as the most formidable challenge that ever confronted the democratic world; and in fact the challenge *is* formidable, for never before in history have the enemies of human liberty possessed such monstrous weapons of mass destruction as are today available to the Communists.

In line with the wisdom of the oft-quoted saying that "it is better to light a candle than to curse the darkness," the editor of this volume also believes that a sound and intelligent understanding of the theory and practice of Soviet Communism is among the surest means to protect our democratic liberties. With this objective in mind the volume is designed (1) to serve either as an independent *primary* text or as *supplementary* source material to accompany any standard textbook on the U.S.S.R.; (2) to offer the general reader an opportunity to acquaint himself in a systematic and comprehensive manner with the many facets of Soviet theory, politics and government; and (3) to serve as a basic source of readings for organized adult education programs and discussion groups.

The selections were made with an eye on promoting an understanding of Soviet Communism—its geographical, historical and theoretical background, its organizational structure and governmental functions, its one-party totalitarian characteristics and techniques of control, its method of international expansion, and its goal of world domination through "communization." They were envisioned also to demonstrate directly or indirectly the applicability of the Marxist critique of capitalism to contemporary Communism and to help generate a healthy skepticism about Communist promises by highlighting the mythological elements inherent in the Marxist–Leninist doctrine and focusing attention on the theory, strategy and tactics of the Communist road to power.

With the exception of Sections I and XII, which include only one selection each, the sections or sub-sections contain two or more articles deliberately juxtaposed to enable the mature reader to judge for himself the merits of the Soviet and Western views. Since, as a consequence, a considerable percentage of the material is of Communist origin and as such propaganda-laden, those less initiated in the arts of Communist wordsmanship will find a key to Soviet semantics in Section C of the Selected Bibliography (p. 604). In addition, each section is preceded by succinct introductory editorial notes.

All of the Western authors are widely known experts in their respective fields. An attempt has been made to include their articles in full; however, the realities of production and cost factors necessitated some occasional abridgments which, it is hoped, have not diminished their value. The selections from British sources were left in their original spelling. The articles reflecting the Soviet view of the structure and functions of the government in the

U.S.S.R. were taken primarly from the treatise by A. Denisov and M. Kirichenko—Soviet government experts—for two reasons: (1) the work represents the post-Stalin conception of the Soviet leaders and as such supersedes, so to speak, Andrei Vyshinsky's *The Law of the Soviet State*, heretofore the authoritative treatise on the subject; (2) it was felt desirable to have some uniformity in style, especially since the views of the Soviet experts on the subject are by necessity almost identical.

Whatever merits this volume may have are due primarily to the excellence of the authors whose articles were included. For permission to use their material I am gratefully indebted to them and their publishers. I owe a special debt to my friends and colleagues Cyril E. Black of Princeton University and Erich Goldhagen of Hunter College for their constructive criticism and invaluable suggestions. I am also indebted to Professor Alexander Erlich of Columbia University for his valuable observations on the economic section. For his help in the technical processing of some of the material I am grateful to Imre Kardashinetz of the Free Europe Committee. I must acknowledge with thanks the wholehearted cooperation received from the staff of the College Department of Alfred A. Knopf, Inc., especially its Editor in Chief Dr. Clifford Mortimer Crist, Mrs. Leonore Hauck, and Miss Anne D. Murphy.

New York, N.Y. *Randolph L. Braham*

Contents

Charts and Figures

SOVIET POLITICS
and
GOVERNMENT
A Reader

SECTION I

The Geographical and Historical Setting

It is a truism to state that the nature of the Soviet state and government has to a large extent been determined by the geographical and historical framework in which the U.S.S.R. was born. The specific geographical features of Russia left a deep imprint on the political physiognomy of both the Tsarist and Soviet regimes, and the historical heritage of the Soviet Union has had a determining influence on the evolution of the form and content of Soviet political life.

The triumph of the proletarian dictatorship, contrary to Marx's expectations, in a socially and economically backward, primarily agricultural country with a high rate of illiteracy was a unique consequence of the interplay of a variety of historical circumstances. While the Tsarist heritage created a series of special problems of government, the tradition of autocracy and centralism, among other things, simplified considerably some of the major political and economic tasks confronting the new rulers. The following study by Professor Towster discusses the various geographical and historical factors that have determined the political development of the U.S.S.R.

The Geography and Historical Heritage
of the U.S.S.R.

JULIAN TOWSTER[*]

Geography

The extent and character of the territory, population, and resources of the Soviet Union have had much to do with the nature
of government in the Soviet state and with its position in the
world system of states.

AREA. The U.S.S.R. is a country of continental dimensions. Its
vast expanse approximates 8,500,000 square miles, one sixth of the
land surface of the globe. Embracing the northern third of Asia
and the eastern half of Europe, the territory of the Soviet Union
extends some 6,000 miles from west to east and between 1,800 and
2,800 miles from south to north. It stretches from the Baltic Sea,
the Carpathians, and the Black Sea to the Pacific Ocean, from the
deserts of Central Asia and the Tien Shan, Sayan, Altai, and Pamir
mountains to the Arctic Ocean. With frontier lines (excluding
those of countries occupied by the military forces) exceeding
37,500 miles in length, the U.S.S.R. borders on almost a dozen
states in Europe and Asia, including Norway, Finland, Poland,

* Professor of Political Science at the University of California, Berkeley, Dr.
Towster is the author of *Political Power in the U.S.S.R., 1917–1947* (1948)
and many other books and articles on the Soviet Union.

Abridged from "The Soviet Orbit: The Union of Soviet Socialist Republics"
by Julian Towster in *European Political Systems* edited by Taylor Cole, pp.
541–560, by permission of Alfred A. Knopf, Inc. New York: Alfred A. Knopf,
Inc., 1959. Copyright 1953, 1959 by Alfred A. Knopf, Inc. For footnote
references, see original source.

Czechoslovakia, Hungary, Rumania, Turkey, Iran, Afghanistan, and China. In its Eurasian mass the Soviet Union exceeds in area the combined territories of the United States, together with those of the United Kingdom and India, the states of Western Europe, and the Near and Middle East. It is the largest single state in the world to occupy such an immense, continuous area.

POPULATION. In 1956 the population of the U.S.S.R. was officially declared to be 200,200,000. In January, 1946, one official Soviet estimate gave the figure as 193,000,000. By comparison with an expected population of around 215,000,000 by that date, this estimate would indicate a wartime population loss of around 22,000,000, i.e., an approximate birth deficit of 8,000,000 and war casualties of some 14,000,000 persons probably evenly divided between military personnel and civilians. . . .*

RESOURCES. In natural resources the U.S.S.R. is one of the richest countries in the world, second only to the United States. It possesses vast reserves of a large variety of raw materials, including those that figure high among the components of state power. The Soviet Union claims to have a higher percentage than any other state of certain of the world's known resources, i.e., water power (280 million kilowatts, or 28 per cent of the world's total); deposits of oil (8 billion tons, or 55 per cent); peat (151 billion tons, or probably 50 per cent); manganese (742.5 million tons, or 30 per cent); apatite (2,000 million tons, or 75 per cent); and others, including chrome ores, gold, and platinum. Second place among states has been claimed for its deposits of coal (1,654 billion tons, or 21 per cent) and of iron ore (10,900 million tons, or 53.5 per cent). Even if some of these estimates are unduly high, there is no doubt that the U.S.S.R. possesses these resources in abundance. It has also deposits of nickel, zinc, lead, copper, bauxite, vanadium, molybdenum, wolfram, and many other metals and minerals, but it lacks tin and natural rubber. It ranks high in the production of salt, potash, magnesite, asbestos, and aluminum. Though still far behind the United States in the production of

* Ed. note: In 1965, the U.S.S.R. had an estimated population of 228,000,- 000. See also pp. 272–274.

steel, pig iron, coal, and oil, the Soviet Union is assuming second place in the world's production of these vital elements of strength. . . .

These geographic factors have made possible the rise of the Soviet Union to the status of a super-power in the short space of three decades. They have enabled the U.S.S.R. to establish new economic bases in Asiatic Russia and generally to attain a high degree of economic self-sufficiency. They were responsible in no small degree for the Soviet "defense in depth" in the recent war, which served again, as it did in the Napoleonic War of 1812, as the means of achieving ultimate victory, despite great initial losses of territory and population. Although possible new elements of vulnerability will exist in future atomic warfare, waged across polar spaces, they do not detract from the present significance of the geographic factors in the political and economic plans and activities of the U.S.S.R.

THE GEOGRAPHIC CONFIGURATION. Another factor of geography that strongly influenced the tsarist polity and is reflected in the government and politics of its successor is the configuration of the land: the Eurasian plain, the absence of secure outlets to the sea and of natural frontiers in the west, and the central geographic location of the U.S.S.R.

THE LANDLOCKED PLAIN. Probably the most important single geographic influence in Russian history is the great Eurasian plain. Five main lateral zones mark the highly diversified topography of the U.S.S.R. from north to south: 1) the treeless *tundra* belt along the Arctic Ocean, comprising 12–15 per cent of the Soviet land; 2) the *forest* zone, which merges into the tundra, embracing over 50 per cent of the territory of the Soviet Union and consisting of coniferous trees in the northern part (the taiga) and mixed forests of coniferous and deciduous trees in its southern belt; 3) the grassy, treeless *steppe*, extending from the western Ukraine to the Altai Mountains over some 964,000 square miles, or 12 per cent of the Soviet area, and including the rich belt of black soil; 4) the *desert* and *semidesert* zone north of the Caspian Sea and including large areas of Central Asia, approximating 18 per cent of the territory of the Soviet Union; and 5) the *subtropical* zone, covering small areas along the Black Sea coast and in the far eastern regions of the Amur and southern Ussuri.

The vast plain embraces the forest, steppe, and desert zones, of which the steppe has been of particular significance. Together with the river system, the plain gives geographic unity to the land, since the great mountain chains are situated on the periphery, and the Urals—often referred to as the dividing line between European and Asiatic Russia—are not in fact high enough to constitute a physical barrier of consequence. Despite the fact that 80 per cent of the U.S.S.R. falls within the temperate zone, the climate prevailing over the plain is severe. It is characterized by inadequate rainfall and extremes of long, cold winters and hot summers because of the distance of the Soviet Union from the Atlantic, the barrier of the mountain ranges on the Pacific coast, and the open face of the country on the north along the Arctic Ocean. In the past the severity of the climate has not only affected Russia's agriculture but also has had a marked influence upon the character of the people.

Surrounded by mountain ranges on the east, south, and southwest, the plain is open on the west and extends into east Central Europe, without any sharp topographic demarcation such as large bodies of water, mountains, or other physical barriers traditionally regarded as natural frontiers and bulwarks of defense. The U.S.S.R. has an extensive seacoast and is constructing a series of canals to connect its major rivers with its twelve seas, eight of which constitute direct outlets to the Arctic or Pacific Ocean. Yet the Soviet Union is properly considered landlocked, since most of its ports are not ice-free during the greater part of the year, whereas the outlets from the Baltic and Black seas (the Skagerrak and Kattegat and the Dardanelles straits) are controlled by the other powers.

THE WAVES OF INVASION AND EXPANSION. These geographic features have contributed to a number of events in Russia's history that have left a deep imprint on the political physiognomy of the land. The steppe invited invasion from Asia. It served as the road of numerous migrations of Asiatic tribes into Europe, including the Mongol hordes that invaded Russia in the thirteenth century under descendants of Ghengis Khan and imposed their rule over the country for nearly two and a half centuries. The open western frontier was a beckoning gate for raids and annexations by border states, including such large-scale penetrations as the Polish occupation of Moscow in 1610, the Ukrainian operations of King Charles XII of Sweden at the opening of the eighteenth century, Napoleon's march into Russia in 1812, and the German invasions of the country in the course of the two world wars.

Paradoxically enough, these geographic features contributed greatly to Russia's own expansion. Once Mongol power had begun to disintegrate, Russian colonists and adventurers encountered little resistance in pushing eastward until they reached the Pacific, while the Russian rulers relentlessly sought to find natural frontiers in the west and to secure warm-water ports in every possible direction. In this process of continuous expansion central Siberia was secured for Tsar Ivan the Terrible (1533–84) by the Cossack Yermak in 1582, and the Baltic countries of Estonia, Latvia, and Lithuania were annexed in the reigns of Peter the Great (1682–1725) and Catherine the Great (1762–96). Catherine also obtained the areas of south Russia, the Crimea, and the lands that are now called western Ukraine and western Byelorussia, as well as a large part of Poland proper during its three partitions in 1772, 1795, and 1796. Tsar Alexander I (1801–25) rounded out the empire's acquisitions in the Baltic by taking Finland from Sweden, and he continued his predecessors' encroachments on Turkish possessions by obtaining Bessarabia. Although the Russian drive for Constantinople and the Turkish Straits was stopped by the defeat of Nicholas I (1825–55) in the Crimean War of 1853–54, his son Alexander II (1855–81) succeeded in adding the Transcaspian region and Transcaucasia to the tsarist domain. He also acquired Turkestan, as well as the Maritime Provinces and Sakhalin, thus firmly establishing Russia's position in the Far East. This position was bolstered further by the acquisition of special rights in Manchuria at the end of the last century.

To be sure, some of these rights had to be yielded in 1905 to Japan, which also obtained the cession of southern Sakhalin; and, by the end of the civil war period in 1920, Soviet Russia had lost the Baltic States, Finland, Bessarabia, the western Ukraine, and western Byelorussia. Except for Finland—from which the U.S.S.R. received the Petsamo area and other strategic points—all of these territories, as well as Russia's former special rights in Manchuria, were recovered by the Soviet Union in the course of World War II. In addition the U.S.S.R. was ceded the Carpatho-Ukraine by treaty with Czechoslovakia, and also acquired the Kurile Islands from Japan and the Königsberg area in Eastern Germany under the terms of the Yalta and Potsdam agreements, respectively. It is estimated that, between the Crimean War and World War I, tsarist Russia gained over 971,000 square miles of territory. Up to the end of 1951 the latest territorial acquisitions during and since World War II have added close to 300,000 square miles to the former limits of the Soviet Union.

The recurring foreign invasions and Russia's expansionist drives have placed a premium on concentrated political authority to keep the sprawling empire and its scattered peoples together; with much justification historians have traced the roots of Russia's centralized and dictatorial system of rule, and of its population's predisposition for disciplined unity in crisis, to the enduring effect of these prolonged national experiences. . . .

Historical Heritage

PRECEDENTS AND PARALLELS. Next in importance to the geographical factors, the heritage that the Soviet regime received from Russia's historical past has been a potent, if not always a conscious, influence in its political development.

In many respects this heritage created special problems of government. Thus the numerous nationalities absorbed by the tsarist empire in its process of expansion posed acute problems of ethnic friction and separatist sentiments. The general backwardness of Russian society, the underdeveloped state of its economy, and the lethargy and ignorance of its masses created difficult tasks of education, training, and organization that entailed a remolding of the life and attitudes of the entire populace.

At the same time this heritage simplified some serious problems of government for the new rulers. Although their purposes and motivations differed radically from those of their predecessors, there was much in the culture that they finally took over to facilitate the use of the tools and techniques of governance they came to employ. Centralized power and excessive utilization of propa-

ganda and violence as instruments of government, the symboliza-
tion of an acclaimed highest leader, a popular predisposition for
submission to authority, suspicion of foreign intentions, and alternating or converging tendencies toward isolationism and messianism—all these factors find precedents and parallels in the position and role of the autocracy, church, and police under the old
regime; in the peasants' faith in the infallibility and benevolence
of the tsar; in the sporadic efforts at reform by the Moscow rulers;
in Russia's periodic aloofness from Europe; and in the recurring
missionary note in her Orthodoxy, Pan-Slavism, and other cultural
currents, as well as in her foreign policy.

THE TRADITION OF AUTOCRACY AND CENTRALISM.   Autocracy and
centralism have a long tradition in Russia. Although the first Russian state was the Kiev principality, founded in 882, autocracy had
its formal beginning in Russia when, following the fall of Constantinople (the "Second Rome") to the Turks in 1453, the grand
duke of Muscovy, Ivan III, or "the Great" (1462–1505), assumed
the Byzantine title of autocrat in 1472. He thus claimed succession
to the last of the Eastern emperors and the role of defender of
Orthodox Christendom, with Moscow becoming the "Third
Rome." Ivan IV, or "the Terrible" (1533–84), followed up the
claim by assuming the title of tsar (Caesar) in 1547, and Peter the
Great in 1721 added the title of emperor.

By the Fundamental Laws of the empire the tsar was "an autocratic and unlimited monarch" to whom obedience "not only from
fear but from conscience, God himself has commanded." Russian
constitutionalists found hope in the omission of the word "unlimited" from this article in the 1906 version of the Fundamental
Laws, following the imperial manifesto of February 20, which
sought to quiet popular revolutionary moods born of the defeat in
the Russo-Japanese War (1904–5) by establishing a state duma
with powers of approval over legislation. In point of fact, however,
another article of the same constitution specifically referred to the
tsar as "unlimited autocrat," and the autocracy found little difficulty in progressively emasculating the supposed constitutional
limitations upon its rule.

The tsar exercised his absolute powers through his council of
ministers at the center and his governors (*gubernatory*) in the

provinces. He was assisted by the Imperial Council, which drafted legislation for his consideration and signature, by a senate, which served as the highest judicial and administrative organ, and by the Holy Synod and its procurator in religious affairs. Over all of these bodies the tsar had complete control, chiefly through his powers of appointment and removal.

In popular lore, as well, the autocracy was regarded as absolute, indispensable, and inevitable almost up to the eve of the revolution in 1917. "It is awe-inspiring, it is frightening, but we cannot do without a tsar," ran a Russian proverb. Other folk sayings emphasized the theme that "everything is in the power of God and the sovereign" and "the sovereign answers only to God," reflecting a reverent and fatalistic acceptance of the autocracy by the masses.

PROCLIVITY FOR CONFORMITY. The Russian autocracy—its theory and practice molded by the triple impact of the Byzantine tradition, the long Tartar domination, and the influence of German authoritarian ideas at the court—was one of the most despotic tyrannies in the world. Under the corrupt bureaucracy through which it ruled, the people endured endless suffering and injustice. Yet, with rare exceptions, they willingly supported the autocracy.

Here one encounters one of the main paradoxes of government in Russia. There was no innate love for authority among the Russian people. On the contrary, the peasant masses were imbued with a deep-seated negativism against all government and a particular hostility against the oppressive officials around them. The philosopher Berdyaev offers this summary: "Among a people who were anarchist in their fundamental bent, there existed a State that developed to a monstrous degree, and an all-powerful bureaucracy surrounding an autocratic tsar and separating him from the people. Such was the peculiarity of the Russian destiny." There appears to be at least some support for the thesis that the Russian people submitted readily to authority because by their very character, influenced by climate and soil and historical experience, they were so much disposed toward anarchy and individualism as to require a strong hand from above to bind them to a common purpose. Centrifugal and parochial tendencies were strong among the scattered communities of the vast land. But survival against the elements within and the enemy without dictated unity. And unity under an autocrat standing above law appeared to make combination easier. In any case, instead of voluntary compromise of individual differences, there was equal submission by all to the one supreme power.

On this foundation there emerged in the peasant mind the symbol of the tsar as the "Little Father"—the last resort and true protector of his people. If the people were suffering cruelties at the hands of the landlords and officials, it was not his fault, for "the tsar does not know what the scribe is doing." He was far away and "the sun cannot warm everybody, nor can the tsar please everybody." But someday he would save his people from their oppressors.

Meantime the imposition of unity from above was matched by pressure for conformity from below in the common faith and common service of God and tsar. Thus submission to authority and conformity became strong habits, deeply ingrained in the culture and life of the Russian people. On the residue of these habits the Communist leaders were able to build when they felt the need. As Berdyaev puts it: "The spirit of the people could very easily pass from one integrated faith to another integrated faith, from one orthodoxy to another orthodoxy, which embraced the whole of life."

CONSOLATION AND COMPULSION. If the tsar could rely on a predominant spirit of loyalty in the people, which was born of fatalism and a sense of collective necessity, he also had at his disposal two major tools to keep his subjects in line, namely, the church and the secret police.

Perhaps nowhere else in the world were the ties between church and state so close, the unity of accepted religion and civil rule, as symbolized in the "Orthodox Tsar," so complete. Russia's acceptance of Christianity from Byzantium is dated from the baptism of Grand Prince Vladimir of Kiev in 988, and his marriage to the Byzantine emperor's sister. From small beginnings, at first under Greek metropolitans appointed by the patriarch of Constantinople, the Russian Church grew into a strong national institution, ecclesiastically autonomous in relation to Constantinople and closely linked to the princes of Muscovy. It played an important role in the struggle against Tartar rule, and its spreading monasteries were a significant factor in Moscow's early territorial expansion.

The Russian church had decisively repudiated the attempted reunion of the Eastern and Western churches at the Council of Florence in 1439, and the only success of the papacy was the Brest-Litovsk Union in 1596, which won over a part of the Orthodox Church to a newly formed Uniat church under its jurisdiction. With the fall of Byzantium, followed by Moscow's claim to its succession, the status of the Orthodox Church reached a new high in "Holy Russia," and in 1589 the Moscow metropolitan assumed the title of patriarch. The influence of the church upon the throne was particularly strong about the time of the election of Mikhail Romanov, the son of Metropolitan Philaret (patriarch, 1619–33), as tsar of Russia in 1613 and during Nikon's occupancy of the Moscow patriarchate from 1652 to 1667. Economically the church prospered to the point where it became one of the largest land-owners and serf owners. By the middle of the sixteenth century the monasteries were estimated to possess about one third of the land, and, at the time of Peter's ascendancy to the throne, about 14 per cent of the peasantry belonged to church lands.

It was the tsars' fear of this economic power, as well as the schism in the church that resulted from Nikon's reforms of the Orthodox ritual and liturgy in 1654, that led to restrictions on the power of the church and to its conversion into an obedient instrument of the autocracy. From the time of Ivan the Terrible, tax and service obligations were increased, and the secularization of church property was fostered. Peter the Great secured the political subordination of the church in 1721 by abolishing the patriarchate and by instituting in its place the tsar-appointed Holy Synod, which subsequently came to be dominated by its lay procurator. The higher clergy, inaccessible to the people and exercising disciplinary jurisdiction over the lower clergy, became the bulwark of the cult of absolutism and, from the time of Alexander I, the pillar of tsarist reaction. At the bottom of the hierarchy the village priests were "shepherds of the Crown" who helped to inculcate the virtues of humility, patience, and obedience in the neglected and maltreated masses. The parish priest, performing the required rites of marriage, birth, and death, and otherwise ministering to the religious needs of his simple flock, and the village church, with the beautiful and semi-mystical symbolism of its ceremonies, were virtually the sole sources of consolation to the peasant in his poverty and grief. And the autocracy did not hesitate to press even the village priests into police service by requiring them to divulge political secrets learned during the confidences of confession. In short, the institution of the church thus became a subordinate and trusted arm of the state.

As an instrument for consolation and persuasion the church provided a strong precedent for the propaganda departments established under Communist rule. In yet another way, it has been suggested, the church may have been an unconscious influence on practices of the present regime through its doctrine of *sobornost*, or "congregationalism." The essence of this doctrine is that truth and love reside in the congregation as a whole, i.e., in the brotherhood of the faithful collectively and not in any of the brethren separately. The opinion of the congregation in its entirety, not that of its individual members, is the measure of truth, and the body of the congregation guards the orthodoxy of its adherents. Only by confessing and renouncing his errors can a deviating member rejoin the communion of the brethren. If the collectivity of the party in the present regime is substituted for that of the Orthodox congregation, the inference of an influence from the past upon the present is strong.

The secret police is by no means a new phenomenon in Russian life. The *Oprichnina*, a separate armed force organized by Ivan the Terrible as his special instrument of control, was only the precursor of police rule in Russia, which grew in importance from the middle of the seventeenth century. Alexander I re-established the secret police organization, which existed under his father, and his successor, Nicholas I (1825–55), set up the dreaded Third Section in his personal chancery to supervise directly the work of a special secret police. Although the Third Section was abolished in 1880 toward the end of the reign of Alexander II, it was not long before the even more notorious *Okhrana* came into existence. Besides recourse to martial law and execution, this political police instituted the practice of infiltrating the labor unions and socialist parties with its own *agents provocateurs*, some of whom (Azev,

Malinovsky, etc.) attained leading positions in the revolutionary movement. The Okhrana was among the first of the tsarist institutions to be abolished in 1917. But in less than a year the Cheka (Extraordinary Commission), with powers of summary arrest and execution, was brought into being by the new regime.

REFORM FROM ABOVE. The outstanding characteristic of reform in Russia is that it has always been effected from above and that it has been piecemeal, inadequate, and too long delayed.

Over the stretch of the centuries a number of Russian rulers charted or experimented with social and political reforms. As early as 1550, Ivan the Terrible established the *Zemsky Sobor*, a representative assembly that played an important role during the great disturbances of the "Time of Troubles" (1584–1613). After the death of Ivan's son, Fedor, pretender followed pretender; the Poles seized and held the Russian throne from 1605 to 1610, when they were dispossessed in a popular rising under Kuzma Minin and Prince Pozharsky. It was this sobor that elected Fedor's father-in-law, Boris Godunov, in 1598, and Mikhail Romanov, the young founder of the Romanov dynasty, in 1613, as tsars of Russia. During the same troubled period the older assembly of the nobles, the Boyars' Duma, likewise asserted itself to a greater extent. Yet the Zemsky Sobor was merely an *ad hoc* body without clearly defined authority, and the Boyars' Duma was a class organ. Neither exercised much power in the face of a strong tsar. And both were discontinued by Peter the Great, whose revolutionary reforms augmented rather than diminished the power of the autocracy and were aimed chiefly at modernization in production and administration.

The Empress Anne (1730–40), Catherine the Great (1762–96), and Alexander I (1801–25) all initially displayed strong liberal ideas and intentions; particularly was this true of Alexander I, who thought of freeing the serfs and restricting the powers of the Crown. In each case the ideas found little if any implementation. Catherine established elective municipal *dumas* (councils) in the cities, but the greatest of all Russian evils—serfdom—actually expanded during her rule. Had the plans of Michael Speransky—drawn up at the special request of Tsar Alexander I—been carried out, Russia would have had a national representative duma, indirectly elected by the people through intermediate stages of local, county, and provincial dumas. Instead only one of his proposals, having no connection with representative government or the limitation of the tsar's prerogatives, was given effect in 1810; a co-ordinating administrative organ, the Imperial Council, was created at that time. The long reign of Alexander's successor, Nicholas I, was one of the darkest periods of reaction and tyrannical rule. Only during the reigns of Alexander II (1855–81) and of the last tsar, Nicholas II (1894–1917), were a few beginnings made on the road to self-government in the *zemstvos* and dumas.

The liberal reforms inaugurated by Alexander II, the "Tsar Liberator," included changes in military service; the judicial legislation in 1864, which made the judges independent of administrative officials and introduced public trial by jury; and, most important, the abolition of serfdom by the imperial edict of March 3–17, 1861. Alexander II even signed a project to include elected representatives of the people in the government's legislative work. Yet so late was the hour in the eyes of the revolutionary wing of the intelligentsia that on the very eve of the intended promulgation of this project in 1881 the tsar was assassinated. This act put an end to all political reform for a quarter of a century.

Even the emancipation of the serfs, great as the achievement seemed, was tragically retarded and inadequate. Serfdom finally had been legalized in Russia by the statute of 1649, when the tsars found it necessary to bind the peasants to the land in order to ensure the services of their landlords in military and administrative posts. And it was ultimately abolished when its usefulness to tsardom had ended and its demoralizing consequences had become obvious to the autocracy itself. Yet the reform did not satisfy the peasantry as a class. At the same time that it gave the serfs their personal freedom it enabled them to receive only half the land for which the landlords were paid by the state, and required them to purchase this land in heavy installments over a forty-nine-year period. The surrendered land, far from sufficient in quantity for the needs of the liberated, became the property, not of the individual peasants, but of the mir, the village community, which through this reform was itself transformed into something like the lowest administrative unit. The mir was responsible for taxes and redemption payments and, consequently, for the peasants' movements, which it controlled by the old passport system.

The subsequent reforms enacted by Prime Minister Stolypin in November, 1906, enabled the peasants to claim their personal holdings (in one place rather than in scattered land strips) by a two-thirds majority vote to divide the village community property. These reforms appealed to an awakened peasant individualism and were potentially beneficial. Yet they did not increase substantially the total amount of land in the possession of the peasantry, which regarded itself as the rightful claimant to all the land. This deep discontent continued to the very eve of the revolution. The intervening years were hardly sufficient to erase the effects of the long serfdom. And on the eve of World War I, Lenin, in comparing the Russian and American emancipations, concluded that the former had been far less thorough than the latter, and that *"therefore now, half a century later, the Russians show many more marks of slavery than the Negroes."*

SPROUTS OF SELF-GOVERNMENT: ZEMSTVOS AND DUMAS. In the somber picture of tsarist political reality the zemstvos, created by Alexander II, and the State Duma, reluctantly conceded by Nicholas II, were among the brightest spots.

Prior to the establishment of the district and provincial zemstvos in 1864 the primitive village mir was virtually the only agency of self-government. The zemstvos were popularly elected bodies, with district councils choosing representatives to the provincial councils. Each zemstvo met only once a year but elected a standing executive committee to act in its place during the interim.

As organs of self-government the zemstvos suffered from several disabilities: elections were so arranged as to assure landlord control; as reaction set in under Alexander III (1881–94), their executive committees were subordinated to the provincial governors; and, above all, their jurisdiction was restricted to such non-political fields as health, highway maintenance, education, and agricultural experimentation. Nevertheless, so great was the need for some popular forum under the autocracy that even these timid bodies could not resist the temptation to speak out against oppression. Indeed, by 1902–04, the informal congress of zemstvo chairmen, meeting annually, felt bold enough to call for equal civil rights, a voice in legislation concerning the localities, and similar liberties.

The State Duma promised by the imperial manifesto of October, 1905, which Nicholas II published to meet the threat of revolution, was designed originally to give Russia a parliamentary government and a responsible executive. The popularly elected representative assembly was to have a real voice in legislation and public expenditure. Instead, the final product delivered by the autocracy appeared singularly shaped to frustrate the people's will. To begin with, a second chamber with equal powers was set up as a check upon the Duma; the Imperial Council was reorganized into the State Council, half of whose members were directly appointed by the tsar. Then, besides reserving certain crucial fields (such as those over fundamental laws and defense) within his exclusive competence, the tsar retained full powers to veto legislation, to dissolve the Duma, and to govern by ukase.

These powers he promptly used at the expense of the first Duma (May 10–July 21, 1906), and of the second Duma (March 5–June 16, 1907), whose liberal composition and bold efforts to discuss vital public matters were not to his taste. Disregarding all constitutional niceties, the autocracy then completely altered the election scheme to deny the vote to various areas and to allot 50 per cent of the representation to the big landowners alone. Packed with reactionaries and conservatives through these and other devices, the third Duma (1907–12) and the fourth Duma (1912–17) were permitted to serve out their terms. Even these dumas became increasingly critical of the inefficiency and corruption of the tsar's administration.

Thus, limited and unrepresentative as they were, the zemstvos and dumas afforded some opportunities for a public airing of accumulated grievances in the stifling atmosphere of the autocracy. Although they were unable to create a strong tradition of popular influence in national administration, they nonetheless offered the people a foretaste of the possibilities of participation in government.

THE LEGACY OF BACKWARDNESS: MATERIAL POVERTY. On February 4, 1931, Stalin told a conference of Soviet industrial managers:

The history of old Russia was one in which she was ceaselessly beaten for her backwardness. She was beaten by the Mongol khans. She was beaten by the Turkish beys. She was beaten by the Swedish feudal lords. She was beaten by the Polish-Lithuanian *pans*. She was beaten by the Japanese barons. All beat her because of her backwardness—for military backwardness, for cultural backwardness, for political backwardness. She was beaten because to beat her was profitable and went unpunished. . . . Do you wish our socialist Fatherland to be beaten . . . ? We are 50 or 100 years behind the advanced countries. We must make up this distance in ten years. Either we do it or we will be wiped out.

A thousand times this cry has been echoed and repeated in official and semiofficial pronouncements, with the main emphasis invariably resting on the backward economy that the Soviet regime had inherited. Although the purpose of the Soviet leaders was to urge the people on to greater production, there was much truth in that plaint. Industrialism came late to Russia, and on the eve of World War I tsarist Russia still held fifth place in industrial production among the states of the world, despite her enormous resources; in certain specific fields, such as electrical energy, she was so far behind the other large states as to hold fifteenth place in world production. In 1913, Russia produced only about four million tons each of pig iron and steel, about nine million tons of oil, and less than thirty million tons of coal. Less than 2 per cent of her coal extraction and only about 6 per cent of her oil extraction were mechanized, and her huge territories were inadequately served by railway lines totaling less than 37,000 miles, while automotive traffic had barely begun.

Whatever the cost also in terms of military security, this economic backwardness spelled, first of all, material poverty for the great majority of Russia's populace. Before the revolution 65 per cent of the peasantry (which was Russia's largest class, constituting three fourths of the population) consisted of poor peasants, and another 20 per cent of middle peasants; only 15 per cent were relatively well-to-do. Of the total number of peasant households 30 per cent had no draft animals, 34 per cent had no agricultural equipment, and 15 per cent had no sowing lands. Tractors and combines were nonexistent. Plows and hoes constituted the main farm tools, and the 1910 census showed that a third of the plows were wooden and that close to eighteen million wooden harrows were in use. Productivity was extremely low, and the primitive nature of much of Russia's agriculture had its counterpart in the underveloped and inefficient state of many branches of industry. In the whole of Russia, for instance, only about 8,500,000 pairs of leather shoes were produced. Similar shortages existed in many other lines.

Facts such as these could but contribute to the socio-political upheaval of 1917. And they continued to pose special problems for the new, Bolshevik rulers, who made initial use of them in attaining power.

MASSES AND CLASSES: INERTIA AND INEPTITUDE. Along with widespread poverty went ignorance and inertia among the masses, irresponsibility and ineptitude among the ruling classes.

Features of Russian society before the revolution that account in no small measure for the lack of progress toward democratic government included the absence of a strong and stable middle class and the wide gulf that separated the upper class of nobles, landlords, higher bureaucracy, and clergy from the vast masses of the peasantry and peasant-derived city proletariat. Official Soviet figures give the percentage of the "bourgeoisie" in 1913—landlords, "big and petty urban bourgeoisie," merchants, and *kulaks*— as 15.9 per cent. In this figure kulaks alone, i.e., rich peasants, accounted for 12.3 per cent. "Workers and employees [i.e., intelligentsia]" comprised at that time 16.7 per cent of the population. Workers alone, who counted no more than a few million at the turn of the century, constituted approximately 14 per cent. It is obvious, then, that the educated urban middle class, traditional champion of constitutionalism and liberalism in government, was exceedingly small. Considerable sections of the similarly small workers' stratum, which was largely peasant in origin, continued to identify their interests with those of the peasantry. Other sections became increasingly attentive to programs offering radical socio-economic and political solutions.

Even more fatal for the cause of free government in Russia was the fact that those at the pinnacle of the social hierarchy—the nobility and bureaucrats who surrounded the tsar and the governors and landlords who ruled in his name—were for the most part corrupt, reactionary, and inefficient. From fairly early days the *boyars* (landed aristocrats) appear to have believed that ordered freedom in a community of equal peers was an impossibility; consequently they preferred common subjection to a tsar. From the time that Ivan the Terrible curbed the unruly boyars and swelled their ranks by establishing the *dvoriane* (court gentry) and *pome-shchiki* (estate owners), all obligated to serve the state in compensation for the land grants they received, the nobility was an estate servile to the tsar. It enjoyed no independent, universally esteemed social position in the land. The table of ranks instituted by Peter the Great merely confirmed and regularized the service status of the nobility vis-à-vis the Crown. As this social stratum developed over the centuries, the nobility as a group, with rare exceptions, showed little vision, initiative, or responsibility; and as landlords and officials it came to be known rather for its abusive selfishness, venality, and marked ineptitude. To be sure, during the nineteenth century some of its members played a leading role in liberal and revolutionary groups. But by that time the tsarist nobility and its cohorts in the bureaucracy, army, and police were firmly identified in the popular mind with blind reaction and oppression.

The base and bulk of the social hierarchy was the huge, amorphous mass of the peasantry—illiterate, lethargic, cautious, and suspicious. It was collectively and individually possessed of an infinite capacity for patience and passivity, skepticism and procrastination, duality and flexibility, in meeting the hardships of nature and the demands and exactions of governors and landlords. Along with the effects of climate and the impact of serfdom, sheer ignorance has had a tremendous influence in shaping the peasant's basic attitudes and reactions. Around the turn of the century 27 per cent of the entire population of Russia (apart from that of her western periphery) was literate; in the rural areas only 23 per cent of the people could be so classified; in the backward regions inhabited by non-Russian nationalities the figure was as low as 13 per cent, and in some localities it was as low as 1 or 2 per cent. On the eve of World War I, despite the splendid efforts of the zemstvos, over 60 per cent, or more than half of Russia's population, was still illiterate. The whole of Russia had then no more than 222 clubs and reading rooms, and of these only 88 functioned in the countryside.

This state of the masses was probably the most difficult of all problems that confronted the Bolshevik rulers. In the light of the grandiose schemes of change proclaimed by them, the human material was inadequate. The biggest task they envisaged was to remold the character of the people, to shake off the age-old lethargy, and to stimulate enough of a desire for growth and initiative to make possible the modernization of Russia, while keeping individual and group aspirations within rigid bounds of political conformity.

FEAR OF THE FOREIGNER: ISOLATIONISM AND MESSIANISM. Another legacy from the past was a well-nigh ingrained fear of the foreigner among the Russian people, despite their innate sociability and strong sense of curiosity. Suspicion of the stranger comes almost naturally to a backward peasant population long wary of its own governors. In this case fear and suspicion fed on memories of past invasions and conquests from east and west. Long before Nazi Germany sought *Lebensraum* in Russia, the Russian people had learned from bitter historical experience that their land was an alluring prize for their neighbors. Physically and spiritually the Russian reaction throughout the centuries has been a sort of dual urge for minimum and maximum security, sometimes seeking safety in retreat and sometimes in attack.

Minimum security lay in seclusion, at times enforced from outside, at other times willingly self-imposed. Mongol, Pole, Turk, Swede, and other peoples as well contributed to Russia's isolation long before the days of the *cordon sanitaire*, erected after World War I, and those of the cold war, which followed World War II. The Russian rulers themselves periodically found isolationism a military bulwark against outside threats. Moreover, spiritual withdrawal was a counterpart of "defense in depth." The unique and solitary position of Russia's Greek Orthodoxy in the world of religion, the calculated obscurantism of Russia's rulers, the cultural self-sufficiency preached by the Slavophiles and other groups in the nineteenth century combined to form a habit of aloofness and apartness that shut the Russian masses off from the cultural currents of the West, despite the "window in the wall" opened by Peter the Great.

Yet, alongside this apartness, there has always existed in Russian culture a strong strain of messianism, which in its more active phases took the form of territorial and ideological expansion. Moscow was "the Third Rome," possessed of "the true faith" in Christendom. As Berdyaev so penetratingly pointed out, there was a wide belief within the masses themselves in the mission of the

Russian people to make social justice and the brotherhood of man a reality. And the woes of the world constituted one of the most pronounced themes in the works of the Russian literati in the nineteenth century. Pan-Slavism and tsarist imperialism were merely facets of Russia's universalist messianism. One of its vital—though for the most part subconscious—underlying assumptions has apparently been that maximum security lies in advance, that is, in the ultimate total victory of Russian ideas.

Here, too, we find potent precedents or germs in the past for the practices of the present, for isolating the Soviet people from contact with the West, and for the minimum safety principle of "socialism in one country," as well as for the maximum security precept of ultimate victory for world communism.

STIRRINGS OF DISCONTENT: REBELS AND REVOLUTIONARIES. Despite the Russian people's general submission to authority Russian history was not free from periodic outbursts of primitive wrath against the oppressive conditions of serfdom, poverty, and maladministration. Besides palace revolutions and the seizure of the throne by impostors, violent peasant revolts occurred from time to time, the most noted of which were the rebellions of Bolotnikov (1606–7), Stenka Razin (1670–71), Bulavin (1707–8), and Pugachev (1773–75). But these large-scale uprisings, marked by extensive pillaging and bloodletting, were more basically social and economic than political in character. In the words of the Cossack Pugachev, they were directed "against the malefactor landowners and the bribetaking officials and judges," not against the autocracy. They failed because they were localized in scope, and the institution of tsardom remained intact.

Only in the revolt of the so-called Decembrists in the nineteenth century was the first assault made upon that institution itself. On December 26, 1825, a group of army officers—all members of the nobility who had contacted liberal political ideas during the Russian campaigns in the west—attempted a coup against the newly ascended Nicholas I and were mercilessly suppressed. This unsuccessful rising, the purposes of which were not even clearly or uniformly understood by the perpetrators themselves, became the prelude to the rise of the radical and revolutionary groups in the second half of the century.

The parent of these groups was the *Narodnik,* or Populist, movement, which sprang up among the students and literati in the sixties. The heart of its beliefs was that Russia, once freed of the autocracy, would attain its own brand of agrarian socialism without the evils of industrialism, and that her salvation lay in a non-capitalist peasant economy based on the communal mir of the village and on small handicraft. Placing their faith in the peasantry as the soul of the nation, the *Narodniki* felt that their purpose was "going to the people" (*Khozhdenie v narod*), living among the peasants, serving them as teachers, nurses, and craftsmen, and spreading the movement's teachings among them. Lack of response on the part of the confused peasantry and repressive measures by the government helped produce dissension over the future tactics of the Narodniki in the late seventies. One group began to pursue a program of terrorism against the autocracy that resulted in the assassination of Alexander II and many tsarist officials. Others continued to carry on underground propaganda work in the villages. Still others—among them Georgii Plekhanov, who formed the Emancipation of Labor group in 1883 and who came to be widely regarded as the father of Russian Marxism—lost faith in the possibility of Russia's salvation through the peasantry and turned to the more strictly Marxist program of reliance on the industrial proletariat. With the growth of industry, factory labor, and education, and with the increased incidence of sporadic strikes in the eighties and nineties, Marxist groups multiplied, until by the end of the century the Narodnik movement had completely disintegrated. To some extent, however, it was succeeded by the Social-Revolutionary party (established in 1901), which likewise centered its program on land and rights for the peasantry and which more than any other group inherited the tradition of individual acts of terrorism.

Other political groups that sought to organize themselves into parties were the Liberals and the Social Democrats. The first group, pursuing a liberal-democratic program, formed the Union of Liberation under the leadership of Paul Miliukov in 1903. It soon was known as the party of the Constitutional Democrats or Cadets, which played a prominent role in the dumas. The second group officially formed the Russian Social Democratic Labor Party (R.S.D.L.P.) at a small, abortive gathering in Minsk in 1898. This meeting was subsequently referred to as the first congress, but the party was actually organized at the second congress in Brussels and London in 1903. At this congress there occurred the momentous split of the newly formed party into majority (*bol'shinstvo*) and minority (*men'shinstvo*) factions, which were thereafter called Bolsheviks (*Bol'sheviki*) and Mensheviks (*Men'sheviki*). This doctrinal schism was to have a profound effect on the destiny of Russia and on that of the rest of the world as well.

DESIGN FOR POWER: THE EMERGENCE OF BOLSHEVISM. As a doctrine and political movement, bolshevism took shape in the writings and struggles of its leaders, not only against Populists, Liberals, and Social-Revolutionaries, but also against various currents in the Russian Social-Democratic movement itself. More than to any other man it owes its emergence to V. I. Ulianov—later known to the world as Nikolai Lenin—who entered upon his revolutionary Marxist career in 1887, following the execution of his brother for complicity in the attempt on the life of Alexander II. With gifted pen and relentless will power Lenin hammered away at all of the other parties: at the so-called Legal Marxists, who preached the possibility of gradual social progress without revolutionary violence and class struggle or the need for the withering away of the state; at the "Economists," who urged the party to forsake political pursuits and concentrate on securing economic benefits for the workers; and at the Mensheviks. The schism between the two factions of the R.S.D.L.P. in 1903 and their subsequent differences over the aims and consequences of the 1905 revolution and over the program to be followed led to a complete organizational break, which resulted in the formation of an independent Bolshevik party, the R.S.D.L.P. (B.), in 1912.

Initially the issue that divided Lenin from his coeditors of the Social Democratic paper *Iskra* (The Spark), L. Martov and Paul Axelrod (who became the leaders of the Menshevik wing and who were subsequently joined by the outstanding theoretician, Georgii Plekhanov), was the party organization. In *Iskra*, from 1900 to 1904, and later in *Vpered* (Forward) and in other journals and pamphlets, Lenin argued for molding the party into a militant, highly centralized, rigidly disciplined organization, composed of a select membership of professional revolutionaries who would be consciously bound by the party program and rules and who would operate under the strict guidance of the highest party leadership. He was against a federal structure for the party, which would recognize nationality differences and grant its ethnic components organizational autonomy; instead he insisted on constituting the party as a single organization rooted in the proletariat. The Mensheviks, led by Martov, opposed these views, contending for a broadly based, decentralized party that would embrace sympathizers no less than activists.

The essence of the rift, which distinguished the Bolsheviks not only from the Mensheviks but also from the Social-Revolutionaries and other groups, involved the central question of the fundamental nature and course of the Russian Revolution. Lenin believed that the proletariat must play a pivotal role in a bourgeois-democratic revolution in Russia, transforming it subsequently into a socialist revolution guided by a dictatorship of the proletariat in alliance with the peasantry. Rejecting individual terrorism as a means of struggle against the autocracy and opposing co-operation with the Liberals as vacillating and perfidious allies, the Bolsheviks urged the employment of the general strike and insurrection to achieve maximum aims in the 1905 revolution. From its failure they quickly drew lessons of a need for greater centralization and for better organized and timed insurrection in the future. With their primary goal of ultimate radical revolution in mind, the Bolsheviks began to take part in the Duma in order to discredit it. They generally combined legal and underground work; and during World War I they advocated conversion of the international armed conflict into internal civil wars and excoriated the "defensists" in the world socialist movement who participated in the war efforts of their respective countries.

By contrast the Mensheviks did not consider the proletariat ready to play the leading role in securing radical change. Believing in social gradualism and in self-government, and visualizing a bourgeois-democratic revolution as the only possibility in Russia for many years ahead, they condemned the Bolshevik tactics in the 1905 revolution and sought to co-operate with the Liberals on a program to replace the autocracy by a constitutional regime that featured parliamentary democracy.

These basic differences determined the respective attitudes of the groups in the crucial period of March–November, 1917. When tsarism collapsed in March of that year under the dead weight of its rotten structure and its crippling wartime inefficiency, a coalition provisional government headed by representatives of the liberal bourgeoisie assumed authority in a sort of duality of power with the spontaneously established soviets, dominated by the Mensheviks and the Social-Revolutionaries. The battle cry of these parties became the convocation of a constituent assembly that would give formal expression to the democratic revolution. To the Bolsheviks, however, these events were merely a consummation of the bourgeois-democratic revolution, of the long-predicted first phase. After a short period of vacillation they came increasingly to believe, under Lenin's relentless pressure following his return to Russia from abroad in April, in the need for transition to the second phase, the socialist revolution. Lenin charted a program of activity designed to exploit the popular discontent for the purpose of undermining the other parties and the government and to establish a republic of soviets in the name of a dictatorship of the proletariat. With the growing economic crisis and the war weariness of the masses making them singularly responsive to the Bolshevik slogans of "land, peace, and bread," and with the winning of the majority in the soviets of the two capitals of Petrograd and Moscow by the end of the summer, the Bolsheviks seized power on November 6, 1917 (October 24, old calendar). On the following day the Second All-Russian Congress of Soviets proclaimed the establishment of Soviet rule.

Thus, if the experiences of the war proved the utter decay of the autocracy and the incompetence of the ruling classes, the legacy of backwardness they left behind, the weakness of the tradition of popular government or political compromise, and the weakness and vacillations of the other political groups made it relatively easy for the resolute group of Bolshevik leaders to step forth as spokesmen for the disaffected masses and to occupy the seat of power.

The Philosophical and Ideological Framework

· 1 ·

THE PHILOSOPHY OF COMMUNISM

In the Soviet Union dialectical materialism is considered an invaluable aid to scientific discovery and a logical guide to the understanding of the objective reasons for the inevitability of the universal triumph of Communism. The principles of dialectical materialism—as interpreted at any given time by the Communist Party—are binding upon both Party members and the artists and scientists of the Communist world.

The principal features of the dialectical method and of philosophical and historical materialism are outlined canonically by Joseph Stalin in the first of the two selections in this section. Although Stalin's stature as both theoretician and state leader diminished considerably during the drive against the cult of personality initiated at the Twentieth Congress of the Soviet Communist Party (February 1956), his basic writings have, so far at least, withstood the Communist test of time. In fact, while denouncing Stalin for the personal regime of terror he instituted in the U.S.S.R., Nikita Khrushchev also referred to him as "one of the strongest Marxists . . . [whose] logic . . . greatly influenced the cadres and Party work."

In the second selection the American philosopher and educator Sidney Hook describes dialectical materialism as the state-philosophy of the U.S.S.R. and the other Communist countries, a phi-

losophy that serves the social and political interests of the Party
and that has "often been invoked to defend control of scientific
research and publication by political decree." In refuting the
Marxists' evaluation of the laws of dialectics as an effective
method of scientific discovery, Professor Hook demonstrates that,
like many theological beliefs in the past, they have been invoked
"to block roads to fresh scientific inquiry and sometimes to contest
scientific theories, like the theory of relativity and the biological
theory of genes, not on grounds of evidence, but because of all sorts
of extra scientific considerations." The canonic propositions of
dialectical materialism about the inevitability of the world victory
of Communism are considered as the expression of an ersatz creed
involving the replacement of "a transcendental religion by an
immanent one."

==========

Dialectical and Historical Materialism

JOSEPH STALIN[*]

==========

Dialectical materialism is the world outlook of the Marxist-Leninist Party. It is called dialectical materialism because its approach to
the phenomena of nature, its method of studying and apprehending them, is *dialectical*, while its interpretation of the phenomena
of nature, its conception of these phenomena, its theory, is
materialistic.

Historical materialism is the extension of the principles of dialectical materialism to the study of social life, an application of the

[*] Former Secretary General of the Soviet Communist Party and Chairman of
the Council of Ministers of the U.S.S.R. Author of *Marxism and the National
Question, Foundations of Leninism*, and *Economic Problems of Socialism in
the U.S.S.R.*

From *Dialectical and Historical Materialism* by Joseph Stalin, selections from
pp. 5–62. Moscow: Foreign Languages Publishing House, 1952.

principles of dialectical materialism to the phenomena of the life of society, to the study of society and of its history.

When describing their dialectical method, Marx and Engels usually refer to Hegel as the philosopher who formulated the main features of dialectics. This, however, does not mean that the dialectics of Marx and Engels is identical with the dialectics of Hegel. As a matter of fact, Marx and Engels took from the Hegelian dialectics only its "rational kernel," casting aside its Hegelian idealistic shell, and developed dialectics further so as to lend it a modern scientific form.

> "My dialectic method," says Marx, "is not only different from the Hegelian, but is its direct opposite. To Hegel, . . . the process of thinking, which, under the name of 'the Ideal,' he even transforms into an independent subject, is the demiurgos (creator) of the real world, and the real world is only the external, phenomenal form of 'the Idea.' With me, on the contrary, the ideal is nothing else than the material world reflected by the human mind, and translated into forms of thought." (K. Marx, Preface to the Second German edition of Volume I of *Capital*.)

When describing their materialism, Marx and Engels usually refer to Feuerbach as the philosopher who restored materialism to its rights. This, however, does not mean that the materialism of Marx and Engels is identical with Feuerbach's materialism. As a matter of fact, Marx and Engels took from Feuerbach's materialism its "inner kernel," developed it into a scientific-philosophical theory of materialism and cast aside its idealistic and religious-ethical encumbrances. We know that Feuerbach, although he was fundamentally a materialist, objected to the name materialism. Engels more than once declared that "in spite of the" materialist "foundation," Feuerbach "remained . . . bound by the traditional idealist fetters," and that "the real idealism of Feuerbach becomes evident as soon as we come to his philosophy of religion and ethics." (K. Marx and F. Engels, Vol. XIV, pp. 652–54.)

Dialectics comes from the Greek *dialego*, to discourse, to debate. In ancient times dialectics was the art of arriving at the truth by disclosing the contradictions in the argument of an opponent and overcoming these contradictions. There were philosophers in ancient times who believed that the disclosure of contradictions in thought and the clash of opposite opinions was the best method of arriving at the truth. This dialetical method of thought, later extended to the phenomena of nature, developed into the dialectical method of apprehending nature, which regards the phenomena of nature as being in constant movement and undergoing constant change, and the development of nature as the result of the development of the contradictions in nature, as the result of the interaction of opposed forces in nature.

In its essence, dialectics is the direct opposite of metaphysics.

1) The principal features of the *Marxist dialectical method* are as follows:

a) Contrary to metaphysics, dialectics does not regard nature as an accidental agglomeration of things, of phenomena, unconnected with, isolated from, and independent of, each other, but as a connected and integral whole, in which things, phenomena are organically connected with, dependent on, and determined by, each other.

The dialectical method therefore holds that no phenomenon in nature can be understood if taken by itself, isolated from surrounding phenomena, inasmuch as any phenomenon in any realm of nature may become meaningless to us if it is not considered in connection with the surrounding conditions, but divorced from them; and that, vice versa, any phenomenon can be understood and explained if considered in its inseparable connection with surrounding phenomena, as one conditioned by surrounding phenomena.

b) Contrary to metaphysics, dialectics holds that nature is not a state of rest and immobility, stagnation and immutability, but a state of continuous movement and change, of continuous renewal and development, where something is always arising and developing, and something always disintegrating and dying away.

The dialectical method therefore requires that phenomena should be considered not only from the standpoint of their interconnection and interdependence, but also from the standpoint of their movement, their change, their development, their coming into being and going out of being. . . .

c) Contrary to metaphysics, dialectics does not regard the process of development as a simple process of growth, where quantitative changes do not lead to qualitative changes, but as a development which passes from insignificant and imperceptible quantitative changes to open, fundamental changes, to qualitative changes; a development in which the qualitative changes occur not gradually, but rapidly and abruptly, taking the form of a leap from one state to another; they occur not accidentally but as the natural result of an accumulation of imperceptible and gradual quantitative changes.

The dialectical method therefore holds that the process of development should be understood not as movement in a circle, not as a simple repetition of what has already occurred, but as an onward and upward movement, as a transition from an old qualitative state to a new qualitative state, as a development from the simple to the complex, from the lower to the higher. . . .

d) Contrary to metaphysics, dialectics holds that internal contradictions are inherent in all things and phenomena of nature, for they all have their negative and positive sides, a past and a future, something dying away and something developing; and that the struggle between these opposites, the struggle between the old and the new, between that which is dying away and that which is being born, between that which is disappearing and that which is developing, constitutes the internal content of the process of development, the internal content of the transformation of quantitative changes into qualitative changes.

The dialectical method therefore holds that the process of development from the lower to the higher takes place not as a harmonious unfolding of phenomena, but as a disclosure of the contradictions inherent in things and phenomena, as a "struggle" of opposite tendencies which operate on the basis of these contradictions. . . .

As to Marxist philosophical materialism, it is fundamentally the direct opposite of philosophical idealism.

2) The principal features of *Marxist philosophical materialism* are as follows:

a) Contrary to idealism, which regards the world as the embodiment of an "absolute idea," a "universal spirit," "consciousness," Marx's philosophical materialism holds that the world is by its very nature *material*, that the multifold phenomena of the world constitute different forms of matter in motion, that interconnection and interdependence of phenomena, as established by the dialectical method, are a law of the development of moving matter, and that the world develops in accordance with the laws of movement of matter and stands in no need of a "universal spirit." . . .

b) Contrary to idealism, which asserts that only our consciousness really exists, and that the material world, being, nature, exists only in our consciousness, in our sensations, ideas and perceptions, the Marxist materialist philosophy holds that matter, nature, being, is an objective reality existing outside and independent of our consciousness; that matter is primary, since it is the source of sensations, ideas, consciousness, and that consciousness is secondary, derivative, since it is a reflection of matter, a reflection of being; that thought is a product of matter which in its development has reached a high degree of perfection, namely, of the brain, and the brain is the organ of thought; and that therefore one cannot separate thought from matter without committing a grave error. . . .

c) Contrary to idealism, which denies the possibility of knowing the world and its laws, which does not believe in the authenticity of our knowledge, does not recognize objective truth, and holds that the world is full of "things-in-themselves" that can never be known to science, Marxist philosophical materialism holds that the world and its laws are fully knowable, that our knowledge of the laws of nature, tested by experiment and practice, is authentic knowledge having the validity of objective truth, and that there are no things in the world which are unknowable, but only things which are still not known, but which will be disclosed and made known by the efforts of science and practice. . . .

3) *Historical Materialism.*

It now remains to elucidate the following question: what, from the viewpoint of historical materialism, is meant by the "conditions of material life of society" which in the final analysis determine the physiognomy of society, its ideas, views, political institutions, etc.?

What, after all, are these "conditions of material life of society," what are their distinguishing features?

There can be no doubt that the concept "conditions of material life of society" includes, first of all, nature which surrounds society, geographical environment, which is one of the indispensable and constant conditions of material life of society and which, of course, influences the development of society. What role does geographical environment play in the development of society? Is geographical environment the chief force determining the physiognomy of society, the character of the social system of man, the transition from one system to another?

Historical materialism answers this question in the negative.

Geographical environment is unquestionably one of the constant and indispensable conditions of development of society and, of course, influences the development of society, accelerates or retards its development. But its influence is not the *determining* influence, inasmuch as the changes and development of society proceed at an incomparably faster rate than the changes and development of geographical environment. . . .

Further, there can be no doubt that the concept "conditions of material life of society" also includes growth of population, density of population of one degree or another, for people are an essential element of the conditions of material life of society, and without a definite minimum number of people there can be no material life of society. Is not growth of population the chief force that determines the character of the social system of man?

Historical materialism answers this question too in the negative.

Of course, growth of population does influence the development of society, does facilitate or retard the development of society, but it cannot be the chief force of development of society, and its influence on the development of society cannot be the *determining* influence because, by itself, growth of population does not furnish the clue to the question why a given social system is replaced precisely by such and such a new system and not by another, why the primitive communal system is succeeded precisely by the slave system, the slave system by the feudal system, and the feudal system by the bourgeois system, and not by some other. . . .

a) What, then, is the chief force in the complex of conditions of material life of society which determines the physiognomy of society, the character of the social system, the development of society from one system to another?

This force, historical materialism holds, is the *method of procuring the means of life* necessary for human existence, the *mode of production of material values*—food, clothing, footwear, houses, fuel, instruments of production, etc.—which are indispensable for the life and development of society.

In order to live, people must have food, clothing, footwear, shelter, fuel, etc.; in order to have these material values, people must produce them; and in order to produce them, people must have the instruments of production with which food, clothing, footwear, shelter, fuel, etc., are produced; they must be able to produce these instruments and to use them.

The *instruments of production* wherewith material values are produced, the *people* who operate the instruments of production and carry on the production of material values thanks to a certain *production experience* and *labour skill*—all these elements jointly constitute the *productive forces* of society.

But the productive forces are only one aspect of production, only one aspect of the mode of production, an aspect that expresses the relation of men to the objects and forces of nature which they make use of for the production of material values. Another aspect of production, another aspect of the mode of production, is the relation of men to each other in the process of production, men's *relations of production*. Men carry on a struggle against nature and utilize nature for the production of material values not in isolation from each other, not as separate individuals, but in common, in groups, in societies. Production, therefore, is at all times and under all conditions *social* production. In the production of material values men enter into mutual relations of one kind or another within production, into relations of production of one kind or another. These may be relations of cooperation and mutual help between people who are free from exploitation; they may be relations of domination and subordination; and, lastly, they may be transitional from one form of relations of production to another. But whatever the character of the relations of production may be, always and in every system, they constitute just as essential an element of production as the productive forces of society. . . .

b) *The first feature* of production is that it never stays at one point for a long time and is always in a state of change and development, and that, furthermore, changes in the mode of production inevitably call forth changes in the whole social system, social ideas, political views and political institutions—they call forth a reconstruction of the whole social and political order. At different stages of development people make use of different modes of production, or, to put it more crudely, lead different manners of life. In the primitive commune there is one mode of production, under slavery there is another mode of production, under feudalism a third mode of production, and so on. And, correspondingly, men's social system, the spiritual life of men, their views and political institutions also vary.

Whatever is the mode of production of a society, such in the main is the society itself, its ideas and theories, its political views and institutions.

Or, to put it more crudely, whatever is man's manner of life, such is his manner of thought.

This means that the history of development of society is above all the history of the development of production, the history of the modes of production which succeed each other in the course of centuries, the history of the development of productive forces and of people's relations of production. . . .

c) *The second feature* of production is that its changes and development always begin with changes and development of the productive forces, and in the first place, with changes and development of the instruments of production. Productive forces are therefore the most mobile and revolutionary element of production. First the productive forces of society change and develop, and then, *depending* on these changes and *in conformity with them,* men's relations of production, their economic relations, change. This, however, does not mean that the relations of production do not influence the development of the productive forces and that the latter are not dependent on the former. While their development is dependent on the development of the productive forces, the relations of production in their turn react upon the development of the productive forces, accelerating or retarding it. In this connection it should be noted that the relations of production cannot for too long a time lag behind and be in a state of contradiction to the growth of the productive forces, inasmuch as the productive forces can develop in full measure only when the relations of production correspond to the character, the state of the productive forces and allow full scope for their development.

Therefore, however much the relations of production may lag behind the development of the productive forces, they must, sooner or later, come into correspondence with—and actually do come into correspondence with—the level of development of the productive forces, the character of the productive forces. Otherwise we would have a fundamental violation of the unity of the productive forces and the relations of production within the system of production, a disruption of production as a whole, a crisis of production, a destruction of productive forces.

An instance in which the relations of production do not correspond to the character of the productive forces, conflict with them, is the economic crises in capitalist countries, where private capitalist ownership of the means of production is in glaring incongruity with the social character of the process of production, with the character of the productive forces. This results in economic crises, which lead to the destruction of productive forces. Furthermore, this incongruity itself constitutes the economic basis of social revolution, the purpose of which is to destroy the existing relations of production and to create new relations of production corresponding to the character of the productive forces.

In contrast, an instance in which the relations of production completely correspond to the character of the productive forces is the socialist national economy of the U.S.S.R., where the social ownership of the means of production fully corresponds to the social character of the process of production, and where, because of this, economic crises and the destruction of productive forces are unknown.

Consequently, the productive forces are not only the most mobile and revolutionary element in production, but are also the determining element in the development of production.

Whatever are the productive forces such must be the relations of production.

While the state of the productive forces furnishes the answer to the question—with what instruments of production do men produce the material values they need?—the state of the relations of production furnishes the answer to another question—who owns the *means of production* (the land, forests, waters, mineral resources, raw materials, instruments of production, production premises, means of transportation and communication, etc.), who commands the means of production, whether the whole of society, or individual persons, groups, or classes which utilize them for the exploitation of other persons, groups or classes?

Here is a rough picture of the development of productive forces from ancient times to our day. The transition from crude stone tools to the bow and arrow, and the accompanying transition from the life of hunters to the domestication of animals and primitive pasturage; the transition from stone tools to metal tools (the iron axe, the wooden plough fitted with an iron coulter, etc.), with a corresponding transition to tillage and agriculture; a further improvement in metal tools for the working up of materials, the introduction of the blacksmith's bellows, the introduction of pottery, with a corresponding development of handicrafts, the separation of handicrafts from agriculture, the development of an independent handicraft industry and, subsequently, of manufacture; the transition from handicraft tools to machines and the transformation of handicraft and manufacture into machine industry; the transition to the machine system and the rise of modern large-scale machine industry—such is a general and far from complete picture of the development of the productive forces of society in the course of man's history. It will be clear that the development and improvement of the instruments of production was effected by men who were related to production, and not independently of men; and, consequently, the change and development of the instruments of production was accompanied by a change and development of men, as the most important element of the productive forces, by a change and development of their production experience, their labour skill, their ability to handle the instruments of production.

In conformity with the change and development of the productive forces of society in the course of history, men's relations of production, their economic relations also changed and developed.

Five *main* types of relations of production are known to history: primitive communal, slave, feudal, capitalist and socialist. . . .

The basis of the relations of production under the capitalist system is that the capitalist owns the means of production, but not the workers in production—the wage labourers, whom the capitalist can neither kill nor sell because they are personally free, but who are deprived of means of production and, in order not to die of hunger, are obliged to sell their labour power to the capitalist and to bear the yoke of exploitation. Alongside of capitalist property in the means of production, we find, at first on a wide scale, private property of the peasants and handicraftsmen in the means of production, these peasants and handicraftsmen no longer being serfs, and their private property being based on personal labour. In place of the handicraft workshops and manufactories there appear huge mills and factories equipped with machinery. In place of the manorial estates tilled by the primitive implements of production of the peasant, there now appear large capitalist farms run on scientific lines and supplied with agricultural machinery.

The new productive forces require that the workers in production shall be better educated and more intelligent than the downtrodden and ignorant serfs, that they be able to understand machinery and operate it properly. Therefore, the capitalists prefer to deal with wage workers, who are free from the bonds of serfdom and who are educated enough to be able properly to operate machinery.

But having developed productive forces to a tremendous extent, capitalism has become enmeshed in contradictions which it is unable to solve. By producing larger and larger quantities of commodities, and reducing their prices, capitalism intensifies competition, ruins the mass of small and medium private owners, converts them into proletarians and reduces their purchasing power, with the result that it becomes impossible to dispose of the commodities produced. On the other hand, by expanding production and concentrating millions of workers in huge mills and factories, capitalism lends the process of production a social character and thus undermines its own foundation, inasmuch as the social character of the process of production demands the social ownership of the means of production; yet the means of production remain private capitalist property, which is incompatible with the social character of the process of production.

These irreconcilable contradictions between the character of the productive forces and the relations of production make themselves felt in periodical crises of overproduction, when the capitalists, finding no effective demand for their goods owing to the ruin of the mass of the population which they themselves have brought about, are compelled to burn products, destroy manufactured goods, suspend production, and destroy productive forces at a time when millions of people are forced to suffer unemployment and starvation, not because there are not enough goods, but because there is an overproduction of goods.

This means that the capitalist relations of production have ceased to correspond to the state of productive forces of society and have come into irreconcilable contradiction with them.

This means that capitalism is pregnant with revolution, whose mission it is to replace the existing capitalist ownership of the means of production by socialist ownership.

This means that the main feature of the capitalist system is a most acute class struggle between the exploiters and the exploited. . . .

d) *The third feature* of production is that the rise of new productive forces and of the relations of production corresponding to them does not take place separately from the old system, after the disappearance of the old system, but within the old system; it takes place not as a result of the deliberate and conscious activity of man, but spontaneously, unconsciously, independently of the will of man. . . .

Here is the formulation—a formulation of genius—of the essence of historical materialism given by Marx in 1859 in his historic Preface to his famous book, *Critique of Political Economy:*

"In the social production of their life, men enter into definite relations that are indispensable and independent of their will, relations of production which correspond to a definite stage of development of their material productive forces. The sum total of these relations of production constitutes the economic structure of society, the real foundation, on which rises a legal and political superstructure and to which correspond definite forms of social consciousness. The mode of production of material life conditions the social, political and intellectual life process in general. It is not the consciousness of men that determines their being, but, on the contrary, their social being that determines their consciousness. At a certain stage of their development, the material productive forces of society come in conflict with the existing relations of production, or—what is but a legal expression for the same thing—with the property relations within which they have been at work hitherto. From forms of development of the productive forces these relations turn into their fetters. Then begins an epoch of social revolution. With the change of the economic foundation the entire immense superstructure is more or less rapidly transformed. In considering such transformations a distinction should always be made between the material trans-formation of the economic conditions of production, which can be determined with the precision of natural science, and the legal, polit-ical, religious, esthetic or philosophic—in short, ideological forms in which men become conscious of this conflict and fight it out. Just as our opinion of an individual is not based on what he thinks of himself, so can we not judge of such a period of transformation by its own consciousness; on the contrary, this consciousness must be explained rather from the contradictions of material life, from the existing conflict between the social productive forces and the rela-tions of production. No social order ever perishes before all the productive forces for which there is room in it have developed; and new, higher relations of production never appear before the material conditions of their existence have matured in the womb of the old society itself. Therefore mankind always sets itself only such tasks as it can solve; since, looking at the matter more closely, it will always be found that the task itself arises only when the material conditions for its solution already exist or are at least in the process of formation." (K. Marx, *Selected Works*, Vol. I, pp. 269–70.)

Such is Marxist materialism as applied to social life, to the his-tory of society.

Such are the principal features of dialectical and historical materialism.

Science and Dialectical Materialism

SIDNEY HOOK[*]

Dialectical materialism may be considered as a system of natural-istic or materialistic philosophy, one of a family of doctrines con-cerning the nature of man and his relation to the world. It may also be considered primarily as the state philosophy of the Soviet Union and its satellite nations.

As a system of naturalistic philosophy the tenets of dialectical materialism have been adumbrated by some forms of evolutionary naturalism in the West which seek to establish certain conclusions about the world, of a generality wider than any to be found in the special sciences. One such conclusion is that wherever values are found they are related to human interest, consciousness or desire, from which the analytic consequence is drawn that truths about the physical world, as a theater of human activity, are politically neutral.

In *this* sense, belief in dialectical materialism is logically com-patible with belief in any social philosophy whatsoever—Commu-nism, Democracy or Fascism. In *this* sense, dialectical materialism, although holding that all forms of consciousness, personal and social, arise, develop, and disappear with changes in the material world, which are the subject matter of the physical sciences, is

---

[*] One of the leading philosophers and educators of America, Professor Hook has written numerous books, including *Reason, Social Myths and Democracy* (1940), *The Hero in History* (1945), *Heresy, Yes—Conspiracy, No* (1953), and *From Hegel to Marx* (1936).

---

opposed to *reductive* materialism. It recognizes the existence of plural levels of organization, emergent qualities, and the efficacy of human thought and action in redetermining some of the conditions of personal and social life. With *this* sense of dialectical materialism, I shall not be concerned.

Dialectical materialism as the system of Soviet state philosophy differs radically from the above in holding that its doctrines entail the validity of communism as a political, social and economic system, and that the validity of communism entails acceptance of the philosophy of dialectical materialism. This is one of the most fateful assertions ever put forward in the history of ideas, for together with certain vague notions concerning the "dialectical" interrelatedness of things, it serves as a theoretical justification, in the eyes of those who accept dialectical materialism, for such propositions as "science, like all culture in modern society, is national in form and class in content." It has often been invoked to defend control of scientific research and publication by political decree. And since similar assertions are being advanced not only in the Soviet Union but in all countries within its political sphere, it is important, even for those who are prone to dismiss this philosophy as a convenient psychological rationalization for the exercise of political power, to understand its claims.

I

According to Lenin, Stalin and other authoritative expositors, the materialistic dialectic is a method "of studying and apprehending" the phenomena of nature: historical materialism is a set of doctrines derived by applying the dialectic method to social phenomena. The dialectic method is therefore central to this philosophy. But just as soon as any authoritative expositor begins to describe the dialectic method, he enunciates statements which are normally found in traditional ontology or metaphysics, e.g., that nature is "a connected and integral whole in which things are organically connected with, dependent on, and determined by, each other"; that nature is in "a state of continuous movement and change," that the movement is from "the lower to the higher"; that "internal contradictions are inherent in all things and phenomena of nature," and so forth. This is just as if someone were to describe the principal features of scientific method merely by reciting the basic laws of dynamics, electromagnetism, genetics, etc., which were discovered by using this method. The whole relation between the dialectical method and scientific method is left in a kind of calculated obscurity. And despite the reiterated statement that the principles of dialectic enter into the development of science no clear and consistent account of the relation can be found.

The relation between the so-called objective laws of dialectic and the sciences of nature and society are characterized in such a way as to suggest (*a*) sometimes that the first are presuppositions of the second in the sense that they are necessary conditions which if denied would involve the denial of valid scientific knowledge; (*b*) sometimes that the laws and features of dialectic are summaries of the results of scientific inquiry; and most often (*c*) that they are broad hypotheses continually confirmed by the progress of science.

(*a*) One difficulty in evaluating the relationship of presupposition is the vagueness and ambiguity of the statements which express the principles of dialectic. Take the statement that "internal contradictions are inherent in all things and phenomena of nature" (Stalin). Ignore for the moment that the usual and only consistent usage of the term "contradiction" makes it a property of assertions or statements, as Aristotle already pointed out. Like the other principles of dialectic it is assumed to have universal validity. But no matter how it is read, it cannot be regarded as a presupposition or necessary condition of any particular piece of scientific knowledge, e.g., that the passage of an electric current under certain conditions induces a magnetic field. For the truth of this scientific statement, or of any other scientific statement, is compatible with the denial of the alleged dialectical law. Even if there were some way of interpreting a specific scientific statement or law as an illustration of the presence or development of internal contradictions, it would in no way be affected by the falsity of the statement about the alleged *universal* validity of this or any other law of dialectic. For some things and processes of nature could have a certain character even if it were false that *all* things and processes have that character. At most the principles of dialectic would be summaries in peculiar language of some characters exhibited by some classes of things and processes.

(b) This would seem to be a reasonable interpretation of what some dialectical materialists mean when they tell us that their philosophy does not stand above the sciences, but that its validity is established step by step within the sciences. From this point of view dialectical materialism would be nothing but a summary, and completely useless, description of the achievements of the sciences at any time. But if this is what is meant, it would be hard to explain why the generalizations of dialectical materialism have remained the same for almost a century, despite the tremendous revolutions in scientific theory and knowledge. It would also make it difficult to understand how at the same time the development of science could be attributed to the fact that scientists were unconsciously following the principles of dialectic in their inquiry. Any method that gave correct or fruitful results would be dialectical by definition, and the notion that dialectics is in any way a guide to discovery of new knowledge would be patently false.

(c) "Nature," writes Stalin quoting Engels, "is the test of dialectics, and it must be said for modern natural science that it has furnished extremely rich and daily increasing materials for this test. . . ." It is interesting to observe that nature is characterized as the test of *dialectics* not of materialism. Now a "test," in any usage of the term, is a trial, a question, which theoretically can be answered in more than one way. If nature is a test of dialectics, then the principles or laws of dialectics must be something more than general summaries of results already won in the past. They must assert something testable about the future. They must function as hypotheses no matter how broadly conceived. We are therefore justified in asking: what would the behavior of things have to be, what would we have to discover, what would we in principle have to observe, in order to reach the conclusion that dialectics *fails* to pass the test of nature?

Dialectical materialists have never been able to tell us, because no matter what is observed in nature, no matter what happens, they can square it as easily with the so-called laws of dialectic as a pious believer can square any event that occurs with his belief that everything happens by the will of God, or that it fulfills some Providential cosmic plan. Since no specific conditions are indicated under which the laws of genuine dialectic would be refuted or abandoned there is no test—and illustrations of the law are confused with proof—so that actually they do not function as hypotheses at all. There is no evidence that they have ever even served as aids to scientific discovery. On the contrary, like many theological beliefs of the past, they have been invoked to block roads to fresh scientific inquiry and sometimes to contest scientific theories, like the theory of relativity and the biological theory of genes, not on grounds of evidence, but because of all sorts of extra scientific considerations.

It is important to point out that the taboos and prescriptions against *specific* scientific theories, like finitistic conceptions of space and time, or psychoanalytic doctrines, do not follow *logically* from the principles of dialectic, for the latter are either irrelevant to the entire enterprise of scientific inquiry or so indeterminate as to be compatible with any scientific detail. The real explanation, therefore, of the restrictive practices associated with dialectical materialism must come from some other source, usually social or political. This is practically admitted in the doctrine of *partinost* according to which not only is the philosophy of dialectical materialism a partisan, class and party-philosophy, but the findings of science, the alleged applications of the laws of dialectic, have this character, too. It is made explicit not only in the demands imposed on Soviet scientists but in the proclamations of faithful Communists throughout the world. "Dialectical materialism," writes the English Communist, Maurice Cornforth, "asks to be judged and will be judged by whether it serves as an effective instrument to show the way out of capitalist crises and war. . . ." Since the validity of the applications of dialectical materialism are to be judged in the same way, it is clear that the bearings of a doctrine for the conquest and retention of political power replace ordinary scientific evidence as ultimately probative in determining which doctrines are to be accepted.

All this indicates that statements which are *logically* or scientifically irrelevant to practice may nonetheless have a profound influence on practice because of their relation to personal or psychological interests, and social or historical interests. This is sometimes denied. Bertrand Russell, for example, has written that "The belief that metaphysics has any bearing upon political affairs is a proof of logical incapacity." What he should have written is that the belief that metaphysics has any *logical* bearing upon practical affairs is a proof of logical incapacity. But there are other bearings which metaphysical doctrines may have on practical affairs that do not follow from their logical meaning or cognitive content. The history of dialectical materialism in the Soviet Union is a good illustration of this. From time to time the Central Committee of the Communist Party has intervened in philosophical and scientific debates, to settle by decree which principles are to be emphasized in dialectical materialism, and what doctrines or tendencies are to be taught in fields ranging from art and agronomy to zoology. At one time the role of chance will be played down; at another it will be played up, for, after all, if Lenin or Stalin are truly great men, they cannot be explained *merely* by the mode of production or any other common environmental phenomenon. At one time language will be considered a part of the cultural superstructure, and therefore a field in which the class struggle is reflected. At another, language is decreed to be part of the common social inheritance, and it therefore becomes nonsensical to speak of a "class language" or "grammar." At one time formal logic is driven out of the curriculum as a mode of metaphysical thinking, and therefore an enemy class science; at another it is reinstated as a non-class science with the resolution "to put the science of logic at the service of the Soviet people, to make it a sharply pointed ideological weapon in the struggle against the survivals of the past in the consciousness of people, in the struggle against the bourgeois ideology alien to us."

A variety of causes probably accounts for these different shifts from one doctrine to another. It has been asserted that the rehabilitation of formal logic at the expense of dialectical logic, as well as the fact that Stalin failed even to mention the dialectical law of "the negation of the negation" in his authoritative exposition of "Dialectical and Historical Materialism," can be explained by a desire to use logic as a support of the present status quo in the U.S.S.R. and to dismiss as relatively unimportant the potential dynamism of dialectical thinking with its stress on the mutability of all things and institutions. It is hard to determine how much truth there is in such an interpretation but since Stalin uses language synonymous with the expression of the law of "the negation of the negation" it seems doubtful. It must be admitted, however, that all governments when safely in power tend to be on the side of eternity. But I am confident that if political facts are often decisive, they are not exclusive, causes in the turns and zig-zags of philosophical and scientific doctrine. Nationalism and national pride obviously, even if foolishly, entered. Stalin's own personal tastes and prejudices which in art and music did not differ from the crude, untutored judgments of philistines in the West, were probably an independent factor. His condemnation of Deborin as a "Menshevizing idealist" may have been merely the result of his failure to understand Deborin's philosophical vocabulary. Certainly, the condemnation of the music of Shostakovitch and Prokofiev cannot be explained only in the light of Stalin's politics. His ear had a lot to do with it. After Stalin's death the ban against their "formalist" works was lifted without modifying the principles of dialectic and the right of the Central Committee of the Communist Party to pass upon the political validity of musical works.

Nor is there any convincing evidence that the imposition of the philosophy of dialectical materialism on Soviet scientists is actually justified in the eyes of the Kremlin by the practical results won in consequence. For although the past achievements of Russian scientists in philosophy and psychology in the undialectical days of the Czars are lauded to the skies, the present activities of Soviet scientists in these fields are constantly under attack. The current canonization of Pavlov, and the strictures against Soviet scientists in physiology and psychology for not developing his work, are eloquent testimony on this point. Why should Russian scientists who were not dialectical materialists have achieved so much more in the past, in contradistinction to Soviet scientists today, who, although they all profess dialectical materialism, are urged strenuously not only to live up to the achievements of their non-dialectical forbears but even to catch up with, and overtake, the achievements of their non-dialectical contemporaries in the decadent West?

A favorite reply to this is that good scientists anywhere, to the extent that they make valid discoveries, are unconsciously using the dialectical method. A possible corollary of this reply would be that in the interests of fruitfulness and the chances of developing Pavlovs, Lorentzes and other pre-Bolshevik scientists approved by the pundits of dialectical materialism, Soviet scientists should be permitted to become *unconscious* of dialectical materialistic philosophy, instead of having it driven into them by implicit threats of the use of sanctions against them.

II

The really baffling thing about dialectical materialism of the Soviet variety is not its validity, for to the extent that it can be intelligibly stated, it consists either of a series of commonplaces, completely irrelevant to the work of science, or of downright falsities and absurdities. It is obvious that a doctrine which holds that all things are dialectically interrelated cannot be a logical guide to any scientific inquiry or experiment which holds that *some* things are irrelevant to any particular phenomena we are exploring. The scientists can only establish connections and interrelations between *specific* states of affairs and must in practice deny that everything is relevant to everything else. That he must search for some connections follows from his desire to find explanation; he therefore doesn't need a philosophy to enjoin him, in misleading language, to search for such connections when he is already embarked on a quest for understanding.

We have already seen that as a philosophy, dialectical materialism cannot justify itself as a fruitful, heuristic method of scientific discovery. Nobody knows the causes of scientific discovery, and it is conceivable that just as some literary men find tobacco or alcohol an aid in their creative labors (or imagine they do), so scientists might get on the track of new knowledge in virtue of their commitment to some private over-beliefs, like Fechner's belief in a world soul or Kepler's view that angels helped move the planets. In the absence of any evidence of statistical correlation between metaphysical belief and scientific discovery, any report by an individual scientist that such a belief played a fruitful role in his thinking would have to be considered as an interesting item in his autobiography, like J. B. S. Haldane's claim many years ago that a reading of Lenin's *Imperialism* cured him of stomach ulcers which, even if true, would hardly warrant its acceptance as a valid technique of medical therapy. Nothing in these remarks should be construed as a denial of the possibility that the private conceits of any scientist might be helpful to him in his work or that he should be discouraged from holding them. But to convert such private conceits into public law or articles of mandatory belief is a good definition of cultural barbarism.

Why, then, should the rulers of the Soviet Union set such store on the acceptance of dialectical materialism by Soviet scientists? I should like to suggest that the most decisive reason is their mistaken belief that the political strategy and social system of Communism depends upon the establishment of certain propositions about nature presumably derived by the laws of dialectic. And further, that this mistaken belief functions in such a way as to give them the illusory assurance that the cosmic process itself, as well as history, is on their side and guarantees the inevitability of Communist victory. In this sense dialectical materialism is an *Ersatz* religion.

(1) That the corollaries drawn from the laws of dialectic are political and social is most clearly seen in Stalin's writings. "If the passing of slow quantitative changes into rapid and abrupt qualitative changes is a law of development, then it is clear that revolutions made by oppressed classes are a quite natural and inevitable phenomenon." Similarly, if development takes place through the mechanisms of objective contradiction, this is presumably the basis of the belief that class struggle and revolutionary dictatorship are "natural and inevitable phenomena."

We have already seen that *formally* this relation is a logical non-sequitur, and that the laws may be false and the specific phenomena may be true (although in *fact* the latter are false, too). Concretely, however, there is evidence that revolutions took place long before "the law of the transformation of quantity into quality" was ever formulated just as it was known that parturition takes place suddenly after nine months of gradual development. The alleged law adds not a particle of information to our knowledge about any subject matter. Indeed, the very meaning of the expression "sudden transformation of slow quantitative changes into rapid qualitative ones" alters as we go from field to field, and no generalizations about the critical points of the changes can be even remotely helpful in practice. Irritation bursts into anger, a volcano into eruption, an altercation into a brawl, a solid into gas or liquid, a retreat into a rout, and discontent into revolution. At this level of crude analogy and vague, inexact statement only the poet is licensed to instruct or entertain us by his references to them. And even he knows that not all irritations burst into anger, not all solids into gases or liquids, etc. Just as soon as we wish scientifically to understand anything about any of these specific phenomena, we court confusion unless we can dissociate ourselves from the cluster of connotations and fancies which adhere to the original analogies of our experience.

Note that the laws of dialectic are supposed to make these social phenomena "natural" as if the fact that they happened was by itself not sufficient to give them a natural status. But since the absence of these phenomena (say, revolutions) is also natural, the so-called law is irrelevant. Actually, "natural" in physics and "natural" in society do not have the same meanings. Anything which happens in physics is "natural," according to the dialectical materialists, but not everything which happens in society and history is "natural," since measures are recommended on the ground that to carry them out would be "natural," while *not* to carry them out would be "unnatural." Laws of nature cannot be violated, but presumably laws of history and social revolution can. This confusion between physics and ethics is not restricted to dialectical materialism; it goes back in Western thought at least to the Stoics and ultimately to the Platonic "form of the good." But dialectical materialism is one of the most conspicuous and persistent illustrations of this confusion since the rise of modern science. Nor are dialectical materialists unique in seeking to use applications of alleged ontological or metaphysical principles in the field of nature as a support of their social views. Some Western philosophers have argued that the sudden leap of an electron from one orbit to another is evidence for freedom of the human will. Dialectical materialists indignantly and properly deny this; they then go on to argue as if it constituted evidence for naturalness and inevitability of the Communist revolution.

The attempt to derive social laws from physical laws is legitimate even if the history of the effort until now has been a history of failure. The validity of a social law, however, can be established independently of the validity of any more general physical law from which it is presumably to be derived, just as the laws of genetics can be established as valid independently of the success or failure of the effort to show that they are derivable from physico-chemical laws. At the very most all one can say today is that no set of social arrangements is possible which violate any valid scientific or biological generalization. But even if this be granted, *it does not follow that men will not try to achieve such a social system.* We may predict that a social ideal based upon the postulate of the indefinite fertility of the soil, or on universal, absolute chastity, or any other aim incompatible with tested scientific knowledge, will be unrealizable. But human beings may attempt the impossible, even though it may lead to rack and ruin. Now if an indefinite variety of social systems is compatible with basic physical laws, how much greater variation is allowed by dialectical or ontological laws which, granted for a moment their cognitive import, either have a wider generality than any physical laws, if metaphysics has a specific subject matter, or are as tautologous as the laws of logic, if metaphysics has no specific subject matter.

The valid arguments for democracy, capitalism, Socialism, Fascism and Communism do not rest on any metaphysics, ontology, or dialectical laws. This is true even for the ethical components and imperatives of social systems, since no ethical statement is derivable from philosophical premises unless a value term or attitude is implicit in such premises or in the situation which we accept as a point of departure. Nor, as we have seen, can social systems be derived from physical generalizations and certainly not the attempts of men to achieve such systems. It is a canonic proposition of dialectical materialism, however, that the struggle for Communism and its universal triumph are equally inevitable.

(2) Since scientific statements are corrigible, and since all predictive statements are conditional, no scientific judgment can guarantee the future. That is why the dialectical method is employed to win a kind of "truth" which is either outside the scope of science or incompatible with its very method. The more narrowly empirical Marxist-Leninist *political* strategy is, the more opportunistic its tactics, the more resolutely does it affirm that "sooner or later" the Communist goal will be achieved. One of the psychological conseqences of this belief is an indifference to alternative means and methods of social change, a denial that such means and methods determine the actual ends reached in history, rather than conversely. Another is a callous disregard of the human costs of social action, since moral responsibility is shifted from human beings to the historical process working itself out with the alleged automatism of natural law. No matter what man's limitations are, no matter what his ignorance or cowardice, no matter how sustained his defeats, they cannot hold up the dialectical

march of the productive forces to a Communist society. But the dialectic in history needs to be supplemented by a *Naturdialektik,* for the history of man is also a part of the history of the cosmos. Tidal waves, earthquakes, extremes of weather have their historical effects, too, and the historical process alone cannot guarantee that a cosmic event—an accident from the standpoint of human history—may not put an end to man's career on earth. Natural development, despite all setbacks and catastrophes is, in Stalin's language, from "the lower to the higher," and the dialectical laws of development, universal and inevitable, give the emotional assurance, which history alone cannot give, that the ideal of Communism will not be defeated. Dialectical materialists believe that if human life is destroyed on this earth, then somewhere else life will develop and resume its advance to the predestined goal.

One may regard it as a politicalized version of early nineteenth-century *Naturphilosophie* with the dialectical process cast in the role of an instrument of Hegel's *List der Vernunft.* It is not accidental, to borrow a favorite expression of this school of thought, that an English Communist, Professor H. Levy, speaks soberly of "fascism in nature" when discussing mechanics. That dialectics gives guarantees is often *explicitly* claimed by dialectical materialists. Thus, one Soviet philosopher, subsequently sent to Hungary on the heels of the Red Army, writes:

> Dialectics not only point out to the proletariat its historical task, but it gives the proletariat the certainty of victory, it is to a certain extent the *guarantee of this victory.*

Whoever understands the universe properly then, i.e., from the standpoint of dialectical materialism, will see (*a*) that the world of nature and society could not have been different from what it is and the victory of communism still be possible, and (*b*) that the structure of the universe is such that victory is logically already involved in the relationships discovered by dialectics. This is the promise of creation. The stars in their courses proclaim it; the ocean floor supports it; and man in his brief career realizes it. Even if life on this planet were destroyed, this philosophy offers the assurance that it would arise somewhere else and begin its pilgrimage to that one far-off event—or succession of events—towards which the cosmos is striving. Communism, it is sometimes admitted, will disappear but the same natural processes which insure its disappearance *necessitate* its coming.

> *But what passes away at one point of the universe, develops anew at another.* One solar system passes away, new ones develop. Life passes away from the earth, it arises elsewhere anew. *In this sense,* dialectical materialism asserts an eternal development; what exists evolves. It evolves because the dialectical self-movement of every thing which exists is a driving force towards development. *Decay holds in general for special cases; the endlessness of development holds only for the infinite universe sub specie eternitatis.*

This not only suggests the familiar consolations of religion; it is an outright expression of the theology of absolute idealism with all its attendant logical difficulties. What an ironic illustration of the alleged dialectic law of the transformation of a thesis into its opposite! Dialectical materialism, which is presumably militant atheism, is here presented as a kind of sentimental theology! The indignant repudiation of this charge by Rudas and other orthodox dialectical materialists is only a measure of their inconsistency and of their failure to grasp the essence of the religious attitude. Because they eschew the use of the word *God* or *Absolute Spirit* and insist that there is no external source of movement, but that every movement is self-movement, they feel that they have escaped religion when all they have done is to replace a transcendental theology by an immanent one. For what is essential to religion is not the use of the term "God" but the belief that the universe is somehow friendly to man and human purpose, that natural processes are such that they must realize the highest human ideals (e.g., Communism, if one believes in it), that these processes cannot be adequately understood without such reference, and that despite momentary defeats and setbacks the victory of the highest human ideals (i.e., the classless society) is guaranteed by the mechanisms of nature and society. To inspire this belief in the minds and hearts of its adherents is the precise function of the theology of orthodox dialectical materialism.

Whether dialectical materialism is an expression of the secular hunger for metaphysics or religion, it is undoubtedly a quest for certainty, a quest for what William James called "a sumptuosity of security" which no scientific philosophy can give. The animus against all deviant philosophical ideas, against technical scientific doctrines like the theory of resonance in chemistry which have not the slightest political implications, can be explained only as a fear that in some way the revolutionary faith that both inspires and consoles is being undermined if philosophy and science are given autonomy to develop as philosophers and scientists in the uncoerced quest for truth see fit to develop them.

What is new about the philosophy of dialectical materialism is not its doctrine of two truths, the ordinary scientific truth, sometimes called metaphysical, and the higher dialectical truth. It is the extent and intensity of political control of the arts and sciences to which this quest for security has gone. It is as if despairing of a rational defense of their political program with its needless sacrifice of untold millions for a problematic future which does not promise to be much better than the past and in many ways threatens to be far worse, the rulers of the Soviet Union must fall back on the authority of a mystical doctrine to whose keys they alone possess the key. "Plechanov and even Bukharin," wrote a party philosopher before the Moscow Trials, "were not in a position to give an unexceptionable exposition of dialectical materialism in the last resort also because they did not have an unexceptionable line in politics." And who has an unexceptionable line in politics? Obviously whoever commands the state security troops.

No matter what else they differ about, the vocation of all scientists in the free world *as scientists* is threatened by the extension of Soviet power and its stock of ideological strait jackets. No matter what school of philosophy to which they belong, all philosophers will be compelled to bow to political decrees in epistemology, logic and methodology. The administration of philosophy will become one of the duties of the police. This is no Orwellian fantasy of the future. For it is a recapitulation of the fate of philosophy in the Soviet Union.

· 2 ·

THE IDEOLOGY OF COMMUNISM

The first three selections in this group represent three important theoretical assessments of the world situation during some of the most crucial periods in the history of the world Communist movement.

The *Manifesto of the Communist Party* was first published in London in February, 1848, in response to a request made a year before by the International Communist League for the elaboration of a statement of policy. Published under the joint authorship of Marx and Engels shortly before the outbreak of revolution in France and elsewhere, the Manifesto is regarded as one of the most significant political pamphlets ever written. Its language and style reflect the authors' basic concern for the application of the philosophy of dialectical materialism to concrete historical situations. Written at a time when "the specter of Communism was haunting Europe," the Manifesto includes, among other things, a general theory of history, a biting analysis of bourgeois society and a program of action for a consciously revolutionary proletariat.

The Manifesto sets forth as a theory of history "the natural phases of evolution," which are considered to unfold under the internal drive of dialectics and expected to culminate in the inevitable victory of the proletariat. The key offered for the understanding of this process and of "all hitherto existing society" is the class struggle.

The ideas of Marxism as incorporated in the Manifesto underwent a series of changes under the impact of the concrete conditions under which the Communist movements had to operate in various parts of the globe.

One of Lenin's great theoretical contributions to Marxism is believed to have been its adaptation to the particular conditions that prevailed in Russia. A socially and economically backward country, Russia proved curiously receptive to radical Western ideas. But as the product of Western industrial conditions Marxism envisaged the establishment of a new social order on the basis of the conscious actions of a large and mature proletariat. The Communist Party as a political organization was expected merely to provide the needed theoretical and organizational leadership and not to substitute itself for the proletariat.

Realizing the fundamentally feudalistic nature of Russian society and doubting the ability of the working class to ever achieve the spontaneous class consciousness depicted by Marx, Lenin asserted the primacy of the Party as the formulator of goals and strategy. Envisaged to be composed of "professional revolutionaries," the Party was expected to serve as a midwife of history in hastening the transformation of the feudal society by the amalgamation of the bourgeois and proletarian revolutions under its aegis.

Marxism-Leninism, as the new theory came to be called, underwent a further change in the wake of the establishment of the U.S.S.R. The victory of the Stalinist policy of "socialism in one country" eventually led to the recognition of the primacy of the U.S.S.R. in the world Communist movement. The Communist Party of the Soviet Union emerged as the chief guardian of the faith whose tenets became binding on all parties through the intermediacy of the Communist International (Comintern).

With the emergence of several new Communist states in the post-World War II period, however, the primacy of the Soviet Union came to be challenged and some of the tenets of Marxism-Leninism-Stalinism were questioned. The myth that wars and international conflicts were characteristic only of the capitalist-imperialist state system was first shattered in 1948 when Marshal Tito refused to subordinate the interests of socialist construction in Yugoslavia to the requirements of reconstruction in the Soviet Union. The upheavals of the post-Stalin era destroyed whatever survived of this myth until 1956.

The denigration of Stalin that year was followed by some fundamental revisions of Communist doctrine. Under the impact of the development of nuclear and thermonuclear weapons of mass destruction and the perfection of the rocket and missile delivery systems, Khrushchev revised the traditional Marxist-Leninist concept as to the inevitability of war in the era of imperialism. He argued that the "epoch-making changes of the last decades"—the growth of the Communist camp, the existence of a large number of non-Communist countries which were opposed to war, the strengthening of the working class movements in the capitalist countries, and the flourishing of the international peace movement—entailed that wars were no longer "fatalistically inevitable." Advancing the policy of "peaceful coexistence" between states with different social and political orders, Khrushchev brought about a second major modification of Marxism-Leninism. He asserted that the weakening of capitalism and the commensurate increase in the power of the "socialist camp" meant that it might be possible to introduce Communist rule in various countries by parliamentary rather than revolutionary means. He accepted the Titoist interpretation of the Leninist thesis as to the right of each country to pursue the building of socialism in accordance with the particular conditions prevailing in the respective country.

But the events which took place in Poland and Hungary in consequence of these countries' attempt to exploit the political climate created by the Twentieth Congress and the Soviet-Yugoslav ideological Party-agreement of June 1956, called for both the reaffirmation of the leadership of the U.S.S.R. and the confirmation of Khrushchev's theoretical innovations. This was achieved by the *Moscow Declaration of November* 1957 which was signed by representatives of twelve Communist states (excluding Yugoslavia) who were in the Soviet capital for the celebration of the fortieth anniversary of the Bolshevik Revolution.

The international developments of the post-1957 period revealed increasingly the clashing national interests of the two Communist colossi. Khrushchev's policy of direct approach to the United States (the "Spirit of Camp David") and his courting of China's potential adversaries in South and South-East Asia—a region of the world which the Chinese regarded as geographically within their sphere of influence—added further venom to the resentment of the Chinese for the failure of the Russians to help them become a nuclear power.

The dispute gradually erupted in full-scale ideological warfare. At first, the battle was fought over the ideological positions of Albania and Yugoslavia. In attacking the Russians, the Chinese criticized the revisionism of Yugoslavia; the Russians, in turn, counter-attacked by condemning Albanian dogmatism. With the widening of the ideological dispute, the Chinese openly challenged the standing of the Soviet Communists as the fountainhead of doctrinal orthodoxy for the world Communist movement. The exacerbation of the ideological conflict necessitated the convening of an international conference of Communist Party representatives from all over the world to settle the dispute.

The *Statement of Eighty-one Communist and Workers Parties,* issued by the participants at the Moscow conference of November, 1960, reflected a temporary compromise between the ideological positions of China and Russia. Divided into six sections, it includes an outline of the major features of the present historical era emphasizing that the existence of the "world socialist system" was the "decisive factor in the development of society." It reasserts the inevitability of the "complete triumph of socialism" and characterizes U.S. imperialism as the "chief bulwark of world reaction, . . . an international gendarme . . . and the enemy of the peoples of the whole world."

Discussing the development and experiences of the U.S.S.R. and the other "socialist" and "people's democratic" states, the Statement claims confidently that "the restoration of capitalism has been made socially and economically impossible" in these countries. With regard to the universal problem of war and peace, U.S. imperialism is again labeled as "the main force of aggression and war" and the policy of "peaceful coexistence" and the military and economic power of the Communist world are depicted as the chief guardians of peace. Though the Statement asserts the possibility of the "peaceful transition" from capitalism to socialism, it also emphasizes the need of bearing in mind the necessity of the non-peaceful transition also. While both "revisionism" and "dogmatism" are condemned, the Soviet Communist Party is no longer referred to as the "leader" but merely as the "vanguard" of the world Communist movement. In the light of the deterioration of Sino-Soviet relations in the 1960's it appears that though the Statement succeeded in ironing out some of the initial ideological differences, it marked merely the end of one phase in the power struggle between the two Communist colossi.

The next two selections discuss the essence of contemporary Communism and the importance of Marxist-Leninist doctrine in the formulation and implementation of Soviet policy.

Western scholars seem to disagree on their evaluation of the relationship between Marxist theory and Soviet practice. While some of them claim that ideological considerations have been decisive in shaping the policies and attitudes of the Communist leaders, others seem to attach an overriding importance to such elements as "power" and "national interest" as the primary factors determining Soviet policy.

There is little doubt that Marxist theory played an important role in the period preceding the Bolshevik Revolution. The oft-quoted statement of Lenin that "without a revolutionary theory there can be no revolutionary movement" is an eloquent testimony to this effect. But the realities of political life after the acquisition of state power in 1917 have often induced the Soviet leaders to reformulate the doctrine and, when necessary, ignore it altogether.

As an ideology, Marxism developed in the economically advanced countries of the West in response to the negative consequences of the industrial revolution. But when Communism came to power in the relatively backward and predominantly agricultural Russia of 1917, it became, according to Djilas, the well-known former leader of Yugoslav Communism, "an exploiting system opposed to most of the interests of the proletariat itself."

Djilas characterizes contemporary Communism as a type of totalitarianism in which ideology is used together with power and ownership as a means of controlling the people by the oligarchy of the "new class," the Party. But while Communism as an ideology is considered to have mainly run its course, Communist power is depicted as "a power which unites within itself the control of ideas, authority, and ownership, a power which has become an end in itself."

Mr. Carew Hunt argues, on the other hand, that while "the present generation does not react to the formal ideology with the same fervor as did its forbears who made the revolution," the Soviet leaders are fortified in their conviction of the soundness of the principles on which bases they claim to rule "by the very nature of their creed." He claims that these leaders have been nurtured in the creed of Marxism-Leninism from birth and that "it would be strange indeed if they had remained unaffected." While he illustrates historically the interpenetration of ideological and non-ideological factors in the determination of Soviet policy, he also cautions about the lack of a reliable yardstick which would permit the measurement "of the exact relationship between power politics and ideology in the policies which result."

Manifesto of the Communist Party (1848)

KARL MARX AND FRIEDRICH ENGELS

A spectre is haunting Europe—the spectre of Communism. All the Powers of old Europe have entered into a holy alliance to exorcise this spectre: Pope and Czar, Metternich and Guizot, French Radicals and German police-spies.

Where is the party in opposition that has not been decried as Communistic by its opponents in power? Where the Opposition that has not hurled back the branding reproach of Communism, against the more advanced opposition parties, as well as against its reactionary adversaries?

Two things result from this fact.

I. Communism is already acknowledged by all European Powers to be itself a Power.

II. It is high time that Communists should openly, in the face of the whole world, publish their views, their aims, their tendencies, and meet this nursery tale of the Spectre of Communism with a Manifesto of the party itself.

To this end, Communists of various nationalities have assembled in London, and sketched the following Manifesto, to be published in the English, French, German, Italian, Flemish and Danish languages.

Bourgeois and Proletarians

The history of all hitherto existing society is the history of class struggles.

From *Manifesto of the Communist Party* by Karl Marx and Friedrich Engels, Introduction and Part I, pp. 46–71. Moscow: Foreign Languages Publishing House. Translation is by Samuel Moore (1888) from the original German text of 1848 and edited by Friedrich Engels. For footnote references, see original source.

Freeman and slave, patrician and plebeian, lord and serf, guild-master and journeyman, in a word, oppressor and oppressed, stood in constant opposition to one another, carried on an uninterrupted, now hidden, now open fight, a fight that each time ended, either in a revolutionary re-constitution of society at large, or in the common ruin of the contending classes.

In the earlier epochs of history, we find almost everywhere a complicated arrangement of society into various orders, a manifold gradation of social rank. In ancient Rome we have patricians, knights, plebeians, slaves; in the Middle Ages, feudal lords, vassals, guild-masters, journeymen, apprentices, serfs; in almost all of these classes, again, subordinate gradations.

The modern bourgeois society that has sprouted from the ruins of feudal society has not done away with class antagonisms. It has but established new classes, new conditions of oppression, new forms of struggle in place of the old ones.

Our epoch, the epoch of the bourgeoisie, possesses, however, this distinctive feature: it has simplified the class antagonisms. Society as a whole is more and more splitting up into two great hostile camps, into two great classes directly facing each other: Bourgeoisie and Proletariat.

From the serfs of the Middle Ages sprang the chartered burghers of the earliest towns. From these burgesses the first elements of the bourgeoisie were developed.

The discovery of America, the rounding of the Cape, opened up fresh ground for the rising bourgeoisie. The East-Indian and Chinese markets, the colonisation of America, trade with the colonies, the increase in the means of exchange and in commodities generally, gave to commerce, to navigation, to industry, an impulse never before known, and thereby, to the revolutionary element in the tottering feudal society, a rapid development.

The feudal system of industry, under which industrial production was monopolised by closed guilds, now no longer sufficed for the growing wants of the new markets. The manufacturing system took its place. The guild-masters were pushed on one side by the manufacturing middle class; division of labour between the different corporate guilds vanished in the face of division of labour in each single workshop.

Meantime the markets kept ever growing, the demand ever rising. Even manufacture no longer sufficed. Thereupon, steam and machinery revolutionised industrial production. The place of manufacture was taken by the giant, Modern Industry, the place of the industrial middle class, by industrial millionaires, the leaders of whole industrial armies, the modern bourgeois.

Modern industry has established the world market, for which the discovery of America paved the way. This market has given an immense development to commerce, to navigation, to communication by land. This development has, in its turn, reacted on the extension of industry; and in proportion as industry, commerce, navigation, railways extended, in the same proportion the bourgeoisie developed, increased its capital, and pushed into the background every class handed down from the Middle Ages.

We see, therefore, how the modern bourgeoisie is itself the product of a long course of development, of a series of revolutions in the modes of production and of exchange.

Each step in the development of the bourgeoisie was accompanied by a corresponding political advance of that class. An oppressed class under the sway of the feudal nobility, an armed and self-governing association in the mediaeval commune; here independent urban republic (as in Italy and Germany), there taxable "third estate" of the monarchy (as in France), afterwards, in the period of manufacture proper, serving either the semi-feudal or the absolute monarchy as a counterpoise against the nobility, and, in fact, cornerstone of the great monarchies in general, the bourgeoisie has at last, since the establishment of Modern Industry and of the world market, conquered for itself, in the modern representative State, exclusive political sway. The executive of the modern State is but a committee for managing the common affairs of the whole bourgeoisie.

The bourgeoisie, historically, has played a most revolutionary part.

The bourgeoisie, wherever it has got the upper hand, has put an end to all feudal, patriarchal, idyllic relations. It has pitilessly torn asunder the motley feudal ties that bound man to his "natural superiors," and has left remaining no other nexus between man and man than naked self-interest, than callous "cash payment." It has drowned the most heavenly ecstasies of religious fervour, of chivalrous enthusiasm, of philistine sentimentalism, in the icy water of egotistical calculation. It has resolved personal worth into exchange value, and in place of the numberless indefeasible chartered freedoms, has set up that single, unconscionable freedom—Free Trade. In one word, for exploitation, veiled by religious and political illusions, it has substituted naked, shameless, direct, brutal exploitation.

The bourgeoisie has stripped of its halo every occupation hitherto honoured and looked up to with reverent awe. It has converted the physician, the lawyer, the priest, the poet, the man of science, into its paid wage-labourers.

The bourgeoisie has torn away from the family its sentimental veil, and has reduced the family relation to a mere money relation.

The bourgeoisie has disclosed how it came to pass that the brutal display of vigour in the Middle Ages, which Reactionists so much admire, found its fitting complement in the most slothful indolence. It has been the first to show what man's activity can bring about. It has accomplished wonders far surpassing Egyptian pyramids, Roman aqueducts, and Gothic cathedrals; it has conducted expeditions that put in the shade all former Exoduses of nations and crusades.

The bourgeoisie cannot exist without constantly revolutionising the instruments of production, and thereby the relations of production, and with them the whole relations of society. Conservation of the old modes of production in unaltered form, was, on the contrary, the first condition of existence for all earlier industrial classes. Constant revolutionising of production, uninterrupted disturbance of all social conditions, everlasting uncertainty and agitation distinguish the bourgeois epoch from all earlier ones. All fixed, fast-frozen relations, with their train of ancient and venerable prejudices and opinions are swept away, all new-formed ones become antiquated before they can ossify. All that is solid melts into air, all that is holy is profaned, and man is at last compelled to face with sober senses, his real conditions of life, and his relations with his kind.

The need of a constantly expanding market for its products chases the bourgeoisie over the whole surface of the globe. It must nestle everywhere, settle everywhere, establish connexions everywhere.

The bourgeoisie has through its exploitation of the world market given a cosmopolitan character to production and consumption in every country. To the great chagrin of Reactionists, it has drawn from under the feet of industry the national ground on which it stood. All old-established national industries have been destroyed or are daily being destroyed. They are dislodged by new industries, whose introduction becomes a life and death question for all civilised nations, by industries that no longer work up indigenous raw material, but raw material drawn from the remotest zones; industries whose products are consumed, not only at home, but in every quarter of the globe. In place of the old wants, satisfied by the productions of the country, we find new wants, requiring for their satisfaction the products of distant lands and climes. In place of the old local and national seclusion and self-sufficiency, we have intercourse in every direction, universal interdependence of nations. And as in material, so also in intellectual production. The intellectual creations of individual nations become common property. National one-sidedness and narrow-mindedness become more and more impossible, and from the numerous national and local literatures, there arises a world literature.

The bourgeoisie, by the rapid improvement of all instruments of production, by the immensely facilitated means of communication, draws all, even the most barbarian, nations into civilisation. The cheap prices of its commodities are the heavy artillery with which it batters down all Chinese walls, with which it forces the barbarians' intensely obstinate hatred of foreigners to capitulate. It compels all nations, on pain of extinction, to adopt the bourgeois mode of production; it compels them to introduce what it calls civilisation into their midst, *i.e.*, to become bourgeois themselves. In one word, it creates a world after its own image.

The bourgeoisie has subjected the country to the rule of the towns. It has created enormous cities, has greatly increased the urban population as compared with the rural, and has thus rescued a considerable part of the population from the idiocy of rural life. Just as it has made the country dependent on the towns, so it has made barbarian and semi-barbarian countries dependent on the civilised ones, nations of peasants on nations of bourgeois, the East on the West.

The bourgeoisie keeps more and more doing away with the scattered state of the population, of the means of production, and of property. It has agglomerated population, centralised means of production, and has concentrated property in a few hands. The necessary consequence of this was political centralisation. Independent, or but loosely connected, provinces with separate interests, laws, governments and systems of taxation, became lumped together into one nation, with one government, one code of laws, one national class-interest, one frontier and one customs-tariff.

The bourgeoisie, during its rule of scarce one hundred years, has created more massive and more colossal productive forces than have all preceding generations together. Subjection of Nature's forces to man, machinery, application of chemistry to industry and agriculture, steam-navigation, railways, electric telegraphs, clearing of whole continents for cultivation, canalisation of rivers, whole populations conjured out of the ground—what earlier century had even a presentiment that such productive forces slumbered in the lap of social labour?

We see then: the means of production and of exchange, on whose foundation the bourgeoisie built itself up, were generated in feudal society. At a certain stage in the development of these means of production and of exchange, the conditions under which feudal society produced and exchanged, the feudal organisation of agriculture and manufacturing industry, in one word, the feudal relations of property became no longer compatible with the already developed productive forces; they became so many fetters. They had to be burst asunder; they were burst asunder.

Into their place stepped free competition, accompanied by a social and political constitution adapted to it, and by the economical and political sway of the bourgeois class.

A similar movement is going on before our own eyes. Modern bourgeois society with its relations of production, of exchange and of property, a society that has conjured up such gigantic means of production and of exchange, is like the sorcerer, who is no longer able to control the powers of the nether world whom he has called up by his spells. For many a decade past the history of industry and commerce is but the history of the revolt of modern productive forces against modern conditions of production, against the property relations that are the conditions for the existence of the bourgeoisie and of its rule. It is enough to mention the commercial crises that by their periodical return put on its trial, each time more threateningly, the existence of the entire bourgeois society.

In these crises a great part not only of the existing products, but also of the previously created productive forces, are periodically destroyed. In these crises there breaks out an epidemic that, in all earlier epochs, would have seemed an absurdity—the epidemic of over-production. Society suddenly finds itself put back into a state of momentary barbarism; it appears as if a famine, a universal war of devastation had cut off the supply of every means of subsistence; industry and commerce seem to be destroyed; and why? Because there is too much civilisation, too much means of subsistence, too much industry, too much commerce. The productive forces at the disposal of society no longer tend to further the development of the conditions of bourgeois property; on the contrary, they have become too powerful for these conditions, by which they are fettered, and so soon as they overcome these fetters, they bring disorder into the whole of bourgeois society, endanger the existence of bourgeois property. The conditions of bourgeois society are too narrow to comprise the wealth created by them. And how does the bourgeoisie get over these crises? On the one hand by enforced destruction of a mass of productive forces; on the other, by the conquest of new markets, and by the more thorough exploitation of the old ones. That is to say, by paving the way for more extensive and more destructive crises, and by diminishing the means whereby crises are prevented.

The weapons with which the bourgeoisie felled feudalism to the ground are now turned against the bourgeoisie itself.

But not only has the bourgeoisie forged the weapons that bring death to itself; it has also called into existence the men who are to wield those weapons—the modern working class—the proletarians.

In proportion as the bourgeoisie, *i.e.*, capital, is developed, in the same proportion is the proletariat, the modern working class, developed—a class of labourers, who live only so long as they find work, and who find work only so long as their labour increases capital. These labourers, who must sell themselves piecemeal, are a commodity, like every other article of commerce, and are consequently exposed to all the vicissitudes of competition, to all the fluctuations of the market.

Owing to the extensive use of machinery and to division of labour, the work of the proletarians has lost all individual character, and, consequently, all charm for the workman. He becomes an appendage of the machine, and it is only the most simple, most monotonous, and most easily acquired knack, that is required of him. Hence, the cost of production of a workman is restricted, almost entirely, to the means of subsistence that he requires for his maintenance, and for the propagation of his race. But the price of a commodity, and therefore also of labour, is equal to its cost of production. In proportion, therefore, as the repulsiveness of the work increases, the wage decreases. Nay more, in proportion as the use of machinery and division of labour increases, in the same proportion the burden of toil also increases, whether by prolongation of the working hours, by increase of the work exacted in a given time or by increased speed of the machinery, etc.

Modern industry has converted the little workshop of the patriarchal master into the great factory of the industrial capitalist. Masses of labourers, crowded into the factory, are organised like soldiers. As privates of the industrial army they are placed under the command of a perfect hierarchy of officers and sergeants. Not only are they slaves of the bourgeois class, and of the bourgeois State; they are daily and hourly enslaved by the machine, by the over-looker, and, above all, by the individual bourgeois manufacturer himself. The more openly this despotism proclaims gain to be its end and aim, the more petty, the more hateful and the more embittering it is.

The less the skill and exertion of strength implied in manual labour, in other words, the more modern industry becomes developed, the more is the labour of men superseded by that of women. Differences of age and sex have no longer any distinctive social validity for the working class. All are instruments of labour, more or less expensive to use, according to their age and sex.

No sooner is the exploitation of the labourer by the manufacturer, so far, at an end, that he receives his wages in cash, than he is set upon by the other portions of the bourgeoisie, the landlord, the shopkeeper, the pawnbroker, etc.

The lower strata of the middle class—the small tradespeople, shopkeepers, and retired tradesmen generally, the handicraftsmen and peasants—all these sink gradually into the proletariat, partly because their diminutive capital does not suffice for the scale on which Modern Industry is carried on, and is swamped in the competition with the large capitalists, partly because their specialised skill is rendered worthless by new methods of production. Thus the proletariat is recruited from all classes of the population.

The proletariat goes through various stages of development. With its birth begins its struggle with the bourgeoisie. At first the contest is carried on by individual labourers, then by the workpeople of a factory, then by the operatives of one trade, in one locality, against the individual bourgeois who directly exploits them. They direct their attacks not against the bourgeois conditions of production, but against the instruments of production themselves; they destroy imported wares that compete with their labour, they smash to pieces machinery, they set factories ablaze, they seek to restore by force the vanished status of the workman of the Middle Ages.

At this stage the labourers still form an incoherent mass scattered over the whole country, and broken up by their mutual competition. If anywhere they unite to form more compact bodies, this is not yet the consequence of their own active union, but of the union of the bourgeoisie, which class, in order to attain its own political ends, is compelled to set the whole proletariat in motion, and is moreover yet, for a time, able to do so. At this stage, therefore, the proletarians do not fight their enemies, but the enemies of their enemies, the remnants of absolute monarchy, the landowners, the nonindustrial bourgeois, the petty bourgeoisie. Thus the whole historical movement is concentrated in the hands of the bourgeoisie; every victory so obtained is a victory for the bourgeoisie.

But with the development of industry the proletariat not only increases in number; it becomes concentrated in greater masses, its strength grows, and it feels that strength more. The various interests and conditions of life within the ranks of the proletariat are more and more equalised, in proportion as machinery obliterates all distinctions of labour, and nearly everywhere reduces wages to the same low level. The growing competition among the bourgeois, and the resulting commercial crises, make the wages of the workers ever more fluctuating. The unceasing improvement of machinery, ever more rapidly developing, makes their livelihood more and more precarious; the collisions between individual workmen and individual bourgeois take more and more the character of collisions between two classes. Thereupon the workers begin to form combinations (Trades' Unions) against the bourgeois; they club together in order to keep up the rate of wages; they found permanent associations in order to make provision beforehand for these occasional revolts. Here and there the contest breaks out into riots.

Now and then the workers are victorious, but only for a time. The real fruit of their battles lies, not in the immediate result, but in the ever-expanding union of the workers. This union is helped on by the improved means of communication that are created by modern industry and that place the workers of different localities in contact with one another. It was just this contact that was needed to centralise the numerous local struggles, all of the same character, into one national struggle between classes. But every class struggle is a political struggle. And that union, to attain which the burghers of the Middle Ages, with their miserable highways, required centuries, the modern proletarians, thanks to railways, achieve in a few years.

This organisation of the proletarians into a class, and consequently into a political party, is continually being upset again by the competition between the workers themselves. But it ever rises up again, stronger, firmer, mightier. It compels legislative recognition of particular interests of the workers, by taking advantage of the divisions among the bourgeoisie itself. Thus the ten-hours' bill in England was carried.

Altogether collisions between the classes of the old society further, in many ways, the course of development of the proletariat. The bourgeoisie finds itself involved in a constant battle. At first with the aristocracy; later on, with those portions of the bourgeoisie itself, whose interests have become antagonistic to the progress of industry; at all times, with the bourgeoisie of foreign countries. In all these battles it sees itself compelled to appeal to the proletariat, to ask for its help, and thus, to drag it into the political arena. The bourgeoisie itself, therefore, supplies the proletariat with its own elements of political and general education, in other words, it furnishes the proletariat with weapons for fighting the bourgeoisie.

Further, as we have already seen, entire sections of the ruling

classes are, by the advance of industry, precipitated into the proletariat, or are at least threatened in their conditions of existence.
These also supply the proletariat with fresh elements of enlightenment and progress.

Finally, in times when the class struggle nears the decisive hour,
the process of dissolution going on within the ruling class, in fact
within the whole range of old society, assumes such a violent,
glaring character, that a small section of the ruling class cuts itself
adrift, and joins the revolutionary class, the class that holds the
future in its hands. Just as, therefore, at an earlier period, a section
of the nobility went over to the bourgeoisie, so now a portion of
the bourgeoisie goes over to the proletariat, and in particular, a
portion of the bourgeois ideologists, who have raised themselves to
the level of comprehending theoretically the historical movement
as a whole.

Of all the classes that stand face to face with the bourgeoisie
today, the proletariat alone is a really revolutionary class. The
other classes decay and finally disappear in the face of modern
industry; the proletariat is its special and essential product.

The lower middle class, the small manufacturer, the shopkeeper,
the artisan, the peasant, all these fight against the bourgeoisie, to
save from extinction their existence as fractions of the middle
class. They are therefore not revolutionary, but conservative. Nay
more, they are reactionary, for they try to roll back the wheel of
history. If by chance they are revolutionary, they are so only in
view of their impending transfer into the proletariat, they thus
defend not their present, but their future interests, they desert
their own standpoint to place themselves at that of the proletariat.

The "dangerous class," the social scum, that passively rotting
mass thrown off by the lowest layers of old society, may, here and
there, be swept into the movement by a proletarian revolution; its
conditions of life, however, prepare it far more for the part of a
bribed tool of reactionary intrigue.

In the conditions of the proletariat, those of old society at large
are already virtually swamped. The proletarian is without property;
his relation to his wife and children has no longer anything in
common with the bourgeois family relations; modern industrial
labour, modern subjection to capital, the same in England as in
France, in America as in Germany, has stripped him of every trace

of national character. Law, morality, religion, are to him so many bourgeois prejudices, behind which lurk in ambush just as many bourgeois interests.

All the preceding classes that got the upper hand, sought to fortify their already acquired status by subjecting society at large to their conditions of appropriation. The proletarians cannot become masters of the productive forces of society, except by abolishing their own previous mode of appropriation, and thereby also every other previous mode of appropriation. They have nothing of their own to secure and to fortify; their mission is to destroy all previous securities for, and insurances of, individual property.

All previous historical movements were movements of minorities, or in the interest of minorities. The proletarian movement is the self-conscious, independent movement of the immense majority, in the interest of the immense majority. The proletariat, the lowest stratum of our present society, cannot stir, cannot raise itself up, without the whole superincumbent strata of official society being sprung into the air.

Though not in substance, yet in form, the struggle of the proletariat with the bourgeoisie is at first a national struggle. The proletariat of each country must, of course, first of all settle matters with its own bourgeoisie.

In depicting the most general phases of the development of the proletariat, we traced the more or less veiled civil war, raging within existing society, up to the point where that war breaks out into open revolution, and where the violent overthrow of the bourgeoisie lays the foundation for the sway of the proletariat.

Hitherto, every form of society has been based, as we have already seen, on the antagonism of oppressing and oppressed classes. But in order to oppress a class, certain conditions must be assured to it under which it can, at least, continue its slavish existence. The serf, in the period of serfdom, raised himself to membership in the commune, just as the petty bourgeois, under the yoke of feudal absolutism, managed to develop into a bourgeois. The modern labourer, on the contrary, instead of rising with the progress of industry, sinks deeper and deeper below the conditions of existence of his own class. He becomes a pauper, and pauperism develops more rapidly than population and wealth. And here it becomes evident, that the bourgeoisie is unfit any longer to be the ruling class in society, and to impose its conditions of existence upon society as an over-riding law. It is unfit to rule because it is incompetent to assure an existence to its slave within his slavery, because it cannot help letting him sink into such a state, that it has to feed him, instead of being fed by him. Society can no longer live under this bourgeoisie, in other words, its existence is no longer compatible with society.

The essential condition for the existence, and for the sway of the bourgeois class, is the formation and augmentation of capital; the condition for capital is wage labour. Wage labour rests exclusively on competition between the labourers. The advance of industry, whose involuntary promoter is the bourgeoisie, replaces the isolation of the labourers, due to competition, by their revolutionary combination, due to association. The development of Modern Industry, therefore, cuts from under its feet the very foundation on which the bourgeoisie produces and appropriates products. What the bourgeoisie, therefore, produces, above all, is its own gravediggers. Its fall and the victory of the proletariat are equally inevitable.

"The Manifesto of 1957"

DECLARATION OF COMMUNIST AND WORKERS' PARTIES
OF SOCIALIST COUNTRIES

Representatives of the Albanian Party of Labor, the Bulgarian Communist Party, the Hungarian Socialist Workers' Party, the Vietnamese Working People's Party, the Socialist Unity Party of Germany, the Communist Party of China, the Korean Party of Labor, the Mongolian People's Revolutionary Party, the Polish

From *Declaration of the Twelve Communist and Workers' Parties, Meeting in Moscow, USSR, Nov. 14–16, 1957, on the Occasion of the Fortieth Anniversary of the Great October Revolution*. New York: New Century Publishers, 1957. By permission of New Century Publishers.

United Workers' Party, the Rumanian Workers' Party, the Communist Party of the Soviet Union and the Communist Party of Czechoslovakia discussed their relations, current problems of the international situation and the struggle for peace and socialism.

The exchange of opinions revealed identity of views of the parties on all the questions examined at the meeting and unanimity in their assessment of the international situation. In the course of the discussion the meeting also touched upon general problems of the international Communist movement. In drafting the declaration the participants in the meeting consulted with representatives of the fraternal parties in the capitalist countries. The fraternal parties not present at this meeting will assess and themselves decide what action they should take on the considerations expressed in the declaration.

I

The main content of our epoch is the transition from capitalism to socialism which was begun by the great October Socialist Revolution in Russia. Today more than a third of the population of the world—over 950,000,000 people—have taken the road of socialism and are building a new life. The tremendous growth of the forces of socialism has stimulated the rapid extension of the anti-imperialist national movement in the post-war period. During the last twelve years, besides the Chinese People's Republic, the Democratic Republic of Vietnam and the Korean People's Democratic Republic, over 700,000,000 people have shaken off the colonial yoke and established national independent states.

The peoples of the colonial and dependent countries, still languishing in slavery, are intensifying the struggle for national liberation. The progress of socialism and of the national liberation movement has greatly accelerated the disintegration of imperialism. With regard to the greater part of mankind imperialism has lost its one-time domination. In the imperialist countries society is rent by deep-going class contradictions and by antagonisms between those countries, while the working class is putting up increasing resistance to the policy of imperialism and the monopolies, fighting for better conditions, democratic rights, for peace and socialism.

In our epoch, world development is determined by the course and results of the competition between two diametrically opposed social systems. In the past forty years socialism has demonstrated that it is a much higher social system than capitalism. It has insured development of the productive forces at a rate unprecedented and impossible for capitalism, and the raising of the material and cultural levels of the working people.

The Soviet Union's strides in economics, science and technology and the results achieved by the other Socialist countries in Socialist construction are conclusive evidence of the great vitality of socialism. In the Socialist states the broad masses of the working people enjoy genuine freedom and democratic rights. People's power insures political unity of the masses, equality and friendship among the nations and a foreign policy aimed at preserving universal peace and rendering assistance to the oppressed nations in their emancipation struggle. The world Socialist system, which is growing and becoming stronger, is exerting ever greater influence upon the international situation in the interests of peace and progress and the freedom of the peoples.

While socialism is on the upgrade, imperialism is heading toward decline. The positions of imperialism have been greatly weakened as a result of the disintegration of the colonial system. The countries that have shaken off the yoke of colonialism are defending their independence and fighting for economic sovereignty, for international peace.

The existence of the Socialist system and the aid rendered by the Socialist nations to these countries on principles of equality and cooperation between them and the Socialist nations in the struggle for peace and against aggression help them to uphold their national freedom and facilitate their social progress.

In the imperialist countries the contradictions between the productive forces and production relations have become acute. In many respects modern science and engineering are not being used in the interests of social progress for all mankind, because capitalism fetters and deforms the development of the productive forces of society.

The world capitalist economy remains shaky and unstable. The relatively good economic activity still observed in a number of capitalist countries is due in large measure to the arms drive and other transient factors. However, the capitalist economy is bound to encounter deeper slumps and crises. The temporary high business activity helps to keep up the reformist illusions among part of the workers in the capitalist countries.

In the post-war period some sections of the working class in the more advanced capitalist countries, fighting against increased exploitation and for a higher standard of living, have been able to win certain wage increases, though in a number of these countries real wages are below the pre-war level. However, in the greater part of the capitalist world, particularly in the colonial and dependent countries, millions of working people still live in poverty. The broad invasion of agriculture by the monopolies and the price policy dictated by them, the system of bank credits and loans and the increased taxation caused by the arms drive have resulted in the steady ruin and impoverishment of the main mass of the peasantry.

There is a sharpening of contradiction, not only between the bourgeois and the working class but also between the monopoly bourgeoisie and all sections of the people, between the United States monopoly bourgeoisie on the one hand and the peoples, and even the bourgeoisie of the other capitalist countries on the other.

The working people of the capitalist countries live in such conditions that, increasingly, they realize that the only way out of their grave situation lies through socialism. Thus, increasingly favorable conditions are being created for bringing them into the active struggle for socialism.

The aggressive imperialist circles of the United States, by pursuing the so-called "positions of strength" policy, seek to bring most countries of the world under their sway and to hamper the onward march of mankind in accordance with the laws of social development. On the pretext of "combating communism," they are angling to bring more and more countries under their dominion, instigating destruction of democratic freedoms, threatening the national independence of the developed capitalist countries, trying to enmesh the liberated peoples in new forms of colonialism and systematically conducting subversive activities against the Socialist countries.

The policy of certain aggressive groups in the United States is aimed at rallying around them all the reactionary forces of the capitalist world. Acting in this way they are becoming the center of world reaction, the sworn enemies of the people. By this policy these anti-popular, aggressive imperialist forces are courting their own ruin, creating their own grave-diggers.

So long as imperialism exists there will always be soil for aggressive wars. Throughout the post-war years the American, British, French and other imperialists and their hirelings have conducted and are conducting wars in Indochina, Indonesia, Korea, Malaya, Kenya, Guatemala, Egypt, Algeria, Oman and Yemen.

At the same time the aggressive imperialist forces flatly refuse to cut armaments, to prohibit the use and production of atomic and hydrogen weapons, to agree on immediate discontinuation of the tests of these weapons; they are continuing the "cold war" and arms drive, building more military bases and conducting the aggressive policy of undermining peace and creating the danger of a new war. Were a world war to break out before agreement on prohibition of nuclear weapons is reached, it would inevitably become a nuclear war unprecedented in destructive force.

In West Germany militarism is being revived with United States help, giving rise to a hotbed of war in the heart of Europe. The struggle against West German militarism and revanchism, which are now threatening peace, is a vital task facing the peace-loving forces of the German people and all the nations of Europe. An especially big role in this struggle belongs to the German Democratic Republic—the first worker-peasant state in German history—with which the participants in the meeting express their solidarity and which they fully support.

Simultaneously the imperialists are trying to impose on the freedom-loving peoples of the Middle East the notorious "Eisenhower-Dulles Doctrine," thereby creating the danger of war in this area. They are plotting conspiracies and provocations against independent Syria. The provocations against Syria and Egypt and other Arab countries pursue the aim of dividing and isolating the Arab countries in order to abolish their freedom and independence.

The SEATO aggressive bloc is a source of war danger in East Asia.

The question of war or peaceful coexistence is now the crucial question of world policy. All the nations must display the utmost vigilance in regard to the war danger created by imperialism.

At present the forces of peace have so grown that there is a real possibility of averting wars, as was demonstrated by the collapse of the imperialist designs in Egypt. The imperialist plans to use the counter-revolutionary forces for the overthrow of the people's democratic system in Hungary have failed as well.

The cause of peace is upheld by the powerful forces of our era: the invincible camp of Socialist countries headed by the Soviet Union; the peace-loving countries of Asia and Africa taking an anti-imperialist stand and forming, together with the Socialist countries, a broad peace zone; the international working class and above all its vanguard, the Communist parties; the liberation movement of the peoples of the colonies and semi-colonies; the mass peace movement of the peoples; the peoples of the European countries who have proclaimed neutrality, the peoples of Latin America and the masses in the imperialist countries are putting up increasing resistance to the plans for a new war.

An alliance of these mighty forces could prevent war, but should the bellicose imperialist maniacs venture, regardless of anything, to unleash a war, imperialism will doom itself to destruction, for the peoples will not tolerate a system that brings them so much suffering and exacts so many sacrifices.

The Communist and Workers' parties taking part in the meeting declare that the Leninist principle of peaceful coexistence of the two systems, which has been further developed and brought up to date in the decisions of the Twentieth Congress of the Soviet Communist Party, is the sound basis of the foreign policy of the Socialist countries and the dependable pillar of peace and friendship among the peoples. The idea of peaceful coexistence coincides with the five principles advanced jointly by the Chinese People's Republic and the Republic of India and with the program adopted by the Bandung Conference of African-Asian countries. Peace and peaceful coexistence have now become the demands of the broad masses in all countries.

The Communist parties regard the struggle for peace as their foremost task. They will do all in their power to prevent war.

II

The meeting considers that in the present situation the strengthening of the unity and fraternal cooperation of the Socialist countries, the Communist and Workers' parties and the solidarity of the international working class, national liberation and democratic movements acquire special significance.

In the bedrock of the relations between the countries of the world Socialist system and all the Communist and Workers' parties lie the principles of Marxism-Leninism, the principles of proletarian internationalism which have been tested by life. Today the vital interests of the working people of all countries call for their support of the Soviet Union and all the Socialist countries who, pursuing a policy of preserving peace throughout the world, are the mainstay of peace and social progress. The working class, the democratic forces and the working people everywhere are interested in tirelessly strengthening fraternal contacts for the sake of the common cause, in safeguarding from enemy encroachments the historic political and social gains effected in the Soviet Union—the first and mightiest Socialist power—in the Chinese People's Republic and in all the Socialist countries, in seeing these gains extended and consolidated.

The Socialist countries base their relations on principles of complete equality, respect for territorial integrity, state independence and sovereignty and non-interference in one another's affairs. These are vital principles. However, they do not exhaust the essence of relations between them. Fraternal mutual aid is part and parcel of these relations. This aid is a striking expression of Socialist internationalism.

On a basis of complete equality, mutual benefit and comradely mutual assistance, the Socialist states have established between themselves extensive economic and cultural cooperation that plays an important part in promoting the economic and political independence of each Socialist country and the Socialist commonwealth as a whole. The Socialist states will continue to extend and improve economic and cultural cooperation among themselves.

The Socialist states also advocate all-round expansion of economic and cultural relations with all other countries, provided they desire it, on a basis of equality, mutual benefit and non-interference in each other's internal affairs.

The solidarity of the Socialist countries is not directed against any other country. On the contrary, it serves the interests of all the peace-loving peoples, restrains the aggressive strivings of the bellicose imperialist circles and supports and encourages the growing forces of peace. The Socialist countries are against the division of the world into military blocs. But in view of the situation that has taken shape, with the Western powers refusing to accept the proposals of the Socialist countries for mutual abolition of military

blocs, the Warsaw Pact Organization, which is of a defensive nature, serves the security of the peoples of Europe and supports
peace throughout the world, must be preserved and strengthened.

The Socialist countries are united in a single community by the
fact that they are taking the common Socialist road, by the common class essence of the social and economic system and state
authority, by the requirements of mutual aid and support, identity
of interests and aims in the struggle against imperialism, for the
victory of socialism and communism and by the ideology of Marxism-Leninism which is common to all.

The solidarity and close unity of the Socialist countries constitute a reliable guarantee of the sovereignty and independence of
each. Stronger fraternal relations and friendship between the Socialist countries call for a Marxist-Leninist internationalist policy
on the part of the Communist and Workers' Parties, for educating
all the working people in the spirit of combining internationalism
with patriotism and for a determined effort to overcome the survivals of bourgeois nationalism and chauvinism. All issues pertaining to relations between the Socialist countries can be fully settled
through comradely discussion, with strict observance of the principles of socialist internationalism.

III

The victory of socialism in the U.S.S.R. and progress in Socialist
construction in the People's Democracies find deep sympathy
among the working class and the working people of all countries.
The ideas of socialism are winning additional millions of people.
In these conditions the imperialist bourgeoisie attaches increasing
importance to the ideological molding of the masses; it misrepre-
sents socialism and smears Marxism-Leninism, misleads and con-
fuses the masses. It is a prime task to intensify Marxist-Leninist
education of the masses, combat bourgeois ideology, expose the
lies and slanderous fabrications of imperialist propaganda against
socialism and the Communist movement and widely propagate in
simple and convincing fashion the ideas of socialism, peace and
friendship among nations.

The meeting confirmed the identity of views of the Communist
and Workers' Parties on the cardinal problems of the Socialist
revolution and Socialist construction. The experience of the Soviet

Union and the other Socialist countries has fully borne out the correctness of the Marxist-Leninist proposition that the processes of the Socialist revolution and the building of socialism are governed by a number of basic laws applicable in all countries embarking on a socialist course. These laws manifest themselves everywhere, alongside a great variety of historic national peculiarities and traditions which must by all means be taken into account.

These laws are: Guidance of the working masses by the working class, the core of which is the Marxist-Leninist party in effecting a proletarian revolution in one form or another and establishing one form or other of the dictatorship of the proletariat; the alliance of the working class and the bulk of the peasantry and other sections of the working people; the abolition of capitalist ownership and the establishment of public ownership of the basic means of production; gradual Socialist reconstruction of agriculture; planned development of the national economy aimed at building socialism and communism, at raising the standard of living of the working people; the carrying out of the Socialist revolution in the sphere of ideology and culture and the creation of a numerous intelligentsia devoted to the working class, the working people and the cause of socialism; the abolition of national oppression and the establishment of equality and fraternal friendship between the peoples; defense of the achievements of socialism against attacks by external and internal enemies; solidarity of the working class of the country in question with the working class of other countries, that is, proletarian internationalism.

Marxism-Leninism calls for a creative application of the general principles of the Socialist revolution and Socialist construction depending on the concrete conditions of each country, and rejects mechanical imitation of the policies and tactics of the Communist parties of other countries.

Lenin repeatedly called attention to the necessity of correctly applying the basic principles of communism, in keeping with the specific features of the nation, of the national state concerned. Disregard of national peculiarities by the proletarian party inevitably leads to its divorce from reality, from the masses, and is bound to prejudice the cause of socialism and, conversely, exaggeration of the role of these peculiarities or departure, under the pretext of national peculiarities, from the universal Marxist-Leninist truth on the Socialist revolution and Socialist construction is just as harmful to the Socialist cause.

The participants in the meeting consider that both these tendencies should be combated simultaneously. The Communist and Workers' Parties of the Socialist countries should firmly adhere to the principle of combining the above universal Marxist-Leninist truth with the specific revolutionary practice in their countries, creatively apply the general laws governing the Socialist revolution and Socialist construction in accordance with the concrete conditions of their countries, learn from each other and share experience. Creative application of the general laws of Socialist construction tried and tested by experience and the variety of forms and methods of building socialism used in different countries, represent a collective contribution to Marxist-Leninist theory. . . .

Of vital importance in the present stage is intensified struggle against opportunist trends in the working class and Communist movement. The meeting underlines the necessity of resolutely overcoming revisionism and dogmatism in the ranks of the Communist and Workers' parties. . . .

IV

The Communist and Workers' Parties are faced with great historic tasks. . . .

The defense of peace is the most important world-wide task of the day. . . .

The working class and the peoples of many countries are still confronted with the historic tasks of struggle for national independence against colonial aggression and feudal oppression. What is needed here is a united anti-imperialist and anti-feudal front of the workers, peasants, urban petty bourgeoisie, national bourgeoisie and other patriotic democratic forces. Numerous facts show that the greater and stronger the unity of the various patriotic and democratic forces, the greater the guarantee of victory in the common struggle. . . .

In those capitalist countries where the American monopolies are out to establish their hegemony and in the countries already suffering from the U.S. policy of economic and military expansion, the objective conditions are being created for uniting, under the leadership of the working class and its revolutionary parties, broad sections of the population to fight for peace, the defense of national independence and democratic freedoms, to raise the standard of living, to carry through radical land reforms and to overthrow the rule of the monopolies who betray the national interests. . . .

The forms of the transition of socialism may vary for different countries. The working class and its vanguard—the Marxist-Leninist party—seek to achieve the Socialist revolution by peaceful means. This would accord with the interests of the working class and the people as a whole as well as with the national interests of the country.

Today in a number of capitalist countries the working class headed by its vanguard has the opportunity, given a united working-class and popular front or other workable forms of agreement and political cooperation between the different parties and public organizations, to unite a majority of the people, to win state power without civil war and ensure the transfer of the basic means of production to the hands of the people. It has this opportunity while relying on the majority of the people and decisively rebuffing the opportunist elements incapable of relinquishing the policy of compromise with the capitalists and landlords. The working class then, can defeat the reactionary, anti-popular forces, secure a firm majority in parliament, transform parliament from an instrument serving the class interests of the bourgeoisie into an instrument serving the working people, launch a non-parliamentary mass struggle, smash the resistance of the reactionary forces and create the necessary conditions for peaceful realization of the socialist revolution.

All this will be possible only by broad and ceaseless development of the class struggle of the workers, peasant masses and the urban middle strata against big monopoly capital, against reaction, for profound social reforms, for peace and socialism.

In the event of the ruling classes resorting to violence against people, the possibility of non-peaceful transition to socialism should be borne in mind. Leninism teaches, and experience confirms, that the ruling classes never relinquish power voluntarily. In this case the degree of bitterness and the forms of the class struggle will depend not so much on the proletariat as on the resistance put up by the reactionary circles to the will of the overwhelming majority of the people, on these circles using force at one or another stage of the struggle for socialism.

The possibility of one or another way to socialism depends on the concrete conditions in each country.

In the struggle for better conditions for the working people, for preservation and extension of democratic rights, winning and maintaining national independence and peace among nations, and also in the struggle for winning power and building socialism, the Communist Parties seek cooperation with the Socialist parties. Although the Right-Wing Socialist Party leaders are doing their best to hamper this cooperation, there are increasing opportunities for cooperation between the Communists and Socialists on many issues. The ideological differences between the Communist and the Socialist parties should not keep them from establishing unity of action on the many pressing issues that confront the working-class movement. . . .

The Communist and Workers' Parties have a particularly important responsibility with regard to the destinies of the world Socialist system and the International Communist movement. The Communist and Workers' Parties represented at the meeting declare that they will tirelessly promote their unity and comradely cooperation with a view to further consolidating the commonwealth of Socialist states and in the interests of the international working-class movement, of peace and socialism.

The meeting notes with satisfaction that the International Communist movement has grown, withstood numerous serious trials and won a number of major victories. By their deeds the Communists have demonstrated to the working people on a worldwide scale the vitality of the Marxist-Leninist theory and their ability not only to propagate the great ideals of socialism, but also to realize them in exceedingly strenuous conditions.

Like any progressive movement in human society, the Communist movement is bound to encounter difficulties and obstacles. However . . . contrary to the absurd assertions of imperialism about a so-called crisis of communism, the Communist movement is growing and gathering strength. . . .

"The Manifesto of 1960"

STATEMENT OF EIGHTY-ONE COMMUNIST
AND WORKERS' PARTIES

Representatives of the Communist and Workers' Parties have discussed at this Meeting urgent problems of the present international situation and of the further struggle for peace, national independence, democracy and socialism.

The Meeting has shown unity of views among the participants on the issues discussed. The Communist and Workers' Parties have unanimously reaffirmed their allegiance to the Declaration and Peace Manifesto adopted in 1957. These program documents of creative Marxism-Leninism determined the fundamental positions of the international Communist movement on the more important issues of our time and contributed in great measure toward uniting the efforts of the Communist and Workers' Parties in the struggle to achieve common goals. They remain the banner and guide to action for the whole of the international Communist movement.

The course of events in the past three years has demonstrated the correctness of the analysis of the international situation and the outlook for world development as given in the Declaration and Peace Manifesto, and the great scientific force and effective role of creative Marxism-Leninism.

The chief result of these years is the rapid growth of the might and international influence of the world socialist system, the vigorous process of disintegration of the colonial system under the

From *Statement of Eighty-one Communist and Workers' Parties Meeting in Moscow, USSR, 1960.* New York: New Century Publishers, 1961. By permission of New Century Publishers.

impact of the national-liberation movement, the intensification of class struggles in the capitalist world, and the continued decline and decay of the world capitalist system. The superiority of the forces of socialism over those of imperialism, of the forces of peace over those of war, is becoming ever more marked in the world arena.

Nevertheless, imperialism, which is intent on maintaining its positions, sabotages disarmament, seeks to prolong the cold war and aggravate it to the utmost, and persists in preparing a new world war. This situation demands ever closer joint efforts and resolute actions on the part of the socialist countries, the international working class, the national anti-imperialist movement, all peace-loving countries and all peace champions, to prevent war and assure a peaceful life for people. It demands the further consolidation of all revolutionary forces in the fight against imperialism, for national independence, and for socialism.

I

It is the principal characteristic of our time that the world socialist system is becoming the decisive factor in the development of society. . . .

Today it is the world socialist system and the forces fighting against imperialism, for a socialist transformation of society, that determine the main content, main trend and main features of the historical development of society. Whatever efforts imperialism makes, it cannot stop the advance of history. A reliable basis has been provided for further decisive victories for socialism. The complete triumph of socialism is inevitable. . . .

The world capitalist system is going through an intense process of disintegration and decay. Its contradictions have accelerated the development of monopoly capitalism into state-monopoly capitalism. By tightening the monopolies' grip on the life of the nation, state-monopoly capitalism closely combines the power of the monopolies with that of the state with the aim of saving the capitalist system and increasing the profits of the imperialist bourgeoisie to the utmost by exploiting the working class and plundering large sections of the population. . . .

The decay of capitalism is particularly marked in the United States of America, the chief imperialist country of today. U.S.

monopoly capital is clearly unable to use all the productive forces at its command. The richest of the developed capitalist countries of the world—the United States of America—has become a land of especially big chronic unemployment. Increasing under-capacity operation in industry has become permanent in that country. Despite the enormous increase in military appropriations, which is achieved at the expense of the standard of life of the working people, the rate of growth of production has been declining in the post-war years and has been barely above the growth of population. Over-production crises have become more frequent. The most developed capitalist country has become a country of the most distorted, militarized economy. More than any other capitalist country, the United States drains Asia, and especially Latin America, of their riches, holding up their progress. U.S. capitalist penetration into Africa is increasing. *U.S. imperialism has become the biggest international exploiter. . . . International developments in recent years have furnished many new proofs of the fact that U.S. imperialism is the chief bulwark of world reaction and an international gendarme, that it has become an enemy of the peoples of the whole world. . . .*

A new stage has begun in the development of the general crisis of capitalism. This is shown by the triumph of socialism in a large group of European and Asian countries embracing one-third of mankind, the powerful growth of the forces fighting for socialism throughout the world and the steady weakening of the imperialists' positions in the economic competition with socialism; the tremendous new upsurge of the national-liberation struggle and the mounting disintegration of the colonial system; the growing instability of the entire world economic system of capitalism; the sharpening contradictions of capitalism resulting from the growth of state-monopoly capitalism and militarism; the increasing contradictions between monopolies and the interests of the nation as a whole; the curtailment of bourgeois democracy and the tendency to adopt autocratic and fascist methods of government; and a profound crisis in bourgeois politics and ideology. . . .

II

A new stage has begun in the development of the world socialist system. The Soviet Union is successfully carrying on the full-scale construction of a communist society. Other countries of the socialist camp are successfully laying the foundations of socialism, and some of them have already entered the period of construction of a developed socialist society. . . .

Today the restoration of capitalism has been made socially and economically impossible not only in the Soviet Union, but in the other socialist countries as well. The combined forces of the socialist camp reliably safeguard every socialist country against encroachments by imperialist reaction. Thus the rallying of the socialist states in one camp and the growing unity and steadily increasing strength of this camp ensure complete victory for socialism within the entire system. . . .

The experience of development of the socialist countries is added evidence that mutual assistance and support, and utilization of all the advantages of unity and solidarity among the countries of the socialist camp, are a primary international condition for their achievements and successes. Imperialist, renegade and revisionist hopes of a split within the socialist camp are built on sand and doomed to failure. All the socialist countries cherish the unity of the socialist camp like the apple of their eye.

The world economic system of socialism is united by common socialist relations of production and is developing in accordance with the economic laws of socialism. Its successful development requires consistent application, in socialist construction, of the law of planned, proportionate development; encouragement of the creative initiative of the people; continuous improvement of the system of international division of labor through the co-ordination of national economic plans, specialization and co-operation in production within the world socialist system on the basis of voluntary participation, mutual benefit and vigorous improvement of the scientific and technological standard. It requires study of collective experience; extended co-operation and fraternal mutual assistance; gradual elimination, along these lines, of historical differences in the levels of economic development, and the provision of a material basis for a more or less simultaneous transition of all the peoples of the socialist system to communism.

Socialist construction in the various countries is a source of collective experience for the socialist camp as a whole. A thorough study of this experience by the fraternal parties, and its proper utilization and elaboration with due regard to specific conditions and national peculiarities are an immutable law of the development of every socialist country.

In developing industrial and agricultural production in their countries at a high rate in keeping with the possibilites they have, the Communist and Workers' Parties of the socialist countries consider it their internationalist duty to make full use of all the advantages of the socialist system and the internal resources of every country to carry out, by joint effort and as speedily as possible, the historic task of surpassing the world capitalist system in overall industrial and agricultural production and then outstrip the economically most developed capitalist countries in per capita output and in the standard of living. To carry out this task, it is necessary steadily to improve political and economic work, continuously to improve the methods of economic management and to run the socialist economy along scientific lines. This calls for higher productivity of labor to be achieved through continuous technical progress, economic planning, strict observance of the Leninist principle of providing material incentives and moral stimuli to work for the good of society by heightening the political consciousness of the people, and for control over the measure of labor and consumption.

To provide a material basis for the transition of the socialist countries to communism, it is indispensable to achieve a high level of production through the use of the latest techniques, electrification of the national economy, and mechanization and automation of production, without which it is impossible to provide the abundance of consumer goods required by a communist society. On this basis, it is necessary to develop communist social relations, vigorously promote the political consciousness of the people and educate the members of the new, communist society.

The socialist camp is a social, economic and political community of free and sovereign peoples united by the close bonds of international socialist solidarity, by common interests and objectives, and following the path of socialism and communism. It is an inviolable law of the mutual relations between socialist countries strictly to adhere to the principles of Marxism-Leninism and socialist internationalism. Every country in the socialist camp is ensured genuinely equal rights and independence. Guided by the principles of

complete equality, mutual advantage and comradely mutual assistance, the socialist states improve their all-round economic, political
and cultural co-operation, which meets both the interests of each
socialist country and those of the socialist camp as a whole.

One of the greatest achievements of the world socialist system is
the practical confirmation of the Marxist-Leninist thesis that
national antagonisms diminish with the decline of class antagonisms. In contrast to the laws of the capitalist system, which is
characterized by antagonistic contradictions between classes, nations and states leading to armed conflicts, there are no objective
causes in the nature of the socialist system for contradictions and
conflicts between the peoples and states belonging to it. Its development leads to greater unity among the states and nations and
to the consolidation of all the forms of co-operation between
them. Under socialism, the development of national economy,
culture and statehood goes hand in hand with the strengthening
and development of the entire world socialist system, and with an
ever greater consolidation of the unity of nations. The interests of
the socialist system as a whole and national interests are harmoniously combined. It is on this basis that the moral and political unity of all the peoples of the great socialist community has
arisen and has been growing. . . .

III

The problem of war and peace is the most burning problem of
our time.

War is a constant companion of capitalism. . . .

The peoples must now be more vigilant than ever. As long as
imperialism exists there will be soil for wars of aggression.

*The peoples of all countries know that the danger of a new
world war still persists. U.S. imperialism is the main force of aggression and war.* Its policy embodies the ideology of militant
reaction. The U.S. imperialists, together with the imperialists of
Britain, France and West Germany, have drawn many countries
into NATO, CENTO, SEATO and other military blocs under the
guise of combating the "communist menace"; it has enmeshed the
so-called "free world," that is, capitalist countries which depend
on them, in a network of military bases spearheaded first and
foremost against the socialist countries. . . .

The time has come when the attempts of the imperialist aggressors to start a world war can be curbed. World war can be prevented by the joint efforts of the world socialist camp, the international working class, the national-liberation movement, all the countries opposing war and all peace-loving forces.

The development of international relations in our day is determined by the struggle of the two social systems—the struggle of the forces of socialism, peace and democracy against the forces of imperialism, reaction and aggression—a struggle in which the superiority of the forces of socialism, peace and democracy is becoming increasingly obvious. . . .

The peace movement is the broadest movement of our time, involving people of diverse political and religious creeds, of diverse classes of society, who are all united by the noble urge to prevent new wars and to secure enduring peace.

Further consolidation of the world socialist system will be of prime importance in preserving durable peace. So long as there is no disarmament, the socialist countries must maintain their defence potential at an adequate level.

In the opinion of Communists the tasks which must be accomplished first of all if peace is to be safeguarded are to stop the arms race, ban nuclear weapons, their tests and production, dismantle foreign war bases and withdraw foreign troops from other countries, disband military blocs, conclude a peace treaty with Germany, turn West Berlin into a demilitarized free city, thwart the designs of the West-German revanchists, and prevent the revival of Japanese militarism. . . .

The Communist Parties regard the fight for peace as their prime task. They call on the working class, trade unions, co-operatives, women's and youth leagues and organizations, on all working people, irrespective of their political and religious convictions, firmly to repulse by mass struggles all acts of aggression on the part of the imperialists.

But should the imperialist maniacs start war, the peoples will sweep capitalism out of existence and bury it.

The foreign policy of the socialist countries rests on the firm foundation of the Leninist principle of peaceful coexistence and economic competition between the socialist and capitalist countries. In conditions of peace, the socialist system increasingly reveals its advantages over the capitalist system in all fields of economy, culture, science and technology. The near future will bring the forces of peace and socialism new successes. The U.S.S.R. will become the leading industrial power of the world. China will become a mighty industrial state. The socialist system will be turning out more than half the world industrial product. The peace zone will expand. The working-class movement in the capitalist countries and the national-liberation movement in the colonies and dependencies will achieve new victories. The disintegration of the colonial system will become completed. The superiority of the forces of socialism and peace will be absolute. *In these conditions a real possibility will have arisen to exclude world war from the life of society even before socialism achieves complete victory on earth, with capitalism still existing in a part of the world.* The victory of socialism all over the world will completely remove the social and national causes of all wars.

The Communists of all the world uphold peaceful coexistence unanimously and consistently, and battle resolutely for the prevention of war. The Communists must work untiringly among the masses to prevent underestimation of the possibility of averting a world war, underestimation of the possibility of peaceful coexistence and, at the same time, underestimation of the danger of war.

In a world divided into two systems, the only correct and reasonable principle of international relations is the principle of peaceful coexistence of states with different social systems advanced by Lenin and further elaborated in the Moscow Declaration and the Peace Manifesto of 1957, in the decisions of the 20th and 21st Congresses of the C.P.S.U., and in the documents of other Communist and Workers' Parties. . . .

The policy of peaceful coexistence is a policy of mobilizing the masses and launching vigorous action against the enemies of peace. Peaceful coexistence of states does not imply renunciation of the class struggle as the revisionists claim. The coexistence of states with different social systems is a form of class struggle between socialism and capitalism. In conditions of peaceful coexistence favorable opportunities are provided for the development of the class struggle in the capitalist countries and the national-liberation movement of the peoples of the colonial and dependent countries.

In their turn, the successes of the revolutionary class and national-liberation struggle promote peaceful coexistence. The Communists consider it their duty to fortify the faith of the people in the possibility of furthering peaceful coexistence, their determination to prevent world war. They will do their utmost for the people to weaken imperialism and limit its sphere of action by an active struggle for peace, democracy and national liberation.

Peaceful coexistence of countries with different social systems does not mean conciliation of the socialist and bourgeois ideologies. On the contrary, it implies intensification of the struggle of the working class, of all the Communist Parties, for the triumph of socialist ideas. But ideological and political disputes between states must not be settled through war. . . .

IV

National-liberation revolutions have triumphed in vast areas of the world. About forty new sovereign states have arisen in Asia and Africa in the fifteen post-war years. The victory of the Cuban revolution has powerfully stimulated the struggle of the Latin-American peoples for complete national independence. A new historical period has set in in the life of mankind: the peoples of Asia, Africa and Latin America that have won their freedom have begun to take an active part in world politics.

The complete collapse of colonialism is imminent. The breakdown of the system of colonial slavery under the impact of the national-liberation movement is a development ranking second in historic importance only to the formation of the world socialist system . . .

The United States is the mainstay of colonialism today. The imperialists, headed by the U.S.A., make desperate efforts to preserve colonial exploitation of the peoples of the former colonies by new methods and in new forms. . . .

The urgent tasks of national rebirth facing the countries that have shaken off the colonial yoke cannot be effectively accomplished unless a determined struggle is waged against imperialism and the remnants of feudalism by all the patriotic forces of the nations united in a single national-democratic front. The national democratic tasks on the basis of which the progressive forces of the nation can and do unite in the countries which have won their freedom, are: the consolidation of political independence, the carrying out of agrarian reforms in the interest of the peasantry, elimination of the survivals of feudalism, the uprooting of imperialist economic domination, the restriction of foreign monopolies and their expulsion from the national economy, the creation and development of a national industry, improvement of the living standard, the democratization of social life, the pursuance of an independent and peaceful foreign policy, and the development of economic and cultural co-operation with the socialist and other friendly countries.

The working class, which has played an outstanding role in the fight for national liberation, demands the complete and consistent accomplishment of the tasks of the national, anti-imperialist, democratic revolution, and resists reactionary attempts to check social progress.

The solution of the peasant problem, which directly affects the interests of the vast majority of the population, is of the utmost importance to these countries. Without radical agrarian reforms it is impossible to solve the food problem and sweep away the remnants of medievalism which fetter the development of the productive forces in agriculture and industry. The creation and extension on a democratic basis of the state sector in the national economy, particularly in industry, a sector independent from foreign monopolies and gradually becoming a determining factor in the country's economy, is of great importance in these countries.

The alliance of the working class and the peasantry is the most important force in winning and defending national independence, accomplishing far-reaching democratic transformations and ensuring social progress. This alliance is called upon to be the basis of a broad national front. The extent to which the national bourgeoisie participates in the liberation struggle also depends to no small degree upon its strength and stability. A big role can be played by the national-patriotic forces, by all elements of the nation prepared to fight for national independence, against imperialism. . . .

The Communist Parties are working actively for a consistent completion of the anti-imperialist, anti-feudal, democratic revolution, for the establishment of national democracies, for a radical improvement in the living standard of the people. They support those actions of national governments leading to the consolidation of the gains achieved and undermining the imperialists' positions. . . .

V

The new balance of world forces offers the Communist and Workers' Parties new opportunities of carrying out the historic tasks they face in the struggle for peace, national independence, democracy and socialism. . . .

The main blow in present conditions is directed with growing force at the capitalist monopolies, which are chiefly responsible for the arms race and which constitute the bulwark of reaction and aggression, at the whole system of state monopoly capitalism, which defends their interests. . . .

The working class, peasantry, intellectuals and the petty and middle urban bourgeoisie are vitally interested in the abolition of monopoly domination. Hence there are favorable conditions for rallying these forces.

Communists hold that this unity is quite feasible on the basis of the struggle for peace, national independence, the protection and extension of democracy, nationalization of the key branches of economy and democratization of their management, the use of the entire economy for peaceful purposes in order to satisfy the needs of the population, implementation of radical agrarian reforms, improvement of the living conditions of the working people, protection of the interests of the peasantry and the petty and middle urban bourgeoisie against the tyranny of the monopolies.

These measures would be an important step along the path of social progress and would meet the interests of the majority of the nation. All these measures are democratic by nature. They do not eliminate the exploitation of man by man. But if realized, they would limit the power of the monopolies, enhance the prestige and political weight of the working class in the country's affairs, help to isolate the most reactionary forces and facilitate the unification of all the progressive forces. As they participate in the fight for dramatic reforms, large sections of the population come to realize the necessity of unity of action with the working class and become more active politically. It is the prime duty of the working class and its Communist vanguard to head the economic and political struggle of the masses for democratic reforms, for the overthrow of the power of the monopolies, and assure its success.

Communists advocate general democratization of the economic and social scene and of all the administrative, political and cultural organizations and institutions.

Communists regard the struggle for democracy as a component of the struggle for socialism. In this struggle they continuously strengthen their bonds with the masses, increase their political consciousness and help them understand the tasks of the socialist revolution and realize the necessity of accomplishing it. This sets the Marxist-Leninist Parties completely apart from the reformists, who consider reforms within the framework of the capitalist system as the ultimate goal and deny the necessity of socialist revolution. Marxists-Leninists are firmly convinced that the peoples in the capitalist countries will in the course of their daily struggle ultimately come to understand that socialism alone is a real way out for them.

Now that more sections of the population are joining in an active class struggle, it is of the utmost importance that Communists should extend their work in trade unions and cooperatives, among the peasantry, the youth, the women, in sports organizations, and the unorganized sections of the population. There are new opportunities now to draw the younger generation into the struggle for peace and democracy, and for the great ideals of communism. Lenin's great behest—to go deeper into the masses, to work wherever there are masses, to strengthen the ties with the masses in order to lead them—must become a major task for every Communist Party. . . .

The decisive role in the struggle of the popular masses of capitalist countries for the accomplishment of their tasks is played by the alliance of the working class and the working peasantry, which represents the main motive force of social revolution.

The split in the ranks of the working class, which the ruling classes, the Right-wing Social-Democratic leadership and reactionary trade-union leaders are interested to maintain on a national and international scale, remains the principal obstacle to the accomplishment of the goals of the working class. Communists work resolutely to eliminate this spirit. . . .

The imperialist reactionaries, who seek to arouse distrust for the Communist movement and its ideology, continue to intimidate the masses by alleging that the Communists need wars between states to overthrow the capitalist system and establish a socialist system. The Communist Parties emphatically reject this slander. The fact that both world wars, which were started by the imperialists, ended in socialist revolutions by no means implies that the way to social revolution goes necessarily through world war, especially now that there exists a powerful world system of socialism. Marxists-Leninists have never considered that the way to social revolution lies through wars between states.

The choice of social system is the inalienable right of the people of each country. Socialist revolution is not an item of import and cannot be imposed from without. It is a result of the internal development of the country concerned, of the utmost sharpening of social contradictions in it. *The Communist Parties, which guide themselves by the Marxist-Leninist doctrine, have always been against the export of revolution. At the same time they fight resolutely against imperialist export of counter-revolution. They consider it their internationalist duty to call on the peoples of all countries to unite, to rally all their internal forces, to act vigorously and, relying on the might of the world socialist system, to prevent or firmly resist imperialist interference in the affairs of any people who have risen in revolution.*

The Marxist-Leninist Parties head the struggle of the working class, the masses of working people, for the accomplishment of the socialist revolution and the establishment of the dictatorship of the proletariat in one form or another. The forms and course of development of the socialist revolution will depend on the specific balance of the class forces in the country concerned, on the organization and maturity of the working class and its vanguard, and on the extent of the resistance put up by the ruling classes. Whatever form of dictatorship of the proletariat is established, it will always signify an extension of democracy, a transition from formal, bourgeois democracy to genuine democracy, to democracy for working people.

The Communist Parties reaffirm the propositions put forward by the Declaration of 1957 with regard to the forms of transition of different countries from capitalism to socialism. . . .

VI

The world Communist movement has become the most influential political force of our time, a most important factor in social progress. As it fights bitterly against imperialist reaction, for the interests of the working class and all working people, for peace, national independence, democracy and socialism, the Communist movement is making steady headway, is becoming consolidated and steeled.

There are now Communist Parties active in 87 countries of the world. Their total membership exceeds 36,000,000. This is a signal victory for Marxism-Leninism and a tremendous achievement of the working class. Like-minded Marxists are rallying in the countries which have shaken off colonial tyranny and taken the path of independent development. Communist Parties consider it their internationalist duty to promote friendship and solidarity between the working class of their countries and the working-class movement of the countries which have won their freedom in the common struggle against imperialism.

The growth of the Communist Parties and their organizational consolidation, the victories of the Communist Parties in a number of countries in the struggle against deviations, elimination of the harmful consequences of the personality cult, the greater influence of the world Communist movement open new prospects for the successful accomplishment of the tasks facing the Communist Parties.

Marxist-Leninist Parties regard it as an inviolable law of their activity steadfastly to observe the Leninist standards of Party life in keeping with the principle of democratic centralism; they consider that they must cherish Party unity like the apple of their eye, strictly to adhere to the principle of Party democracy and collective leadership, for they attach, in keeping with the organizational principles of Leninism, great importance to the role of the leading party bodies in the life of the Party, to work indefatigably for the strengthening of their bonds with the Party membership and with the broad masses of the working people, not to allow the personality cult, which shackles creative thought and initiative of Communists, vigorously to promote the activity of Communists, and to encourage criticism and self-criticism in their ranks.

The Communist Parties have ideologically defeated the revision-ists in their ranks who sought to divert them from the Marxist-Leninist path. Each Communist Party and the international Communist movement as a whole have become still stronger, ideologically and organizationally, in the struggle against revision-ism, Right-wing opportunism.

The Communist Parties have unanimously condemned the Yugoslav variety of international opportunism, a variety of modern revisionist "theories" in concentrated form. After betraying Marx-ism-Leninism, which they termed obsolete, the leaders of the League of Communists of Yugoslavia opposed their anti-Leninist revisionist program to the Declaration of 1957; they set the L.C.Y. against the international Communist movement as a whole, sev-ered their country from the socialist camp, made it dependent on so-called "aid" from U.S. and other imperialists, and thereby ex-posed the Yugoslav people to the danger of losing the revolu-tionary gains achieved through a heroic struggle. The Yugoslav revisionists carry on subversive work against the socialist camp and the world Communist movement. Under the pretext of an extra-bloc policy, they engage in activities which prejudice the unity of all the peace-loving forces and countries. Further exposure of the leaders of Yugoslav revisionists and active struggle to safeguard the Communist movement and the working-class movement from the anti-Leninist ideas of the Yugoslav revisionists, remains an essen-tial task of the Marxist-Leninist Parties.

The practical struggles of the working class and the entire course of social development have furnished a brilliant new proof of the great all-conquering power and vitality of Marxism-Leninism, and have thoroughly refuted all modern revisionist "theories."

The further development of the Communist and working-class movement calls, as stated in the Moscow Declaration of 1957, for continuing a determined struggle on two fronts—against revision-ism, which remains the main danger, and against dogmatism and sectarianism.

Revisionism, Right-wing opportunism, which mirrors the bour-geois ideology in theory and practice, distorts Marxism-Leninism, emasculates its revolutionary essence, and thereby paralyzes the revolutionary will of the working class, disarms and demobilizes the workers, the masses of the working people, in their struggle against oppression by imperialists and exploiters, for peace, democracy and national-liberation, for the triumph of socialism.

Dogmatism and sectarianism in theory and practice can also become the main danger at some stage of development of individual parties, unless combated unrelentingly. They rob revolutionary parties of the ability to develop Marxism-Leninism through scientific analysis and apply it creatively according to the specific conditions; they isolate Communists from the broad masses of the working people, doom them to passive expectation or Leftist, adventurist actions in the revolutionary struggle, prevent them from making a timely and correct estimate of the changing situation and of new experience, using all opportunities to bring about the victory of the working class and all democratic forces in the struggle against imperialism, reaction and war danger, and thereby prevent the peoples from achieving victory in their just struggle.

At a time when imperialist reaction is joining forces to fight communism it is particularly imperative vigorously to consolidate the world Communist movement. Unity and solidarity redouble the strength of our movement and provide a reliable guarantee that the great cause of communism will make victorious progress and all enemy attacks will be effectively repelled.

Communists throughout the world are united by the great doctrine of Marxism-Leninism and by a joint struggle for its realization. The interests of the Communist movement require solidarity in adherence by every Communist Party to the estimates and conclusions concerning the common tasks in the struggle against imperialism, for peace, democracy and socialism, jointly reached by the fraternal Parties at their meetings.

The interests of the struggle for the working-class cause demand ever closer unity of the ranks of each Communist Party and of the great army of Communists of all countries; they demand of them unity of will and action. It is the supreme internationalist duty of every Marxist-Leninist Party to work continuously for greater unity in the world Communist movement.

A resolute defence of the unity of the world Communist movement on the principles of Marxism-Leninism and proletarian internationalism, and the prevention of any actions which may undermine that unity, are a necessary condition for victory in the struggle for national independence, democracy and peace, for the successful accomplishment of the tasks of the socialist revolution and of the building of socialism and communism. Violation of these principles would impair the forces of communism.

All the Marxist-Leninist Parties are independent and have equal rights; they shape their policies according to the specific conditions in their respective countries and in keeping with Marxist-Leninist principles, and support each other. The success of the working-class cause in any country is unthinkable without the internationalist solidarity of all Marxist-Leninist parties. Every party is responsible to the working class, to the working people of its country, to the international working-class and Communist movement as a whole.

The Communist and Workers' Parties hold meetings whenever necessary to discuss urgent problems, to exchange experience, acquaint themselves with each other's views and positions, work out common views through consultations and co-ordinate joint actions in the struggle for common goals.

Whenever a Party wants to clear up questions relating to the activities of another fraternal Party, its leadership approaches the leadership of the Party concerned; if necessary, they hold meetings and consultations.

The experience and results of the meetings of representatives of the Communist Parties held in recent years, particularly the results of the two major meetings—that of November, 1957 and this Meeting—show that in present-day conditions such meetings are an effective form of exchanging views and experience, enriching Marxist-Leninist theory by collective effort and elaborating a common attitude in the struggle for common objectives.

The Communist and Workers' Parties unanimously declare that the Communist Party of the Soviet Union has been, and remains, the universally recognized vanguard of the world Communist movement, being the most experienced and steeled contingent of the international Communist movement. The experience which the C.P.S.U. had gained in the struggle for the victory of the working class, in socialist construction and in the full-scale construction of communism, is of fundamental significance for the whole of the world Communist movement. . . .

The Essence of Contemporary Communism

MILOVAN DJILAS[*]

1

None of the theories on the essence of contemporary Communism treats the matter exhaustively. Neither does this theory claim to do so. Contemporary Communism is the product of a series of historical, economic, political, ideological, national, and international causes. A categorical theory about its essence cannot be entirely accurate.

The essence of contemporary Communism could not even be perceived until, in the course of its development, it revealed itself to its very entrails. This moment came, and could only come, because Communism entered a particular phase of its development—that of its maturity. It then became possible to reveal the nature of its power, ownership, and ideology. In the time that Communism was developing and was predominantly an ideology, it was almost impossible to see through it completely.

Just as other truths are the work of many authors, countries, and movements, so it is with contemporary Communism. Communism has been revealed gradually, more or less parallel to its develop-

[*] A partisan hero of the anti-Nazi war and Vice President of Yugoslavia under the Tito regime, Mr. Milovan Djilas was expelled in January 1954 from the League of Communists, as the Yugoslav Communist Party is known, for having appealed for "democratization." Hailing the Hungarian uprising of 1956 as "the beginning of the end of Communism," he was sentenced to three years at hard labor in Mitrovica prison.

From *The New Class: An Analysis of the Communist System* by Milovan Djilas, selections from pp. 164–170. New York: Frederick A. Praeger, Inc., 1957. By permission of the publisher.

ment; it cannot be looked upon as final, because it has not completed its development.

Most of the theories regarding Communism, however, have some truth in them. Each of them has usually grasped one aspect of Communism or one aspect of its essence.

There are two basic theses on the essence of contemporary Communism.

The first of them claims that contemporary Communism is a type of new religion. We have already seen that it is neither a religion nor a church, in spite of the fact that it contains elements of both.

The second thesis regards Communism as revolutionary socialism, that is, something which was born of modern industry, or capitalism, and of the proletariat and its needs. We have seen that this thesis also is only partially accurate: contemporary Communism began in well-developed countries as a socialist ideology and a reaction against the suffering of the working masses in the industrial revolution. But after having come into power in underdeveloped areas, it became something entirely different—an exploiting system opposed to most of the interests of the proletariat itself.

The thesis has also been advanced that contemporary Communism is only a contemporary form of despotism, produced by men as soon as they seize power. The nature of the modern economy, which in every case requires centralized administration, has made it possible for this despotism to be absolute. This thesis also has some truth in it: modern Communism is a modern despotism which cannot help but aspire toward totalitarianism. However, all types of modern despotism are not variants of Communism, nor are they totalitarian to the degree that Communism is.

Thus whatever thesis we examine, we find that each thesis explains one aspect of Communism, or a part of the truth, but not the entire truth.

Neither can my theory on the essence of Communism be accepted as complete. This is, anyway, the weakness of every definition, especially when such complex and living matters as social phenomena are being defined.

Nevertheless, it is possible to speak in the most abstract theoretical way about the essence of contemporary Communism, about what is most essential in it, and what permeates all its manifestations and inspires all of its activity. It is possible to penetrate deeper into this essence, to elucidate its various aspects; but the essence itself has already been exposed.

Communism, and likewise its essence, is continuously changing from one form to another. Without this change it cannot even exist. Consequently, these changes require continuous examination and a deeper study of the already obvious truth.

The essence of contemporary Communism is the product of particular conditions, historical and others. But as soon as Communism becomes strong, the essence itself becomes a factor and creates the conditions for its own continued existence. Consequently, it is evident that it is necessary to examine the essence separately according to the form and the conditions in which it appears and is operating at a given moment.

2

The theory that contemporary Communism is a type of modern totalitarianism is not only the most widespread, but also the most accurate. However, an actual understanding of the term "modern totalitarianism" where Communism is being discussed is not so widespread.

Contemporary Communism is that type of totalitarianism which consists of three basic factors for controlling the people. The first is power; the second, ownership; the third, ideology. They are monopolized by the one and only political party, or— according to my previous explanation and terminology—by a new class; and, at present, by the oligarchy of that party or of that class. No totalitarian system in history, not even a contemporary one— with the exception of Communism—has succeeded in incorporating simultaneously all these factors for controlling the people to this degree.

When one examines and weighs these three factors, power is the one which has played and still continues to play the most important role in the development of Communism. One of the other factors may eventually prevail over power, but it is impossible to determine this on the basis of present conditions. I believe that power will remain the basic characteristic of Communism.

Communism first originated as an ideology, which contained in its seed Communism's totalitarian and monopolistic nature. It can certainly be said that ideas no longer play the main, predominant role in Communism's control of the people. Communism as an ideology has mainly run its course. It does not have many new things to reveal to the world. This could not be said for the other two factors, power and ownership.

It can be said: power, either physical, intellectual, or economic, plays a role in every struggle, even in every social human action. There is some truth in this. It can also be said: in every policy, power, or the struggle to acquire and keep it, is the basic problem and aim. There is some truth in this also. But contemporary Communism is not only such a power; it is something more. It is power of a particular type, a power which unites within itself the control of ideas, authority, and ownership, a power which has become an end in itself.

To date, Soviet Communism, the type which has existed the longest and which is the most developed, has passed through three phases. This is also more or less true of other types of Communism which have succeeded in coming to power (with the exception of the Chinese type, which is still predominantly in the second phase).

The three phases are: revolutionary, dogmatic, and non-dogmatic Communism. Roughly speaking, the principal catchwords, aims, and personalities corresponding to these various phases are: Revolution, or the usurpation of power—Lenin. "Socialism," or the building of the system—Stalin. "Legality," or stabilization of the system—"collective leadership."

It is important to note that these phases are not distinctly separate from one another, that elements of all are found in each. Dogmatism abounded, and the "building of socialism" had already begun, in the Leninist period; Stalin did not renounce revolution, or reject the dogmas, which interfered with the building of the system. Present-day, non-dogmatic Communism is only non-dogmatic conditionally; it just will not renounce even the minutest practical advantages for dogmatic reasons. Precisely because of such advantages, it will at the same time be in a position to persecute unscrupulously the minutest doubt concerning the truth or purity of the dogma. Thus, Communism, proceeding from practical needs and capabilities, has today even furled the sails of revolution, or of its own military expansion. But it has not renounced one or the other.

This division into three phases is only accurate if it is taken roughly and abstractly. Clearly separate phases do not actually exist, nor do they correspond to specific periods in the various countries.

The boundaries between the phases, which overlap, and the forms in which the phases appear are varied in different Communist countries. For example, Yugoslavia has passed through all three phases in a relatively short time and with the same personalities at the summit. This is obvious in both precepts and method of operation.

Power plays a major role in all three of these phases. In the revolution it was necessary to seize power; in the building of socialism, it was necessary to create a new system by means of that power; today power must preserve the system.

During the development, from the first to the third phase, the quintessence of Communism—power—evolved from being the means and became an end in itself. Actually power was always more or less the end, but Communist leaders, thinking that through power as a means they would attain the ideal goal, did not believe it to be an end in itself. Precisely because power served as a means for the Utopian transformation of society, it could not avoid becoming an end in itself and the most important aim of Communism. Power was able to appear as a means in the first and second phases. It can no longer be concealed that in the third phase power is the actual principal aim and essence of Communism.

Because of the fact that Communism is being extinguished as an ideology, it must maintain power as the main means of controlling the people.

In revolution, as in every type of war, it was natural to concentrate primarily on power: the war had to be won. During the period of industrialization, concentrating on power could still be considered natural: the construction of industry, or a "socialist society," for which so many sacrifices had been made, was necessary. But as all this is being completed, it becomes apparent that in Communism power has not only been a means but that it has also become the main, if not the sole, end.

Today power is both the means and the goal of Communists, in order that they may maintain their privileges and ownership. But since these are special forms of power and ownership, it is only through power itself that ownership can be exercised. Power is an end in itself and the essence of contemporary Communism. Other classes may be able to maintain ownership without a monopoly over power, or power without a monopoly over ownership. Until now, this has not been possible for the new class, which was formed through Communism; it is very improbable that it will be possible in the future.

Throughout all three of these phases, power has concealed itself as the hidden, invisible, unspoken, natural and principal end. Its role has been stronger or weaker depending on the degree of control over the people required at the time. In the first phase, ideas were the inspiration and the prime mover for the attainment of power; in the second phase, power operated as the whip of society and for its own maintenance; today, "collective ownership" is subordinated to the impulses and needs of power.

Power is the alpha and the omega of contemporary Communism, even when Communism strives to prevent this.

Ideas, philosophical principles and moral considerations, the nation and the people, their history, in part even ownership—all can be changed and sacrificed. But not power. Because this would signify Communism's renunciation of itself, of its own essence. Individuals can do this. But the class, the party, the oligarchy cannot. This is the purpose and the meaning of its existence.

Every type of power besides being a means is at the same time an end—at least for those who aspire to it. Power is almost exclusively an end in Communism, because it is both the source and the guarantee of all privileges. By means of and through power the material privileges and ownership of the ruling class over national goods are realized. Power determines the value of ideas, and suppresses or permits their expression.

It is in this way that power in contemporary Communism differs from all other types of power, and that Communism itself differs from every other system.

The Importance of Doctrine

R. N. CAREW HUNT[*]

The term ideology is one which is more often used than defined. As the present study will be concerned with what the Russian Communists, and Communists in general, mean by it, a definition taken from a Soviet source is in order. The *Filosoficheskii Slovar* (Philosophical Dictionary, 1954 ed.), calls ideology "a system of definite views, ideas, conceptions and notions adhered to by some class or political party," and goes on to say that it is always "a reflection of the economic system predominant at any given time." In a class-divided society the ideology will be that of one or another of the struggling classes, but under socialism, when there is no longer any class division, it will be that of society as a whole. A quotation from Lenin is added to the effect that there can be no "middle way" between the ideology of the bourgeoisie and that of the proletariat. The one is false and the other true.

Such a summation, albeit neat, is not altogether satisfactory. Broadly speaking, Marx was right in contending that the ideology of a society—the complex of ideas which determine its "way of life"—will be that of its dominant class, that is, of those whose abilities (whether used rightly or wrongly is irrelevant in this context) have raised them above the common herd. But this sociological fact applies equally to the Soviet Union, where the party

* Formerly on the faculty of St. Antony's College, Oxford University, Mr. Carew Hunt is the author of *Calvin* (1933), *The Theory and Practice of Communism* (1957), *Marxism: Past and Present* (1954), and A *Guide to Communist Jargon* (1957).

From "The Importance of Doctrine" by R. N. Carew Hunt, *Problems of Communism*, Washington, D.C., Vol. VII, No. 2, March–April 1958, selections from pp. 10–15. Reprinted by permission.

certainly constitutes such a class and indeed is assigned the duty of fertilizing the masses with its ideas. Undoubtedly the current Soviet ideology is intended to strengthen the party and reinforce its claim to rule. But one must probe further to explain why the party should have adopted the particular body of doctrine that it has. The fact is that the ideology has been largely determined by the type of collective society which has been established in the Soviet Union.

The authors of the October Revolution were Marxists, and were thus committed to abolishing the capitalist system and replacing it by a nationwide planned economy. For a brief period the experiment of allowing the workers to take charge was tried out, but, when this led to chaos, the party assumed control and has ever since retained it.

If a Communist regime is to be set up in a backward country, the first prerequisite, as Lenin saw, is industrialization; this is likely to be carried out as rapidly as possible since the quicker the country is developed, and particularly its war potential, the stronger will be the position of its rulers. The execution of such a program of necessity demands the centralization of power in the hands of a small group of leaders, along with the adoption of such unpopular measures as the fixing of wages, the direction of labor and the prohibition of strikes. And as large-scale planning geared to an expanding economy is impracticable if the plan is liable to be upset at any moment by a vote in a popular assembly, it is not to be expected that the planners will long tolerate any opposition. Furthermore, they will be tempted to interfere in one branch of human activity after another, seeing that all can be so manipulated as to assist the execution of their grand design.

All this has happened in the Soviet Union, and the outcome has been an ideology which derives from the logic of collectivism. Its basic principles are to be found in Marx's revolutionary doctrine, the implications of which were spelled out by Lenin and Stalin when confronted with the practical problem of setting up the type of social order Marx had advocated. Communist literature and propaganda have made us familiar with the doctrine, and there is no need to analyze it here even if space permitted. The issue to be decided is what role ideology plays today, and how far it influences Soviet policy.

Myths and the Masses

Virtually all analysts would agree that in the years of struggle before the October Revolution the Bolsheviks took the theory which lay behind their movement in deadly earnest; there is also general agreement that in the 1920's the doctrine acted as a stimulus to the workers, who took pride in building up their country. In the 1930's, however, the situation changed. Stalin assumed absolute power. The machinery of the state and of the secret police was greatly strengthened, and all prospect of establishing a genuine classless society disappeared. With the Stalin-Hitler Pact, if not before, the Soviet Union entered an era which can plausibly be represented as one of naked power politics, perpetuated after World War II in the aggressive and obstructive policies pursued by the regime. Hence it is sometimes argued that Communist ideology has now ceased to possess any importance; that it is simply a top-dressing of sophistries designed to rationalize measures inspired solely by Soviet interests; and that apart from a few fanatics, such as may be found in any society, no one believes in the doctrine any longer, least of all the leaders themselves.

Yet such unqualified assertions are erroneous. Consider, first, the outlook of the ordinary Soviet citizen *vis-à-vis* the ideology. Day in, day out, he is subjected to intensive and skillfully devised propaganda through every known medium, designed to demonstrate that the ideology on which the Soviet Union is based makes it the best of all possible worlds, and that on this account it is encircled with jealous enemies bent on its destruction. The Soviet leadership has always considered it essential that every citizen possess as deep an understanding of Communist principles as his mind is capable of assimilating, and those holding positions of consequence are obliged recurrently to pass through carefully graded schools of political instruction.

It is significant that whenever the leaders feel themselves in a tight corner—as in the recent aftermath of destalinization and the intervention in Hungary—their invariable reaction is to intensify indoctrination in an attempt to refocus public attention on "first principles." As hard-headed men they would certainly not attach such importance to indoctrination if they did not know that it paid dividends—and experience has proved that the persistent repetition of a body of ideas which are never challenged is bound to influence the minds of their recipients. Of course, the present generation does not react to the formal ideology with the same fervor as did its forebears who made the revolution, and there are doubtless those who view official apologetics with a large degree of cynicism. But between total commitment and total disillusionment there are many intermediate positions; it is quite possible for a man to regard much of what he is told as nonsense while still believing that there is something of value behind it, especially if he identifies that "something" with the greatness of his country as "the first socialist state" and believes in its historic mission.

Leadership Credence—a Hope or a Habit?

More significant, in the present context, than the attitude of the ordinary citizen is that of the ruling elite which is responsible for policy. What its top-ranking members believe is a question which no one, of course, can answer positively. But before surmising, as do some analysts, that the Soviet leadership cannot possibly believe in the myths it propounds, we should remind ourselves that no class or party ever finds it difficult to persuade itself of the soundness of the principles on which it bases its claim to rule.

The Soviet leaders are fortified in this conviction by the very nature of their creed. They have been nurtured in it from birth, and it would be strange indeed if they had remained unaffected. It has become second nature to these men to regard history as a dialectical process—one of incessant conflict between progressive and reactionary forces which can only be resolved by the victory of the former. The division of the world into antagonistic camps, which is an article of faith, is simply the projection onto the international stage of the struggle within capitalistic society between the bourgeoisie, which history has condemned, and the proletariat, whose ultimate triumph it has decreed. The leaders seem to be confident that history is on their side, that all roads lead to communism, and that the contradictions of capitalism must create the type of situation which they can turn to their advantage.

Democratic governments desirous of recommending a certain

policy normally dwell upon its practical advantages. But in the Soviet Union this is not so. Any important change of line will be heralded by an article in *Pravda,* often of many columns, purporting to show that the new policy is ideologically correct because it accords with some recent decision of a party congress, or with Lenin's teaching, or with whatever other criterion may be adopted. How far the policy in question will have been inspired by considerations of ideology as opposed to others of a more mundane nature can never be precisely determined. This, however, is not an exclusive feature of the Communist system; in politics, as for that matter in personal relations, it is seldom possible to disentangle all the motives which determine conduct. The policies of any party or government are likely to reflect its political principles even if they are so framed as to strengthen its position, and there is no reason why the policies adopted by the Soviet leaders should constitute an exception.

Analysts of the "power politics" school of thought hold that the Kremlin leaders are concerned solely with Soviet national interest, and merely use the Communist movement to promote it. Yet here again the difficulty is to disengage factors which are closely associated. The future of the Communist movement cannot be disassociated from the fortunes of the Soviet Union. If the Soviet regime were to collapse, that movement would count for little, and whether it would long survive even in China is doubtful. Recognizing this, non-Russian Communist parties generally have remained subservient to Moscow even when threatened with large-scale defections of rank-and-file members in the face of particularly odious shifts in the Moscow line.

The "Separate Paths" Issue

The quarrel between the Soviet and the Yugoslav Communist parties—which an intergovernmental agreement of June 1956 has failed to resolve—is a good example of the interpenetration of ideological and non-ideological factors in policy determinations. The immediate occasion of the quarrel was Tito's unwillingness to allow the spread of Soviet influence through the presence of Soviet military officers and technological experts on Yugoslav soil. As a result Stalin determined to crush Tito, and resorted to various political and economic measures in an unsuccessful attempt to do so. It was at least a year before the struggle was extended to the ideological plane. But that it should have been was inevitable. One may well sympathize with Tito's desire for independence and hope that other national leaders will follow his example. Yet from the Communist point of view, if the movement is to be an international one, it must have an international center, and upon historical grounds alone Moscow has a strong claim to the mantle. Ever since Communist parties were formed, it was in fact to Moscow that their internal disputes were referred for settlement, just as it was Moscow which directed their general policy. Whether this role was performed well or ill is beside the point.

Hence the principle of "separate paths to socialism," approved by the Twentieth CPSU Congress for tactical reasons, is one which Moscow can accept only with reservations. If it merely means that in establishing communism in a given country consideration must be given to local conditions, and that every country's experience adds to the common store, then it is not only unobjectionable but is a salutary corrective to the earlier dogmatism which insisted on the universal applicability of the Russian experience. Such is the attitude nowadays expressed by Soviet theoreticians, though they insistently stress the dangers of exaggerating the importance of national characteristics, denying "the common laws of socialist development," or playing down the October Revolution. The official Soviet position is best expressed in an article in *New Times*, March 1956, which states that "while *serving as an example* to other working class parties, the CPSU *draws upon their experience and formulates it in general theoretical principles* for the benefit of all working class parties."

Clearly the Soviet leaders are on the defensive in this matter. They recognize that concessions must be made, but will make no more than they can help. The desire to perpetuate their own power doubtless influences their stand, but considering the fact that communism professes to be a world movement, it would be unreasonable to conclude that either national or personal interests are the sole factors motivating them.

Inefficiency—an Index of Ideology

Indeed, if the analysis given earlier in this article of the genesis of the Communist ideology is correct, the attitude of the Soviet leaders *must* be attributed, at least in part, to the theoretical principles which distinguish Communist regimes from other forms of dictatorship. Certainly the leaders shape and phrase their domestic and foreign policies to fit the general framework established by these principles, and the latter often do not allow much room for maneuver. In fact, their application may sometimes weaken rather than strengthen the country.

To take a simple example, much waste would be avoided if small traders were permitted to operate on a profit basis; the fishmonger, for instance, would have an incentive to put his fish on ice, which he frequently fails to do to the discomfort of the public. Allowance of profits, however, would constitute a return to private enterprise, which cannot be tolerated.

Similarly, in the Communist view it has long been regarded as indefensible to subordinate a higher to a lower form of socialized enterprise. Thus, while it has been apparent for years that Soviet agriculture would be more efficient if the Machine Tractor Stations were handed over to the collective farms, the issue has been consistently dodged, because the MTS are fully state-owned organs and therefore "higher" than the farms, which still belong in part to the peasants. When the economist Venzher advocated this measure some years ago, he was slapped down at once by Stalin, the fact that it had already been adopted in Yugoslavia only making his suggestion the more objectionable. Just two years ago Khrushchev launched an extensive program to strengthen the organization and power of the MTS. Very recently, however, he indicated that the regime was—at long last—prepared to yield to practical necessity on this point; in a speech on farm policy, he advocated the transfer of farm machinery to the collectives, and although his proposals are not yet legalized, it would appear that a number of MTS have already been dissolved.*

The principle of hierarchy has not been repudiated, however, and still governs other aspects of agricultural organization—for example, the relative status of the two forms of agricultural enter-

* Ed. note: By virtue of a law of the Supreme Soviet of the U.S.S.R. of March 31, 1958, the MTS (*Mashinno-Traktornye Stantsii*: Machine and Tractor Stations) sold their stock to the *kolkhozy* (collective farms). Some of the MTS continue to operate as repair shops and trade centers for gasoline and spare parts. These are now known as RTS (*Remontno-Tekhnicheskie Stantsii*: Technical-Repair Stations).

prise. From the standpoint of productive efficiency the collective farms are bad, but the state farms are worse. Nonetheless, the latter represent a "higher type" of organization, and thus the present virgin lands campaign has been based upon them.

Dogmatism in Foreign Policy

The same point can be scored by examining the Soviet Union's treatment of its satellites. Poland affords a good example. With the country at its mercy after World War II, the Soviet regime decided, among other measures, to integrate the Polish economy with its own. Now had Poland been regarded merely as a colony to be exploited, the operation would have been viewed primarily as a business proposition, and due attention would have been paid to such questions as the nature of the country's resources and the aptitudes of its people. The need to proceed with caution was very evident. The traditional hostility of the Poles to everything Russian should have been taken into account, as well as the fact that the Polish Communist Party had no public support (due in part to the liquidation of its established leaders during the Great Purges). Yet it was decided that the country must pass through, in shorter time intervals, precisely those stages of development which the Soviet Union had traversed. The result was a serious disruption of the economy through the erection of a top-heavy industrial structure on the basis of a depressed agriculture. This policy cannot be attributed to Stalin alone as it was continued after his death. It proved disastrous, and is only intelligible on the assumption that it was primarily motivated by ideological considerations.

The argument can be carried further. By its behavior throughout its history, the Soviet Union has incurred the hostility, or at least the suspicion, of the entire free world. Yet there was no practical reason why it should have done so. After the October Revolution the Bolshevik regime was faced with appalling domestic problems, and it had nothing to gain by courting the animosity of the West. The Soviet leaders might well have built up their country in accordance with the principles to which they were committed without exciting such widespread hostility. What governments do at home is commonly regarded as their own affair. Fundamentally, the regime in Yugoslavia is as Communist as that of the Soviet Union, and was established with an equal ruthlessness. But Tito, having asserted his independence from Moscow, has muffled his attacks on the West, and in turn the Western governments have demonstrated their desire—albeit tempered with caution—to believe in his good faith.

What no country will tolerate is the attempt, deliberately engineered by a foreign power, to overthrow its form of government; this has been the persistent aim and effort of the Soviet regime in defiance of its express diplomatic guarantees of non-interference. It is hard to see how this strategy has assisted the development of Soviet Russia, and that it has never been abandoned cannot be dissociated from those messianic and catastrophic elements in the Communist creed which influence, perhaps impel, the Soviet drive for world power.

In conclusion, it is frequently stated that communism has created an ideological cleavage between the West and the Soviet bloc. Yet this statement would be meaningless if the issue today were, as some believe, simply one of power politics. An ideology is significant only if it makes those who profess it act in a way they would not otherwise do. The fact that large numbers of persons accept communism would not constitute a danger if it did not lead them to support policies which threaten the existence of those who do not accept it. It is true that many people, especially in backward countries, call themselves Communists without having any clear idea of what it means. Yet the movement would not be the force it has become were there not in every country men and women who sincerely believe in the ideas behind it, which form collectively what we call its ideology.

To represent this ideology as a species of opium with which the Soviet leaders contrive to lull the people while taking care never to indulge in it themselves is to attribute to them an ability to dissociate themselves from the logic of their system—an ability which it is unlikely they possess. For the concepts which make up that system, fantastic as many of them appear to be, will be found on examination to be interrelated, and to be logical extensions of the basic principles to which all Communists subscribe.

To turn it the other way around, Communists claim a theoretical justification for the basic principles in which they believe. But these principles must be translated into appropriate action; and action, if directed by the rulers of a powerful country like the Soviet Union, will take the form of *Realpolitik*. There is no yardstick which permits a measure of the exact relationship between power politics and ideology in the policies which result; but surely neither factor can be ignored.

· 3 ·

THE PROGRAM OF THE COMMUNIST PARTY OF THE SOVIET UNION

The Third Program of the Communist Party of the Soviet Union was adopted in October 1961 by the Twenty-second Congress of the Party. As a doctrinal manifesto it reflects to a large extent Nikita S. Khrushchev's emergence as the ideological interpreter and political leader of world Communism.

By its timing the Program was intended to serve simultaneously as a review and restatement of Marxist-Leninist theory and practice, a rationalization of current domestic and international policies, a blueprint for future action, a guide for the world Communist movement, and an introduction to the Twenty-Year Plan for economic development. The last-named is designed to bring about the attainment of the first phase of Communism in the U.S.S.R. by 1980.

Although the Third Program reiterates the aspirations and illusions of the ideological stereotypes included in the first (1903) and second (1919) Party programs, it also incorporates many of the doctrinal innovations associated with the Khrushchev era. Thus it includes the doctrine of peaceful coexistence, denying implicitly the validity of the traditional Leninist assumptions on the inevitability of war. Describing the feasibility of "peaceful and parliamentary roads to socialism," the Program places special emphasis on the new concept of "national democracy" as a path to socialism in countries permitting the participation of Communists in coalition governments.

While the characteristics of the first phase of Communism are defined in relatively concrete terms, the Program leaves the functions traditionally attributed to the Soviet state and Party basically unchanged. The coming era of economic well-being notwithstanding, the state is not expected to "wither away" until the complete victory of Communism over capitalism "in the international arena." Nevertheless, says the Program, the Soviet state is no longer a dictatorship of the proletariat but a state in the service of a classless society made possible by the "full and irrevocable" establishment of socialism in the U.S.S.R. In such a state, the Program emphasizes, the dictatorship and its "coercive organs" can gradually give way to "Communist self-government which will embrace the Soviet trade unions, cooperatives, and other mass organizations of the people."

In spite of this change in the official view of the Soviet state, the supremacy of the Party has been neither challenged nor diminished. On the contrary, the "need for a further enhancement of the role and importance of the Party as the leading and guiding force of Soviet society" has been re-emphasized.

In the second article of this section Professor Rudolf Schlesinger analyzes the historical and international aspects of the Third Program and the assumptions underlying its conceptions of Communism.

The Road to Utopia:

THE THIRD PROGRAM OF
THE SOVIET COMMUNIST PARTY

Introduction

The Great October Socialist Revolution ushered in a new era in the history of mankind, the era of the downfall of capitalism and the establishment of communism. Socialism has triumphed in the

From *Program of the Communist Party of the Soviet Union.* (Adopted by the Twenty-second Congress of the C.P.S.U., October 31, 1961), selections from pp. 7–142. New York: Crosscurrents Press, Inc., 1961. Reprinted by permission.

Soviet Union and has achieved decisive victories in the People's Democracies; socialism has become the practical cause of hundreds of millions of people, and the banner of the revolutionary movement of the working class throughout the world. . . .

Today the Communist Party of the Soviet Union (C.P.S.U.) is adopting its third Program, a program for the building of communist society. The new Program is a constructive generalization of the experience of socialist development, it takes account of the experience of the revolutionary movement throughout the world and, giving expression to the collective opinion of the Party, defines the main tasks and principal stages of communist construction.

The supreme goal of the Party is to build a communist society on whose banner will be inscribed: "From each according to his ability, to each according to his needs." The Party's motto, "Everything for the sake of man, for the benefit of man," will be put into effect in full. . . .

PART ONE *The Transition from Capitalism to Communism Is the Road of Human Progress*

I. THE HISTORICAL NECESSITY OF THE TRANSITION
FROM CAPITALISM TO SOCIALISM

The epoch-making turn of mankind from capitalism to socialism, initiated by the October Revolution, is a natural result of the development of society. Marxism-Leninism discovered the objective laws of social development and revealed the contradictions inherent in capitalism, the inevitability of their bringing about a revolutionary explosion and of the transition of society to communism.

Capitalism is the last exploiting system. Having developed its productive forces to an enormous extent, it became a tremendous obstacle to social progress. Capitalism alone is responsible for the fact that the twentieth century, a century of colossal growth of the productive forces and of great scientific progress, has not yet put an end to the poverty of hundreds of millions of people, has not provided an abundance of material and spiritual values for all men on earth. The growing conflict between productive forces and production relations imperatively demands that mankind should break the decayed capitalist shell, release the powerful productive forces created by man and use them for the good of society as a whole. . . .

Capitalism had entered its final stage, the stage of monopoly capitalism, of imperialism. . . . Imperialism is decaying and moribund capitalism; it is the eve of the socialist revolution. *The world capitalist system as a whole is ripe for the social revolution of the proletariat.*

II. THE HISTORIC SIGNIFICANCE OF THE OCTOBER REVOLUTION AND OF THE VICTORY OF SOCIALISM IN THE U.S.S.R.

The Great October Revolution breached the imperialist front in Russia, one of the world's largest countries, firmly established the dictatorship of the proletariat and created a new type of state—the Soviet socialist state, and a new type of democracy—democracy for the working people.

Workers' and peasants' power, born of the revolution, took Russia out of the bloodbath of the imperialist war, saved her from the national catastrophe to which the exploiting classes had doomed her, and delivered her peoples from the danger of enslavement by foreign capital.

The October Revolution undermined the economic basis of a system of exploitation and social injustice. Soviet power nationalized industry, the railways, banks, and the land. It abolished the landlord system and fulfilled the peasants' age-long dream of land.

The October Revolution smashed the chains of national oppression; it proclaimed and put into effect the right of nations to self-determination, up to and including the right to secede. The Revolution completely abolished the social-estate and class privileges of the exploiters. For the first time in history, it emancipated women and granted them the same rights as men.

The socialist revolution in Russia shook the entire structure of world capitalism to its very foundations; the world split into two opposing systems. . . .

What are the principal lessons to be learned from the experience of the Soviet people?

Soviet experience has shown that the peoples are able to achieve socialism only as a result of *the socialist revolution and the establishment of the dictatorship of the proletariat*. . . .

Soviet experience has fully borne out the Marxist-Leninist theory that *the Communist Party plays a decisive role* in the formation and development of socialist society. Only a party that steadfastly pursues a class, proletarian policy, and is equipped with progressive, revolutionary theory, only a party solidly united and closely linked with the masses, can organize the people and lead them to the victory of socialism.

Soviet experience has shown that fidelity *to the principles of Marxism-Leninism, of proletarian internationalism*, their firm and unswerving implementation and defense against all enemies and opportunists, are imperative conditions for the victory of socialism.

The world's greatest revolution and the socialist reorganization of society, which has attained unprecedented heights in its development and prosperity, have confirmed in practice *the historical truth of Leninism* and have delivered a crushing blow to social-reformist ideology.

As a result of the devoted labor of the Soviet people and the theoretical and practical activities of the Communist Party of the Soviet Union, *there exists in the world a socialist society that is a reality and a science of socialist construction that has been tested in practice. The highroad to socialism has been paved*. Many peoples are already marching along it, and it will be taken sooner or later by all peoples.

III. THE WORLD SOCIALIST SYSTEM*

The Soviet Union is not pursuing the tasks of communist construction alone but in fraternal community with the other socialist countries.

The defeat of German fascism and Japanese militarism in the Second World War, in which the Soviet Union played the decisive part, created favorable conditions for the overthrow of capitalist and landlord rule by the peoples in a number of European and Asian countries. . . .

A new form of political organization of society, *people's democracy*, a variety of the dictatorship of the proletariat, emerged. It

* Ed. note: See also pp. 79–81, 88–91.

reflected the distinctive development of socialist revolution at a time when imperialism had been weakened and the balance of forces had tilted in favor of socialism. It also reflected the distinctive historical and national features of the various countries.

There emerged a world socialist system, a social, economic and political community of free sovereign peoples pursuing the socialist and communist path, united by an identity of interests and goals and the close bonds of international socialist solidarity. . . .

The world socialist system is *a new type of economic and political relationship between countries.* The socialist countries have the same type of economic basis—social ownership of means of production; the same type of political system—rule of the people with the working class at their head; a common ideology—Marxism-Leninism; common interests in the defense of their revolutionary gains and national independence from encroachments by the imperialist camp; and a great common goal—communism. This socioeconomic and political community constitutes the objective groundwork for lasting and friendly inter-governmental relations within the socialist camp. The distinctive features of the relations existing between the countries of the socialist community are complete equality, mutual respect for independence and sovereignty and fraternal mutual assistance and cooperation. In the socialist camp or, which is the same thing, in the world community of socialist countries, none have, nor can have, any special rights or privileges. . . .

IV. CRISIS OF WORLD CAPITALISM*

Imperialism has entered the period of decline and collapse. An inexorable process of decay has seized capitalism from top to bottom—its economic and political system, its politics and ideology. Imperialism has forever lost its power over the bulk of mankind. The main content, main trend and main features of the historical development of mankind are being determined by the world socialist system, by the forces fighting against imperialism, for the socialist reorganization of society. . . .

The economic and with it the political and military center of imperialism, has shifted from Europe to the United States. U.S. monopoly capital, gorged on war profits and the arms race, has

* Ed. note: See also pp. 76–78.

seized the most important sources of raw materials, the markets and the spheres of investment, has built up a unique kind of colonial empire and become the biggest *international exploiter*. Taking cover behind spurious professions of freedom and democracy, U.S. imperialism is in effect performing the function of *world gendarme*, supporting reactionary dictatorial regimes and decayed monarchies, opposing democratic, revolutionary changes and launching aggressions against peoples fighting for independence.

The U.S. monopoly bourgeoisie is the mainstay of international reaction. . . .

V. THE INTERNATIONAL REVOLUTIONARY MOVEMENT OF THE WORKING CLASS*

The international revolutionary movement of the working class has achieved epoch-making victories. *Its chief gain is the world socialist system.* The example of victorious socialism is revolutionizing the minds of the working people of the capitalist world; it inspires them to fight against imperialism and greatly facilitates their struggle.

Social forces that are to ensure the victory of socialism are taking shape, multiplying and becoming steeled in the womb of capitalist society. . . .

The world situation today is more favorable to the working class movement. . . .

General democratic struggles against the monopolies do not delay the socialist revolution but bring it nearer. *The struggle for democracy is a component of the struggle for socialism. . . .*

The working class and its vanguard—the Marxist-Leninist parties—seek to accomplish the socialist revolution *by peaceful means.* This would meet the interests of the working class and the people as a whole, it would accord with the national interests of the country. . . .

Where the exploiting classes resort to violence against the people, the possibility of a *non-peaceful transition to socialism* should be borne in mind. Leninism maintains, and historical experience confirms, that the ruling classes do not yield power of their own free will. . . .

The success of the struggle which the working class wages for

* Ed. note: See also pp. 99–102.

the victory of the revolution will depend on how well the working class and its party master the use of *all forms* of struggle—peaceful and non-peaceful, parliamentary and extra-parliamentary—and how well they are prepared for any swift and sudden replacement of one form of struggle by another form of struggle. While the principal law-governed processes of the socialist revolution are common to all countries, the diversity of the national peculiarities and traditions that have arisen in the course of history creates specific conditions for the revolutionary process, the variety of forms and rates of the proletariat's advent to power. This predetermines the possibility and necessity, in a number of countries, of *transition stages* in the struggle for the dictatorship of the proletariat, and a *variety of forms* of political organization of the society building socialism. But whatever the form in which the transition from capitalism to socialism is effected, that transition can come about only through revolution. However varied the forms of a new, people's state power in the period of socialist construction, their essence will be the same—*dictatorship of the proletariat*, which represents genuine democracy, democracy for the working people. . . .

Overcoming the split in its ranks is an important condition for the working class to fulfil its historic mission. No bastion of imperialism can withstand a closely-knit working class that exercises unity of action. The Communist parties favor cooperation with the Social-Democratic parties. . . .*

At the same time Communists criticize the ideological positions and Right-wing opportunist practice of Social-Democracy and expose the Right Social-Democratic leaders, who have sided openly with the bourgeoisie and renounced the traditional socialist demands of the working class. . . .

The Communist movement grows and becomes steeled as it fights against various opportunist trends. Revisionism, Right opportunism, which is a reflection of bourgeois influence, is the chief danger within the Communist movement today. . . . The revisionists deny the historical necessity of the socialist revolution and of the dictatorship of the proletariat. They deny the leading role of the Marxist-Leninist party, undermine the foundations of proletarian internationalism, and drift to nationalism. The ideology of

* Ed. note: See also pp. 85, 97.

revisionism is most fully embodied in the program of the League of Communists of Yugoslavia.

Another danger is dogmatism and sectarianism, which cannot be reconciled with a creative development of revolutionary theory, which lead to the dissociation and isolation of Communists from the masses, doom them to passive expectation or incite them to Leftist adventurist actions in the revolutionary struggle, and hinder a correct appraisal of the changing situation and the use of new opportunities for the benefit of the working class and all democratic forces. Dogmatism and sectarianism, unless steadfastly combated, can also become the chief danger at particular stages in the development of individual parties. . . .

VI. THE NATIONAL-LIBERATION MOVEMENT*

The world is experiencing a period of stormy national-liberation revolutions. Imperialism suppressed the national independence and freedom of the majority of the peoples and put the fetters of brutal colonial slavery on them, but *the rise of socialism marks the advent of the era of emancipation of the oppressed peoples.* . . .

Consistent struggle against imperialism is a paramount condition for the solution of national tasks. Imperialism seeks to retain one-time colonies and semi-colonies within the system of capitalist economy and perpetuate their underprivileged position in it. *U.S. imperialism is the chief bulwark of modern colonialism.* . . .

A national-liberation revolution does not end with the winning of political independence. Independence will be unstable and will become fictitious unless the revolution brings about radical changes in the social and economic spheres and solves the pressing problems of national rebirth.

The working class is the most consistent fighter for the consummation of this revolution, for national interests and social progress. . . .

In many countries, the liberation movement of the peoples that have awakened proceeds under the flag of nationalism. Marxist-Leninists draw a distinction between the nationalism of oppressed nations and that of the oppressor nations. The nationalism of an oppressed nation contains a *general democratic element* directed

* Ed. note: See also pp. 94–96.

against oppression, and Communists support it because they consider it historically justified at a given stage. That element finds expression in the striving of the oppressed peoples to free themselves from imperialist oppression, to gain national independence and bring about a national renascence. But the nationalism of an oppressed nation has yet another aspect, one expressing the ideology and interests of the reactionary exploiting top stratum. . . .

The C.P.S.U. considers fraternal alliance with the people who have thrown off the colonial or semi-colonial yoke to be a cornerstone of its international policy. This alliance is based on the common vital interests of world socialism and the world national-liberation movement. The C.P.S.U. regards it as its internationalist duty to assist the peoples who have set out to win and strengthen their national independence, all peoples who are fighting for the complete abolition of the colonial system.

VII. THE STRUGGLE AGAINST BOURGEOIS
AND REFORMIST IDEOLOGY

A grim struggle is going on between two ideologies—communist and bourgeois—in the world today. . . . *Bourgeois ideology is experiencing a grave crisis* . . . The chief ideological and political weapon of imperialism is *anti-communism*, which consists mainly in slandering the socialist system and distorting the policy and objectives of the Communist parties and Marxist-Leninist theory. . . .

VIII. PEACEFUL COEXISTENCE AND THE
STRUGGLE FOR WORLD PEACE*

The C.P.S.U. considers that the chief aim of its foreign-policy activity is to provide peaceful conditions for the building of a communist society in the U.S.S.R. and developing the world socialist system, and together with the other peace-loving peoples to deliver mankind from a world war of extermination. . . .

The issue of war and peace is the principal issue of today. Imperialism is the only source of the war danger. . . . *The main thing is to ward off a thermonuclear war, to prevent it from breaking out.* This can be done by the present generation. . . .

* Ed. note: See also pp. 78–79, 91–94, 480–491.

Socialism has offered mankind the only reasonable principle of maintaining relations between states at a time when the world is divided into two systems—the principle of the peaceful coexistence of states with different social systems, put forward by Lenin.

Peaceful coexistence of the socialist and capitalist countries is an *objective necessity* for the development of human society. *War cannot and must not serve as a means of settling international disputes.* Peaceful coexistence or disastrous war—such is the alternative offered by history. Should the imperialist aggressors nevertheless venture to start a new world war, the peoples will no longer tolerate a system which drags them into devastating wars. They will sweep imperialism away and bury it.

Peaceful coexistence implies renunciation of war as a means of settling international disputes, and their solution by negotiation; equality, mutual understanding and trust between countries; consideration for each other's interests; non-interference in internal affairs; recognition of the right of every people to solve all the problems of their country by themselves; strict respect for the sovereignty and territorial integrity of all countries; promotion of economic and cultural cooperation on the basis of complete equality and mutual benefit.

Peaceful coexistence serves as a basis for the peaceful competition between socialism and capitalism on an international scale and constitutes a specific form of class struggle between them. As they consistently pursue the policy of peaceful coexistence, the socialist countries are steadily strengthening the positions of the world socialist system in its competiton with capitalism. Peaceful coexistence affords more favorable opportunity for the struggle of the working class in the capitalist countries and facilitates the struggle of the peoples of the colonial and dependent countries for their liberation. Support for the principle of peaceful coexistence is also in keeping with the interests of that section of the bourgeoisie which realizes that a thermonuclear war would not spare the ruling classes of capitalist society either. The policy of peaceful coexistence is in accord with the vital interests of all mankind, except the big monopoly magnates and the militarists.

The Soviet Union has consistently pursued, and will continue to pursue, the policy of the peaceful coexistence of states with different social systems.

PART TWO *The Tasks of the Communist Party of the Soviet Union in Building a Communist Society*

COMMUNISM—THE BRIGHT FUTURE OF ALL MANKIND

The building of a communist society has become an immediate practical task for the Soviet people. The gradual development of socialism into communism is an objective law; it has been prepared by the development of Soviet socialist society throughout the preceding period.

What is communism?

Communism is a classless social system with one form of public ownership of the means of production and full social equality of all members of society; under it, the all-round development of people will be accompanied by the growth of the productive forces through continuous progress in science and technology; all the springs of cooperative wealth will flow more abundantly, and the great principle "From each according to his ability, to each according to his needs" will be implemented. Communism is a highly organized society of free, socially conscious working people in which public self-government will be established, a society in which labor for the good of society will become the prime vital requirement of everyone, a necessity recognized by one and all, and the ability of each person will be employed to the greatest benefit of the people.

A high degree of communist consciousness, industry, discipline, and devotion to the public interest are qualities typifying the man of communist society.

Communism ensures the continuous development of social production and rising labor productivity through rapid scientific and technological progress; it equips man with the best and most powerful machines, greatly increases his power over nature and enables him to control its elemental forces to an ever greater extent. The social economy reaches the highest stage of planned organization, and the most effective and rational use is made of the material wealth and labor reserves to meet the growing requirements of the members of society.

Under communism there will be no classes, and the socio-economic and cultural distinctions, and differences in living conditions, between town and countryside will disappear; the countryside will rise to the level of the town in the development of the productive forces and the nature of work, the forms of production relations, living conditions and the well-being of the population. With the victory of communism mental and physical labor will merge organically in the production activity of people. The intelligentsia will no longer be a distinct social stratum. Workers by hand will have risen in cultural and technological standards to the level of workers by brain. . . .

In defining the basic tasks to be accomplished in building a communist society, the Party is guided by Lenin's great formula: *"Communism is Soviet power plus the electrification of the whole country."*

The C.P.S.U. being a party of scientific communism, proposes and fulfills the tasks of communist construction in step with the preparation and maturing of the material and spiritual prerequisites, considering that it would be wrong to jump over necessary stages of development, and that it would be equally wrong to halt at an achieved level and thus check progress. The building of communism must be carried out by successive stages.

In the current decade (1961–70) the Soviet Union, in creating the material and technical basis of communism, will surpass the strongest and richest capitalist country, the U.S.A., in production per head of population; the people's standard of living and their cultural and technical standards will improve substantially; everyone will live in easy circumstances; all collective and state farms will become highly productive and profitable enterprises; the demand of Soviet people for well-appointed housing will, in the main, be satisfied; hard physical work will disappear; the U.S.S.R. will have the shortest working day.

The material and technical basis of communism will be built up by the *end of the second decade* (1971–80), ensuring an abundance of material and cultural values for the whole population; Soviet society will come close to a stage where it can introduce the principle of distribution according to needs, and there will be a gradual transition to one form of ownership—public ownership. Thus, *a communist society will in the main be built in the*

U.S.S.R. The construction of communist society will be fully completed in the subsequent period. . . .

I. THE TASKS OF THE PARTY IN THE ECONOMIC FIELD
AND IN THE CREATION AND PROMOTION
OF THE MATERIAL AND TECHNICAL
BASIS OF COMMUNISM

The main economic task of the Party and the Soviet people is to create *the material and technical basis of communism* within two decades. This means complete electrification of the country and perfection on this basis of techniques, technologies, and organization of social production in all the fields of the national economy; comprehensive mechanization of production operations and a growing degree of their automation; widespread use of chemistry in the national economy; vigorous development of new, economically effective branches of production, new types of power and new materials; all-round and rational utilization of natural, material and labor resources; organic fusion of science and production, and rapid scientific and technical progress; a high cultural and technical level for the working people; and substantial superiority over the more developed capitalist countries in productivity of labor, which constitutes the most important prerequisite for the victory of the communist system. . . .

II. THE TASKS OF THE PARTY IN IMPROVING
THE LIVING STANDARD OF THE PEOPLE

The heroic labor of the Soviet people has produced a powerful and versatile economy. There is now every possibility to improve rapidly the living standards of the entire population—the workers, peasants, and intellectuals. The C.P.S.U. sets the historically important task of *achieving in the Soviet Union a living standard higher than that of any of the capitalist countries*.

This task will be effected by: (a) raising individual payment according to the quantity and quality of work done, coupled with reduction of retail prices and abolition of taxes paid by the population; (b) increase of the public consumption fund intended for the satisfaction of the requirements of members of society irrespective of the quantity and quality of their labor, that is, free of charge (education, medical treatment, pensions, maintenance of children at children's institutions, transition to cost-free use of public amenities, etc.). . . .

III. THE TASKS OF THE PARTY IN THE SPHERES
OF STATE DEVELOPMENT AND THE FURTHER
PROMOTION OF SOCIALIST DEMOCRACY

The dictatorship of the proletariat, born of the socialist revolution, played an epoch-making role by ensuring the victory of socialism in the U.S.S.R. In the course of socialist construction, however, it underwent changes. After the exploiting classes had been abolished, the function of suppressing their resistance ceased to exist. The chief functions of the socialist state—organization of the economy, culture and education—developed in full measure. The socialist state entered a new period of its development. The state began to grow over into a nation-wide organization of the working people of socialist society. Proletarian democracy was growing more and more into a socialist democracy of the people as a whole.

The working class is the only class in history that does not aim to perpetuate its power. Having brought about the complete and final victory of socialism—the first phase of communism—and the transition of society to the full-scale construction of communism, the dictatorship of the proletariat has fulfilled its historic mission and has ceased to be indispensable in the U.S.S.R. from the point of view of the tasks of internal development. The state, which arose as a state of the dictatorship of the proletariat, has in the new, contemporary stage, become a state of the entire people, an organ expressing the interests and will of the people as a whole. Since the working class is the foremost and best organized force of Soviet society, it plays a leading role also in the period of the full-scale construction of communism. The working class will have completed its role of leader of society after communism is built and classes disappear.

The Party holds that the dictatorship of the working class will cease to be necessary before the state withers away. The state as an organization of the entire people will survive until the complete victory of communism. Expressing the will of the people, it must organize the building up of the material and technical basis of communism, and the transformation of socialist relations into communist relations, must exercise control over the measure of work and the measure of consumption, promote the people's welfare, protect the rights and freedoms of Soviet citizens, socialist law and order and socialist property, instill in the people conscious discipline and a communist attitude to labor, guarantee the defense and security of the country, promote fraternal cooperation with the socialist countries, uphold world peace, and maintain normal relations with all countries.

All-round extension and perfection of socialist democracy, active participation of all citizens in the administration of the state, in the management of economic and cultural development, improvement of the government apparatus, and increased control over its activity by the people constitute the main direction in which socialist statehood develops in the period of building of communism. As socialist democracy develops, the organs of state power will gradually be transformed into organs of public self-government. The Leninist principle of democratic centralism, which ensures the proper combination of centralized leadership with the maximum encouragement of local initiative, the extension of the rights of the Union republics and greater creative activity of the masses, will be promoted. It is essential to strengthen discipline, constantly control the activities of all the sections of the administrative apparatus, check the execution of the decisions and laws of the Soviet state and heighten the responsibility of every official for the strict and timely implementation of these laws. . . .

IV. THE TASKS OF THE PARTY IN THE FIELD OF NATIONAL RELATIONS

Under socialism the nations flourish and their sovereignty grows stronger. The development of nations does not proceed along lines of strengthening national strife, national narrow-mindedness and egoism, as it does under capitalism, but along lines of their association, fraternal mutual assistance and friendship. . . .

Obliteration of distinctions between classes and the development of communist social relations make for a greater social homogeneity of nations and contribute to the development of common communist traits in their culture, morals and way of living, to a further strengthening of their mutual trust and friendship.

With the victory of communism in the U.S.S.R., the nations will draw still closer together, their economic and ideological unity will increase and the communist traits common to their spiritual make-up will develop. However, the obliteration of national distinctions, and especially of language distinctions, is a considerably longer process than the obliteration of class distinctions.

The Party approaches all questions of national relationships arising in the course of communist construction from the standpoint of proletarian internationalism and firm pursuance of the Leninist nationalities policy. The Party neither ignores nor over-accentuates national characteristics.

The Party sets the following tasks in the sphere of national relations:

(a) to continue the all-round economic and cultural development of all the Soviet nations and nationalities, ensuring their increasingly close fraternal cooperation, mutual aid, unity and affinity in all spheres of life, thus achieving the utmost strengthening of the Union of Soviet Socialist Republics. . . .

(b) in the economic sphere, it is necessary to continue the line of comprehensive development of the economies of the Soviet republics. . . .

(c) to work for the further all-round development of the socialist cultures of the peoples of the U.S.S.R. The big scale of communist construction and the new victories of communist ideology are enriching the cultures of the peoples of the U.S.S.R., which are socialist in content and national in form. . . .

V. THE TASKS OF THE PARTY IN THE SPHERES
OF IDEOLOGY, EDUCATION, INSTRUCTION,
SCIENCE, AND CULTURE

Soviet society has made great progress in the socialist education of the masses, in the molding of active builders of socialism. But even after the socialist system has triumphed there persist in the minds and behavior of people survivals of capitalism, which hamper the progress of society.

In the struggle for the victory of communism, ideological work becomes an increasingly powerful factor. . . .

The Party considers that the paramount task in the ideological field in the present period is to educate all working people in a spirit of ideological integrity and devotion to communism, and cultivate in them a communist attitude to labor and the social economy; to eliminate completely the survivals of bourgeois views and morals; to ensure the all-round, harmonious development of the individual; to create a truly rich spiritual culture. Special importance is attached by the Party to the molding of the rising generation. . . .

VI. COMMUNIST CONSTRUCTION IN THE U.S.S.R. AND COOPERATION OF THE SOCIALIST COUNTRIES

The C.P.S.U. regards communist construction in the Soviet Union as a component of the building of communist society by the peoples of the entire world socialist system.

The fact that socialist revolutions took place at different times and that the economic and cultural levels of the countries concerned are dissimilar, predetermines the non-simultaneous completion of socialist construction in those countries and their non-simultaneous entry into the period of the full-scale construction of communism. Nevertheless, the fact that the socialist countries are developing as members of a single world socialist system and utilizing the objective laws and advantages of this system *enables them to reduce the time necessary for the construction of socialism and offers them the prospect of effecting the transition to communism more or less simultaneously, within one and the same historical epoch.* . . .

The C.P.S.U., in community with the Communist parties of the other socialist countries, regards the following as its tasks:

in the *political* field, the utmost strengthening of the world socialist system; promotion of fraternal relations with all the socialist countries on lines of complete equality and voluntary cooperation; political consolidation of the countries of the socialist community for joint struggle against imperialist aggressors, for universal peace and for the complete triumph of communism;

in the *economic* field, expansion of trade between the socialist countries; development of the international socialist division of labor; increasing coordination of long-range economic plans of the socialist countries to ensure a maximum saving of social labor and an accelerated development of the world socialist economy: the promotion of scientific and technical cooperation;

in the *cultural* field, steady development of all forms of cultural cooperation and intercourse between the peoples of the socialist countries; exchanges of cultural achievements; encouragement of joint creative effort by scientists, writers and artists; extensive measures to ensure the mutual enrichment of national cultures and bring the mode of life and the spiritual cast of the socialist nations closer together. . . .

VII. THE PARTY IN THE PERIOD OF
FULL-SCALE COMMUNIST CONSTRUCTION

As a result of the victory of socialism in the U.S.S.R. and the consolidation of the unity of Soviet society, the Communist Party of the working class has become the vanguard of the Soviet people, a Party of the entire people, and extended its guiding influence to all spheres of social life. The Party is the brain, the honor and the conscience of our epoch, of the Soviet people, the people effecting great revolutionary transformations. It looks keenly into the future and shows the people scientifically-motivated roads along which to advance, arouses titanic energy in the masses and leads them to the accomplishment of great tasks.

The period of full-scale communist construction is characterized by a further *enhancement of the role and importance of the Communist Party* as the leading and guiding force of Soviet society.

Unlike all the preceding socio-economic formations, communist society does not develop spontaneously, but as a result of the conscious and purposeful efforts of the masses led by the Marxist-Leninist Party. The Communist Party, which unites the foremost representatives of the working class, of all working people, and is closely connected with the masses, which enjoys unbounded prestige among the people and understands the laws of social development, provides proper leadership in communist construction as a whole, giving it an organized, planned and scientifically based character.

The enhancement of the role of the Party in the life of Soviet society in the new stage of its development derives from:

the growing scope and complexity of the tasks of communist construction, which call for a higher level of political and organizational leadership;

the growth of the creative activity of the masses and the participation of fresh millions of working people in the administration of state affairs and of production;

the further development of socialist democracy, the enhancement of the role of social organizations, the extension of the rights of the Union republics and local organizations;

the growing importance of the theory of scientific communism, of its creative development and propaganda, the necessity for improving the communist education of the working people and struggling to overcome the survivals of the past in the minds of people.

There must be a new higher stage in the development of the Party itself and of its political, ideological, and organizational work that is in conformity with the full-scale building of communism. The Party will continuously improve the forms and methods of its work, so that its leadership of the masses, of the building of the material and technical basis of communism, of the development of society's spiritual life will keep pace with the growing requirements of the epoch of communist construction.

Being the vanguard of the people building a communist society, the Party must also be in the van in the organization of internal Party life and serve as an example and model in developing the most advanced forms of public communist self-government.

Undeviating observance of the Leninist standards of Party life and the principle of collective leadership, enhancement of the responsibility of Party organs and their personnel to the Party rank and file, promotion of the activity and initiative of all Communists and of their participation in elaborating and realizing the policy of the Party, and the development of criticism and self-criticism, are a law of Party life. This is an imperative condition of the ideological and organizational strength of the Party itself, of the unity and solidarity of Party ranks, of an all-round development of inner-Party democracy and an activization on this basis of all Party forces, and of the strengthening of ties with the masses.

The cult of the individual, and the violations of collectivism in leadership, of inner-Party democracy and socialist legality arising out of it, are incompatible with the Leninist principles of Party life. The cult of the individual belittles the role of the Party and the masses and hampers the development of the ideological life of the Party and the creative activity of the working people. . . .

The Party will continue to strengthen the unity and solidarity of its ranks, and to maintain the purity of Marxism-Leninism. The Party preserves such organizational guarantees as are provided by the Rules of the C.P.S.U. against all manifestations of factionalism and group activity incompatible with Marxist-Leninist Party principles. *The unshakable ideological and organizational unity of the Party is the most important source of its invincibility, a guarantee for the successful solution of the great tasks of communist construction. . . .*

The CPSU Program: A Critique

RUDOLF SCHLESINGER*

I) The CPSU Programme: Historical and International Aspects

BACKGROUND AND MAIN CHARACTERISTICS

The new programme of the CPSU adopted by the XXII Party Congress is intended as a document dealing with all basic aspects of international life and with all the complex tasks facing Soviet society. Inherent criticism even of all its major aspects would require the writing of a book, since the programmatic statements would have to be discussed in connection not only with their

* On the faculty of the University of Glasgow, Professor Schlesinger is co-editor of *Soviet Studies* and the author of *The Spirit of Post-War Russia. Soviet Ideology, 1917–1946* (1947), *Marx, His Times and Ours* (1950), and of many other well-known works.

From "The CPSU Programme: Historical and International Aspects" and "The CPSU Programme: The Conception of Communism" by Rudolf Schlesinger, *Soviet Studies*, London, Vol. XIII, No. 3, January 1962, pp. 303–317, and No. 4, April 1962, pp. 386–406. Reprinted by permission of the author, editors, and publisher, Basil Blackwell & Mott Ltd. For footnote references, see original sources.

ideological background but also with present conditions and possible developments. . . .

The new programme is the third in the history of the Bolshevik party, after those adopted by the II Congress in 1903 and by the VIII Congress in 1919. The length of the last interval, embarrassing though it was in view of the central importance of a programme for party-political education, is explicable by the fact that a programmatic embodiment of some of the innovations of the later Stalin period in the field of social policies would have involved a politically undesirable going back on some of the promises of the 1919 programme. The gap is also explicable by the theoretical sterility of that period. Near the end of his life Stalin wrote his Economic Problems of Socialism with a view that it might serve as the basis for a new programme, and the XIX Party Congress decided accordingly, Stalin himself heading the Commission elected by the Congress for elaborating the new programme. If this commission had come into operation, the CPSU would now have had a programme envisaging, as an immediate task, the gradual replacement of market relations by direct commodity exchange and, in a slightly longer perspective, the nationalization of the collective farms; of course it would have had to amend it.

A party programme, in particular that of a party in power, is neither a systematic reformulation of basic theory nor a comprehensive plan of practical action: it is a meeting place between established party ideology (in the Soviet case, of the bodies professionally concerned with political indoctrination) and the requirements of practical policies (including, in particular, the definite demands requiring satisfaction in order to make a regime more popular and effective). The former tend to preserve as much as possible of the formulae to which they are accustomed and on the continuity of which, in their opinion, the party's authority depends: the latter fill the old formulae, even if preserved, with new content. For the student as well as for the practical politician the element of change counts more than the continuity of certain given tenets. Particular efforts may be required in order to overrule these tenets. The form in which this can be done may vary between: (a) delay of application—or correction—of some tenet by postponement of its tackling (this way has been pursued, in the present programme, as regards the eventual fusion of the two types of socialist property, the eventual 'withering away' of money incentives, and the distribution of output according to needs beyond a point which still may be described as a radical variety of the welfare state); (b) intentional vagueness of formulations so as to allow for future restatements of theory (this holds, for example, true as regards non-orthodox possibilities of the transition of underdeveloped countries to socialism); and (c) straightforward dropping of a traditional tenet, such as the inevitability of major wars as long as monopoly capitalism survives, or the necessity of proletarian dictatorship for the whole transition period from capitalism to communism.

The institutional function of the programme as an instrument of political indoctrination makes for its homogeneity and systematic nature. These qualities are far superior in the new programme to that of the 1919 programme—which only too clearly showed the traces of the emergency conditions in which it was drafted and the paucity of practical experience on which its introduction of new concepts had to operate. These requirements have caused, on the other hand, tiresome repetitions in the 1961 document, which tries to find some place, fitting or otherwise, for every statement in traditional use. There is also a tendency of government departments to get programmatic sanction for their current activities and to increase their appeal to students choosing their future careers; quite a few of the amendments suggested in the course of a very modest discussion point in the same direction.

Apart from the requirements of party-political education, developments since the XX Party Congress called for an authoritative definition of policies and general prospects. These topical problems may be brought under three main headings:

(1) Effective agrarian policies require a clarification of the party's approach to the future of the kolkhoz system, and the closely associated question of whether the transition to communism requires an immediate or only a very gradual fusion of the two forms of socialist property. After a period of intense discussion and experiment (which may represent the major *internal* contribution to the shaping of the new programme) a very gradual step, transferring the main transition to the second decade of the plan period and preserving meanwhile even the private plot, has been adopted in the new programme.

(2) During the last six years, the feel of an insufficiency of the existing planning methods developed: from the very start the current seven-year plan was conceived as a transitional link between the traditional five-year plans and the continuous planning then aimed at and now explicitly required in the new programme. Already in his report to the XX Party Congress Khrushchev envisaged that the new party programme should be drafted together with a long-term economic plan: this combination makes sense from the standpoint of bringing party aims (in particular the 'transition to communism') closer to reality, and from that of improving planning. The association of the improvements promised in the programme with an elaborate plan for the development of the resources available for fulfilling them resulted in an extreme paucity, in the published part of the discussion preceding the party congress, of suggestions exceeding the scope of explanation or of departmental self-assertion. Most of the exceptions concern improvement of institutional arrangements for the implementation of principles already elaborated in the draft programme. Suggestions made in the course of the discussion in the party organizations and accepted in Khrushchev's report include precisions on the draft as regards the location of one of the new metallurgical bases in the Kursk area and as regards the housing programme: existing substandard and overcrowded accommodation is to be replaced during the next decade. Khrushchev sharply rejected suggestions from the 'dogmatic' ideological side which were directed against the programme statements about the obsoleteness of the proletarian dictatorship in the U.S.S.R. and against the continuation of the kolkhoz market.

(3) At least as important as the internal are the *international* urges towards a programmatic clarification of the party's attitude. Partly, these reflect a consciousness of the conditioning of all progress possible in the U.S.S.R. by what is happening in the world as a whole and in particular by the preservation of peace, which is impossible without a combination of those forces all over the world which oppose attempts to undo the changes which followed World War II as well as military interference with developments in the uncommitted countries. The two issues are closely associated in that nations sympathetic to a final settlement of the German question, to China's admission to UNO, etc., dislike

being confronted, for their own development, with the sole alternative between the American and the Soviet way. Western readers, who are used to regarding it as unfair that West Germany will have to pay for its adherence to an alliance directed against the U.S.S.R. by a final acceptance of the *status quo*, or that Laotian neutrality is being defined as non-alignment with either bloc yet not as an exclusion of any possible ways of internal development, should keep in mind that each of these solutions has also an aspect less agreeable from the communist point of view and hence open to criticism within the Soviet bloc.

There is, however, no need to look for anti-'Maoist' implications of the self-reliance with which the Soviet way of building socialism is treated as the typical one, or of the very sharp rejection of the 'personality cult', directed not solely against the dead individual Stalin but against any replacement of the authority of the collective by any individual, however outstanding. Polycentrism has sufficiently developed in the communist camp to enable the Chinese leaders to by-pass even such features of the new programme as its failure to mention the 'People's Communes'. (Presumably the Soviet leaders assume that the Chinese, having to face the same difficulties as the Russians met in 1929–31, also repeat the ideological mistakes current in those days. In general, enormous difficulties, requiring from those who have to overcome them superhuman efforts, tend also to produce Leftist ideologies.) But although I have met, in diverse lands, young communists who brought what I would describe as revolutionary impatience under the heading of 'Maoism', I find it difficult to guess rational objections which Mao, or any other Marxist sharing his general views on dialectics and on the dynamics of revolutions in underdeveloped countries, could raise against the statements of the programme (Chapter V) about the peaceful transition to socialism, possible in some countries by democratic means (still described as a variety of the dictatorship of the proletariat), or those in Chapter VI on peaceful coexistence, defined as a rejection of war as a means of settling international disputes and as the prevention of thermonuclear war. Surely, such a war is particularly abhorrent for a nation with an enormous population concentration in large cities and without a nuclear deterrent of its own. Even from the ideological standpoint, concepts of an alleged inevitability of major war are hardly relevant for the leaders of a party which even less than the CPSU accepts the reality of the 'affluent society' in the West and which glances mainly at the underdeveloped countries, where revolutions for internal reasons are obviously in the cards. As to dogmatics, the authors of the new programme are clearly right when stating, in Chapter V, that the communists never based all their revolutionary expectations on a new war.

But differences were bound to arise, and may continue, on the interpretation of the likely development tendencies of the new uncommitted states: a chain of disagreeable experiences from Kerala to Egypt, though in Marxist terms explicable as due to the unavoidable vacillations of the national bourgeoisie, may look different from the angle of observers convinced that they can build the new society by their own unaided efforts and from that of politicians who gained power by what was, all in all, a successful peasant revolution directed against the national bourgeoisie. The current disagreements on the assessment of international developments made their impact upon the drafting process as well as upon the shape of the programme. Nearly all that is known about its preparation centres on the discussions between the diverse communist parties which were concluded by the adoption, by the Conference held in November 1960, of a document containing all the basic statements now embodied in the first, general, part of the CPSU programme. This procedure sharply contrasts with that observed at least since 1924 in Comintern, the Congresses of which were to be convened after the Russian but before the other national party congresses, and thus were intended to serve as an agency of transmitting Russian policy decisions to the other parties.

The new programme is more orientated towards the analysis of international relations than were any of its predecessors. In spite of its own extension, caused by a more elaborate detailed approach, the second, practical, part of the new programme occupies just slightly more than half the total length (in the programme of 1903 it occupied three-fifths, in that of 1919 more than three-quarters). Within the general part the economic analysis of capitalism and its tendencies, which fully occupied this part in 1903 and still dominated it in 1919, now occupies only two of the eight chapters. The shift of emphasis to international relations, in itself shared by all students of social relations who wish to rise above a parochial standpoint, is particularly important in a document intended to serve as the basis of Marxist thought for a period of decades: it ends the predominant emphasis on domestic issues characteristic of the century during which Marxism, up to now, has operated as a guidance of the socialist movement. . . .

THE WORKING-CLASS MOVEMENT IN THE CAPITALIST COUNTRIES
(CHAPTERS IV AND V OF THE PROGRAMME)

The association of the programme with party-political education helps to broaden its outlook beyond the traditional Marxist pre-occupation with labour conditions but becomes a handicap in the treatment of those traditional subjects: a machine catering for homogeneity of doctrine is likely to combine the diverse past stages of doctrinal development in a way which reminds one of geological strata, without much bother about the relevance of those strata for the present. This shortcoming is most in evidence where the authors have to assert the inherent necessity of socialist revolutions (not necessarily violent) in the old-established capitalist countries (no particular difficulties are encountered in our days in demonstrating the inherent necessity of anti-colonial revolutions).

The drafters of the 1903 programme, like those of all the pre-1917 socialist programmes, believed that a mere demonstration of the inherent contradictions of capitalism, plus the necessarily increasing weight of the industrial proletariat, amounted to a demonstration of its tendency eventually to overthrow capitalism. (The classical elaboration of this concept is Chapter XXIV of the first volume of *Capital*.) Without suggesting that the overthrow of capitalism would necessarily occur in consequence of an economic depression, the programme of 1903 concluded its description of the economic cycle with the statement that slumps 'even quicker [than the normal course of capitalist development] lead to a relative [in relation to the rising incomes of the capitalists] and sometimes even to an absolute deterioration of the conditions of the working class'. This statement was repeated without change in the 1919 programme and is repeated, again without change, in the present programme. In 1903 it was treated only as one important element amongst those aspects of capitalist society which increase the workers' class-consciousness (as slumps undoubtedly do): yet the immediate task facing the Russian working class was then described as overthrowing Tsarism—and a democratic revolution was surely on the cards. In 1919 the statement, like all the definitions of capitalism taken over from the 1903 programme, was intended to show that capitalism had not lost its basic features. But the revolution which had meanwhile taken place in Russia, and those which were expected in other lands, could easily be explained by the general disruption caused by the war, independently of the effects of the economic cycle.

When subsequently being confronted with a stabilization of capitalist relationships the communists, unwilling to base all their revolutionary prospects on a new war, had to look for tendencies to a depression of working-class conditions even in 'normal' post-war capitalism. As early as 1922 Bukharin asserted the existence of *absolute* pauperization in the capitalist system as a whole (i.e. leading capitalist countries plus the colonies exploited by them): he reproached Kautsky for having confused the issue by his emphasis on a merely *relative* pauperization of the working class in the leading capitalist countries (i.e. a lagging of the increase in its standard of life behind the rise of profits). Readers of the new programme, having found in the mentioned re-quotation from the 1903 programme a documentation of Marxist attitudes before World War I, will find the attitudes of the period between the wars revived in Chapter IV, where a discussion of unemployment and of the conditions of the masses in underdeveloped countries is followed by the statement that the decay of world capitalism does not imply full standstill nor exclude the growth of capitalist economies in individual periods and individual countries. Yet the position of the working class in the capitalist world as a whole is said to deteriorate, notwithstanding the occurrence of individual successes in its economic struggle. In our days, the conditions of Negro workers in the South African gold mines or in the Rhodesian copper belt play a more immediate part in a world-wide conception of revolutionary developments than they could in the twenties. But a statement such as that quoted can hardly make a relevant contribution to the interpretation of the behaviour of the workers of the leading capitalist countries. Readers of the programme get no positive help in assessing the new phenomena.

Of post-war capitalist developments only state-monopoly capitalism gets a treatment of some length: this is almost exclusively devoted to the rejection of assertions about its allegedly near-socialist character and about a possibility of overall planning and of overcoming the contradictions of capitalist society without abolishing private ownership in the basic means of production, etc. At the end of these paragraphs it is, however, said that state-monopoly capitalism represents the complete material preparation for socialism. In the following chapter (V) it is stated that the proletariat demands far-reaching nationalization measures under conditions as favourable to the people as possible, the nationalized industries and all the economic activities of the state being subject to control by parliament, by the trade unions and by representative bodies. The reservations of Chapter IV against nationalizations as strengthening the power positions of monopoly capitalism are thus being reduced to an emphasis on the impossibility of achieving a socialist planned economy without a radical change of government. The progress of automation and of other aspects of the present technical revolution is narrowed down by capitalist relations of production; even in so far as it can take place in these conditions, it is bound to increase unemployment and to pauperize the small producers.

In the two chapters here under discussion, there are no straightforward references to advances made in capitalist countries in social services and to transfers of income (i.e. to the phenomena usually described in the West as the Welfare State, not necessarily with a tendency to idealization but in opposition to earlier conceptions of the state as not concerned with social security problems). In Chapter V, in the most general terms, it is said that the bourgeoisie, having drawn some lessons from the October Revolution 'applies new means to cover the ulcers and diseases of the capitalist system: these means, although they complicate the activity of the revolutionary forces in the capitalist countries, cannot weaken the antagonism between capital and labour'. The programme explicitly mentions the Welfare State only in Chapter VII (which is devoted to the struggle against hostile ideologies) as an ideological tool of anti-communism, i.e. of defamation of the socialist system and falsification of its aims and policies, apart from really propagandist theories such as assertions of an alleged 'people's capitalism', 'dispersion of capital ownership', equalization of incomes, etc. The authors appear to ignore the topical issues of political struggle in the USA and in Britain, or anti-communist literature in the ordinary sense of the word which, since Kravchenko's days, uses the denunciation of Soviet socialism as a convenient means to attack social reforms nearer home. One feels the sectarian blinkers of the professional propagandist who regards the political disputes of our days as essentially conducted between communists on one side and Social Democrats, Yugoslav Revisionists etc. on the other side. It is this approach—with its counterpart on the Western side of the 'curtain'—which in our days makes so much for ignorance of conditions in the 'opposite' part of the world.

The extreme reserve with which the economic issues allowing for day-to-day reform are tackled may be associated with a fear of loss of identity in the broad political combinations recommended by the programme. In the issue of war and peace these combinations have to include all reasonable strata of the bourgeoisie; broad strata of the lower middle classes should help to form a front against the big monopolies, the mainstays of armaments and, in some countries, of fascist threats. To the Social Democratic parties—presumably the left-wing variety, since the right-wing Social Democrats are regarded as the main supporters of the rejected concepts of a possible democratization of monopoly capitalism— even fuller collaboration is offered 'not only in the struggle for peace, for the improvement of the workers' living conditions, for the preservation and extension of their democratic rights, but also for the conquest of power and the construction of a socialist society'. The programme states that the communists prefer to establish a working class regime '*by peaceful means** without civil war': if the ruling classes, however, violently oppose the will of an overwhelming majority of the people (destroy the parliamentary institutions, outlaw communist parties, etc.) the conquest of power by violent means has to be envisaged. But after a further consolidation of the socialist system (on the international stage) the bourgeoisie of some countries may voluntarily accept nationalization, if compensation is paid to the former owners of the means of production. The forms of transition and its institutional setting thus will differ from country to country, but whatever their shape, they are interpreted as varieties of the dictatorship of the prole-

* *Italics in the original.*

tariat. In practical terms, this appears to mean that the transition, once carried out, would be irreversible.

The remarkable thing about this approach is, not that it has been formulated with such frankness (in substance, it was contained in Khrushchev's report to the XX Party Congress in 1956) but that it appears to meet only moderate objections within the world communist movement. These objections are (a) that in the present setting the achievement of working-class aims short of a conquest of power is impossible (and hence the issue of further progress towards a socialist transformation would not arise), and (b) that the struggle against the capitalist monopolies (including partial nationalization measures) and for the defence, or restoration, of democratic institutions might form, not a preparatory step on the road to socialism but a means of consolidating a slightly reformed bourgeois regime. As to (a), the programme states, positively, that the working class of many countries, if rallying broad strata of the working people

> can force the ruling circles to stop the preparation for a new world war, to waive the initiation of local wars, to use the national economy for peaceful purposes; it can defeat the attacks of the fascist reaction, achieve a realization of a national peace programme, of national independence, of democratic rights, and of some improvement in the people's living conditions.

As to objection (b), the programme says, apparently in polemic against internal critics, that 'the common democratic struggle against the monopolies does not delay the socialist revolution but brings it nearer. *The struggle for democracy is an inherent part of the struggle for socialism.*'

THE SOCIALIST SYSTEM AND THE EMANCIPATION MOVEMENTS IN THE UNDERDEVELOPED COUNTRIES

In development of accepted communist concepts the programme describes the international setting discussed in its general part as the third stage of the general crisis of capitalism (the first one was associated with the October revolution, the second with the extension of the communist system over a whole group of countries). This third phase, as the authors of the programme emphasize, did *not* develop in connection with a world war; Khrushchev's now familiar argument is elaborated in Chapter VIII which puts the struggle for peace into the centre of the efforts of all reasonable people. The *possibility* of war cannot be excluded but, with the strengthening of the socialist system and the colonial emancipation movements the imperialist powers (more precisely, the most aggressive of the monopolies urging towards war) are deprived of reasonable prospects of success in a world war: if the peace forces remain vigilant, the great transformations of our days can proceed without interruption by other than local conflicts which are sometimes unavoidable in the course of colonial emancipation movements (still, Ghana and Guinea, which achieved their independence by peaceful means, are regarded as truly national democracies). The programme excludes from the process of the extension of the socialist system to other countries even local wars other than those fought in self-defence of the socialist states against 'export of counter-revolution'. 'The revolution does not proceed by order: it cannot be imposed on a people from outside: it arises in consequence of the deep internal and international contradictions of capitalism. A victorious working class cannot impose any blessings on an alien people without thereby undermining its own victory.' This statement is supported by the mention, in Chapter III, of national prejudices and of the residua of former national hatred, as one of the most stubborn and persistent obstacles to progress in the socialist part of the world: clearly, these difficulties would increase by successful 'exports of revolution'.

The concept of 'peaceful competition' of states with different social systems, by which the U.S.S.R. wishes to replace the 'cold war', is elaborated in Chapter VIII: it involves, not an abrogation of class conflict (which, according to basic Marxist tenets, is in any way beyond the powers of negotiators) but its being shifted to the more civilized rails of propaganda by example and economic help. In particular in the atomic age, 'War cannot, and must not, serve as the means of deciding international disputes'. . . .

The changes suggested to [end the possibility of the new sovereign nations becoming the subject of international exploitation] are treated on three successive levels:

(1) National independence can become a reality only if politi-

cal sovereignty is supplemented by breaking the power of the foreign monopolies and of the feudal strata within the countries collaborating with them, and only if it is strengthened by the people's active participation in government. . . .

(2) A nation which has achieved national independence has the choice between the capitalist and the non-capitalist ways of development. . . .

(3) Having defined the non-capitalist way of development of former colonial countries, the programme recommends the State of National Democracy, based on a bloc of all progressive and democratic forces, as the institutional framework for the completion of a consistently anti-imperialist, anti-feudal and democratic revolution. Presumably intentionally, the formula is loose in that it does not answer the question whether the State of National Democracy is a mere framework within which the choice between the two possible ways of industrializing a backward country has to be made, or is already the institutional setting established once question (2) has been decided in favour of the non-capitalist way; nor does it answer the question whether this institutional setting provides a specific form of building a socialist society, with implications as regards the general validity of the concept of proletarian dictatorship. . . .

Indirect conclusions on the attitude of the authors of the programme to efforts at achieving socialism by unorthodox methods may be drawn from their description of the essential features of the existing socialist camp, keeping in mind that any admission of the possibility of different ways is likely to enter their statements by omission of possible negative argument rather than in positive terms. Chapter III of the first part, which deals with the emergence of the world socialist system as one of the elements in the international transition from capitalism to communism, enumerates the existing members of the camp, adding that Yugoslavia, too, has entered the socialist road but that her leaders by their revisionist policy put the country in opposition to the world socialist movement; thereby they are said to have brought about the danger of a possible loss of the revolutionary achievements. In the further course of the chapter the argument about the political and economic dangers involved in attempts to construct socialism in isolation from the socialist camp is repeated without specific reference to Yugoslavia. It appears that, in the opinion of the authors of the programme, an effort to build socialism without the direct help of the camp does not imply a contradiction in terms; it may be suggested that heterodoxies of a level comparable with the Yugoslav ones, if originating from a country without claims to present the true interpretation of Marxism-Leninism (and hence without appeal to deviationist tendencies in the existing communist parties) would be more charitably dealt with, however obvious might be the dependence of joint economic planning on the achievement of some degree of political unity. Chapter VI of the second part, dealing with the Cooperation of the Socialist Countries, recommends a development of coordinated planning and specialization as well as an increase in commercial exchanges: a future development in which all of the then existing socialist states might share in the second but only a nucleus in both forms of economic coordination, would not exceed the intellectual framework of the programme.

Too broad an interpretation of the geographical scope of the socialist camp to be expected in a near future is contradicted by the prospects for the transition to communism developed in that chapter. The time lags existing between the socialist revolutions in the diverse bloc countries and their different levels of economic development are said to preclude a simultaneous entrance into the period of communist construction; yet by coordination of their economic efforts and full use of the experience achieved by the more advanced of them 'the time required for the building of socialism may be shortened to such an extent that the transition to communism may take place more or less simultaneously, within the limits of one historical period'. Concepts such as 'one historical period' and, as we shall later see, 'transition to communism', are too loose to allow for precise delimitations; still it is clear that the authors of the programme (a) expect the transition to communism to take place in some parts of the world while, in others, capitalism still survives, and (b) regard socialism, that is to say a state of things in which the new attitudes to work can develop on the basis of full nationalization of the means of production yet still under the impact of the familiar material incentives, as a necessary transition stage to communism. From these two premises it follows that during the later stage of the transition period, alongside with capitalist and communist, there will be socialist systems, some of them fairly advanced but some very backward, applying non-capitalist methods for carrying out their industrialization. . . .

II) *The CPSU Programme: The Conception of Communism*

An analysis of present Soviet concepts of communist society, as distinct from the socialist one regarded as already established, has to start from the fact that the authors of the new party programme describe its construction as 'the immediate practical task of the Soviet people'. By 1980, 'in the U.S.S.R. a communist society will be built in essentials' (*v osnovnom*); its construction will be completed during the following period. Such a definition of the tasks of the next period implies a definition of a communist society as the aggregate of those reforms which, during the twenty-year period, can be carried out or, at least, be approached to such an extent that their tackling during the subsequent years immediately follows from what will have been achieved by 1980. This interpretation of the time-table is supported by Khrushchev's argument, in his address to the Party Congress, against comrades who had suggested a shorter time-limit: this would be unrealistic and harm the authority of communism. For communism, he says, means abundance. Moreover, the programme concludes with the solemn promise that 'the present generation of Soviet people will live under communism'.

Yet communism implies not only a system of measures intended to increase welfare (to which we shall later return) but definite changes in social relationships. The programme envisages that by the end of the twenty-year period the collective and state farm systems will be fused into a higher form of socialist enterprises on the basis of a rise in the rewards of collective farmers to a point where the private plot is no longer needed: for our basic argument it is not essential whether, because of an over-optimistic formulation of the productivity targets in the agricultural field, the period should in fact be a few years longer. But the abolition of a social differentiation between industrial workers and peasants does not yet mean the disappearance of all social differentiations. For this also an equalization of the status of the *intelligentsia* and the former manual workers would be required: as Gatovski explains in

Kommunist (1961 no. 17) this depends on full automation of production which (in particular if the position of agriculture is kept in mind) is possible only many decades after the end of the programme period. The communism envisaged by Khrushchev as a programme task is hence a society with greatly improved living standards but not yet free of social differentiations. . . .

Their present use of the term [Communism] is conditioned by the earlier description of the society which had to be defended in World War II as 'socialist' and by tendency, during the difficult years of construction, to promise the realization of those aspects of traditional socialism which exceed the mere needs of growth for a communist future. In 1955 Molotov, critical of his late master's terminology yet faithful to his political testament, questioned the completion of more than the foundations of socialism in the U.S.S.R. From the continuation of his struggle up to the enactment of the new programme it is clear that he regarded, and presumably still regards, the building of *socialism* as incomplete as long as the kolkhoz system, distinct from the nationalized state industry, survives and as long as distribution is dominated by money circulation, as distinct from *produkto-obmen* (direct exchange of goods) as suggested in Stalin's Economic Problems of Socialism. In terminology, Molotov was more moderate than the majority of the Presidium (he asked for a mere completion of *socialist* construction where Khrushchev, now, speaks of 'transition to communism') but in practical policies he was more radical. While Khrushchev started a whole series of reforms intended to make the working of the kolkhoz system conform with its asserted character, Molotov apparently wished to attack it, reserving the term 'communism' for something going much further than the practical suggestions (as distinct from quotations from the classics) contained in the present programme. In 1955, the issue was decided against Molotov; the concept he had stood for was defeated in the winter of 1960–1, when it became clear that the kolkhoz system had to be preserved for a long period.

Since the term 'socialism'—including its completion—had already been used, the comprehensive formula for the new stage had to be 'communism'. If the authors of the programme are right in their assertion that the carrying out of the reforms envisaged for the twenty-year period will result in a social need for the further steps traditionally associated with 'the higher stage of a communist society', their successors will meet no particular difficulty in drafting, about 1980, another programme headed 'the completion of the building of communism'. If, however, their assumption should prove incorrect, the present programme may be followed by others envisaging still shorter hours, more free services, even better education for all, etc., without advocating a social structure different from that by then in operation. There would still remain the need for some anticipating body, influencing decisions about the use of the increasing social product from the standpoint of long-term prospects as conceived by it: society as a whole (as distinct from individual citizens, who may eventually be conditioned by social education to make no demands exceeding the possibilities of a truly affluent society) will always have to face scarcity, though on increasingly higher levels. But social decisions can be initiated in various ways: the party's particular function would come to an end when it would no longer stand for progress to a different social structure.

Progress *within* the given structure is obviously decisive for the outcome of the international competition; notwithstanding some verbal tribute paid to long-term prospects, it attracts the predominant attention of the programme. We shall have to discuss the changes envisaged in the field of production relations (in particular, as regards the evolution of the kolkhoz system), in the formation of the cultural and social services so far as these affect the conditions and outlook of the citizen as a producer and the associated questions of the use of the distributable part of the national income, and finally the political structure of the envisaged society. The availability of the material resources on which the authors of the programme rely may be taken for granted on the condition, obvious in itself and made explicit in the concluding passages of Chapter II of that part, that internal reconstruction will not be delayed by international complications. Their availability may be taken for granted if the present rate of growth can be maintained during the twenty-year period: there remains the question of how far their intended use will involve structural changes.* . . .

* Ed. note: The changes envisaged in the field of production relations, the formation of cultural and social services, and the limits within which the development of the latter can, for the foreseeable future, approach a distributor according to needs, are discussed by the author on pp. 385–395 of the source.

POLITICAL ORGANIZATION

Where the programme deals with economic prospects, a careful though far-seeing formulation of practical aims is combined with a preservation of traditional formulae: as soon as we enter the realm of political institutions, a straightforward revision of tenets hitherto regarded as basic for Marxist-Leninist theory is coupled with an avoidance of innovations exceeding the reforms already well under way. The key sentence of Chapter III of the second part—and, perhaps, of the programme as a whole—is the statement that the proletarian dictatorship

> by securing the full and final victory of socialism, the first stage of communism, and the transition of society to the developed building of communism, has fulfilled its historical mission and, from the standpoint of internal development, has ceased to be necessary in the U.S.S.R. The state which originated as a state of the dictatorship of the proletariat has been transformed into an all-national state, an organ expressing the interests and the will of the whole people. . . .

The restriction to 'the standpoint of the internal development of the U.S.S.R.' represents one of the various compromises arrived at in the drafting committee: in his speech at the Congress, Mikoyan implicitly argued against it by observing that a state need not be a dictatorship in order to defend itself against external foes: the all-national state (i.e. the people's state, in the sense of all citizens having equal rights and obligations) envisaged by the programme could perform this function as well as the proletarian dictatorship of an earlier period had done. This argument, but also the formulation given in the programme, were repeated in an (unsigned) official commentary, published in *Pravda*, 5 December 1961. The programmatic statement announces that the state, being a coercive institution, will no longer have to apply its powers against social groups as distinct from individual lawbreakers: there is an obvious connection with Khrushchev's peasant policies, and in particular with the dropping of any intention to bring about a premature, and hence non-voluntary, assimilation of the kolkhoz to state enterprises. The statement (against which the protests of Molotov and his 'dogmatist' friends were apparently directed) has some inherent association with the denunciation, at the Congress, of their participation in Stalin's terror. By implication Khrushchev says: these things have happened because we have carried out the collectivization of agriculture by violent means. This may have been necessary at the time but no violent acceleration of the peasant's progress to socialism is necessary any more; hence our state no longer needs to be a dictatorship.

Still the party is, and intends to remain, the leading force in state and society: it intends to direct further developments in the direction of greater socialization. Moreover, it remains interested in a sensible proportion, amongst its members, of workers (and peasants) since these are not, like managerial staff, attracted to membership by their very position. In order to express these interests, the statement about the obsoleteness of the proletarian dictatorship in the U.S.S.R. is supplemented by another, saying that the working-class, being the leading and most organized force in Soviet society, will continue to play a leading part up to the full disappearance of classes under communism. Yet Chapter VII opens with the statement that the party, historically grown as the party of the working class, 'has . . . become the party of the whole people'.

The more we feel the struggle of conflicting trends, the more impressive is the fact that the one which prevailed was strong enough to secure the acceptance of what amounts to a basic change in Marxist theory. It is acknowledged (a) that the state is not necessarily an instrument of class rule: in a particular stage of social development, there can be states which serve the people as a whole, and (b) that the proletarian dictatorship represents an intermediate stage not, as was assumed by revolutionary Marxists since Marx's criticism of the 1875 Programme of German Social Democracy, between a state ruled by the bourgeoisie and the stateless communist society of the future (presumably based on voluntary cooperation) but between the bourgeois state based upon private ownership of the means of production and the all-national state of a society in which such private property, and hence class-divisions, have been overcome. This theoretical shift is more fundamental than Stalin's acknowledgement, in 1938, of the possibility of a survival of the state under communism in view of the capitalist environment, the main task of this state being conceived as the struggle against this encirclement and its agents (it would not be a very democratic state): the new programme expects the state to continue independently of the international setting (for example in the case of general disarmament and, for a while at least, even after a world-wide triumph of socialism) because it is necessary for the coordination of economic construction and for the education of the builders of communism. Yet Khrushchev's state of the period of communist construction, as distinct from Stalin's 'communism in one country', is characterized by 'all-sided development and perfection of socialist democracy, active participation of all citizens in government, in leading economic and cultural construction work, improvement of the work of the state apparatus and strengthening of popular control over its activities'.

There are, in principle, three lines on which such an evolution may be brought about: (a) making the existing Soviet system more representative by allowing the individual citizen more scope in influencing the composition of the Soviets and determining their policies; (b) broadening the opportunities available to Soviet members and other interested citizens to influence legislation and to supervise administration; (c) transfer of state functions to voluntary bodies bringing thus, in cooperation with the Soviets, new forms of direct democracy into being. Although the authors of the programme expect the eventual withering away of the state to proceed along the lines of (c), the practical suggestions made in this direction hardly exceed what is already accepted in laws and official directives. A strong case can be made in favour of first transferring existing enactments such as about the participation of trade unions in factory management into reality: in his report to the Congress Khrushchev remarked that a far-reaching replacement of the full-time trade union apparatus by the voluntary activities of unpaid workers would result in a more active participation of their members in public life. But this very state of things shows that 'the higher stage of a communist society' in the field of administration is at least as remote a Utopia as it is in the field of distribution.

Nor is substantial progress announced in securing some initiative to the Soviet electorate. A 'broad and all-sided discussion in meetings and in the press of the personal and business qualities of candidates' is required but, if the present system of plebiscite-type elections is preserved, this can hardly imply more than an additional 'scourge against inefficient officials': the party-controlled press is unlikely to publish criticism of the policies supported by candidates unless it is an issue of their failing to conform with authoritatively accepted policies. Supporters of the new formulation take for granted the continuation of the existing practice of 'recommending' party nominees for nomination by electors' meetings and hail the new formula as a means of preventing the most obvious misuses. If, however, the party at some stage should dissociate its authority from the fate of individual candidates and not be afraid of the implications of contested elections, less than 98% votes, etc., then the discussion of the merits of individual candidates—and even of individual measures advocated by them—could be free. This would involve a difficult transition: national referendums on issues regarded by the CPSU as most important may not just offer the most suitable starting point, but there might be more scope for genuinely democratic decision if referendums were held within individual administrative units on issues facing local governments. On the other hand, it may be unfair to look in an official programme for declarations of a kind which would destroy the authority of the existing election system before an alternative has been successfully tried on a local scale, so as to allow for generalization in public.

The rules governing the systematic rejuvenation of the Soviet bodies actually lag behind existing practices. They may just prevent claims of the professional Soviet hierarchy to lifelong tenure of administrative office: failure to be re-elected for a fourth term would imply no straightforward disapproval (and hence would not prevent the party from appointing the official concerned to another position of responsibility) but a mere indication that the man was not quite the ideal type for this post. But the law would allow two-thirds of the members of any body to be re-elected as long as they can command the support of a three-quarters majority, which would surely be available except in the event of a major scandal.

The programme takes a more positive approach to the rights of local and regional (including the Republican) Soviets, and to the broadening of the participation in their work of other than their leading members. Local Soviets are to be granted final decision power on all issues of merely local importance; higher up, the members of the Permanent Commissions of the Supreme Soviets of the Union and the Union Republics should continuously supervise the work of the individual ministries and sovnarkhozy. (They enjoyed similar powers in the first years of the Soviet régime but had little time to exercise them and, perhaps, were even insufficiently qualified in relation to the senior civil servants whose work they had to check: now, their qualifications have certainly improved, and, according to the programme, they are to be granted such leave from their ordinary jobs as required for the performance of their duties.) In the lower links, voluntary participation of active citizens in the work of the soviet organs is sought, with a prospect of bringing, eventually, the civil service as a particular profession to an end. Such information as we have about the work of 'unpaid (*vneshtatniye*) Departments' of City and Provincial Soviets refers to the supervision of trade, education and health, i.e. to activities which in any conceivable system must be managed by professionals. Most of the active citizens concerned are, presumably, themselves doctors, teachers or cooperative officials: even so they may represent a useful check against the civil service element. None of the measures suggested in the programme points to any 'withering away of the state'—unless 'the state' is identified with bureaucracy. But it is true that the concept of a 'withering away of the state' was developed by Marx in a polemic against the Prussian State-socialists, applied by Lenin, and revived after Stalin's death, in the particular conditions of Russia, Prussia as well as Russia being well-developed samples of the bureaucratic state.

For any foreseeable future, the party expects its rôle in the Soviet policy to be strengthened, partly in consequence of the ever increasing importance of foresight and planning in the building of a communist society, and partly because the pluralistic elements of the intended reforms (such as the increasing autonomy of the individual republics, the increasing scope of the activities of local Soviets and voluntary bodies) require, as their supplement, the activity of a force 'which represents the interests of the whole people and is not associated with the interests of any individual group or government department' (*gruppovymi ili vedomstvennymi interesami*). Not less than before, the problem of Soviet democracy centres on the question of internal party democracy. The programme recognizes this straightforwardly when stating that the party being the vanguard of a people building a communist society must also go ahead in the organization of its internal life, giving an example and model of the elaboration of the most accomplished forms of communist social self-government.

The basic norm of party life is the immovable observance of its Leninist conception and of the principle of collective leadership, the increasing responsibility of the party organs and of their individual officials before the rank and file, the securing of the rise of the activity and initiative of all communists, of their participation in the elaboration and in the carrying out of party policies, in the development of criticism and self-criticism. . . .

The counterpart of such collective shaping of the party's activities is the personality cult. This is no longer a circumscription of a man (in his reply to the debate Khrushchev criticized not only Stalin but also excessive praise devoted to himself or any other living leader): the denunciation of the man may have been regarded by most of the delegates as a solemn promise, to quote a Leningrad delegate, that 'these things will never again be repeated; there is no return to the past'. In the programme, as in all decisions of the congress, the personality cult is treated as a disorder of the body politic which can arise whenever the Leninist rules of party life are neglected, even if no leaders of more than local standing, newspaper editors, etc. are involved. It is connected 'with violations of the principle of collective leadership, of democracy within the party, and of socialist legality. The personality cult leads to a lowering of the rôle of the party and of the masses of the people, restricts the development of the party's *ideiny* life and of the creative activities of the workers'. In art. 28 of the Rules the warning against 'the personality cult and the violations of intra-party democracy associated with it', is repeated; they are described as 'incompatible with the Leninist principles of party life'. In his speech introducing the programme Khrushchev, in the most solemn forms, explained these statements as an expression of the party's undertaking 'to apply all measures necessary in order to close for ever the doors to any personality cult'. If the dramatic manifestations of the struggle against the personality cult at and after the end of the Congress had been conditioned by unexpectedly strong resistance from internal and external dogmatists against the allegedly 'revisionist' approach of the programme, they would the more have manifested the inherent logic of events.

In the field of party organization just as in the field of state administration, strong shifts in approach are coupled with comparatively minor suggestions for at least their first implementation. The provisions for periodical rejuvenation of the leading bodies need hardly, at the top, provide more than an honourable ground for some Furtseva or Mukhitdinov to leave the Presidium while still being employed in high state or party office. (The Central Committee is the only party body to which re-election is permissible for an unlimited number of election periods; even officials retired on grounds of health or old age may thus continue to tender advice in what has in substance become a kind of party parliament.) In the middle ranks the new provisions for rejuvenation do not exceed what has become current even in Provinces and Republics where no major reshuffle of the leadership occurred. They may, however, be quite efficient in the lowest links, i.e. the primary organizations, where the party has to meet the danger of loss of control of management by the formation of cliques cooperating with it: as a rule, the secretaries of such organizations cannot be re-elected for more than two consecutive years. The participation of a much increasing proportion of the party membership in the holding of lower party office can be expected and professional officialdom is likely to be cut down in its lower links. A party official's failure to make of his holding of elected office a success (such failures, of course, are more frequent at the primary level than higher up) would involve no loss in personal authority (and so would not harm his professional prospects); hence the possibilities of attracting non-careerist minded people to these essential but in many cases thankless posts should increase.

Slightly higher up, the participation of a comparatively broad body of active members in organizational work might follow from the prescription for rotation in committee membership and from the programme's demand for 'a consistent restriction of the paid apparatus and a broader participation of party members [in the work of the machine] as unpaid officials, as a social activity'. The term recalls the conditions of the early twenties, when every member of the party (still conceived as a body of conscious revolutionaries with high political qualifications) was expected to shoulder, apart from his duties on his job, some extra social activity (*nagruzka*), the full-time party machine being in theory still regarded as an apparatus auxiliary to the work performed by the party as a whole.

By now, even the best party organizations are far from these conditions. . . .

[This] may herald a state of things in which, apart from extraordinary cases and from what is required to keep the leading officials in
touch with the life of the primary organizations, the ordinary party
member will get most of his political guidance from someone who,
like himself, performs an ordinary job instead of being a mere link
in the party machine. This may mean a lot, in particular when it is
a question of the realistic, or otherwise, character of the demands
made on the primary organizations, and also as regards the prospects that those who perform this day-to-day guidance speak
frankly with those who issue their directives; in connection with
the new prescriptions for regular rotation in the higher party committees it may also promote a recruitment of those bodies from
people whose primary ambitions are not directed to advancement
within the machine.

All this may help to realize the repeated demand that the party
organization should guide but not administer, and to bring it
closer to the nation's life. In substance, such closeness and the
implied opportunity to reduce the full-time apparatus in a more
than statistical sense, depend on the character of the policies pursued, organizational arrangements being mere channels through
which social processes can flow. In this sense, the realistic policies
recommended in this programme may bring the state and society
closer together than can the steps envisaged to restrict bureaucracy
in party and state.

SECTION III

The Communist Concept of the State

Lenin's *State and Revolution* is perhaps one of the most persuasive political tracts ever published. Written in 1917, it is basically an eclectic summary of the views of Marx and Engels on the historical role of the state. Considering Marxism as a theory of revolutionary tactics, it characterizes the state as "the product of the irreconcilability of class antagonisms." The state, according to this theory, is the superstructural reflection of society's economic base, which serves as an instrument of suppression of one class by another. The bourgeois state, whatever form it may assume, is depicted as essentially a dictatorship of the bourgeoisie. While it is expected to be swept away by a violent revolution and replaced by a proletarian state, the latter is expected gradually to "wither away" as an instrument of class repression. The dictatorship of the proletariat is characterized as the transitional period between capitalism and communism, a period of "immense expansion of democracy . . . for the poor . . . and not democracy for the rich folk." The transition itself will take place in two distinct phases. During the first or lower phase of communism (socialism), justice and equality will not yet prevail and differences in wealth will continue, even though "exploitation of man by man will have become impossible." These injustices and differences will supposedly disappear with the attainment of the second, higher phase of Communist society, which will be guided by the motto "From each according to his ability; to each according to his needs." The "hows" and "whens" of this attainment are left generally unanswered.

In the second article Professor Daniels traces the historical evolution of the Marxist conception of the state and the institutional and ideological innovations that followed the acquisition of state power by the Bolsheviks. He demonstrates that while Lenin's *State and Revolution*, in contrast to the author's previous and subsequent writings, does not reflect his pervasive preoccupation with the central position of the Party as the determining factor in any "progressive" revolutionary movement, it also reveals Lenin's failure to grasp the basic rationale of Marx's thesis about smashing the state—"the protection of society against the dangerous independence of the state machinery." Since he had a narrow, class-determined conception of the state and an almost fanatical conviction about the indispensability of the Party as the determining historical factor in the transitional period between capitalism and communism, Lenin is claimed to have vitiated Marx's program of mass control over the exercise of political power.

Under the impact of the realities of organizing and defending acquired state powers, the Communists' preoccupation with the "withering away" of the state gradually gave way to the rising of the Party to the forefront of Marxist-Leninist theory. While the conception of the "withering away" of the state was theoretically still upheld, the "scope of 'state' and 'withering' were being progressively constricted." Dismissing the necessity of formally limiting political authority from below and characterizing the Party as the vanguard of the proletariat and, as such, as the prime mover of history, the new doctrine now extolled the state as "the highest form of social organization and a great creative force." As the state of the working class, the Soviet State was by definition considered incapable of perpetrating the crimes usually attributed to a state whose powers were not derived from the consent of the governed.

This "enrichment" of the Marxist-Leninist doctrine of the state was primarily the work of Stalin following the consolidation of power in his hands. The new theory incorporates Stalin's conceptions of "socialism in one country" and "the capitalist encirclement of the U.S.S.R." and considers the Soviet State as "the most democratic in the world, the chief instrument for the overcoming of class differences and for the preparation of the material and spiritual prerequisites for the transition to Communism."

This view of the Soviet State has been upheld even in the post-Stalin era of the "thaw," sanctifying, so to speak, the "socialist" version of the Leviathan which Marx, Bukharin and other visionaries held as historically and logically inherently impossible.

State and Revolution

V. I. LENIN

The State as the Product of the Irreconcilability of Class Antagonisms

. . . Let us begin with the most popular of Engels' works, *The Origin of the Family, Private Property, and the State.* . . . Summarising his historical analysis Engels says:

> The state is therefore by no means a power imposed on society from the outside; just as little is it "the reality of the moral idea," "the image and reality of reason," as Hegel asserted. Rather, it is a product of society at a certain stage of development; it is the admission that this society has become entangled in an insoluble contradiction with itself, that it is cleft into irreconcilable antagonisms which it is powerless to dispel. But in order that these antagonisms, classes with conflicting economic interests, may not consume themselves and society in sterile struggle, a power apparently standing above society becomes necessary, whose purpose is to moderate the conflict and keep it within the bounds of "order"; and this power arising out of society, but placing itself above it, and increasingly separating itself from it, is the state.

Here we have, expressed in all its clearness, the basic idea of Marxism on the question of the historical rôle and meaning of the state. The state is the product and the manifestation of the *irreconcilability* of class antagonisms. The state arises when, where, and to the extent that the class antagonisms *cannot* be objectively

From *State and Revolution* by V. I. Lenin, selections from pp. 8–16, 20–23, 31, and 71–80. New York: International Publishers, 1932. By permission of International Publishers Company, Inc.

reconciled. And, conversely, the existence of the state proves that the class antagonisms *are* irreconcilable. . . .

According to Marx, the state is an organ of class *domination*, an organ of *oppression* of one class by another; its aim is the creation of "order" which legalises and perpetuates this oppression by moderating the collisions between the classes. But in the opinion of the petty-bourgeois politicians, order means reconciliation of the classes, and not oppression of one class by another; to moderate collisions does not mean, they say, to deprive the oppressed classes of certain definite means and methods of struggle for overthrowing the oppressors, but to practice reconciliation. . . .

That the state is an organ of domination of a definite class which *cannot* be reconciled with its antipode (the class opposed to it)—this petty-bourgeois democracy is never able to understand. . . .

What is forgotten or glossed over is this: if the state is the product of the irreconcilable character of class antagonisms, if it is a force standing *above* society and "increasingly separating itself from it," then it is clear that the liberation of the oppressed class is impossible not only without a violent revolution, *but also without the destruction* of the apparatus of state power, which was created by the ruling class and in which this "separation" is embodied. . . .

Engels develops the conception of that "power" which is termed the state—a power arising from society, but placing itself above it and becoming more and more separated from it. What does this power mainly consist of? It consists of special bodies of armed men who have at their disposal prisons, etc.

We are justified in speaking of special bodies of armed men, because the public power peculiar to every state is not "absolutely identical" with the armed population, with its "self-acting armed organisation." . . .

A state is formed, a special power is created in the form of special bodies of armed men, and every revolution, by shattering the state apparatus, demonstrates to us how the ruling class aims at the restoration of the special bodies of armed men at *its* service, and how the oppressed class tries to create a new organisation of this kind, capable of serving not the exploiters, but the exploited. . . .

The State as an Instrument for the Exploitation of the Oppressed Class

. . . [Engels says:]

As the state arose out of the need to hold class antagonisms in check; but as it, at the same time, arose in the midst of the conflict of these classes, it is, as a rule, the state of the most powerful, economically dominant class, which by virtue thereof becomes also the dominant class politically, and thus acquires new means of holding down and exploiting the oppressed class. . . .

Not only the ancient and feudal states were organs of exploitation of the slaves and serfs, but

the modern representative state is the instrument of the exploitation of wage-labour by capital. By way of exception, however, there are periods when the warring classes so nearly attain equilibrium that the state power, ostensibly appearing as a mediator, assumes for the moment a certain independence in relation to both. . . .

In a democratic republic, Engels continues, "wealth wields its power indirectly, but all the more effectively," first, by means of "direct corruption of the officials" (America); second, by means of "the alliance of the government with the stock exchange" (France and America).

At the present time, imperialism and the domination of the banks have "developed" to an unusually fine art both these methods of defending and asserting the omnipotence of wealth in democratic republics of all descriptions. . . .

We must also note that Engels quite definitely regards universal suffrage as a means of bourgeois domination.

The petty-bourgeois democrats . . . share, and instil into the minds of the people, the wrong idea that universal suffrage "in the *modern* state" is really capable of expressing the will of the majority of the toilers and of assuring its realisations. . . .

A detailed analysis of all the falseness of this idea, which Engels brushes aside, is given in our further account of the views of Marx and Engels on the "modern" state.

A general summary of his views is given by Engels in the most popular of his works in the following words:

The state, therefore, has not existed from all eternity. There have been societies which managed without it, which had no conception of the state and state power. At a certain stage of economic development, which was necessarily bound up with the cleavage of society into classes, the state became a necessity owing to this cleavage. We are now rapidly approaching a stage in the development of production at which the existence of these classes has not only ceased to be a necessity, but is becoming a positive hindrance to production. They will disappear as inevitably as they arose at an earlier stage. Along with them, the state will inevitably disappear. The society that organises production anew on the basis of a free and equal association of the producers will put the whole state machine where it will then belong: in the museum of antiquities, side by side with the spinning wheel and the bronze axe.

The "Withering Away" of the State and Violent Revolution

Engels' words regarding the "withering away" of the state:

. . . The proletariat seizes state power, and then transforms the means of production into state property. But in doing this, it puts an end to itself as the proletariat, it puts an end to all class differences and class antagonisms, it puts an end also to the state as the state. Former society, moving in class antagonisms, had need of the state, that is, an organisation of the exploiting class at each period for the maintenance of its external conditions of production; therefore, in particular, for the forcible holding down of the exploited class in the conditions of oppression (slavery, bondage or serfdom, wage-labour) determined by the existing mode of production. The state was the official representative of society as a whole, its embodiment in a visible corporate body; but it was this only in so far as it was the state of that class which itself, in its epoch, represented society as a whole: in ancient times, the state of the slave-owning citizens; in the Middle Ages, of the feudal nobility; in our epoch, of the bourgeoisie. When ultimately it becomes really representative of society as a whole, it makes itself superfluous. As soon as there is no longer any class of society to be held in subjection; as soon as, along with class domination and the struggle for individual existence based on the former anarchy of production, the collisions and excesses arising from these have also been abolished, there is nothing more to be repressed, and a special repressive force, a state, is no longer necessary. The first act in which the state really comes forward as the representative of society as a whole—the seizure of the means of production in the name of society—is at the same time its last independent act as a state. The interference of a state power in social relations becomes superfluous in one sphere after another, and then becomes dormant of itself. Government over persons is replaced by the administration of things and the direction of the processes of production. The state is not "abolished," *it withers away*. It is from this standpoint that we must appraise the phrase "people's free state"—both its justification at times for agitational purposes, and its ultimate scientific inadequacy—and also the demand of the so-called Anarchists that the state should be abolished overnight.

The replacement of the bourgeois by the proletarian state is impossible without a violent revolution. The abolition of the proletarian state, *i.e.*, of all states, is only possible through "withering away." . . .

The state is a special organisation of force; it is the organisation of violence for the suppression of some class. What class must the proletariat suppress? Naturally, the exploiting class only, *i.e.*, the bourgeoisie. The toilers need the state only to overcome the resistance of the exploiters, and only the proletariat can direct this suppression and bring it to fulfilment, for the proletariat is the only class that is thoroughly revolutionary, the only class that can unite all the toilers and the exploited in the struggle against the bourgeoisie, in completely displacing it.

The exploiting classes need political rule in order to maintain exploitation, *i.e.*, in the selfish interests of an insignificant minority, and against the vast majority of the people. The exploited classes need political rule in order completely to abolish all exploitation, *i.e.*, in the interests of the vast majority of the people, and against the insignificant minority consisting of the slaveowners of modern times—the landowners and the capitalists. . . .

The overthrow of the bourgeoisie is realisable only by the transformation of the proletariat into the *ruling class*, able to crush the inevitable and desperate resistance of the bourgeoisie, and to organise, for the new economic order, *all* the toiling and exploited masses.

The proletariat needs state power, the centralised organisation of force, the organisation of violence, both for the purpose of crushing the resistance of the exploiters and for the purpose of *guiding* the great mass of the population—the peasantry, the petty-bourgeoisie, the semi-proletarians—in the work of organising Socialist economy. . . .

The forms of bourgeois states are exceedingly variegated, but their essence is the same: in one way or another, all these states are in the last analysis inevitably a *dictatorship of the bourgeoisie*. The transition from capitalism to Communism will certainly bring a great variety and abundance of political forms, but the essence will inevitably be only one: *the dictatorship of the proletariat*. . . .

Transition from Capitalism to Communism

. . . [In his *Critique of the Gotha Programme*, Marx writes:]

> Between capitalist and Communist society—Marx continues—lies the period of the revolutionary transformation of the former into the latter. To this also corresponds a political transition period, in which the state can be no other than *the revolutionary dictatorship of the proletariat*.

This conclusion Marx bases on an analysis of the rôle played by the proletariat in modern capitalist society, on the data concerning the evolution of this society, and on the irreconcilability of the opposing interests of the proletariat and the bourgeoisie. . . .

What, then, is the relation of this dictatorship to democracy? . . .

In capitalist society, under the conditions most favourable to its development, we have more or less complete democracy in the democratic republic. But this democracy is always bound by the narrow framework of capitalist exploitation, and consequently always remains, in reality, a democracy for the minority, only for the possessing classes, only for the rich. Freedom in capitalist society always remains just about the same as it was in the ancient Greek republics: freedom for the slave-owners. The modern wage-slaves, owing to the conditions of capitalist exploitation, are so much crushed by want and poverty that "democracy is nothing to them," "politics is nothing to them"; that, in the ordinary peaceful course of events, the majority of the population is debarred from participating in social and political life. . . .

Democracy for an insignificant minority, democracy for the rich—that is the democracy of capitalist society. If we look more closely into the mechanism of capitalist democracy, everywhere, both in the "petty"—so-called petty—details of the suffrage (residential qualification, exclusion of women, etc.), and in the technique of the representative institutions, in the actual obstacles to the right of assembly (public buildings are not for "beggars"!), in the purely capitalist organisation of the daily press, etc., etc.—on all sides we see restriction after restriction upon democracy. These restrictions, exceptions, exclusions, obstacles for the poor, seem slight, especially in the eyes of one who has himself never known want and has never been in close contact with the oppressed classes in their mass life (and nine-tenths, if not ninety-nine hundredths, of the bourgeois publicists and politicians are of this class), but in their sum total these restrictions exclude and squeeze out the poor from politics and from an active share in democracy.

Marx splendidly grasped this *essence* of capitalist democracy, when, in analysing the experience of the Commune, he said that the oppressed were allowed, once every few years, to decide which particular representatives of the oppressing class should be in parliament to represent and repress them!

But from this capitalist democracy—inevitably narrow, subtly rejecting the poor, and therefore hypocritical and false to the core—progress does not march onward, simply, smoothly and directly, to "greater and greater democracy," as the liberal professors and petty-bourgeois opportunists would have us believe. No, progress marches onward, *i.e.*, towards Communism, through the dictatorship of the proletariat; it cannot do otherwsie, for there is no one else and no other way to *break the resistance* of the capitalist exploiters.

But the dictatorship of the proletariat—*i.e.*, the organisation of the vanguard of the oppressed as the ruling class for the purpose of crushing the oppressors—cannot produce merely an expansion of democracy. *Together* with an immense expansion of democracy which *for the first time* becomes democracy for the poor, democracy for the people, and not democracy for the rich folk, the dictatorship of the proletariat produces a series of restrictions of liberty in the case of the oppressors, the exploiters, the capitalists. We must crush them in order to free humanity from wage-slavery;

their resistance must be broken by force; it is clear that where there is suppression there is also violence, there is no liberty, no democracy.

Engels expressed this splendidly in his letter to Bebel when he said, as the reader will remember, that "as long as the proletariat still *needs* the state, it needs it not in the interests of freedom, but for the purpose of crushing its antagonists; and as soon as it becomes possible to speak of freedom, then the state, as such, ceases to exist."

Democracy for the vast majority of the people, and suppression by force, *i.e.*, exclusion from democracy, of the exploiters and oppressors of the people—this is the modification of democracy during the *transition* from capitalism to Communism.

Only in Communist society, when the resistance of the capitalists has been completely broken, when the capitalists have disappeared, when there are no classes (*i.e.*, there is no difference between the members of society in their relation to the social means of production), *only then* "the state ceases to exist," and "*it becomes possible to speak of freedom.*" Only then a really full democracy, a democracy without any exceptions, will be possible and will be realised. And only then will democracy itself begin to *wither away* due to the simple fact that, freed from capitalist slavery, from the untold horrors, savagery, absurdities and infamies of capitalist exploitation, people will gradually *become accustomed* to the observance of the elementary rules of social life that have been known for centuries and repeated for thousands of years in all school books; they will become accustomed to observing them without force, without compulsion, without subordination, without the *special apparatus* for compulsion which is called the state. . . .

First Phase of Communist Society

. . . Marx undertakes a *concrete* analysis of the conditions of life of a society in which there is no capitalism, and says:

What we are dealing with here [analysing the programme of the party] is not a Communist society which has *developed* on its own foundations, but, on the contrary, one which is just *emerging* from capitalist society, and which therefore in all respects—economic, moral and intellectual—still bears the birthmarks of the old society from whose womb it sprung.

And it is this Communist society—a society which has just come into the world out of the womb of capitalism, and which, in all respects, bears the stamp of the old society—that Marx terms the "first," or lower, phase of Communist society.

The means of production are no longer the private property of individuals. The means of production belong to the whole of society. Every member of society, performing a certain part of socially-necessary work, receives a certificate from society to the effect that he has done such and such a quantity of work. According to this certificate, he receives from the public warehouses, where articles of consumption are stored, a corresponding quantity of products. Deducting that proportion of labour which goes to the public fund, every worker, therefore, receives from society as much as he has given it.

"Equality" seems to reign supreme. . . .

"Equal right," says Marx, we indeed have here; but it is *still* a "bourgeois right," which, like every right, *presupposes inequality*. Every right is an application of the *same* measure to *different* people who, in fact, are not the same and are not equal to one another; this is why "equal right" is really a violation of equality, and an injustice. In effect, every man having done as much social labour as every other, receives an equal share of the social products (with the above-mentioned deductions).

But different people are not alike: one is strong, another is weak; one is married, the other is not; one has more children, another has less, and so on.

. . . With equal labour—Marx concludes—and therefore an equal share in the social consumption fund, one man in fact receives more than the other, one is richer than the other, and so forth. In order to avoid all these defects, rights, instead of being equal, must be unequal.

The first phase of Communism, therefore, still cannot produce justice and equality; differences, and unjust differences, in wealth will still exist, but the *exploitation* of man by man will have become impossible, because it will be impossible to seize as private property the *means of production*, the factories, machines, land, and so on. . . .

Marx not only takes into account with the greatest accuracy the inevitable inequality of men; he also takes into account the fact that the mere conversion of the means of production into the common property of the whole of society ("Socialism" in the generally accepted sense of the word) *does not remove* the defects of distribution and the inequality of "bourgeois right" which *continue to rule* as long as the products are divided "according to work performed."

But these defects—Marx continues—are unavoidable in the first phase of Communist society, when, after long travail, it first emerges from capitalist society. Justice can never rise superior to the economic conditions of society and the cultural development conditioned by them.

And so, in the first phase of Communist society (generally called Socialism) "bourgeois right" is *not* abolished in its entirety, but only in part, only in proportion to the economic transformation so far attained, *i.e.*, only in respect of the means of production. "Bourgeois right" recognises them as the private property of separate individuals. Socialism converts them into common property. *To that extent*, and to that extent alone, does "bourgeois right" disappear.

However, it continues to exist as far as its other part is concerned; it remains in the capacity of regulator (determining factor) distributing the products and allotting labour among the members of society. "He who does not work, shall not eat"—this Socialist principle is *already* realised; "for an equal quantity of labour, an equal quantity of products"—this Socialist principle is also *already* realised. However, this is not yet Communism, and this does not abolish "bourgeois right," which gives to unequal individuals, in return for an unequal (in reality unequal) amount of work, an equal quantity of products.

This is a "defect," says Marx, but it is unavoidable during the first phase of Communism; for, if we are not to fall into Utopianism, we cannot imagine that, having overthrown capitalism, people will at once learn to work for society *without any standards of right*; indeed, the abolition of capitalism *does not immediately lay* the economic foundations for *such* a change.

And there is no other standard yet than that of "bourgeois

right." To this extent, therefore, a form of state is still necesssary, which, while maintaining public ownership of the means of production, would preserve the equality of labour and equality in the distribution of products.

The state is withering away in so far as there are no longer any capitalists, any classes, and, consequently, no *class* can be suppressed.

But the state has not yet altogether withered away, since there still remains the protection of "bourgeois right" which sanctifies actual inequality. For the complete extinction of the state, complete Communism is necessary.

Higher Phase of Communist Society

Marx continues:

In a higher phase of Communist society, when the enslaving subordination of individuals in the division of labour has disappeared, and with it also the antagonism between mental and physical labour; when labour has become not only a means of living, but itself the first necessity of life; when, along with the all-round development of individuals, the productive forces too have grown, and all the springs of social wealth are flowing more freely—it is only at that stage that it will be possible to pass completely beyond the narrow horizon of bourgeois rights, and for society to inscribe on its banners: from each according to his ability; to each according to his needs! . . .

We have a right to speak solely of the inevitable withering away of the state, emphasising the protracted nature of this process and its dependence upon the rapidity of development of the *higher phase* of Communism; leaving quite open the question of lengths of time, or the concrete forms of withering away, since material for the solution of such questions is *not available.*

The state will be able to wither away completely when society has realised the rule: "From each according to his ability; to each according to his needs," *i.e.*, when people have become accustomed to observe the fundamental rules of social life, and their labour is so productive, that they voluntarily work *according to their ability.* . . .

Until the "higher" phase of Communism arrives, the Socialists demand the *strictest* control, *by society and by the state,* of the quantity of labour and the quantity of consumption; only this control must *start* with the expropriation of the capitalists, with the control of the workers over the capitalists, and must be carried out, not by a state of bureaucrats, but by a state of *armed workers.* . . .

The State and Revolution: A Case Study in the Genesis and Transformation of Communist Ideology

ROBERT V. DANIELS*

By common agreement among virtually all political complexions, Lenin's *State and Revolution* is accepted as the core of his doctrine of revolution and the proletarian dictatorship. A striking indication of the importance and contemporary relevance attributed to the work has been its use as evidence in the trials of the leaders of the American Communist party for conspiring to overthrow the government. And to the present Soviet commentator no less than to his bitterest adversary, *State and Revolution* sets up the premises from which the Soviet reality of today is considered to be the logical conclusion.

Yet this reasoning cannot be sustained on the basis of logic alone. *State and Revolution* is a work conforming neither to

* On the faculty of the University of Vermont, Professor Daniels is the author of a number of books and scholarly articles on Marxism and Soviet affairs, among them A *Documentary History of Communism* (1962), *The Conscience of the Revolution: Communist Opposition in Soviet Russia* (1960), and *The Nature of Communism* (1962).

From "The State and Revolution: A Case Study in the Genesis and Transformation of Communist Ideology" by Robert V. Daniels, *The American Slavic and East European Review*, New York, Vol. XIII, No. 1, January 1953, selections from pp. 22–43. By permission of the author and publisher. For footnote references, see original source.

Lenin's previous thought nor to his subsequent practice. It stands as a monument to its author's intellectual deviation during the year of revolution, 1917. Nevertheless, the ideas of *State and Revolution*, permeated with an idealistic, almost utopian spirit, were made to serve as the reference point for rationalizing the subsequent evolution of the Soviet State in an entirely different direction.

In *State and Revolution* Lenin developed in detail for the first time a political program to be followed by the proletarian dictatorship after the expected revolutionary victory. The plan was not complicated in its outlines. It comprised three main provisions for the ordering of the new body politic: 1) the destruction of the repressive machinery of the bourgeois state; 2) the establishment of a real democracy of the working class, with political representatives strictly subordinate to the will of the masses; 3) transference of the tasks of administration directly into the hands of the masses. Lenin summarized the new regime thus:

> The workers, having conquered political power, will break up the old bureaucratic apparatus, they will shatter it to its very foundations, until not one stone is left upon another; and they will replace it with a new one consisting of these same workers and employees, *against* whose transformation into bureaucrats measures will at once be undertaken, as pointed out in detail by Marx and Engels: 1) not only electiveness, but also instant recall; 2) payment no higher than that of ordinary workers; 3) immediate transition to a state of things when *all* fulfill the functions of control and superintendence, so that *all* become "bureaucrats" for a time, and *no one*, therefore, can become a "bureaucrat."

Such would be the constitution of the regime which would liquidate the remnants of the bourgeois order, superintend the socialist reorganization of the economy, and pave the way for the transition to the stateless society of communism.

State and Revolution, the most developed product of Lenin's thought in 1917, stands in sharp contrast to the main substance of "Leninism" expressed previously and subsequently. This is suggested by the fact that in *State and Revolution* the "party" in the abstract, as an element in the theory of the revolutionary process, is mentioned exactly *once*, and then only obliquely. The central position which the party otherwise usually held in Lenin's thought hardly needs to be stressed. A glance at Lenin's earlier writings readily reveals his accustomed emphasis on the role of the party in the revolutionary movement, and indicates moreover the contrast in organizational spirit with *State and Revolution*. In his famous pamphlet *Čto delat'?* (What Is to Be Done?) Lenin declared, ". . . the spontaneous struggle of the proletariat will not become a genuine 'class struggle' until it is led by a strong organization of revolutionaries," i.e., the party. The party was characteristically for Lenin the key element in the process of revolution. Within it, ". . . as regards the ideological and practical direction of the movement and the revolutionary struggle of the proletariat, the greatest possible centralization is necessary. . . . To lead the movement we must have the smallest possible number of the most single-minded groups, of professional revolutionaries tested by experience." Far removed is this from the faith in the masses of 1917.

Lenin's characteristic post-revolutionary attitude was typified in the theses which he presented on behalf of the Central Committee of the Communist Party to the Ninth Party Congress in March, 1920—"iron discipline," "obedience of labor," "centralization of economic administration," were terms in which he described the only course he saw open to the proletarian dictatorship in Russia. He declared frankly that ". . . the elective principle must be replaced by the principle of *selection*." A year later, at the Tenth Congress, Lenin summed up his current political philosophy in a single phrase, as he denounced the criticisms of the Workers' Opposition: ". . . the dictatorship of the proletariat is impossible except through the Communist Party."

These remarks are only cited as illustrations of the prevailing patterns of Lenin's political thought at various times. They should show sufficiently the extent to which *State and Revolution* is an aberration. The change in Lenin in 1917 was not, however, confined to theory; in his day-to-day political activity, his ideas of tactics, and in his relations with his fellow-revolutionaries in the Bolshevik party, Lenin displayed a shift in 1917 closely corresponding to the temporary modification of his over-all political outlook.

Understanding this extensive political change in Lenin is difficult within the limits of the usual conception of the history of the Bolshevik party. Ordinarily the party's pattern of development is seen as a straight line of unfolding Leninist strategy, flanked in either direction by deviations which split off. These in the early period dissipate themselves or rejoin the main stream, while in the later period they come to final grief in physical liquidation. This scheme is superficial and inadequate; actually, it corresponds closely to the official Communist picture of the history of the party. More accurately the party should be understood as comprising two fairly distinct lines of thought and policy, extending almost from the inception of the party to the political destruction of the Left Opposition in 1927. The dominant stream of Bolshevism was the Leninist—the familiar doctrine and organization which the party's founder represented up until 1917 and from 1918 on, and of which Stalin inherited the headship. The other ideological and political tendency was represented by various left-wing groups. From this designation it should not be assumed that the Leninist wing was particularly "rightist"; the latter was rather distinguished by its organizational "hardness." Essentially the Leninist and leftist streams of thought originated in separate though partially coincident splits from the prevailing Social-Democratic orthodoxy in two different dimensions—organizational hardness, and programmatic leftism. For a time many followers of these two tendencies believed themselves to be in the same camp, until disagreements arose after the revolution of 1905. However, a large number of future Left Oppositionists, from Trotsky on down, remained outside the Bolshevik ranks as late as 1917.

Between the two wings of the party there were clear-cut and consistent differences of outlook. The leftists stressed the egalitarian and anarchistic social goals of the revolution and pressed for their rapid realization; the Leninists stressed the means of struggle and the organization of power which they considered necessary for the attainment of the goals. The leftists were revolutionary idealists, the Leninists revolutionary pragmatists. In their backgrounds, the leftists tended to be middle class intellectuals; the Leninists, proletarian or peasant and non-intellectual; the Leninists were less likely to have had experience as émigrés in the West. Understandably, then, the leftists tended toward a theoretical and international outlook, the Leninists toward a practical and national view.

Although the leftist tendency did not enjoy such strength or continuity as did the Leninist, it was nevertheless expressed fairly consistently over the years by a succession of opposition groups—the Otzovists, Ultimatists, and Vperëdists during the period 1907–1912, the "Left Bolsheviks" during the war years, the Left Communists in 1918, the Democratic Centralists and the Workers' Opposition during the period of War Communism, the Trotskyists in 1921 and again from 1923 to 1927. In 1917, the leftist group for a time stepped out of its oppositionist role, and became the dominant force in the party. This was due not only to the revolutionary situation and the influx of the non-Bolshevik leftists, but also to the fact that Lenin himself shifted from the Leninist wing to the leftist wing of the party! This is why Lenin's April Theses were such a shock to the cautious Leninism of the majority of the people from the underground Bolshevik organization. Proceeding and gaining momentum, the leftist upsurge carried the party through 1917 and, overriding objections on the part of some of Lenin's formerly closest disciples, consummated the victory of October. *State and Revolution,* placed in its proper context as the most complete formulation of the leftist program, begins to make some sense.

What were the sources of the egalitarian and anarchistic program set forth by Lenin in *State and Revolution,* and in particular why did he stress so much the question of "smashing" the bourgeois state? Up until 1916 Lenin, in company with most of his Social-Democratic contemporaries, had given little or no attention to the problems treated in *State and Revolution,* or to the works of Marx and Engels in which they were originally discussed. Quite suddenly, in late 1916 and early 1917, he developed an avid interest in these matters, and commenced the study and writing which eventually took published form in *State and Revolution.* This sudden focus of attention on the theory of the revolutionary state immediately preceded Lenin's shift over to the leftist stream of Bolshevik thought, and was apparently instrumental in precipitating his change of outlook.

The principal credit for inspiring the new trend in Lenin's political thought belongs to Nikolaj Bukharin, later an eminent Communist theoretician, leader of the Right Opposition against Stalin, and finally shot in 1938. Up to 1918 Bukharin was the chief leader of the left-wing Bolsheviks. In 1916 he wrote a number of extremely interesting articles on the relation of the state to the Socialist revolution. The influence which these had on Lenin was indicated in the collection of Lenin's notes and miscellaneous writings, *Leninskij Sbornik* (Lenin Collection), published in 1924, in an editorial note appended to the materials relating to this period:

> Under the pseudonym of "Nota Bene" N. I. Bukharin placed in No. 6 of the journal "The Youth International" [Jugendinternationale] an article on the question of the state, in which he subjected to criticism the "commonly held" but in fact Kautskian interpretation of the teaching of Marx on the state. It was precisely this article which induced Vladimir Il'ich to occupy himself more closely with the corresponding question. From the article prepared by Vladimir Il'ich . . . arose his work *State and Revolution.*

In the body of his letter to Alexandra Kollontay of February 17, 1917, to which the above note referred, Lenin wrote:

> I am preparing . . . an article on the question of the relation of Marxism to the state. I have already come to conclusions more sharply against Kautsky than against Bukharin. . . .

The article by Bukharin to which Lenin referred was "Der imperialistische Raubstaat," which appeared in *Jugendinternationale* on December 1, 1916. It was one of a series of articles in which Bukharin developed the idea that a fundamental task of the proletarian revolution was the literal destruction of the existing bourgeois state. The rationale of this program Bukharin set forth most profoundly in another article, where he revealed what in retrospect can be seen as amazing prophetic insight. This was "Teorija imperialisticeskogo gosudarstva" (The Theory of the Imperialist State), an essay so apt as an analysis of a major social trend of the twentieth century that its virtual oblivion imperatively should be remedied.

Bukharin in this article advanced the thesis that in the era of imperialism a new form of political and social organization was evolving out of bourgeois society. "Militaristic state capitalism," he termed this incipient new order, under which

> the state power . . . sucks in almost all areas of production; it not only embraces the general conditions of the exploitative process; the

state becomes more and more a direct exploiter, which organizes and directs production, as a collective capitalist.

The ultimate result of this tendency would be ". . . a new Leviathan, in comparison with which the fantasy of Thomas Hobbes seems like child's play." Socialism, in Bukharin's mind, had nothing in common with the totalitarian, bureaucratic state whose possible evolution he foresaw.

Socialism is the regulation of production directed by *society*, not by the state. . . . it is the abolition of class contradictions, not their intensification.

The proletarian revolution is not simply the midwife of the new socialist society which is bound to come forth at some moment from the shell of capitalist society; there are two alternative successors to capitalism—"militaristic state capitalism," under which the whole force of social organization bears down on the proletariat to exploit it, where "the worker is transformed into a slave"—*or* socialism.

Theoretically, there can be two possibilities here: either the workers' organizations, like all the organizations of the bourgeoisie, will merge into the state-wide organization and be transformed into a simple appendage of the state apparatus, or they will outgrow the framework of the state and burst it from within, as they organize their own state power (the dictatorship [of the proletariat]).

The proletarian revolution was assigned the crucial task of forcing the development of society out of the course toward state capitalism, and into the course toward socialism. (Bukharin, to his personal misfortune, was of course unaware of the possibility that a successful proletarian revolution might fail to divert the course of history and, under certain conditions, actually accelerate the evolution of the Leviathan which he so feared.)

The tactical conclusion which Bukharin derived from his theory of contemporary social evolution was ultra-radical, ". . . a general attack on the ruling bandits. In the developing revolutionary struggle the proletariat destroys the state organization of the bourgeoisie. . . ." This dictum was echoed by Lenin in *State and Revolution*: "A revolution must not consist in a new class ruling, governing with the help of the *old* state machinery, but in this class *smashing* this machinery and ruling, governing by means of *new* machinery."

With this attitude toward the old political order Bukharin and Lenin were following in the footsteps of certain left-wing European Marxists, notably the Dutch Social-Democrat Anton Pannekoek, an astronomer by profession, but by avocation a revolutionary theorist. Pannekoek posed the thesis that

> The state power is not a simple neutral object in the class struggle; it is a weapon and a fortress of the bourgeoisie, the strongest support, without which the bourgeoisie could never retain its place.

This view was the basis for his contention that

> The struggle of the proletariat is not simply a struggle against the bourgeoisie *over* the state power as an object, but a struggle *against* the state power. . . . The content of this revolution is the destruction and dissolution of the state's means of force by the proletariat's means of force.

Underlying the emphasis which Pannekoek, Bukharin, and (following them) Lenin placed on revolution as an act of smashing the state, was an aspect of Marxian political theory which was subject to a great deal of misunderstanding. This was the question of the relation of the state machinery to the class struggle; specifically, was the existence of the political power exclusively a product of the class struggle? As popularly understood the doctrine of Marxism is simple; the state is nothing more than the organ of the ruling class to suppress the masses and maintain the conditions of exploitation. Bukharin, for example, even in "The Theory of the Imperialist State," defined the state thus:

> From the point of view of Marxism, the state is nothing other than the greatest general organization of the ruling classes, the basic function of which consists of the preservation and extension of the exploitation of the oppressed classes.

Lenin, in *State and Revolution*, is on this point quite clear: no class conflict, no state.

Reference to the original sources of the theory, however, reveals a different implication. Engels, in *The Origin of the Family, Private Property, and the State*, explained the development of political institutions thus:

The state, then, is by no means a power forced on society from the outside. . . . It is simply a product of society at a certain stage of evolution. It is the confession that this society has become hopelessly divided against itself, has entangled itself in irreconcilable contradictions which it is powerless to banish. In order that these contradictions, these classes with conflicting economic interests, may not annihilate themselves and society in a useless struggle, a power becomes necessary that stands apparently above society and has the function of keeping down the conflicts and maintaining "order." And this power, the outgrowth of society, but assuming supremacy over it and becoming more and more divorced from it, is the state.

Engels made here a point that most of his successors never really grasped: that the class struggle explains the *origin* of the state, but not necessarily its *continued existence*. Once established, the state organization tends to become its own *raison d'être*, and can exist more and more independently of the conditions which originally produced it. To be sure, the state continues to play a role in the class struggle:

The state is the result of the desire to keep down class conflicts, but having arisen amid these conflicts, it is as a rule the state of the most powerful economic class that by force of its economic supremacy becomes also the ruling political class and thus acquires new means of subduing and exploiting the oppressed masses.

This and other tasks which the state is called upon to perform simply increase the power, scope, and independence of the state organization:

This public power of coercion . . . increases in the same ratio in which the class antagonisms become more pronounced, and in which neighboring states become larger and more populous. A conspicuous example is modern Europe, where the class struggles and wars of conquest have nursed the public power to such a size that it threatens to swallow the whole society. . . .

Here Engels took account of a particularly important aspect of the modern state—as a unit in an anarchistic international society, with the consequent pressures of defense and/or aggrandizement—an aspect ignored almost totally in most Marxist thought on the state, but an aspect which nevertheless played a key role in Soviet political rationalizations after the revolution.

Marx himself employed the idea that the state can become an independent source of evil in society, apart from any given ruling class. This was the tendency which he observed in France, whose government until 1848 had been

> . . . a mere tool in the hands of the dominant class. Not until the second Bonaparte rose to power, does the State seem to have become completely independent. As against bourgeois society, the State machine has fortified itself so thoroughly that the chief of the So-ciety of December the Tenth [Louis Bonaparte's brownshirts] can function as its director. . . .

Later on, Marx analyzed the Bonaparte dictatorship of the Second Empire as an instance of the particular independence which the state power was able to acquire at a time when the contending social classes, in this case bourgeoisie and proletariat, were nearly evenly balanced in strength.

> . . . it was the only form of government possible at a time when the bourgeoisie had already lost, and the working class had not yet acquired, the faculty of ruling the nation.

The interesting point here lies in Marx's reference to "ruling the nation," which by the implication of this context represents some kind of a social function which has to be carried on entirely apart from the class struggle. This suggests that the class struggle theory of the state was all along supposed to be understood in a limited sense, as referring only to that aspect of social organization which concerned the means by which one class repressed another. Close analysis of *State and Revolution* reveals that Lenin, by way of the restricted definitions which he employs, made precisely this tacit assumption.

Proceeding from the recognition that the state power could become dangerously independent, Marx drew upon the experience of the Paris Commune for a prescription of the course of action which should be taken to ensure a successful proletarian revolu-tion. In *The Civil War in France* he outlined the measures which would have to be taken in order to end permanently the threat to the proletariat posed by the old state institutions, and to

> . . . restore to the social body all the forces hitherto absorbed by the state parasite feeding upon, and clogging the free movement of, society.

Complete democratic control over all political functions was to be assured by election of all officials, the right of immediate recall of elected officials, limitation of the salaries of all government officials to the level of workmen's wages, local and municipal autonomy as far as practicable, and above all the replacement of all police and military formations by the national guard, i.e., the collectivity of the population, the "armed people."

Marx commented on the program of the Commune itself:

> The few but important functions which still would remain for a central government . . . were to be discharged by Communal, and therefore strictly responsible agents. . . . While the merely repressive organs of the old governmental power were to be amputated, its legitimate functions were to be wrested from an authority usurping pre-eminence over society itself, and restored to the responsible agents of society. Instead of deciding once in three or six years which member of the ruling class was to represent the people in Parliament, universal suffrage was to serve the people, constituted in Communes, as individual suffrage serves every other employer in the search for the workmen and managers in his business. . . . nothing could be more foreign to the spirit of the Commune than to supersede universal suffrage by hierarchic investiture.
>
>   . . . the Commune . . . was a thoroughly expansive political form, while all previous forms of government had been emphatically repressive. Its true secret was this. It was essentially a working-class government, the product of the struggle of the producing against the appropriating class, the political form at last discovered under which to work out the economic emancipation of Labor.

Engels, in his 1891 introduction to *The Civil War in France*, went even further in his political conclusions:

> The Commune was compelled to recognize from the outset that the working class, once come to power, could not carry on business with the old state machine; that, in order not to lose again its own position of power which it had but just conquered, this working class must, on the one hand, set aside all the old repressive machinery previously used against itself, and on the other, *safeguard itself against its own deputies and officials* by declaring them all, without any exception, subject to recall at any moment. . . . What had been the characteristic attribute of the former state? Society had created its own organs to look after its common interests, originally through simple division of labor. But these organs at whose head

was the state power, had in the course of time, in pursuance of their own special interests, transformed themselves from the servants of society into the masters of society. . . .

In this manner Engels derived from his conception of the independent existence of the state an imperative directive for action to protect the socialist society. The state is not ultimately a derivative of the class struggle, but was (in Engels' Rousseauan phraseology) "created" by "society" "to look after its common interests." The class aspect is an auxiliary feature, acquired in the course of history. Hence there is no reason to conclude that with the termination of the class struggle by a proletarian revolution, the state will necessarily wither away; it simply ceases to be an organ of *class* repression, because there are no more classes to be repressed by each other. Not only does the state still exist; it continues to be a threat to the successful establishment of a socialist society because of the possibility of "transforming itself into the master of society." Therefore it is imperative for the proletariat to take the measures which Marx outlines, in order that the institutions which must exist to carry out necessary social functions will not be able to dominate the population which they are supposed to serve.

> Against this transformation of the state and the organs of the state from servants of society into masters of society—a process which had been inevitable in all previous states—the Commune made use of two infallible remedies. In the first place, it filled all posts—administrative, judicial, and educational—by election on the basis of universal suffrage of all concerned, with the right of these electors to recall their delegate at any time. And in the second place, all officials, high or low, were paid only the wages received by other workers.

This action by the Commune Engels hailed as the "shattering of the former state power and its replacement by a new and really democratic state."

Lenin had no sooner acquainted himself with the program of smashing the bourgeois state than he incorporated it wholeheartedly into his scheme of the revolutionary process. The idea of smashing the state proved quickly to be irresistible to Lenin as a set of political tactics. However, he failed to grasp the basic rationale of the smashing dictum—protection of society against the dangerous independence of the state machinery—and as a result he allowed the entire program of mass control over the exercise of political power to be vitiated after his party came to power. Lenin did not go beyond the narrow class-determined conception of the state. This simple view, justifying all the rigorous measures taken in the name of the dictatorship of the proletariat, and assuring the ultimate prospect of the withering away of the state and political coercion, was the generally accepted premise of the political doctrine of the Communist Party. (The subtleties of Marx and Engels about the broader aspects of political institutions have remained in a convenient oblivion as far as Communist theoreticians have been concerned.)

In *State and Revolution* Lenin followed Engels on the withering of the narrowly conceived state:

> . . . once the majority of the people *itself* suppresses its oppressors, a "special force" for suppression is *no longer necessary*. In this sense the state *begins to wither away*. Instead of a privileged minority . . . the majority can itself directly fulfill all these functions; and the more the discharge of the functions of state power devolves upon the people generally, the less need is there for the existence of this power.

It was, however, only to the state in the narrow sense, as an instrument for class repression, that Lenin applied the dicta of smashing and democratic controls (measures originally designed for application to the state in the broad sense to keep it from becoming the "master of society"). His shift after the October Revolution to his characteristically greater emphasis on pragmatic and power considerations was foreshadowed even in *State and Revolution* as he revealed his readiness to yield, outside the realm of the narrowly "political," to pressures for the maintenance of a strong institutional authority and for the retention of the old bureaucratic and managerial personnel. The anarchistic ideal, he reasoned, was rendered utopian in economic affairs by the actual development of the conditions of production under industrialism:

> Take a factory, a railway, a vessel on the high seas . . . is it not clear that not one of these complex technical units, based on the use of machines and the ordered cooperation of many people, could function without a certain amount of subordination and, consequently, without some authority or power?

Lenin was frank in recognizing the preferred position which this requirement conferred on trained technical and managerial personnel inherited from the old regime:

> We need good organizers in banking, and in the work of combining enterprises (in these matters the capitalists have more experience, and work is done more easily with experienced people); we need more and more engineers, agronomists, technicians, scientific experts of every kind. . . . Probably, we shall only gradually bring in equality for all work, leaving a temporary higher rate of pay for such specialists during the transition period, but we shall put them under an all embracing workers' control. . . . As for the organizational form of the work, we do not invent it, we take it ready-made from capitalism. . . .

The prospects for a flourishing institutional structure outside the context of the withering political state were indicated by Lenin in his speech to the First Congress of Economic Councils in May, 1918:

> There is no doubt that the further the conquests of the October Revolution advance . . . the greater and higher will become the role of the economic councils, which alone among all state institutions will preserve for themselves a lasting place that will become all the more permanent the nearer we come to the establishment of a socialist system, the less we need a purely administrative apparatus engaged only in government, strictly speaking. This apparatus, an apparatus engaged only in government, strictly speaking. This apparatus is doomed, after the resistance of the exploiters has definitely been smashed, after the toilers have learned to organize socialist production—this apparatus of administration in the proper, narrow, restricted sense of the word, this apparatus of the old state is doomed to die; but an apparatus of the type of our Supreme Economic Council is destined to grow, develop, and become strong, fulfilling all principal active functions of an organized society.

This was yet another effort to reconcile the narrow, strictly class conception of the state with the patent necessity of over-all social organization and authority to direct the growingly complex affairs of modern society. The "state" might wither away, to be sure, but the scope of "state" and "withering" were being progressively constricted.

Very rapidly after the October Revolution the dominant orientation of the party and its leadership shifted from program and ideals to the problems of organizing and defending political power; the party again rose to the forefront in the Bolshevik system of thought. Most party members ceased to take the program of *State and Revolution* seriously, at least not in their day-to-day activity. This neglect became general under the pressure of the civil war. The soviets, supposedly embodying the control measures of the 1917 program, fell into abeyance, as the locus of real political power shifted to the party and especially to the higher organs of the party. Military and economic stress, the practical and military orientation of the party, the necessity of recourse to bureaucratic methods to make the government, economy, and army function, and the limitations in the program itself as understood, all combined to defeat the democratic spirit of the revolutionary ideology and to facilitate the formation of a new bureaucratic, hierarchical political order.

A rearguard action, hopeless under these conditions, was fought by the leftist opposition groups in the party—the Workers' Opposition and the Democratic Centralists—to defend the spirit of *State and Revolution* against the bureaucratic expediencies which the majority of the party was freely condoning. All thought of formally limiting political authority from below was dismissed by most Communists. Strong state power, under the firm control of the party as the vanguard of the proletariat, was held to be the indispensable instrument of the dictatorship of the proletariat in carrying through the socialist revolution and suppressing the resistance of the dispossessed classes.

The theory of the state as the instrument of the dictatorship of the proletariat in the period of transition, consolidation, and building of socialism served effectively to put out of mind the real problems of the relation of the state to society and the dangers of the state becoming independent of mass control and the "master of society." It was in this theoretical context, or lack of context, that the Soviet State, independent of any popular control or class domination, did in fact become the "master of society," realizing more accurately that one could ever expect the fears expressed by Marx and Bukharin.

This institutional evolution has been mirrored in ideology. Changes in the field of political theory provide a striking illustration of the post-revolutionary transformation in Soviet thinking. From the view of the state as a necessary evil destined to wither away from the revolutionary social transformation was accomplished, party doctrine has shifted around 180 degrees, to extol the state as the highest form of social organization and a great creative force.

Like most of the theoretical content of party ideology, the doctrine of the state remained substantially unchanged from the Revolution to 1929. The extensive evolution in political practice and institutions which took place up to that time, the decline of the soviets and the rise of the party, were subsumed under the category of the dictatorship of the proletariat, which was still officially expected to lead into the withering away of the state when the resistance of remnants of the exploiting classes had been finally overcome. The one potentially significant development was Stalin's theory of socialism in one country, which, in asserting the possibility of socialism being achieved under conditions of capitalist encirclement, contained in embryo a justification for the retention of the state under socialism to meet the needs of defense.

Some foretaste of the state of mind which was later to prevail was provided by developments on the theory of the political role of the party, which accompanied the consolidation of power in the hands of Stalin and the party secretariat. The dynamic scheme whereby the revolution was to be made in the ultimate interest of the whole population, by the workers, under the leadership of the vanguard of the proletariat, the party, was transformed into a static pattern for the organization of the revolutionary regime in a sharply stratified and hierarchical form.

> . . . the party is not only indispensable to the proletariat for the establishment of the dictatorship. It becomes even more necessary after the seizure of power in order to maintain the dictatorship of the proletariat, to consolidate and enlarge it with a view to inaugurating a completely socialized order. . . . The proletarian masses must be imbued with the spirit of discipline and organization; . . . the proletarian masses must be inoculated against the harmful influence of the petty bourgeoisie, must be prevented from acquiring petty-bourgeois habits and customs.

Thus did Stalin demonstrate his distrust of the masses, who could not be relied on to behave in a socialist fashion without external compulsion. Stalin was in practice coming to consider the party, and conscious top-level political leadership, as the prime mover of history (a not unnatural attitude toward the role which he himself was coming to play). It was the party, rather than spontaneous economic evolution, which must be looked to primarily for the preparation of "the conditions for the inauguration of socialist production."

In 1930 Stalin first explicitly modified the doctrine of the withering-away of the state.

> We are in favor of the state dying out, and at the same time we stand for the strengthening of the dictatorship of the proletariat, which represents the most powerful and mighty authority of all forms of state which have existed up to the present day. The highest possible development of the power of the state, with the object of preparing the conditions of the dying out of the state: that is the Marxist formula. Is it "contradictory"? Yes, it is "contradictory." But this contradiction is a living thing, and completely reflects Marxist dialectics.

Four years later, Stalin strengthened this view by incorporating the experience of the violent imposition of central power which characterized the period of the first Five Year Plan and collectivization:

> It goes without saying that a classless society cannot come of itself, spontaneously, as it were. It has to be achieved and built by the efforts of all the working people, by strengthening the organs of the dictatorship of the proletariat, by intensifying the class struggle, by abolishing classes, by eliminating the remnants of the capitalist classes, and in battles with enemies both internal and external.

Worries about the state power becoming dangerously independent were dispersed by the narrow class conception of the state which Marxists by this time accepted almost universally. The Soviet State was the state of the working class, and hence by definition could do naught but serve the interests of the proletariat. The stronger the state and the party, the better would the interests of the proletariat be served. From this it followed that the idealistically-minded oppositionists in the party who from time to time ventured to protest the growing centralization of power were "objectively" undermining the revolutionary cause and rendering themselves liable to appropriate measures of discipline. As to the ultimate disposition of the state with its manifest bureaucratic tendencies, the final achievement of communism would automatically cause the withering of the state and all its problems. Evidently there were growing misgivings in the party over this, for Stalin found it necessary to discredit the concern felt by some Bukharinists, apparently over the failure of the state to begin to show signs of withering away. Referring to "a little confusion and . . . unhealthy sentiments among a section of party members," he asserted:

> . . . they began to reason in this way: If it is classless society, then we can relax the class struggle, we can relax the dictatorship of the proletariat, and get rid of the state altogether, since it is fated to die out soon in any case. They dropped into a state of moon-calf ecstasy, in the expectation that soon there will be no classes, and therefore no class struggle, and therefore no cares and worries, and therefore we can lay down our arms and retire—to sleep and to wait for the advent of classless society. (General laughter.) It goes without saying that if this confusion of mind and these non-Bolshevik sentiments obtained a hold over the majority of our Party, the Party would find itself demobilized and disarmed.

In accord with actual political developments, the role of political power and organization was moving to the forefront of Communist theory.

It was on the basis of the above pronouncements of Stalin that party spokesmen were able to argue the continued need to strengthen the state when, with the introduction of the Constitution of 1936, socialism was declared to have been achieved. ". . . all the exploiting classes have now been eliminated," Stalin declared; there remained three cooperating groups, workers, peasants, and the "Soviet intelligentsia."

Nevertheless, the struggle against the remnants of the exploiting classes had to be intensified:

> The specific gravity of the hostile elements in our Soviet structure is unusually low, almost equal to zero, but even so these elements can resort to the sharpest forms of struggle with us.

"Vigilance against the enemies of the Soviet State" provided the theoretical heading under which was subsumed in all its ramifications the Great Purge.

For a definitive new theory of the state, the party had to wait until Stalin got around to making a statement. This he did at the Eighteenth Party Congress in 1939. He was faced with the problem of developing a more convincing rationalization for the obviously permanent Leviathan state whose construction had just been completed, a political order which blatantly contravened the withering prognosis of Marxian theory.

At the Congress, Stalin casually and sketchily indicated the outlines of his new theory of the Soviet state. Once he had spoken, his words were seized upon in the now familiar pattern, and broadcast, amplified, elaborated upon, interpreted, and canonized into the body of infallible revolutionary truth: "Comrade Stalin raised the Marxist-Leninist doctrine of the state to a new, higher level," was the theme running through all these commentaries.

Comrade Stalin certainly did raise the Marxist-Leninist doctrine of the state to a new, higher level. He raised it from the level of a superstructural dependence on economic forces and class contradictions, a temporarily necessary evil from the standpoint of revolution, to the level of a prime mover of history and a positive social good. We now have, at every turn in Soviet writings, "The Soviet state, a state of a new type, the most democratic in the world, the chief instrument for the overcoming of class differences and for the preparation of the material and spiritual prerequisites for the transition to communism."

By one of the typically labored feats of common sense which pass for genius in the Soviet Union, Stalin brought the Marxian theory of the state down to Soviet earth by recalling some of the most prosaic aspects of the state which had been abstracted out of the realm of the political by the restricted class conception of the state.

Without the pretentiousness which the significance of his remarks might have justified, Stalin began his cursory re-examination of the political theory of the Soviet state by considering the obvious question, why has the state not begun to wither away? The very posing of such a question, he asserted, indicated an erroneous approach to the whole problem, by people who followed theory too literally without regard to the complexities of practice. Vyshinsky had in an article published shortly before been much harsher with the questioners; treachery, he termed it, to suppose that

. . . the process of the withering of the state will be realized not through the maximum strengthening of the state power of the proletariat, but through the weakening of this power.

Stalin had particularly in mind the implications of the international context in which socialism was being built in the Soviet Union; the necessity of the state for national defense was obvious. Whether consciously or not, he was taking advantage of one of the serious weaknesses of the ordinary narrow Marxist view of the state; he pointed to very real considerations—such as defense—which were not taken into account in the narrow class theory of the state, but which could hardly be denied. These considerations he used to justify political developments which would seem inexplicable if not intolerable from the old point of view. In this way Stalin undertook to correct the doctrine of the withering of the state as formulated by Engels. He contended that Engels had reasoned in abstraction from the international context, with his assumption of the simultaneous victory of socialism in most or all states. However, Stalin was either partially ignorant of Engels' views, or chose to distort them. Engels had specifically referred to international pressures in accounting for the growth of the supra-class aspects of the state as the master of society. The socialist revolution would necessarily have to be international, in order to eliminate the needs of defense which so encouraged the tendency toward bureaucracy. This point, however, had been entirely overlooked in all the discussions on socialism in one country.

Having established the orthodoxy of the socialist revolution in national isolation, Stalin was able to justify all the features of the traditional state which were associated with national security—he referred particularly to the army, intelligence service, and penal institutions. In fact, the whole of Stalin's new political theory can be described as the shift from the narrow class theory of the state back to the broad conception of the state as an institution of social service, compulsion, and action, standing above classes (though of course influenced by the class structure of society). Stalin was simply recognizing the emergence of the supra-class state which Marx, Engels, and Bukharin warned against. But in his evaluation of this state he differed diametrically with them.

An almost conventional and common-sense attitude was suggested in Stalin's description of the development of the Soviet state and its functions, a development which he broke down into two phases: phase one, to the elimination of the exploiting classes; phase two, afterwards. The state in phase one had three functions: 1) the familiar work of the dictatorship of the proletariat, suppressing the exploiting classes; 2) national defense—following logically from the doctrine of socialism in one country; 3) a new idea—the beginnings of "the economic-organizing and cultural-educational work of the organs in our state, which had as its goal the development of the sprouts of a new, socialist economy and the reeducation of people in the spirit of socialism." (Here we can see the complete divergence from Marxism, in conceiving of economic and cultural development as the results of political organization and action.) This positive role of the state was completely foreign to the narrow class view of the state. The functions described here had earlier been thought of as the non-political administrative operations which would devolve upon society as the state withered away; this was, for example, the course envisaged by Lenin in his speech on the economic councils in May, 1918.

In phase two,

> The function of military suppression within the country fell off, died away, for the exploiters were annihilated, there are no more exploiters left to suppress. In place of the function of suppression the state has taken on the function of defense of socialist property from thieves and embezzlers of the people's goods.

Even if euphemistically, Stalin was forced to recognize in his theoretical system the extreme tensions in Soviet society and the need for the regime to rely on police repression. The second function, defense, continues under phase two, while the third, the development of the economy and educational work by the state, becomes fully extended.

Finally, Stalin asked himself the crucial question:

> Will we also retain the state even in the period of communism?
>
> Yes, it will be retained, if the capitalist encirclement is not liquidated. . . .
>
> No, it will not be retained but will die away, if the capitalist encirclement is liquidated, if it is replaced by a socialist encirclement.
>
> Thus do matters stand on the question of the socialist state.

And thus have matters stood ever since, with innumerable commentaries on Stalin's brief statement, but with no positive contributions to the theory save Stalin's own contained in his article

"On Marxism in Linguistics" in June, 1950. Earlier constructions of Marxist political theory have been recast in the spirit of Stalin's broad conception of the state as independent of class society and charged with a variety of positive roles. Typical of this effort to reinterpret Communist doctrine is a recent article by one V. V. Nikolaev, which amounted to an exercise in tying together in a chain of historical logic both the present Soviet regime and the Bolshevik program of 1917. As is characteristic in the application of Communist ideology to the rationalization of the Soviet regime, the connection was established with the use of broad ideological categories—"socialism," "democracy," "classless," "mass participation"—terms which were always loose and whose practical content was subjected to drastic change. This accomplished the formal identification of present practice and the ideal of *State and Revolution*. Effectively suppressed were the vast substantive differences between them which had resulted from two decades of the most rapid social change.

The new Stalinist conception of the state was an adaptation of theory to reality, a correction of the narrow Marxist approach which had been overwhelmed by events. In the Soviet Union there was a state, independent of classes and the class struggle, growing more powerful as "class" (though not "strata") differences were supposed to be disappearing; moreover, this state was not the mere product or reflection of deeper economic and social conditions—it had become a prime mover of history. Accordingly, Stalin could revise the basic Marxist conception of the social process and revolution, as he did in discussing the problem of base and superstructure (referring especially to the political organs of society) in relation to language:

> The superstructure is generated by the base, but this by no means signifies that it merely reflects the base, that it is passive, neutral and indifferent to the fate of its base, to the fate of classes, to the character of the system. On the contrary, having put in an appearance, it then becomes a most active force which has contributed vigorously to the formation and consolidation of its base, takes all steps to assist the new order to drive the old base and the former classes into the dust and liquidate them.

Marx has been turned on his head. Bukharin has been shot. The Leviathan has come into its own.

The Ultimate Source of Power:
The Party

· 1 ·

THE PROFESSIONAL REVOLUTIONARY

AND THE PARTY

If Lenin's *State and Revolution* refers only obliquely to the role of the Party in the theory of the revolutionary process, his *What Is to Be Done?*, excerpts from which comprise the first article in this section, attaches paramount importance to it. Stressing the need for a centralized revolutionary organization for the planned political struggle against the "oppressors of the proletariat," Lenin emphasized the necessity of developing the political class consciousness of the workers. This, he argues, can be achieved "*only from without*, that is, only from outside of the economic struggle . . . between workers and employers." By its own effort alone the working class, in his view, is able to develop only trade union consciousness and organizations. But while the broad trade union organizations are considered capable of becoming "a very important auxiliary to political agitation and revolutionary organization," they are also deemed unsuitable by their very nature for the application of the "methods of strict secrecy" required by the clandestine conditions of the political struggle. These can be applied, in Lenin's view, only by a conspiratorial, highly centralized (though not necessarily extensive) organization composed of disciplined full-time *professional revolutionaries*.

Though Lenin's conception of the Party and its relation to the proletariat was formulated in the light of the autocratic conditions that prevailed in Tsarist Russia, it implicitly denied the Marxian assumption that the capitalist relations of production and distribution, rather than forces from without, determine both the political class consciousness of the workers and the characteristics of revolutionary ideology. In the words of Plekhanov, the great Russian Marxist theoretician, Lenin confused "the dictatorship of the proletariat with the dictatorship *over* the proletariat."

Writing later under the conditions of Soviet power in Russia, Stalin considers the Party as the "vanguard of the working class" designed "to lead the proletariat, and not follow in the tail of the spontaneous movement." In his article, *The Party* (pages 209–216), based on a lecture he delivered at the Sverdlov University of Moscow in April 1924, Stalin associates the Party with the General Staff of an army, emphasizing the indispensability of both. The Party is considered not only as the "organized detachment" and the "highest form of class organization of the proletariat," but as the central, policy-determining organ of all non-Party mass organizations as well. But above all, Stalin argues, the Party is "an *instrument* in the hands of the proletariat *for* achieving the dictatorship where that has not yet been achieved and *for* consolidating and expanding the dictatorship where it has already been achieved." As an instrument of this type, the Party is required to establish an iron discipline and bring about the complete and absolute "unity of action" of its members. The disease of "factionalism and opportunism"—obviously as diagnosed by the upper Party hierarchy—is to be eradicated by periodic purges.

In his book *The New Class* (pages 216–219) Milovan Djilas, who once served as Vice President of Yugoslavia under the Tito regime, refutes the Leninist-Stalinist conception of the Party as the vehicle of progress guiding the working class on the road to Utopia. As the main force of the Communist state, the Party tends "to unite within itself the new class, the government, ownership, and ideas." The ideals professed before the acquisition of power are gradually perverted after the revolution when the Party hierarchy gets to control all power.

What Is to Be Done?

V. I. LENIN

"Everyone agrees" that it is necessary to develop the political consciousness of the working class. The question is, *how* is that to be done, what is required to do it? The economic struggle merely "brings home" to the workers questions concerning the attitude of the government towards the working class. Consequently, *however much we may try* to "lend the economic struggle itself a political character" *we shall never be able* to develop the political consciousness of the workers (to the level of Social-Democratic political consciousness) by keeping within the framework of the economic struggle, for *that framework is too narrow.* . . .

Class political consciousness can be brought to the workers *only from without*, that is, only from outside of the economic struggle, from outside of the sphere of relations between workers and employers. The sphere from which alone it is possible to obtain this knowledge is the sphere of relationships between *all* the classes and strata and the state and the government, the sphere of the interrelations between *all* the classes. For that reason, the reply to the question: what must be done in order to bring political knowledge to the workers? cannot be merely the one which, in the majority of cases, the practical workers, especially those who are inclined towards Economism, mostly content themselves with, i.e., "go among the workers." To bring political knowledge to the *workers* the Social-Democrats must *go among all classes of the population*, must dispatch units of their army *in all directions.* . . .

The . . . assertions . . . that the economic struggle is the most widely applicable means of political agitation and that our

From *What Is to Be Done?* by V. I. Lenin, selections from pp. 132–232. Moscow: Foreign Languages Publishing House, 1952.

task now is to lend the economic struggle itself a political character, etc., express a narrow view not only of our political, but also of
our *organizational* tasks. The "economic struggle against the employers and the government" does not in the least require—and
therefore such a struggle can never give rise to—a . . . centralized
organization that will combine, in one general onslaught, all and
every manifestation of political opposition, protest and indignation,
an organization that will consist of professional revolutionaries and
be led by the real political leaders of the whole people. This is but
natural. The character of any organization is naturally and inevitably determined by the content of its activity. . . .

The political struggle of Social-Democracy is far more extensive
and complex than the economic struggle of the workers against the
employers and the government. Similarly (and indeed for that
reason), the organization of a revolutionary Social-Democratic
party must inevitably be of a *different* kind than the organizations
of the workers designed for this struggle. A workers' organization
must in the first place be a trade organization; secondly, it must be
as broad as possible; and thirdly, it must be as little clandestine as
possible (here, and further on, of course, I have only autocratic
Russia in mind). On the other hand, the organizations of revolutionaries must consist first, foremost and mainly of people who
make revolutionary activity their profession (that is why I speak of
organizations of *revolutionaries*, meaning revolutionary Social-
Democrats). In view of this common feature of the members of
such an organization, *all distinctions as between workers and intellectuals*, and certainly distinctions of trade and profession, must be
utterly obliterated. Such an organization must of necessity be not
too extensive and as secret as possible. Let us examine this three-
fold distinction.

In countries where political liberty exists the distinction between a trade union and a political organization is clear enough, as
is the distinction between trade unions and Social-Democracy.
The relation of the latter to the former will naturally vary in each
country according to historical, legal and other conditions—it may
be more or less close, complex, etc. (in our opinion it should be as
close and simple as possible); but there can be no question of
trade union organizations being identical with the Social-Democratic Party organizations in free countries. . . .

The workers' organizations for the economic struggle should be trade union organizations. Every Social-Democratic worker should as far as possible assist and actively work in these organizations. That is true. But it is not at all to our interest to demand that only Social-Democrats should be eligible for membership in the "trade" unions: that would only narrow down our influence over the masses. Let every worker who understands the need to unite for the struggle against the employers and the government join the trade unions. The very aim of the trade unions would be unattainable if they failed to unite all who have attained at least this elementary degree of understanding, and if they were not very *wide* organizations. And the wider these organizations are, the wider our influence over them will be—an influence due not only to the "spontaneous" development of the economic struggle but also to the direct and conscious effort of the socialist trade union members to influence their comrades. But a broad organization cannot apply the methods of strict secrecy (since the latter demands far greater training than is required for the economic struggle). How is the contradiction between the need for a large membership and the need for strictly secret methods to be reconciled? How are we to make the trade unions as little clandestine as possible? Generally speaking, there can be only two ways to this end: either the trade unions become legalized (and in some countries this preceded the legalization of the Socialist and political unions), or the organization is kept a secret one, but so "free" and amorphous, *lose* as the Germans say, that the need for secret methods becomes almost negligible as far as the bulk of the members is concerned. . . .

Trade union organizations can be not only of tremendous value in developing and consolidating the economic struggle, but can also become a very important auxiliary to political agitation and revolutionary organization. . . . A small, compact core of the most reliable, experienced and hardened workers, with responsible representatives in the principal districts and connected by all the rules of strict secrecy with the organization of revolutionaries, can, with the widest support of the masses and without any formal organization, perform *all* the functions of a trade union organization, and perform them, moreover, in a manner desirable to Social-Democracy. Only in this way can we secure the *consolidation* and development of a *Social-Democratic* trade union movement, in spite of all the gendarmes.

It may be objected that an organization which is so loose that it is not even definitely formed, and which even has no enrolled and registered membership, cannot be called an organization at all. That may very well be. I am not out for names. But this "organization without members" will do everything that is required, and from the very outset guarantee the closest contact between our future trade unions and Socialism. Only an incorrigible utopian would want a *broad* organization of workers, with elections, reports, universal suffrage, etc., under the autocracy.

The moral to be drawn from this is a simple one: if we begin with the solid foundation of a strong organization of revolutionaries, we can guarantee the stability of the movement as a whole and carry out the aims of both Social-Democracy and of trade unions proper. If, however, we begin with a broad workers' organization, supposed to be most "accessible" to the masses (but as a matter of fact most accessible to the gendarmes and making the revolutionaries most accessible to the police), we shall achieve neither one nor the other of these aims. . . .

I assert that it is far more difficult to wipe out a dozen wise men than a hundred fools. And this position I shall defend no matter how much you instigate the crowd against me for my "antidemocratic" views, etc. As I have already said time and again that by "wise men," in connection with organization, I mean *professional revolutionaries*, irrespective of whether they are trained from among students or workingmen. I assert: 1) that no revolutionary movement can endure without a stable organization of leaders that maintains continuity; 2) that the wider the masses spontaneously drawn into the struggle, forming the basis of the movement and participating in it, the more urgent the need of such an organization, and the more solid this organization must be (for it is much easier for demagogues to sidetrack the more backward sections of the masses); 3) that such an organization must consist chiefly of people professionally engaged in revolutionary activity; 4) that in an autocratic state, the more we *confine* the membership of such an organization to people who are professionally engaged in revolutionary activity and who have been professionally trained in the art of combating the political police, the more difficult will it be to wipe out such an organization, and 5) the *greater* will be the number of people of the working class and of the other classes of society who will be able to join the movement and perform active work in it. . . .

The question as to whether it is easier to wipe out "a dozen wise men" or "a hundred fools" reduces itself to the question we have considered above, namely, whether it is possible to have a mass *organization* when the maintenance of strict secrecy is essential. We can never give a mass organization that degree of secrecy without which there can be no question of persistent and continuous struggle against the government. But to concentrate all secret functions in the hands of as small a number of professional revolutionaries as possible does not mean that the latter will "do the thinking for all" and that the crowd will not take an active part in the *movement*. On the contrary, the crowd will advance from its ranks increasing numbers of professional revolutionaries; for it will know that it is not enough for a few students and for a few working-men waging the economic struggle, to gather together and form a "committee" but that it takes years to train oneself to be a professional revolutionary; the crowd will "think" not of amateurish methods alone but of such training. The centralization of the secret functions of the *organization* by no means implies the centralization of all the functions of the *movement*. The active participation of the widest mass in the illegal press will not diminish because a "dozen" professional revolutionaries centralize the secret functions connected with this work; on the contrary, it will *increase* tenfold. In this way, and in this way alone, will we ensure that reading of illegal literature, writing for it, and to some extent even distributing it, will *almost cease to be secret work,* for the police will soon come to realize the folly and futility of setting the whole judicial and administrative machine into motion to intercept every copy of a publication that is being broadcast in thousands. This applies not only to the press, but to every function of the movement, even to demonstrations. The active and widespread participation of the masses will not suffer; on the contrary, it will benefit by the fact that a "dozen" experienced revolutionaries, trained professionally no less than the police, will centralize all the secret aspects of the work—drawing up leaflets, working out approximate plans and appointing bodies of leaders for each urban district, for each factory district and for each educational institution, etc. . . .

The centralization of the most secret functions in an organization of revolutionaries will not diminish, but rather increase the extent and quality of the activity of a large number of other organizations which are intended for a broad public and are therefore as loose and as non-secret as possible, such as workers' trade unions, workers' self-education circles and circles for reading illegal literature, socialist and also democratic circles among *all* other sections of the population, etc., etc. We must have such circles, trade unions and organizations everywhere in *as large a number as possible* and with the widest variety of functions; but it would be absurd and dangerous to *confuse* them with the organization of *revolutionaries*, to obliterate the border line between them, to dim still more the masses' already incredibly hazy appreciation of the fact that in order to "serve" the mass movement we must have people who will devote themselves exclusively to Social-Democratic activities, and that such people must *train* themselves patiently and steadfastly to be professional revolutionaries. . . .

In order to unite all these tiny fractions into one whole, in order not to break up the movement while breaking up its functions, and in order to imbue the people who carry out the minute functions with the conviction that their work is necessary and important, without which conviction they will never do the work, it is necessary to have a strong organization of tried revolutionaries. The more secret such an organization is, the stronger and more widespread will be the confidence in the Party, and, as we know, in time of war, it is of the utmost importance to imbue not only one's own army with confidence in its strength, but it is important also to convince the enemy and all *neutral* elements of this strength; friendly neutrality may sometimes decide the issue. . . .

[The] first and most imperative duty is to help to train working-class revolutionaries who will be on the same level *in regard to Party activity* as the revolutionaries from amongst the intellectuals (we emphasize the words "in regard to Party activity," because although necessary, it is neither so easy nor so imperative to bring the workers up to the level of intellectuals in other respects). Therefore, attention must be devoted *principally* to *raising* the workers to the level of revolutionaries. . . . The worker-revolutionary must also become a professional revolutionary. . . .

As the spontaneous rise of the working-class masses becomes wider and deeper, they promote from their ranks not only an increasing number of talented agitators, but also talented organizers, propagandists and "practical workers" in the best sense of the term (of whom there are so few among our intelligentsia who, for the most part, in the Russian manner, are somewhat careless and sluggish in their habits). When we have detachments of specially trained worker-revolutionaries who have gone through extensive preparation (and, of course, revolutionaries "of all arms"), no political police in the world will then be able to contend against them, for these detachments of men absolutely devoted to the revolution will themselves enjoy the absolute confidence of the widest masses of the workers. . . .

The spontaneous struggle of the proletariat will not become its genuine "class struggle" until this struggle is led by a strong organization of revolutionaries. . . .

In *form* such a strong revolutionary organization in an autocratic country may also be described as a "conspiratorial" organization, because the French word *"conspiration"* is tantamount to the Russian word *"zagovor"* ("conspiracy"), and we must have the utmost secrecy for an organization of that kind. Secrecy is such a necessary condition for this kind of organization that all the other conditions (number and selection of members, functions, etc.) must be made to conform to it. . . .

The objection may be raised: such a powerful and strictly secret organization, which concentrates in its hands all the threads of secret activities, an organization which of necessity is centralized, may too easily rush into a premature attack, may thoughtlessly intensify the movement before the growth of political discontent, the intensity of the ferment and anger of the working class, etc., have made such an attack possible and necessary. To this we reply: speaking abstractly, it cannot be denied, of course, that a militant organization *may* thoughtlessly commence a battle, which *may* end in defeat, that might have been avoided under other circumstances. But we cannot confine ourselves to abstract reasoning on such a question, because every battle bears within itself the abstract possibility of defeat, and there is no other way of *reducing* this possibility than by organized preparation for battle. . . .

The "economic struggle against the employers and the government" can *never* satisfy revolutionaries, and because opposite extremes will always arise here and there. Only a centralized, militant organization that consistently carries out a Social-Democratic policy, that satisfies, so to speak, all revolutionary instincts and strivings, can safeguard the movement against making thoughtless attacks and prepare attacks that hold out the promise of success.

A further objection may be raised, viz., that the views on organization here expounded contradict the "principles of democracy." . . .

Everyone will probably agree that "broad democratic principles" presuppose the two following conditions: first, full publicity, and second, election to all offices. It would be absurd to speak about democracy without publicity, that is, a publicity that is not limited to the membership of the organization. . . .

In politically free countries, this condition is taken for granted. "Membership of the Party is open to those who accept the principles of the Party program and render the Party all possible support"—reads clause I of the rules of the German Social-Democratic Party. And as the entire political arena is as open to the public view as is a theatre stage to the audience, this acceptance or non-acceptance, support or opposition, is known to all from the press and public meetings. . . .

Just try to put this picture into the frame of our autocracy! Is it conceivable in Russia for all those "who accept the principles of the Party program and render the Party all possible support" to control every action of the revolutionary working in secret? Is it possible for all the revolutionaries to elect one of their number to any particular office, when, in the very interests of the work, he *must* conceal his identity from nine out of ten of these "all"? Ponder a little over the real meaning of the high-sounding phrases to which the *Rabocheye Dyelo* gives utterance, and you will realize that "broad democracy" in Party organization, amidst the gloom of the autocracy and the domination of gendarme selection, is nothing more than a *useless and harmful toy*. It is a useless toy because, as a matter of fact, no revolutionary organization has ever practised, or could practise, *broad* democracy, however much it desired to do so. It is a harmful toy because any attempt to practise the "broad democratic principles" will simply facilitate the work of the police in carrying out large-scale raids, it will perpetu-

ate the prevailing amateurishness, divert the thoughts of the practical workers from the serious and imperative task of training
themselves to become professional revolutionaries to that of drawing up detailed "paper" rules for election systems. Only abroad,
where people who have no opportunity of doing real live work
gather together very often, could this "playing at democracy" develop here and there, especially in various small groups. . . .

The only serious organizational principle for the active workers
of our movement should be the strictest secrecy, the strictest selection of members and the training of professional revolutionaries.
Given these qualities, something even more than "democracy"
would be guaranteed to us, namely, complete, comradely, mutual
confidence among revolutionaries. . . .

The Party

JOSEPH STALIN

1) The Party as the Vanguard of the Working Class

The Party must be, first of all, the *vanguard* of the working
class. The Party must absorb all the best elements of the working
class, their experience, their revolutionary spirit, their selfless devotion to the cause of the proletariat. But in order that it may really
be the vanguard, the Party must be armed with revolutionary
theory, with a knowledge of the laws of the movement, with a
knowledge of the laws of revolution. Without this it will be incapable of directing the struggle of the proletariat, of leading the
proletariat. The Party cannot be a real party if it limits itself to

From *Foundations of Leninism* by Joseph Stalin, selections from pp. 109–123.
New York: International Publishers, 1939. By permission of International
Publishers Company, Inc.

registering what the masses of the working class feel and think, if it follows in the tail of the spontaneous movement, if it is unable to overcome the inertness and the political indifference of the spontaneous movement, if it is unable to rise above the momentary interests of the proletariat, if it is unable to elevate the masses to the level of the class interests of the proletariat. The Party must stand at the head of the working class; it must see farther than the working class; it must lead the proletariat, and not follow in the tail of the spontaneous movement. . . .

Only a party which takes the standpoint of the vanguard of the proletariat and is able to elevate the masses to the level of the class interests of the proletariat—only such a party can divert the working class from the path of trade unionism and convert it into an independent political force. The Party is the political leader of the working class. . . . No army at war can dispense with an experienced General Staff if it does not want to court certain defeat. Is it not clear that the proletariat can still less dispense with such a General Staff if it does not want to give itself up to be devoured by its mortal enemies? But where is this General Staff? Only the revolutionary party of the proletariat can serve as this General Staff. The working class without a revolutionary party is an army without a General Staff. The Party is the General Staff of the proletariat.

But the Party cannot be only a *vanguard* detachment. It must at the same time be a detachment of the *class*, part of the class, closely bound up with it by all the fibres of its being. The distinction between the vanguard and the main body of the working class, between Party members and non-Party people, cannot disappear until classes disappear; it will exist as long as the ranks of the proletariat continue to be replenished with newcomers from other classes, as long as the working class as a whole lacks the possibility of rising to the level of the vanguard. But the Party would cease to be a party if this distinction were widened into a gap, if it shut itself up in its own shell and became divorced from the non-Party masses. The Party cannot lead the class if it is not connected with the non-Party masses, if there is no bond between the Party and the non-Party masses, if these masses do not accept its leadership, if the Party enjoys no moral and political credit among the masses. . . .

2) *The Party as the Organized Detachment of the Working Class*

The Party is not only the *vanguard* of the working class. If it desires really to direct the struggle of the class it must at the same time be the *organized* detachment of its class. The Party's tasks under the conditions of capitalism are extremely serious and varied. The Party must direct the struggle of the proletariat under the exceptionally difficult conditions of internal and external development; it must lead the proletariat in the offensive when the situation calls for an offensive; it must lead the proletariat in retreat when the situation calls for retreat in order to ward off the blows of a powerful enemy; it must imbue the millions of unorganized non-Party workers with the spirit of discipline and system in the struggle, with the spirit of organization and endurance. But the Party can fulfil these tasks only if it is itself the embodiment of discipline and organization, if it is itself the *organized* detachment of the proletariat. Without these conditions there can be no talk of the Party really leading the proletarian millions. The Party is the organized detachment of the working class. . . .

But the Party is not merely the *sum* of Party organizations. The Party at the same time represents a single *system* of these organizations, their formal amalgamation into a single whole, with higher and lower leading bodies, with subordination of the minority to the majority, with practical decisions binding on all members of the Party. Without these conditions the Party cannot be a single organized whole capable of exercising systematic and organized leadership in the struggle of the working class. . . .

3) *The Party as the Highest Form of Class Organization of the Proletariat*

The Party is the organized detachment of the working class. But the Party is not the only organization of the working class. The proletariat has also a number of other organizations, without which it cannot properly wage the struggle against capital: trade unions, cooperative societies, factory and works organizations, parliamentary groups, non-Party women's associations, the press, cultural and educational organizations, youth leagues, revolutionary fighting organizations (in times of open revolutionary action), Soviets of deputies as the form of state organization (if the proletariat is in power), etc. The overwhelming majority of these organizations are non-Party, and only a certain part of them adhere directly to the Party, or represent its offshoots. All these organizations, under certain conditions, are absolutely necessary for the working class, for without them it would be impossible to consolidate the class positions of the proletariat in the diverse spheres of struggle; for without them it would be impossible to steel the proletariat as the force whose mission it is to replace the bourgeois order by the socialist order. But how can single leadership be exercised with such an abundance of organizations? What guarantee is there that this multiplicity of organizations will not lead to divergency in leadership? It might be argued that each of these organizations carries on its work in its own special field, and that therefore these organizations cannot hinder one another. This, of course, is true. But it is also true that all these organizations should work in one direction, for they serve *one* class, the class of the proletarians. The question then arises: who is to determine the line, the general direction, along which the work of all these organizations is to be conducted? Where is that central organization which is not only able, because it has the necessary experience, to work out such a general line, but, in addition, is in a position, because it has sufficient prestige for that, to induce all these organizations to carry out this line, so as to attain unity of leadership and to preclude the possibility of working at cross purposes?

This organization is the Party of the proletariat.

The Party possesses all the necessary qualifications for this because, in the first place, it is the rallying centre of the finest elements in the working class, who have direct connections with the non-Party organizations of the proletariat and very frequently lead them; because, secondly, the Party, as the rallying centre for the finest members of the working class, is the best school for training leaders of the working class, capable of directing every form of organization of their class; because, thirdly, the Party, as the best school for training leaders of the working class, is by reason of its experience and prestige the only organization capable of centralising the leadership of the struggle of the proletariat, thus transforming each and every non-Party organization of the working class into an auxiliary body and transmission belt linking the Party with the class. The Party is the highest form of class organization of the proletariat. . . .

4) *The Party as the Instrument of the Dictatorship of the Proletariat*

The Party is the highest form of organization of the proletariat. The Party is the principal guiding force within the class of the proletarians and among the organizations of that class. But it does not by any means follow from this that the Party can be regarded as an end in itself, as a self-sufficient force. The Party is not only the highest form of class association of the proletarians; it is at the same time an *instrument* in the hands of the proletariat *for* achieving the dictatorship where that has not yet been achieved and *for* consolidating and expanding the dictatorship where it has already been achieved. The Party could not have risen so high in importance and could not have overshadowed all other forms of organization of the proletariat, if the latter were not confronted with the problem of power, if the conditions of imperialism, the inevitability of wars, and the existence of a crisis did not demand the concentration of all the forces of the proletariat at one point, the gathering of all the threads of the revolutionary movement into one spot in order to overthrow the bourgeoisie and to achieve the dictatorship of the proletariat. The proletariat needs the Party first of all as its General Staff, which it must have for the successful seizure of power. . . .

But the proletariat needs the Party not only to achieve the dictatorship; it needs it still more to maintain the dictatorship, to consolidate and expand it in order to achieve the complete victory of socialism. . . .

Now, what does it mean to "maintain" and "expand" the dictatorship? It means imbuing the millions of proletarians with the spirit of discipline and organization; it means creating among the proletarian masses a cementing force and a bulwark against the corrosive influences of the petty-bourgeois elements and petty-bourgeois habits; it means enhancing the organizing work of the proletarians in re-educating and re-moulding the petty-bourgeois strata; it means helping the masses of the proletarians to educate themselves as a force capable of abolishing classes and of preparing the conditions for the organization of socialist production. But it is impossible to accomplish all this without a Party which is strong by reason of its solidarity and discipline.

> "The dictatorship of the proletariat," says Lenin, "is a persistent struggle—sanguinary and bloodless, violent and peaceful, military and economic, educational and administrative—against the forces and traditions of the old society. The force of habit of millions and tens of millions is a most terrible force. Without an iron party tempered in the struggle, without a party enjoying the confidence of all that is honest in the given class, without a party capable of watching and influencing the mood of the masses, it is impossible to conduct such a struggle successfully." (*Selected Works*, Vol. X, p. 84.)

The proletariat needs the Party for the purpose of achieving and maintaining the dictatorship. The Party is an instrument of the dictatorship of the proletariat.

But from this it follows that when classes disappear and the dictatorship of the proletariat withers away, the Party will also wither away.

5) *The Party as the Embodiment of Unity of Will, Incompatible with the Existence of Factions*

The achievement and maintenance of the dictatorship of the proletariat is impossible without a party which is strong by reason of its solidarity and iron discipline. But iron discipline in the Party is inconceivable without unity of will, without complete and absolute unity of action on the part of all members of the Party. This does not mean, of course, that the possibility of contests of opinion within the Party is thereby precluded. On the contrary, iron discipline does not preclude but presupposes criticism and contest of opinion within the Party. Least of all does it mean that discipline must be "blind." On the contrary, iron discipline does not preclude but presupposes conscious and voluntary submission, for only conscious discipline can be truly iron discipline. But after a contest of opinion has been closed, after criticism has been exhausted and a decision has been arrived at, unity of will and unity of action of all Party members are the necessary condition without which neither Party unity nor iron discipline in the Party is conceivable. . . .

The existence of factions is incompatible either with the Party's unity or with its iron discipline. It need hardly be proved that the existence of factions leads to the existence of a number of centres, and the existence of a number of centres connotes the absence of one common centre in the Party, the breaking up of the unity of will, the weakening and disintegration of discipline, the weakening and disintegration of the dictatorship. . . . The Party represents unity of will, which precludes all factionalism and division of authority in the Party. . . .

6) *The Party Is Strengthened by Purging Itself of Opportunist Elements*

The source of factionalism in the Party is its opportunist elements. The proletariat is not an isolated class. It is constantly replenished by the influx of peasants, petty bourgeois and intellectuals who have become proletarianized by the development of capitalism. At the same time the upper stratum of the proletariat, principally trade union leaders and labour members of parliament who are fed by the bourgeoisie out of the super-profits extracted from the colonies, is undergoing a process of decay.

"This stratum of bourgeoisified workers, of the 'labour aristocracy,'" says Lenin, "who are quite philistine in their mode of life, in the size of their earnings, and in their outlook, serves as the principal prop of the Second International, and, in our days, the principal social (not military) *prop of the bourgeoisie*. They are the real *agents of the bourgeoisie in the labour movement*, the labour lieutenants of the capitalist class, real channels of reformism and chauvinism." (*Selected Works*, Vol. V, p. 12.)

In one way or another, all these petty-bourgeois groups penetrate into the Party and introduce into it the spirit of hesitancy and opportunism, the spirit of demoralization and uncertainty. It is they, principally, that constitute the source of factionalism and disintegration, the source of disorganization and disruption of the Party from within. To fight imperialism with such "allies" in one's rear means to expose oneself to the danger of being caught between two fires, from the front and from the rear. Therefore, ruthless struggle against such elements, their expulsion from the Party, is a prerequisite for the successful struggle against imperialism.

The theory of "overcoming" opportunist elements by ideological struggle within the Party, the theory of "outliving" these elements within the confines of a single Party, is a rotten and dangerous theory, which threatens to condemn the Party to paralysis and chronic infirmity, threatens to make the Party a prey to opportunism, threatens to leave the proletariat without a revolutionary party, threatens to deprive the proletariat of its main weapon in the fight against imperialism. . . . Proletarian parties develop and become strong by purging themselves of opportunists and reformists, social-imperialists and social-chauvinists, social-patriots and social-pacifists. The Party becomes consolidated by purging itself of opportunist elements. . . .

The Party of the New Class

MILOVAN DJILAS

The party is the main force of the Communist state and government. It is the motive force of everything. It unites within itself the new class, the government, ownership, and ideas.

The totalitarian dictatorship of the Communist Party oligarchy in the Communist system is not the result of momentary political relations, but of a long and complex social progress. A change in it would not mean a change in the form of government in one and the same system, but a change in the system itself, or the beginning of a change. Such a dictatorship is itself the system, its body and soul, its essence.

From *The New Class: An Analysis of the Communist System* by Milovan Djilas, selections from pp. 78–82. New York: Frederick A. Praeger, Inc., 1957. By permission of the publisher. For biographical note see p. 103.

The Communist government very rapidly becomes a small circle of party leaders. The claim that it is a dictatorship of the proletariat becomes an empty slogan. The process that leads to this develops with the inevitability and uncontrollability of the elements, and the theory that the party is an *avant-garde* of the proletariat only aids the process.

This does not mean that during the battle for power the party is not the leader of the working masses or that it is not working in their interests. But then, the party's role and struggles are stages and forms of its movement toward power. Although its struggle aids the working class, it also strengthens the party, as well as the future power-holders and the embryonic new class. As soon as it attains power, the party controls all power and takes all goods into its hands, professing to be the representative of the interests of the working class and the working people. Except for short periods during the revolutionary battle, the proletariat does not participate or play a greater role in this than any other class.

This does not mean that the proletariat, or some of its strata, are not temporarily interested in keeping the party in power. The peasants supported those who professed the intention to rescue them from hopeless misery through industrialization.

While individual strata of the working classes may temporarily support the party, the government is not theirs nor is their part in the government important for the course of social progress and social relations. In the Communist system nothing is done to aid the working people, particularly the working class, to attain power and rights. It cannot be otherwise.

The classes and masses do not exercise authority, but the party does so in their name. In every party, including the most democratic, leaders play an important role to the extent that the party's authority becomes the authority of the leaders. The so-called "dictatorship of the proletariat," which is the beginning of and under the best circumstances becomes the authority of the party, inevitably evolves into the dictatorship of the leaders. In a totalitarian government of this type, the dictatorship of the proletariat is a theoretical justification, or ideological mask at best, for the authority of some oligarchs.

Marx envisioned the dictatorship of the proletariat as democracy within and for the benefit of the proletariat; that is, a government in which there are many socialist streams or parties. The only dictatorship of the proletariat, the Paris Commune of 1871, on which Marx based his conclusions, was composed of several parties, among which the Marxist party was neither the smallest nor the most significant. But a dictatorship of the proletariat which would be directly operated by the proletariat is a pure Utopia, since no government can operate without political organizations. Lenin delegated the dictatorship of the proletariat to the authority of one party, his own. Stalin delegated the dictatorship of the proletariat to his own personal authority—to his personal dictatorship in the party and in the state. Since the death of the Communist emperor, his descendants have been fortunate in that through "collective leadership" they could distribute authoirty among themselves. In any case, the Communist dictatorship of the proletariat is either a Utopian ideal or a function reserved for an elite group of party leaders.

Lenin thought that the Russian soviets, Marx's "ultimate discovery," were the dictatorship of the proletariat. In the beginning, because of their revolutionary initiative and because of the participation of the masses, the soviets did seem to be something of this kind. Trotsky also believed that the soviets were a contemporary political form just as parliaments, born in the struggle against absolute monarchs, have been. However, these were illusions. The soviets were transformed from revolutionary bodies into a form suitable for the totalitarian dictatorship of the new class, or the party.

This was also the case with Lenin's democratic centralism, including both that of the party and of the government. As long as public differences are tolerated in the party, one can still speak of centralism—even though it is not a very democratic form of centralism. When totalitarian authorty is created, centralism disappears and the naked despotism of the oligarchy takes over.

We may conclude from this that there is a constant tendency to transform an oligarchic dictatorship into a personal dictatorship. Ideological unity, the inevitable struggle at the top of the party, and the needs of the system as a whole tend toward personal dictatorship. The leader who succeeds in getting to the top, along with his assistants, is the one who succeeds in most logically expressing and protecting the interests of the new class at any given time.

There is a strong trend toward personal dictatorship in other historical situations: for instance, all forces must be subordinated to one idea and one will when industrialization is being pressed or when a nation is at war. But there is a specific and pure Communist reason for personal dictatorship: authority is the basic aim and means of Communism and of every true Communist. The thirst for power is insatiable and irresistible among Communists. Victory in the struggle for power is equal to being raised to a divinity; failure means the deepest mortification and disgrace.

The Communist leaders must also tend to personal extravagance—something which they cannot resist because of human frailty and because of the inherent need of those in power to be recognizable prototypes of brilliance and might.

Careerism, extravagance, and love of power are inevitable, and so is corruption. It is not a matter of the corruption of public servants, for this may occur less frequently than in the state which preceded it. It is a special type of corruption caused by the fact that the government is in the hands of a single political group and is the source of all privileges. "Care of its men" and their placement in lucrative positions, or the distribution of all kinds of privileges, becomes unavoidable. The fact that the government and the party are identical with the state, and practically with the holding of all property, causes the Communist state to be one which corrupts itself, in that it inevitably creates privileges and parasitic functions.

· 2 ·

THE PARTY AND THE SOVIETS

In 1905 when the first revolutionary councils emerged, and later when the Soviets of Workers', Soldiers', and Peasants' Deputies probably came closer to expressing popular aspirations than did the new government which succeeded the downfall of the Tsar, the Bolsheviks believed that these bodies corresponded to Marx's image of the dictatorship of the proletariat. They were convinced that the soviets were a contemporary political form as revolutionary in scope as were the parliaments which succeeded the overthrow of absolute monarchies in the West. But while the Soviets may have had much popular support under the particular conditions that prevailed in the Russia of 1917, the acquisition and consolidation of power by the Bolsheviks saw their gradual transformation from popular revolutionary bodies into instruments serving the interests of the Party.

The authors of the first selection—A. Denisov and M. Kirichenko, two leading Soviet political scientists of the post-Stalin era—present contemporary Communist conceptions of the role of the Soviets in the U.S.S.R. While they consider the Soviets as a direct expression of the dictatorship of the proletariat, they also recognize the supremacy of the Party in "guiding" their activities. The Party, they admit, not only "directs the selection, distribution and training of the personnel of the Soviet state apparatus [i.e., the Soviets], it also checks the activity of the organs of state power and state administration." In fact, "not a single decision is taken by the Soviet state organs without preliminary guiding directions and advice from the Party." Nevertheless, the authors claim that the Soviet state is distinct from the Party. In their view, the Soviet state is an organization which "embraces the whole population of the country through the compulsory subordination of all citizens to the will of the state power representing the interests and will of the people as a whole. . . . [while] the Communist Party is the leading core of the power of the working people."

Professor Towster's article presents a succinct historical review of the evolution of the relationship between the Party and the soviets. He demonstrates that while during the early phase of "war Communism" in the U.S.S.R., an attempt was still made to juxtapose the soviets and the Party, on the assumption that the former constituted the "state power" while the latter was only the "core of the state power." In this context the Party was expected merely to "guide the activity of the Soviets, not to supplant them." But as the Bolsheviks gradually transformed themselves from a ruling minority into a dominating "majority," the identification of the Party and the state became ever more discernible. Beginning with the gradual operational integration of the Party-soviet pyramids, the process culminated in the "amalgamation of the summits" characterized by the fusion of the powers of the state and Party in the hands of the upper hierarchy of the Party.

The Soviets and the Party

A. DENISOV AND M. KIRICHENKO

The Political Foundation of the Soviet State

Soviet society has established the genuine sovereignty of the working people who exercise their power through competent representative organs—the Soviets of Working People's Deputies.

These Soviets, constituting the political foundation of the U.S.S.R. and of the Union and Autonomous Republics, developed and consolidated as a result of the overthrow of the power of the landlords and capitalists, and of the establishment of the dictatorship of the proletariat. . . .

The Soviets are a direct expression of the dictatorship of the proletariat. This means that all measures aimed at consolidating the dictatorship of the working class and building a communist society are effected through these organs. Through the Soviets the working class exercises its state guidance of the peasantry. As state organs, the Soviets link the working people of town and country with the Communist Party.

Soviet power is a state power of a new, higher type: it signifies a new type of democracy (for the working class and the working people in general) and a new type of dictatorship (directed against the exploiters and oppressors of the people). Soviet power acts in the interests of the working majority of the people. It functions through a state apparatus consisting of the best representatives of the people, it is near and dear to the workers, peasants and labouring intelligentsia. . . .

From *Soviet State Law* by A. Denisov and M. Kirichenko, selections from pp. 138–144. Moscow: Foreign Languages Publishing House, 1960.

Figure 1. THE STRUCTURE OF SOVIETS IN THE U.S.S.R.

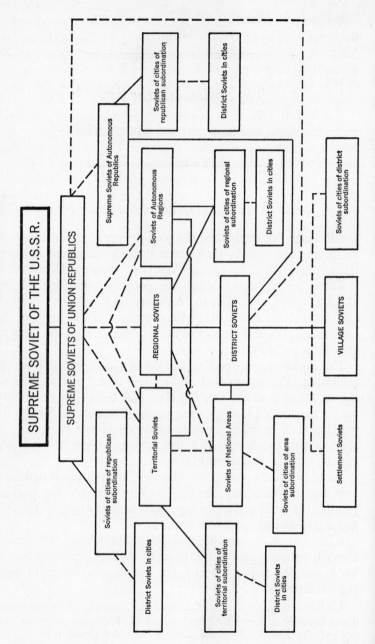

The strength of the Soviets lies in the fact that they constitute the most all-embracing mass organizations of the working class. They are the only organizations which unite all the working people of town and country. The Soviets enable the working class to exercise more easily and fully its state guidance of the struggle of the masses to build a communist society. . . .

The various links of the Soviet representative system are closely interconnected; for example, all the village Soviets within the territory of a District are subordinate to the District Soviet, all the District Soviets within the territory of a Region—to the Regional Soviet, and the latter—to the Supreme Soviet of the Union Republic. Thus, the higher Soviets direct the activities of the lower Soviets, check on the lawfulness of their acts and are responsible for their work.

The Soviets are guided by the Communist Party of the Soviet Union which is closely connected with the people and consistently defends the interests of the people.

It is the leadership of the Party which ensures the successful work of the Soviets. The Party takes an active part in the formation of the state organs. Its organization, like all other public organizations and societies of the working people, have been granted the right to nominate candidates for the Soviets. *The Communist Party directs the selection, distribution and training of the personnel of the Soviet state apparatus; it checks the activity of the organs of state power and state administration. Not a single important decision is taken by the Soviet state organs without preliminary guiding directions and advice from the Party. In this way the Communist Party of the Soviet Union imparts a planned and purposeful character to the work of the entire Soviet state apparatus.* *

The Soviets have set up numerous central and local administrative, economic, cultural and other establishments which function under their direction.

The Communist Party—the Leading and Directing Force of Soviet Society

The Soviets, as a political form of organization of the working masses, is one of the greatest gains of the working class. This form,

* Italics supplied.

however, is not decisive in itself. Of prime importance is the content, i.e., the character and direction of the activity of the Soviets. Without a revolutionary Marxist party the Soviets cannot perform the role of organs of the dictatorship of the proletariat. This is testified to by the experience of the revolutions in Russia, Hungary and some other countries.

The Communist Party of the Soviet Union should not be confused with the Soviet state. As distinct from the Party, which is a voluntary militant union of like-minded people—Communists—the Soviet state is an organization which embraces the whole population of the country through the compulsory subordination of all citizens to the will of the state power representing the interests and will of the people as a whole. The Communist Party is the leading core of the power of the working people. This, however, does not mean that the leading role of the Party organs is identified with the state organs. The Programme of the Party adopted in 1919 specially emphasized that the functions of the Party bodies should by no means be confused with the functions of the state organs, and that the Party must carry out its decisions through the state organs by directing their activity and in no way by supplanting them.

The source of the authority of the Communist Party lies in the confidence shown it by the working people which it has won as a result of its correct policy, devotion to the working class and labouring peasantry, its close connection with the working people of town and country, and ability to convince the masses of the people of the correctness of its political appeals. Persuasion is the principal method by which the Party influences the working people and rallies them around itself.

Thus, the policy of the Communist Party which expresses the interests of the working people of the Soviet land constitutes the vital foundation of the whole Soviet socialist system.

The Evolution of the Party-Soviets Relationship

JULIAN TOWSTER

1) The Relationship of the First Years

THE ORIGINAL AMBIGUITY OF THE RELATIVE SPHERES OF ACTIVITY.
The development of the theory of the relationship between the
Party and the soviets, which gave substance to this conception, falls
into several distinct phases. By the Revolution of November 1917
the Bolshevik Party was transformed from an underground or opposition party, pursuing primarily propaganda and agitation, into
a ruling party, gaining for the first time the material and technical
means to play such a role. The leaders of the Party, from Lenin
down, had all taken posts in the Soviet government. But the intensity of the civil war kept the Party leaders from clearly defining
the relation between the Party and the soviet structure, especially
since the latter structure was itself being hewed out at the time.

2) The Demarcation of Party-Soviet Functions

THE DEFINITION OF THE PARTY-SOVIETS RELATIONSHIP. A definition of relationship providing for a demarcation of the respective
functions of the Party and the soviets was first offered by the
Eighth Party Congress, in March 1919:

> The Communist Party poses as its task the conquest of a most
> decisive influence and complete direction in all the organizations of

From *Political Power in the U.S.S.R.* by Julian Towster, pp. 178–183. New
York: Oxford University Press, 1948. Copyright 1948 by Oxford University
Press, Inc. Reprinted by permission. For footnote references, see original
source. For biographical note, see p. 4.

toilers: trade unions, co-operatives, village communes, et cetera. The Communist Party seeks especially the realization of its program by and [the achievement of] its complete dominance in the contemporary state organizations—the soviets . . . By practical, daily, self-sacrificing work in the soviets, by putting forth its most stable and devoted members for all soviet posts, the R.C.P. must conquer for itself undivided political dominance in the soviets and actual control over all their work.

But the functions of the Party collectives must on no account be confused with the functions of the state organs—the soviets. Such confusion would produce fatal results, especially in military affairs. The Party must carry out its decisions through the soviet organs, *within the frame of the Soviet constitution.* The Party should endeavor to guide the activity of the soviets, not to supplant them.

Similar statements were made at several subsequent Party congresses against action that would tend to erase the lines of demarcation between the Party and the soviet organs, i.e. to make the Party compete with the soviets rather than guide them. Yet in these same years, the leadership in control fought determinedly against all attempts to juxtapose the soviets and the Party, repeatedly and unequivocally asserting the supremacy of the Party's directing role in the soviets, and incessantly calling for further expansion of that role.

THE DISTINCTION BETWEEN THE RESPECTIVE ROLES OF THE PARTY AND THE SOVIETS.   Theoretically, therefore, the problem of this relationship resolved itself into a demand not to confuse the Party with the soviets—the 'core of the state power' with 'the state power'—and into a double injunction against either 'commanding' or 'tailism' (following, instead of showing initiative) in the Party's exercise of its prerogatives of leadership within the soviets. As regards the first, Stalin sought a conclusive clarification of the subject in a statement on 25 Janurary 1926:

The Party realizes the dictatorship of the proletariat. 'The Party is the direct governing vanguard of the proletariat; it is the leader.' (Lenin.) In this sense the Party *takes* power, the Party *governs* the country. But this does not yet mean that the Party realizes the dictatorship of the proletariat separately from and without the state power; that the Party governs the country apart from the soviets, and not through them. But this does not yet mean that the Party can be identified with the soviets, with the state power. The Party is the core of this power, but it is not and cannot be identified with the state power itself. 'As the ruling party,' writes Lenin, 'we could not but merge the "upper stratum" of the Party with the "upper stratum" of the soviets; we have merged them, and they will continue so.' . . . But he never stated that the Party is the state power, that the soviets and the Party are one and the same. The Party . . . leads the soviets, with their national and local ramifications . . . but it cannot and should not replace them by itself.

As for the second, a series of warnings were issued by the higher Party organs to Party bodies and fractions at all the levels of the pyramid that they should endeavor to guide, lead, teach, and correct the errors and shortcomings of the soviets in which they operate, and not command and order them around. At the same time the Party bodies were warned that they must under no circumstances find themselves dragging behind, at the tail end of the procession, in the operation of the soviets, that they must never forget their primary objective of leading in the promotion, stimulation, and initiation of desirable action by the soviets.

Such was the theoretical position concerning the Party-soviets relationship, at least up to the early 'thirties, with its chief reflection in practice in the official separation of Party directives from the laws and enactments of the soviet government organs, and in the formal distinction between the operation of the Party and soviet pyramids. It is important to point out here, however, that in his own time Lenin was not at all against a progressively greater fusion of Party and soviet functions, wherever it seemed necessary for the good of the cause; that the effort to keep the two separate was to a large extent a concession to various oppositions of the earlier period; that admitted exceptions to the theory of separation of the Party and government functions were known at least in several instances: the Politbureau-Sovnarkom, Politbureau-Narkomindel, and the Central Control Commission-Rabkrin working combinations; and that, as in all other fields, the Party reserved for itself full freedom to alter the forms of its own organization, operation, and relationships.

3) *The Operative Integration of the Pyramids*

MOUNTING FUNCTIONAL FUSION OF THE PARTY AND THE SOVIETS. In 1929–30, about the time when the industrialization and collectivization programs went into full swing, a more open fusion of the Party and government began to emerge. First, there appeared the frequent public association of the Party and government in authoritative Party pronouncements. Then, a number of resolutions directed specifically to higher government bodies, commissariats, and various government enterprises were issued by the Party Central Committee, calling upon them for certain action. These resolutions were followed as a rule by simultaneously promulgated official laws covering the same points, though at times they took full effect entirely by and of themselves. Lastly and even more significantly, since January 1931, numerous formal laws and enactments have been published in the official Gazette and Collection of Laws in the joint name of the Council of People's Commissars and the Central Committee of the C.P.S.U.(B), signed by Molotov as Chairman of the Council and Stalin as Secretary of the Central Committee. No precise criteria have been publicly suggested in regard to the nature or subject matter of the laws that were to be so promulgated, though practice indicates that this form was, in the majority of cases, used to underscore the primacy of certain legislation or the vital current urgency of the items embraced by these laws.

THE AMALGAMATION OF THE SUMMITS. The cycle was completed in 1941, with Stalin's assumption of the chairmanship of the Council of People's Commissars on 7 May. Enactments promulgated in the joint name of the government and the Party for a time bore the sole signature of Stalin as 'Chairman of the Council of People's Commissars and Secretary of the Central Committee of the C.P.S.U.(B).' Stalin—like Lenin before him —[was] both the acknowledged highest leader of the Party and the official head of the government.* And even more than during Lenin's earliest tenure, the Party and government are publicly associated and closely amalgamated in personnel, operation, and performance of the all-embracing function of preparation and promulgation of general and fundamental, as well as current and specific, activity-guiding norms.

* Ed. note: This was also the case of Khrushchev's rule between 1958 and 1964.

The Rationalization of Terror

Leon Trotsky, one of the great figures of the Bolshevik Revolution, lived to see the realization of the great fears he had expressed during the early congresses of the Russian Social Democratic Labor Party, as the first version of the Communist Party was known. Opposing at the time (1903–1905) Lenin's program, which emphasized the supremacy of the Party of "professional revolutionaries" over the proletariat, Trotsky argued that if the Bolshevik view were adopted, the "Party [would be] replaced by the organization of the Party, the organization by the Central Committee, and finally the Central Committee by the Dictator." The historical processes that led to the fulfilment of this prophecy were detailed in 1936 in Trotsky's *The Revolution Betrayed*.

But the height of terror of the totalitarian regime was yet to come. An authentic description of the Stalin era in Soviet history is given on pages 231–242 by the person who came to inherit the dictator's mantle, Nikita S. Khrushchev. Speaking to a closed session of the Twentieth Congress of the Communist Party of the Soviet Union (February 24–25, 1956), Khrushchev submitted a "secret" report which contained an extensive and harsh indictment of Stalin and a biting criticism of the sycophantic "personality cult" that flourished during his regime. The report presents an intimate inside view of the formulas and techniques employed in the elimination of the actual and potential opponents of the regime—formulas and techniques which, though considerably toned down, still form part and parcel of the Soviet system.

Professor Hazard's article (pages 242–254) discusses the use of terror as an instrument of government in the Soviet Union. He shows that although terror is primarily a means for the preservation of Communist power, the Soviet rulers have quite effectively rationalized its employment, especially during Stalin's time. In absolute control of the media of mass communication and of a vast and complex network of propaganda, the Communists succeeded in establishing "in the public mind the Marxist tenet of the desirability of state ownership of the productive forces and the Communist tenet of the desirability of a strong and skilled leadership. . . ."

But while the Marxist tenet continued to be upheld in the post-Stalin era, the justification of terror as an instrument of government has been seriously questioned. Opposition came primarily from the members of the "new class"—technocrats, managers, Party functionaries, etc.—who worried about the safety of their own positions. The change in Party and state leadership brought about a dramatic shift from the use of naked terror to more subtle means for the preservation of Soviet power. But while the numerous reform measures adopted after 1953 eliminated many of those features of Soviet law which permitted the disguise of terror in legal form, there is no doubt that political terror is still one of the most important weapons for the preservation of Communist rule in the Soviet Union. In the Soviet formula of government, political terror continues to play a dual role—the prevention of opposition and resistance and the consolidation and reinforcement of personal power through the constant elimination of all actual and potential enemies of the dictators. Indeed, one cannot really speak of the elimination of this form of terror so long as opposition to a given "party line" is all but impossible. This is but one of the many features of Soviet political reality which keeps alive the fear that terror as once known may be reintroduced, should this be found necessary by the regime. And as Harold J. Berman, an American expert on the Soviet legal system, has remarked, "the fear of a return of terror is itself a form of terror."

"The Crimes of Stalin"

NIKITA S. KHRUSHCHEV[*]

Comrades! In the report of the Central Committee of the party at the 20th Congress, in a number of speeches by delegates to the Congress, as also formerly during the plenary CC/CPSU [Central Committee of the Communist Party of the Soviet Union] sessions, quite a lot has been said about the cult of the individual and about its harmful consequences.

After Stalin's death the Central Committee of the party began to implement a policy of explaining concisely and consistently that it is impermissible and foreign to the spirit of Marxism-Leninism to elevate one person, to transform him into a superman possessing supernatural characteristics, akin to those of a god. Such a man supposedly knows everything, sees everything, thinks for everyone, can do anything, is infallible in his behavior.

Such a belief about a man, and specifically about Stalin, was cultivated among us for many years.

The objective of the present report is not a thorough evaluation of Stalin's life and activity. Concerning Stalin's merits, an entirely sufficient number of books, pamphlets and studies had already

[*] Former Chairman of the Council of Ministers of the U.S.S.R. and First Secretary of the Soviet Communist Party.

From the *Special Report to the Twentieth Congress of the Communist Party of the Soviet Union (Closed Session, February 24–25, 1956)* by Nikita S. Khrushchev. Reprinted by permission from the special edition of *The New Leader*: "The Crimes of the Stalin Era," selections from pp. 52–67. This edition was annotated by Boris I. Nicolaevsky, formerly of the Marx-Engels Institute of Moscow, and the author of *Letter of an Old Bolshevik*. The authenticity of the Report on the "cult of the individual" has not been acknowledged by Soviet sources. The text was released by the State Department on June 4, 1956, as "obtained from a confidential source."

been written in his lifetime. The role of Stalin in the preparation and execution of the Socialist Revolution, in the Civil War, and in the fight for the construction of socialism in our country, is universally known. Everyone knows this well.

At present, we are concerned with a question which has immense importance for the party now and for the future—with how the cult of the person of Stalin has been gradually growing, the cult which became at a certain specific stage the source of a whole series of exceedingly serious and grave perversions of party principles, of party democracy, of revolutionary legality.

Because of the fact that not all as yet realize fully the practical consequences resulting from the cult of the individual, the great harm caused by the violation of the principle of collective direction of the party and because of the accumulation of immense and limitless power in the hands of one person, the Central Committee of the party considers it absolutely necessary to make the material pertaining to this matter available to the 20th Congress of the Communist Party of the Soviet Union. . . .

When we analyze the practice of Stalin in regard to the direction of the party and of the country, when we pause to consider everything which Stalin perpetrated, we must be convinced that Lenin's fears were justified. The negative characteristics of Stalin, which, in Lenin's time, were only incipient, transformed themselves during the last years into a grave abuse of power by Stalin, which caused untold harm to our party. . . .

Stalin acted not through persuasion, explanation and patient cooperation with people, but by imposing his concepts and demanding absolute submission to his opinion. Whoever opposed this concept or tried to prove his viewpoint and the correctness of his position was doomed to removal from the leading collective and to subsequent moral and physical annihilation. This was especially true during the period following the 17th Party Congress, when many prominent party leaders and rank-and-file party workers, honest and dedicated to the cause of Communism, fell victim to Stalin's despotism. . . .

Stalin originated the concept "enemy of the people." This term automatically rendered it unnecessary that the ideological errors of a man or men engaged in a controversy be proven; this term made possible the usage of the most cruel repression, violating all norms of revolutionary legality, against anyone who in any way disagreed with Stalin, against those who were only suspected of hostile intent, against those who had bad reputations. This concept "enemy of the people" actually eliminated the possibility of any kind of ideological fight or the making of one's views known on this or that issue, even those of a practical character. In the main, and in actuality, the only proof of guilt used, against all norms of current legal science, was the "confession" of the accused himself; and, as subsequent probing proved, "confessions" were acquired through physical pressures against the accused. This led to glaring violations of revolutionary legality and to the fact that many entirely innocent persons, who in the past had defended the party line, became victims.

We must assert that, in regard to those persons who in their time had opposed the party line, there were often no sufficiently serious reasons for their physical annihilation. The formula "enemy of the people" was specifically introduced for the purpose of physically annihilating such individuals. . . .

Arbitrary behavior by one person encouraged and permitted arbitrariness in others. Mass arrests and deportations of many thousands of people, execution without trial and without normal investigation created conditions of insecurity, fear and even desperation.

This, of course, did not contribute toward unity of the party ranks and of all strata of working people, but, on the contrary, brought about annihilation and the expulsion from the party of workers who were loyal but inconvenient to Stalin. . . .

Stalin's willfulness *vis-à-vis* the party and its Central Committee became fully evident after the 17th Party Congress which took place in 1934.

Having at its disposal numerous data showing brutal willfulness toward party cadres, the Central Committee has created a party commission under the control of the Central Committee Presidium; it was charged with investigating what made possible the mass repressions against the majority of the Central Committee members and candidates elected at the 17th Congress of the All-Union Communist Party (Bolsheviks).

The commission has become acquainted with a large quantity of materials in the NKVD archives and with other documents and has established many facts pertaining to the fabrication of cases against Communists, to false accusations, to glaring abuses of socialist legality, which resulted in the death of innocent people. It became apparent that many party, Soviet and economic activists, who were branded in 1937–1938 as "enemies," were actually never enemies, spies, wreckers, etc., but were always honest Communists; they were only so stigmatized and, often, no longer able to bear barbaric tortures, they charged themselves (at the order of the investigative judges—falsifiers) with all kinds of grave and unlikely crimes.

The commission has presented to the Central Committee Presidium lengthy and documented materials pertaining to mass repressions against the delegates to the 17th Party Congress and against members of the Central Committee elected at that Congress. These materials have been studied by the Presidium of the Central Committee.

It was determined that of the 139 members and candidates of the party's Central Committee who were elected at the 17th Congress, 98 persons, *i.e.*, 70 per cent, were arrested and shot (mostly in 1937–1938). (Indignation in the hall.) What was the composition of the delegates to the 17th Congress? It is known that 80 per cent of the voting paticipants of the 17th Congress joined the party during the years of conspiracy before the Revolution and during the civil war; this means before 1921. By social origin the basic mass of the delegates to the Congress were workers (60 per cent of the voting members).

For this reason, it was inconceivable that a congress so composed would have elected a Central Committee a majority of whom would prove to be enemies of the party. The only reason why 70 per cent of Central Committee members and candidates elected at the 17th Congress were branded as enemies of the party and of the people was because honest Communists were slandered, accusations against them were fabricated, and revolutionary legality was gravely undermined.

The same fate met not only the Central Committee members but also the majority of the delegates to the 17th Party Congress. Of 1,966 delegates with either voting or advisory rights, 1,108 persons were arrested on charges of anti-revolutionary crimes, *i.e.*, decidedly more than a majority. This very fact shows how absurd, wild and contrary to common sense were the charges of counter-revolutionary crimes made out, as we now see, against a majority of participants at the 17th Party Congress. (Indignation in the hall.)

We should recall that the 17th Party Congress is historically known as the Congress of Victors. Delegates to the Congress were active participants in the building of our socialist state; many of them suffered and fought for party interests during the pre-Revolutionary years in the conspiracy and at the civil-war fronts; they fought their enemies valiantly and often nervelessly looked into the face of death.

How, then, can we believe that such people could prove to be "two-faced" and had joined the camps of the enemies of socialism during the era after the political liquidation of Zinovievites, Trotskyites, and rightists and after the great accomplishments of socialist construction? This was the result of the abuse of power by Stalin, who began to use mass terror against the party cadres.

What is the reason that mass repressions against activists increased more and more after the 17th Party Congress? It was because at that time Stalin had so elevated himself above the party and above the nation that he ceased to consider either the Central Committee or the party.

While he still reckoned with the opinion of the collective before the 17th Congress, after the complete political liquidation of the Trotskyites, Zinovievites and Bukharinites, when as a result of that fight and socialist victories the party achieved unity, Stalin ceased to an ever greater degree to consider the members of the party's Central Committee and even the members of the Political Bureau. Stalin thought that now he could decide all things alone and all he needed were statisticians; he treated all others in such a way that they could only listen to and praise him.

After the criminal murder of Sergei M. Kirov, mass repressions and brutal acts of violation of socialist legality began. On the evening of December 1, 1934 on Stalin's initiative (without the approval of the Political Bureau—which was passed two days later, casually), the Secretary of the Presidium of the Central Executive Committee, Yenukidze, signed the following directive:

1. Investigative agencies are directed to speed up the cases of those accused of the preparation or execution of acts of terror.
2. Judicial organs are directed not to hold up the execution of

death sentences pertaining to crimes of this category in order to consider the possibility of pardon, because the Presidium of the Central Executive Committee of the U.S.S.R. does not consider as possible the receiving of petitions of this sort.

3. The organs of the Commissariat of Internal Affairs are directed to execute the death sentences against criminals of the above-mentioned category immediately after the passage of sentences.

This directive became the basis for mass acts of abuse against socialist legality. During many of the fabricated court cases, the accused were charged with "the preparation" of terroristic acts; this deprived them of any possibility that their cases might be re-examined, even when they stated before the court that their "confessions" were secured by force, and when, in a convincing manner, they disproved the accusations against them . . .

The majority of the Central Committee members and candidates elected at the 17th Congress and arrested in 1937–1938 were expelled from the party illegally through the brutal abuse of the party statute, because the question of their expulsion was never studied at the Central Committee plenum.

Now, when the cases of some of these so-called "spies" and "saboteurs" were examined, it was found that all their cases were fabricated. Confessions of guilt of many arrested and charged with enemy activity were gained with the help of cruel and inhuman tortures.

At the same time, Stalin, as we have been informed by members of the Political Bureau of that time, did not show them the statements of many accused political activists when they retracted their confessions before the military tribunal and asked for an objective examination of their cases. There were many such declarations, and Stalin doubtless knew of them.

The Central Committee considers it absolutely necessary to inform the Congress of many such fabricated "cases" against the members of the party's Central Committee elected at the 17th Party Congress. . . .

In those years repressions on a mass scale were applied which were based on nothing tangible and which resulted in heavy cadre losses to the party.

The vicious practice was condoned of having the NKVD prepare lists of persons whose cases were under the jurisdiction of the

Military Collegium and whose sentences were prepared in advance. Yezhov would send these lists to Stalin personally for his approval of the proposed punishment. In 1937–1938, 383 such lists containing the names of many thousands of party, Soviet, Komsomol, Army and economic workers were sent to Stalin. He approved these lists.

A large part of these cases are being reviewed now and a great part of them are being voided because they were baseless and falsified. Suffice it to say that from 1954 to the present time the Military Collegium of the Supreme Court has rehabilitated 7,679 persons, many of whom were rehabilitated posthumously. . . .

Facts prove that many abuses were made on Stalin's orders without reckoning with any norms of party and Soviet legality. Stalin was a very distrustful man, sickly suspicious; we know this from our work with him. He could look at a man and say: "Why are your eyes so shifty today?" or "Why are you turning so much today and avoiding to look me directly in the eyes?" The sickly suspicion created in him a general distrust even toward eminent party workers whom he had known for years. Everywhere and in everything he saw "enemies," "two-facers" and "spies." Possessing unlimited power, he indulged in great willfulness and choked a person morally and physically. A situation was created where one could not express one's own will.

When Stalin said that one or another should be arrested, it was necessary to accept on faith that he was an "enemy of the people." Meanwhile, Beria's gang, which ran the organs of state security, outdid itself in proving the guilt of the arrested and the truth of materials which it falsified. And what proofs were offered? The confessions of the arrested, and the investigative judges accepted these "confessions." And how is it possible that a person confesses to crimes which he has not committed? Only in one way—because of application of physical methods of pressuring him, tortures, bringing him to a state of unconsciousness, deprivation of his judgment, taking away of his human dignity. In this manner were "confessions" acquired.

When the wave of mass arrests began to recede in 1939, and the leaders of territorial party organizations began to accuse the NKVD workers of using methods of physical pressure on the arrested, Stalin dispatched a coded telegram on Jaunary 20, 1939 to the committee secretaries of *oblasts* and *krais*, to the central committees of republic Communist parties, to the People's Commissars of Internal Affairs and to the heads of NKVD organizations. This telegram stated:

> The Central Committee of the All-Union Communist Party (Bolsheviks) explains that the application of methods of physical pressure in NKVD practice is permissible from 1937 on in accordance with permission of the Central Committee of the All-Union Communist Party (Bolsheviks) . . . It is known that all bourgeois intelligence services use methods of physical influence against the representatives of the socialist proletariat and that they use them in their most scandalous forms.
>
> The question arises as to why the socialist intelligence service should be more humanitarian against the mad agents of the bourgeoisie, against the deadly enemies of the working class and of the *kolkhoz* workers. The Central Committee of the All-Union Communist Party (Bolsheviks) considers that physical pressure should still be used obligatorily, as an exception applicable to known and obstinate enemies of the people, as a method both justifiable and appropriate.

Thus, Stalin had sanctioned in the name of the Central Committee of the All-Union Communist Party (Bolsheviks) the most brutal violation of socialist legality, torture and oppression, which led as we have seen to the slandering and self-accusation of innocent people. . . .

The power accumulated in the hands of one person, Stalin, led to serious consequences during the Great Patriotic War. . . .

The threatening danger which hung over our Fatherland in the first period of the war was largely due to the faulty methods of directing the nation and the party by Stalin himself. . . .

All the more monstrous are the acts whose initiator was Stalin and which are rude violations of the basic Leninist principles of the nationality policy of the Soviet state. We refer to the mass deportations from their native places of whole nations, together with all Communists and Komsomols without any exception; this deportation action was not dictated by any military considerations.

Thus, already at the end of 1943, when there occurred a permanent breakthrough at the fronts of the Great Patriotic War benefiting the Soviet Union, a decision was taken and executed concerning the deportation of all the Karachai from the lands on which they lived.

In the same period, at the end of December 1943, the same lot befell the whole population of the Autonomous Kalmyk Republic. In March 1944, all the Chechen and Ingush peoples were deported and the Chechen-Ingush Autonomous Republic was liquidated. In April 1944, all Balkars were deported to faraway places from the territory of the Kabardino-Balkar Autonomous Republic and the Republic itself was renamed the Autonomous Kabardian Republic.

The Ukrainians avoided meeting this fate only because there were too many of them and there was no place to which to deport them. Otherwise, he would have deported them also. (Laughter and animation in the hall.)

Not only a Marxist-Leninist but also no man of common sense can grasp how it is possible to make whole nations responsible for inimical activity, including women, children, old people, Communists and Komsomols, to use mass repression against them, and to expose them to misery and suffering for the hostile acts of individual persons or groups of persons. . . .

The willfulness of Stalin showed itself not only in decisions concerning the internal life of the country but also in the international relations of the Soviet Union.

The July plenum of the Central Committee studied in detail the reasons for the development of conflict with Yugoslavia. It was a shameful role which Stalin played here. The "Yugoslav affair" contained no problems which could not have been solved through party discussions among comrades. There was no significant basis for the development of this "affair"; it was completely possible to have prevented the rupture of relations with that country. This does not mean, however, that the Yugoslav leaders did not make mistakes or did not have shortcomings. But these mistakes and shortcomings were magnified in a monstrous manner by Stalin, which resulted in a break of relations with a friendly country.

I recall the first days when the conflict between the Soviet Union and Yugoslavia began artificially to be blown up. Once, when I came from Kiev to Moscow, I was invited to visit Stalin, who, pointing to the copy of a letter lately sent to Tito, asked me, "Have you read this?"

Not waiting for my reply, he answered, "I will shake my little finger—and there will be no more Tito. He will fall." . . .

But this did not happen to Tito. No matter how much or how little Stalin shook, not only his little finger but everything else that he could shake, Tito did not fall. Why? The reason was that, in this case of disagreement with the Yugoslav comrades, Tito had behind him a state and a people who had gone through a severe school of fighting for liberty and independence, a people which gave support to its leaders.

You see to what Stalin's mania for greatness led. He had completely lost consciousness of reality; he demonstrated his suspicion and haughtiness not only in relation to individuals in the U.S.S.R., but in relation to whole parties and nations.

We have carefully examined the case of Yugoslavia and have found a proper solution which is approved by the peoples of the Soviet Union and of Yugoslavia as well as by the working masses of all the people's democracies and by all progressive humanity. The liquidation of the abnormal relationship with Yugoslavia was done in the interest of the whole camp of socialism, in the interest of strengthening peace in the whole world. . . .

The cult of the individual acquired such monstrous size chiefly because Stalin himself, using all conceivable methods, supported the glorification of his own person. This is supported by numerous facts. One of the most characteristic examples of Stalin's self-glorification and of his lack of even elementary modesty is the edition of his *Short Biography*, which was published in 1948. . . .

The cult of the individual has caused the employment of faulty principles in party work and in economic activity; it brought about rude violation of internal party and Soviet democracy, sterile administration, deviations of all sorts, covering up the shortcomings and varnishing of reality. Our nation gave birth to many flatterers and specialists in false optimism and deceit.

We should also not forget that, due to the numerous arrests of party, Soviet and economic leaders, many workers began to work uncertainly, showed overcautiousness, feared all which was new, feared their own shadows and began to show less initiative in their work. . . .

If we sharply criticize today the cult of the individual which was so widespread during Stalin's life and if we speak about the many negative phenomena generated by this cult which is so alien to the spirit of Marxism-Leninism, various persons may ask: How could it be? Stalin headed the party and the country for 30 years and many victories were gained during his lifetime. Can we deny this? In my opinion, the question can be asked in this manner only by those who are blinded and hopelessly hypnotized by the cult of the individual, only by those who do not understand the essence of the revolution and of the Soviet state, only by those who do not understand, in a Leninist manner, the role of the party and of the nation in the development of the Soviet society.

The Socialist Revolution was attained by the working class and by the poor peasantry with the partial support of middle-class peasants. It was attained by the people under the leadership of the Bolshevik Party. Lenin's great service consisted of the fact that he created a militant party of the working class, but he was armed with Marxist understanding of the laws of social development and with the science of proletarian victory in the fight with capitalism, and he steeled this party in the crucible of revolutionary struggle of the masses of the people. . . .

Some comrades may ask us: Where were the members of the Political Bureau of the Central Committee? Why did they not assert themselves against the cult of the individual in time? And why is this being done only now?

First of all, we have to consider the fact that the members of the Political Bureau viewed these matters in a different way at different times. Initially, many of them backed Stalin actively because Stalin was one of the strongest Marxists and his logic, his strength and his will greatly influenced the cadres and party work.

It is known that Stalin, after Lenin's death, especially during the first years, actively fought for Leninism against the enemies of Leninist theory and against those who deviated. Beginning with Leninist theory, the party, with its Central Committee at the head, started on a great scale the work of socialist industrialization of the country, agricultural collectivization and the cultural revolution.

At that time Stalin gained great popularity, sympathy and support. The party had to fight those who attempted to lead the country away from the correct Leninist path; it had to fight Trotskyites, Zinovievites and rightists, and the bourgeois nationalists. This fight was indispensable.

Later, however, Stalin, abusing his power more and more, began to fight eminent party and Government leaders and to use terroristic methods against honest Soviet people. . . .

Attempts to oppose groundless suspicions and charges resulted in the opponent falling victim of the repression. . . .

It is clear that such conditions put every member of the Political Bureau in a very difficult situation. And, when we also consider the fact that in the last years the Central Committee plenary sessions were not convened and that the sessions of the Political Bureau occurred only occasionally, from time to time, then we will understand how difficult it was for any member of the Political Bureau to take a stand against one or another unjust or improper procedure, against serious errors and shortcomings in the practices of leadership.

Terror and Its Rationalization

JOHN N. HAZARD[*]

Terror has always been an instrument of government in the Soviet system. From the earliest days of 1917, members of classes that owned productive property, as well as priests, monks, policemen of the Tsarist government, and members of the royal family, were considered to be enemies of the government and were terrorized accordingly. In a sense they were outlaws, although no formal law

[*] Professor of Public Law at Columbia University, Dr. Hazard is the author of *Soviet Housing Law* (1939), *Law and Social Change in the U.S.S.R.* (1953), *Settling Disputes in Soviet Society* (1960), and many other scholarly publications.

Reprinted from *The Soviet System of Government* by John N. Hazard, selections from pp. 62–75, by permission of The University of Chicago Press. Copyright 1961 by the University of Chicago Press. Chicago: The University of Chicago Press, 1961.

declared them subject to arrest and execution if apprehended. Punishment was to be meted out to citizens only when there was crime, yet in practice the "class enemy" could expect no leniency if he aroused the hostility of anyone in authority.

The exclusion of a part of the population from participation in government was formally accomplished by the Third Congress of Soviets in a resolution of January, 1918. The first Constitution of the Russian Republic, adopted in July, 1918, made the rule specific by listing in detail the classes of people who could not vote or hold office. They were, in effect, second-class citizens, subject to all the obligations of citizenship but denied any share in the determination of policy or in the administration of the state.

The first law establishing a Soviet court system to replace the courts of the Tsar created a special bench called a "revolutionary tribunal" to try allegations of opposition to the bolshevik regime. Contemporary accounts indicate that although these tribunals were supposed to act with some semblance of legal procedure, they reached quick decisions on limited evidence whenever they had before them a member of the enemy classes. There appeared two yardsticks of criminality, one for the worker and peasant, and another for the property owner and the priest.

As if this double standard of justice were not enough to protect the regime, there was created an "Extraordinary Committee" called the *Cheka*, with power to ferret out conspiracies against the state and with authorization to take immediate action, even to the point of execution, to prevent a new revolution. During the winter of 1917–18 the Minister of Justice opposed the extensive powers granted to the *Cheka*, because he, as a member of the Socialist Revolutionary party, anticipated that the apparatus would turn eventually against the leaders of the state itself. But his voice went unheeded. Ardent supporters of the new regime seemed to feel that the *Cheka* could be kept within bounds and directed solely against the class enemy. The records of the time show no signs that any definable group within the government except the Socialist Revolutionaries anticipated what was eventually to come. Only the Socialist Revolutionaries feared that the *Cheka* would turn upon some of its masters.

As the day loomed, and *Cheka* agents infiltrated into the activities of workers and peasants, and finally into the ranks of the

Communist party itself, the bolshevik commissar of justice who had succeeded the Socialist Revolutionary incumbent began to appreciate the danger and to struggle for the supremacy of his own commissariat in maintaining order. By December, 1921, hostility to the lawlessness of the *Cheka* even in dealing with supporters of the regime had gone so far that the Ninth Congress of Soviets voted its abolition and the assumption of most of its duties by the revolutionary tribunals and the regular courts. Only its investigatory functions were to be left, and these were given in February, 1922, to a newly created State Political Administration known as the G.P.U.

The terrorizing apparatus did not keep its place. The G.P.U. arrogated to itself greater authority than it had been given, and it was soon trying people in its own tribunals without publicity or benefit of counsel.

Stalin seems to have found this terrorizing apparatus a convenient instrument. Although the people became so restless under the lash of the G.P.U. that he found it necessary in 1934 to abolish it and transfer its functions in limited form to the Ministry of Internal Affairs, this Ministry was rarely restrained in performing its task. Even today, its role is important in the Soviet system of government, although its power has been reduced considerably since Stalin's death.

The Terrorizing Apparatus

From an examination of evidence brought to light by those who have escaped from the U.S.S.R., the pattern of terrorizing and its part in the system of government have become clear. The instruments are the Ministry of Internal Affairs and a companion agency that has sometimes been within the Ministry and sometimes outside it as a Ministry of State Security. The Ministry of State Security has had the task of ferreting out potential threats to the stability of the regime and investigating them. These investigations have been exposed by the Soviet authorities themselves, since Stalin's death, as characterized by the practice of physical and psychological torture to obtain confessions of guilt. With such confessions, or even without them, the Ministry of State Security has made a report, and a decision has then been made, presumably by the Prosecutor General of the U.S.S.R. or his representative, either to prosecute before a court or to permit the case to be handled by a special board of the Ministry of Internal Affairs.

The special boards in the Ministry of Internal Affairs were created by statute. They were not required to hold their proceedings in public, nor to provide any of the procedural guarantees of the constitution such as right to counsel, nor to follow the procedural provisions of the criminal code. According to the testimony of some whose fate has been settled by one or another of them, they often heard cases in the absence of the accused. Under a 1934 statute, they were permitted to sentence persons found to be "socially dangerous" to five-year terms in remote places in the U.S.S.R. or in concentration camps. No definition of social danger was set in the statute, and, from what is known from refugees, the provisions and definitions of the criminal code did not bind the special boards to prove a charge. On the contrary, their primary task was to apply terrorizing methods when there was no specific crime involved. They had no function if crime could be proved, for in such circumstances the case was tried by a criminal court in accordance with the code of criminal procedure and the constitutional guarantee of counsel.

Documents stolen from files of the Ministry of Internal Affairs in the Baltic states indicate that the terrorizing process has been applied to frighten into submission communities in which opposition to the regime was of serious proportion. To arrive at this effect, local representatives of the Ministry were instructed to arrest and deport to camps in the Russian Republic specified numbers of persons of given categories, but no specific individuals were named. The categories were those of prospective enemies, such as army officers of the former Latvian army, estate owners, factory owners, and merchants. The local official determined which persons within the given categories were the most likely enemies and proceeded to arrest them under conditions as mysterious and dramatic as possible. The entire operation was designed to strike fear into the hearts of those who remained and thus to silence them, lest they be next. Some of the effectiveness of the system would be lost if it were not arbitrary, that is, if one could predict where its hand would fall. Apparently, it is in popular insecurity that the regime's security has been thought to lie.

The Ministry of Internal Affairs and its security police, sometimes organized as a separate security agency, were given a privileged position under Stalin. Although the central office operated through ministries in each of the republics, its chain of command was completely centralized below that level in that the on-the-spot officials were free from any influence of local soviets. These officials were appointed or dismissed by the Ministry in Moscow, and they were beyond the reach even of local Communist politicians. Only the Prosecutor-General of the U.S.S.R. had administrative authority over the Ministry of Internal Affairs and its security agents.

As an element of post-Stalin reform, the privileged position of the Ministry of Internal Affairs was abolished, in part, in that its officials at the province level were made department chiefs in the executive committees of the provincial soviets, thus having to answer to provincial officials as well as to the Ministers in the republic capitals and in Moscow. The security police, however, retained their independence of provincial officials. This was done by separating them from the Ministry and placing them under a Committee for State Security, known as the KGB, created in the Council of Ministers of the U.S.S.R., and in the Council of Ministers in each of the Republics. By this move there was re-emphasized the desirability of separating the investigative function from any possibility of local interference.

Instances in which the Ministry has exceeded its authority have been disclosed in the past. The Minister of Internal Affairs, Henry Yagoda, was purged by Stalin in 1938 because he seems to have tried to make himself a threat to the inner circle of Stalin's associates. His successor then overdid his assignment by pressing the purge begun by Stalin into every corner of the industrial and state apparatus, and he himself was purged. Finally, after Stalin's death, his friend Lavrenti Beria, who had been for many years supervisor of the security apparatus, was arrested and executed as a traitor under circumstances said by those who have fled his Ministry to havens abroad to have been related to his desire to seize power.

To facilitate its work the Ministry of Internal Affairs has found it desirable to enlist large numbers of informers from the rank and file of the population. Through them, much information is obtained about unwary neighbors, and the expectable presence of such informers in every group enhances the terror of those who have reason to fear the hand of the state.

Terrorizing is obviously a weapon that was designed by the Soviet leadership to maintain itself in power, but events since Stalin's death suggest that it may be losing value in the eyes of the new leaders. Fearing that the structure of their power might disintegrate in a wave of mass opposition to the severity of the regime during Stalin's declining years, Stalin's heirs promised to redraft the criminal code, to make it less severe, and they amnestied many prisoners. Also, they declared false the allegations brought against the Kremlin doctors during Stalin's final weeks of life. These doctors had been indicted only a short while before on the strength of their alleged confessions to composing a revolutionary band planning to kill the Kremlin leaders by malpractice, and the new leaders branded the confessions as untrue because they had been obtained through torture.

Stalin's heirs promised that in the post-Stalin era enemies of the state would be tried in accordance with the rules of Soviet law and that "justice" would be done in the administration of the state. This series of events has been read by foreign observers as evidence that terrorizing is not now conceived by Soviet leaders as a desirable weapon. Yet it is noteworthy that at the very time that new general principles for criminal law and criminal procedure were adopted in December, 1958, there was emerging a new instrument of social control permitted to function outside the law. This was the "social assembly," created in a few border republics in 1957 but increased in number so that by 1959 eight of the fifteen union republics contained them.

In structure the social assembly is a gathering of citizens living together in a large apartment house, on a city street, or on a farm. It is convened on call of the community's public order committee, composed of Communist party members and other community leaders. It hears charges leveled by the Communist Youth League, a trade union, or other public organization against a citizen of conduct showing "an anti-social, parasitic way of life." This is not defined except to indicate that it is evidenced by evading socially useful work or by living on unearned income. This covers speculators in scarce commodities on the public markets.

The vote on the charge is by a show of hands, and the penalty may be banishment for periods up to five years to a remote area within the republic. There is no appeal, although the executive committee of the local soviet must confirm the sentence and must have someone present at the hearing. No rules of procedure are specified, except that the accused be present, unless he refuses to attend.

Practice has shown that these bodies have heard charges not only against speculators but against those who listen to foreign broadcasts. It is evident that the bodies have a political function. Since gatherings of citizens bound to observe no codes and unfamiliar with legal principles can be tyrannical in any society, especially when whipped to a frenzy by able agitators such as the Communist party can provide under circumstances in the U.S.S.R., the social assembly must be categorized among the agencies suited to the terrorizing process. Insufficient time has elapsed to indicate whether they will arrogate power as arbitrarily as the *Cheka* and its successors did, but the potentiality is present.

The Rationalization of Terror

Although the written record and refugees' verbal accounts of terrorizing activities in the U.S.S.R. might lead an American to suppose that restless Soviet millions must seethe on the verge of revolt, very few students of the Soviet system believe that such a conclusion is justified. To understand this apparent paradox, one must consider the unusual phenomenon of a people who appear, in the main, to have accepted terror during Stalin's time as a necessary evil. In short, one must understand that terrorizing as a technique of government was rationalized by Stalin for most Soviet citizens. Appreciation of this fact is important for those who attempt to measure the strength of the Soviet regime, for it is likely that opposition could come only from the very leadership group to which the necessity for the policy of terror has been imparted.

In a Western democracy, where there is no "official" philosophy of government and no monopoly of the press and the public platform, it is incredible that any governmental propaganda line would have universal or nearly universal acceptance. There is always a powerful opposition newspaper to act as critic of the government and of its propaganda. As has been seen, the Soviet system has eliminated the possibility of an opposition party, and the media of information and propaganda remain completely subject to the Communist party's control. These media, augmented by compulsory study groups for all members of the population, are employed to convince the people of the correctness of certain propositions. These propositions bear examination, because it is through their acceptance that the Soviet leaders expect to reduce and in some quarters even eliminate opposition to the policies of the regime, including terrorizing.

The foundation of the Soviet government's propaganda line is that its program rests upon scientifically proved fact. To twentieth-century man in any land an aura attaches to a thesis said to rest upon scientifically proved fact, and Soviet leaders can exploit this situation by quoting Marx and Engels, who claimed to be always scientific in evolving their doctrine of revolution and the dictatorship of the proletariat. The strongest card played by these nineteenth-century writers, on whom Lenin based his own thinking, was the claim that the process of historical development had finally been analyzed correctly and the key to the process found. It could then be argued that it was now possible for man to control the future course of history. . . .

The Effectiveness of the Rationalization

All Soviet citizens have been made to memorize the Marxian interpretation of the course of history. Those who are less tutored or incapable of grasping the detail are taught but the simple thesis: that a scientific analysis of history leads to the conclusion that the Soviet system of government is the highest type of state. It also claims to be the most democratic type of state, the logical final stage in the development of an economic and social system designed to come closer to satisfying man's wants than has any society in the past. It alone is said to make possible, through state ownership of land, factories, mines, means of communication, and means of distribution, the quantity of production necessary to meet man's needs. It alone claims to be structured in such a way that the workmen, and their allies the peasants, may determine policy and hence claim the position of masters of their own fates.

It alone claims to be preparing the way for the ultimate withering away of repression, when men will perform their social duties without need of compulsion and when production will be sufficient to distribute goods to men in full accordance with their needs.

Western students can point out effectively that the Marxist thesis is oversimplified and untrue, that the Soviet state is structured so that in the name of democracy there have been eliminated the fundamentals of democracy because the general public cannot control the formulation of policy. Western economists can also prove that a workman in a private enterprise economy is much more productive and better paid than in the U.S.S.R. The iron-curtain policy of closing Soviet frontiers to the foreign press and to foreign speakers has been designed in part to prevent the foreign view, and even the facts of Western economic life, from reaching the ears of the masses of Soviet workmen and peasants.

The success of Soviet propagandists in preaching their line can now be measured by means of interviews with those who have escaped. These interviews, conducted by teams organized by Harvard University, have indicated marked success in certain fields, which is the more remarkable because they were held with people who had come to dislike the Soviet system so much that they were willing to flee, often at risks to themselves and to the families they left behind.

It is generally true of all those interviewed that they have been convinced by Soviet schooling, press, and radio that production for maximum public benefit is possible only when factories, natural resources, and means of transportation and distribution are state owned. In short, private enterprise as a way of life has been rejected even by those who hated the Stalin regime. The key to long-range prosperity has come to be for most Soviet citizens, whatever their political persuasion, state ownership of the means of production.

This acceptance of state ownership as the key to prosperity has extended even to the peasants, although among these there is divided opinion. Among the older farmers in the displaced-persons camps of Europe in which most of the interviews occurred, there was found strong opposition to state ownership and to its hand-maiden, collective-farm operation of the land, on the ground that such communal use of the land was not right. The younger farmers, on the other hand, as reported by Alice C. Rossi, seemed to have accepted their Soviet education. While these younger people thought that the collective farms had been bad, their criticism was of management rather than of the system. All, both young and old, were agreed that there must never be a return to the system of estates under which large landowners owned the land and employed peasants to work it.

With mass acceptance of the basic tenet of Marxism—that there is no room in modern society for private ownership of productive resources—the Soviet leaders have scored their major victory. They do not have to worry about any serious opposition to the fundamental principle of their society. No large group of persons is likely to try to restore private enterprise in relation to the primary sources of wealth. There will be individuals who will want to make a profit on the sale of homemade products or of homegrown vegetables or meat, and there will even be individuals who want to steal state property and sell it on the open market, particularly during periods of short supply when the price is high. But there is not to be expected a demand for a basic change from the policy of state ownership of the means of production. The basic principle behind the implementation of this tenet—the principle that workmen require leadership to reach the goal of abundance— is also generally accepted. Respect for education is high, and leadership based upon superior skills, whether in operating a factory or in conducting the affairs of the state, is revered.

Here Marxist doctrine has helped the Communists especially, for it relates political parties to class interests. It teaches that in Western democracies one party will normally represent the landowners, another the peasants, a third the wealthy industrialists and their associates, a fourth the shopkeepers and small producers, and a fifth the working class; then, that class lines are clearly drawn in the differences between political parties, whence it can be argued logically that multiple political parties develop to represent the different economic interests existent in a given society. Conversely, where instead of multiple economic interests there is but a single economic interest, there need be only a single party. Soviet society is said by the Communists to have reached the stage where there is only one economic interest, that of the "toilers," whether these be workmen, clerks, or farmers. In consequence, there need be only a single political party to provide the leadership which all agree to be necessary. Since both refugees from, and recent American travelers in, the U.S.S.R. say that belief in a necessity for multiple parties has lessened there with the years, it is probable that most Soviet citizens accept this tenet of Communist doctrine.

It is probable that most accept also the idea that they can have a democratic system under conditions of state ownership when there is only one political party. What doubt there has been within the U.S.S.R. has centered on the desirability of permitting factions or organized voting blocs to exist within the single party. Stalin thought it necessary to preservation of his own power to stamp out with violence those of his colleagues who wanted to retain factions within the Communist party, but it is uncertain how successful he was in eradicating the lingering desire to form them.

Since Stalin's death factions have emerged within the party, and public notice of the fact was provided in June, 1957, when one group tried to oust Khrushchev from the Presidium, only to be answered by his successful exclusion of the group from the party's governing circle. It seems likely, as a result of this action, that the no-faction rule will not be questioned soon again. Unless the desire to influence policy through group action is stimulated again by some extreme change of policy, such as that introduced by Khrushchev in the field of industrial management and agriculture in 1957, it can be supposed that there will be no challenge in the foreseeable future to Stalin's contribution—a no-faction monopoly party—to Marxist political lore.

The Beginning of Disbelief

Having established in the public mind the Marxist tenet of the desirability of state ownership of the productive forces and the Communist tenet of the desirability of a strong and skilled leadership, it has not been hard for Soviet leaders to claim convincing reason for a policy of terror. It has been necessary only to relate the objects of the policy to a stand opposing the Marxist definition of social progress. So long as elements of the old regime remained in Soviet society, this relationship was usually established on the domestic scene. For example, middle-class farmers called "kulaks" were ordered liquidated as a class in the early 1930's for their opposition to the collectivization of agriculture. In the propaganda line, emphasis was placed on the fact that these farmers were natural enemies: they had employed labor on their farms, they favored private ownership of land, and, in short, they had been capitalists. It must have been expected that this was sufficient indictment in peasant eyes to justify terrorizing the rich as enemies of social progress.

When the remnants of the private enterprisers of pre-Soviet days were no more, or almost no more, it became necessary to relate those marked for imprisonment to the capitalists of other lands. First, the opposition was linked with the French, as the archcapitalists of Europe, and then with the British. Before the war with Hitler, the purge trials linked Stalin's opposition with Hitler and with his efforts to march to the Urals. Since the war, persons marked for execution in the U.S.S.R. have been called "American spies" and have been linked with "capitalist powers" generally, as was the case with Beria.

Only since Stalin's death has there begun to appear some hostility toward the argument that terrorizing is justified as an instrument of government. The opposition seems to come from the newly educated workmen and peasants forming the ranks of the technical and managerial class. It has already been suggested . . . that these new intellectuals are probably exerting pressure on the Communist party leaders to expand the circle of policy-makers at the very top of the party hierarchy. While they probably support wholeheartedly the economic system of state ownership and the idea of one-party government, it may well be that they now oppose terrorizing because it threatens predictability of tenure of office among members of the technical and managerial class. The managers of today witnessed the prewar purge, when those who were then their superiors were blacklisted as capitalist agents and placed in concentration camps or executed. They do not want this to happen to them. They are sufficiently well educated to question the accuracy of the "capitalist" label placed by Stalin upon their former colleagues. It may be that this group is now pressing for a relaxation of terrorizing, in the interest of greater personal stability, and that for them, at least, the Stalinist rationalization is wearing thin.

Such an explanation may lie at the base of the seeming reduction in importance of the Ministry of Internal Affairs since Stalin's death and, in particular, since Beria's execution. The regular army is said to have absorbed the border patrol troops of the Ministry of Internal Affairs. The special boards of the Ministry of Internal Affairs are reported to have been abolished in September, 1953, and their field of jurisdiction transferred to the military tribunals under the supervision of the Supreme Court of the U.S.S.R. Such a change is of some importance because the military courts are required on pain of Supreme Court reversal to observe procedural codes and constitutional guarantees.

Some of the instability of life seems to be slipping away for the managerial class, but it is still too early to say whether it has gone for good for the population as a whole. The social assemblies created in 1957 are ominous reminders that Communist party officials are not yet prepared to tie their hands with legal procedures from which they cannot depart.

While the changes in policy relating to terrorizing are beginning to be impressive, the end is not yet. Khrushchev used the twentieth party congress to denounce the excesses of Stalin's terrorizing apparatus, but he told his fellow party members at the same time that the agents of the Ministry of Internal Affairs were still necessary. The terrorizing apparatus is to remain, although there seems to be a desire to make its presence less evident.

SECTION VI

Soviet Constitutionalism

The most important single factor in constitutionalism, according to Western democratic standards, is the concept of *limited government*. This principle has little, if anything, to do with the existence or absence of a formal constitutional text; it implies primarily a balance between governmental *authority* and personal *freedom*. From this point of view, therefore, we can hardly speak of constitutionalism in the Soviet context. Yet Soviet "constitutionalists" insist that the fundamental document of the U.S.S.R. is not only more "advanced" but also more "democratic" than its Western counterparts which, in their view, merely assure "democracy for the strong, democracy for the propertied minority."

The merits of the Soviet constitution were outlined authoritatively by Joseph Stalin—"the father of the constitution"*—in his report to the Special Eighth All-Union Congress of Soviets (November 25, 1936). Characterized as a landmark in the transitional period between capitalism and communism, the Constitution of 1936 is claimed to mark the attainment of "socialism." The constitution, in Stalin's view, reflected the great changes that were made in the transformation of Russia from a backward, "bourgeois-landlord-dominated" state into an advanced "socialist" power. The fundamental law of the U.S.S.R., consequently, is viewed as a flexible document designed to take account of the advancements made in Soviet life and not "merely to record formal rights." As can be seen from the interpretations of Denisov and Kirichenko in the first selection of this section, the denigration of Stalin has in no way altered the "Stalinist" conception of the nature of Soviet constitutionalism.

* According to an announcement made early in 1962, a new constitution is being prepared in the Soviet Union. By the end of 1964, however, no date had yet been given for its presentation.

A Western view of the rationale and functions of constitutional documents in the U.S.S.R. is provided in the selection by Professor Fainsod.

Soviet Constitutionalism

A. DENISOV AND M. KIRICHENKO

The Soviet Constitution is the fundamental law of the socialist state. It gives legislative embodiment to the social and state system of the country, defines the principles underlying the organization and activity of the state organs, records the fundamental rights and duties of Soviet citizens and establishes the country's electoral system. It reflects the achievements scored in the building of the first socialist state in the world—the historic gains of the Soviet people in economic, political and cultural life.

The distinctive feature of the Soviet Constitution is that it mirrors the real correlation of class forces in the country—the class structure of society, the actual position of the existing classes and their relationships, the degree and forms of democracy in various spheres of activity.

In its class nature the Soviet Constitution in no way differs from other laws passed by the Soviet state. Yet it must not be identified with them.

The Constitution differs from current laws primarily in its content, for it records what has already been achieved and establishes the general framework of the state structure (the administrative-territorial division of the country, its system of organs of state power, state administration, courts and the Procurator's Office, the entire legislative activity, etc., are based on the Constitution).

The Soviet Constitution possesses specific juridical powers, since

From *Soviet State Law* by A. Denisov and M. Kirichenko, pp. 19–22. Moscow: Foreign Languages Publishing House, 1960.

all current legislation is exercised in full conformity with the Constitution and no law can contradict it. Thus, in a sense it predetermines the character of all other laws of the Soviet state. /

One of the features distinguishing the Soviet Constitution from current laws is the specific, more complicated procedure for amending it. This procedure is defined in the Constitution itself.

The Constitution of the Soviet country came into being as a result of the victory of the October Revolution in 1917; its evolution is indissolubly bound up with the tasks and functions of the Soviet state which in its development effected the transition from capitalism to socialism, entering the period of socialism already before the Second World War.

The evolution of the Soviet Constitution reflects all the changes which have taken place in the social and state structure, in the system of state organs, in the fundamental rights and duties of citizens and the electoral system of the country. It is manifested not only in the modification of the Constitution within the limits of the fundamental constitutional principles, i.e., without adopting a new constitution, but also in the replacement of one Soviet constitution by another, for example, of the 1918 Constitution of the R.S.F.S.R. by the 1925 Constitution of the R.S.F.S.R., or of the 1924 Constitution of the U.S.S.R. by the 1936 Constitution of the U.S.S.R.

The history of the Soviet Constitution reflects the law-governed process of the consolidation of the dictatorship of the working class, the development and extension of socialist democracy, the introduction of new guarantees of democratic freedoms and rights of the working people in the course of socialist construction.

It shows how the national policy of the Communist Party is being put into practice, how it has made for friendship and cooperation among all the peoples of the country.

It exposes the insinuations of the enemies of socialism who assert that Soviet power allegedly pursues a policy of forcible russification of all Soviet Republics.

It testifies to a constant perfection of the forms of state structure, of the administrative-territorial division and system of the Soviet organs of state power, state administration, courts and the Procurator's Office.

Finally, it conclusively proves the superiority of the Soviet social and state system, of the Soviet form of democracy over the capitalist social and state system, over bourgeois democracy.

The evolution of the Soviet Constitution graphically shows that:

1. The Soviet Constitution was drawn up *with the active and decisive participation of the working people and their representative institutions.* It embodies the will of all nations, national groups and nationalities of the country. This determines the truly popular character of the Soviet Constitution, which is expressed in the fact that it records: a) the socialist and democratic gains of the working masses and of all the peoples of the country, and b) the practical experience and forms of political, economic and cultural organization of the working people of town and country. It is also expressed in the simple and lucid style of the Constitution, which eliminates the need to decipher any of its provisions.

The elaboration and steady improvement of the fundamental law of the Soviet state was inspired and guided by the Communist Party. But while directing this work, the Communist Party in no way substituted the higher state organs which are empowered to adopt the fundamental law. It proceeded from the Leninist proposition according to which ". . . every representative of the masses, every citizen must be placed in conditions which would enable him to participate in the discussion of the state laws, in the election of his representatives and in putting the state laws into practice."

Thus, the elaboration and adoption of the Soviet Constitution was the result of collective creative effort and the common will of the working masses and of all peoples of the Soviet Union.

2. When working out the fundamental principles of the Constitution, the progressive forces of Soviet society, guided by the Communist Party, had to overcome the resistance of reactionary forces—of the class enemies, bourgeois nationalists and all those who attempted to hamper the constitutional development of the U.S.S.R., to distort the socialist essence and democratic character of the Soviet Constitution, to weaken its influence on all spheres of social life.

3. Both in the period of the transition to socialism and after the creation of a socialist society the Communist Party has waged a consistent struggle for a proper interpretation and application of

Soviet constitutional principles, for overcoming the errors and distortions in this field. The Central Committee of the Communist Party of the Soviet Union resolutely condemned the personality cult and its consequences which led to certain violations of constitutional norms, democracy and the law.

The cult of personality is utterly alien to the very nature of the Soviet state. The errors and shortcomings arising from this cult have not changed and could not, of course, change the socialist essence and democratic character of the Soviet state and of its Constitution.

The Nature of Soviet Constitutionalism

MERLE FAINSOD[*]

In Western eyes, constitutions exist to impose limits on the governments which they create. Whether embodied in formal documents or in customary usage, they attempt to confine each branch of government to its prescribed role, to safeguard citizens against abuse of power by officialdom, and to enforce the continuing responsibility of the governing authorities to the electorate. In more positive terms, they seek to liberate political energies by creating a forum in which competing political forces find free expression, in which the government of the day is subject to a constant flow of criticism from its opponents, and in which changes of government and shifts in public policy may be achieved by registering the

* Professor of Government at Harvard University, Dr. Fainsod is the author of *International Socialism and the World War* (1935), *Smolensk Under Soviet Rule* (1958), and many other scholarly publications.

Reprinted by permission of the publishers from Merle Fainsod, *How Russia Is Ruled,* from pp. 349–350, revised edition. Cambridge, Mass.: Harvard University Press. Copyright 1953, 1963, by the President and Fellows of Harvard College.

shifting preferences of the voting constituency. Where constitutionalism is incorporated in the living texture of society, it generates respect for the dignity of the individual. Men walk in freedom and dare to dissent from the views of their rulers.

This conception of constitutionalism is alien to the Soviet Union. Its ruling group is self-perpetuating, and it cannot be dislodged save by revolution. Its powers are all-embracing and without limit. So-called "constitutional" arrangements derive such force as they possess from its sanction; the whole apparatus of government and administration is subject to its dictates. The leaders of the regime enforce a standard of orthodoxy from which there can be no dissent. Opposition is outlawed and invested with the stamp of treason. Citizens have duties and obligations; such rights as they exercise depend on the precarious beneficence of the ruling group. Freedom is equated with obedience. Individual values must conform to the system of values prescribed by the top leadership. Men walk in subservience and bow to a power which they dare not defy.

From the point of view of the Soviet rulers, the constitutional documents of the U.S.S.R. and the union republics perform several useful functions. In the first place, they make the formal governmental structure explicit. No dictatorship can escape the problem of devising a system of central and local authorities which will be responsive to its will. By incorporating these arrangements in pseudo-constitution form, the ruling group gives them an air of legitimacy and stability which no series of administrative ukases can ever communicate. In the second place, the constitutions play an important propaganda role both at home and abroad. The emphasis in the constitutions on mass mobilization of the electorate and mass participation in the proceedings of the Soviets is designed to evoke an illusion of monolithic support for the dictatorship. The manipulated unanimity of "plebiscitory democracy" is intended to demonstrate that opposition to the regime has ceased to exist and that the ruling group is the living incarnation of its people's aspirations. From this platform the regime's spokesmen go on to claim that their constitution is the most democratic in the world, that Western constitutions serve as mere camouflage for the dictatorship of monopoly capital, and that only the Soviet Constitution guarantees the advancement of mass welfare. The utilization of the Constitution as an instrument of propaganda is not limited to domestic audiences. The Constitution of the U.S.S.R. has been carefully drafted to feature the economic security which the Soviet system is alleged to provide, to leave the impression that ultimate power resides in the hands of the toilers rather than in a narrow ruling clique, and to implant a vision of an idyllic society in which all conflicts have been resolved and all problems can be solved. It seeks to rally support for the Soviet cause in non-Soviet lands by appealing to the dissatisfied, the frustrated, and the gullible whose perceptions of the inadequacies of the societies in which they live can readily be transformed into an idealization of the virtues of a social system which they have not experienced.

SECTION VII

Structure and Functions
of Government

· 1 ·

THE STATUS OF NATIONALITIES
AND THE FEDERAL SYSTEM

Perhaps no other issue concerning Soviet life has evoked so much controversy as that of the treatment of national minorities in the U.S.S.R. Protagonists of the Soviet system claim that the political measures and institutional arrangements adopted in the U.S.S.R. have successfully resolved the national problem that plagued Tsarist Russia and which continues to plague many countries of the world today. They depict the U.S.S.R. as a model of a multinational state which assures in practice the equality and friendship of all the peoples inhabiting it. Opponents, on the other hand, argue that the Communist-imposed "solution" merely brought about a political *Gleichschatung* which in fact resulted in the Russification, if not obliteration, of the cultural characteristics of the many national and ethnic groups living in the U.S.S.R. Furthermore, they claim that the Soviet leaders have not hesitated to uproot a number of national groups, showing no regard for age and sex or individual guilt or innocence, if this was found politically necessary or expedient. As their authority they cite Khrushchev, who in his famous "secret" report on the "cult of the individual" of February 25, 1956, admitted that "rude violations of the basic Leninist principles of the nationality policy" were committed in the U.S.S.R. He referred to the mass deportations of

1943–44 involving the Karachai, the Chechen and Ingush, the Balkar and the Volga Germans.*

What, then, are the realities of the successes and failures of Soviet nationality policy? The authoritative pro-Soviet account is presented by Denisov and Kirichenko (pages 266–270). In their view, the "victory of socialism" and the concomitant elimination of the bourgeois seeds of national discontent made possible the establishment of a new Soviet culture which is "national in form and socialist in content." The political-institutional solution of the question of nationalities was found in the establishment of a "federal state" based on the principles of "national sovereignty, voluntary unification and equal rights of the federated subjects." Moreover, the coequality of the national and ethnic groups is claimed to be assured by their proportionate representation in the Soviet of Nationalities, one of the two houses of the Supreme Soviet.

Professor Inkeles' article outlines the demographic and historical background of the nationalities problem in Russia and evaluates the Leninist formula adopted for its solution in the Soviet Union. He is concerned particularly with answering the following questions:

1. To what extent does the country's nationality policy provide for gradual transition to separate statehood for the major national minorities whose culture, history, and socio-political and economic maturity make them reasonable candidates for such status?

2. To what degree are the minorities permitted and facilitated the free expression of their cultural heritage?

3. To what extent is Soviet nationality policy non-discriminatory —that is, to what extent does it offer members of the minority nationalities equal access to such benefits as the society provides for average citizens?

4. Has there been any economic exploitation of minority regions, by depletion of the land or other natural resources, by the carrying off of wealth produced in the area without sufficient compensation, or by the development of the region's economy in so special or limited a way as to subordinate it unduly to the productive needs and interests of the dominant majority?

The special characteristics of the Soviet federal system are described in the article by Professor Hazard. He demonstrates the historical and political factors which induced the Bolsheviks to adopt the federal scheme as the one best suited for the advance-

* See pp. 238–239.

ment of their own interests. Exploiting the hostility felt by the national minorities toward the oppressive Russification policies of the Tsars, the Bolsheviks advanced the principle of self-determination, proclaiming the right of each ethnic and national group to determine its own political destinies. While they did not view favorably the possible disintegration of a "progressive," that is, a Communist-controlled, country, they were fully aware of the tactical advantages inherent in the principle. The Bolsheviks relied, of course, on the "unifying" powers of the Party, which transcended national barriers. And, in fact, as the leadership of the various ethnic and national groups fell gradually into the hands of the Bolsheviks during and after the Revolution, the originally manifested tendencies toward secession were halted and the various "independent" republics were brought back into a "voluntary" Union of Soviet Socialist Republics. The idea of "narrow, bourgeois nationalism" gradually gave way to the idea of "socialist patriotism" and "proletarian internationalism."

The drive for the unification of the various territorial units was enhanced by historical circumstances that necessitated a united stand against invading enemy armies. After the consolidation of the regime, the need for unity in peacetime was "demonstrated" by the logic of the requirements of centralized economic planning. The formula of federalism seemed enticing both for political and practical reasons. But while both the 1924 and 1936 constitutions*

* For the constitutional provisions concerning the federal state structure of the U.S.S.R., see Articles 13–29 of the 1936 Constitution. The trend toward the establishment of a unitary state based on a single "Communist culture," as envisaged in the Third Program of the Communist Party of 1961, has been discernible for the past few years. The Soviet Union was pressing a far-reaching plan aimed to convert the present structure of national republics into a system of regional federations that would de-emphasize the distinctiveness of non-Russian ethnic groups. The principles underlying these political units are to be defined in the new constitution which is being drafted to replace the Stalin Constitution of 1936. The first steps toward the implementation of the plan were taken in 1962 when the four Soviet union republics of Central Asia —the Uzbek, Turkmen, Tadzhik and Kirghiz—were placed under a single Communist Party command and a single system of economic management. This was followed by similar changes involving the union republics of Armenia, Georgia and Azerbaijan. The acceleration of the trend was portended by the conference of sociologists, economists, lawyers and linguists held in October 1963 in Frunze, the capital of the Kirghiz Republic. The conference recommended, *inter alia*, that "scholarly study groups be formed in Central Asia, Transcaucasia and the Baltic Region to devise ways for establishing new

provided for a state structure with powers neatly "divided" between the central and union republican governments and guarantees for the rights of the national minorities, in reality they merely camouflaged the all-inclusive powers of the Communist Party. In fact, the supremacy of the Party in the Soviet state acquired an aura of "legitimacy" by virtue of Articles 126 and 141 of the 1936 Constitution.

As for the Soviet approach toward the minorities' cultural self-expression, the history of the U.S.S.R. leaves little doubt that tolerance of cultural diversity has been dependent upon the given ideological or political needs of the regime.

The National Minorities
and the Soviet State Structure

A. DENISOV AND M. KIRICHENKO

The all-round collaboration of the nations, national groups and nationalities inhabiting the Soviet Union, as well as the ideology of equality, friendship and brotherhood among them have long been established within the Soviet federative state. This new type of relations between nations arose as a result of the victory of socialism in the Soviet Union. They were made possible by: 1) the establishment and consolidation of the dictatorship of the working class, which is an irreconcilable opponent of national and racial oppression, and is the vehicle of the ideas of socialist international-

---

federations in those areas." After the ouster of Khrushchev in October 1964, however, the trend seems to have reversed. In December 1964, the new Soviet leadership restored the economic powers of the four Central Asian republics by abolishing the consolidated agencies established in 1962–1963.

From *Soviet State Law* by A. Denisov and M. Kirichenko, selections from pp. 147–154. Moscow: Foreign Languages Publishing House, 1960.

ism; 2) the abolition of the exploiting classes (landlords and capitalists)—instigators and fomenters of enmity between nations and races; 3) the mutual aid rendered by the socialist nations which ensure the great successes achieved in the political and economic life of the country and brought about a new culture, *national in form and socialist in content.**

The Soviet Union, a multinational state, originated and developed into a mighty socialist power on the basis of the solidarity of all its peoples, on the basis of the principles of proletarian internationalism. Proletarian internationalism implies the recognition of and respect for the principle of national equality, and the basic common interests of the working people of all nations and races. . . . In its national policy the Party has always proceeded from the Leninist thesis that Socialism does not eliminate national features but ensures the all-round economic and cultural development of all nations and nationalities.

The peoples of the Soviet Union consider that the determination of forms of state structure is their internal affair. The nations of other countries have the same right to this. Soviet people do not attempt to force on anybody any form of state structure. This, however, does not preclude or diminish in any way the influence exerted by the Soviet forms of state structure upon the state systems of other countries. The Soviet forms of state structure are regarded by the broad masses in a number of countries as an example of how the national problem and the problem of truly democratic co-operation of different nations within a single multinational state have been solved on socialist lines.

The U.S.S.R. as a Union State

The concept of the state structure of the U.S.S.R. covers a broad range of state and law phenomena. It includes the principles governing the unification of the Soviet socialist republics in a single multinational state, the delimitation of powers vested in the U.S.S.R. and in the Union Republics, the legal status of the Autonomous Republics, Autonomous Regions and the National Areas in the system of the U.S.S.R. and the corresponding Union Republics, the administrative and territorial division of the Republics as well as Soviet citizenship.

The Soviet Union is a federal state formed by the Union

* Italics supplied.

Republics with a view to jointly exercising their functions in the economic and political spheres, and in military defence. It is a voluntary union of the equal Soviet Socialist Republics possessing the rights that correspond to the aims and tasks of this association.

The *economic foundation* of the Soviet federation is the socialist system of economy and the socialist ownership of the instruments and means of production. Socialist ownership makes for community of economic interests of the working people of all nations, cultivates feelings of fraternal solidarity among workers, peasants and intellectuals irrespective of their nationality or race. This guarantees the exceptional strength and stability of the Soviet federation, which is based on the *dictatorship of the working class*.

The Soviet federation is a union of *state formations* which differ in the national composition of their population. It has been formed to solve the national questions and the problems of fraternal co-operation of the nations in all spheres of life and expresses both the common interests of the working people of all the nations and the specific interests of each nation.

The Soviet federation is organized along the lines of *democratic centralism*. The keynote of this federation is recognition and observance of the principles of the *national sovereignty, voluntary unification and equal rights of the federated subjects*.

The voluntary union of the Soviet Republics, on which the U.S.S.R. has been founded since its inception, is one of the sources of the strength and stability of the multinational socialist state. This principle follows from the right of nations to self-determination including the right to secession and the formation of independent states. This right negates any forcible interference in the internal life of peoples. In other words, nobody has the right to limit or violate national sovereignty.

Solution of the question of what form of state structure best suits this or that nation depends on its specific economic, political and cultural conditions.

The logical conclusion to be drawn from the fact that the Soviet Union is built on the principle of voluntary union is that every Union Republic has the right to decide the question of secession from the Soviet Union. From this it is clear that within the U.S.S.R. violence cannot be used by one republic or nation against another.

Figure 2. NATIONAL STATE STRUCTURE OF THE U.S.S.R.

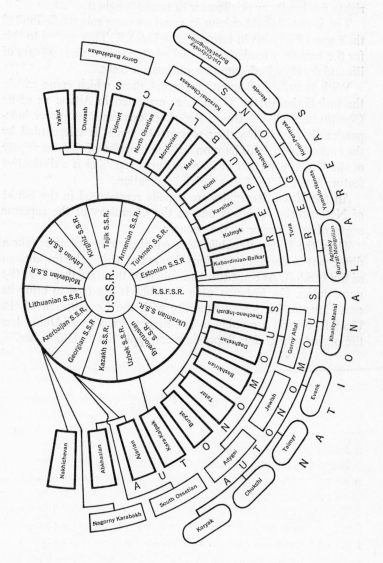

Not a single Union Republic is discriminately limited in its rights, nor has it any privileges with regard to others.

The Union Republics have in equal measure voluntarily limited their sovereign rights in favour of the U.S.S.R. They agreed to this for the benefit of rendering mutual assistance in various spheres of life and deciding both common and specific tasks.

With regard to all questions except those which come within the jurisdiction of the U.S.S.R. as expressed in Article 14 of its Constitution, all the Union Republics exercise state power independently. Herein lies their sovereignty which is safeguarded by the entire Union. This harmonious combination of the sovereignty of the Union with that of its constituent republics is a distinctive feature of the U.S.S.R. as a socialist federation.

All the Union Republics are equally represented in the Soviet of Nationalities, which is one of the Chambers of the supreme organ of state power in the country.

Thus, the Union Republics through their representatives take a direct part in deciding questions that come within the jurisdiction of the U.S.S.R. As constituent members of the state they have the same duties. For instance, each Republic is expected to bring its own Constitution into conformity with the Constitution of the U.S.S.R. Should a republican law diverge from an all-Union law the organs of a Union Republic must apply the all-Union law.

Soviet Nationality Policy in Perspective

ALEX INKELES[*]

In the current atmosphere of "peaceful competition between systems," increasing emphasis is placed on the economic factor of production and consumption levels in comparisons of Soviet and non-Soviet achievement. In the process some observers have all but lost sight of the fundamental political, social and cultural characteristics that continue to differentiate the two systems. Among relevant issues one of importance is the status of the national and racial minorities in the Soviet Union. At a time when the Western democracies are granting full independent statehood to one after another of the formerly subject peoples of Africa and Asia, it seems particularly appropriate to inquire into the position of the Soviet minorities. Unfortunately, this subject has received less attention than it deserves, perhaps because many have uncritically accepted Moscow's claim that any issues of nationality and race have long since been successfully resolved. If this were true, Soviet policy would still merit close examination. The fact is, however, that despite some substantial attainments, the Soviet regime has far from solved the problem of minority status either to the satisfaction of the groups themselves or to the particular credit of the Soviet system.

In order to assess Soviet nationality policy intelligently, it is

[*] A prominent American sociologist on the faculty of Harvard University, Professor Inkeles is the author of *Public Opinion in Soviet Russia* (1950), and co-author of *How the Soviet System Works* (1956), and *The Soviet Citizen* (1959).

From "Soviet Nationality Policy in Perspective" by Alex Inkeles, *Problems of Communism*, Washington, D.C., Vol. IX, No. 3, May–June 1960, selections from pp. 25–34. Reprinted by permission.

necessary to know certain distinctive historical and demographic facts about the minorities.

Population Patterns

While the Great Russians are the single largest group in the Soviet Union, they hold only a precariously slim margin of numerical superiority over the combined population of the national minorities. Indeed, as a result of the rapid expansion of the Tsarist Empire, the Russians were formerly in a minority, comprising only 45 percent of the population in the 1897 census. The loss of certain territories during the Revolution and the Civil War somewhat redressed the balance, and by the 1926 census the Great Russians emerged as 52.9 percent of the total. With the apparent aim of widening this slight margin, the basis of classification was changed in the 1939 census: people were no longer asked what they regarded as their "ethnic origin" (*narodnost*), but rather what they thought of as their "nationality," the Russian term for which (*natsionalnost*) is closer in meaning to culture or citizenship than to race. With the aid of this device the regime was able to report a Russian majority of 58 percent in 1939.

The 1959 census . . . reveals a new downward ratio, undoubtedly due to the incorporation of the Baltic states, a section of Poland, and part of Bessarabia (Moldavia) since 1939. Today somewhat under 55 percent of the Soviet people think of themselves as Russian by nationality, and even fewer designate Russian as their native language.

The minorities generally live in homogeneous and compact groups on the outer edge of the central land mass which is the territory of the Great Russians. This basic demographic structure persists despite a great increase in the dispersion of peoples—especially of Russians—into other nationality areas during World War II and its aftermath. The 15 national republics strung around the outer borders of the Soviet Union constitute the overwhelming bulk, 80 percent or more, of the country's national minorities. In the northwest, the three Baltic republics include close to five million Latvians, Lithuanians and Estonians. On the western frontier there are some eight million Belorussians, and 37 million Ukrainians who, when added to the Russians, give the Soviet

Union its overwhelmingly Slavic majority. On the same frontier are two and a quarter million Moldavians, in the republic of the same name, and almost one and a half million Poles, who for obvious reasons have no identifying territorial unit. Further to the south and east, along the Black Sea and in the Caucasus, there are numerous nationalities distributed in a complex pattern of settlement. These include the Georgians, Armenians and Azerbaijanians, each in their own republic and each more than two and a half million strong—as well as several million Tatars. In Central Asia, the four republics of the Turkmen, Uzbeks, Tadzhiks and Kirghiz, along with the people of adjoining Kazakhstan, contribute some 13 million Turkic people of Moslem faith. Other Moslems, living in areas further in from the border, include several million Volga Tatars and almost a million of the closely related Bashkirs. A neighboring area contains close to a million and a half Chuvash, a Christian and often Russianized remnant of the old Bolgar Empire on the Volga. Of the remaining larger nationalities, only the million and a quarter Mordvians and the two and a quarter million Jews are widely dispersed.

Some 85 percent of all the Great Russians live in the vast, sprawling Russian Soviet Federated Socialist Republic. The rest are spread throughout the surrounding ring of nationality areas, usually living in enclaves in the cities within a countryside that is solidly non-Russian. In this limited sense minority status is at least as typical of the Russian as any other Soviet nationality. Collectively, Russian groups constitute a median proportion of 13.5 percent of the population in the 14 republics other than the RSFSR. In certain areas, however, the influx of Russians has been far greater. In Kazakhstan, for example, the Russians are now the most numerous group (43 percent) of the population; together with other Slavic residents, the Ukrainians and Belorussians, they constitute a majority of the republic. Thus, the Kazakhs have become a minority in the area presumably set aside for them as a national home, and by [a] process over which they have had little say and less control.

Most of the important minorities represent separate and distinct nationalities, with their own language and literature, and in many cases an earlier history of independent existence as a nation-state. Their sense of separate identity is intensified by the fact that ethnicity is generally linked with religious identification, without the cross-cutting of religion and race found in some lands. Thus, to be Russian is to be Orthodox, to be Polish, Catholic; Armenians are in the Armenian National Church and Georgians in the Georgian Church; and the Asiatic peoples, especially the Turkic, are overwhelmingly Moslem. It seems fairly clear that the last thing these people wish is the loss of identity as separate nationalities through absorption into the larger homogeneous culture of the Russian nation. Indeed, although there are often important historical ties which bind them to the center in Moscow, the nationalities seldom share much in common with other peoples of the Soviet Union beyond their minority status. How, then, did these diverse peoples all come together in common Soviet citizenship? The answer is not to be found, as in some other ethnically heterogeneous nations, in voluntary emigration or incorporation into Russia. It must be sought in the history of Russian state policy going back many centuries.

Tsarist Expansionism

Following their subjugation by the Khans, the Russian people lived for centuries under the rule of the Tatar hordes, compressed into a modest area in central Russia and cut off from other major Slavic groups such as the Poles and Ukrainians, who were variously under domination by peoples from the West, Scandinavia and the Baltic. The starting point of Russian colonialism may be taken as 1552, when Ivan the Terrible took Kazan, and thus liquidated the Tatar Khanate. The expansion of the previously small Muscovite state thus began with the incorporation of large numbers of Turkic peoples, especially from along the Volga and its tributaries. About a century later a comparable major movement to the west was completed when the left-bank regions of the Dnieper were established as a protectorate, bringing Cossack and Ukrainian peoples under Russian hegemony. Peter the Great added the peoples along the coast of the Baltic Sea. In her turn Catherine the Great made further acquisitions in the west, including parts of Poland, and drove all the way to the Black Sea in the south. The Caucasus was added later, and most of the rest of Turkestan was acquired by Alexander II to complete the movement by the end of his reign in 1881.

This extraordinary territorial expansion was estimated to have proceeded at the rate of 50 square miles a day over a period of 400 years, from the end of the 15th to the end of the 19th centuries. As pointed out earlier, it brought the Russians to the status of being a minority in the land they ruled. To speak of Russia as having a minority problem in the usual sense is therefore misleading. Russia was a huge colonial empire; but in distinction to the other empires of Europe, her colonial possessions were contiguous to the homeland. Thus she *incorporated* her possessions, her dependencies and satellites, within one continuous border, with the captive nations strung around the outer limits of the solid Great Russian core. It is impossible to understand the nationality problem in the Soviet Union without always keeping in mind that the Soviet regime inherited this "prison of nations" from the Tsars when it took power, and it had to operate within the framework thus set by history.

The Leninist Formula

In this situation, the Soviet regime has adopted an essentially dualistic attitude toward Tsarist expansionism: on the one hand, it has generally treated the conquest and incorporation of the minorities as an "historically progressive" policy; on the other hand, it has encouraged the myth that Tsarist treatment of the captive peoples was uniformly harsh, oppressive and reactionary, and that it was designed to destroy the character and individuality of the many groups which had come under the empire's sway. Actually Tsarist policy toward the subject minorities varied considerably at different times, depending on the political philosophy of the different rulers. It also varied with respect to different areas and groups. Most modern impressions of this policy tend to concentrate on the period of intensive suppression starting after the accession of Alexander III in 1881 and lasting until the revolution in 1905, after which a considerable liberalization again ensued. The depredations of Alexander's reign, especially the marked efforts at Russification and the virtual driving undergound of local cultural movements, left a lasting mark not only on world opinion but on the national groups, and this fact was soon to be of great importance to the as yet unborn Soviet government.

Considering how obvious a source of grievance against the Tsarist regime here lay ready for exploitation, it is striking that the

Bolsheviks were so slow to realize its potentialities as an instrument for shaking the old order. But their whole philosophy inclined them to gloss over the nationality problem. It was a basic belief of Marxists that the path of history would lead toward ever larger, more homogeneous, centralized, industrial, political units which in time would yield to a world-wide "proletarian" society. The slogan "the proletariat has no fatherland" expressed the belief that nationalism, patriotism, regionalism, and similar attachments were part and parcel of the social pattern of bourgeois capitalism, which would somehow be outlived and sloughed off once socialism and then communism came to the world. Lenin himself gave virtually no attention to the nationality problem until 1913, when he was forced to turn to it both because of the growing popularity of the Bauer-Renner program and because of his own growing awareness that the success of his plans must reckon with the fact of national loyalties and aspirations.

The Bauer-Renner program, conceived to meet the multinational situation facing the political parties in the Austro-Hungarian empire, proposed an unusual degree of autonomy for minorities in the conduct of their own affairs; had it been put into effect, it would have permitted a great multiplication of small and more-or-less exclusive national, religious and ethnic units. Lenin naturally viewed this program as a challenge to the principle of centralization which he had steadfastly espoused; but he was equally opposed to the alternative idea of federalism, again on grounds that it weakened the chances for the development of a truly international proletarian power. Forced to take a stand, he went to what he thought was the absolute heart of the matter, by basing his policy squarely *and exclusively* on the right of each nationality to so-called "self-determination." He was unwilling to consider any compromises which might weaken the power of a central Communist government. Any people or nation—theoretically, at least—had the right to secede from the larger society, but if it chose to remain it must accept the general system in its entirety, without demanding special status or privilege and without asking for a federal union:

> The right to self-determination is an exception to our general thesis, which is centralism. This exception is absolutely necessary in the face of the Black Hundred type of Great Russian nationalism.

. . . But a broad interpretation may not be made of an exception. There is *nothing*, absolutely nothing here, and there must be nothing here, but the *right* to secede.

Lenin felt that this acknowledgement of the abstract "right" to secede was necessary as a political maneuver. But at the same time—in a contradiction that no amount of esoteric language could hide—he held that any attempt at *actual* secession would be retrograde, anti-proletarian, bourgeois counterrevolution. He assumed, in short, that no one would want to *exercise* the right of secession should there be a proletarian revolution.

He proved completely wrong, although in this he had the company of most of the other political groups in Russia, all of whom inadequately assessed both the effect of Tsarist policy in hardening national feeling against *any* central Russian government, and the effect of the rapid social and cultural changes which were increasing national consciousness in many of the minority areas. In any event, the Bolshevik regime found, to its great embarrassment, that in most of the national areas of the former empire the local political leaders took their right of secession quite seriously. Even where complete separation was not their prime objective, the local leaders viewed themseleves as equals with the leaders in Moscow, entitled on that basis to negotiate the nature of their nationality's participation in the new state.

The Bolsheviks did not hesitate to use the force of arms to meet this upsurge of independence, sending their Red Armies to regain control over most of the provinces of the former empire. Finland was allowed to slip away without any particular struggle, and Poland and the Baltic States were abandoned after unsuccessful military campaigns. But under the command of such well-known Communist figures as Frunze and Kuibyshev in Central Asia, Kirov and Ordzhonikidze in the north Caucasus, Kaganovich in Belorussia, and Mikoyan in Azerbaijan, almost all the other territories were recaptured by Soviet troops and turned over to the control of the local Communist parties, reliable subordinates of the central party apparatus in Moscow. The army which entered Georgia on February 16, 1921, and by February 25th once again placed the Communist flag over the capital Tiflis, fought the last major round in the effort to reintegrate the rebellious national areas.

The need for force to win back control of these areas brought home to the Soviet leaders the crucial nature of the nationality problem, and it is largely to this realization that we owe the particular forms which the so-called nationality policy of the Soviet Union has assumed. Rather than attempting to relate the explicit history of the policy, the writer will turn directly to a consideration of its overall features, giving the historical context as seems necessary. Perhaps the best approach is to pose four questions which would be important in evaluating the policy of any large-scale colonial power.

Self-Determination: A Paper Right

1). The first question in such an assessment would be: to what extent does the country's nationality policy provide for gradual transition to separate statehood for the major national minorities whose culture, history, and socio-political and economic maturity make them reasonable candidates for such status?

The attainment of a condition of self-government and national independence has come to be accepted as a fundamental goal and an inalienable right of people all over the world. Since World War II we have witnessed a tremendous socio-political movement as virtually all the major colonial dependencies of the former British Empire, and to a lesser but striking degree of the French Empire, have achieved national independence. Any nation which tries to maintain control over a colonial area—or even to slow down the pace toward independence—invites serious criticism and often serious trouble. . . . It seems not at all inappropriate, therefore, to address the above question to the Soviet Union, particularly since it takes so much pride in pointing to the provision in its constitution which grants each of the constituent republics the ultimate right "freely" to secede from the Union. What, if anything, is done to implement this right in practice?

It may seem superfluous to observe, in the first place, that the Soviet regime in no way acts to encourage the secession of the minorities. In fact, one might well argue that no central government could be expected to take an active part in urging its constituent parts to achieve independence. The point is made here because there are those who apply a double standard on this score, criticizing other colonial powers for their lack of encouragement to independence movements, while turning a blind eye to Soviet practice.

It is of course one thing for a central government to encourage some part of a larger union to detach itself, and quite another to ask simply that minority peoples have the right to advocate and work peacefully for their eventual independence. Since the right of secession is constitutionally guaranteed in the Soviet Union, the right to pursue that goal would logically seem to follow. Yet even to advocate, let alone to work toward, the political independence of any area in the Soviet Union is unthinkable for the Soviet citizen. Such action is identified, both by law outside the constitution and by long practice of the secret police, as a counterrevolutionary crime against the state, warranting severe punishment. Almost every major purge trial has involved charges that the accused conspired to separate some national area from the Union. At various stages of Soviet history hundreds and thousands of officials, teachers, writers and other members of the intellectual classes of different national republics have been purged from the party and state apparatus, and/or sent into forced labor on charges of harboring "bourgeois nationalist leanings," the official term for identifying with the interests of one's national group and resisting abject subordination to the interests of the Moscow center.

In short, what the constitution says about the national question bears virtually no relationship to Soviet practice. Any lingering doubts on this score should have been destroyed by the action of the Soviet regime during World War II, when it simply erased from the map and from the face of the earth four autonomous socialist republics—the Volga German, the Crimean Tatar, the Kalmyk, and the Chechen-Ingush. Although there was an announcement in the case of the Volga Germans that this action was taken in the interest of national security, and a belated statement that the Chechen and Crimean Tatars had collaborated with the Germans, not even this much explanation was given with regard to the Kalmyks.

Not only were the republics liquidated as political entities, but their millions of people were dispersed to distant regions of the Soviet Union. There were wide repercussions and revulsion against this act; among others, Tito of Yugoslavia went so far as to accuse the Soviet Union of genocide. Certainly the indiscriminate mass dispersion of a whole population because of acts of individuals, no matter how numerous, violated basic standards of humanity and made a mockery of Stalin's assertion that "the national question and the problem of collaboration among nations have been settled better [in the USSR] than in any other multinational state." It was not until after Stalin's death that some members of these nationalities were rehabilitated and partially restored to their former status.

Cultural Survivals

2). The second broad question may be phrased: To what degree are the minorities permitted and facilitated in the free expression of their cultural heritage? First and foremost, this involves the right to use one's native tongue in all types of public and private communication and in the education of youth. Cultural expression also includes the preservation and further development of folk and tribal ways, including art forms, ceremonial and religious customs, the national costume, *etc*. In addition, some hold that free cultural expression should include the right to have economic and political forms of organization which are distinctive to a particular culture.

That the Soviet approach toward the cultural self-expression of the minorities has been unique is beyond doubt; whether it has been as liberal as is claimed is quite another question. The doctrinal explanation of Soviet policy rests in the distinction which is made between the content and the form of culture, expressed in the well-worn formula "national in form, socialist in content." In theory, this phrase means that the values and ideas of the socialist society should be uniform in every culture, though the means by which they are expressed may be—indeed, should be—of a traditional and indigenous nature. The vagueness of this formula, however, has left wide leeway in its application, and like most Soviet slogans it has become quite meaningless in practice.

Obviously it is important to know *which* institutions and distinctive cultural forms are allowed to persist, and how crucial to the integrity of the original culture are those which have been suppressed because they fall in the realm where "socialist" uniformity is required. In the Soviet totalitarian system, the model for society as developed in Moscow is so rigid and all-pervasive that very little has in fact been left that could qualify as being "national" without conflicting with what must be "socialist."

The outstanding survival has been the native languages. With one exception (Yiddish), the Soviet regime has made no attempt to eradicate local tongues; they are used in the educational system, in communications media, and in indigenous literature. Generally distinctive literary forms associated with the languages in such spheres as poetry; epic writing and drama have also been permitted. Another class of survivals which has suffered comparatively little interference is folk arts, including folk handicrafts and native art forms. Nor has there been much effort made to alter distinctive modes of native dress (except in the case of the Moslem veil for women, against which a rather successful campaign has been waged). These policies, it might be pointed out, parallel the practice adopted by most colonial powers.

If the Soviet attitude with respect to these several fundamentals of cultural expression has been generally permissive—and certainly represents a vast reform over the depredatory Russification efforts of Alexander III—there is nevertheless much on the record to indicate that tolerance extends only as far as it suits the interests of the central authorities. Even in the matter of language, Moscow's actions have in some cases profoundly affected an indigenous culture. Much is made of the fact that the Soviets provided alphabets for several dozen languages which previously could not be written down, paving the way for newspapers and other literature in these tongues. Less is known of the fact that the Soviet regime used its power, against the overwhelming opposition of the local population, to force the abandonment of the religiously-sanctioned Arabic script used by the millions of Soviet Moslems. Not once but twice they did this, first introducing the Latin alphabet, and then in 1939 substituting the Cyrillic. Even the Tsars never dreamed of attempting such a victory for Russian culture among their subject Moslems.

Folk literature and art, too, have been subjected to interference and suppression whenever Moscow chose to see in their various forms any manifestations of "bourgeois nationalism." Frequently the regime has seized on old or new folk writings, dramas, operas, *etc.*, condemning them for deviation from the official line, forbidding their production, and taking reprisals against their authors. The writing or presentation of native history in particular has suffered from intervention by the authorities, who insist that the Tsarist subjugation of the nationality areas be treated as "historically progressive." Among many such acts of repression, one of the more glaring examples was the dissolution of the entire cultural apparatus of the Soviet Jews—including their native theater, newspapers, publishing houses and writers' association—during the postwar wave of officially-inspired anti-Semitism; despite regime claims that no discrimination is practiced, nothing has ever been done to rectify this situation.

All of the minority religions have, of course, been the object of repressive measures. The fact that these moves have, from a doctrinal point of view, been part of the Communist campaign against religious belief *per se* (including the Russian Orthodox faith) has made little difference to peoples whose religion and nationality are closely identified. For them, the attack on religion has been simply another example of the effort of an alien regime to encroach on indigenous cultural patterns and to shackle national development.

In short, the Soviet attitude toward "national forms" in the cultural sphere has been one of tolerance when—but only when—tolerance has not interfered with the ideological or practical needs of the regime.

System and Sacrifice

Outside of the specific areas of cultural expression mentioned above, few of the traditional ways of the minorities have been allowed to survive. In the political, economic, and generally the social spheres, the uniform institutions of Soviet society prevail in the form of the supreme ruling party, the bureaucratic administrative apparatus, the planned and centrally-controlled industrial economy, the collectivized peasant agriculture, and the ubiquitous instruments of ideological indoctrination and control. Thus Soviet nationality policy has allowed no recognition of the fact that economic, political and social forms of organization may be distinctive and indeed crucial elements in a particular national culture.

The imposition of the Soviet system involved a social and cultural revolution throughout Soviet-held territory. Among the more settled European or Europeanized populations, whose culture was already somewhat geared to the patterns of industrial society, the process of Sovietization was highly disruptive, but no more so than for the majority of the Great Russians—and perhaps even less so in the case, say, of Armenian traders than of the Russian peasants. But among the peoples of the more isolated, underdeveloped areas—mainly in Asia—the depredations caused by Sovietization and the enforced departure from traditional ways were of enormous magnitude.

An outstanding example is the case of the Kazakh people. Before collectivization the Kazakhs were either nomads, who relied extensively on the use of horses on the great Central Asian steppe, or recently-settled cattle and sheep herders. Their whole way of life was regulated by and within the tribal structure, especially the clan system. The attempt blindly to impose the pattern of collectivization on these people in the early 1930's met with intensive resistance, leading to an open struggle with the regime. The loss of life was staggering. While some of the Kazakhs escaped with their herds over the border into Chinese Sinkiang, the huge decimation of the population during this period was mainly due to deaths in the fighting or through starvation. Census figures for 1926 and 1939 show that in the interim the Kazakh population dropped from 3.967 to 3.098 million, an absolute decline of 869 thousand, or 22 percent. Calculating in what would have been an expectable rate of population growth under normal circumstances (on the basis of 15 percent for the Soviet population as a whole), the survivors in Kazhakstan were one and a half million fewer by 1939 than they should have been, a staggering deficit considering the overall size of the population. Moreover, in the course of the bitter struggle the greater part of the livestock on which the local economy had rested was lost, through retaliative slaughter on the part of the desperate natives, neglect of the herds while the men were off fighting, or in minor part migration. Taking the stocks in 1928 as a base, by 1934 only 25 to 50 percent of the cattle, 13 percent of the sheep, and 12 percent of the horses remained.

Although the stark statistics above are from official sources, the Soviet regime has never put forward any explanation of this chapter of its history. Unfortunately the statistics are little known to

the world, and are seldom weighed in the balance when glib estimates are made in praise of "enlightened" Soviet nationality
policy. Yet this case represents a relentless fulfillment of Stalin's
instruction to the Communist Party in 1923, when he urged that
Turkestan—which included Kazakhstan—be transformed into a
model republic because of its revolutionary significance for Soviet
Russia's eastern policy. He declared: "We have to fulfill this task
whatever the price, without sparing efforts and without shrinking
from sacrifices. . . ." Stalin, certainly, could never be accused of
having shrunk from sacrifices in Kazakhstan.

Equal Opportunity

3). Turning to the third question under consideration, to what
extent is Soviet nationality policy non-discriminatory—that is, to
what extent does it offer members of the minority nationalities
equal access to such benefits as the society provides for average
citizens? Are opportunities for education, work, pay, social mobility, freedom of movement, and choice of residence the same for
all or does the dominant group enjoy a favored status?

On the whole the record of the Soviet Union in these respects is
good. The data which support this evaluation are based on republics as a whole, not on pure ethnic or national groups, so that the
presence of large Russian and Ukrainian minorities in some of the
national republics—and conversely of non-Russian minorities in
the RSFSR—may distort the picture of Soviet accomplishment to
some degree. Still, on the basis of a large number of indices, it
seems clear that members of all nationalities (including the Great
Russian) have received broadly equal treatment with respect to
personal economic and social—if not political—opportunities. Allowance must be made, of course, for the fact that many of the
minorities live in predominantly rural or backward regions whose
development has expectably lagged behind that of more urban or
industrial areas; however, the *relative* position of these groups has
improved greatly since the prerevolutionary era.

Important among the indices considered here is the striking
spread of literacy among all groups of the Soviet population. In
the intercensus period from 1926 to 1939 the overall literacy rate
in the Soviet Union rose from 51 to 81 percent. In certain national
republics the low base at start made the rise much more dramatic.

For example, in the Central Asian Tadzhik republic the rate of literacy increased from 4 to 72 percent, and in the Azerbaijan republic from 25 to 73 percent. The preliminary release on the 1959 census does not provide data on literacy by nationality, but since the All-Union rate is now reported to be 98.5 percent, it must be assumed that the nationality areas have continued to advance in this respect. While the Soviet definition of literacy is based on a very rudimentary level of learning, and while some area improvement can be attributed to the influx of Russian and other literates, the record of accomplishment is nevertheless substantial.

Data on improvements in education are closely related. In the area of the five Central Asian Republics (including Kazakhstan) there were in 1914–15 only 136,000 pupils in elementary and secondary schools, representing less than half of one percent of the 9.6 million pupils in all Russia. By 1955–56 the parallel enrollment was 3.59 million, an increase by more than 25-fold; this figure constituted about 13 percent of the total student enrollment in the same grades, which is about the weight of the population of the Central Asiatic republics in the Soviet population as a whole. Similar progress has been made in higher education: whereas before the Revolution there were virtually no higher school establishments in these areas, by 1955 local institutions had an enrollment of 155 thousand students, or about 9 percent of the total higher school population in the USSR.

There are many other ways in which the Soviet regime has accorded equal treatment to the minorities. Available data show that facilities such as libraries, medical clinics, movie and dramatic theaters, sports stadia, clubs, newspapers and journals, radio and television stations, *etc.*, have been provided in the nationality areas at close to the same per capita rate as in the Great Russian area.

The sum indication of such statistical evidence is that minority members (again, with the striking exception of Soviet Jews) do not suffer from any discrimination insofar as educational training, economic opportunity, and social benefits are concerned. This impression is supported by the testimony of Soviet refugees. In the Harvard Project on the Soviet Social System, in which this writer participated, questionnaires were submitted to several hundred Ukrainians and to smaller groups of other nationalities—along with Russians—all of whom had escaped from the Soviet Union. The replies showed that people whose occupations had been on a comparable level had, regardless of their nationality, been in very similar circumstances with respect to income, opportunities for education, job satisfaction, and the general rate of social mobility. Such similarity in living conditions produced similarity in values, attitudes and opinions, again cutting across national lines. In other words, class status rather than national identification determined what people found praiseworthy in the Soviet system and what they condemned. The Russian peasant described and criticized his life very much as did the Ukrainian, Georgian, Tatar of Kazakh peasant; similarly, professional people of different nationality evaluated their life situations in like terms and shared the same criticisms of the system. Such differences as did emerge between nationalities were largely a reflection of the varying class composition—in particular, the proportion of peasants—from group to group.

Unequal Inopportunity

There was, however, one distinctive complaint voiced by those in the minority nationalities, and this on an issue of profound importance. The reader may have noted that all of the above examples of nondiscrimination have been confined to the economic and social spheres. In the political realm—in the structure of rule—a very different picture emerges. The crucial protest voiced in common by refugees from the minorities was that their people did not share equally in the direction of society and were not free to shape their culture along lines in keeping with native or indigenous traditions. Many saw themselves as still essentially vassals of a foreign power, as ruled by the alien Russian. The basis of these feeelings is not just a matter of the sharp restrictions which, as we have seen, the regime places on the development of local nationalism. Just as important is the fact that the institutions of governance, both at the center and within the republics, have not included a proportionate representation of the minorities. The Communist Party has been predominantly a Russian party, with only a weak representation of the nationalities, while in the republics themselves the influence and indeed control of Russians and other outsiders sent in from Moscow has been painfully evident.

The composition of the supreme council of the party has reflected this imbalance during most of its history. Up to the time of its reorganization in 1952, the Politburo had altogether 28 members, of whom 16 were Russians and 8 more Russified Jews or Georgians. The people of 13 national republics, containing some 80 million of the population, never had representation on that body, including the third largest nationality, the Belorussians, and some 16 to 20 million Moslems. The 30 to 40 million Ukrainians were not represented after 1938, when the purges claimed the leading figures of Ukrainian nationality. The membership of the Presidium, which replaced the Politburo in 1952, has been somewhat more in proportion, but not markedly so. Of the 33 people who have served on the Presidium only 8—including Stalin before his death—have been non-Russians. The others are Beria (also Georgian), Kaganovich (Jewish), Mikoyan (Armenian), Korotchenko and Kirichenko (Ukrainians), Kuusinen (Finnish), and Mukhitdinov (Uzbek). A number of minority members, however, have been appointed as candidate (alternative) members of the Presidium.

The fact that Stalin himself was a Georgian by birth counts for little, since like many of these leaders he thoroughly identified himself with the Russians, a trait reflected in his extraordinary toast at the end of World War II:

> I should like to propose a toast to the health of our Soviet people, and above all of our Russian people. I drink in particular to the health of the Russian people because it is the most outstanding of all the nations of the Soviet Union. . . .

The weakness of national representation has been evident not only at the top of the power hierarchy, but in the rank-and-file of the party. In proportion to population, the Communist Party is strongest in the predominantly Great Russian areas, weakest in the nationality regions. In Moscow and Leningrad, for example, the ratio of local to total party membership is more than twice that of local to total population; in republics like Tadjikistan the reverse applies. In fact, however, the disproportion is much greater, since within the nationality areas, the party is not only small but includes a substantial number of non-natives, preponderantly Russians. The exact ratios are hard to estimate, since the party generally stopped publishing data according to nationality by 1938. It is known, however, that as late as 1935 Tadzhiks and Turkmen—for example—constituted 75 percent of the population in the republics bearing their names, but only about 50 percent of the party organizations.

Within the lower and middle ranks of the national parties, both the rank-and-file and their officials are predominantly of native stock and speak the native language (the same is even truer of the governmental apparatus). But in the large urban centers, at the seats of power, the Russian image looms large. Access to positions of power is comparatively limited to the native, except insofar as he has become Russified—and in this case he is considered a nonnational who may be transferred to work anywhere within the Soviet Union.

The fact that the party chief in the national areas has often been someone sent in from the outside has been perhaps the most important affront to national pride and symbol of the alien nature of the party. The best example in this respect is the Ukraine, where the First Secretary of the Communist Party has almost always been a non-Ukrainian, even though sometimes vaguely connected with the Ukrainian area or nationality. Kaganovich, who held the post in 1925–28, was a Russified Jew born in Belorussia. Kossior, who followed, was a Pole. The rest were Russians, and many never even learned to speak Ukrainian with fluency, despite the fact that it was the national tongue of some 40 million subjects. The only exception in the line of rule was Khrushchev's chosen successor in the post—his Ukrainian assistant Kirichenko (who later rose to the Presidium but is now in disgrace).

Economic Development Policy

To pose the fourth and last question: has there been any economic exploitation of minority regions, by depletion of the land or other natural resources, by the carrying off of wealth produced in the area without sufficient compensation, or by the development of the region's economy in so special or limited a way as to subordinate it unduly to the productive needs and interests of the dominant majority?

In the Soviet case the answer to these questions is clear-cut: the regime's economic policy as a whole does not discriminate against the minority areas and their economic development in favor of the Great Russians. Soviet industrialization was, of course, based on forced savings, which the government extracted for investment at the cost of popular consumption. But the minorities were not asked to bear a disproportionate share of the resulting hardships of a depressed living standard. The burden fell on all; in fact, it might be argued that the Great Russian majority initially made the greater sacrifice in order to permit the development of the capital-hungry, economically backward areas.

One economist has estimated, for example, that while the all-Union living standard fell markedly during the 1930's, in the four republics of Central Asia (not counting Kazakhstan), it may actually have improved to a slight degree. At the time the local economy was undergoing rapid change, as indicated by the fact that industrial output, which had been negligible, multiplied between six and nine times over between 1928 and 1937. Such an increase could only have been accomplished by the substantial investment of capital drawn from other parts of the country and by the application of new technology. Such help was even more important to the agriculture of the region.

In the initial stage of European colonial development, substantial capital was invested in the colonies, but often only in order to create a one-crop economy that in the long run was economically disadvantageous to the local people. There was an element of this approach in the Soviet regime's insistence on the expansion of cotton acreage in Central Asia, usually at the expense of existing wheat crops. But the area was not treated simply as a vast cotton plantation for the rest of the Soviet Union. On the contrary, existing resources of other kinds were widely developed. A hydroelectric power industry was developed, the output of which increased 8.5 times over in the period 1928–37. Earlier virtually all cotton had been shipped to Russia to be made into textiles, which in turn had to be shipped back, but in the 1930's a substantial textile industry was established in Tashkent. Leather shoe-making was established to utilize the hides from the region's extensive herds. These efforts make it evident that capital was retained in the area and not syphoned off for accumulation at the center. The data already cited on the growth of education and other cultural and social facilities similarly indicate that a goodly share of the returns accrued from exploitation of the region's natural wealth was reinvested in raising standards in the region.

Although the central Asian case may be one of the more outstanding examples, it reflects the general pattern of Soviet policy in the economic development of backward areas. The allocation of investment during the process of economic expansion has not in any significant degree been guided by considerations of nationality, but rather by those of economic efficiency or the defense needs of the country. And the benefits—as well as the burdens—which have resulted from economic development have been more or less equally shared by all peoples of the Soviet Union.

A Summary View

The main features of Soviet nationality policy sketched above have been consistently manifested since at least the early 1930's. Although the program as a whole is often identified as "Stalinist" nationality policy, only minor modifications have taken place in the post-Stalin era. In line with the general relaxation of terror in the USSR, the most repressive policies *vis-à-vis* certain nationalities have been abandoned and some of the iniquities of Stalin's reign (*e.g.*, the dispersion of the Chechen-Ingush, Kalmyks, and so on) have been rectified. In addition, Khrushchev has shown more awareness of the requirements of good "public relations" by such gestures as personal visits to the nationality areas, the appointment of a Ukrainian to the top post in the Ukraine, and the nomination of representatives of the Central Asian peoples to the higher councils of the ruling Communist Party.

In all other respects, however, the present leadership has followed the pattern of the past. On the credit side of the record, this has generally meant equality of social and economic opportunity for the individual of minority status. On the whole it has also meant equal treatment of national groups with regard to the exploitation of resources and economic development on the one hand, and to the elaboration of certain cultural institutions on the other.

Against these features, other factors must be weighed. First, if equality of treatment has been the general rule in the above respects, the exceptions and departures have been numerous enough and in some cases so glaring as to demonstrate that the application of nationality policy remains a matter of arbitrary and expedient decision on the part of the regime. More important, however, are the moral and political issues which underlie the question of minority rights. The basic fact—and no amount of achievement can obscure it—is that Soviet nationality policy has constituted a forceful imposition of social, political and economic forms by a powerful center upon a host of colonial subjects. If these people had little part in choosing their path of national development, they have as little freedom today to alter it.

The Soviet Federal System

JOHN N. HAZARD

Democratic institutions have sometimes been said to depend upon a federal system of government. The experience of the United States has made its impress upon the world, and federations have appeared in countries such as Brazil, Mexico, Argentina, Venezuela, Canada, Australia, India, Indonesia, Burma, and Yugoslavia. The reorganized German Federal Republic was consciously shaped in the form of a federation so as to improve its chances for the development of firm democratic institutions. It was thought that its *länder* might provide grass-roots democracy that would restrain any trend toward authoritarianism at the center. To many people who shared in the planning for Germany, a centralized government spelled potential dictatorship, even though the history of France, with her great centralization, had indicated that a centralized state could also be democratic.

Reprinted from *The Soviet System of Government* by John N. Hazard, pp. 76–90, by permission of The University of Chicago Press. Copyright 1961 by The University of Chicago Press. Chicago: The University of Chicago Press, 1961. For biographical note, see p. 242.

The Soviet leaders have made much of the fact that the U.S.S.R. is also a federation. They have claimed that through the federal form the various peoples of the U.S.S.R. have obtained control over their own affairs, and that they have more privileges than states in other federations. The status of the various Soviet republics that make up the U.S.S.R. is said to be further proof of the democratic base upon which the Soviet system rests.

In spite of the familiar terminology used to describe the relationship among the various peoples of the U.S.S.R., the Soviet federation has some special characteristics. It is not as loose a federation as that of the United States, and by no means as decentralized as Canada or Australia. The Soviet leaders have characterized their system as being a federation that is "national in form but socialist in substance." An examination of its details will indicate what is meant.

The federal structure of the U.S.S.R. grew out of the efforts of the bolsheviks to win friends to their revolutionary plans. The Tsarist empire, unlike the United States, had been a territory in which large numbers of persons of different races, religions, languages, and cultures lived in self-contained pockets rather than diffused throughout the empire. In addition to the Great Russians, representing the most numerous of the Slavic branch of mankind, there were large numbers of Ukrainians and Byelorussians, who were also within the Slavic group but had cultures and languages differing from the Russian. There were the Latvians, Lithuanians, Estonians, and Finns, who had quite different cultures and religions from those of the Slavs. In the areas south of the Caucasus there were the ancient Armenians and Georgians, and in Central Asia and Siberia the numerous Turkic peoples and some Mongol peoples.

Tsarist practice had been to give the underdeveloped peoples of the non-Slavic groups in Central Asia and Siberia considerable cultural autonomy, but for all peoples the official language of the empire had been Russian, the positions of prestige were given primarily to Russians, and the empire had been administered in a completely centralized manner, except for the Grand Duchy of Finland. Even Finland had been closer to union with the Russians than the Finns had been willing to admit. Because of the policy of centralized government and what seemed to the minority peoples to be a policy of "Russification" of culture as well, considerable hostility toward Russian domination had developed by the turn of the twentieth century. Lenin decided to play upon this hostility in winning friends for his program. In 1912 he set Stalin to work to write a program for the national minorities that would enlist them in bolshevik ranks on the basis of the subject of their dreams, namely, independence. Stalin, being himself a Georgian, was well fitted to dramatize the willingness of the Russian Lenin to accede to the wish for independence expressed by the national minority groups.

Stalin's Concept of Self-determination

In Stalin's book, which subsequently became the bolshevik propaganda manual for dealing with the minority peoples, the position is taken that ethnic groups have the right to self-determination, that is, they have the right to determine their own political future. Stalin knew that all of them had but one desire, and that was to be independent. He knew that in taking his position he was inciting revolution against the Tsar and dismemberment of the empire.

Stalin anticipated the trouble which might befall his bolshevik party in the event of ultimate victory in the revolution. The newly independent national minority peoples might go their own ways and become splinter groups so weak as to be absorbed by another empire. He argued, therefore, that while each people had the indubitable right of self-determination, the party for which he was writing would oppose the exercise of self-determination if it did not represent a step toward what the Marxists called "progress," namely, communism. Stalin warned that his party would not agree to the passing over of the minority peoples, once they were free from the bonds of the Russian Empire, to a capitalist camp hostile to what was to be the new Russia.

When the Revolution had been won in the capital of the Russian Empire, Petrograd, the bolsheviks found themselves tested in their policy toward the peoples who had been the national minorities of the old empire. The right of self-determination had been promised, and it had to be offered, at least to the peoples who were sufficiently numerous to present a problem in control if it were denied. In some cases, as with the Finns, it meant losing them for the Soviet system, yet they, and the Ukrainians, the Byelorussians, the Armenians, Azerbaijanians, Georgians, and Baltic peoples, were permitted to break away. The Central Asian principalities that had been in close union with, but not a part of, the empire were likewise permitted to establish their own states. Yet, for the peoples of Buryat Mongol, Yakut, Bashkir, and Tartar stock, no such privileges were granted. They were kept within the new Russian state, although it was called a "federation" to indicate that they were to have at least token autonomy.

Lenin could not afford to fail to fulfil his party's promises of self-determination to the really vocal minorities. He probably thought that in fulfilling these promises he was gaining more in good will than he was risking in ultimate loss of these peoples and of the territories they controlled. Lenin had two reasons to expect that the newly emancipated peoples would eventually return to his fold. One reason was the Communist party, and the other was force of circumstances.

The Communist party had been organized as a unitary body soon after its permanent creation in 1903. The minority peoples who had asked that they be permitted to create their own party organizations and to federate them with the Russian organization had been denied that privilege. In consequence, the members of the Communist party who lived in the territories of what had become the new Ukrainian and Byelorussian and other republics were under orders from the highly centralized headquarters of the Communist party. Their task was to bring back into close association with Lenin's new Russian Republic the peoples with whom they lived. Their ideal was "internationalism" of the working class, and not nationalism. They knew full well that their party had bowed to the demand for self-determination in order to win friends and that it was their task to bring back the various new republics into the fold as soon as possible. In most cases they proved themselves competent to the task.

Force of circumstances greatly aided the Communists in their effort to reunify the republics. The Revolution had taken place in November, 1917, a year before the Germans, Austro-Hungarians, Bulgarians, and Turks were finally defeated by the allied and associated powers in the First World War. The German army was still a very powerful force on the Russian front, and it continued to press its advantage as the Russian troops disintegrated. The republics on the fringes of what had been the Russian Empire were being overrun. The peace of Brest Litovsk in the spring of 1918 brought only a respite, for there soon began a merciless civil war in which those who remained loyal to the past sought to unseat the bolsheviks. This civil war raged most prominently in the Ukraine, and the forces hostile to the bolsheviks finally captured all but a small part of it in mid-1919. Various foreign powers participated in the civil war, the most effective being the Poles, who marched into the Ukraine and captured its capital in 1920. It was a time when the Ukraine and the other fringe areas could conclude with reason that their future as independent states depended upon military and economic support from the Russians.

The lesson that unity was necessary for survival in war was reinforced by the lesson that unity was necessary for economic development in peace. The empire, quite naturally, had developed its economy without thought of ethnic boundaries. Railroads ran where the terrain was best, crossing and recrossing what had now become the new ethnic frontiers. Raw materials from one province had been used to supply industry in another. After the Revolution, these provinces were often separated by what was in law an "international" boundary. It was clear that if the boundaries were not to be eradicated, a very difficult economic readjustment would become necessary, and in this readjustment productive capacity would be reduced. Unification within one state was the obvious solution to the problem.

Creating a Soviet Federation

Playing upon the growing realization of most of the minority peoples, fanned by the Communist party in each republic, that there must be a new unity within what had been the Russian Empire, Lenin and Stalin planned a federation. Communist party delegates from the various republics that had adopted the Soviet system of government, frequently under the pressure of military operations, met during the late summer of 1922 and evolved a draft constitution that called for a federation of four republics. Three of these already existed as the Russian, Byelorussian, and Ukrainian republics. The fourth was created by bringing together in a new Transcaucasian Republic the three existing republics of Azerbaijan, Armenia, and Georgia.

While each of the latter was to retain its own republic structure, it was to be within a federation which, in turn, would join the larger federation of the U.S.S.R. The reason given later for the subfederation of the Transcaucasian Republic was that the peoples south of the Caucasus had to be forced into a mold of co-operation because of their long history of conflict with one another. Presumably it was easier to do so with them than with the more numerous Ukrainians and the Byelorussians. One can speculate that if the Ukrainians had been more pliable and less nationalistic in outlook, they also might have been brought closer to the Russians than was done in 1922.

Having secured agreement among the Communist party members living in the various republics, the Russian party leaders had to take only a step to obtain formal agreement among representatives of the four republics that were to join in federation. A constitutional congress was held in Moscow at the end of December, 1922, and the delegates from the four republics accepted the treaty of union that had been drafted. They then declared themselves the new All-Union Congress of Soviets, which was to be the body bringing together delegates from the whole territory of the new U.S.S.R. A constitution was ordered prepared; it was completed and adopted provisionally in July, 1923, and when the Congress of Soviets of the U.S.S.R. met in a second session in January, 1924, the Constitution was ratified.

Where was the federal principle to be found in the governmental structure of the new Union? As in all federal constitutions, there were clauses allocating powers to the federal government and clauses reserving powers to the states that had come together to form the federation. Those who know the history of the Constitutional Convention in the United States know of the struggles between those who wished to reserve to the states significant powers and those who urged greater federal powers. There is no indication that such a struggle occurred in the Communist party group that formulated the first draft of the Constitution, nor in the drafting committee of the Congress of Soviets which prepared the formal document for adoption. The Communist party seems already to have become sufficiently sure of its power and of the acceptance of its leadership by the minority peoples to plan for much more centralism than was acceptable to the Founding Fathers in Philadelphia.

The federal government in the U.S.S.R. was granted by the Constitution some powers familiar to the system in the United States. The federal government alone could coin money, maintain a postal service, establish standards of weights and measures, regulate citizenship in the Union, and settle disputes among republics. The federal government also had sole power to declare war, conclude treaties, and conduct diplomatic relations. At this point similarity ends, for the Soviet Constitution gives additional powers to the federal government, of which the Founding Fathers in the United States had not even heard.

This grant of additional powers stems from the Marxist doctrine of what is necessary to achieve maximum production. As has been seen, the Marxists deny that private enterprise can produce as much as state-owned enterprise. One of their professed reasons for such a belief is that the workman will labor harder when he anticipates payment in full for his work rather than payment of only that part which is left from the value he produces after the private enterpriser's profit has been siphoned off. Another reason, one which has been elaborated by the Soviet leadership on the basis of limited implication by Marx, is that economic planning will save waste and duplication. In a planned economy there should be no surpluses seeking customers.

For both these reasons, economic planning has become one of the major tenets of present-day Soviet leadership, and the reflection of this view is to be found in the first federal Constitution of 1923. The first Constitution empowered the federal government to develop a general plan for the entire national economy; to establish general principles for the development and use of the soil, mineral deposits, forests, and waters; to direct transport and telegraph services; and to conduct trade.

Special Features of the Soviet Federation

While the Soviet federal Constitution transferred far more economic power to the federal government than did the United

States Constitutional Convention in 1787, there were some notable omissions in other areas. The Soviet federal Constitution included no bill of rights, such as did the United States Constitution in its first group of amendments. The Soviet bills of rights, such as they were, existed in the constitutions of the republics that had formed the Union, and it was decided, apparently, to leave them in these constitutions alone. It was also left to the republics to develop their own electoral law. No federal provisions declared who might vote and who might not vote. Finally, the federal Constitution left unmolested the civil, criminal, family, land, and labor codes, and the codes of criminal and civil procedure, as these had developed in the republics before federation. While some of these codes might be affected by such general principles for the use of the soil, mineral deposits, forests, and waters as the federal government might adopt, the Communist party seems to have preferred to rely upon the unifying influence of its members in the various republic legislatures rather than to require the republics to accept a system of federal codes.

The concept of federation found reflection in the structure of the Central Executive Committee of the U.S.S.R., which, under constitutional provision, was to be elected by the Congress of Soviets to legislate and generally to supervise the administrative and judicial arms of government during the year-long intervals between meetings of the Congress of Soviets. The Central Executive Committee was made bicameral: one chamber was to be chosen on the basis of population representation alone, while the other chamber was to be chosen on the basis of representation from each national minority group within the U.S.S.R.

The chamber in which each national minority group was to be represented seems to have been the major concession made to the minority peoples in the federation. It may also have been introduced into the Soviet system of government to appeal to other peoples outside the U.S.S.R. In 1922 it was still anticipated that revolution of the Soviet type would occur in Europe and in Asia in the foreseeable future. It was equally anticipated that German and other Western European Communists, who were by this time sending delegations to a Communist International with its seat in Moscow and having as its goal world revolution, might be sufficiently proud to want a share, in any future union, equal to that of the very numerous Russians. The bicameral Central Executive Committee could serve as proof to national groups outside the U.S.S.R. that they would not be submerged in a sea of Slavs.

The second chamber of the Central Executive Committee was to contain representatives not only from the constituent republics that had formed the Union in December, 1922, but also from other national minority groups as well. The Communists had to think of the sensibilities of the Azerbaijanians, the Armenians, and the Georgians, who had started as independent states after the revolutions organized in each and thus had been of equal status with the Russians, Ukrainians, and Byelorussians. While these three peoples south of the Caucasus had been brought into the federation as a subfederation, they were proud, and each was therefore given the same number of seats in the chamber of nationalities as each of the three larger republics, rather than only a one-third share of the seats which might have been given to their subfederation. Then there were the Buryat Mongolians, the Yakuts, the Tatars, the Bashkirs, and the Volga Germans, as well as some less numerous peoples who had been, since the Revolution, given the title of republics within the Russian Republic. These peoples had, apparently, expressed through party channels in 1922 the feeling that if the Byelorussians and Ukrainians were to be brought into the Union on an equal basis with the Russians, there was no reason why they should be one step removed from the top level and required to channel their relations with the federal government through the Russian Republic.

A Place for Small Minorities

Stalin reported at the constitutional convention of 1922 that some thought had been given to the status of the small ethnic groups within the Russian Republic. He said that he believed that their relationship with the Russian Republic had been established on a satisfactory basis and that to put them on the level of a constituent republic would be to take a step backward and to loosen a bond which had been tightened. In making this remark, Stalin indicated the direction in which he intended to move and clarified the reason why the federal rather than the unitary form of state was being adopted. The reason was simply that no closer bond than that provided by federation was politically possible at the time.

As a concession to the pride of the Tatars and of the other peoples within the Russian Republic who had cultural minority status as "Autonomous Republics" but not the higher political status of a constituent republic, the Communists offered them a number of seats equal to that of the Russians and of the constituent republics in the chamber of nationalities of the Central Executive Committee. With this provision there appeared the curious form of representation that has become a peculiarity of the Soviet federal system: subordinate parts of the republics that comprise the Union send representatives to the highest body of the federation, somewhat as if the Pennsylvania Dutch had a representative in the United States Senate alongside the senators from the Commonwealth of Pennsylvania. Even the Eskimos and other very small national minority groups were given seats in the chamber of nationalities, though not in the same number as the larger groups. In consequence, the chamber of nationalities contained a large number of representatives of non-Russian peoples. To the minority groups, and to the world at large, it looked as if the Russians were prepared to share power with their small neighbors in the U.S.S.R.

Yet, in assessing this situation, the role of the Communist party must be kept in mind. Throughout each national group there were Communists, required to think of themselves as internationalists and subject to strict discipline originating at the center. These might even be nationals of groups other than the one in which they were ordered to make their home. Further, they had been trained in the party to propose only those programs which central party officials favored. Under their influence, the representatives of the national minority groups have never expressed a special interest in any but very limited local policy matters, such as the allocation of funds for irrigation in Central Asia or for housing in Georgia. The minority representatives have always voted unanimously for any program presented by the party, and it has never been necessary to reconcile through reconciliation procedure any contrary views of the chamber of nationalities and the chamber composed of representatives selected on the basis of population alone, although the Constitution provides for such an eventuality.

The very real contrast between the Soviet legislature and those of Western democracies is indicated by the fact that there has never been a public difference of opinion between the chambers.

The Influence of the Years

With the passage of time, the local nationalism of the minorities seems to have been reduced, although events in Georgia in 1956 suggest that it may still be aroused by signs of discrimination against a minority people. Soviet text writers declare that a lessening of local patriotism is inevitable, since these minority groups have found that no "Russification" of their cultures is occurring. However, such a declaration does not accord with the facts. It is true that Soviet law does not require that Russian be the sole language spoken in schools, government offices, and courts. On the contrary, the law guarantees that both schools and government business will be conducted in the language of the local ethnic community. Nevertheless, Russian is compulsory as a second language, and any young man or woman who wants to achieve a position of prominence in the U.S.S.R. learns Russian to the best of his or her ability because it is a key to social and geographic mobility. Knowledge of Russian opens doors to the highest professional schools, where it is the language of instruction. Knowledge of Russian enables a man to communicate both in any part of the country to which the party orders him and also on the international scene. The Russian language has become a political and social asset, and the ambitious Ukrainian, Georgian, or other minority representative cultivates the use of it. Thus, today, anyone who visits the U.S.S.R. will find that Russian is commonly used throughout the land, although it is often noted that in outlying districts, and even on Ukrainian farms, no one but the farm officials speaks it with facility.

While minority cultures are fostered, if need be through Russian subsidization of their opera, drama, and literature, local authors are admonished not to be "chauvinistic" in their art. Some of them have even been criticized and disgraced within the Communist party for alleged preaching of national pride and of hostility toward the Russian culture. Since Stalin's death, insufficient respect for national minority susceptibilities has been declared to have been one of his shortcomings, and his heirs, setting out early to rectify the balance, assigned Beria to the job. This assignment has complicated the situation, however, for on Beria's arrest he was accused, among other things, of fostering national animosities, and it may be that he went farther than the rest of Stalin's heirs were willing to go in placating minority restlessness following upon Stalin's glorification of the Great Russians for their major part in winning the Second World War.

Federal Changes in the 1936 Constitution

In the second federal Constitution, adopted in 1936, the powers reserved to the republics were somewhat reduced. A federal bill of rights and electoral law were introduced, and it was also provided that civil and criminal codes, and codes of civil and criminal procedure, should be established by the federal government rather than by the republics. No federal codes were completed in Stalin's time, although the existing codes were brought into increasing uniformity by federal acts made compulsory for the republics.

The second federal Constitution also changed the state structure, which had been headed by the Congress of Soviets of the U.S.S.R. and its Central Executive Committee. The unicameral Congress of Soviets was abolished and the former Central Executive Committee was made into the new bicameral Supreme Soviet. The general powers of this body have already been discussed, but it remains to indicate the extent to which it reflects the principle of federation.

The Supreme Soviet of the U.S.S.R., like the preceding Central Executive Committee established by the first federal Constitution, has two chambers, one representing the population generally and called the "Soviet of the Union," the other representing the national minority groups and called the "Soviet of Nationalities." This latter body is not composed in precisely the same manner as was its predecessor, for now only the constituent republics have the same number of delegates as the Russian Republic, that is, twenty-five. The lesser minority peoples organized in what are known as "Autonomous Republics"—the Tatars, Yakuts, Bashkirs, and Buryat Mongolians—now have only eleven delegates and, thus, a relatively lesser position, as measured by number of deputies, than before. The still smaller ethnic groups, those organized into "Autonomous Regions," have five deputies, and the even smaller ethnic groups, those organized into "National Districts," only one. Thus all peoples who number more than a handful and who can claim to be of unique ethnic stock have representation, but in quantity graduated according to population.

The varying levels of representation and of prestige that resulted from the provisions of the federal Constitution of 1936 gave rise, apparently, to new criticism from the Tatars and Bashkirs, if not from other national minority groups. When Stalin was explaining the state structure to the constitutional congress called to adopt the 1936 Constitution, he dwelt at some length on the reason for placing some of the national minority groups into what appeared to be the favored category of "union" republic while others, just as numerous and as culturally mature, were left out. In so doing, he stressed that the distinction between republics in the "union" and "autonomous" categories was based not only on size and on maturity of cultural development but also, and in some cases more importantly, on location. He argued that location was crucial because the Constitution gave only "union" republics the right to secede from the U.S.S.R., and, if secession were to be more than a paper right, a people exercising this right should not find themselves completely surrounded by the U.S.S.R. from which they had seceded and, therefore, would have to be situated on a border of the U.S.S.R. in the first place.

To foreign students of Stalin's writings, such an explanation sounds strained. The right of secession had been guaranteed since the first federal Constitution, presumably to placate the last diehards among the minority groups that were not yet sufficiently under Communist party control to accept permanent federation. The right of secession may even have been included in the Constitution to please Germans and other non-Soviet peoples who would have been reluctant to enter a permanent union. Whatever the reason for making the right of secession part of the Constitution, in the view of foreign students the right lacked reality.

Limitations on the Rights of Republics

Both in his 1912 manual and in subsequent statements, Stalin had made it clear that he felt that the Communist party should oppose any movement for secession if it meant that a people would return to the capitalist form of economy, for, in Marxist terms, a return to capitalism was a retrogressive step and, by definition, should be opposed by Communists. With Communist opposition assured against any effort to secede, it seemed to foreigners inconceivable that any republic could exercise the right successfully.

Stalin's argument for categorizing peoples in "union" or "autonomous" republics seems especially empty in the light of his writings on secession. The argument can have been thought to have value only for propagandizing the peoples who live on the frontiers of the U.S.S.R., such as the Iranians, the Afghans, the Latvians, the Poles, and others. At the time of his utterance, Stalin probably had not anticipated that some of these territories could be brought within the Soviet orbit so soon by military action rather than by the subversion to which his argument might be said to have appealed.

The limited nature of the powers reserved to the republics in the Soviet federal system is most clearly demonstrated in the law governing the budget of the U.S.S.R. Annually, the Supreme Soviet of the U.S.S.R. adopts a budget for the entire Union that is broken down republic by republic in its totals. No republic has its own source of revenue subject to its own control, and no republic can spend on its institutions any funds except those allocated by the federal budget. Only after the Supreme Soviet has adopted the budget for the entire country do the supreme soviets of each of the union republics meet in annual session to adopt their budgets. The total for a republic has to be the total established by the federal budget for that republic, but the republic may divide that total among its various provinces as it thinks fit. Obviously, the federal planners have drafted the federal budget with knowledge of the needs and possibilities of each province in each republic, but a republic's government can provide some variation. It can, through the budget debate, give to the deputies from the various provinces and from the various "autonomous republics," "autonomous regions," and "national districts" within the republic some sense of participation in the process of government. As has been seen, this sense of participation is probably one of the primary reasons why the Communist party has maintained the system of soviets alongside its own institutions.

To the outsider who knows the jealousy with which the states in the United States have guarded their budgets from federal encroachment, it is evident that one of the bases on which the autonomy that is still maintained by the American states rests is the power of the purse. In relinquishing this power to their federal government, the republics of the U.S.S.R. have given away the key to much of the independence possible within a federal system.

Of recent years, Soviet leaders have sought to enhance the appearance of independence in their republics by amending the clause in their federal Constitution that relates to the division of powers between federal and republic governments. In 1944 the Supreme Soviet of the U.S.S.R. extended to each of the then existing sixteen union republics the power to conduct its foreign relations, within the limits of policy established by the federal government, and to establish military formations of its own, within limits established by the federal government. The republics were permitted to organize ministries of foreign affairs and of defense to administer their affairs in these areas, but federal ministries of the same names were retained to co-ordinate policy. Further, the federal government was charged with "the representation of the Union in international relations, conclusion and ratification of treaties with other states, and the establishment of the general procedure in the mutual relations between the Union Republics."

Various reasons have been suggested for the changes of 1944. The most cogent is that Stalin was preparing to ask for sixteen seats in the United Nations, which was then being planned. He made such a request of the planning group at Dumbarton Oaks and, again, at the Yalta Conference. The world now knows the compromise that was accepted by Franklin D. Roosevelt and by Winston Churchill, under which the Byelorussian and Ukrainian republics received membership in the United Nations along with the U.S.S.R. while the other fourteen republics received no international recognition. The voting and debating records of these two Soviet republics in the United Nations since that time indicate that the federal government of the U.S.S.R. sets policy on all matters, as its Constitution requires it to do.

An additional reason for the 1944 amendments may lie in their possible appeal to the U.S.S.R.'s neighbors in Asia. For example, the Afghan government could deal directly with the governments of the Central Asian republics on border matters, though, when any cession of territory is made, as was the case in 1955 when territory was ceded to Iran, the treaty is made with the U.S.S.R. The republics concerned indicated their formal consent to the Presidium of the Supreme Soviet of the U.S.S.R. There was no negotiation between Iran and the two republics whose territory was affected.

After Stalin's death the trend toward centralization was accentuated by the reduction of the Karelo-Finnish Republic's status from that of a union republic to that of an autonomous republic within the Russian Republic. This event of mid-1956, which marked the first occasion in Soviet history of reduction of a union republic's status, provides a possible explanation of the real criteria used in 1936 and subsequently to determine which ethnic groups shall have union republic status within the federation. Stalin may have conceded union republic status to the minority peoples on the federation's frontiers not for the reasons he gave publicly but to improve the power of each people to entice their blood brothers across the frontiers in Poland, Rumania, Turkey, Iran, Afghanistan, China, and Finland to withdraw in revolt from the states in which they lived and to join the Soviet federation.

The reduction in status of Karelo-Finland in 1956 may have occurred because Stalin's heirs no longer shared the expectation which Stalin had evidenced as late as the war with Finland in 1940 that the citizens of Finland would join the Soviet federation as a part of the Karelo-Finnish Republic if given an opportunity. Stalin's heirs may have decided that it was time to be realistic and to incorporate the Karelo-Finnish minority within the Russian Republic to which they were already closely bound economically. Efficient administration may be easier when all matters can be handled through the apparatus of an autonomous republic rather than channeled through the relatively more cumbersome procedures of a union republic.

The Karelo-Finnish case was shown to be an exception to the plans of Stalin's heirs for the federation as a whole by events of 1957. At that time constitutional amendments were introduced into the federal and republic constitutions, returning to the republics some of the authority of which they had been deprived by

Stalin. Notably, the drafting of codes of law became again the task of the republics, as it had been prior to 1936. The federal government returned to its former position of guide in that it dictated the general principles to be followed by the draftsmen. The republics were also authorized to draw the administrative boundaries of their internal subdivisions, their provinces and counties. Previously these had been dictated from the center in accordance with directions of the planning authorities.

Changes in the relationship between federal authority and that of the republics occurred in the administration of industry within a few months of the constitutional amendments, and the administrative apparatus of secondary and higher education followed suit in 1958. Industrial and educational reorganization had to do primarily with public administration where operations and not policy were concerned.

· 2 ·

THE ORGANS OF STATE POWER
AND ADMINISTRATION

According to what Julian Towster calls the Soviet "nuclear theory of authority," the soviets represent "the state power" while the Party is "merely the core of state power" in the U.S.S.R. In the light of the presently available evidence, however, there is little doubt that the soviets and the other governmental organs have gradually been transformed into instruments of Party policy. The identification of the state and Party is symbolized by the merger of the upper layers of the Party and governmental hierarchies (see Fig. 3).

The fundamental position of the Party in the Soviet governmental system is also admitted by Denisov and Kirichenko, the Soviet authors of the first selection in this section. While the Soviet state apparatus is depicted as a positive factor in the establishment of a new and more "advanced" societal order, it is also considered unable to fulfill its functions effectively without the "guiding force [of] the Communist Party and its militant headquarters, the Central Committee." The Party "guides" the state organs, according to these authors, by filling the key governmental positions with loyal Party members who, in turn, are guided in

Figure 3. THE SOVIET PARTY STATE: THE INTERLOCKING LEADERSHIP

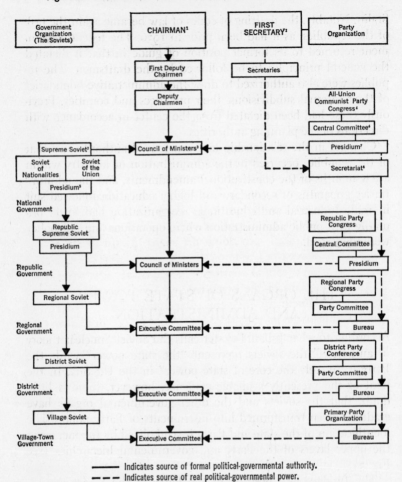

———— Indicates source of formal political-governmental authority.
– – – – Indicates source of real political-governmental power.

1. Up to 1965 the offices of Chairman of the Council of Ministers and First Secretary [Secretary General] of the Party had been held by one man during two periods: by Stalin from 1941 to 1953 and by Nikita S. Khrushchev from 1958 to October 1964.

2. The Legislature, which is nominally the supreme governmental authority but which meets only rarely, primarily to ratify the Presidium's acts taken in the interim between its sessions.

3. The Cabinet, or chief executive organ, theoretically appointed by the Supreme Soviet but actually by the Party. It is composed of the top leaders of the Party.

4. Theoretically the highest Party authority, actually just a forum for pronouncements of the Party line.

5. The "inner legislature" which issues decrees and orders having the force of law on instructions from the Party.

6. Organ directing Party between Congresses on the basis of decisions taken by the Party Presidium.

7. The highest authority on policies and appointments in the Party, and thus in the Soviet Union. The members are chosen by the Central Committee.

8. Chief executive organ of the Party, dealing with problems of organization and the execution of policies.

their work by the principle of "democratic centralism." The principle theoretically implies the elective character of the various governmental organs and the responsibility and accountability of the lower state organs to the higher state organs. In reality, however, the Communist Party, as the authors frankly admit, "not only plays a decisive role in the preparation and adoption of decisions by Soviet state organs, but systematically controls the fulfillment of these decisions."

Professor Towster's article describes the all-embracing scope of the Soviet legislative and executive-administrative system. Formal constitutional provisions notwithstanding, Soviet public administration involves in reality "the conscious and deliberate organization of the entire population by the Party for the production and distribution of all goods and services, with everyone exhorted, induced and coerced into doing his share toward attaining the goals set in successive 'Economic Plans.'"

Indeed, from a formal constitutional point of view,* the structure and functions of the executive and legislative organs of the Soviet Government are in many respects identical with those of their counterparts in the Western democracies. But while the Supreme Soviet is characterized as "the highest organ of the state power" having "exclusive" legislative prerogatives and the Council of Ministers is depicted as "the highest executive and administrative organ of state power," in reality both these branches of government are overshadowed by the predominant position of the Party in Soviet life.

Unlike the Congress of the United States or the legislative bodies of any Western democracy, the Supreme Soviet is primarily a rubber-stamp agency that approves unanimously the decisions taken by the Party-controlled Presidium during the interim between its sessions. Convened for brief sessions twice a year, the Supreme Soviet is actually an assembly of notables who were nominated (*ergo* elected) by the Party organizations as a reward for loyalty and proficiency. The recent establishment of "permanent commissions" notwithstanding, there seems to be little doubt that the proceedings of the Supreme Soviet are largely per-

---

* For the constitutional provisions concerning the organs of state power and administration in the U.S.S.R., the Union Republics and the Autonomous Republics, see Articles 30–93.

functory, merely "legalizing" the actions taken in its name by the Party.

The same observations cannot be made with regard to the Council of Ministers (known as the Council of People's Commisars or *Sovnarkom*). It is in fact the most powerful organ in the formal political hierarchy of the U.S.S.R., primarily because of the intimate relationship between the Council and the Party leadership. For, indeed, the leading figures of the Party are always the leading members of the Soviet Government.

The System of Soviet State Organs

A. DENISOV AND M. KIRICHENKO

The Soviet state apparatus is an absolutely new system of state organs, previously unknown in the history of class society. It is organized on broad democratic principles. The backbone are the Soviets, the organs of state power which historically evolved as a result of the creative activity of the working people. . . .

The Soviet state apparatus includes not only the Soviets themselves as representative organs of power, but also the whole system of executive and administrative organs (the Government, Ministries and local organs of state administration), as well as the judicial institutions and organs of the Procurator's Office. . . .

At all stages of development of the socialist state the activity of the Soviet state apparatus has been subordinated to the accomplishment of the tasks and functions of the dictatorship of the working class. The Soviet state apparatus is a vivid embodiment of the unity of economic and political administration. It is an important instrument in transforming the old society into a new one,

---

From *Soviet State Law* by A. Denisov and M. Kirichenko, selections from pp. 189–281. Moscow: Foreign Languages Publishing House, 1960.

in building communism; it ensures the implementation of the policy of the Communist Party. . . .

Basic Principles of the Organization and Activity of Soviet State Organs

The principles underlying the organization and activity of the Soviet state organs are determined by the Soviet social and state structure of the U.S.S.R. and of the Union and Autonomous Republics.

The economic foundation of the organization of Soviet state organs is the socialist system of economy and the socialist ownership of the instruments and means of production; its juridical foundation is the Constitution of the U.S.S.R. and other laws defining the order of formation and activity of the state organs. . . .

With the steady advance of the Soviet people towards communism and with the continuous growth of the creative initiative and activity of the people, a number of functions now performed by state bodies will be taken over by public organizations. . . .

The transfer of certain state functions to public bodies does not at all imply weakening the role of the socialist state in the building of communism. On the contrary, the state will be in a position to concentrate still greater attention on developing the national economy. As long as aggressive imperialist blocs exist, the Soviet Union will continue to strengthen its Armed Forces and the state security organs whose functions are spearheaded primarily against foreign agents smuggled into the U.S.S.R. At the same time new functions are now assumed by the state. . . .

A characteristic feature of the system of Soviet state organs is the unity and interconnection of all of its component parts. The Soviet state organs do not oppose each other, are not isolated and self-contained organizations; on the contrary, they are in constant interaction.

The activity of the Soviet state organs is closely bound up with the functions of the socialist state. . . .

One of the most important principles underlying the work of the Soviet state organs is solicitude for the material and cultural well-being of Soviet people, for the protection of their rights and interests. . . .

The system of Soviet state organs is notable for its democratism. The work of each of its links expresses the interests of the working people of town and country. . . .

The system of Soviet state organs fully reflects the federative character of the U.S.S.R. Their structure and activity are based on the principle of internationalism which is one of the fundamental principles of the Soviet multinational state. Both the central and local organs of the Soviet state include representatives of all nations and nationalities inhabiting the country. In their work these organs take strict account of the specific requirements and national peculiarities of all the peoples of the U.S.S.R. . . .

Socialist legality plays an important part in the activity of all Soviet state organs; it signifies strict observance of the laws of the U.S.S.R. and of the Union and Autonomous Republics, as well as of all other normative acts.

Democratic centralism is the main organizational principle on which the system of Soviet state organs is based.

This principle takes the following concrete forms in the organization and activity of the state organs:

1) electivity of all organs of state power, of the majority of executive and administrative organs and of all courts;

2) responsibility and accountability of lower state organs to higher ones;

3) obligatory nature of the directives of higher organs for lower ones;

4) control by the working people of the activity of state organs, officials and especially, deputies; the right of the electors to recall any elected representative who has not justified the confidence of the people;

5) full conformity of the acts issued by lower state organs to those issued by higher state organs;

6) extensive development of local initiative by every state organ within the bounds of its powers with the aim of better disclosing and utilizing local resources and potentialities;

7) application of the system of dual subordination, especially in the work of executive and administrative organs, which is of extreme importance for securing a harmonious combination of local interests with the interests of the state as a whole. . . .

Definite stages of development of the Soviet state necessitated the strengthening of the principle of centralism to meet the internal or international situation. . . .

The state organs of the U.S.S.R. and the corresponding organs of the Union and Autonomous Republics are essentially uniform, but each of them possesses its own powers and is consequently to some degree independent in deciding questions within its jurisdiction. . . .

The supreme principle of activity of the Soviet state organs is the principle of collective (collegial) guidance worked out by the Communist Party and verified in practice in the course of many years. It stems from the socialist nature of the Soviet state. . . .

The principle of collegial guidance in no way means absence of personal responsibility for the work entrusted. The entire activity of the Soviet state organs is based on the well-known Leninist principle of "collective discussion and personal responsibility." . . .

The Leninist principles underlying the organization and activity of the Soviet state apparatus were violated to a great extent in the last years of Stalin's life. The cult of personality depreciated the role of the Party and of the masses of the people in Soviet state activity and belittled the practical significance of collective guidance; it led to grave omissions in the entire work of the state apparatus, to violations of socialist legality and democratic centralism. In view of this, the Twentieth Party Congress resolutely came out against the personality cult as absolutely alien to Marxism-Leninism and enjoined the Central Committee of the Communist Party to carry out a number of measures which would ensure the liquidation of the consequences of this cult in all spheres of Party and state activity, and to steadily implement the principles of Party and state guidance. . . .

Types of Soviet State Organs

The system of Soviet state organs includes organs of state power, organs of state administration, judicial organs and organs of the Procurator's Office.

The Soviets of Working People's Deputies are the organs of state power; they are divided into *higher* and *local* organs. The higher organs of state power include the Supreme Soviet of the U.S.S.R. and its Presidium, the Supreme Soviets of the Union and

Figure 4. STRUCTURE OF THE SUPREME SOVIET OF THE U.S.S.R.

SUPREME SOVIET OF THE U.S.S.R.

SOVIET OF THE UNION

SOVIET OF NATIONALITIES

PRESIDIUM OF SUPREME SOVIET OF THE U.S.S.R.

Credentials Committee

Standing Commissions

Foreign Affairs

Budgetary

Legislative Proposals

Economic

Credentials Committee

Standing Commissions

Foreign Affairs

Budgetary

Legislative Proposals

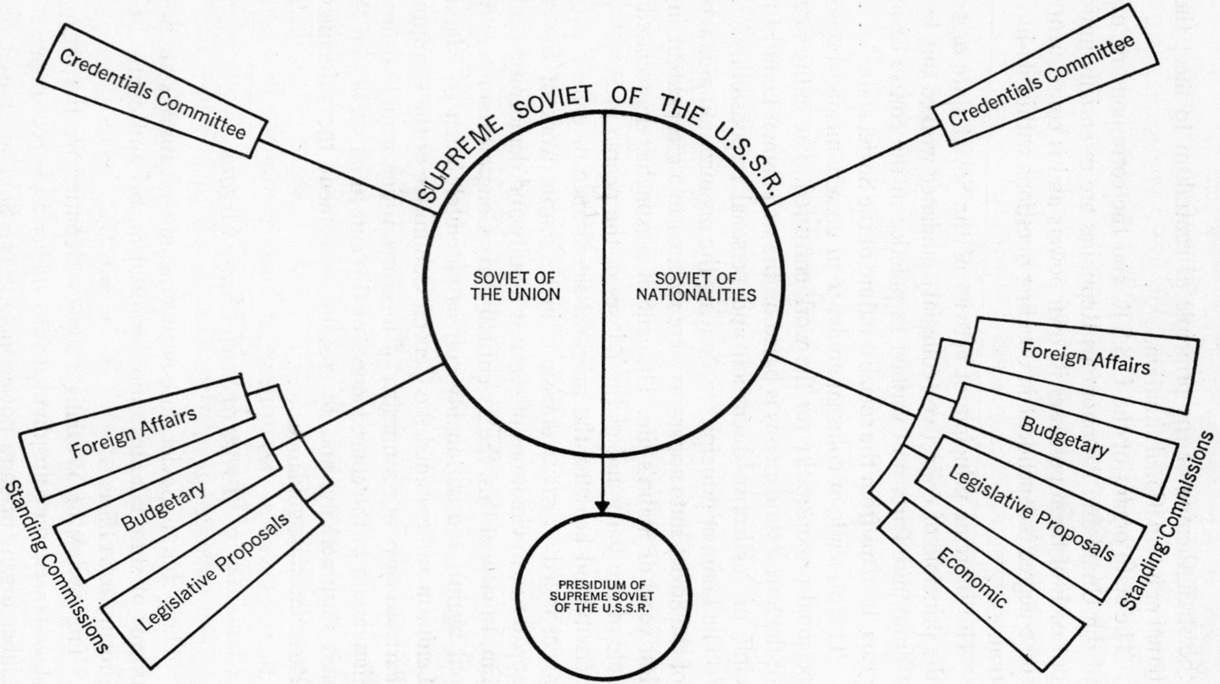

Autonomous Republics and their Presidiums; the local organs include the Soviets of Working People's Deputies of Territories, Regions, Areas, Districts, cities and rural localities.

The Supreme Soviets exercise state power within the bounds of the corresponding Republics, and the local Soviets—within Territories, Regions, Areas, Districts, cities, villages or settlements.

Executive and administrative activity, i.e., activity connected with the direct guidance of various branches of life, is carried out by the organs of state administration. From the point of view of the territorial limits of this activity, the organs of state administration are divided into higher, central and local organs. The higher organs of state administration are the Council of Ministers of the U.S.S.R. and the Councils of Ministers of the Union and Autonomous Republics. The central organs include the Ministries of the U.S.S.R., the Ministries of the Union and Autonomous Republics and other central all-Union or republican departments. The local organs include: the Executive Committees of the Soviets of Territories, Regions, Areas, Districts, cities and rural localities, as well as local organs of certain Ministries and departments (for example, local administrations of communication).

As regards their jurisdiction, the organs of state administration are divided into general organs and those which direct individual branches of state activity. The general organs unite and direct the management of all, or at least of many branches of the economy and culture; they are: the Council of Ministers of the U.S.S.R., the Councils of Ministers of the Union and Autonomous Republics, and the Executive Committees of the local Soviets of Working People's Deputies. Among organs directing separate branches of state activity are: Ministries, Committees, Central Administrations, as well as departments and administrations of Executive Committees of local Soviets.

The judicial organs of the U.S.S.R. are divided into all-Union and republican. The all-Union judicial organs include the Supreme Court of the U.S.S.R. and the military tribunals. The judicial organs of the Union Republics include the Supreme Courts of the Union and Autonomous Republics, the Territorial, Regional, Area Courts and the People's Courts. The system of organs of the Procurator's Office in the main corresponds to the administrative-territorial division of the country and is headed by the Procurator-

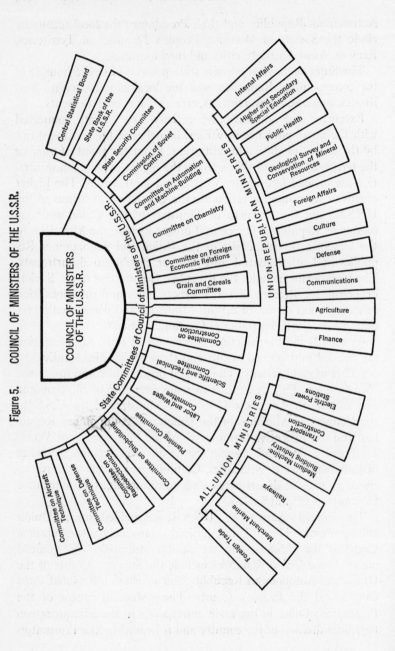

Figure 5. COUNCIL OF MINISTERS OF THE U.S.S.R.

COUNCIL OF MINISTERS OF THE U.S.S.R.

State Committees of Council of Ministers of the U.S.S.R.

UNION-REPUBLICAN MINISTRIES

- Internal Affairs
- Higher and Secondary Special Education
- Public Health
- Geological Survey and Conservation of Mineral Resources
- Foreign Affairs
- Culture
- Defense
- Communications
- Agriculture
- Finance

State Committees of Council of Ministers of the U.S.S.R.

- Central Statistical Board
- State Bank of the U.S.S.R.
- State Security Committee
- Commission of Soviet Control
- Committee on Automation and Machine-Building
- Committee on Chemistry
- Committee on Foreign Economic Relations
- Grain and Cereals Committee
- Committee on Construction
- Scientific and Technical Committee
- Labor and Wages Committee
- Planning Committee
- Committee on Shipbuilding
- Committee on Radioelectronics
- Committee on Defense Technique
- Committee on Aircraft Technique

ALL-UNION MINISTRIES

- Electric Power Stations
- Transport Construction
- Medium Machine-Building Industry
- Railways
- Merchant Marine
- Foreign Trade

General of the U.S.S.R. Besides, this system includes the military and transport Procurator's Offices.

Leading Role of the Communist Party in the Activity of the Soviet State Organs

The efficient and well co-ordinated work of the Soviet state organs would be impossible without a single guiding and organizing force. This guiding force is the Communist Party and its militant headquarters, the Central Committee.

The leading role of the Communist Party in the whole system of Soviet state organs does not at all mean that the Party supplants these organs. The Communist Party forms the leading core of all state organs.

Its guidance of the state organs is expressed first of all in the fact that it promotes the best Party members to key positions and through them carries out its political line in all state organs. It keeps check on the work of the state organs, lays bare the mistakes and shortcomings in their activity and thus strengthens and improves the state apparatus. Finally, every state organ is guided by the directives of the Party when planning its work.

The congresses and conferences of the Communist Party and the plenary meetings of the Central Committee of the Party regularly discuss questions relating to the organization and activity of the Soviet state organs. In this way the Party guides the work of the state organs without supplanting them. . . .

The Communist Party not only plays a decisive role in the preparation and adoption of decisions by Soviet state organs, but systematically controls the fulfillment of these decisions. . . .

The Soviet Legislative and Executive System

JULIAN TOWSTER

The Federal Supreme Soviet:
The Fiction of Exclusive Legislation

Of all the federal organs the Supreme Soviet of the U.S.S.R. is
depicted in Soviet constitutional theory as the most important.
The constitution calls it "the highest organ of state power in the
U.S.S.R." and declares that it alone exercises the legislative power
of the Union (Arts. 30, 32). Since the prerogatives of the Supreme
Soviet are supposed to embrace all the powers assigned to the
Union by Article 14 of the constitution, in so far as they do not
fall within the specific jurisdiction of the federal Presidium, Council of Ministers, or ministries (Art. 31), the formal competence
of the Supreme Soviet is indeed imposing. In practice, however,
the role of the Supreme Soviet is quite different.

The Supreme Soviet is a bicameral body composed of two
chambers: a Council of the Union, elected on the basis of one
deputy per 300,000 people, and a Council of Nationalities, elected
on the basis of twenty-five deputies from a union republic, eleven
from an autonomous republic, five from an autonomous region,
and one from a national area. Its regular term of office is four
years. The Presidium of the Supreme Soviet, which convenes the
Supreme Soviet twice a year, can call extraordinary sessions at its
own discretion or on demand of a union republic. Also, in case of

Abridged from "The Soviet Orbit: The Union of Soviet Socialist Republics" by Julian Towster in *European Political Systems* edited by Taylor Cole,
pp. 647–661, by permission of Alfred A. Knopf, Inc. New York: Alfred A.
Knopf, Inc., 1959. Copyright 1953, 1959 by Alfred A. Knopf, Inc. For footnote references, see original source. For biographical note, see p. 4.

persistent disagreement between the chambers (a contingency that has never arisen and is very unlikely to occur), the Presidium is empowered to dissolve the Supreme Soviet and to order new elections. The two chambers are accorded equal powers. Their sessions begin and end simultaneously. Each elects a chairman and four vice-chairmen (prior to June, 1950, only two vice-chairmen), who are required to conduct the proceedings of the respective chambers, and the chairmen take turns in presiding over joint sittings. The passage of a law entails approval of both chambers by a simple majority vote in each. The same procedure is followed for constitutional amendments, except that a majority of not less than two thirds of the votes in each chamber is required for passage.

The procedure of the Supreme Soviet has become quite standardized. The first session of a newly elected Supreme Soviet differs from later sessions only in that it has the additional duties of electing a Presidium and Council of Ministers. Generally a session lasts about a week. As a rule the two chambers convene separately for the first meeting. In each council an opening speech by a veteran deputy is followed by the selection of the chairmen, approval of the procedure and agenda for the session, and election of a credentials commission and three standing commissions: a budget commission of twenty-six members, a legislative commission of nineteen members, and a foreign-affairs commission of eleven persons. The second meeting is a joint session of the two chambers, at which the minister of finance is called upon to report on the annual budget for the coming year (and every second year also on the fulfillment of the budget for the two preceding years). This meeting has become a special occasion, with the Party Presidium members in attendance and the government box filled with party dignitaries and members of the Supreme Soviet Presidium and Council of Ministers. At later meetings half of the Party Presidium members attend the sessions of the Council of the Union and the other half those of the Council of Nationalities.

The finance minister's report includes a statement of past and projected progress, sprinkled with references to the international position of the U.S.S.R. and denunciations of foreign opponents. The third meeting of the Supreme Soviet, when the report of the credentials commission is approved, is usually taken up with a "co-report" on the budget presented in each chamber by the chairman of its budget commission. As a rule this co-report proposes an increase in revenues through taxation, notes the petitions by various deputies for greater appropriations, and also criticizes some aspects of the work of different ministries. The following two or three meetings of the separate chambers are devoted to a discussion of the budget, which is one of the approved outlets for permissible types of criticism. Various deputies, probably instructed in advance, speak of progress as well as inadequacies in the fulfillment of plans in their respective areas, criticize some specific actions of ministries, and point out needed expenditures or sources of additional revenues. A number of ministers answer these criticisms, confess "defects," and promise improved performance in the future. At the end of the discussions the finance minister makes a virtually identical closing report in each chamber, accepting proposals for increasing the revenue and indicating that suggestions of individual members will subsequently be considered in detail by the ministries concerned. The brief report is followed by unanimous approval of the budget and an article-by-article vote on the budget law.

At one meeting the list of interim decrees issued by the Presidium of the Supreme Soviet is read. This list, which includes decrees involving changes in the ministries as well as appointment and removal of ministerial personnel, is presented by the secretary of the Presidium before each chamber and is unanimously approved without any discussion. If constitutional changes are proposed, the secretary submits a special bill embodying those changes. Separate laws, formally initiated for the first time in the Supreme Soviet, are presented infrequently and are passed without any serious debate.

The final meeting is a joint session of the two chambers that unanimously elects the federal Presidium by confirming the list suggested on behalf of the Council of Elders (steering committee) of each chamber and also "elects" the Council of Ministers by voting to approve its work and to instruct it to continue to discharge its duties. It also passes sundry resolutions, designed as a rule for specific internal or external propaganda purposes. In 1951 the joint final session of the chambers was devoted to the presentation of a "peace law" sponsored by the "World Congress of the Partisans of Peace." This was an obviously staged performance, highlighted by numerous speeches concerning the "peace efforts" of the Soviet Union and the "warmongering" of the Western democracies.

To summarize, the Supreme Soviet of the U.S.S.R. is not the powerful organ or source of authority that Soviet theory would make it. It is an assembly of notables, of persons whose membership in the Supreme Soviet is a reward for loyalty and proficiency and who, at most, serve as an added means of contact between localities and local interests and Moscow. The proceedings of the Supreme Soviet are largely perfunctory, and there is little evidence that its permanent commissions play more than a nominal role. The size of its membership and the manner of its election lend it the superficial appearance of a representative organ. As such it is used both as a formal ratifying body, which the regime can claim as an organ of "popular" rule, and as a sounding board for official propaganda. Since legal norms are produced in volume by the Presidium of the Supreme Soviet and by the Council of Ministers, and since interim Presidium decrees are not even debated prior to their approval by the Supreme Soviet, it is clear that the claim of "exclusive legislative powers" by the latter is mere fiction.

Presidium of the Supreme Soviet

Although first established by the new constitution, the Presidium of the Supreme Soviet, which began functioning in January, 1938, reflects in its operation the role performed earlier to a lesser degree by the Central Executive Committee and to a greater extent by the Executive Committee's Presidium. During the proceedings that led to adoption of the 1936 constitution an amendment was proposed that the chairman of the Presidium be elected by the people. Stalin objected to the proposal on the ground that an "individual president" elected by the entire population on an equal basis with the Supreme Soviet "might essay to stand out against the Supreme Soviet," and he concluded that the U.S.S.R. must have a "collective" president chosen by the Supreme Soviet, namely, the Presidium of the Supreme Soviet. Thus the official conception to date is that the Presidium is the "collective president" of the Soviet Union. In practice, however, the chairman of the Presidium often acts as the titular head of the state in dealings with foreign countries, and consequently he has occasionally been referred to abroad as "the Soviet President."

Under the provisions of the constitution the Presidium is elected every four years at a joint sitting of the two chambers of the Supreme Soviet (Art. 48). During World War II, however, such election was delayed until 1946. The membership of the Presidium, which numbered forty-three persons earlier, was reduced to thirty-three by a law adopted on March 19, 1946—and later incorporated in the constitution—that prescribed the following composition: a chairman, fifteen vice-chairmen, a secretary, and sixteen members. . . . In its structure and composition it reflects several established principles and customs. In as much as the Presidium is deemed to reflect, not only the interests of the entire populace, but the special interests of the separate nationalities, it has become customary to fill the posts of the vice-chairmen of the Presidium with the chairmen of the presidia of the fifteen union republics. It was also customary—in part, no doubt, for purposes of liaison, surveillance, and co-ordination—to have several members of the Politburo among the Presidium membership. This custom carries over to the newly created Party Presidium, seven of whose members and candidates are also on the Presidium of the Supreme Soviet. On the other hand, several practices that prevailed in the composition of the Presidium of the Central Executive Committee were not continued after 1936. For example, the inclusion of ministers in the membership of the Presidium is now considered improper on the ground that the new constitution has clearly delimited the respective functions of the Council of Ministers and the Presidium and has made the first body responsible and accountable to the second. . . . The chairmen and vice-chairmen of the two chambers of the Supreme Soviet are not placed in the Presidium on the ground that these officers preside over the body to which the Presidium is constitutionally accountable. One or two members of the high command of the Soviet Army have also sat on the Presidium. . . .

The Presidium is listed in the constitution as one of the "highest organs of state power," although it is at the same time declared answerable for its acts to the other "highest organ," i.e., the Supreme Soviet (Art. 48). The Presidium has no veto power over Supreme Soviet legislation, and, except in the special case of disagreement between its two chambers, it has no authorization to dissolve the Supreme Soviet.

Nevertheless, the avowed primacy of the Supreme Soviet in the Soviet structure notwithstanding, the Presidium is vested by the constitution (Art. 49) with an impressive array of functions. These functions include executive duties, such as convening sessions of the Supreme Soviet, setting election dates, instituting and awarding decorations and medals, exercising the right of pardon, issuing decrees, and dissolving the Supreme Soviet in event of disagreement between its chambers. Executive functions of a military nature include the establishment of military titles, appointment and removal of the higher command of the armed forces, and proclamation of martial law and of general or partial mobilization. The Presidium is the chief Soviet organ for the conduct of foreign relations, as is evidenced by its powers to appoint and receive diplomatic representatives and to ratify and denounce treaties. Judicial functions are also assigned by the constitution to the Presidium; in particular, it interprets the laws of the U.S.S.R. in force and annuls decisions and ordinances of the Council of Ministers of the U.S.S.R. and of the councils of ministers of the union republics in case of non-conformance to law. Also, the Presidium acts for the Supreme Soviet in the period between sessions of the latter in the appointing and dismissal of members of the Council of Ministers, in proclaiming a state of war in event of armed attack, or in carrying out international treaty obligations. Finally, the Presidium may on its own initiative or upon the request of a union republic conduct referendums.

Of particular importance is the Presidium's decree-issuing power, since, despite the emphasis on the exclusive competence of the Supreme Soviet with regard to legislation, many of the Presidium's decrees are legislative in character and in fact become effective long before they are confirmed by the Supreme Soviet. In addition to decrees issued in pursuance of its functions under Article 49 of the constitution, the Presidium has issued decrees on subjects of U.S.S.R. jurisdiction not specifically assigned to it and on matters explicitly or implicitly within the competence of the Supreme Soviet, such as the alteration of union-republic boundaries and formation of new regions and autonomous republics. Recent examples of the types of decrees passed by the Presidium are found in the lists confirmed by the Supreme Soviet in 1956 that comprise enactments reorganizing governmental organs, including ministries; appointments and dismissals of ministers; constitutional amendments; approval of territorial-administrative changes, such as the conversion of the Karelo-Finnish Union Republic into the Karelian Autonomous Republic. It may be remembered also that during World War II, when a State Defense Committee vested with "the full plentitude of power in the state" was created, the Presidium continued to issue decrees on many important matters. Presidium decrees, like laws of the Supreme Soviet, are issued over the signatures of the chairman and secretary of the Presidium.

Unlike its predecessor under the old constitution the Presidium of the Supreme Soviet has no authority to annul or suspend decisions of the supreme soviets or presidia of the union republics. It is, however, the sole organ now vested by the constitution with the power to interpret laws, a power that under the earlier federal constitution was possessed, not only by the Presidium of the Central Executive Committee, but also by the Supreme Court of the U.S.S.R.

Thus the Presidium has operated as an organ for the conduct of foreign relations, performed duties of a titular executive, and served as a legislative body in the Soviet system. It would be a mistake, however, to conclude that the Presidium is an independent policy-determining organ. The Party Presidium, as earlier the Politburo, has many arms in both the party and the Soviet structures to carry out its will and to implement its decisions through particular methods and on different levels. The Presidium of the Supreme Soviet is merely one of them. Another such instrument is the Council of Ministers.

Council of Ministers of the U.S.S.R.

The Council of Ministers was called the Council of People's Commissars, or *Sovnarkom*, until March 19, 1946. At that time the terms "commissar" and "commissariat" were abandoned in the U.S.S.R. and the union republics in favor of terms "minister" and "ministry." The earlier Sovnarkom dated from one of the first acts of the Bolshevik revolutionary regime, having been created by a decree of the Second Congress of Soviets on November 8, 1917.

The official conception of the council's role was changed in the mid-thirties. The decree creating the Sovnarkom, with power to govern the country until the meeting of a constituent assembly (which convened but was dispersed by the Bolsheviks in January, 1918), declared that the "governmental power belongs to . . . the Council of People's Commissars." The constitution of 1918 made the council responsible and accountable to the Congress of Soviets and Central Executive Committee (Arts. 35–38, 40, 46). Likewise the Union constitution of 1924 designated the council as the "executive and administrative organ" of the Central Executive Committee and made it responsible to the committee and the Presidium (Arts. 37, 38, 40, 41). Yet, under each constitution, the council was vested with broad legislative powers, and in both constitutional theory and practice it was actually regarded as a legislative agency no less than an executive and administrative one.

Since the adoption of the 1936 constitution the legislative role of the council has been formally de-emphasized in consonance with the emphasis placed in theory upon the Supreme Soviet as *the* legislative organ. Decisions and ordinances issued by the Council of Ministers, called the highest "executive and administrative" organ of state power, are said to be enacted solely "on the basis and in pursuance of the laws in operation" (Arts. 64–66). In practice, however, the role of the council as a legislative organ has not decreased. It takes an active part in the preparation of all legislation, including drafts of laws brought before the Supreme Soviet. And even though its decisions may be annulled or suspended by the Presidium, it is clear from the volume and range of its enactments that the Council of Ministers is actually the greater producer of compulsory and enforceable rules in the governmental system.

The council is endowed with broad powers by the constitution. According to Article 68, the council exercises the following functions: it co-ordinates and directs the work of the ministries and other institutions under its jurisdiction and directs the sovnarkhozi through the councils of ministers of the union republics; it adopts measures to implement the economic plan, budget, credit and monetary system, and to maintain public order and protect state interests and citizens' rights; it exercises general guidance in the sphere of foreign relations and directs the general organization of the armed forces; and whenever necessary it sets up special committees and central administrations for economic, cultural, and defense purposes. Moreover, it has the power to check on the execution of its decisions and orders; and with respect to branches of administration and economy under the jurisdiction of the U.S.S.R., the Councils of Ministers may suspend decisions and orders of the union-republic councils of ministers and sovnarkhozi and annul orders and instructions of ministers of the U.S.S.R. (Art. 69).

As of March, 1959, the council consisted of its chairman, two first deputy chairmen, three deputy chairmen, the chairman of the State Planning Committee (who is one of the deputy chairmen), the ministers, and the chairmen of the following state committees: Labor and Wages, Construction Affairs, State Security, Foreign Economic Ties, Defense Technology, Aviation Technology, Shipbuilding Technology, Radio and Electronic Technology, Automation and Machine Building, Chemical Industry, Grain Products, and the Scientific-Technical Committee; and in addition the chairman of the Soviet Central Control Commission, the chairman of Administration of the State Bank, and the chief of the Central Statistical Administration.* In addition the council of

---

* Ed. note: The state committees came into prominence in 1957, following the adoption of Khrushchev's recommendations to the Central Committee Plenum (February 1957) on the reorganization of the central governmental apparatus. The original "decentralization" scheme involved the abolition of the 25 central ministries engaged in industry and construction and the transfer of their functions to the then established regional *sovnarkhozy* (*sovety narodnogo khozyastva*: councils of national economy). Directed by an All-Union *Sovnarkhoz*, the originally established 104 regional *sovnarkhozy*—apparently not fulfilling the hopes attached to them—were gradually amalgamated and their activities synchronized first through the establishment of all-republic *sovnarkhozy*, with broad coordinating powers (1960), and then through the division of the nation into 17 large economic regions for purposes of territorial planning (1961). The trend toward centralization became more evident at the end of 1962, when the Party-State Control Committee was established to serve as a central auditing-inspection organ of the Party and Government. By this time the number of *sovnarkhozy* was reduced to about 40. In a major reversal of Khrushchev's policies, the new Kremlin leadership recentralized in March 1965 the management of the defense industries by converting the state committees for aircraft, defense technology, radio, shipbuilding, electronics and medium machinery into full-fledged ministries. It appears (Spring

Ministers includes the chairmen of the council of ministers of the fifteen union republics as members ex officio, and the chairman of the Council of Ministers of the U.S.S.R. may request the Supreme Soviet to appoint deputies of the chairman of Gosplan and chiefs of its basic branches as ministers within the council. These officials are voting members of the council, whose membership is formally "approved" by the Supreme Soviet for a term of approximately four years. The episode in 1938, when three names were dropped from the proposed list of ministers on the basis of criticisms voiced in the Supreme Soviet, was never repeated, and Supreme Soviet approval has become a matter of routine. Between sessions of the Supreme Soviet individual changes in the council's membership are made by a formal vote of the Presidium at the instance of the chairman of the council. Later they are placed before the Supreme Soviet for confirmation.

The extent to which the activities of the Council of Ministers pervade Soviet governmental life, placing this organ in a class by itself in the structure of the Soviets, can be seen from its composition. The post of chairman has always been filled by persons from the summit of the party hierarchy: Lenin until 1924, Rykov until 1930, Molotov until 1941, Stalin until March, 1953, Malenkov until February, 1955, Bulganin until 1958, and Khrushchev [until October 1964].

Within each ministry there is a collegium, consisting of the leading departmental officials and the minister, and a large council to serve as a liaison between the center and the field. The minister operates on the "one-man management principle," first advocated by Lenin but given fullest expression with the inauguration of the Five Year plans. To emphasize the minister's role the collegia were abolished in 1934, but they were restored in 1936 to serve as consulting bodies within the ministries. The minister's decisions are final, but in case of disagreement the collegium of his ministry has a formal right of appeal to the Council of Ministers and the party's Central Committee.

The Council of Ministers exercises control over each minister

1965) that the post-Khrushchev leadership adopted a compromise decision under which the lesser consumer-goods industries would continue operating under regional control.

and on occasion has annulled departmental acts. In official theory the minister carries a dual responsibility. He is a "servant of the people"; consequently, both he and the Council of Ministers are responsible to the Supreme Soviet and must be ready to answer questions addressed to them by a Supreme Soviet deputy within a three-day period (Art. 71). The minister is also "a pupil of Lenin," deemed to owe supreme allegiance to the party and its highest leadership. Actually the second responsibility is by far the more important. And by virtue of the intimate relationship between the Council of Ministers and party leadership the Council of Ministers is in fact the most powerful organ in the formal Soviet political hierarchy.

Public Administration in the Soviet Union

Public administration in the U.S.S.R. is unique in character. Its over-all preoccupation, as in public administration of other countries, is to get things done in an efficient manner and at minimum cost, but the achievement of this objective is affected by many peculiar problems because all governmental activities in the U.S.S.R. are conditioned by requirements of theoretical dogma, on the one hand, and are subject to the shifting strategy of the party leaders, on the other.

Soviet administration has dealt with such customary problems as the proper division of labor and of liaison between the center and the localities, financial solvency, administrative efficiency, and training of reserves of skilled personnel. It has sought to meet the first of these through the graded territorial-administrative structure of the soviets, with its system of dual subordination of administrators at every level, and through the three grades of ministries: All-Union, Union-Republic, and Republic, the last of which has no counterpart on the Union level. Here is an administrative solution that fundamentally emphasizes centralized policy determination and control, occasionally permitting a measure of decentralized operative supervision. Financial solvency is supposed to be ensured by the work of the Ministry of Finance through its budget and bank-credit controls and its inspection machinery, and by the Commission of State Control through its periodic check on expenditures of state funds. The State Commission on the Civil Service seeks to promote administrative efficiency by preparing organizational charts, job classifications, suggestions for ceilings on personnel, and rationalized procedures in order to eliminate duplicated operations and to reduce surplus staffs. Although the Chief Administration of Labor Reserves trains the yearly contingents of recruits as skilled workers for Soviet economic enterprises, each sector of industry and administration maintains its own system of schools and institutes to train higher technical personnel and administrators. The combined efforts of these activities are obviously designed to produce a large pool of skilled personnel.

In addition public administration in the U.S.S.R. has been confronted with such unorthodox problems as the maintenance of the party's primacy in all spheres, the planning of all activities, the focusing of responsibility within each unit of administration, the periodic utilization of mass pressure devices over the lower bureaucracy, and the permanent guardianship of the political loyalty of all public employees. The activities of party organizations at all levels and those of the Gosplan provide Soviet solutions for the first two problems; the "one-man management" principle, the concentration of responsibility in the head of the administrative unit or enterprise, is designed to counteract the earlier tendency toward an escape from responsibility under the "collegial management" practice. The controlled practice of "criticism and self-criticism" is intended partly as an extra check against lethargy, nepotism, and ineffectiveness, and it is designed also as a "sop" to the populace. Finally, representatives of the security organs, operating within all branches of administration and the economy, are presumed to ensure the fealty of public service and the security of the regime.

Taken together, all these techniques and devices are designed to provide a comprehensive check on performance in the Soviet system of administration. Despite the multiplicity of controls, however, many bureaucratic features are in evidence. These characteristics of Soviet administration are rooted in the extraordinary scope of state activity and in the extreme degree of centralization that prevail in the U.S.S.R., conditions that are not likely to change appreciably in the foreseeable future.

· 3 ·

LOCAL GOVERNMENT: THE SOVIETS

The theory and practice of the local soviets in the over-all political and governmental structure of the U.S.S.R. have undoubtedly been among the most neglected areas of Western scholarship on the Soviet system. Conceived by Communist apologists as schools of government for the masses, the local soviets have been depicted as institutions of popular rule wielding sovereign powers. In reality, they play a secondary but highly utilitarian role in Soviet life, serving as transmission belts for the implementation of Party directives. In this capacity they act with the same unanimous alacrity characteristic of the other Soviet governmental organs. Nevertheless, the mass participation of people in administration seems to have engendered a high degree of identification with the regime, a political attitude not only encouraged but constantly reinforced by the incessant propoganda pronouncements of the Party. Constitutional provisions notwithstanding,* the autonomy of the local soviets is restricted not only by their direct accountability to the hierarchically superior soviets (acting through their respective executive organs) but also by the predominance of the Party.

The theoretical and legal bases of, and the elements of continuity and change in, Soviet local government are described by Professor Churchward. He shows that while the local soviets continue to rely on the "guidance" of the Party and the activities of a vast bureaucracy composed primarily of amateurish but loyal functionaries, they have also undergone a number of significant changes in recent years. Professor Churchward pays special attention to four of these changes: "increased popular participation in local government; greater insistence on socialist legality; reduction of the size of the administrative apparatus; and enlargement of the scope of local government activities, especially in the fields of industrial control and social services."

---

* For the constitutional provisions concerning the local organs of state power in the U.S.S.R., see Articles 94–101.

Local Organs of State Power

A. DENISOV AND M. KIRICHENKO

The local organs of state power in the U.S.S.R. are a component part of the Soviet state apparatus; they constitute the foundation of the unitary system of Soviet state organs. The unity of this system is based on the common aims and tasks of all Soviet state organs and on the unity of the political and economic structure of the Soviet state.

There are not, and cannot be any contradictions between local and central state organs in the Soviet state.

The Soviets of Working People's Deputies, as an aggregate of political institutions of the state, form a harmonious, democratically centralized system of organs of state power in the U.S.S.R.

The proper organization of the system of Soviets, the establishment of the proper relationship between them, the definition of their powers and delimitation of these powers between the various Soviets have always been an important and complex problem of Soviet state law. It is not fortuitous, therefore, that these problems occupy a prominent place in the Soviet constitutions, and in the decisions of the congresses and conferences of the Communist Party of the Soviet Union and of plenary meetings of its Central Committee.

In a speech to the Congress of the Chairmen of the Gubernia Soviets on July 30, 1918, Lenin emphasized that one of the essential features of the first Soviet Constitution was that it ". . . clarified the relation of the volost authorities to the authorities of the uyezds, of the uyezd authorities to those of the gubernias, and of the latter to the centre."

From *Soviet State Law* by A. Denisov and M. Kirichenko, selections from pp. 275–295. Moscow: Foreign Languages Publishing House, 1960.

This feature of the 1918 Constitution of the R.S.F.S.R. was of great importance in the early years of Soviet power, when the local authorities exhibited marked tendencies towards separatism. Lenin pointed out that, although as regards the desire for creative activity there was much common sense and good will in these tendencies, ". . . only constructive work which will be accomplished according to a large-scale general plan striving to utilize all economic values evenly can be worthy of being called socialist." At the same time Lenin stated that Soviet power in no way intended to belittle the role of the local authorities or to suppress their independence and initiative, especially because the peasantry, which was then the overwhelming majority of the population, also appreciated, as a result of its experience, the need for centralism.

The organizational and legal relationships and interconnections between the various Soviets, both central and local, were later regulated by the 1924 Constitution of the U.S.S.R. and by the corresponding Constitutions of the Union Republics.

These relationships are now governed by the 1936 Constitution of the U.S.S.R. and the Constitutions of the Union and Autonomous Republics. Local organs of state power have been set up and are functioning in Territories, Regions, Autonomous Regions, National Areas, Districts, cities and rural localities. The network of local organs of state power is extensive, their total number being about 60,000.

The local Soviets of Working People's Deputies, more than any other state organs, have the assistance of public-spirited citizens. For millions of working people they are good schools of state administration.

In addition to the many citizens directly participating in the work of the local Soviets and their standing commissions and executive organs, the general public have been drawn into various forms of public activity. Varied democratic institutions have been set up by the working people which give day-to-day assistance to the local organs of state power in the carrying out of their economic, cultural and political tasks.

These include street and block commissions of citizens, parents' commissions in the schools, the commissions which assist the system of state credit and savings banks, the commissions which help to organize public services and to plant greenery in towns

Figure 6. TERRITORIAL (REGIONAL) ORGANS OF STATE POWER AND ADMINISTRATION

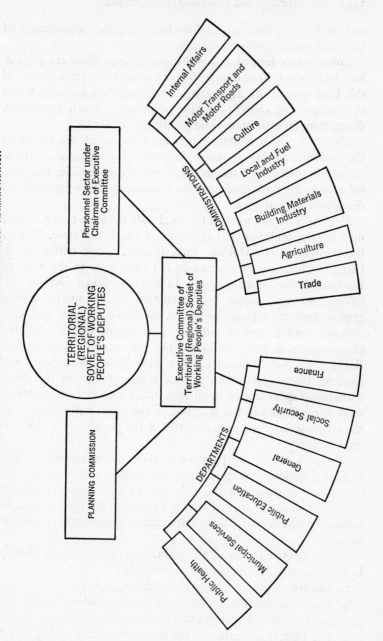

and settlements, the commissions furthering the development of trade and public catering and many others.

Commissions formed at house-management offices are particularly widespread. For example, in 1955 alone 2,263 commissions of this kind were set up in Moscow. Their members included scores of thousands of citizens—mostly people with much experience, drawn from different trades and different social strata.

The local organs of state power are those which are closest to the workers. Owing to their frequent re-constitution (accomplished by democratic means) they are highly flexible; this contributes to the rapid and effective elimination of all bureaucratic distortions in their work.

The structure and work of the local state organs is closely bound up with the multinational character of the Soviet state. Within the territory of the U.S.S.R. there is not a single nation or nationality whose representatives do not participate in the work of the local organs of state power. In every territorial division (including primary) where the population has its specific ethnographic features, all administrative, economic, cultural and educational work is carried out with due regard for the national characteristics of the population. The Autonomous Regions, National Areas and National Districts have their own national systems of state organs which include representatives of the given nations and nationalities. In all state institutions and organizations work is conducted in the language of the given nationality or in the language known to the majority of the population within the given territory.

The work of the local organs of state power throughout the U.S.S.R., beginning with villages and ending with Regions and Territories, is based on the principle of democratic centralism which underlies the work of all other organs of the Soviet state. As applied to the work of local state organs, democratic centralism means:

1. The elective nature of all local organs of state power directly by the people on broad democratic principles;

2. The accountability of lower to higher organs;

3. The all-round development of local initiative within the framework of the tasks confronting the body concerned;

4. The obligatory nature of the directives (acts) of higher for lower organs;

5. The extensive application of the principle of dual subordination in the system of executive bodies of the local Soviets. This ensures the harmonious combination of local interests with those of the state as a whole.

The local organs of state power are the supports of the central state organs: they translate into reality the directives of the Communist Party and of the higher organs of state power and state administration, not only in their own work and in the work of the subordinate organs, but also in the activity of all officials and citizens. Thus, within a given administrative and territorial division, the local state organs are the vehicles of socialist legality.

Local Soviets of Working People's Deputies

According to the 1936 Constitution of the U.S.S.R. and the Constitutions of the Union and Autonomous Republics, the local Soviets of Working People's Deputies are sovereign state organs acting within Territories, Regions, Autonomous Regions, National Areas, Districts, cities and rural localities (kishlaks, auls, etc.).

All these local Soviets are elected on the basis of universal, equal and direct suffrage by secret ballot for a term of two years.

The system of local organs of state power has been reconstituted seven times on the basis of the democratic principles of Soviet state law. In 1957 more than 1,500,000 deputies representing all strata of Soviet society were elected to local Soviets (Sixth Convocation) in all the Union Republics.

The basis of representation on local Soviets is established by the Constitutions of the Union and Autonomous Republics and is concretized by special Regulations Governing Elections. For example, according to the Constitution of the R.S.F.S.R. and the Regulations Governing Elections to Local Organs of State Power of the R.S.F.S.R., one deputy is elected to Territorial Soviets—for every 11,000–15,000 citizens (depending on the population of the given Territory); to Regional Soviets for every 8,000–30,000 citizens; to District Soviets for every 1,000 citizens (but not more than 60 deputies) if the population exceeds 35,000; Districts with a population of less than 35,000 elect 35 deputies. Deputies to City Soviets are elected on the basis of one deputy per 350 citizens (but not more than 250 deputies) if the population numbers from 12,000–100,000; in towns with a population of 100,000–150,000 elections are carried out on the basis of one deputy for every 400 citizens (however, not more than 300 deputies may be elected), etc. In Moscow and Leningrad one deputy is elected per 6,000 citizens; in towns with a population of less than 12,000 35 deputies are elected.

Elections to Village and Settlement Soviets are conducted on the following basis: on territories of village Soviets and settlements with a population of more than 1,500 citizens—one deputy for every 100 citizens (but not more than 35 deputies), while on territories of village Soviets and settlements with a population of less than 1,500 citizens 15 deputies are elected.

Today, when socialism has triumphed in the U.S.S.R. and when the country has entered upon a new and highly important stage in its development—the period of the comprehensive building of a communist society—it is necessary to make a number of amendments and additions to the Constitution of the U.S.S.R. reflecting the most substantial changes which have taken place in the country's political and economic life. In particular, today, when the activity of the masses of the people is continuously growing, the role of the Soviets of Working People's Deputies is becoming immeasurably greater. In order to improve the work of the Soviets, to strengthen their ties with the people, to raise Soviet democracy to a still higher level and to extend the participation of the working people in the work of the Soviets, the Supreme Soviets of the Union Republics have increased the number of deputies on the local Soviets (in the election campaign of March 1959) by nearly 350,000.

The local Soviets of Working People's Deputies function through their *sessions*. Under the terms of the Constitutions of the Union Republics, sessions of Territorial and Regional Soviets are convened not less than four times a year, sessions of District Soviets—not less than six times a year, and sessions of the Soviets of cities and rural localities—not less than once a month.*

The powers of the local Soviets are extensive and varied. According to Article 97 of the Constitution of the U.S.S.R., they direct local economic and cultural activity, draw up local budgets, ensure the maintenance of public order, the observance of Soviet laws

* According to recent decisions, in some Union Republics sessions of the Soviets of cities and rural localities are convened at least six times a year.

Figure 7. DISTRICT ORGANS OF STATE POWER AND ADMINISTRATION

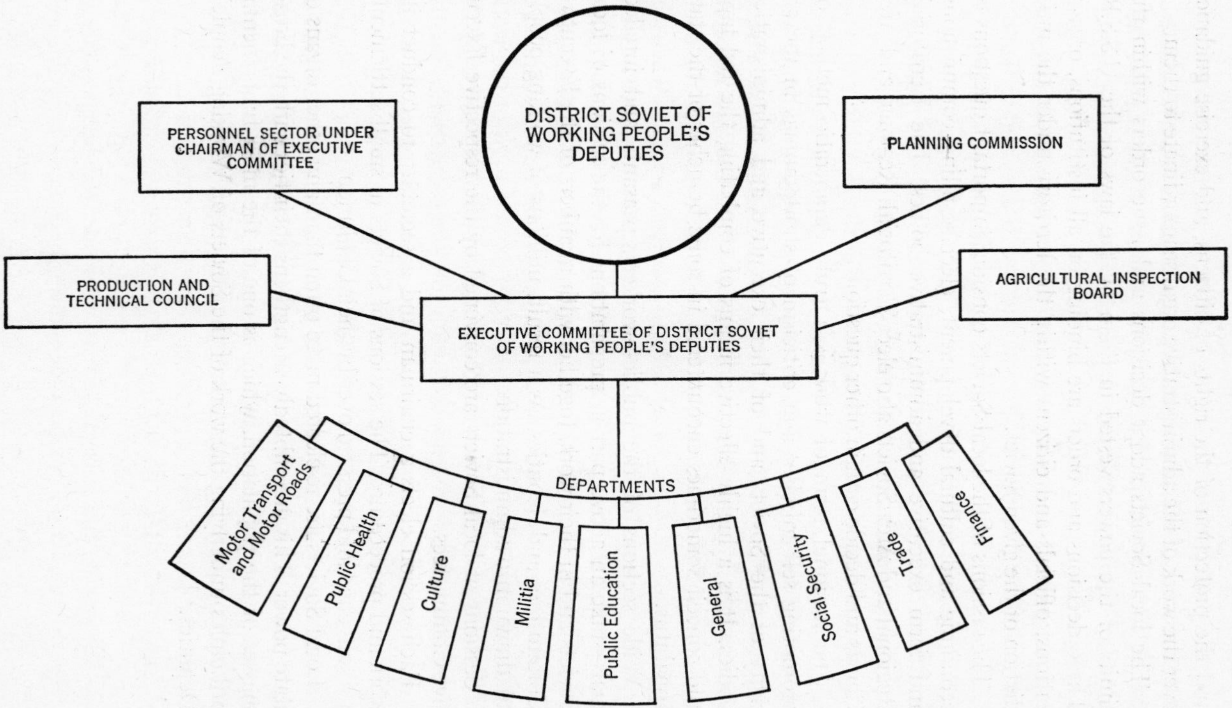

DISTRICT SOVIET OF WORKING PEOPLE'S DEPUTIES

PLANNING COMMISSION

AGRICULTURAL INSPECTION BOARD

PERSONNEL SECTOR UNDER CHAIRMAN OF EXECUTIVE COMMITTEE

PRODUCTION AND TECHNICAL COUNCIL

EXECUTIVE COMMITTEE OF DISTRICT SOVIET OF WORKING PEOPLE'S DEPUTIES

DEPARTMENTS

Finance

Trade

Social Security

General

Public Education

Militia

Culture

Public Health

Motor Transport and Motor Roads

and the protection of the rights of citizens, and exercise guidance over the work of the administrative organs subordinate to them.

The local Soviets adopt decisions and issue orders within the limits of the powers vested in them by the laws of the U.S.S.R. These decisions and orders are binding on all institutions, organizations, officials and citizens within the territory under the jurisdiction of the given Soviet.

The sessions of the local Soviets consider important questions of economic and cultural development, elect standing commissions, and form executive and administrative bodies. The Territorial, Regional and Area Soviets also elect Territorial, Regional and Area Courts and decide certain other questions.

The sessional form of work is a truly democratic method of promoting self-criticism and criticism of shortcomings in the activity of the Soviets and of their executive and administrative bodies. It is a highly effective means of combating the red tape and conceit sometimes encountered in some branches of the state apparatus.

Wide sections of the public—workers, peasants and intellectuals—take an active part in preparations for the sessions of local Soviets and in their work, together with members of the Executive Committees and deputies. As a result, millions of working people are drawn into administration.

Sessions of local Soviets are convened by the respective Executive Committees.

Each session elects a chairman and a secretary to conduct its work and proceedings. The sessions of Soviets in small settlements are convened and presided over by their Chairmen.

Local Soviets are re-elected more often than any other organs of state power. This undoubtedly strengthens their ties with the broad masses of the population, which is one of the most fundamental principles underlying the work of the Soviets of Working People's Deputies.

Continuity and Change in Soviet Local Government

L. G. CHURCHWARD[*]

Most Western writers on Soviet government ignore the role of local government organs. This attitude reflects their preoccupation with power structures, their concentration on the central policy-making organs of the party and state, and their belief that local organs are merely agencies for the carrying out of central policies and decisions. . . .

The Structure of Soviet Local Government

The concept of "local government" as it is used in the Soviet Union actually covers several levels of the administrative structure. All levels of government excepting the All-Union, Union Republic, and Autonomous Republic levels are included in the concept of local government as defined in the constitution of the U.S.S.R. (Chapter VIII). This means in effect that three levels of local government are included. The highest of these levels includes all administrative units which are directly subordinate to the Republic government: namely, the krais (territories, existing only

* Senior Lecturer in Political Science at the University of Melbourne, Professor Churchward is the editor of *The Australian Labor Movement, 1850–1907* (1960), and is the co-author of *Policy Making in the U.S.S.R., 1953–1961: Two Views* (1962). He is also the author of numerous scholarly articles and is currently completing a textbook on *Contemporary Soviet Government*.

From "Continuity and Change in Soviet Local Government" by L. G. Churchward, *Soviet Studies*, London, Vol. IX, No. 3, January 1958, selections from pp. 256–285, with the statistical figures on local Soviets revised to January 1, 1963 and a few minor changes made by the author. Reprinted by permission of the author, editors, and publisher, Basil Blackwell & Mott Ltd. For footnote references, see original source.

in the Russian Republic and Kazakhstan), oblasts (provinces), autonomous oblasts and national okrugs (areas), and the larger cities.

The second level of local government administration includes the rural and industrial raions (districts) and towns and cities of krai, oblast and autonomous oblast supervision.

The third level of local government includes village Soviets, settlement Soviets, city district Soviets and small town Soviets (those subject to district and city supervision).

At the beginning of 1963 there were 47,915 local Soviets—210 at the highest level, 2,720 at the intermediate level and 44,985 at the lowest level. Except in certain territories and provinces where separate industrial and agricultural Soviets operate, there is only one Soviet for each administrative unit.

Theoretical Basis of Soviet Local Government

One of the factors producing a neglect and underestimation of the role of Soviet local government by Western scholars is their use of Western standards of local government as criteria for evaluating the Soviet system and the consequent refusal to examine the theoretical basis of Soviet local government. Soviet writers list various principles of local government but they seldom present a complete statement of these principles. I would formulate these basic principles as follows:

1. Democratic centralism.
2. Direct election of all Soviets.
3. Recognition of nationality in the structure of local government.
4. Socialist planning of the economic and social development of the community.
5. Participation of the citizens in the actual process and work of government agencies.
6. Socialist legality in the work of the state apparatus.
7. Communist Party direction and leadership of all activities of local government.

These principles are basic to Soviet government at all levels, but before examining the work of Soviet local government agencies in recent years it will be necessary to see how these general principles apply to the specific field of local government.

The concept of "democratic centralism" has been copied in the Soviet state structure from the structure of the Communist Party. The extent to which local government organs serve to carry out central government decisions seems so alien to Western conceptions of the relationship between local and central government that many Western writers dismiss entirely the Soviet claim that they have local government. This difficulty of drawing the usual division between central and local government in the Soviet system reflects the principle of democratic centralism under which the entire government structure, from the highest to the lowest organs, is considered as forming one united system of state power, or, as it is often put, all government organs are links in one continuous chain of state power. Under this system the local organs of state power are not and are not intended to be law making agencies in the full sense of the term. They act more as directing agencies for the central government. Local Soviets may take decisions, including obligatory decisions, but these will be designed to fulfil central government policy, for example, in housing construction or in crop expansion. Local Soviets may collect auxiliary revenue from local taxes but the types and amounts of the taxes, and often the uses to which such income may be put, are laid down by the central government. In conformity with the principles of democratic centralism higher organs of government may direct lower organs and Executives of lower Soviets are responsible not only to their Soviet but to the Executive Committee of the next higher Soviet. Thus the Executive Committee of a village Soviet is responsible both to the village Soviet and to the *raiispolkom* (Executive Committee of Raion Soviet). The raiispolkom is responsible not merely to the raion Soviet but also to the *Oblispolkom* (Executive Committee of Oblast Soviet), and so on. Not only may lower Soviets and the Executive Committees be directed and overruled by higher Soviets (and their Executive Committees) but the departments of the Executive Committee of a lower Soviet may be directed by the relevant department of a higher Executive. Thus the educational department of a raiispolkom may be directed or overruled by the educational department of the oblispolkom. Representatives of higher Soviet Executive Committees (or their departments) often take part in the proceedings of lower Soviets. Thus the instructors belonging to the Organizational-Instructional Department of the Oblispolkom usually attend meetings of the raion Soviets under their supervision, while members of the raiispolkom frequently sit in on village Soviet meetings.

The second principle, the direct election of all Soviets and all Executive Committees, is a development in the Soviet system only since 1936. Since the elections of 1939 all local government elections have been direct elections. Citizens have voted for all levels of local government at the one time on the basis of universal adult (over 18 years) suffrage and single-member electorates of varying size according to the level of Soviet being elected. Elections to all levels of local government are held every two years. All local Soviets elect their chairman, deputy-chairmen, secretary and members of the Executive Committee at the first Soviet meeting after the election. Soviets also elect the members of their Standing Commissions, although the Executive Committee and not the Soviet elects the members of the Departments of the Executive Committee.

The recognition of nationality as a criterion for governmental administration is taken further in the Soviet Union than in any western country. Not only are national groupings given a graded representation in the Supreme Soviet (within the Soviet of Nationalities) but national groupings where they exist are recognized as sufficiently important to provide the basis of government at all levels down to the level of local government, for the Soviet constitution provides not only for Union Republics and Autonomous Republics but for Autonomous Oblasts (Provinces) and National Okrugs (Areas). Both Union Republics and Autonomous Republics have their own constitutions and Supreme Soviets; both autonomous oblasts and national okrugs are directly responsible to the Republic government and are not legally subordinate to any other division of local government, such as an oblast or a krai Soviet. At the present time there are 20 Autonomous Republics, 8 Autonomous Oblasts, and 10 National Okrugs in the U.S.S.R.

Socialist planning is fundamental to Soviet society and it is the fulcrum of the entire activity of the local Soviets and their Executive organs. The local Soviets give substance to the general economic plan, the perspectives of which are prepared by the higher central government and the details of which are filled in as they reach nearer to the point of execution. The local plan, which is merely a section of the national plan for economic and cultural development, provides the basis for all the decisions and all the organizing of the local Soviet. To fulfil this plan all sections of local government, Executive Committees, departments and boards, standing commissions, etc. are required to work strictly to annual, quarterly, and monthly plans. Because of this the key departments in the structure of any local government are inevitably the Budget Department and the Planning Commission.

The principle of the participation of the citizens in the actual work of government was hailed by Lenin in 1918 as one of the distinguishing characteristics and advantages of the Soviet system of government. The point was frequently re-emphasized by Stalin, for example in 1925 when he said that

> The Soviet state structure does not consist only of Soviets. The Soviet state structure, in the deepest meaning of these words, consists of the Soviets plus millions in organizations, uniting in each and all non-party and party people, binding the Soviets with the deepest 'roots', merging the government apparatus with the masses, and destroying step by step every barrier between government apparatus and population.

Whatever the value of such a measure as a check on bureaucracy or even as an expression of democracy there is no gainsaying the fact that many millions are actively engaged in working in or assisting local government. Thus there are nearly 2 million deputies of local Soviets, plus 2½ million 'activists' serving on more than 250,000 standing commissions of local Soviets, and many millions assisting in the work of street committees, parents' committees, etc., not to mention 6 millions serving on the election commissions which supervise the actual conduct of the elections. The high turn-over of deputies helps to extend the percentage of the Soviet public with experience in the actual work of local government. It is still characteristic of Soviet local government, as it was in the thirties, that it depends far less than most western countries on the skilled specialist and far more on the enthusiasm of masses of amateurs.

The principle of socialist legality means more than conformity to the letter of the law. It insists that Soviet government organs must act in the interests of Soviet socialist society and defend the dictatorship of the working class. . . .

The principle of Communist Party leadership in the local Soviets, as in the state generally, is frequently acknowledged in broad terms but is seldom examined concretely by Soviet authors. Very few Soviet writers go into detail on this question. In fact, the party and state structures at the level of local government, as at the centre, are closely inter-linked. Party directives are sometimes issued direct to local Soviets, without the usual procedure of being issued jointly by the Central Committee of the CPSU and the Council of Ministers (or the Presidium) of the Supreme Soviet. At the level of the raion the first secretary of the *raikom* (raion party committee) is usually a member of the *raiispolkom*, and in fact the two Executive Committees, party and state, are usually housed in the same building. Party meetings anticipate and guide the work of the village Soviet, the raion Soviet and the oblast Soviet, and they prepare slates of candidates for the election of the Executive Committees. It would seem that, at least in many rural raions, it is the raikom rather than the raiispolkom that really constitutes the agency of local govenment.

Legal Basis of Soviet Local Government

The legal basis of Soviet local government is unusually complex since it consists not merely of sections of the constitution of the U.S.S.R. and the Republics, but of acts, decrees, and decisions of the central government, directives of the Central Committee of the CPSU, and decisions of higher levels of local government. . . .

Continuity in Soviet Local Government

It is necessary to emphasize at the outset the elements of continuity in the system which provide the framework within which the system is changing.

The first and decisive factor of stability in the system of Soviet local government is its continued control by the Communist Party.

This factor alone marks Soviet local government off as distinct from what we know in the west, in Britain, the United States or in Australia. The element of inter-party struggle which occurs in most capitalist states even when the ideal of 'no-partisanship in local politics' is most revered, is totally lacking in the Soviet Union. The whole purpose, and certainly the reality of the election system, is not to choose persons holding different views from those of the Communist Party but simply to strengthen Communist leadership in the local Soviets by the election of active non-party people who fully accept the leadership and politics of the Communist Party. Although the electoral law itself would seem to allow for choice by the voter between several candidates, the practice of the ballot reduces that choice to the alternative of supporting or not supporting the single official candidate. Nor is there any sign that this practice is likely to be modified in the immediate future. . . .

A second element of continuity in the system is the continuity of the principle of 'democratic centralism'. Notwithstanding certain definite increases in local autonomy the local Soviets are still primarily agencies for carrying out central government and party policy in the localities. . . .

A third element of continuity in the Soviet local government system is that of bureaucratic practices. Indeed bureaucracy and red tape would seem to be endemic in the Soviet governmental structure. In part this may result from the complexity and the depth of the administrative structure. The Soviet villager may well have four or five levels of government—village, raion, oblast and Republic—between himself and the central government. Such a network is a paradise for the buck-shoving local official and a source of perennial exasperation for the ordinary citizen who is apt to find that a simple request such as the application for a tax reduction, made to the local Soviet, is referred two steps up the administrative ladder and is lost for months or even years, or if it is granted locally is countermanded some months later by the oblispolkom. Then again, the insistence on regular checking of decisions and supervision of public money and property and on plan fulfilment has put a premium on book work and book-keepers and has fostered excessive red tape. This bureaucracy and red tape in local government has been sharply criticized in recent years and the criticism has produced countless examples in the Soviet press which seem lifted directly out of the pages of Gogol. . . .

Fourthly, and this may sound surprising in view of the above, Soviet local government continues to rely very largely on amateurs. The whole system of Soviet local government could not work were it not for the enthusiastic and active assistance which millions of Soviet citizens give to the 2 million members of local Soviets. . . .

Change in Soviet Local Government

If so much of the old pre-war structure of local government continues, what precisely has changed in recent years? I would suggest that at least four important changes are in process at the moment: increased popular participation in local government; greater insistence on socialist legality; reduction of the size of the administrative apparatus; and enlargement of the scope of local government activities, especially in the fields of industrial control and social services.

Increased popular participation is evident in many aspects of Soviet local government work. The material published in the Soviet press reveals this. Whereas the material published in the early post-war years (up to about 1952) concentrated mainly on explaining the role of local Soviets, the powers of Standing Commissions, the relationships between Executive Committees and Soviets, the conduct of Soviet meetings, etc., the material published since 1952, both at the editorial level and in contributions by the public and by experts, has been increasingly critical of the shortcomings of local government. It is reflected in the increased interest on the part of citizens in the local elections and in the activities of local government. Whereas a decade ago it was sometimes difficult for agitators even in the larger cities to fill their meetings, the main problem now in some areas at least is to find halls sufficiently large to hold the attendance. It is evident in the increased attention being given by local Soviets to the regular reporting back of deputies to their electors. . . .

The concept of socialist legality which is now regarded by Soviet writers as a basic principle in the operation of the government system, was until recently more honoured in the breach than in the observance. In the days of collectivization drive and even more during the war years and the years of frantic reconstruction that followed, the stress in local government organization was on achievement rather than on the process of achievement. In these years the man who gained recognition was the man who produced results. . . .

The present drive for socialist legality in the function of local government is also reflected in the increasing activity of local divisions of the Procurator's office in protesting against illegal acts on the part of local government and economic agencies. . . .

The campaign for socialist legality in the work of local government organs has also been taken up by the Soviets themselves. City and oblast Soviets have discussed the problem in their sessions and organized their deputies and activists to carry out mass explanatory work in the raions. Members of the local Soviets are becoming increasingly alert to detect and protest against any illegal actions on the part of their Executive or any interference with their rights of electing their Executive by a higher Soviet Executive Committee. During 1955 the Presidium of the Supreme Soviet of the RSFSR adopted a decree 'Concerning Instances of Violation of Socialist Legality in the Work of Local Soviet Executive Committees in the Russian Republic', which directed local Soviets and Executives to a closer effort at acting within the limits of Soviet law, and on the basis of which specific oblast Executive Committees have been directed to eliminate shortcomings of local government organs within their territory.

Yet another indication of the strengthening of the demand for socialist legality on the part of local government organs is the frequent demand for legal clarification of local Soviet powers. . . .

The reduction in the numbers serving in the local govermental apparatus has developed since 1954 as a response to the demand of the central government. Khrushchev reported to the XX Congress a reduction in the size of the Soviet administrative and managerial apparatus of practically 750,000 persons. The bulk of this reduction, no doubt, was at the central and Republican levels, but the structure of local government, right down to the raion level, was clearly affected. Throughout the Moscow Oblast the administrative structure was reduced by 5 per cent in 1955 and by a further 10 per cent in 1956, and this figure may be taken as fairly typical of the extent of reduction in local government administrative structure throughout the country. This reduction has been brought about mainly by the streamlining of the existing apparatus, eliminating obvious overlapping in departments and in some cases by the abolition of unnecessary divisions in the local government structure (as by the merging of adjoining raions). Duplication of departments frequently existed at places where two levels of local government organization happened to be situated, as for example in towns which had a town Soviet (responsible to the oblispolkom) and were at the same time the centre of a rural raion administration; or where a raion and an oblast administration were centred in the same town. . . .

The final change that has occurred in Soviet local government over recent years is the enlargement of its scope. The most significant increase in local government powers has been in relation to industrial supervision. The early phases in the recent industrial decentralization program did not have any major impact on the industrial powers of local Soviets. During 1954–55 over 11,000 industrial establishments were transferred from All-Union to Republican control. The only change to local government powers at this time was the granting to local Soviets in 1955 of the right to amalgamate or separate local industrial establishments. In a few of the larger cities, Leningrad and Tashkent for example, several constructional agencies were transferred from Ministries and consolidated into Construction Trusts under the control of the City Soviet. The second phase in this program (May 1956—May 1957), which saw the transfer of a further large group of enterprises to the control of the Republics, this time accompanied by a major reconstruction of the industrial Ministries, did not greatly increase the industrial powers of local Soviets.

The third phase in the industrial decentralization program, the dissolution of most of the industrial Ministries and the establishment of the Sovnarkhozy, has certainly extended the industrial competency of local governments, especially at the oblast level. . . .

Most of the industrial establishments released by the dissolution of the industrial Ministries were handed over to the control of the Sovnarkhozy. In Russia in June 1957 the Sovnarkhozy controlled 75 per cent of all industry, while in Moldavia they controlled 73 per cent. But a considerable number of industrial establishments of local significance were transferred to the control of local Soviets. . . .*

The increased industrial power of local Soviets is closely linked with other recent extensions in their powers, especially with their newly enlarged responsibility for public housing in their areas and with the present drive for housing construction that is going on in the larger cities throughout the U.S.S.R. And local Soviets are doing more and more to meet the cultural and material needs of the Soviet people.

Perhaps also connected with the new industrial powers of local Soviets are the proposals (already law in some Republics) to give local Soviets the power to expel from their territory any persons capable of work who refuse to work. These proposals, which would seem to grant quasi-judicial powers to the local Soviets, have been criticized by some lawyers in the U.S.S.R. but they seem to have the approval of most local Soviets.

The most significant development of the police powers of local Soviets was the merging in March 1957 of the administration of the Ministry of Internal Affairs and the regional and territorial militia and the placing of these departments under the control of the Executive Committees of the Krai and Oblast Soviets, as well as under the supervision of the central Ministry. The reform not merely strengthened the powers of local Soviets but allowed for a considerable reduction of staff in the police departments throughout the U.S.S.R. . . .

It is likely that the recent increase in industrial responsibilities of local Soviets will soon be followed by further increases in their financial powers. . . .

The Dynamic of Change in Soviet Local Government

In conclusion, I should like to raise the question of why these changes are occurring in Soviet local government at the present time.

How far are they connected with the death of Stalin? It cannot be argued that the changes began in March 1953, since they were already discernible during 1952 and even earlier. The most that

* Ed. note: See note, pp. 326–327.

can be said is that Stalin's death intensified the process since it allowed for a much more thorough-going campaign for socialist legality, collective leadership and extended democracy in local government. The criticism of individual leadership at the level of local Soviets and local party organs developed very sharply in the years after 1953, especially at the hands of writers such as Ehrenburg, Nikolayeva, Ovechkin, and others. That the Central Committee campaign for industrial decentralization and broader powers for local government, which developed after 1954, was met with some opposition within the ranks of the Communist Party itself is clear not only from the admissions of the Central Committee in July 1957 but also from the contributions to the public debate on the 30th March theses and to other reports in the Soviet press.

Various other theses might be advanced to explain recent changes in Soviet local government. However, it seems to me that the basic factor producing these changes—changes which have been supervised and controlled throughout by the party leadership—is the dynamic of economic development. By 1950 the Soviet economy had largely made good the war losses and the volume of industrial production was well above the level of 1940. Each year since 1950 has seen significant gains in the industrial strength and maturity of the Soviet economic system and this economic maturity produced at once the necessity for and the confidence required to make significant changes in the Soviet political and administrative structure. The connection between changes in material economic conditions and modifications in the administrative structure is very clear. Thus the consolidation of the collective farms in 1950, a consolidation produced primarily by economic considerations, was followed a few years later by the consolidation of the village Soviets, the essence of which was a restoration (although incomplete) of a harmony between the basic economic unit in the countryside and the lowest level governmental unit, the village Soviet. Similarly, the redistribution of responsibility between the rural raion and the MTS (1953–55) was simply an administrative recognition of the economic facts of kolkhoz life, namely that the MTS, because of its economic relationship and proximity of the kolkhoz, was in a much better position to direct kolkhoz production than the Agricultural Department of the Raiispolkom. Again, the determination of the

Soviet government (since 1954) to reduce the size of its governmental apparatus at all levels is also at basis a response to the
growing shortage of skilled labour in both agricultural and industrial production, a shortage that is primarily due to the losses
sustained by the U.S.S.R. during the recent war.

The establishment of the Economic Regional Councils was
primarily designed to bring the organization of administration of
industry closer to the industrial enterprises and plants, and to
promote industrial efficiency. As has already been noted, the establishment of the Regional Economic Councils was accompanied by
a significant expansion of the industrial competency of local
Soviets. It is also very clear that the main pressure for modification
of the top-level pattern of Soviet local administration is provided
by the Sovnarkhozy. The pressure is already on for bringing the
political administrative structure into line with the economic
administrative structure. . . .

Finally, the economic maturing of Soviet industry since about
1950 has made it possible for the first time in the history of the
U.S.S.R. for the Soviet government to place emphasis on the
production of consumer goods. Although the priority of investment into capital goods industry over investment into consumer
goods industry is still held as an immutable part of Marxian economics, the gap between these two broad types of investment is
narrowing. This increased emphasis on consumer goods industry is
the economic basis for the extension of the number of economic
establishments controlled by local Soviets, for a high proportion of
consumer goods industries are classified as local industry whereas
most capital goods industry cannot be classified as local industry.
Consequently as the curve of consumer goods goes up in future
years so the present distribution of industry between Sovnarkhozy
and local Soviets will tend to alter in favour of local Soviets,
though it is unlikely that they will control a greater amount of
industry than the Sovnarkhozy in the conceivable future. As has
already been stated, the increased control by local Soviets over
local industry, especially over construction agencies, means that for
the first time since industrialization the local Soviets have effective
control over housing and social welfare construction programmes.
This extension of local Soviet activities in particular has been
responsible for the increased interest of Soviet citizens in the

process of local government. This public demand for more results in terms of houses, hospitals, schools, transport, water supply and sewerage, consumer goods, etc., has itself become a potent factor in the present trend towards enlarged powers and more local initiative in local government, towards more democracy and less centralism. In Marxist terms the superstructure of local government is being modified by changes in the economic basis of society, and the changing superstructure of government apparatus and public opinion is reacting on the economic basis itself.

· 4 ·

LAW AND JUSTICE IN THE U.S.S.R.

According to Marxist-Leninist theory, the legal institutions of any given society are but the superstructural manifestations of the realities of the economic base determined by the prevailing modes of production and distribution. Law and justice in this respect are considered as instruments in the hands of the dominating class, that is, the class which controls the economic base.

Ever since the establishment of the U.S.S.R., law has been conceived as a major instrument for achieving the goals outlined by the Communist Party. It has been used not only as a device for the attainment of "socialist justice" but also as a primary means of educating the Soviet people and for molding their conduct, character and "socialist morality." "Socialist justice" is viewed as one of the most effective tools for the training of Soviet citizens "in the spirit of patriotism and loyalty to the cause of Communism."

From the constitutional point of view,* the Soviet judicial organs are obliged to safeguard the social and political structure of the "socialist" state, the personal and property rights of citizens and the interests of state and public institutions. The "democratic bases" of Soviet law and justice, according to the Third Program of the Communist Party of the Soviet Union, are assured by the "election and accountability of the judges and people's assessors, the right to recall them before expiration of their term, publicity of court proceedings, and participation of social prosecutors and

---

* For the constitutional provisions concerning the administration of justice in the U.S.S.R. and the courts and the procurator's office, see Articles 102–117.

defenders in the work of the courts, with the courts and investigating and prosecuting bodies strictly observing legality and all procedural norms."

The nature of "socialist justice" and the mechanics and institutional structure of the Soviet judiciary are described from the Soviet point of view by A. Denisov and M. Kirichenko.

The character and significance of the legal reforms inaugurated in the post-Stalin era are reviewed in the following article by Professor Berman of the Harvard Law School. The coexistence of law and terror that characterized the Stalin regime of the mid-1930's has gradually been overshadowed by the law reform movement which began in 1953. This movement, according to Professor Berman, "may prove to have been the most significant aspect of Soviet social, economic, and political development in the decade after Stalin's death." He presents a composite picture of Soviet law reforms by depicting the major tendencies that characterized them.

In their drive to tone down, if not completely eliminate, the Stalinist dualism of law and terror, the successors of Stalin established a more humane and rational legal system which undoubtedly produced a more tolerant political climate. Nevertheless, as Professor Berman points out,

> the Soviet legal system remained Stalinist in its basic structure and its basic purposes. The organization and functions of lawmaking, law-enforcing, and law-practicing agencies—of the legislature, the Procuracy, the courts, the administrative organs, the bar—were not essentially different ten years later from what they were when Stalin died. . . .
>
> Also, if one looks behind the structure to the purposes of Soviet law, it remained a totalitarian law, in the sense that it sought to regulate all aspects of economic and social life. . . . It remained the law of a one-party state. It remained the law of a planned economy. It remained a law whose primary function is to discipline, guide, train, and educate Soviet citizens to be dedicated members of a collectivized and mobilized social order.

The Soviet Administration of Justice:
The Courts and the Procurator's Office

A. DENISOV AND M. KIRICHENKO

The courts and the Procurator's Office with their own particular forms of work are designed to protect socialist legality and socialist law and order. . . .

The judicial organs administering socialist justice and the Procurator's Office vested with supervisory power to ensure the strict observance of the law are obliged to safeguard:

1) the social and state system of the U.S.S.R. enacted by the Constitution of the U.S.S.R. and by the Constitutions of the Union and Autonomous Republics, as well as the socialist system of economy and socialist property;

2) the political, labour, housing and other personal and property rights and interests guaranteed to citizens by the Constitution of the U.S.S.R. and Constitutions of the Union and Autonomous Republics;

3) the rights and interests of state institutions, enterprises, collective farms, co-operative and other public organizations protected by the law.

Justice in the U.S.S.R. is designed to ensure the strict observance of the laws by all institutions, organizations, officials and citizens of the U.S.S.R. . . .

Socialist Justice and Its Fundamental Tasks

Soviet justice has from the very first days of its existence made an important contribution to the formation and consolidation of

From *Soviet State Law* by A. Denisov and M. Kirichenko, selections from pp. 300–318. Moscow: Foreign Languages Publishing House, 1960.

the socialist system of society and to the successful accomplishment of the tasks of the proletarian dictatorship.

Socialist justice educates Soviet citizens in the spirit of patriotism and loyalty to the cause of communism, in the spirit of strict adherence to the Soviet Constitution and Soviet laws. It inculcates solicitude and concern for socialist property, strict labour discipline, an honest attitude towards their duties to the state and society and respect for the rules of socialist intercourse. By imposing penalties on offenders, the Soviet court strives not only to punish them, but also to reform and re-educate.

Judicial power is a form of state power. "The court is an organ of power," wrote Lenin. "This is sometimes forgotten by the liberals. But a Marxist commits a sin if he forgets it." In his work *The Immediate Tasks of the Soviet Government*, Lenin pointed out that judicial work was one of the functions of state administration. But at the same time he stressed that this activity should be clearly distinguished from the work of the organs of state administration.

"We need a state," Lenin said, "we need compulsion. It is the Soviet courts which must serve as organs of the proletarian state effecting such compulsion." The specific feature of the courts, as distinct from other organs of the socialist state, is that they administer justice. This means that a court, before pronouncing its decision (i.e., before it acquits the defendant or inflicts a penalty upon him, before it rejects a claim or satisfies it) tries the case according to the law and to the existing legal rules. In other words, it considers criminal and civil cases in accordance with the procedure laid down by the law and decides them on the basis of operative legal rules.

The Organs of Socialist Justice

The court of the socialist state is a system of bodies entrusted with the administration of socialist justice.

In general, the Soviet system of judicial bodies corresponds to the form of state structure in the U.S.S.R. and to the administrative and territorial division of the Union and Autonomous Republics.

The following organs administer justice in the Soviet Union: the Supreme Court of the U.S.S.R., the Supreme Courts of the

Union and Autonomous Republics, the Territorial, Regional and City Courts, the Courts of the Autonomous Regions and National Areas, the District (City) People's Courts and Military Tribunals.

The strict definition of their *jurisdiction*, i.e., of the range of cases which come within the powers of the given institution, is of great importance to the proper functioning of judicial bodies.

The entire system is divided into courts of first instance and courts of second instance. The former include those which directly hear criminal and civil cases. Such cases are tried in courts consisting of a judge and two people's assessors. The courts of second instance hear appeals and protests against judgements and sentences pronounced by lower courts. The hearing of these appeals and protests is conducted by courts consisting of three members. The courts of second instance also function as courts of first instance when trying cases of which they are given jurisdiction by the law.

The main link of the judicial system of the socialist state is the *People's Court*, which tries most of the criminal and civil cases. It functions only as a judicial body of first instance.

As distinct from the People's Courts, the Regional, Territorial Courts, the Courts of the Autonomous Regions and National Areas, and the Supreme Courts of the Union and Autonomous Republics perform the functions not only of courts of first instance directly trying cases, but also of courts of second instance hearing appeals against sentences and judgements of lower courts. Each of these courts consist of a civil collegium, a criminal collegium, and a Presidium.

The Supreme Court of a Union Republic is its highest judicial organ. As a court of first instance, it tries cases with the participation of a presiding judge and two people's assessors. As a court of second instance, it exercises its supervisory functions with the participation of three members of the court or the Presidium.

The highest judicial organ of the U.S.S.R. is the Supreme Court of the U.S.S.R. It supervises the judicial activities of the judicial organs of the U.S.S.R. and of the Union Republics within the limits established by the Statute on the Supreme Court of the U.S.S.R. endorsed by the Supreme Soviet of the U.S.S.R. on February 12, 1957. The Supreme Court of the U.S.S.R. is vested with the right to initiate legislation. . . .

The Soviet judicial organs are elected and perform their functions in conformity with the general principles of socialist democracy.

The democratic character of the Soviet judicial system manifests itself, above all, in the fact that the courts are elected organs. The people's judges are elected on the basis of universal, direct and equal suffrage by secret ballot for a term of five years. Every eligible citizen who has reached the age of twenty-five may be elected a people's judge or people's assessor. People's assessors are elected by meetings of working people at their places of work or residence for a term of 2 years.

The Soviet people elect those who have not only the formal, but also the moral right to administer justice.

The Supreme Court of the U.S.S.R. is elected by the Supreme Soviet of the U.S.S.R., and the Supreme Courts of the Union and Autonomous Republics by the Supreme Soviets of these Republics. The Courts of Territories, Regions, Cities, Autonomous Regions and National Areas are elected by the respective Soviets of Working People's Deputies. All these judicial bodies are elected for a term of five years.

The institution of *people's assessors* has been inherent in the Soviet court from the very first days of its existence. This institution is established by Article 103 of the Constitution of the U.S.S.R.: "In all courts cases are tried with the participation of people's assessors, except in cases specially provided for by law."

The people's assessors perform their duties in rotation and have the rights of judges when the court is sitting. Factory and office workers functioning as people's assessors are paid their normal wages during the whole term of their service in the court. In all other cases expenses connected with their performance of their duties are paid for in the manner laid down by the laws of the Union Republics.

The democratic character of the Soviet judicial system is also manifest in the right of the electors to *recall* any judge or people's assessor *prior to the expiry of their term of office*, and also in the fact that the people's judges are *accountable* to their electors for their work and for the work of their respective courts.

Along with the elective nature of the courts and the participation of people's assessors in the hearing of cases, the organization and activity of the Soviet judicial institutions are based on the constitutional democratic principle that *judges are independent and subject only to the law*. . . .

The equality of all citizens before the court is another constitutional democratic principle underlying the Soviet judicial system. The Soviet court applies the same criminal, civil and procedural legislation to all citizens of the U.S.S.R.

One of the principles of socialist justice embodied in the Constitution of the U.S.S.R., is *the public character of all court proceedings*. This means that the general public have free access to the courtrooms, where civil and criminal cases are tried in public. Thus, the work of the courts is placed under the control of the citizens. This assists the struggle of the working people for the strengthening of socialist legality and socialist law and order.

The Constitution of the U.S.S.R. grants the accused the *right to defence*. In order to ensure this right, an institution of advocates has been set up in the country.

Representatives of public organizations may also be allowed to participate in court hearings as defenders.

Finally, the democratism of the Soviet court is characterized by the fact that *judicial proceedings are conducted in the language* of the population of the given Union or Autonomous Republic, or Autonomous Region. . . .

The Soviet Procurator's Office

. . . The Statute on the Supreme Court of the U.S.S.R. adopted shortly after the formation of the Soviet Union set up the post of Procurator of the Supreme Court of the U.S.S.R., appointed by the Presidium of the Central Executive Committee of the U.S.S.R. The practice of building socialism, however, necessitated a further strengthening of legality. Hence, on June 20, 1933, the Central Executive Committee and the Council of People's Commissars of the U.S.S.R. passed a decision on the establishment of the Procurator's Office of the U.S.S.R. as an independent state organ. According to this decision, the Procurator-General of the U.S.S.R. was charged with the following functions: a) to see that orders and regulations issued by official bodies of the U.S.S.R., the Union Republics and local authorities are consistent with the Con-

Figure 8. SYSTEM OF ELECTIONS TO JUDICIAL ORGANS OF THE U.S.S.R.

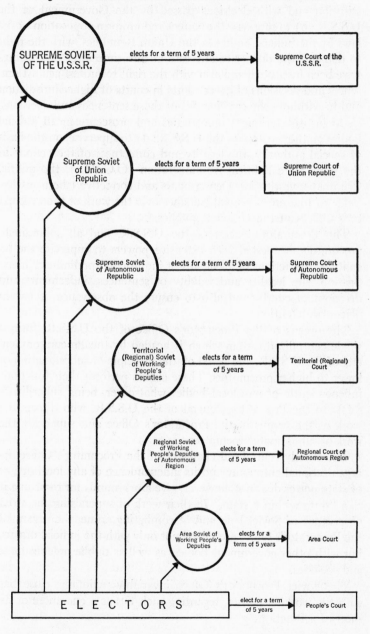

stitution and with decisions passed by the Government of the U.S.S.R.; b) to supervise the correct and uniform application of the laws by the judicial bodies of the Union Republics, with the right to demand the dossier of any case at any time after proceedings have been instituted, and also with the right to protest against sentences and decisions of lower courts in courts of higher jurisdiction and to withhold the carrying out of those sentences and decisions; c) to institute criminal proceedings and prosecute in all judicial bodies on the territory of the U.S.S.R.; d) to supervise, on the basis of special authority, the legality and correctness of the actions of the Joint State Political Administration (O.G.P.U.), the militia, Criminal Investigation Departments and corrective labour institutions; e) to exercise general guidance over the work of the Procurator's Offices of the Union Republics. . . .

The Procurator-General of the U.S.S.R. and all subordinate procurators are vested with extensive powers to supervise the legality of the actions of all organs of inquiry and preliminary investigation, the legality and validity of sentences, judgements and decisions of courts, and also to ensure the observance of law in places of detention.

The organs of the Procurator's Office of the U.S.S.R. form a single centralized system which is headed by the Procurator-General of the U.S.S.R. and based on the principle of subordination of lower to higher procurators. These organs perform their functions independently of any local bodies whatsoever, being subordinate solely to the Procurator-General of the U.S.S.R. who directs the work of the organs of the Procurator's Office and supervises the work of subordinate procurators. . . .

The strictly centralized character of the Procurator's Office, its organizational autonomy and its independence of any local organs of state power does not, however, give any grounds for regarding it as a "state within a state." In their work of supervising the strict observance of Soviet laws and of combating crime, the organs of the Procurator's Office are linked not only with the judicial organs, but with other government bodies, as well as public organizations and societies.

The Soviet Procurator's Office invariably maintains close ties with the working masses, regarding such ties as a guarantee of its successful functioning.

Figure 9. ORGANS OF THE PROCURATOR'S OFFICE OF THE U.S.S.R.

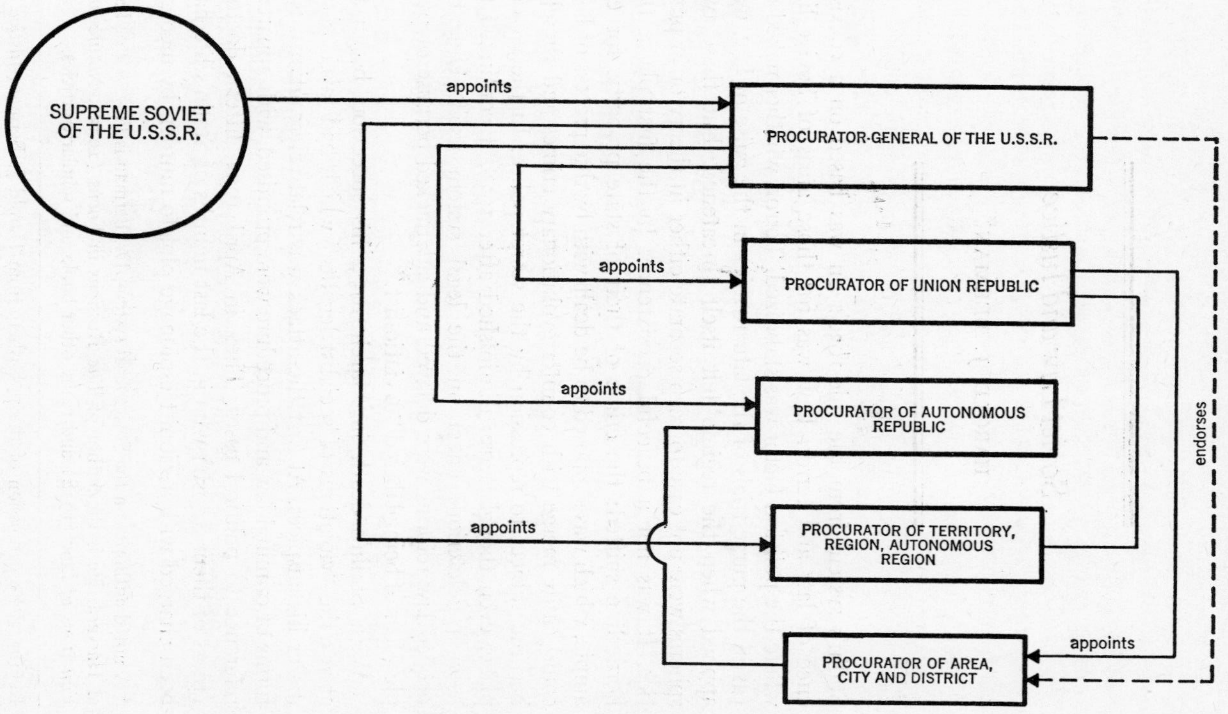

Soviet Law and Justice

HAROLD J. BERMAN[*]

Stalin's system from the mid-1930's on was based on a coexistence of law and terror. Law was for those areas of Soviet life where the political factor was stabilized. Terror, whether naked or (as in the purge trials of the late 1930's) in the guise of law, was applied when the regime felt itself threatened. But these two spheres were not easy to keep separate either in theory or in practice. It was not a peaceful coesixtence. In the first place, the borderline shifted: the crime of theft of state property, for example, which was supposed to be dealt with by due process of law, could easily merge with counterrevolutionary crimes and thereby become subject to repression by the secret police. In the second place, even though terror diminished after 1938, it continued to have a deleterious effect on the legal system itself. Urgently needed law reforms were delayed and sidetracked because of people's fear of being labeled "deviationist."

With Stalin's death in March 1953, his successors began to attack the "violations of socialist legality" which had taken place under his auspices. At first the attack was relatively cautious. Reforms of criminal law and procedure were promised, with apparent reference to political cases. Then in April 1953, fifteen doctors (most of them Jewish) who in the last months of Stalin's life had been charged with a Zionist espionage plot to murder, by medical

[*] A noted authority on the Soviet legal system, Dr. Berman is Professor of Law at Harvard. He is the author of *The Russians in Focus* (1953), *Nature and Functions of Law* (1958) and many other books and scholarly articles.

Reprinted by permission of the publishers from Harold J. Berman, *Justice in the U.S.S.R.: An Interpretation of Soviet Law*, pp. 66–96. Cambridge, Mass.: Harvard University Press. Copyright, 1959, 1963, by The President and Fellows of Harvard College. For footnote references, see original source.

means, a whole series of top Soviet leaders, were exonerated, and leading security officials were charged with "impermissible procedures" in extorting confessions from them. The exposure of the "Doctors' Plot," which some have supposed Stalin had trumped up as a signal for a new wave of purges, was accompanied by articles in the press proclaiming the "inviolability" of Soviet law. After the arrest of Beria in July 1953, some of the excesses of Stalinist terror were attributed not to the dictator, but to his chief of secret police. This deception gradually wore thin, however, and in February 1956 N. S. Khrushchev, who a year earlier had succeeded in bringing about the resignation of G. M. Malenkov as head of the Soviet state, attacked Stalin by name at the 20th Congress of the Communist Party, denouncing him for the "cult of [his own] personality" and for persecution of loyal party members in violation of their legal rights. In October and November 1961, at the 22nd Party Congress, the attacks on Stalin were renewed with even greater vigor. Vyshinsky's name was added to Stalin's as co-author of a legal system which permitted falsification and distortion of legality for the persecution of people innocent of any crime.

The attack upon Stalinist terror facilitated the introduction of wholesale reforms in almost every branch of Soviet law. Indeed, the law reform movement which started in 1953 and gathered increasing momentum throughout the following years may prove to have been the most significant aspect of Soviet social, economic and political development in the decade after Stalin's death.

In interpreting this reform movement, however, one must start with Stalin—however much his successors would have liked to expunge his name from the memory of their people. For despite the very substantial changes which they introduced, the Soviet legal system remained Stalinist in its basic structure and its basic purposes. The organization and functions of the lawmaking, law-enforcing, and law-practicing agencies—of the legislature, the Procuracy, the courts, the administrative organs, the bar—were not essentially different ten years later from what they were when Stalin died. The main outlines of Soviet criminal law and procedure, civil law and procedure, labor law, agrarian law, family law, administrative law, constitutional law, and other branches of the Soviet legal tree—remained basically the same as before.

Also, if one looks behind the structure to the purposes of Soviet law, it remained a totalitarian law, in the sense that it sought to regulate all aspects of economic and social life, including the circulation of thought, while leaving the critical questions of political power to be decided by informal, secret procedures beyond the scrutiny or control either of legislative or judicial bodies. It remained the law of a one-party state. It remained the law of a planned economy. It remained a law whose primary function is to discipline, guide, train, and educate Soviet citizens to be dedicated members of a collectivized and mobilized social order.

If this is so, it may be asked, what is the significance of the post-Stalin reforms? Indeed, many Western observers treated each successive development in Soviet law after Stalin's death as mere smoke without fire—or even as a smokescreen designed to conceal the absence of any fire. Others viewed the reforms as half-hearted concessions designed to appease the appetite of the Soviet people without really satisfying their hunger. These grudging responses are reminiscent of Soviet interpretations of American law reforms: the New Deal, we are told by Soviet writers, did not really alter the fundamental nature of the American capitalist system; the Supreme Court decision in the School Segregation cases did not end discrimination against Negroes; American law remains "bourgeois."

Viewed from a sufficiently lofty height, the scene never changes. This may only mean, however, that the viewer does not see what is really going on. To give an example: in December 1958, the Supreme Soviet enacted new Fundamental Principles of Criminal Law which, among other things, reduced the maximum period of detention of criminals from 25 to 15 years. This was part of a general movement toward greater leniency in penal policy. In 1961 and 1962, however, the death penalty (which previously had been restricted in peacetime to certain crimes against the state and to first-degree murder) was extended to a wide variety of other crimes, including certain non-violent crimes such as counterfeiting and bribery. One of the main reasons for the excessive harshness of 1961–1962 was the disappointment of the Soviet leaders in the results of the excessive softness of 1958, for in fact the rate of serious crimes increased in 1959, 1960 and 1961. The point is that those Western observers who did not take seriously the earlier policy of leniency are in a poor position to evaluate the later policy of repression.

Of course, if the observer abandons all elevation and descends into the midst of the events, he loses all perspective and sees only flux. The foreign journalist in Moscow—and the readers of his articles at home—tend to see a whirling, eddying stream. The only solution is to seek a composite picture, from various perspectives.

Such a composite picture would reveal at least seven major tendencies in Soviet law reform in the decade after March 1953.

First, there was a tendency toward the elimination of political terror.

Second, there was a tendency toward the liberalization both of procedures and of substantive norms.

Third, there was a tendency toward the systematization and rationalization of the legal system.

Fourth, there was a tendency toward decentralization and democratization of decision-making.

Fifth, there was a tendency to introduce popular participation in the administration of justice.

Sixth, there was a tendency in 1961 and 1962 to threaten those who will not co-operate in building communism with harsh criminal and administrative penalties.

Seventh, there was developed a new Soviet theory of state and law which rejected some of the Stalinist innovations in Leninist doctrine.

The Tendency Toward the Elimination of Terror

Important steps were taken after March 1953 to eliminate those features of the previous Soviet law which permitted the disguise of terror in legal form.

First, the Special Board of the Ministry of Internal Affairs was abolished. It was this Special Board which had been the chief instrument of terror. It was a three-man administrative committee—the Russians called it a troika—which was empowered by a 1934 statute to send people to labor camps without a hearing, in a secret administrative procedure, without right of counsel and without right of appeal.

Second, the security police were deprived of the power to conduct investigations of crimes under their own special rules without supervision by the Procuracy.

Third, the special procedures for court cases involving the most serious anti-state crimes were abolished. The laws of 1934 and 1937 permitting persons charged with certain such crimes to be tried secretly, in absentia, and without counsel, were repealed.

Fourth, the military courts, which had previously had a wide jurisdiction over civilians, particularly in the case of political crimes, were deprived of all jurisdiction over civilians except for espionage.

Fifth, the law permitting punishment of relatives of one who deserts to a foreign country from the armed forces—though they knew nothing of the desertion—was abolished.

Sixth, Vyshinsky's doctrine that confessions have special evidentiary force in cases of counterrevolutionary crimes—based on the transparently false notion that people will not confess to such crimes unless they are actually guilty—was repudiated; confessions were now treated as having no evidentiary force in themselves, and the matters contained in a confession must be corroborated by other evidence.

Seventh, Vyshinsky's doctrine that the burden of proof shifts to the accused in cases of counterrevolutionary crimes was also repudiated. The new Soviet codes place the burden of proving the guilt of the accused squarely on the prosecutor. Although the phrase "presumption of innocence" is avoided in the codes, all that American jurists generally mean by that phrase is spelled out in Soviet law.

Eighth, Vyshinsky's broad definition of complicity, borrowed from the Anglo-American doctrine of conspiracy, was repudiated. Persons may no longer be held liable for acts of their associates unless they intended those acts to take place.

Ninth, the law on so-called "counterrevolutionary crimes" was slightly narrowed and made a little less vague. The term "counterrevolutionary" was eliminated and the term "state" (*i.e.*, anti-state) substituted. The crime of "terrorist acts," which hitherto had been interpreted to include any violent act against a state or Party official, or, indeed, his close relatives, whatever the motive, was restricted to murder or serious bodily injury of the official himself committed for the purpose of overthrowing or weakening the Soviet authority. The law on State secrets was substantially relaxed—though it is still far wider in its scope than most Americans would consider tolerable—and a new list of information constituting a state secret was enacted which is less broad and more precise than the earlier list.

Finally, there took place from 1955 to 1957 a systematic re-examination of all cases of persons previously convicted of counterrevolutionary crimes and the release from labor camps of the overwhelming majority of such persons, with full rehabilitation.

The restoration of procedural due process of law in political cases is a signal achievement of the post-Stalin regime. The Soviet citizen is now protected against police terror, false charges and faked trials to a far greater extent than ever before in Soviet history. No longer need he fear the midnight knock on the door as a prelude to transportation to a Siberian labor camp without a fair hearing.

Yet one cannot speak of the total elimination of political terror so long as open opposition to Communist Party policy—the "Party line"—can lead to criminal sanctions, however "objectively" and "correctly" imposed. The 1958 Statute on State Crimes carries over from the earlier law on counterrevolutionary crimes the provision against "agitation or propaganda" directed against the Soviet system. To defame the Soviet political and social system, or even to possess written materials of such defamatory nature, if for the purpose of weakening Soviet authority, is punishable by deprivation of freedom of up to seven years.

The law of anti-Soviet agitation and propaganda is only one of many features which keep alive the fear of Soviet citizens that the terror may return. This fear, and the conditions which give rise to it, will be discussed more fully below. But it is important to stress at this point that the fear of a return to terror is itself a form of terror. Therefore, one must view the developments of the ten years after Stalin's death as reflecting only a tendency—though an extremely important tendency—toward the elimination of terror.

The Liberalization of Soviet Law

Even apart from political crimes, Soviet law underwent substantial liberalization after Stalin's death. It would be impossible to list the hundreds, indeed thousands, of needed reforms which were introduced. A brief account of some of the most important may suffice, however, to indicate the direction and scope of the tendency toward liberalization.

In criminal law and procedure, the "tightening up" of the rules with respect to burden of proof, the evaluation of confessions, and the doctrine of complicity, which have already been mentioned in the discussion of political crimes, gave increased protection to persons accused of other crimes as well. In addition, the right to counsel prior to trial, though still limited, was significantly extended; time for supervisory review of an acquittal in a criminal case, formerly unlimited, was reduced to one year; powers of search and seizure were somewhat restricted; the doctrine of analogy, whereby a person who committed a socially dangerous act not specifically made punishable by law could be sentenced under a law proscribing an analogous act, was finally eliminated, penalties were substantially lightened for many crimes—for example, new laws imposing lighter sentences for petty rowdyism ("hooliganism") and petty theft of state or public property removed the necessity of many long years in labor camps for such trivial offenses; some crimes were eliminated altogether—for example, abortion and also absenteeism from work and quitting one's job without permission. Large-scale amnesties of 1953 and 1957 released all except those sentenced for, or charged with, the most serious offenses.

With respect to the system of detention, a 1957 law eliminated the term "labor camp," substituting "labor colony" for all places of confinement (except prisons, which are used only for temporary detention or, very rarely, for the most serious crimes) and introduced a new regime for prisoners which permits far more leniency in their treatment. Those convicted of less serious crimes are permitted to have their wives (or husbands) visit and stay with them from time to time; they are paid substantial wages for their work and are required to send home allotments to their dependents. Also liberal parole provisions were introduced.

Liberalization was not confined to criminal policy. After 1953, and especially after 1955, there was a re-examination of every branch of law and a weeding out of many of the harshest features. For example, a new civil right was created to obtain a court order for public retraction of a newspaper libel. In labor law, the rights of trade unions were enhanced and the procedures for settlement of workers' grievances were improved. Similar examples could be multiplied from many other fields of law.

In 1961 and 1962 there was a contrary trend, away from liberalization, in certain areas. These backward steps, however, did not stop the liberal momentum of the post-Stalin reforms.

Systematization and Rationalization

The tendency toward liberalization of law generally is, of course, an important supporting buttress of the tendency toward elimination of political terror. For such tendencies to have permanence, however, deeper foundations are required in the legal system as a whole. From that standpoint, the efforts of the post-Stalin regime to systematize and rationalize the Soviet legal system are of great significance.

The Stalin Constitution of December 1936, and the Vyshinsky jurisprudence which surrounded it, rehabilitated the various republican criminal, civil, labor and family codes of the NEP period of the 'twenties which had largely fallen into disrepute in the period from 1928 to 1936. Of course the NEP codes, designed for a transition period of mixed capitalism-socialism, were inadequate for the new period of full socialism with its planned economy. The Stalin Constitution therefore called for the creation of all-union codes to replace the earlier republican codes. But until such new all-union codes were adopted, the earlier ones were to prevail, together with the thousands of statutory and administrative changes introduced into them.

During the remaining sixteen years of Stalin's reign, however, new all-union codes were not adopted, although many drafts were produced. Only with the removal of the political and ideological pressure of Stalinist autocracy did it become possible to introduce new codes, and, together with them, a reorganization of the entire system of legal administration.

The first major event in this development was the adoption in August 1955, of a new Statute on Procuracy Supervision. The Procuracy is the cornerstone of the Soviet legal system. It combines functions of our Department of Justice, Congressional investigating committees, and grand juries. It not only investigates and prosecutes crimes, but it supervises the entire system of administration of justice, and has power to investigate and protest to higher authorities (whether administrative or judicial) any abuse of law which comes to its attention. Until 1955 it operated on the basis of a 1922 statute upon which were encrusted many legislative and administrative modifications. The 1955 statute clarified and consolidated its supervisory powers over judicial and administrative acts. Incidentally, the new statute also added sanctions against officials of the Procuracy for negligence in failing to expose illegal practices in places of detention of criminals.

The second major event was the removal of certain aspects of Ministry of Justice control over the courts and the reorganization of the Supreme Court of the U.S.S.R. and of the republican and regional courts. This took place in 1956 and 1957. The result was a streamlining of the court system and an increase in its independence.

In December 1958 the Supreme Soviet of the U.S.S.R. adopted a series of Fundamental Principles of various branches of law—Fundamental Principles of Criminal Law, Fundamental Principles of Criminal Procedure, and Fundamental Principles of Court Organization—together with new comprehensive Statutes on State Crimes, Military Crimes, and Military Tribunals. Subsequently, in December 1961, the Supreme Soviet adopted Fundamental Principles of Civil Law and of Civil Procedure. As of 1962, Fundamental Principles of Family Law and of Labor Law were in preparation; indeed, a Statute on the Procedure for the Hearing of Labor Disputes adopted in 1957 was itself a systematization of many aspects of labor law.

On the basis of the various Fundamental Principles, the republics adopted their own new codes of criminal law and criminal procedure and in 1962 were in the last stages of work on new codes of civil law and civil procedure.

Of the many other important pieces of legislation of the first post-Stalin decade, mention should also be made of the 1961 statute on administrative commissions of local municipal councils, which restricted the powers of administrative bodies to impose fines and established a procedure for appealing from such fines; the 1960 Statute on State Arbitrazh, which reorganized the procedures for hearing the hundreds of thousands of contract disputes which arise each year between state economic enterprises; and the new statutes on the organization of the legal profession in the various republics, which strengthen the independence of the advocate and his responsibility to his client.

Two other items deserve mention in connection with the systematization of Soviet law. The Juridical Commission of the Council of Ministers of the U.S.S.R. was given the function of determining which laws have lost their force in the light of the new legislation. In the twenty years between 1937 and 1958, the U.S.S.R. Supreme Soviet enacted over 7,000 statutes, edicts and decrees, and the U.S.S.R. Council of Ministers issued about 390,000 decrees and regulations. Few of these were formally declared to have lost their force. Yet in 1960 only about 15,000 of these approximately 397,000 normative acts actually remained in force. The Juridical Commission has attempted to cleanse the Augean stables of Soviet legislation by systematically listing, little by little, those laws and other normative acts which are no longer valid.

In connection with this, it is important to note a 1958 law on the publication of laws. Of the more than 7,000 laws of the Supreme Soviet enacted between 1937 and 1958, only some hundreds were published. Of the 390,000 decrees and regulations of the Council of Ministers, only some thousands were published. The rest were merely distributed to the appropriate officials concerned with their enforcement and to other authorized persons. The 1958 law attempted to increase the publicity of laws by requiring that all laws and acts of the U.S.S.R. Supreme Soviet and all edicts and decrees of its Presidium which have "general significance" or are of a "normative character" be published in the Journal of the Supreme Soviet. Also decrees of the Council of Ministers which are of general significance or have a normative character are required to be published in the Collected Decrees of the Government of the U.S.S.R.

The systematization and rationalization of Soviet law is not something which can be accomplished in a few years. Indeed, it is something which must go on continually. The recognition of its importance, and the very great efforts devoted to it, are an encouraging sign of the determination of the post-Stalin regime to establish a far higher degree of legal security than that which existed in the past.

The Tendency Toward Decentralization and Democratization

Implicit in the tendencies toward an all-embracing, liberalized and systematic legality is the belief in the possibility of a wide decentralization of decision-making and a still wider participation of the public in the formulation of issues for decision.

Two qualifications must be made at the outset, however, in discussing the tendency of the post-Stalin period of Soviet history toward greater decentralization and democratization. The first is that there has been no sign that the present Soviet leadership has any intention of allowing this tendency to go beyond its power to control it. The limits of decentralized decision-making and democratization are set by the central authorities. The second qualification is that this theory of "democratic centralism"—centralization of authority combined with decentralization of operations—was also Stalin's theory. The difference since his death is a difference in degree.

The tendency toward decentralization and democratization was greatly accelerated after Stalin's death, however, by the very nature of the tendencies toward elimination of political terror, toward liberalization, and toward systematization and rationalization of the law. Apart from all other considerations, these tendencies have imposed an absolute requirement of help from hundreds of thousands of people at various levels of the official hierarchy and in various parts of the Soviet Union. In addition, the main purpose of these tendencies—to overcome the rigidities of the system inherited from Stalin, to stimulate local and individual initiative and enthusiasm—has necessitated the enlistment of maximum cooperation from the maximum number of people.

When one thinks of America one thinks of one hundred and eighty million people of diverse outlooks, diverse traditions, and diverse interests, scattered across a great continent which includes not only New York City and Washington, D.C., but also Texas and California and Mississippi and Vermont and a host of other very different kinds of communities. But too many, when they think of the Soviet Union, stop with the Kremlin. It should not need demonstration that even if one imagined the entire Soviet population to be a disciplined army, the Commander-in-Chief would be greatly in need of subordinate units of command with considerable autonomy of action. He could not run the lives of 220 million people, including thirty or forty major nationalities, spread across one-sixth of the earth's surface—by pushbutton from Moscow. When an American scholar presented the "pushbutton" theory to a leading Soviet jurist some years ago, he merely replied: "It would take too many pushbuttons!"

This is not to say that centralization is not the major fact of the Soviet political and economic system. "Bolsheviks are centralists by conviction," said John Maynard in 1948. Under Stalin this Bolshevik conviction was strengthened by fear of "the leader" (*vozhd'*), who often urged decentralization but did not hesitate to crack down when it tended toward deviation.

The decision in 1957 to abandon the rule of the 1936 Constitution calling for all-union codes and to substitute a rule calling for separate codes in each of the fifteen Soviet republics, based, however, on All-Union Fundamental Principles; the earlier decision to dissolve the All-Union Ministry of Justice into separate republican ministries of justice, and the later decision to do the same with the Ministry of Internal Affairs; and, most important of all, the decision in 1957 to split the economy of the country into about 100 economic regions, each with its own Council of National Economy, and to divide among these regional councils some of the functions of the former economic ministries with their central offices in Moscow*—these decisions in the direction of decentralization were called for by the enormous bureaucratization of Soviet social and economic life, which had become almost too stifling to endure.

Yet decentralization in itself is not democratization; it may be, and to a certain extent it has been, simply a moving of the center to the localities, a stretching of the chain of command. It has also been more than that, however. The lower links in the chain have unquestionably been given more initiative. And even where ultimate decisions have been reserved for Moscow, a far greater hearing has been given to the voices of the localities.

This is illustrated by the process of law reform itself. Khrushchev and his immediate associates could give the word that the

* Ed. note: See note, pp. 326–327.

time had come for substantial law reforms and could indicate the lines along which the reforms should run. But the word could not become a reality without an enormous effort on the part of the people who would be directly affected by these reforms. These include not only the professional lawyers who would have to draft them and the officials who would have to administer them, but also the various people who would have to live under them.

The comprehensive legislation enacted in the late 1950's and early 1960's were worked on by representatives of hundreds, indeed thousands, of organizations. All the major governmental agencies expressed detailed views on their various provisions. There was endless discussion of them in the universities, in research institutes, in economic organizations of various kinds, in scholarly journals, and in the daily press.

In addition, popular participation in lawmaking has been stimulated by the expansion of the committee system of the Supreme Soviet of the U.S.S.R. and of the Supreme Soviets of the fifteen republics. Tens of thousands of expert consultants have reported to these committees. And apart from major all-union and republican legislation, there has been a substantial increase in the powers of the local municipal councils and a vast amount of activity of local governmental organizations, involving the participation of literally hundreds of thousands of Soviet citizens.

Of course it would be a mistake to suppose that Soviet federalism and Soviet democracy involve—as ours do—a struggle between opposing political units and groups, a competition for political leadership. In the Soviet Union all power resides in the Communist Party, which remains, as stated in the Constitution, the "central core" of all organizations, whether they be state organizations or social organizations. Despite the development of greater intra-Party democracy after 1953, the Party remains a disciplined elite, subservient to its leadership. Decentralization and democratization of decision-making in the spheres of government, law, and economic administration is not a threat to Party supremacy; indeed, it is required by the Party as a means of maintaining its supremacy.

Yet Party control is, in a much deeper sense, challenged by the development of autonomous centers of discussion and initiative, even though it remains the "central core" of such centers. The cohesion of Soviet jurists, for example, is striking. Whether they are judges, procurators, Ministry of Justice officials, law professors, research workers, legal advisers of state institutions and enterprises, advocates, or notaries, the seventy to eighty thousand jurists in the Soviet Union are bound together by the closest professional ties. They meet together in many different kinds of activity; they discuss and debate common problems; they work together; and they are bound not only by their common legal education but also by their common vested interest in the preservation of legality. As a class, they have grown greatly in importance during the years after Stalin's death.

Popular Participation in the Administration of Justice

In describing the movement away from political terror, harshness of punishment, chaos and irrationality of legislation, and overcentralization of decision-making, one runs the risk of leaving the false impression that the Soviet legal system is becoming just like ours. It is true that Stalin's successors have sought to eliminate the dualism of law and terror which formerly characterized the Soviet system, and in so doing they have taken important steps in the direction of a more humane, more rational and more democratic legal system. Yet they have sought to do this without abandoning the dynamic revolutionary development of the Soviet state and of Soviet society; indeed, their purpose has been to instill new vitality into that revolutionary development by softening the motive force of fear and strengthening the motive force of common effort, common struggle, common enthusiasm. The Soviet people are now being asked voluntarily to make sacrifices which formerly were evoked from them in part by threat of force. No doubt both the leaders and the people are greatly relieved at the decrease in emphasis upon terror and coercion and the increase in emphasis upon the liberal, rational and democratic elements in their legal system. But these elements are not—for the leaders, at least—ends in themselves, but rather a means toward lifting their society to new heights of economic progress, political power and social solidarity.

Law is conceived as a major instrument for achieving these goals. Law is conceived, above all, as a means of educating Soviet people to be the type of socially conscious, dedicated members of society which are required if socialism is to be maintained and if communism is to be achieved.

This concept of the dynamic function of law in molding not merely the conduct of men but also their morality and their very characters . . . is perhaps the greatest challenge which Soviet law presents to the West. One aspect of this concept is the greatly increased participation of ordinary Soviet citizens—of society, the public, *obshchestvennost'*, as Soviet terminology has it—in the administration of justice.

It is Soviet theory that under communism the functions of state organizations (which operate in part by coercion) will be turned over entirely to social organizations (which operate only by persuasion). In anticipation of this glorious day, the role of social organizations was greatly increased from about 1959 on. Neighborhood and factory meetings were convened for a variety of purposes and were given certain semi-judicial functions. Also a voluntary auxiliary police force was organized—the so-called *druzhiny*, or bands—to help keep order; they direct traffic, take drunks into custody, and in general attempt to enforce law and order among the people on the streets. In addition many special volunteer commissions have been formed and given semi-official status—to observe conditions in the labor colonies and to make recommendations, to report to municipal councils on housing questions, to report on local observance of "socialist legality," and for a host of similar purposes. Trade unions and the Young Communist League (Komsomol) are also considered to be social organizations, and their functions have been extended.

Many of the functions of Soviet social organizations are also performed in the United States by volunteer workers and social organizations. Indeed, probably no country in the world can match the United States in the amount of public-spirited activity of volunteer social organizations. Yet there is a difference in kind between Soviet social organizations and their American counterparts—a difference which is striking. In part it is a difference in the scope of the activities of Soviet social organizations and especially their powers over the lives of their members; in part it is a difference in the amount of official pressure that can be brought upon them, due especially to their links with the state through the Communist Party.

For example, the Komsomol organizations in the universities call for student volunteers to work during the summer holidays in the so-called "virgin lands" of the East. The volunteers are recruited, however, by lists posted on bulletin boards, and refusal to go courts expulsion from the Komsomol and probably—at least it is so assumed by the students—from the university.

A second example may be found in the activities of the "Comrades' Courts," now operating under a 1960 statute, which meet in apartment houses or in factories to consider minor offenses committed by neighbors or fellow-workers. Their punitive powers are limited to a ten-ruble fine.* Mostly they issue reprimands and warnings. However, they may also recommend eviction from the apartment or disciplinary action (including demotion but not discharge) by the factory management. Such eviction or disciplinary action may be resisted through regular court proceedings, but nevertheless the recommendation of the Comrades' Court is a serious matter.

One other example: Soviet courts sometimes go "on circuit," so to speak, to apartments or factories, to hear criminal cases involving persons in those places. The purpose is to demonstrate to the entire "collective" and to the public the social danger of the offenses charged and to educate people in the requirements of the law. But the tendency to convict and to mete out harsh punishment is very strong when such an educational purpose is in the forefront of the procedure itself.

Some Western students of the Soviet scene have exaggerated the evils of this kind of new "social justice." To evaluate them properly, one must put oneself in the Soviet situation, where true social co-operation in informal voluntary groups, entirely independent of the state, hardly exists. The Comrades' Courts in

---

* A ruble is now officially valued at $1.11. On January 1, 1961, a currency reform resulted in the substitution of one new ruble for ten old rubles, with corresponding ten-fold reductions in prices, wages, and all other accounts. References in this book to "old" rubles and "new" rubles refer to the pre-1961 and post-1961 ruble respectively. [By a decree of March 1965, the "Comrades' Courts" were authorized to impose fines of up to 50 rubles and to demand full repayment on damaged property. The power of these quasi-judicial, irregular citizens' courts seems to have been increased in an effort to combat petty thefts of Government property.—Ed.]

action have impressed outside observers by the good spirit with which they are received. Especially important is the fact that their powers are very limited and that these limits are enforced by the courts and by the legal system.

The great danger, of course, is the potentiality of abuse of these social organizations by the Communist Party and the state. The still greater danger is the dream of a far-off time when there will be no legal system and no state but only one vast social organization, one vast Communist Party. It is, no doubt, a dream which can never be realized; but so long as it is held it inhibits the achievement of true legal security.

The Return to Harsh Criminal and Administrative Penalties

A sixth major tendency in Soviet law in the post-Stalin period was the return in 1961 and 1962 to harsh criminal and administrative penalties against those who refuse to cooperate in building communism.

In May and June 1961, the three largest republics, comprising three-fourths of the Soviet population, finally enacted the notorious anti-parasite law which had been first proposed for public discussion in 1957 and later adopted in the smaller republics during 1957 to 1960. This law, in its final form, provides for "resettlement" (*vyselenie*) in "specially designated localities," for two to five years, of persons who "are avoiding socially useful work and are leading an anti-social parasitic way of life." Money or property acquired by such persons "by non-labor means" is subject to confiscation. Persons may be sentenced under this law by the judges of the regular courts in a summary procedure and without the usual guarantees of the criminal law and without right of appeal, or else by general meetings in the factories or collective farms with review by the local municipal council.

To a Western lawyer, and—judging from private conversations —to many Soviet lawyers as well, the antiparasite laws contradict the provision of the 1958 Fundamental Principles of Criminal Procedure that no person may be punished for a crime except by sentence of a court. Official Soviet doctrine, however, has reconciled these laws with the Fundamental Principles on the more-than-tenuous theory that the offender is not being punished for a crime, nor is he being confined; he is simply "resettled" in another place where he must take a socially useful job! This is considered an "administrative," not a "penal," measure.

In the first year of the operation of this law in the R.S.F.S.R., according to a statement made by the Minister of Justice at a public lecture in Moscow in May 1961, 10,000 people in Moscow were charged under the antiparasite law; 8,000, he said, received only warning; 2,000 were sent out of Moscow; of these, only a small number were subjected to confiscation of property. It may be inferred from the relatively few instances of confiscation that the law is principally a device for getting rid of vagrants and putting them to work.

Also, the extension of the death penalty in 1961 and 1962 to a wide variety of crimes, many of them economic crimes not involving violence, reflected the regime's determination to take extreme measures against those who most flagrantly violate the tenets of communist morality. In May 1961, the death penalty (which had been abolished altogether in 1947, and restored in 1950 for treason, espionage, wrecking, terrorist acts and acts of banditry, and in 1954 for murder committed under aggravating circumstances) was extended to theft ("plunder") of state or social property in especially large amounts, counterfeiting money or securities for profit, and the commission of violent attacks in places of detention by especially dangerous recidivists or persons convicted of serious crimes. In July 1961, the death penalty was extended to speculation in foreign currency. In February 1962, it was extended to attempts upon the life of a policeman or volunteer auxiliary policeman (*druzhinnik*) on duty, to rape committed by a group or by an especially dangerous recidivist or entailing especially grave consequences or committed on a minor, and to the taking of bribes under aggravating circumstances by an official who holds a responsible position or who has been previously tried for bribery or has taken bribes repeatedly.

In a case tried in July 1961, the statute imposing the death penalty for foreign currency speculation was applied retroactively by a special decree of the Presidium of the Supreme Soviet authorizing the retroactive application "as an exception" in the specific case. (The decree was never published as it was not considered to be "of general significance.") There is reason to believe that there were other such cases of retroactive application of the death sentence, specially authorized by similar edicts. The 1961 law was the first example of a Soviet criminal law expressly made retroactive, so far as the author has been able to discover, since 1929.

Judging from Soviet press accounts of individual trials, probably over 250 Soviet citizens were executed for economic and other crimes in the year from May 1961 to May 1962, and probably an equal or greater number were executed from June to December 1962. One can only say "probably" because Soviet crime statistics are a state secret! (In 1961, 43 persons were executed in the United States.)

This harsh policy was also reflected in increased penalties for lesser crimes. Soviet jurists have publicly criticized the tendency of some procurators and courts to treat the imposition of the death penalty for serious crimes as a signal for reversing the entire trend toward liberalization.

What significance should we attach to these developments? As is so often the case with violations of basic principles of judicial procedure, the particular individual victims do not command our affection. They were, presumably, scoundrels. It is rather the abuse of the integrity of the legal process that concerns us, for one abuse suggests another.

During the years after Stalin's death much was heard of "the thaw"—to use the title of Ilya Ehrenburg's 1954 novel—that is, the unfreezing of Soviet life, the reduction of terror, the increased freedom to criticize, the greater encouragement of individual initiative, the relaxation of tensions. But the *long-range* problem of government in the Soviet Union is whether the Soviet leaders are willing and able to establish not merely a season, or a climate, or a policy, of freedom and initiative, but also a legal and institutional foundation which will make freedom and initiative secure from their own intervention. Until that problem is solved, the fear of a return to Stalinist terror will haunt the Soviet people, and especially the intellectuals. In research institutes and universities, as well as among educated people generally, debates rage over the "liquidation of the consequences of the cult of personality," which is Party jargon for preventing a recurrence not only of violence but also of all the rigidities that went with it. Nobody—presumably from Khrushchev on down—wants such a recurrence. But nobody can guarantee that it won't happen.

In 1957, Deputy Procurator General P. I. Kudriavtsev, responding to a series of questions on guarantees against a return to Stalinist terror, said to the author: "Do not forget that we have in the Soviet Union the dictatorship of the proletariat, and that law must serve the state authority." To the question: "Suppose the law conflicts with the interests of the state, which prevails?"—he replied, "The interests of the state." He amplified: "Compulsion may be necessary. The Special Board of the MVD was necessary in its time, in the late 'thirties. Only it was later abused. The Cheka, which Lenin introduced, was entirely justified. No revolution is bloodless—ours is the most bloodless revolution in history, far more bloodless than the French or English revolutions." I asked: "When will your revolution be over?" He replied: "We live in an age of war and revolution. The revolution goes on." And then, to make crystal clear the connection between this basic historical perspective and the law reforms we had been discussing, he said: "If it becomes necessary we will restore the old methods. But I think it will not be necessary."

In addition to preserving the possibility of a return to physical terror "if it becomes necessary," Khrushchev replaced the Stalinist dualism of law and terror by a new dualism of law and social pressure: one is free from arbitrary arrest by the secret police, but one is not free from the social pressure of the "collective"— whether it be the more innocuous pressure of the collective of the neighbors in the crowded apartment houses or the less innocuous pressure of the factory, one's co-workers, or the local Party organization. The new dualism still stands in the shadow of the old.

Yet it would be a great mistake to assume that the "thaw" ended with the harsher methods adopted in 1961 and 1962. Such an assumption underestimates the importance of the legal and institutional changes which had in fact taken place. The law reforms had already counted. They had acquired a momentum which was hard to stop. A vast structure of procedures and rights had been built, and though its foundations needed to be greatly strengthened, it was not something which could easily be toppled.

The Reform of Soviet Theory of State and Law

Stalin's successors have denounced their former leader for the terror which he unleashed, and have declared many of the policies which he sponsored, as well as many of his theories, to be a betrayal of Leninism. They have created a new political, economic and social climate in the Soviet Union, which is far more tolerant of experimentation and of dissent. The strengthening of the legal system has played an important part in effectuating this change in the atmosphere of Soviet society. It is true that the legal system, and the political-economic-social system of which it is a part, remains Stalinist in its basic structure and outlines; but here the old French proverb is applicable in reverse—the more it stays the same, the more it changes.

In many respects the post-Stalin regime is less conservative than its predecessor. It places somewhat less theoretical emphasis upon historic continuity with the pre-revolutionary Russian tradition, upon the stability of the family, upon toleration of religion; it has sought to reduce inequalities of income and possibilities for acquiring personal wealth, and to subordinate even further the economic autonomy of producing units to the central planning authorities; it has re-emphasized the supremacy of the Party over the state and has sought to revive the "popular" and "revolutionary" aspects of Soviet law. There is something of the dynamic spirit of the early 'thirties in this—in law, something of the spirit of Pashukanis rather than of Vyshinsky, although officially Pashukanis' theories still remain in limbo.

As leader of both Party and state, Khrushchev has sought to establish his own legitimacy as well as the legitimacy of his policies by tracing their derivation to Lenin rather than to Stalin. He continually attacks the dead dictator for his betrayal of truly Leninist principles. The effect of this, however, is often a return to the more volatile ideas and policies which Stalin supported in the first phase of the development of the Soviet state, prior to 1936, but which he later denounced.

Yet basically Khrushchev has introduced a third phase of development, which is different from both the first and the second phases though it builds on both. This third phase was officially termed in 1959, at the twenty-first Party Congress, "the period of expanded construction of communism" (*period razvernutogo stroitel'stra kommunizma*). Although this phrase is often translated "transition to communism," it is meant to add something to the Stalinist doctrine that socialism (achieved in 1936) is itself a stage of gradual transition to communism. (Lenin, following Marx, had said socialism *is* the first stage of communism.) Now Khrushchev says that the "full and final victory of socialism" has been achieved, and a new period of "expanded" construction will lead to the eventual attainment of communism. However, communism itself is now divided into stages. The 1961 Party Program calls for the achievement of the first stage of communism in twenty years.

From the point of view of political and legal theory, the principal difference between the present phase as defined by Khrushchev and the earlier socialist phase as defined by Stalin is that Stalin taught that before the state begins to wither away it must get stronger and stronger. Only the strongest possible state, in Stalin's view, could pave the way for ushering in the stateless society. In connection with this, Stalin also said that the class struggle becomes sharper and sharper as communism draws nearer and nearer—chiefly because of the existence of a hostile capitalist-imperialist world which will do all in its power to prevent communism from arriving. The dictatorship of the proletariat therefore always had to stand guard over the progress of the Soviet Union toward communism, although, except for Soviet people who had fallen under the evil influence of the capitalist world-outlook, there were supposedly no antagonistic classes left even under socialism.

After Stalin's death, Khrushchev denounced the doctrine of the increasing intensification of the class struggle under socialism, which he rightly called merely an excuse for repressions against those whom Stalin considered potential enemies. The 1961 Party Program states that in the Soviet Union "the dictatorship of the proletariat has ceased to be a necessity." And the state must begin now—not in the distant future—to be replaced by voluntary social cooperation; coercion must begin more and more to give way to persuasion as the proletarian dictatorship has been replaced by an "all-people's state" and as this state itself begins to turn over its functions to "social organizations."

To American ears, these doctrines sound more pleasant than the older ones, but equally difficult to take at face value. Of course it is possible theoretically to imagine a society in which there would be no need for coercion; the Christian Church has always preached such a kingdom. But to suppose that any existing political community, and especially the Soviet, is ready for such a transformation strains credulity. One is drawn inescapably to the conclusion that the doctrines, though perhaps believed in a very general sense, are primarily designed to symbolize a policy. That policy is, first, to extend the influence of the Communist Party, which is *the* "social organization" par excellence in the Soviet Union, defined as a social organization in the Constitution and also described therein as the "central core" of all other social organizations; and, second, to draw into public administration more and more people, in order to strengthen the society and eliminate the shortcomings of a rigid bureaucratism.

The theoretical question of the nature and functions of law during and after the period of transition to communism is one that has exercised the ingenuity of Soviet jurists. The definition of law given by Vyshinsky in 1938, which of necessity was accepted in all published legal writings thereafter, stressed three elements: the source of law in the will of the state (ruling class), the sanction for law in the coercive power of the state, and the nature of law as a body of rules. Except for its reference to class interests, this definition does not differ essentially from positivist definitions familiar to Western legal thought, although in the gloss on Vyshinsky's definition it was possible to detect strong elements of a natural-law philosophy, since in Soviet society it was assumed that law corresponded to the needs and interests of the whole people (there being no class antagonism).

Until the 22nd Party Congress it was possible for Soviet jurists to continue to repeat Vyshinsky's definition. Stalin's crimes, they said, consisted partly in his disregard of the very rules which he had been responsible for enacting, and partly in his insistence upon the enactment of some bad rules. With the end of his tyranny, the bad rules could be replaced by good ones. And with the development of the new "people's state" and the gradual replacement of coercive sanctions by persuasion, law would help to become (in many of its aspects, at least) more lenient and more permissive and would help to pave the way for its own very gradual disappearance once the first stage of communism was achieved.

At the 22nd Party Congress in 1961, however, Vyshinsky was singled out for special attack and Soviet jurists were charged with being still under the influence of the cult of his (and not merely Stalin's) personality. Specifically, they were attacked for not having found a new and better definition of law to replace Vyshinsky's, which was linked with Stalin's terror. After that time a series of discussions took place in which Soviet jurists debated what exactly was wrong with the definition and what should be substituted for it.

Much of this debate was in terms very familiar to a Western lawyer. It was said by some that certain Stalinist laws (*zakony*) lacked the essential qualities of "legality" (*zakonnost'*) and therefore could not be called "law" (*pravo*). Examples are the laws of 1934 and 1937 establishing a special summary secret procedure for the trial of certain counterrevolutionary crimes. Others countered that "a law is a law," and the trouble with those laws was simply that they were bad laws, not that they were not law. If we deny the quality of "law" to bad laws, it was argued, a person may simply refuse to obey a law of which he does not approve.

In supporting a new definition of law which would stress "legality" as an essential element, some Soviet jurists have contended that a sharp distinction between the "is" and the "ought" is foreign to Marxism. Legal rules, they say, must be understood not merely as factual descriptions of commands or standards laid down by the state, but also as statements of goals, to be intepreted in the light of these goals. It has also been contended by some that law includes much more than commands; it may consist of administrative recommendations, for example, or of procedures for voluntary settlement of disputes by negotiation or arbitration.

The question of the nature of law bears directly, of course, upon the role it is to play in a society conceived of as moving away from institutions of coercion toward institutions of persuasion and cooperation. If those who tend toward the narrower concept of law reflected in Vyshinsky's definition win the day, it would appear that law will continue to be under the theoretical cloud of the "withering away" doctrine. If the broader concept gains the favor of the Communist Party leadership, the sharp distinction between the coercive functions of law and the cooperative nature of the ideal society will be blunted and law will be considered to have not merely a temporary but a permanent value for communist society.

The Party Program of 1961, and statements of Party leaders supporting the Program, leave this question open. The Program is warm enough in its support of law and legality during the transition period. It states:

"The further *strengthening of the socialist legal order* and the perfecting of norms of law which regulate economic-organizational and cultural-educational work and which contribute to the accomplishment of the tasks of communist construction and to the all-round flourishing of personality are very important.

"*The transition to communism means the fullest extension of personal freedom and the rights of Soviet citizens.* Socialism has given and has guaranteed to the working people the broadest rights and freedoms. Communism will bring the working people great new rights and opportunities.

"The Party sets the objective of enforcing strict observance of socialist legality, of eradicating all violations of the legal order, of abolishing crime and removing all its causes.

"Justice in the U.S.S.R. is exercised in full conformity to law. It is built on truly democratic foundations: election and accountability of the judges and people's assessors, the right to recall them before expiry of their term, publicity of court proceedings, and participation of social prosecutors and defenders in the work of the courts, with the courts and investigating and prosecuting bodies strictly observing legality and all procedural norms. The democratic foundations of justice will be developed and improved."

Yet even this endorsement of law and legality contains an inherent ambiguity. For the development of the "democratic foundations" of justice—by which is meant principally the increase in the role of social organizations (*e.g.,* through members who are deputized to appear in criminal cases alongside the regular prosecutor and defense counsel as "social" prosecutors and "social" defenders)—is a threat to the independence of the courts.

Moreover, in proclaiming the doctrine of the gradual transformation of "socialist statehood" into "communist self-administration," the Party Program leaves open the question of the role of law once communism is achieved. Khrushchev, in reporting on the Party Program at the 22nd Party Congress, stated that "the fact that the dictatorship of the proletariat has ceased to be necessary in no way means any weakening of the social order and legality. . . . Law, freedom, honor and the dignity of Soviet man will be strictly protected by society and the state." But neither he nor the Party Program indicates what will happen to law when the state disappears. However academic such a question may appear, it has a strong bearing on the attitudes of Soviet people—both leaders and led—toward the absolute value of law. If law is defined as norms enacted by the state and enforced by the coercive sanctions of the state, it is destined, like the state, to find its way ultimately into the "museum of antiquities" (to use Engels' phrase). If, however, law is defined as an institutional process of resolution of conflicts, based on general standards objectively applied—a definition which many Americans would endorse and toward which some Soviets are groping—then it is not inconsistent with the "unified, generally recognized rules of communist social life," observance of which will become the "inner need and habit of all people" under communism, according to the Party Program.

If one compares the controversy of the early 1960's over the role of law in Soviet society with that which raged in the mid-1930's, one is struck by certain similarities and some very sharp differences. In both cases, there was a search for a single orthodox theory of law, a single orthodox definition of its origin and destiny, its nature and functions. In both cases there was an effort to found such a theory on Marxism-Leninism, and by the same token to make it an instrument for the building of a certain type of political-economic-social system as well as for justifying the existing regime. Although the participants in the debates were for the most part law professors and legal scholars, they were acting—in the 1960's as in the mid-1930's—under general instructions of the leaders of the Communist Party and were highly conscious of the immediate political implications of every word which they uttered. The clash of ideas was not conceived primarily as a means of discovering truth; it was rather like a legislative debate over the enactment of a statute, with the parties grouped in various blocs, than like an academic debate about the nature of social reality.

However, the spirit of the later debate was one of far greater moderation than that of the earlier one. There was no Vyshinsky to dominate it, and no Stalin in the background. Those who were publicly attacked for heresy did not, as before, expect to disappear to Siberia, or worse. Even Vyshinsky, though denounced, was not made the subject of ridiculous accusations of being a traitor, "wrecker," and capitalist agent—as Pashukanis, Krylenko and others were in the 1930's.

Moreover, the style of the debate in the 1960's was more rational. There was much less reliance on phrases and texts taken from Marx, Lenin and their political successors. The chanting of the Marxist liturgy could still be heard, but it did not dominate as it had earlier. Indeed, one could read whole articles on legal theory which hardly referred to Marxist-Leninist texts, although it was still unthinkable that anyone would propose an explicitly anti-Marxist or anti-Leninist—or, indeed, an explicitly *non*-Marxist, or *non*-Leninist concept.

Soviet jurists, like the Soviet leaders themselves, are striving to create the impression that they have eliminated the Stalinist distortions of Leninist theory and have returned to the true teachings of their master. No doubt many of them think of themselves as true Leninists. Yet their legal theory is at best a distant reflection of Leninism, since Lenin had no developed legal theory. For Lenin, as we have seen, law was accepted as a necessary evil during the temporary period of proletarian dictatorship which preceded, in his view, the imminent advent of classless socialism. If one seeks a historical analogy, one may point to the eschatological world-view (or end-of-the-world-view) of St. Paul; the Roman Catholic Church did ultimately build on Pauline passages reflecting a natural-law theory, and the Protestant Reformation subsequently sought to eliminate what the Reformers thought to be Roman Catholic distortions of Pauline thought. There was both a continuity and a discontinuity between the doctrines of St. Paul, St. Thomas Aquinas and Martin Luther. In a sense, Khrushchev appears as a Soviet Reformer, going back to the original Leninist texts to reinterpret them against his predecessor. But the Leninist texts will not support the actual developments in Soviet law, which are a response to political, economic and social needs that Lenin could not possibly visualize. If we may carry the historical analogy one step further, we may compare the relationship between Soviet law and Khrushchev's Leninism to the relationship between German law in the 16th century and Luther's Paulinism. There is, of course, a relationship; but it is a relationship in terms of outlook and approach and attitude, not a relationship in terms of theory.

We must seek the operative theory of Soviet law, therefore, not in the Leninist texts which Soviet jurists cite, but in the evolution of the law itself. . . .

SECTION VIII

Civil Rights and Liberties
and the State

In his report to the Special Eighth All-Union Congress of Soviets (November 25, 1936), Stalin attempted to demonstrate the "superiority" of the Soviet Constitution over the bourgeois constitutions by emphasizing, *inter alia*, that the new fundamental law of the U.S.S.R. did not "limit itself to recording formal rights of citizens." In contrast to bourgeois practice, he argued, the new "socialist democracy" of the Soviet Union *guaranteed* the enjoyment of fundamental rights and liberties by "providing definite material facilities" for their exercise. According to Article 125 of the Soviet Constitution, the basic civil liberties of Soviet citizens "are ensured by placing at the disposal of the working people and their organizations printing presses, stocks of paper, public buildings, the streets, communications facilities and other material requisites for the exercise of these rights."* But these rights, according to the same article, can be enjoyed only "in conformity with the interests of the working people, and in order to strengthen the socialist system." In other words, the basic freedoms of speech, press and assembly—the essential elements underlying any genuine democratic system—can be "enjoyed" in the U.S.S.R. only for purposes of advancing the interests of the Communist Party.

Soviet apologists justify this practice on the assumption that the Soviet citizen "is the bearer of a new morality based on the strug-

* For the constitutional provisions concerning the fundamental rights and duties of citizens in the U.S.S.R., see Articles 118–133.

gle for the building of a Communist society." As such, in their view, there can be no contradiction between the rights and interests of the Soviet state and those of the Soviet citizen. In this line of reasoning, the political freedoms "enjoyed" by Soviet citizens express the interests of the working class, making possible the management of public affairs by the people, with the Communist Party "merely" exercising "political guidance over all state and public organizations."

Taking cognizance of both Soviet practices and Marxist-Leninist theories, Professor Schuman differentiates between the fictitious and factual rights of citizens in the U.S.S.R. by recalling two of the many basic questions related to the nature of freedom: "freedom *from* what? freedom *for* what?" While recognizing that considerable progress has been made in the realm of personal and social rights, especially since the death of Stalin in March 1953, he also demonstrates that the Soviet state "is still a totalitarian one-Party oligarchy in which competitive political activity is forbidden and 'freedom' of expression is permissible only within the limits of the current 'Party line.'"

Fundamental Rights and Duties of Citizens

A. DENISOV AND M. KIRICHENKO

Introduction

The Soviet state has eliminated the injustice which existed in Russia prior to the October Revolution, when the members of the exploiting classes enjoyed almost all rights, while duties were imposed predominantly upon the working people. The U.S.S.R.

From *Soviet State Law* by A. Denisov and M. Kirichenko, selections from pp. 319–343. Moscow: Foreign Languages Publishing House, 1960.

has abolished any dependence of the legal status of man on private property, social origin, nationality or race, religion, sex, etc. The Soviet citizen is a full and equal member of socialist society. He is the sole master of his country enjoying the fundamental rights and entrusted with the duties set down in the socialist Constitution. He is the bearer of a new morality based on the struggle for the building of a communist society.

New, advanced ideas of justice, freedom, equality, rights and duties of citizens now prevail in the Soviet Union.

Fundamental Rights of Soviet Citizens

The fundamental rights of Soviet citizens are constitutional rights *conforming to the interests of the working people** of town and country.

The subjects of these rights are all the citizens of the U.S.S.R.

When Soviet power was coming into being, not a single Soviet institution restricted any citizen in his democratic rights. The bourgeoisie and the landlords took advantage of this and utilized the freedoms of speech, assembly and the press, together with all other political rights gained as a result of the October Revolution, for their counter-revolutionary ends. In their speeches and newspapers the enemies of the working people slandered the October Revolution and the Soviet Government. They interpreted the right to free association to mean freedom for all exploiters and traitors to set up their counter-revolutionary organizations. Similarly, the bourgeoisie and the landlords utilized the electoral rights for their anti-Soviet activity. They fraudulently infiltrated into the organs of the Soviet state, trying to undermine and corrupt them from within. The Soviet Government detected these criminal machinations of the enemies of the working people in good time and deprived them of political rights.

But those who work were granted all rights from the very first days of Soviet power. With the consolidation of the socialist system, these rights and freedoms, as well as their guarantees, have been considerably extended.

Soviet citizens are working people completely free from the yoke of exploitation and enjoying guaranteed rights in all spheres. . . .

* *Italics supplied.*

All the fundamental rights of Soviet citizens may be divided into three categories: political, socio-economic, and cultural.

Political rights include freedom of speech, freedom of the press, freedom of assembly, including the holding of meetings, freedom of street processions and demonstrations, freedom to unite in public organizations and societies of working people, electoral rights, equality of citizens and freedom of conscience. It is these rights which contribute most to the development of the political activity and creative initiative of the masses of the people.

Socio-economic rights include the right to work, the right to rest and leisure, the right to maintenance in old age and also in case of sickness or disability, the right to personal property and the right to inherit it, and the right of collective-farm households to have their own holdings.

Cultural rights include, above all, the right to education, which enables all Soviet citizens to enjoy the blessings of culture and the achievements of science and art.

The Constitution also provides for such personal freedom as the inviolability of the person, the inviolability of their homes and the privacy of correspondence.

A distinguishing feature of these fundamental rights is that they are guaranteed politically, economically and juridically.

The most substantial guarantee of the fundamental rights of Soviet citizens is Soviet power itself, which does not merely affirm the rights of citizens, but lays special stress on measures for ensuring their implementation. . . .

The fundamental rights and freedoms of Soviet citizens are of great importance and have an outstanding part to play in many spheres of public life. They enable the citizens of the U.S.S.R. to take an active part in the country's economic, governmental, cultural, political and other activity.

Thus, the rights of Soviet citizens do not contradict the interests of the Soviet state, just as the interests of the state do not contradict the rights and freedoms of citizens. . . .

THE RIGHT TO WORK. The Soviet people are engaged in free creative labor for the good of their socialist country. They do not know any threat of unemployment. . . .

The right to work implies, according to the proletarian conception, "the appropriation of the means of production, their subjection to the associated working class and, therefore, the abolition of wage labor, of capital and of their mutual relations." . . .

The Political Freedoms of Soviet Citizens

The political freedoms of the citizens of a socialist state mean their guaranteed democratic rights to participate in state, political and public life with the aim of consolidating the power of the working people, applying this power correctly and developing the organizational initiative and political activity of the masses of the people.

When analyzing the political freedoms of citizens of a socialist state, one must find out: 1) In the interests of which classes these freedoms have been established; 2) what is their concrete essence; 3) what is their role in the life of society.

In the Soviet state and the People's Democracies the *political freedoms** of their citizens *express the interests of the working class** and of all the working people guided by this class. Political freedom means that the working people have been emancipated from the power of the capitalists and landlords, that they are free to raise and solve any questions relating to state and public life, that *the masses of the people themselves rule the state through** their representatives in the organs of state power and through their mass organizations (trade unions, co-operative organizations, the Young Communist League, etc.) and *the Communist Party which exercises political guidance over all state and public organizations of the working people.** . . .

FREEDOM OF CONSCIENCE. This freedom means the right of citizens to practise any form of religion, or not to recognize religion at all and to conduct anti-religious propaganda. . . .

The Soviet Union has never had any laws restricting freedom of conscience or establishing any privileges for citizens on account of their religious beliefs. Soviet power proceeds from the proposition that religious views and beliefs cannot be changed by means of legislative or administrative bans. The religious outlook is being overcome and will be fully overcome in the course of building a communist society as a result of the cultural and educational work

* *Italics supplied.*

of the socialist state and the extensive scientific and atheistic propaganda conducted by the state organs among the population.

Freedom of conscience was established in the Soviet state immediately after the October Revolution. The Soviet power, however, had to wage a resolute struggle against those religious organizations and groups among the clergy which resisted the gains of the October Revolution.

With the triumph of socialism in the U.S.S.R., and as a result of profound changes which took place in the economy and class structure of Soviet society, the social roots of religion disappeared and the very foundation of the church has thus been undermined. This, as well as the rapid development of science and the improvement in the general cultural level of the population of the country, has contributed to the successful liberation of the Soviet people from religious survivals.

At present the clergy are loyal to the Soviet state, and the struggle against religious survivals is a purely ideological struggle of the scientific (materialistic) outlook against the anti-scientific religious (idealistic) outlook. . . .

FREEDOM OF SPEECH.   In accordance with Article 125 of the Constitution of the U.S.S.R., Soviet citizens are guaranteed freedom of speech, which means the right freely to express and advocate their thoughts and convictions on matters of public concern orally or in written form.

When discussing problems of international or domestic life and practical questions relating to the work of factories, state and collective farms and institutions, the citizens of the socialist state thereby exercise their freedom of speech in the interests of the building of communism and the consolidation of peace.

Criticism is one of the basic manifestations of freedom of speech in the U.S.S.R. At their meetings and in the press the citizens of the socialist state reveal shortcomings and errors in the work of undertakings, state and other bodies. Under the guidance of the Communist Party, the working people of the U.S.S.R. are combating harmful and dangerous manifestations of arrogance, ostentation and complacency; along with shortcomings and errors in work, they disclose negative features in the life of society and make suggestions concerning the ways and means in which they can be eliminated.

Such criticism strengthens the rule of the working people, contributes to the building of a new life, educates the state officials and Party workers in the spirit of communism, increases their sense of responsibility for the work entrusted to them, instils intolerance of all shortcomings and is, in general, an important factor in the struggle for overcoming pernicious survivals in the minds of men. . . .

FREEDOM OF THE PRESS. Citizens of the U.S.S.R. are guaranteed freedom of the press, i.e., the right to publish and distribute newspapers, magazines, books, posters, etc., as well as the right freely to express their views in the press.

In a socialist state, freedom of the press means that all printing-houses, paper mills and factories producing printing-inks are fully at the disposal of the working people of town and country. It is mainly this which ensures freedom of the press in the U.S.S.R. . . .

FREEDOM OF ASSEMBLY AND DEMONSTRATION. Citizens of the U.S.S.R. are guaranteed freedom of assembly, including the holdings of meetings and freedom of street processions and demonstrations. These freedoms are ensured by placing at the disposal of the working people all public buildings, streets, squares and other material requisites for the exercise of these rights (Article 125 of the Constitution of the U.S.S.R.). . . .

THE RIGHT OF ASSOCIATION. In conformity with the interests of the working people, and in order to develop the organizational initiative and political activity of the masses of the people, citizens of the U.S.S.R. are guaranteed the right to unite in public organizations. . . .

In the U.S.S.R. voluntary societies are independent organizations of the working people; according to the territorial limits of their activities, they may be of all-Union, republican or local importance. The legal status of these societies is in the main determined by their rules.

All public organizations and societies of working people in the Soviet Union are based on the principles of voluntary association and equality of their members. It is this which determines their democratic character.

They support and assist the Soviet state in the accomplishment of its tasks and functions. They occupy a prominent place and play an outstanding role in the system of the dictatorship of the working class.

The most active and politically conscious citizens from among the ranks of the working class, working peasants and working intellectuals have voluntarily united in the Communist Party of the Soviet Union which is the highest form of working-class political organization. It is the Communist Party which has ensured the historical victories of the Soviet people. The alliance of the working class and peasantry, which as a result of the October Revolution overthrew the power of the capitalists and landlords, established the dictatorship of the working class, abolished capitalism and all forms of exploitation of man by man and built up a socialist society, was created and consolidated under its leadership. *The Communist Party is the vanguard of the working people in their struggle to build a communist society, and is the leading core of all organizations of the working people, both public and state.**

The democratism of the socialist system is clearly manifested in the fact that this system gives birth to numerous public organizations and societies of the working people which, under the guidance of the Communist Party, play an active part in the building of communism, strengthening the defence of the country, and in ensuring security and peace among all nations. . . .

The formation of any fascist or fascist-type organizations, or of any other association whose aims and activities are directed against the social and state system of the workers and peasants, or against socialist law and order, is strictly prohibited in the socialist countries.

Personal Rights of Citizens

The fundamental rights of Soviet citizens include inviolability of the person, inviolability of the home and privacy of correspondence. . . .

Equality of Citizens of the U.S.S.R.

The equality of citizens in all spheres of economic, governmental, public, political and cultural life is an indivisible law of the U.S.S.R.

* *Italics supplied.*

The citizens of the U.S.S.R. enjoy equal rights and discharge equal duties. Any restriction of the rights of citizens, advocacy of hatred and contempt, instigation of enmity or humiliation of citizens on account of their sex, nationality, race or attitude to religion is punishable by law. . . .

The Marxist concept of equality fundamentally differs from the bourgeois interpretation.

The bourgeoisie tries to present equality as a formal similarity of rights and opportunities for all citizens under circumstances in which the diametrically opposing economic and political status of the exploiting minority and the exploited majority is retained in full. Such an interpretation serves to camouflage the inequality which in fact exists.

The ideologists of the bourgeoisie claim that Marxism advocates the abolition of all physical and spiritual differences between people. But Marxism in fact interprets the concept of equality only as equality in the social status of people. From the Marxist point of view, any abolition of differences in the requirements and tastes of people, any levelling of their personal needs and mode of life, is a petty-bourgeois, reactionary absurdity incompatible with scientific socialism.

The equality of Soviet citizens lies in their equal relation to public property. This means that the means and instruments of production belonging to the whole people as represented by the state are equally accessible to every citizen, and that all citizens engaged in socialist economy have an equal right to payment for their work in accordance with its quantity and quality. All citizens equally enjoy the guaranteed political rights and freedoms.

In socialist countries the equality of citizens includes: 1) equality of men and women and 2) equality of citizens of all nationalities and races. . . .

Fundamental Duties of Soviet Citizens

The citizens of the U.S.S.R. not only enjoy guaranteed rights, but also discharge certain duties to the state, the fundamental duties of Soviet citizens have been established by the Constitution of the U.S.S.R. . . .

The fundamental duties bear a strictly personal character: every citizen must discharge them himself and has no right to confide their performance to somebody else. Nor can these duties pass to other persons by right of succession.

The fundamental duties of citizens concern *all* spheres of economic, governmental, political and cultural life of the country; thus, they are the duties of citizens towards society and the state as a whole.

A citizen of a socialist state is a free and competent builder of a new society. His solicitude for the consolidation of the state and of the established law and order are, therefore, quite natural. This explains why Soviet citizens always discharge their constitutional duties voluntarily and readily; thereby they strengthen the political and economic might of the socialist state and its defence potential.

The performance of fundamental duties by citizens is supervised by the corresponding state organs. Coercive measures are applied to those citizens who fail to discharge the duties imposed by the Soviet state. Such compulsion, however, is only used against a minority, since very few violate the rules of behavior established by the Soviet state. . . .

The Rights of Man

FREDERICK L. SCHUMAN[*]

Within the limits of oligarchy, what are the realities and what are the fictions of the "constitutional rights" of Soviet citizens as

[*] Woodrow Wilson Professor of Government at Williams College, Dr. Schuman is the author of *International Politics* (1933), *Night Over Europe* (1941), *Soviet Politics at Home and Abroad* (1946), *The Commonwealth of Man* (1952), and *Government in the Soviet Union* (1961).

---

elaborately set forth in Chapter X and XI of the Charter of 1936? The answer is less simple than many Western commentators have assumed. "Real liberty," declared Stalin to Roy Howard (cf. *Izvestia*, December 8, 1936), "can be had only where exploitation is destroyed, where there is no oppression of one people by another, where there is no unemployment and pauperism, where a person does not shiver in fear of losing tomorrow his job, home, bread. Only in such a society is it possible to have real, and not paper, liberty, personal and otherwise."

This "reality" proved meaningless over many years to the millions of Soviet citizens arrested by agents of the OGPU, NKVD, or MVD and consigned to forced-labor camps in Siberia and the Far North, where only the hardiest survived the rigors of arduous work, meager diet, miserable living conditions, and systematic terrorization and exploitation—pending the amnesties, relaxations, and "mellowing" of the police-state regime since Stalin's death.

Many other rights solemnly guaranteed by the Supreme Law of Sovietland remained "dead letters" during most of the two decades after 1936. Freedom of speech, press, assembly, and association (§§125, 126) and inviolability of persons, homes, and correspondence (§§127, 128) were often honored more in the breach than in the observance, as was acknowledged at Party Congress XX and thereafter. The same was true of intellectual, scientific, and academic freedom, particularly in the black years of Stalin's posturing as the infallible source of all truth and taste—when the *Vozhd* and his agents felt in duty bound to impose "Socialist Realism" on writers, artists, and musicians, Lysenko's fantasies on biologists, "Marxist physics" on other scientists, etc. Political privileges (§§134–42) have been less right than duties, and have, in any case, only a tangential relationship to public policy-making and the selection of representatives. The independence of the courts (§112) and the protection of the individual against arbitrary arrest, imprisonment, or execution (§§111, 127, 128) remained fictitious so long as the MVD possessed the right to punish alleged political offenders without public trial, so long as the criminal code permitted penalization "by analogy" of acts not defined as crimes but held dangerous to the State, so long as the death penalty was prescribed (as in the act of August 7, 1932) for theft of public property, and so long as the full rigors of the criminal code were made applicable (as in the act of April 7, 1935) to juvenile delinquents.

Freedom of conscience and worship (§124), or the lack thereof, have undergone many vicissitudes during the four decades of Soviet power. The sequence began with open persecution by a regime of atheists of many churchmen and believers during the years when the established Orthodox Church, smarting from Soviet disestablishment and dispossession of most of its wealth, championed Autocracy and the cause of the White Armies. The charter of 1936 re-enfranchised the clergy. The "League of the Militant Godless," founded in 1925 and directed by Emilian Yaroslavsky, claimed 10,000,000 members by 1932 but had declined to 3,000,000 by 1940. When Communist efforts to extirpate religion had clearly failed and the new Church patriotically rallied to the defense of the State against the Nazi invaders, the League was dissolved and its publishing facilities were transferred to the Orthodox priesthood. On September 12, 1943, an officially sponsored *Sobor* elected Metropolitan Sergei of Moscow Patriarch of all Russia. Upon his death a new *Sobor* in January 1945 elected Metropolitan Alexei as Patriarch. Meanwhile, in October of 1943 a State Council on Church Affairs, headed by Georgi Karpov, was set up to promote "genuine religious freedom."

Any congregation willing to pay the salary of a cleric and the costs of building maintenance may conduct services in church, mosque, or synagogue. But religious instruction of the young outside of home is still (1957) forbidden. No church receives any financial aid from the State save for the restoration and upkeep of ecclesiastical structures of historic or artistic importance—most of which, however, are without congregations and have been converted into museums. Under these circumstances religious life languishes despite formal freedom of worship.

Soviet citizens enjoy certain other "constitutional rights" that are more substance than shadow. Individual and collective property rights, along with rights of ownership and inheritance of income, personal property, savings, and private houses (§§7–10), appear to be well respected within the limits already indicated. The major social gains of the Revolution are embodied (§§118–20) in the rights to work, to paid vacations, to insurance against illness and old age, and to free dental and medical service, including access to hospitals and sanatoria. The social-insurance system, administered by the trade unions, and socialized medicine, directed by the Ministry of Health, are among the significant contributions of the Soviet State to the welfare of the people. The number of physicians increased from 20,000 in 1913 to 63,000 in 1928, 141,000 in 1941 (January 1), and 299,000 in 1955 (July 1), with lesser health workers, including *feldshers* (medical aides) and nurses, increasing from 393,200 in 1941 to 731,100 in 1955. Death rates declined from 18.3 per thousand population in 1940 to 9.6 in 1950, 9.0 in 1953, and 8.4 in 1955, while birth rates for the corresponding years were reported as 31.7, 26.5, 24.9, and 25.6.

Equality of rights for women, including equal access to all vocations and identical status with men as to salaries, vacations, social insurance, and education, plus "pre-maternity and maternity leave with full pay" (§122), is also a fact and not a fiction. Early Soviet legislation made marriage and divorce simple civil formalities, costing only a few rubles at the Registration bureaus (*Zags*), recognized no distinction between legitimate and illegitimate children, and permitted free abortions in public clinics. In a change of "line," decrees and laws of 1936 forbade abortions except for reasons of health. Under the impact of the fearful blood-letting of World War II, new legislation of 1943–44 made divorce expensive and difficult, imposed special taxes on the unmarried and the childless, and offered monetary rewards and honors to mothers of many children. While these statutes are still in force, abortion was again legalized in 1955. Any Soviet woman, married or unmarried, may by her own decision have an abortion without cost. Meanwhile, Western travelers in the U.S.S.R. are often shocked to see women sweeping streets, working in construction gangs, building houses, and performing other heavy tasks. But this phenomenon is merely visual evidence—along with many policewomen and numerous female bus-drivers, subway-operators, taxi-drivers, etc.—that equality of the sexes is a reality. By 1955, according to the handbook issued in Moscow by the Central Statistical Board, women comprise the following percentages of sundry vocations: health services, 85 (over two-thirds of Soviet physicians are women); restaurant workers, 83; teachers, 68; public administration, 49; industry, 45; transport and communications, 33; and construction, 31.

Amid so mixed a record of failures and successes, of pledges broken and of promises carried out, of rights betrayed and rights achieved, it is fitting to conclude our evaluation with the one duty of the State which has been most adequately fulfilled and is bright with hope for the future. §121: "Citizens of the U.S.S.R. have the right to education. . . ." Freedom from ignorance through the abolition of illiteracy has been achieved via the nation-wide network of ten-year public schools, combining elementary and secondary grades in one sequence and raising the number of pupils in attendance from 7,900,000 in 1914 to 34,800,000 in 1940. Falling birth rates and the decline of population during the years of war reduced the total to 28,200,000 in 1955. All Soviet children were going through seven grades by 1956. All would go through all ten grades by 1960, thus universalizing high-school education even more completely than in the USA. Coeducation, introduced in 1918 and abolished in 1943, was restored in 1956–57. Early experimentation in "progressive" education gave way in the 1930's to an exacting discipline, which has never since been much modified, despite complaints in recent years that school children are overworked.

Mathematics and the natural sciences are the "core" of Soviet education in the upper grades. All pupils are required to choose English, French, or German in the fifth grade (Latin, Greek, Spanish, Italian, and other tongues are not taught below the university level) and to study their choice for six years—with graduates of the ten-year schools usually acquiring a good reading knowledge, though seldom an adequate speaking knowledge, of the language thus selected. German was the most popular choice before 1939. English has been the favorite since 1945. A new network of highly selective "boarding schools" was established in 1956–57 on the model of English "public" and American private schools.

Beyond the ten-year schools Soviet higher education has taken flourishing form in a galaxy of trade schools, technical institutes, research centers, and universities, with the latter planned not for the few, as in Western Europe, but for the many, as in America.

Small tuition fees were introduced in 1940 but were abolished in 1956–57. All Soviet youths with the requisite talents are encouraged to attend universities, granted scholarships and living stipends whenever their needs call for such support, and generously rewarded for outstanding achievement with honors, prizes, and vocational opportunities. Between 1940 and 1955 the graduates of institutes and universities waxed from 908,000 to 2,184,000, with engineers increasing from 289,000 to 585,900, economists and business specialists from 59,300 to 113,800, and teachers, librarians, and other "cultural workers" from 300,400 to 906,400. In 1955, 1,230,000 young people were full-time students at universities, as compared with 850,000 in 1950 and 590,000 in 1940 (USA, 1954: 2,499,750). In 1955, 54,700 books were published in almost a billion copies, with even the most abstruse scientific works, however large the printing, being snatched up by an insatiable public within a few days in the innumerable bookstores and sidewalk stalls throughout the U.S.S.R. Public libraries numbered 277,000 with 527,000,000 books in 1940, and 392,000 with 1,351,000,000 books in 1955.

In short, Russia since 1917 has become educated as well as industrialized and urbanized. Stalin's totalitarian police state brought into being a community that can no longer be governed by the police methods of totalitarianism. In sundry ways, not yet altogether clear in 1957, the "dead letters" of the Constitution of 1936 were in painful process of having some breath of life infused into their empty symbols by the post-Stalin "collective" leadership. It is not fortuitous that, apart from the nearby Kremlin, the most impressive building in central Moscow, 40 years after 1917, is the Lenin State Library, claiming to be, with its 18,000,000 books, pamphlets, and periodicals, the largest library in the world, though singularly devoid of anti-Soviet works in any language. Neither is it accidental that the visitor who comes to Moscow by plane obtains his first glimpse of the Soviet capital, on the horizon of the Lenin Hills between the airport and the city, in the form of the 37-story tower (surrounded by a gigantic "suburban" development of huge apartment blocks, planned to house 200,000 people) of the new building of Moscow State University, opened in 1953. This imposing edifice, along with its adjuncts, is dedicated to physics, chemistry, biology, and allied sciences, with social studies and the humanities housed elsewhere in older academic structures within the city proper. The central citadel of learning, unquestionably the largest university building in the world, contains classrooms, lecture halls, laboratories, gymnasiums, and apartments for all of the faculty and much of the student body of 22,000. The Stalinist State, having in some measure expiated the crimes committed in its name by educating Russia, was in process, four decades after 1917, of ceasing to be a Stalinist State.

SECTION IX

The Electoral Process

One of the basic assumptions underlying democracy as an ideology and as a form of government is that the just powers of the government are derived from the consent of the governed. In a genuinely democratic society decision-making power is normally acquired by virtue of a competitive political struggle waged within the framework of an open marketplace of ideas and the context of freedom of choice. Such a competitive political struggle requires as a *conditio sine qua non* the prior existence of at least two independent political parties. Under these circumstances, the electoral process affords the machinery for both the peaceful transfer of governmental authority and the accountability of the rulers to the governed.

Notwithstanding the supremacy of the Communist Party in both the theory and practice of Soviet Government, adherents of Marxism-Leninism contend that the "one-party system . . . is [in fact] one of the merits of Soviet democracy in general and the Soviet electoral system in particular."*

The extension of the Marxist theory of the state to justify the exclusiveness of the Party is based on the contention that political parties represent economic class interests. With the elimination of the economic bases dividing society into two antagonistic classes, Soviet theorists argue, the interests of the Soviet people, composed of the two friendly classes of workers and peasants, are fully and effectively represented by the vanguard of the working class, the Communist Party. They contend, moreover, that the multiplicity of political parties notwithstanding, Western democracies have in

* For the constitutional provisions concerning the Soviet electoral system, see Articles 134–142.

fact only two parties representing the interests of the two antagonistic classes: the "genuinely democratic" political party—the
Communist Party—representing the interests of the "vast majority
of the exploited masses," and all the other parties which, "irrespective of their names, labels or pseudo-differences," constitute in
fact but one party representing the interests of the bourgeoisie. A
parliament composed of the representatives of such parties, according to Lenin's *State and Revolution*, is merely an instrument of
the "dictatorship of the bourgeoisie . . . given up to talk for the
special purpose of fooling the common people. . . ." In Lenin's
view, "Marx splendidly grasped the *essence* of capitalist democracy, when, in his analysis of the experience of the Commune, he
said that the oppressed are allowed, once every few years, to decide
which particular representatives of the oppressing class are to
represent and repress them in Parliament! . . . "

   If the Party's exclusive role in Soviet life is so rationalized, the
functions of the Soviet electoral processes become more understandable. Although the "elections" traditionally result in the
almost unanimous endorsement of official candidates, the rituals of
the no-contest affairs are extremely important for the Soviet rulers.
Their meaning and consequences of the process of election in the
Soviet Union are discussed in the article by Professors McClosky
and Turner.

The Soviet Electoral System

A. DENISOV AND M. KIRICHENKO

The Soviet electoral system is the aggregate of the democratic
principles which govern the elections to the representative bodies
of the Soviet state. These principles include: universal, equal and

From *Soviet State Law* by A. Denisov and M. Kirichenko, selections from
pp. 351–362. Moscow: Foreign Languages Publishing House, 1960.

direct suffrage by secret ballot; the responsibility and accountability of those elected to their electorate; the right of electors to recall their deputy at any time before his term of office expires, if he has not justified their confidence. The electoral law, i.e., the aggregate of the laws governing the electoral rights of citizens is an integral part of the electoral system.

The Soviet electoral system is consistently democratic in character and is an important means of drawing the working people into the administration of state affairs. It ensures efficient control by the people over the work of the organs of state power and the deputies. . . .

The right to nominate candidates belongs to public organizations of the working people: Communist Party organizations, trade unions, co-operative associations, youth organizations and cultural societies. This right is enjoyed both by the central, republican, territorial, regional, uyezed and district bodies of these organizations and societies and by general meetings of workers and other employees at factories and establishments, servicemen in military units, peasants on collective farms and in villages, and agricultural workers and other employees on state farms. . . .

The Communists nominate candidates jointly with non-Party people. The bloc of Communists and non-Party people is an alliance resulting from struggle which the people have waged against the enemies of the socialist revolution over many years under the leadership of the Communist Party. The Communist Party has consolidated the alliance of the workers and peasants and rallied the masses of non-Party people around it. By building socialist society, educating new people and establishing their moral and political unity, the Party has made this alliance the basis for conducting elections to the organs of power.

Bourgeois propagandists criticize the Soviet electoral system because it proceeds from the existence of one party in the Soviet Union—the Communist Party, which, in their opinion, means that only one candidate can stand in each constituency. True, in the Soviet Union there is a one-party system, which evolved historically. But this is not a shortcoming—on the contrary, it is one of the merits of Soviet democracy in general and the Soviet electoral system in particular. There are no antagonistic classes in the Soviet Union, and therefore there is no basis for the existence of

diametrically opposed political parties. The interests of the workers, peasants and intellectuals are expressed and safeguarded by the
Communist Party of the Soviet Union.

As for the bourgeois propagandists' allegation that the Soviet
electoral system permits only one candidate in each constituency,
it is the result of either ignorance or of deliberate slander. The
Soviet law provides for election of one deputy from each constituency, but does not restrict the rights of organizations and
societies to nominate any number of candidates they desire. It goes
without saying that this right cannot be interpreted as meaning
that these organizations and societies have a duty to nominate not
one, but two or more candidates in each constituency.

The Soviet Electoral Process

HERBERT MCCLOSKY AND JOHN E. TURNER[*]

In a democratic state, elections afford the machinery for transferring political authority peacefully and for holding officials accountable to the voters. The functioning of the electoral process
therefore provides an important clue to the nature of a political
system. Consent and accountability are achieved in a democratic
society through elections in which the voters are free to associate
and to join parties, free to discuss issues, and free to choose among
alternative policies and candidates. If these conditions for registering approval or dissent are absent, democracy cannot even be
approximated.

[*] Professor McClosky is associated with the Survey Research Center at the
University of California (Berkeley); Dr. Turner is Professor of Government at
the University of Minnesota and is the co-author of *The New Japan: Government and Politics* (1956).

Soviet elections are frequently hailed by Communist officials as the "most democratic of any country in the world." In contrast with foreign systems, where elections are alleged to be devices of the ruling class, elections in the U.S.S.R. are described as the expression of *all* the people. Under the present Constitution every Soviet citizen who has reached the age of eighteen is entitled to vote, regardless of nationality, sex, residence, social origin, property holdings, or education (Arts. 134–142). Only the mentally incompetent and those convicted of crime and deprived of their rights by a court are disfranchised. Voting is now on a territorial basis, with deputies directly elected by secret ballot. The Constitution provides that in the exercise of their electoral privileges, citizens are to enjoy freedom of speech, assembly, and demonstration.

Soviet electoral practices are designed to encourage maximum participation by the voters. Elections for the Supreme Soviet of the U.S.S.R., the republic soviets, and the local assemblies are usually held at different times, thereby enabling the regime to conduct as many campaigns as possible. Campaigns are relatively long, often beginning a month or two in advance of an election. Furthermore, elections are scheduled on a "rest day" in order to encourage a large turnout of voters. Voter registration is virtually automatic and occurs merely through the compiling of lists of all eligible voters in each locality. To foster widespread participation in elections, the regime has established a hierarchy of election commissions extending from the precinct to the All-Union level. Each commission consists of representatives of the Party, trade unions, youth organizations, cooperatives, cultural and scientific societies, and similar associations. The commissions, made up at the higher levels chiefly of Communists, are approved by the presidia or executive committees of the soviets. It is the duty of the commissions to administer elections, examine complaints about irregularities, tabulate the votes, and publicize the results. Their most important task is to certify the list of legally nominated candidates, and in exercising this responsibility the lower commissions are bound by the decisions of the higher ones. The extent of popular participation in the administering of elections may be judged from the claim that 7,000,000 people served on election boards in 1939, supervising an election in which nearly 1,300,000 deputies were chosen to the local soviets.

Since only one name appears on the ballot for each office,

nomination is equivalent to election. In the nominating of candidates, the Communist Party, of course, plays the central role, although candidates may also be nominated by such groups as the
trade unions, cooperatives, youth organizations, and cultural societies. The Party, however, is the "leading core" of each of these
organizations and especially dominates their higher echelons,
where decisions affecting the ultimate nomination are made. At
prenomination meetings in factories, farms, and other places of
employment, the name of a candidate is proposed and his qualifications are examined. These meetings are followed by a general
gathering of all nominating organizations in the constituency,
where a local candidate is chosen, usually by a nonsecret and
unanimous vote. The nominee is likely to be a person who has
distinguished himself in some way and whose work has come to
the attention of the Party. In addition to selecting a candidate
from the locality, constituencies sometimes nominate a nationally
prominent Communist for the same office. This prominent leader,
however, allows his name to stand in only one district. Once he
has made his choice, each constituency that had nominated him
thereupon deletes his name and designates the local hero as its
official nominee. With rare exceptions, therefore, each constituency presents only one candidate to the voters, the justification
being that only a single candidate is needed to represent the *single
interest* of "harmonious" classes.

Such unanimity in a country of widely divergent interests and
cultures leaves little doubt that most nominations have been
prearranged. In the event that more than one candidate is proposed for nomination, the election commission is free to withhold
certification from all but the preferred candidate. A decision refusing certification may be appealed, but only to the next higher
election commission whose determination is final. Disputes over
nominations are not subject to judicial review. In the 1937 election, thirty-seven candidates disappeared and were replaced by
other nominees between the time of nomination and election
day—a development in which the required nomination procedures
were apparently bypassed entirely. During 1937 and 1938, the
regime eliminated some electoral contests by police action, and
since that time the one-candidate ballot has been the rule. Although the Party controls the organizations that participate in the

nominating process, it does not initiate the selection of every candidate. By occasionally permitting the non-Party organizations to nominate their own favored people, the Party is able to learn who the potential leaders are and who should be recruited into its own ranks. No matter how a candidacy is initiated, of course, the Party at some stage approves the nomination.

Since elections in the U.S.S.R. are no-contest affairs, the regime turns the rather lengthy campaign into a vast propaganda drive. Soviet citizens are continuously deluged by propaganda campaigns of one type or another, but an approaching election is the signal for a greatly intensified effort all along the line. The election campaign affords one more occasion for explaining official policies, dramatizing Soviet achievements, and hailing the superiority of the Communist system over its competitors. Voters are told that they can demonstrate their loyalty to the system by casting their ballots unanimously for the single slate of candidates nominated by the Communist Party and the mass organizations. Workers and peasants are encouraged to commemorate the election by engaging in socialist competitions to increase production. The regime sends several million agitators into the field to explain official policies as well as to induce voters to go to the polls. The country is flooded with brochures, books, and speeches on the glories of the Soviet system and the people's obligations to it. Study circles, discussion groups, campaign meetings, house-to-house canvassing, and staged demonstrations are among the many devices used to educate the masses and alert them to their civic duties. During the first campaign held under the new Constitution 100,000 propagandists were at work in Moscow alone, 50,000 in Leningrad, and 50,000 in Kazakhstan. In the 1946 elections for the Supreme Soviet of the U.S.S.R., more than 3 million agitators were engaged in campaign activity, while 50 million books and pamphlets and 12 million political posters were distributed. For a voter to betray apathy toward public issues in the face of this frenzied campaigning is to risk being labeled an undesirable.

On election day the voters troop to the polls in great numbers. The election is made out to be a festive occasion, with bands and demonstrations celebrating the triumph of Soviet democracy. Upon arrival at the polling station, the voter is handed a one-candidate ballot, which he is entitled to mark in the privacy of a booth. His choice, of course, is extremely limited, since he can protest only by crossing off the single name or by failing to vote at all. Unless more than half the voters strike his name from the ballot, a candidate is legally elected. On very rare occasions a candidate for election to one of the lower soviets fails to win a majority, but this eventuality is almost unheard of in elections to higher bodies. The usual practice is for a citizen to cast his vote for the official candidate without troubling to enter the polling booth, since use of the booth might arouse suspicion that he is scratching the ballot. To avoid suspicion many voters go so far as to sign their ballots and some write expressions of adulation and gratitude to Soviet leaders.

Although the Soviet press often complains of poor organization and ineffective agitation in particular election districts, voting statistics show a long-term trend toward unanimity. In the early years the proportion of eligible voters who went to the polls was relatively small. In 1922, for example, only 36.5 per cent of the urban and 22.3 per cent of the rural electors bothered to vote. By 1926 the turnout of voters had risen to 52.0 per cent in the cities and 47.3 per cent in the farm areas, while the comparable figures after 1930 were 79.6 per cent and 70.4 per cent. In the first election for the Supreme Soviet under the present Constitution (1937), 96.8 per cent of the eligible voters cast their ballots, and by 1958 the number had increased to 99.97 per cent. Voter turnout in republic and local elections has increased in approximately the same ratio, with over 99 per cent participating in 1957.

Only the fascist dictatorships have rivaled the U.S.S.R. in the number of voters brought to the polls. Even in countries that have had long experience with democratic institutions, voter turnout rarely exceeds 85 to 90 per cent, and the proportion is frequently much lower. Communist officials point to the overwhelming response of Soviet voters as a manifestation of the unity of the people and their enthusiasm for the new order. The election returns, however, are not a reliable index of the strength of popular support, for they largely result from an effort in which the entire propaganda and organizing machinery of the totalitarian system is brought into operation. With every step in the consolidation of the dictatorship there has been an increase in voter participation. To ensure a large voting turnout Party workers and special election agitators are sent into every locality, and if possible into every home. The press, radio, and other media of mass influence whip up enthusiasm and tirelessly implore the voters to flock to the polls. Neighbors are pressed into service on election day to call upon tardy or recalcitrant citizens and to spur their appearance at the polls. There is thus created an atmosphere of intense movement, which subjects the voter to both obvious and subtle pressures. He quickly becomes aware of the risks he will incur if he fails to go to the polls or refuses to cast his ballot for the approved candidate. It is not surprising, therefore, that astonishing majorities are recorded for the official slate. In the 1958 elections to the Supreme Soviet, for example, the Communist and "non-Party" nominees received 99.7 per cent of the total vote cast, and similar majorities are usually registered in the election of deputies in the republic legislatures.

With several million elective offices to be filled, it is difficult for the regime to find enough Party members who can qualify as candidates. Partly for this reason the Party sponsors the candidacy of some "non-Party" nominees along with the Communist bloc. Since these nominees are carefully hand-picked, the Party and non-Party groups are virtually indistinguishable. "Every non-Party candidate for deputy," we are told, "is also the candidate of the Communists, and every Communist candidate for deputy is also the candidate of the non-Party people." The proportion of Communist candidates rises as the importance of the legislative office increases. Party members may constitute fewer than one-fourth of the candidates for village or town soviets, but in the soviets at the republic or All-Union levels the number of Communists reaches 80 per cent or higher. . . .

Since Soviet elections do not, even in theory, constitute a limitation on the Communist Party but are merely an endorsement of official candidates whose victory is never in doubt, why does the regime conduct such long campaigns and make such a show of carrying out a genuine election? Communist leaders, recognizing the persuasive power of the democratic myth, have tried to incorporate some of the symbols and trappings of democratic procedure into the pattern of dictatorship. Since the regime pretends to base its legitimacy partly on mass support, it is compelled to go through the motions of allowing the people to register their "consent." Elections are also looked upon as a "mighty instrument for further educating and organizing the masses politically" and as the "broadest form of attracting the masses into state administration." The election device, moreover, affords Party rulers the opportunity to discover new leadership or, at the other extreme, to unearth passive or otherwise uncooperative elements. Then, too, as we have seen, an election serves as an occasion for raising the campaign of Communist indoctrination to a new pitch, for publicizing current policies, and for renewing the call to sacrifice. Finally, one of the most important functions of a Soviet election is to demonstrate to people at home and abroad that the Soviet masses are unified and fervently behind the regime. The 1954 election, for example, was characteristically welcomed as an opportunity for a "new and powerful demonstration of the close unity of Party, government and people." Naturally the huge voter turnout and the overwhelming victory of the Communist-sponsored candidates are cited as evidence of Soviet solidarity.

It would seem, then, that Soviet elections do not perform either of the two basic functions listed at the outset of this discussion, neither transferring authority peacefully nor guaranteeing political accountability. No election during the entire history of the U.S.S.R. has ever brought about an actual transfer of power from one group of rulers to another, or even had the slightest discernible influence on the competition for office at the higher levels. Furthermore, since there is only a single candidate for each office, a Soviet election can hardly be considered a device for achieving accountability. The Soviet view of legitimacy does not rest on the right of consent in the electorate alone but assigns the right of final approval to the Party as well. Both the electorate and the Party are thus perceived as the ultimate sources of legitimacy—a contradiction that can be reconciled only by the mystical notion that the Party *is* the people at a more advanced stage.

SECTION X

Government and the Planned Economy

Perhaps no other aspect of Soviet life has been more consistently held up for emulation than the Soviet system of economic planning. The ability of the Soviet leaders to transform a relatively backward, primarily agricultural Russia into the second greatest economic power in the course of a few decades has stirred the imagination of many leaders of the economically underdeveloped newly independent nations of the world. Eager to bring about the rapid industrialization of their countries, these leaders have often tended to rationalize the need for the "temporary" sacrificing of democratic institutions and processes in order to justify certain political and socio-economic measures.

Using the gross national product figures as the most comprehensive indicator of an economy's performance, one is struck by the fact that while the Soviet economy in the early 1960's represented approximately only 46 percent of the size of the United States economy,* it was more than double the size of any third power. This phenomenal expansion of the Soviet economy has undoubtedly been made possible by the state's absolute control over the basic factors of production. The increased allocations of investment funds for the capital goods industries—a primary factor in determining the growth rate of any economy—has been achieved primarily by curtailing the resources allocated for the advancement of consumer welfare.

Yet, paradoxically, in spite of the priorities granted to indus-

---

* The U.S. Gross National Product in billions of current dollars in 1960 was 504.4.

trialization since the inauguration of the first of the Five-Year plans in 1928, and notwithstanding all the efforts made to maintain rapid expansion, the U.S.S.R. is still heavily agricultural. Generating nearly a third of the national income, the agricultural sector of the economy occupies about 43 percent of the labor force (1960) as compared with only 7 percent in the USA. The Achilles' heel of the Soviet economy, agriculture has been plagued by chronic shortcomings ever since the establishment of the U.S.S.R. These shortcomings were dramatized in the Fall of 1963 when the Soviet Union—the world's largest wheat producer—was compelled to buy millions of tons of wheat from Canada and the United States. The low productivity of Soviet agriculture is to a large extent due to both the inherent weaknesses of the collective (*Kolkhozy*) and state farm (*Sovkhozy*) system and the cumulative neglect and periodic disinvestments to which agriculture was subjected during the long period of rapid industrialization. Neglect and disinvestments were reflected especially in the shortage of fertilizers and farm equipment and the inadequacy of the irrigation systems. The consequences of these shortcomings were felt particularly in the 1950's when an ambitious virgin lands program was undertaken to extend the wheat area into the semi-arid territories of Siberia and Kazakhstan.

The persistence of the agricultural and many of the industrial problems has been aggravated by the relatively heavy defense burdens assumed by the U.S.S.R. during the post-World War II period.

To improve the over-all performance of the economy, the Soviet leaders periodically adopted a number of measures calculated to streamline the structure and functions of the various sectors of the economy. The reorganization drive gathered momentum after the death of Stalin without affecting, however, the fundamental principles underlying the Soviet planned economic system.

The persistence of economic shortcomings can be gauged from the great interest attached in both governmental and academic circles to the new economic ideas advanced by Prof. Yevsey G. Liberman of Kharkov University. Originally revealed in September 1962, Prof. Liberman's "Western" ideas called for the introduction of profit-incentives calculated to encourage plant managers to set and attain higher output targets, to introduce new technology and new products, and to improve the over-all quality of production. "Libermanism," as these ideas are popularly referred to, has found a favorable response among many Soviet economists and scientists, including Academicians Vadim A. Trapeznikov and Lev A. Leontyev, and Sergei A. Afanasyev, Chairman of the Industrial Management Council of the Russian SFSR.

Notwithstanding such radical changes as the abolition of the machine-and-tractor stations and the reorganization of industrial management on the basis of the principle of territoriality (1957), however, the machinery of management and planning continues to be considered as "a major instrument of the Communist Party in building a Communist society."

The Soviet viewpoint with regard to the basic principles underlying economic planning and management, the fundamental changes introduced in industrial and agricultural operations, and the structure and functions of the various central, regional and local economic planning agencies is represented in the first selection of this section written by Mr. I. Yevenko.

Professor Gregory Grossman reviews in the second article the nature of the various changes introduced in the structure and organization of the Soviet economy from the Western point of view. He observes that while considerable progress was made by Soviet industry and agriculture, "there is hardly an economic problem that preoccupied the regime twenty-five years ago which does not preoccupy its successor today." Of the multitude of problems confronting the Soviet economy, Professor Grossman emphasizes the following:

(1) Problems pertaining to agriculture: its pronounced lag behind the rest of the economy, its sluggish response to many of the remedial measures, [etc.]; (2) Overcentralization and bureaucratization of the whole economy. . . . (3) Deficiencies of planning. . . . (4) Inadequate attention to economic efficiency (optimization) in planning and management; (5) Chronic and general supply difficulties with regard to producer goods, including equipment; . . . (6) Obstacles to innovation, whether owing to "friction" in the bureaucratic hierarchies or to resistance from below; (7) "Localism" and "departmentalism" of varying degrees of enlightenment or selfishness; . . . (8) The many ills of the construction industry. . . . (9) The consumer's well-known woes: shortages of consumer goods and interruptions in their supply, their poor quality and

limited variety, the lack of both service and services, and the ever-present housing shortage.

The persistence of these problems in spite of the many years of experience in Soviet economic planning and management and the thorough training and indoctrination programs is strong evidence, according to Professor Grossman, "that they are a systemic phenomenon."

Planning in the U.S.S.R.

I. YEVENKO

Basic Principles of Management and Planning of the Economy in the U.S.S.R.

. . . The scientific principles of managing and planning the socialist economy were elaborated by Lenin. He formulated the propositions on the functions of the socialist state in directing the economy; the unity of political and economic leadership; the principles and organisation of national economic planning, accounting and control by the entire people; democratic centralism in economic management and planning; the proper selection of personnel and control of fulfilment of orders and plans; the principles of cost accounting and strict economy; the use in economic management of personal material incentives, etc. The first long-term national economic plans were drawn up under the guidance of Lenin who called them plans of "economic and social development." . . .

Socialist ownership of the means of production creates a solid basis for organising the management and planning of the economy. State management of the economy in socialist society em-

From *Planning in the U.S.S.R.* by I. Yevenko, selections from pp. 7–62. Moscow: Foreign Languages Publishing House.

braces all aspects of extended socialist reproduction—production, distribution, circulation and consumption of the social product— in all the diversity of their interconnections.

Centralised management of production under socialism is a manifestation of the objective law of planned, proportionate development of the national economy, one of its requirements.

The socialist state manages the national economy in accordance with a single long-term plan, which helps to organise and direct the work of millions of people. The great organisational and mobilising role of the Soviet state and of its inspiring and guiding force, the Communist Party, is expressed in that they perform organisational functions, which ensure the continuous development of the socialist economy, science and culture at a fast rate and also the steady advance of the people's living standard.

The socialist state, with the help of its agencies of economic management, planning and accounting, directs the economy and culture and organises social production. Governmental bodies take into account the multifarious requirements of society and, in conformity with them, plan both in the centre and in the periphery the growth and improvement of production, the application of advanced technology, steady rise in the productivity of social labour and increase of socialist accumulations, and also direct capital construction and the geographical distribution of the productive forces.

At each stage, the socialist state determines the concrete tasks of national economic development, the volume of production, sets the directions, rates and proportions of economic growth, allocates the material, labour and financial resources, establishes the volume of home and foreign trade, sets prices, wages, etc. The state also guides the economic activities of co-operative organisations (collective farms, consumer co-operatives) through the system of their elected bodies and its leading agencies.

The state performs other functions: it organises the educational system and the training of personnel and promotes the development of science and art. Thus, the economic, cultural and educational activities of the socialist state and its local bodies embrace all the aspects of society's life.

Planned direction of the national economy is a principal feature of the economic and organising function of the socialist state.

Economic planning is a special function performed by an apparatus set up for this purpose, which is part of the state administration and economic management both in the centre and in the localities.

The apparatus directly in charge of planning economic and cultural development in the Soviet Union plays an important part among the bodies of the socialist state. The intricate functions of management and planning in socialist society demand of the state apparatus deep and diverse technical and economic knowledge and great experience. *The machinery of management and planning is a major instrument of the socialist state and the Communist Party in building communist society.**

Political and economic leadership in the Soviet Union is united. *Economic plans represent a consistent embodiment of the general line of the Communist Party.** They reflect the economic programme of the Party which expresses the basic, vital interests of the working people. Lenin taught us that "politics is the concentrated expression of economics," thus stressing the fact that the tasks of the Party and of the state plans in building the material and technical basis of socialism are inseparable. . . .

Centralised guidance consists first of all in the development of the socialist economy being based on long-term plans. Herein lies the great strength of the socialist planned economy.

Centralised direction in planning creates favourable conditions for the development of the productive forces on a country-wide scale, for rapid progress in all social and economic spheres.

The economy of the Soviet Union is a socially homogeneous gigantic and widely ramified organism functioning over the vast territory of the 15 Union republics, embracing hundreds of different branches and categories of production, hundreds of thousands of enterprises and construction sites.

The Soviet Union has over 200,000 state enterprises, more than 100,000 construction sites, over 2,900 state repair-and-service stations, some 7,500 state farms and about 45,000 collective farms. The state owns a ramified network of railways, over 124,000 km long, 251,000 km of motor roads, air lines and planes, hundreds of thousands of state warehouses and trading establishments (which account for 70 per cent of all retail trade), and also a wide network of cultural and educational establishments (including 739 universi

* *Italics supplied.*

ties and colleges and 3,329 secondary technical schools), banks, foreign trade organisations and scientific institutions.

State property is the dominant form of property in the Soviet Union. It accounts for about 90 per cent of all the production facilities of the country and 94 per cent of the total industrial output. Alongside state industrial enterprises and state farms there are large collective farms and small industrial establishments belonging to them, as well as thousands of small industrial and service establishments belonging to consumer co-operatives.

Centralised state guidance in socialist society, however, does not detract from the role of local bodies in managing the economy, does not hamper their initiative in operating it, with due account of the specific features of each Soviet republic, of each economic administration area.

Administration of the state, management and planning of the economy in socialist society are based on the Leninist principle of *democratic centralism.* Its application makes it possible correctly to combine centralised planned direction of social production by the state with the maximum stimulation of the effort of the masses. . . .

Democratic centralism in economic planning means that state plans set only the main assignments which determine the principal directions, rates and proportions in the development of the economy. At the same time the enterprises, economic councils and republican agencies themselves draw up economic plans in conformity with the general tasks of the state, but with consideration for local possibilities and conditions. . . .

But once the general tasks of the state in developing the economy of the Soviet Union or of a Union republic have been elaborated with the participation of the periphery and approved, fulfilment of the planned assignments becomes obligatory for all managerial and planning bodies at the lower levels, in the Union republics, autonomous republics, territories and regions, down to the enterprises of industry, agriculture, construction, transport, trade—in other words, for all the links in the socialist economy.

Management of a separate enterprise which is an integral part of the national economy is done on the basis of the principles and methods that are general for the entire socialist economy.

One-man management of production is a basic principle of the socialist operation of the economy. It implies the subordination of the personnel to the will of the manager who is vested with the necessary rights and bears full responsibility for the work of the section entrusted to him. . . .

The proper combination of one-man management and collegial leadership, one-man management and control and criticism by the masses, combination of the authority of the leader and the initiative of the people he leads—this is one of the cardinal features of democratic centralism.

State management and planning of the socialist economy are based on a broad and flexible system of the people's participation in operating the economy. Democracy in management and planning is especially manifested in socialist emulation of working people. Emulation is a very important form of drawing the workers into managing the economy and of working for the fulfilment of economic plans. . . .

The system of management of state enterprises in the Soviet Union is based on the principle of the *territorial* organisation of the entire managerial machinery, brought as close to production as possible. This means that management and planning in a given territory are arranged on the basis of the definite production specialisation of the various economic organisations and the territorial location of industry. Economic councils direct all enterprises and construction sites of an area, while boards, combines and trusts, subordinated to economic councils, unite similar or interrelated enterprises located near each other.

Problems of the political organisation of society, of the state structure and administration acquire great importance in the period of the full-scale building of communism.

The building of socialism in the Soviet Union has shown that as socialist society advances to communism, the functions of the state in economic management and planning, far from withering away, steadily grow in scale and importance.

Development and Improvement of the Forms of Management and Planning

. . . On the basis of a deep analysis of the economic development attained and the experience accumulated in economic management, the Soviet Government adopted during the Fifth Five-Year Plan period (1951–55) a number of decisions to eliminate excessive centralisation in economic management. The rights of the Councils of Ministers of the Union republics were extended considerably. Some of the all-Union ministries were reorganised into Union-republican ones, and some Union-republican ministries were abolished.

Important changes were introduced in the system of economic planning in the Union republics; the role of the leading bodies of the republics in planning was enhanced and their responsibility for carrying out state plans raised. Much work was done to improve planning and the central planning machinery.

Essential changes were likewise introduced in the system of planning agriculture. Prior to 1955, the general state plans for agriculture set a great many assignments, including, for example, the areas to be sown to various crops, the head of livestock, etc. Such excessive centralisation of planning frequently led to mistakes in the agricultural plans for the different areas and natural-climatic zones. . . .

A new system of planning in agriculture was introuduced in 1955. The state plans set only targets for the purchases of farm produce by the Government. Planning of agricultural production is done by the state and collective farms themselves with the participation of local administrative bodies. . . .

Prior to mid-1957 industrial enterprises located in the territory of the Russian Federation were directed by 84 all-Union and Union-republican ministries and departments; in the Ukrainian Republic, by 68; in the Uzbek Republic, by 52; in the Georgian Republic, by 50; in the Latvian Republic, by 44, etc.

Such a system of industrial management raised artificial barriers to solving urgent problems, especially to applying rational specialisation and co-ordination among industrial enterprises located in a given area. It hampered the integrated economic development of the Union republics and large economic zones. The subordination of an industrial enterprise to a central body according to the departmental principle tended to weaken and upset normal territorial ties between enterprises of different industries located in the same economic area. In some instances it prevented the local authorities from solving economic problems in a way that would promote the most efficient use of available material, labour and financial resources and especially of productive capacity. A certain contradiction arose between the territorial and economic community of enterprises in a republic, on the one hand, and the departmental division in the direction of their activities, on the other. Departmentalism hindered the adoption of timely decisions to eliminate shortcomings brought to light in the course of plan fulfilment and made it harder to manoeuvre with the resources of a given area.

Bearing in mind the necessity of eliminating all these shortcomings, and taking into consideration the greater scale of production and also the new sweeping tasks of the economic and cultural progress of the Soviet Union as it advances to communism, the Supreme Soviet of the U.S.S.R. adopted in May 1957 a Law on the Further Organisational Improvement of Management of Industry and Construction.

This law brought about a change-over from the management of industry and construction by ministries and departments, which at a definite historical stage played a positive part in economic construction, to new forms of management on the territorial principle (on the basis of economic administration areas and Union republics).

The reorganisation of industrial management resulted in the abolition of more than 140 all-Union, Union-republican and republican ministries which had under their jurisdiction various branches of the national economy. At the same time, the central and republican planning bodies were reorganised. . . .

Throughout the Soviet Union 104 economic administration areas were set up. Their activities are directed by economic councils. In some Union republics the boundaries of the economic areas coincided with the administrative boundaries of the respective republics and for this reason they have only one economic council. In the other republics economic councils were formed in regions, territories and autonomous republics: in the Russian Federation there are 68 economic councils; in the Ukrainian Republic, 11; in the Kazakh Republic, 9; and in the Uzbek Republic, 5.*

* Ed. note: See note, pp. 326–327.

In December 1960, the Supreme Soviet of the U.S.S.R. adopted a law on the establishment of republican economic councils. Such councils function in Union republics which have a considerable number of economic administration areas, and they co-ordinate their activities. The republican economic councils are subordinated directly to the Councils of Ministers of the respective Union republics.

The establishment of a system of economic councils on the territorial principle marked a *new stage in the direction of the economy by the state on the basis of the creative development of the Leninist principles of socialist management.*

The system of economic councils made it possible better to combine centralised state direction of the economy with the enhanced role of the Union republics in solving their economic problems, with the stimulation of the activities of the masses. It opened up broad possibilities for the fuller use of the natural and economic resources of each area, for the acceleration of technical progress, wider dissemination of advanced production experience, for greater specialisation and co-ordination in industry. . . .

The Structure of Economic Planning Agencies and Their Tasks

General direction of national economic planning is effected by the Central Committee of the C.P.S.U.* and the higher organs of state power in the country, the Supreme Soviet of the U.S.S.R. and the Government it forms. The higher organs of state power and state administration guide the work of the Gosplan of the U.S.S.R., the State Economic Research Council (Gosekonomsovet) and other state committees, of the all-Union and Union-republican ministries and departments, guide the economic councils through the republican Councils of Ministers and republican economic councils, and also direct the country's financial and credit system.

The Central Committee of the C.P.S.U. maps out the principal economic and political tasks of the plans. The control figures and directives for national economic development are approved by the

* *Italics supplied.*

congresses of the C.P.S.U. *The Soviet Government,* the highest executive state organ, *applies in its decisions the directives of the Party** and gives single centralised direction to the national economy. The Council of Ministers of the U.S.S.R. examines and endorses the economic plans and state budget of the Soviet Union and submits them for final approval to the Supreme Soviet of the U.S.S.R.

In the Union republics direction of planning is based on the same principle. The republican Council of Ministers, the highest executive organ of a Union republic, co-ordinates and directs the work of the economic councils, the republican ministries and departments, examines and endorses the plans for the development of the republic's economy and culture and submits them for final approval to the republican Supreme Soviet and to the respective all-Union bodies.

A republican Council of Ministers takes measures for carrying out plans, directs and controls the work of the executive committees of the Soviets at all lower levels.

Planning bodies in the Soviet Union at all levels are agencies of the respective executive and economic management bodies, their "economic general staffs." The Council of Ministers of the U.S.S.R. has two all-Union planning agencies, the State Planning Committee (the Gosplan) and the State Economic Research Council (the Gosekonomsovet); the Councils of Ministers of the Union republics have state planning commissions (republican gosplans); the Councils of Ministers of the autonomous republics have planning commissions; the executive committees of Soviets of territories, regions and districts have corresponding planning commissions. Economic councils, committees, ministries, boards, and also industrial enterprises and construction sites and most governmental organisations and institutions have planning departments.

The system of state statistics plays an important part in the drawing up of national economic plans and particularly in the control and analysis of their fulfilment. The Central Statistical Board of the Council of Ministers of the U.S.S.R. is a body exercising centralised direction of accounting and statistics. The Central Statistical Board has a wide network of local statistical agencies—statistical boards of the Union republics, autonomous repub-

* *Italics supplied.*

Figure 10. STRUCTURE OF THE ORGANS OF STATE ADMINISTRATION AND ECONOMIC PLANNING

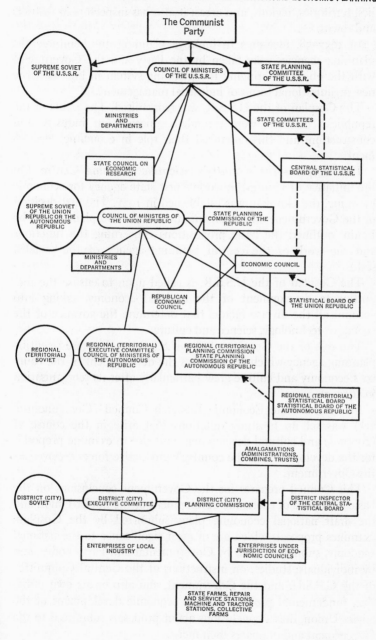

lics, territories, regions, and areas; it also has inspectors in districts and towns. . . .

In 1957–58, measures to improve planning and reinforce the planning agencies were taken by the Party and the Government with the object of bringing the planning system in line with the new organisational forms of industrial management.

The Gosplan of the U.S.S.R. was reorganised. The rights of the republican gosplans were extended, especially in industry and construction, and this enhanced their role in economic development.

The Gosplan—the Country's Scientific Planning Centre. On the initiative of Lenin, the world's first state agency for economic planning, the Gosplan, was established in 1921. The first decision of the Government on the organisation of the Gosplan, signed by Lenin, outlined the basic propositions concerning the functions and the work of the central planning agency of the socialist state. . . .

The Gosplan of the U.S.S.R. is called upon to ensure the proportionate development of the national economy, taking into account all the diverse factors that determine the advance of the economy, technology, science and culture.

The role of the Gosplan of the U.S.S.R. as the state scientific planning agency which co-ordinates the development of the country's economy and culture grew particularly after its reorganisation in 1957–58.

In 1959, a State Economic Research Council (Gosekonomsovet) was set up to study questions that arise in the course of economic and cultural development and also to examine proposals for the development of the country's productive forces received by the Government.

This Council prepares for the Government conclusions on the basic directions of economic development of the Soviet Union and the draft national economic plans submitted by the Gosplan; examines proposals which are of great significance to the national economy, submitted both by Governmental and Party bodies and by individuals; studies, on instructions of the Central Committee of the C.P.S.U. and the Government, and also on its own initiative, fundamental problems of the economic development of the Soviet Union, draws conclusions about proposals submitted to the Government and evaluates their merit.

The main task of the Gosplan and the Gosekonomsovet is to ensure high rates of extended socialist reproduction, the proportionate development of the socialist economy with priority growth of heavy industry, the continuous rise of the productivity of social labour and the rapid advance of all branches of the economy on the basis of the latest technology, the most effective utilisation of the natural wealth and of the material and labour resources of the country. . . .

The Gosplan consists of 30–35 members who include: the Chairman of the Gosplan who is a Vice-Chairman of the Council of Ministers of the U.S.S.R.; Vice-Chairmen of the Gosplan who are Ministers of the Government and are appointed by the Supreme Soviet of the U.S.S.R.; members of the Gosplan, heads of departments who are personally appointed by the Council of Ministers of the U.S.S.R. The Chairman of the Gosplan, the Vice-Chairmen and heads of departments who have the rank of all-Union ministers make up the Collegium of the Gosplan.

The central staff of the Gosplan consists of branch departments and general economic departments. The branch departments are in charge of drafting plans and elaborating the problems pertaining to the respective branches of the economy.

The function of general economic departments is to study general economic problems and to work out the summary sections of the long-term and annual plans for republics and branches. . . .

The Structure and Organization
of the Soviet Economy

GREGORY GROSSMAN[*]

I

An economist has little reason to dispute a political scientist's appraisal of the 1961 Program of the CPSU as a "credo of conservatism," although the economist might qualify the conservatism as a dynamic one. While aiming at the eventual creation of full communism, for the near future the Program eschews all radical departures from established rates and directions of growth and from prevailing socio-economic institutions or the current tendencies in the evolution of these institutions. In this sense the Program codifies the present and projects it into the future. "Maximal Growth with Minimal Change" could well be the epigraph of its economic section.

It is perhaps no surprise that the economist finds no major surprises in the Program. Conservatism is said to have two sources: not wanting change and not knowing how to bring it about. Both partially apply in this case. Surely the progress of the Soviet economy since 1953—the basis for economic comparisons in the

[*] The author of *Soviet Statistics of Physical Output of Industrial Commodities: Their Compilation and Quality* (1960), and "Soviet Agriculture Since Stalin," *The Annals of the American Academy of Political and Social Science*, Vol. CCCIII, January 1956, Professor Grossman is on the faculty of the University of California (Berkeley).

From "The Structure and Organization of the Soviet Economy" by Gregory Grossman, *The Slavic Review*, Seattle, Wash., Vol. XXI, No. 2, June 1962, selections from pp. 203–222. By permission of The American Association for the Advancement of Slavic Studies, Inc. and the author. For footnote references, see original source.

U.S.S.R. nowadays—has been such as to make the party doubt the wisdom of changing courses, and at the same time the difficulties of the Soviet economy are so deeply rooted in its present institutions that any fundamental reform would not be easy to design. Indeed, like any established regime, the post-Stalin Soviet regime has been assiduously avoiding radical solutions. Except possibly for some of the measures in the agricultural sector, such as the abolition of the MTS, its institutional and organizational reforms have tended to be chiefly of a "patchwork" character when minor (e.g., the various measures to spur technological progress), or essentially conservative when major (as in the 1957 reorganization of industry and construction).

That the Program's conservatism is more than matched by the continuity and persistence of the economy's problems is forcefully brought out if one looks back a full quarter of a century. True, the economy's scale is quite different at the end of 1961, the time of this writing, than in 1936–37. Taking the average of the two earlier years as the base, we find that agricultural production has nearly doubled (though the territory has of course expanded), and industrial production has increased by a factor of about nine according to the official index, and by around half as much according to independent estimates.* Yet there is hardly an economic problem that preoccupied the regime twenty-five years ago which does not preoccupy its successor today, or indeed has not plagued the economy and its rulers continuously for at least three decades. The list is a long one; there is no need to recite it fully here. But we may take a look at the more important problems, grouping them in an arbitrary fashion.

(1) Problems pertaining to agriculture: its pronounced lag behind the rest of the economy, its sluggish response to many of the

* Ed. note: Analysts of the Central Intelligence Agency disclosed on January 9, 1964, that the annual economic growth rate of the Soviet Union had slipped to 2.5 per cent during 1962 and 1963. This estimate was indirectly acknowledged by the Soviets when they omitted the statistic on national income from the economic report for 1963. By comparing the national income data of the pre-1963 period as published in official statistics with the one given for 1963 by *Pravda*, the Soviet Party daily, Western economic analysts concluded that the Soviet economic growth rate was about 3 per cent in 1963. According to the *Pravda* article, the national income of the U.S.S.R. in 1963 was 170 billion rubles ($187 billion).

remedial measures, the low productivity of labor, the great dispersion of peasant incomes around a relatively low average, the contrasts between the socialized sector and the private plot.

(2) Overcentralization and bureaucratization of the whole economy, with attendant delays, inefficiencies, and political problems.

(3) Deficiencies of planning: cumbersomeness, great delays in the plans reaching the executants and their frequent revisions; their imperfect internal consistency and balance; poor articulation between production (or investment) planning, supply planning, and financial planning.

(4) Inadequate attention to economic efficiency (optimization) in planning and management; related problems in pricing.

(5) Chronic and general supply difficulties with regard to producer goods, including equipment; and, as the other side of the coin, poor quality, improper assortment, incomplete assembly, and many other defects of the goods themselves.

(6) Obstacles to innovation, whether owing to "friction" in the bureaucratic hierarchies or to resistance from below.

(7) "Localism" and "departmentalism" of varying degrees of enlightenment or selfishness; neglect and pilferage of socialist property; self-serving acts of the greatest variety and ingenuity, not to say ubiquity; and widespread deception of superiors.

(8) The many ills of the construction industry, such as dispersion of funds and resources among too many projects, building without blueprints, great delays in completion and frequent partial noncompletion (the notorious *nedodelki*), a very large amount of resources frozen in the "unfinished construction" and "uninstalled equipment," and the generally low quality of the product. When, at the 22nd Party Congress, Mr. Khrushchev characterized the performance of the contruction industry as "the problem of problems," he was merely attaching a new—and since much popularized—label to a decades-old headache.

(9) The consumer's well-known woes: shortages of consumer goods and interruptions in their supply, their poor quality and limited variety, the lack of both service and services, and the ever-present housing shortage.

While a quarter of a century ago one could attribute these difficulties in good measure to the workers' and peasants' "darkness" (as the Russians might say) and to the planners' and managers' greenness, today their children are hardly wanting in the experience, training, education, indoctrination, and tools to do a much better job of it. The persistence of the problems is strong evidence that they are a systemic phenomenon.

II

Economic systems are best known by the institutions they keep. The undogmatic student nowadays realizes that all classifications are no more than constructs and abstractions, that their function is to be tools of analysis and not its master, and that therefore they ought to be adapted to the object of his study. In examining economic systems from a dynamic standpoint it is useful to look at the factors conditioning their motion in particular phases of their histories, namely, their ideologies (or the ideologies of their governing elites) and the points in economic-historical development marking the beginning of these phases. The latter of course determine the resources on hand, while the ideologies bear on the directions and speed of development, the degree of pressure on the available resources, and the political restraints that might or might not be placed on the single-mindedness of the advance.

Some—notably Alexander Gerschenkron—would argue that the nature and intensity of the ideological commitment to industrialization is related to the country's relative economic backwardness at the beginning of the relevant phase; in other words, that the march of Economic History is not an orderly procession but a grand and inexorable game of catching up. Be that as it may, the U.S.S.R. can be seen as a special case of a country that despite considerable economic backwardness relative to the other great powers (1) enjoyed a favorable resource endowment and had already had its industrial "take-off" decades earlier (in this regard it is very different from many an underdeveloped country today), (2) has been, for various reasons good or bad, in an enormous hurry to industrialize and to build up its military might, and (3) has had a polity providing few checks on the urgent and single-minded policy of industrialization. It is not necessary to accept the dubious thesis that the actual Soviet pattern of development, including its noneconomic aspects, was the only possible one in order to see that this pattern was a consistent product of the logic of haste under conditions of relative backwardness and (to put it mildly) within a highly authoritarian political milieu. The logic of haste is above all a powerful centralizing force in social affairs. In the Soviet instance "centralism" found a ready and most convenient ally in "socialism," however incompatible with some of the European intellectual roots of socialism the total social mobilization in the Soviet case may have been.

The Soviet—or, more exactly, Stalinist—formula for industrialization is by now well known. One of its cornerstones has been, of course, the collectivization of agriculture, which permitted a large unrequited extraction of agricultural surplus while avoiding (or so it was thought) a large-scale withdrawal of effort by the peasants, as happened during War Communism. The extraction of the agricultural surplus in turn allowed a very high rate of investment out of the national product. Physical resources have been "mobilized" for capital construction by virtue of central planning and a tight control over the allocation of materials and foreign exchange. Western technology has been taken over on a vast scale and injected into the economy from above under constant pressure. A large training program has been conducted. Material benefits and social privileges have been offered in a highly selective and differentiated way in order to stimulate labor to maximum self-improvement and best performance on the job. But direct controls were exercised over labor for a long time, too.

Money, of course, remained in use, but in the production sector more "passively," to control compliance and constrain independence, than "actively," to guide performance. The economy has not only been planned centrally (although all effective national planning is by definition "central," and no planning is entirely centralized), and not only has the volume and distribution of investments been centrally determined, but the economy has also been *centrally managed* by dint of a plethora of production directives and allocation orders *in natura*. It is primarily the last of these three features of central direction, rather than the first two, that sets the Soviet-type economy apart from other planned economies such as the Indian, Norwegian, or Yugoslav, and which has produced such appellations as "command economy" and *Zentralverwaltungswirtschaft*. (The Soviets have no name for their own type of economy except "socialist," which is of course quite imprecise.) A command economy, in contrast to a market economy, allocates resources and attempts to attain balance between requirements and availabilities by means of commands (orders, directives) from the center, rather than by the mutual interaction of many decentralized economic units linked together by a market (price) mechanism. A command economy must also be a planned one in the sense that a certain minimal amount of co-ordination between the directives is required lest the economy break down. While a command economy need not be socialist—the Nazi war economy is frequently cited in evidence of this—it is difficult to imagine one except in a highly authoritarian milieu. On the other hand, a market economy can be both planned and socialist, as these words are commonly understood in the West. The Yugoslav economy, and the Soviet economy itself during the NEP era, are the most outstanding examples of "market socialism" with central planning.

It is only with reference to the logic of haste under conditions of relative economic backwardness and of political dictatorship that one understands those crucial features of Soviet industrialization (and the later Chinese industrialization) which go completely counter to Western experience. If in the West industrialization was associated with commercialization and a great extension of the scope of the market mechanism, Soviet industrialization, as we have just seen, all but abolished the market mechanism. If in the West there was a parallel monetization of the economy the Soviet economy was to a considerable degree demonetized. If in the West, and even in Tsarist Russia, restrictions on labor mobility were progressively removed and the individual's relation to society tended to shift "from status to contract," in the Soviet case there was a marked return to restrictions on labor mobility paternalism of a sort, and even labor adscription within the new institutional context. The functional role of the three "M's" of Western in-dustrialization—the market, money, and mobility—are well known: in brief, they afforded the greatest scope and incentive for innovation, accumulation, and growth under essentially decentral-ized initiative and decision-making. *Laissez-faire* is the name we use for the more extreme form of such decentralization. It was only later in the West (at least in the Anglo-Saxon world) that substantial curbs came to be placed on the working of the market mechanism, and trade unions came to impart status privileges to labor as the production ethic gave ground to considerations of welfare, social justice, and economic stability.

Ideologically rooted in the nineteenth-century revolt against *laissez-faire* and politically committed to dictatorship as it was, the new Soviet regime could hardly have been expected to opt for rapid industrialization within a decentralized framework, not to say with private initiative and private property in industry. The rate of accumulation, and hence the rate of growth, and the pattern of investment, and hence the direction of development, could hardly have been left to the despised and dreaded *stikhiinost'* (spontaneous and atomized decision-making). But—not to mention coercion and terror—it is questionable that the (socialist) market mechanism had to be destroyed, the economy partially demonetized, the labor mobility impaired, to the extent that they were. And it is quite understandable that these three "non-M's" would tend to come into progressively sharper conflict with the very development of the economy that they originally were intended to spur—a conflict whose manifestations were repressed by Stalin, but which, together with the closely related problem of agriculture, has dominated the *Problematik* of the post-Stalin era. The fact is that the three "non-M's" clash with some of the most fundamental requirements of a modern economy and society. The lack of a market mechanism, that is, the command principle, obstructs decentralization and thus conflicts with a modern economy's enormous complexity, the need for dispersed initiative to take full advantage of industrialism's productive and growing potential, and the modern consumer's quest for quality and variety of goods and services. Demonetization, albeit partial, stands in the way of effective decentralization and bars the use of a rational calculus even within the framework of the command economy. And lastly, direct controls over labor—trained and educated labor at that—offend against human dignity and the sense of justice. In terms of the historical contrast with the West, the wheel is set for another turn.

III

Labor.—The breaking of the autonomy of the Soviet trade unions at the outset of the Five-Year Plans—more precisely, at the 16th Party Conference in April, 1929—was essential for the consolidation of Stalin's power. Their concern with living standards and distributive justice would have stood in the way of Stalin's industrialization. What followed is well known. Less than a year later began the collectivization drive, a kind of mass enserfment in the name of socialism, an adscription of the peasantry to state-controlled (if not formally state-owned) estates complete with *barshchina* (*corvée*). The impressing of millions into forced labor camps or work at places of banishment was an even harsher kind of adscription, though primarily to industrial and building enterprises. The structure of wages was revised to reward contribution to the industrialization drive above all other considerations.

Toward the end of the first decade of the Plan Era came the notorious measures aimed at limiting the mobility and controlling the activity of free nonpeasant labor: the introduction of labor books on December 20, 1938, penalties against absenteeism and loafing on December 28, 1938, and prohibitions against voluntary quitting and much stiffer penalties against absenteeism on June 26, 1940. In October of the same year appeared decrees empowering authorities to transfer skilled and technical personnel regardless of the individual's wishes and establishing a labor draft (State Labor Reserves) for youths. During the war additional restrictions on labor mobility were decreed in the face of the new and grave emergency.

One must also bear in mind that in all these cases it was the individual's mobility that was being curbed; the state's freedom to move labor was in no way limited. On the contrary, it was enhanced. Where in the West the individual had to be freed to be drawn into new forms of life in the course of industrialization, in the Soviet Union the conflict between curbs on mobility and industrialization did not appear, at least not at that stage. The adscriber and the industrializer were one and the same.

If we cannot approve these developments on ethical grounds, we can at least understand some of them with reference to the logic of haste operating in the particular milieu. But the controls over labor—and especially the concomitant drop in living standards (including "leisure") and the brutalities of the collectivization drive and of the forced labor camps—had a great and lasting negative impact on two of the regime's prime long-run goals: the re-education of man according to the Communist model, and productivity (particularly in agriculture).

More gradually and less dramatically, but in the long run possibly of no smaller importance, there also appeared a situation in which the life of the individual urban worker or employee—not to mention the peasant on the kolkhoz—became closely tied in very many ways to his immediate employer and the closely-related trade union. The individual came to depend largely on the employer and the trade union for housing, recreation, vacations, medical care, cultural activities, and further technical or professional training. This tended, and still tends, to "pigeon-hole" the individual in society along the lines of his job and profession to a greater extent than is usually the case in other industrial systems. In a sense, the regime has striven to maintain some aspects of a rural social structure as well as a village morality while industrializing and urbanizing at unprecedented speed. Convenient as this may have been for the regime for political, educative, and economic purposes, one wonders how well it accords with a more highly developed, urban, industrial society. Or, alternatively, whether it might not hide the seeds of a certain particularism along economic lines.

The post-Stalin developments with regard to labor are far from consistent. In some respects the direct controls over individuals have been tightened, despite the over-all relaxation of terror in the country. This is especially true of the peasants, by now of course a much smaller proportion of the population. Although criminal prosecution for failure to work the required minimum for the kolkhoz was apparently abandoned in October, 1953, beginning with mid-1954 the minimum itself was sharply increased on a farm-by-farm basis. Certain new sanctions were introduced to enforce compliance with the minimum work norms, the most important of which seems to be the curtailment or complete recapture of the private plot. But at the same time, in the usual "carrot and stick" fashion, work for the kolkhoz has been made materially much more attractive. The direction (largely through the Komsomol) of many hundreds of thousands for settlement in the "virgin lands," annually for harvesting, and for construction projects in the East, are other instances of retained or even enlarged direct controls over labor. Graduates of various technical and professional schools are apparently also still administratively assigned to their first jobs. And last, but certainly not least, there are now the "anti-parasite laws," adopted by the various republics in somewhat varying form between 1957 and 1961, and aimed against those deemed not to engage in socially useful activities.

On the other side of the ledger the two major developments are (1) the transformation of at least a large part of the forced labor camps into "correctional labor colonies" and apparently a very large reduction in the number of persons undergoing forced labor, and (2) the repeal in April, 1956, of the 1940 decrees pertaining to penalties for absenteeism and the compulsory transfer of workers. The latter, however, apparently merely recognized the *de facto* situation, since the decrees had not been really enforced for quite a number of years. Simultaneously, a thoroughgoing wage and income reform has been carried out, chiefly for the benefit of the lowest paid workers and employees and of pensioners. Its effect has been to reduce very markedly the extent of income inequality in the nonpeasant sector and, with the relative pulling up of the peasants' earnings, in the society as a whole. The fact that the reduction in wage inequality coincided with the abolition of certain direct controls (outside the village) only served to underline how anachronistic the latter had become by the mid-fifties.

Thus, what a Western economist would consider a rather "normal" labor market has emerged (always excepting the kolkhoz sector). True, the total supply of labor in this market is subject to much greater social and political pressure than exists in other industrial systems, as, for instance, through the medium of the anti-parasite laws. Moreover, chiefly because of inertia, labor exchanges have not yet been organized, though the matter is apparently receiving attention on the part of some economists. Although rate setting is still formally a centralized function, the allocative function of Soviet wages is on the whole the same as in any labor market, and in their slow way they tend to move accordingly.

It is therefore not surprising that the factory trade union committees should be significantly revitalized and should become more actively concerned with questions of fairness as they affect the individual workers. At the same time, the range of these questions is being significantly broadened as mechanization and automation begin to release substantial numbers of workers from their jobs.

But effective trade union independence or local workers' management are something else again. Both imply a degree of pluralism in the society of which there seems to be no sign on the horizon, least of all in the party Program. Workers' management also implies a degree of enterprise autonomy that hardly has a place in the Soviet command economy; it cannot come while management itself, for all its authority in the plant, has hardly any autonomy in relation to the environment.

The party Program is concerned with something quite different, namely, the remaking of man into a "Communist man," that is, into a willing, eager, honest, and highly efficient worker. (Indeed, so eager and willing that the question of autonomy on any level would lose much of its meaning; and we are moreover told that the Communist society will retain the centralized guidance of production.) This is the Program's paramount goal, its center of gravity. In a sense, it is also its most conservative feature: it sets out to change man, not institutions, on the way to "communism." No one will say that the party has set itself an easy target.

IV

Money.—During the period of so-called War Communism, under the double impact of the direct emergency and a misguided doctrine, money lost virtually all its usual functions: as a medium of exchange, unit of account, and store of value. One could even say that it disappeared, were it not for its conspicuous presence in hyperinflated denominations. Under the impact of another dire emergency, and after a painful confrontation of doctrine with reality, its usual roles and functions were restored with the NEP. Then, roughly from 1929 on, as the market mechanism was squeezed out and the command principle enthroned in its place, the Soviet economy was again partially demonetized.

In what ways was the Soviet economy under Stalin partially demonetized? True, money retained the traditional functions cited above, but with many important exceptions. Because of the reliance placed on it for wage payment and consumer goods distribution (chiefly for labor-incentive purposes), money was most in its own in the relations between the state and the household sector and within the household sector itself. Yet even here there were important exceptions: distribution of income within the kolkhoz, most of which was in kind, the maintenance of forced labor, the rationing of urban housing at nominal rents, self-supply in housing and foodstuffs by both the agricultural and the nonagricultural populations, compulsory road labor by the peasantry, and so forth.

Money as a medium of exchange was also removed, or almost removed, from a considerable number of transactions in the production sector. Kolkhozy paid in kind for the services of MTS equipment, and more by way of tribute than by way of fee at that; the state purchased most foodstuffs from the kolkhozy and their members at "procurement prices" which were not far from zero; with insignificant exceptions, nothing was paid by enterprises for the use of natural resources, or of fixed capital and a large part of working capital; the portion of working capital borrowed from the Bank carried only nominal interest rates; the "charter capital" extended by the state to its enterprises was not only interest-free, but was also nonrepayable; certain intangibles were not legally subject to sale or purchase, for example, patents, licenses (except for fiscal levies on some), "goodwill"; tangible capital assets were also generally not subject to sale after having become part of a state enterprise's "basic fund," and after 1941 even surplus equipment could not be easily disposed of. Finally, the use of money by enterprises was circumscribed in many ways (earmarking, rationing of producer goods) so as to minimize the chance of unauthorized claims against resources.

The function of money as a unit of account was equally seriously impaired. What could not be bought or sold generally carried no price at all (land, natural resources, intangibles, the services of capital as a factor of production in most cases), or was often accounted for at rather unrealistic prices (structures and installed equipment). The system of physical success indicators for management and of physical investment-choice indicators for planners, in itself partly a consequence of the demonetization, tended to reduce the role of money in accounting and calculation even further. The result was to render economic calculation often impossible or extremely difficult, quite apart from the rationality of such price parameters as existed. Agriculture, with its crazy quilt of prices and no prices, was only the most conspicuous example of a situation that cut across the whole economy. (Although the discussion in this and the preceding two paragraphs is in the past tense, much of what is said still applies at this writing.)

It would be difficult to assign a single explanation for the partial demonetization of the Soviet economy after 1929. Certainly ideological and doctrinal factors were quite important. Marxian economic analysis attributes more of a distributive than an allocative importance to "value categories" (price, wage, rent, interest), and with the distribution problem "solved" in the new order, there seemed to be little need for attention to them. This view still finds expression among those Soviet economists who see only a very limited connection between "the law of value" and resource allocation by the planning organs. Also, if certain things, such as land, are not for sale, why have prices for them? Why account for them? "Direct" calculation, that is, calculation in physical terms or in labor time, seemed to bring the economy closer to its ultimate goal of full communism—a tendency that was no doubt reinforced by the technocratic biases in Soviet planning.

Technocracy (though not necessarily under its own name)— whether in the earlier decades in the U.S.S.R., in the United States during the Great Depression, or in some underdeveloped countries today—is essentially a response to great economic need, to crisis, in the form of a revolt against conventional methods of problem-solving. It is another expression of the logic of haste. While the technocrat's dismissal of money is irrational, nonetheless long-range planning for a technological and economic revolution of the magnitude of that in the U.S.S.R. in the thirties must rely a good deal on physical criteria, because value magnitudes become too unstable and unpredictable over time under such conditions.

Further, considerations of social control were doubtless also quite important. Money is a form of social power that may lead resources astray and is subject to only imperfect control by political authority. The considerable demonetization of ariculture under Stalin was thus a way of bringing this sector under the most direct political control for the extraction of its surplus. That this demonetization of agriculture, along with other measures applied to it, turned out to be disastrous for its long-run productivity is another matter. And, as we have already seen, the use of money funds by nonagricultural enterprises was also limited in many ways for control purposes.

The post-Stalin period saw a moderate but significant reversal in this regard, especially in agriculture, where relations between producers and the state were largely remonetized, mainly owing to the abolition of the MTS and the considerable reduction in the multiplicity of prices. Yet the kolkhoz's obligation to sell predetermined amounts of produce to the state remains. The relations between the kolkhoz and its members have also been considerably remonetized, chiefly by virtue of much higher farm prices, though payment in kind against labor days and self-supply are still important.

Outside agriculture the progress in remonetization has been less actual than by way of problem-setting and intellectual debate. The official position under Khrushchev has been the opposite of Stalin's—the role of "value categories" is to increase progressively, and the entry into moneyless communism is to be "dialectical" rather than gradual. (It is very convenient indeed to have both dialectical and smooth—*neuklonnyi*—progress in one's intellectual baggage!) The 1961 party Program reitereates this position, although one searches in vain in the literature of recent years for a clear explanation of just what the increased role of "value categories" is to represent henceforth. The answer is probably not yet available. We may note in passing, however, that questions of money, and gold, still tend to be suffused with considerable mysticism in the Soviet economic mind.

One should take note, though, of the partial resolution along rationalist lines of such an important problem as that of "capital efficiency," that is, of allowing explicitly for the scarcity of capital. The resolution is partial because it only legalizes the use of a surrogate for the interest rate and legitimizes established practice; it fails to answer the crucial question of how such a charge is to be determined in fact. However, there are now those who advocate interest payments by enterprises on the capital invested in them by the state, and even repayment of such capital, various types of rent on natural resources, assignment of capital values to subsoil resources, relative valuation of different parcels of land, and even a consistent and integrated system of rational prices for all scarce goods and resources. The fat is in the fire, but clearly major changes must take time. It seems that at this writing the 1962 reform of wholesale prices is to proceed according to rather conventional principles, that is, the principles that shaped such Soviet reforms from 1936 on.

At stake is of course more than monetization; even more than economic calculation, rational prices, and allocative efficiency. At stake is the whole centralized structure of the Soviet economy, the command economy itself, and ultimately, the location and distribution of power in the society. This brings us to what is, with agriculture, one of the two most topical questions in the Soviet economy, the question of centralization-decentralization.

V

Over-all organization.—The Soviet press and economic literature may still eschew the word "decentralization," but they cannot avoid the thought. Many ideas on the subject are clearly abroad in the land. Managers, who often found the sovnarkhozy easier and faster to deal with than the old ministries and *glavki* but who have in fact gained hardly any additional powers since Stalin's death, seem to be bringing their complaints more into the open again. These are the traditional ones: delays in receiving plans, too many plan revisions, too many authorities, chronic supply difficulties, and—foremost—lack of power at the enterprise level and "petty tutelage" from above. The sovnarkhozy plead for more power as against their superiors, and republic authorities ask for more power vis-à-vis union authorities. Judging by the complaints, the situation has changed little on the whole since 1957, despite considerable optimism on this score at the time.*

The complaints are perfectly understandable but should not be dismissed as mere ex parte pleas. The disinterested observer can see great need for decentralization in the Soviet economy, and primarily to the following ends:

(1) To permit far greater modernization and innovation on the basis of dispersed initiative. At the moment such attempts run into serious obstacles not only because of management's conservatism but also because decision with regard to the necessary elements—finances, production of equipment, supply of materials, technological policy—is highly centralized, and co-ordination among them is poor and slow. A kind of "contradiction" has developed between the abundance of skill and talent on the spot and the organizational means for translating this creativity into reality. The much-publicized party and "public" supervisory committees, established mostly after the June, 1959, Plenum of the CC CPSU, can perhaps spur and goad allegedly conservative managers, but can they "fight city hall"?

(2) To permit a certain amount of local investment in response

* See note, pp. 326–327.

to local needs. The argument here is similar. Immediately after the 1957 reorganization there was apparently some thought even in the highest places of turning investment funds over to the sovnarkhozy in lump sums, but manifestations of localism on their part led to progressive re- (not de-) centralization of this function.

(3) To permit greater lateral communication within the economy, a type of communication that necessarily suffers in a command economy. This refers to the sensitivity and responsiveness of production and distribution to demand (for both producer and consumer goods). It also refers to that specifically Soviet problem of trilateral communication between the designers, builders, and users of equipment and structures. The vertical communication that today largely substitutes for lateral communication is long and slow, passes through a large number of intermediate levels, and often involves decisions by a considerable number of authorities even at the highest levels. Better lateral connections would presumably also permit improvement in the success indicators for management.

(4) To alleviate the unfavorable trend of increasing complexity and burden of planning, checking on plan fulfillment, and collecting data. In the case of Soviet-type planning the main burden of the work (especially in production and supply planning) arises from the need to determine the *interrelations* between goods (factors, products, construction jobs) and between economic units (regions, enterprises). Thus, crudely speaking, the amount of planning work is proportional to the square of the product of the number of goods and the number of economic units. (Of course, in very many instances there are no interrelations between given goods or enterprises. This, however, does not affect our conclusion so long as the proportion of such empty cells in our notional matrix remains roughly constant.) It is clear, therefore, that in the absence of major methodological or organizational changes the burden of planning and related work in such a rapidly expanding economy as the Soviet must be growing very fast. Decentralization would seem to be one of the ways in which the burden of this work might be held down.

The "territorialization" of economic organization after the 1957 reform has by now resulted in a considerably more complicated structure than was probably originally intended. First, two additional territorial levels have been created: in mid-1960 republic sovnarkhozy in the three larger republics (RSFSR, Ukraine, Kazakhstan) to supervise the local sovnarkhozy; and in May, 1961, the so-called Councils for Co-ordination and Planning in seventeen newly-created "large economic regions," each embracing on the average about six of the original economic-administrative regions. Secondly, by the end of 1961 there have been established eleven U.S.S.R. State Commissions (*Komitety*) for individual branches of industry and for construction. While the CCP's and the Commissions are presumably less concerned with day-to-day operations than with technological and investment policies, nonetheless the channels of communication within the economy must have been substantially lengthened and complicated.

The limits to decentralization in a command economy such as the Soviet, however, derive not only from the presumably considerable vested interests that might be arrayed against it. (In connection with the latter point, let us recall that the 1957 reorganization was carried out as part of a major power struggle in the Kremlin.) Such limits also stem from (a) the fact that the lower echelons' objectives do not always coincide with objectives at the top, and (b) from the lower echelons' incomplete information. That is to say, "centralism," to use the Soviet term, serves the crucial functions of safeguarding the regime's values and of assuring balance to the economy. The two have in common, *inter alia*, a certain dependence on the extent to which pressure is put on the economy's resources. The greater the haste and the less slack in the economy, the more the regime strives to prevent any unauthorized use (or non-use) of resources, and, at the same time, the sellers' market becomes more acute and the problem of balance arises more urgently. In short, given its political and economic realities, there is generally a substantial recentralizing tendency in the Soviet system, though it usually operates on a piecemeal basis as individual problems are faced and resolved by taking them away from the jurisdiction of lower authorities.

Short of a renunciation of the command economy in favor of a radically different structure, what courses of action are open to reduce the costs of centralization or to decentralize without the disadvantages just mentioned? The one attracting high attention at the moment in the U.S.S.R. (and, by reflection, abroad) is the use of mathematical techniques, primarily input-output matrices, in conjunction with modern computational equipment, to speed up the construction of plans and to permit the preparation of alternative plans. Academician V. S. Nemchinov, a leader in this new trend among Soviet economists, has propounded the more elaborate notion of "economic cybernetics" which would combine the high-speed plan-construction techniques with high-speed, continuous transmission of information to the planning center and of directives from it. This is not the place to analyze at length the promise that input-output or economic cybernetics offer to the Soviet economy. It must be borne in mind, however, that the matrix would have to be very large to supplant the present set of material balances at the Gosplan U.S.S.R. level alone; in planning for 1962, Gosplan U.S.S.R. employed over 14,000 material balances. Even if a matrix of this size were constructed and successfully utilized, and if similar tables were employed at other levels, many of the present difficulties of the Soviet economy—sellers' market, faulty success indicators, faulty prices, and so forth—need not be completely remedied. Nor are the planners very likely to automate entirely their delicate functions (and work themselves out of their own jobs besides).

Secondly, some sectors might be taken out of the command-economy structure and linked to the rest of the economy by means of a price nexus, as, for example, is already the case with the household sector. Steps in this direction have also been taken since Stalin's death (e.g., in 1955 and 1958) with regard to the collective farm sector. It was expected that collective farms would determine their production programs with reference to the prices posted by the state. But delivery quotas were never abolished, and because of the constant pressure from the top, the kolkhozy have been subjected to rather detailed control and guidance by local authorites. Thus, the price mechanism has not been given a chance to be decisive. At any rate, agriculture can be potentially so "separated out" because of its rather small use of current inputs from the rest of the economy. Where the flow of current inputs is much more important in relation to output, the given sector's reciprocal relation with the rest of the economy is greater, and therefore its "separation" by means of the price mechanism is not likely to be viewed with much favor so long as the command principle remains dominant.

Thirdly, a way of meeting some of the problems of the sellers' market is to merge enterprises with their suppliers, thus transforming the problems into intra-enterprise ones and thereby facilitating their solution, as was done in Czechoslovakia in 1958. This was also done for years in the U.S.S.R. in a relatively small number of conspicuous cases (the so-called *kombinaty*). Recently, a merger movement among industrial enterprises was started in the Ukraine. The development bears watching, although the motives in this instance seem to be mixed: many of the mergers are horizontal, having been formed to amalgamate what are regarded to be uneconomically small units.

A more topical issue than greater enterprise self-sufficiency is regional autarky. There is a strong bias under Soviet conditions in this direction, for regional autarky may appeal both to the local interests, by easing supply problems, and to central authorities, by reducing planning complexities. In other words, it shortens the lines of communication, and over time may ease the problem of assuring balance. But of course in the short run it is likely to increase supply difficulties elsewhere, and in the long run may also amount to an uneconomic allocation of resources. An important reason for the creation of the "large economic regions" seems to be the countering of autarkic tendencies on the part of the local sovnarkhozy; yet, autarkic development of the large economic regions may now be stimulated.

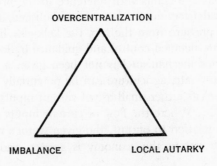

OVERCENTRALIZATION

IMBALANCE   LOCAL AUTARKY

In sum, imbalance is avoided or reduced in the command economy through greater centralization or by permitting more regional or sectoral self-sufficiency. Overcentralization is avoided by risking imbalance or allowing autarky. And the suppression of autarky is bought at the cost of a high degree of centralization, or alternatively, of imbalance. We may therefore speak of the command economy's "triangle of hazards," the vertices of which are the three conditions named. (See Figure.) Moving away from one fault brings the economy closer, though not necessarily in equal degree, to the other two.

The most recent recentralizing trend is probably a response to a multiplicity of factors: the heightened pressure on resources brought about by increased defense commitments, lags in construction of new capacity in a number of sectors, and the unsatisfactory performance of agriculture; autarkic moves by the sovnarkhozy; and lags in technological progress (in relation to intentions).

Neither the text of the party Program nor the speeches by Khrushchev and others at the 22nd Party Congress foreshadows any significant departure from the present system of planning and economic administration; on the contrary, they amount to its reaffirmation. And despite the traditional bows in the direction of "the role of local authorities" and "enterprise initiative," their general tenor suggests, if anything, stronger central controls for the balancing of plans and in investment and technological policy. Perhaps the only important contrary note was struck by Khrushchev when he said, "For the sake of better plan fulfillment it is necessary to give enterprises greater opportunities to dispose of their profits, and to use the latter more amply to stimulate better work by the enterprise's staff and for the enterprise's expansion." It may be noted that this was the only point in the whole part of the speech dealing with planning and organization that elicited applause, according to the official transcript.

VI

The recovery of agricultural production stands out as one of the most noteworthy economic achievements of the regime since

Stalin's death. It was brought about by a combination of measures, on the whole salutary both singly and in combination. One may mention among these the increased investment, the abolition of the MTS and acquisition of their equipment by the kolkhozy, much increased farm prices and the diminution in their multiplicity, certain tax concessions, the introduction of wage-like money pay in the better-to-do kolkhozy, and attempts at cost accounting. The length of this list, if nothing else, indicates determination and considerable flexibility in trying to solve the problem of agriculture. These measures jointly, plus of course the putting of some 100 million acres under the plow, have been instrumental in raising grain production by some 60 per cent, and gross agricultural output by about 55 per cent, between 1953 and 1960. (These percentages are based on official data which may be appreciably exaggerated for a variety of reasons.) Yet per capita agricultural output is only moderately above the 1928 level and seems to have remained on a plateau since 1958.*

Along with the salutary developments a good many doubtful practices have persisted: the imposition of pet projects from above, "campaigning," excessive targets, and, as we have already seen, little change in the authoritarian methods of planning agricultural output and procurements. Similarly, the trend toward kolkhoz "giantism" has continued. By the end of 1960, mostly through amalgamation, the number of kolkhozy was reduced to 44,000— only half as many as at the end of 1955—and the average kolkhoz came to contain nearly 3,000 hectares of plowed land and nearly 400 households.

The party Program in essence pledges to continue the salutary measures mentioned above. Increased money pay, some equalization of incomes among kolkhozy, increased social services to

---

* Ed. note: At its meeting of March 1965, the Central Committee of the Communist Party of the Soviet Union adopted a new farm program providing for more investment in agriculture, higher farm prices, lower rural taxes, and lower prices for consumer goods bought by peasants. These measures were expected to raise the farmers' purchasing power and help reduce the sharp differences in living standards between town and countryside. A joint decree of the Government and the Central Committee issued a month later cancelled the debt, equivalent to more than 2 billion dollars, that the *kolkhozy* owed to the State Bank.

kolkhozniki—these and other policies, if continued, would tend to attenuate the differences between state and collective farms. Nevertheless, the collective farm system is to be retained, according to the Program, for another two decades (though probably progressively diminished in extent), and the private plot is to be similarly preserved. Judging by the Program's targets for agricultural output and productivity, the total agricultural population is to remain virtually stable in absolute numbers over the decade of the sixties, and to decline by 30 to 40 per cent in the succeeding decade. It would thus take considerable resources to raise kolkhoz incomes to sovkhoz levels. It would also be rather costly to abolish the private plot, nuisance though it be to the collective farm. As Newth has shown, as late as 1959 the private sector (of which kolkhoz private plots made up nearly three-fourths the area) still produced about one-third of the total gross agricultural output and nearly one-half of the livestock products. Moreover, crop yields per hectare in the private sector have been 50 to 100 per cent higher than in the socialist (though here too there are questions of statistical reliability).

The agricultural production targets are however so high—2.5-fold increase in gross output by 1970, and 3.5 by 1980—that an aura of unreality surrounds everything the Program and Mr. Khrushchev say about agriculture. If the targets are taken even half seriously by the authorities, we may expect the pressure on the village to mount progressively to the point where the institutional and organizational prospects for agriculture outlined in the Program may well be re-examined. In fact, the implications are more profound. Success or failure in agriculture is bound to affect the pressure on resources in the economy as a whole, the fortunes of the consumer, the rate of urbanization and industrialization, the sense of haste, and the political climate in the country. The gulf between the peasant's behavior and the regime's national and international aspirations may not be as deep as it was thirty or twenty-five years ago, nor do the peasants dominate the domestic picture as much, but the development and structure of the Soviet economy and the fortunes of the Soviet society have not yet cut themselves entirely loose from dependence on the peasant's will and whim. The reality of the whole Program in large measure depends on whether and how this chasm may be bridged.

SECTION XI

The Soviet Union in World Affairs

Western experts on Soviet affairs tend to disagree in evaluating Soviet relations with the external world. Some claim that Soviet foreign relations have traditionally been guided by ideological considerations; others maintain that they tend to reflect primarily the "national interests" of the U.S.S.R.; still others believe that both Soviet domestic and foreign policies are determined exclusively by a political realism defined in terms of power. These conflicting views are reflected in the articles in this section.

W. W. Rostow, Chairman of the Policy Planning Council of the U.S. Department of State in the Kennedy and Johnson administrations, argues that Soviet foreign relations are basically governed by "the same empirical criteria for the exercise of power which evolved in Soviet internal policy." The primacy of domestic power considerations notwithstanding, the foreign policy techniques of the Soviet state, according to the author, have been generally conventional, and its performance, with certain exceptions, "similar to that of other ambitious national states." While during the early phase of Soviet history the leaders of the U.S.S.R. were concerned primarily with the consolidation of domestic political power and economic reconstruction and expansion, in the later phase, especially after World War II, they assumed an increasingly offensive posture. Dr. Rostow discusses the fundamental issues raised by the historical transition from an "essentially defensive pursuit of power from a relatively weak base," to an increasingly offensive position in an era in which the Soviet Union is a major power base. While the Soviet regime aims persistently at the preservation of domestic control and the maximization of external power, it is limited in its designs by the realities of political life and the realization of the possible consequences of wars fought with modern weapons of mass destruction. Although the Soviet regime is prepared, in the author's view, "to exploit fully such possibilities for expanding its power as the world scene may offer . . . [it] is limited consciously in its pursuit of power by the desire to avoid major war and limited unconsciously by the institutionalized methods to which it is attached both in conducting its foreign relations and in controlling its own society."

One of the basic means by which the Soviet leaders of the post-Stalin era strove to maintain and expand the power of the U.S.S.R. and world communism was the advancement of the policy of "peaceful coexistence." This policy reflects to a large extent a traditional Soviet objective to avoid risking the loss of what the Soviet regime had acquired since its establishment in 1917–18 by engaging in doubtful military adventures.

The Communist conception of peaceful coexistence differs radically from the Western interpretation of the term.* From the Communist point of view, peaceful coexistence does not imply the necessity or desire to foster better relations for purposes of bringing about an accommodation between the two major political and military blocs dividing the world; it is conceived rather as a new form of class struggle made necessary by the development of weapons of mass destruction. In this context, peaceful coexistence is a tactical means for the advancement of world communism without the risk of a nuclear war. This policy, however, does not preclude the use of military power for the promotion of political interests, especially in the non-Communist world. With the nuclear might of the Western powers neutralized by the nuclear arsenal of the Soviet Union, the "national liberation wars" of the "oppressed peoples" are to be encouraged and openly or covertly supported by the U.S.S.R.

The pitfalls inherent in the many meanings of peaceful coexistence, especially in their employment for the advancement of Soviet interests, are spelled out in the article by Philip Mosely. The Soviet leadership, he points out, realizes the mutually suicidal character of a nuclear war, but the "Kremlin is not actively interested in bringing nuclear arms under control, and it believes it can

* For the Soviet view of the world situation, including its policy of peaceful coexistence, see pp. 74–102, 119–138.

gain more political advantages by continuing the arms race at a high pitch." Moscow's policy of peaceful coexistence was designed to wrest decisive victories for the cause of world communism by all means short of nuclear holocaust. In spite of the relative relaxation of international tension, this policy may in the long run be more dangerous for the West than was that of Stalin. For, as Professor Mosely observes, "in contrast to Stalin's cautious peripheral probings, Khrushchev's declared ambitions and the current Soviet programs of action now extend to all continents except, perhaps temporarily, Australia. . . . Since Soviet military and economic strength will be growing rapidly in coming years, it is not going to be enough for the countries that cherish freedom to repeat old and tried formulas that have served them well in previous crises. They must seek actively for new ways to bring their great political, economic and strategic resources to bear in the balance if they are going to survive in freedom the multiple challenge that is posed by [the Soviet] program of 'peaceful coexistence.' "

Although this program represented and continues to represent a formidable challenge to the West, its bold advancement in the post-Stalin era also augured one of the great opportunities for the West. While not in itself responsible for the centrifugal pressures that appeared in the Soviet bloc after the death of Stalin, it undoubtedly helped exacerbate the conflict that split the Communist camp. The Marxist-Leninist myth that the destruction of capitalist society and its replacement by a world socialist order would logically lead to the establishment of a new, harmonious supranational community of nations and the permanent abolition of war was first challenged by Yugoslavia's extrication from the Stalinist mold in 1948 and permanently shattered by the ever increasing belligerency noticeable in Sino-Soviet relations. The gradual division of the Communist world into two antagonistic camps seems to have demonstrated the Communists' inability to surmount the limits of nationalism and the nation-state system they set out to destroy (see Figure 11).

The causes of the failure of contemporary Communism to fulfill the "apocalyptic visions of Marx" are analyzed by Professor Shoup. He precedes his analysis by a succinct discussion of the meaning of nationalism and the prewar Communist views on supra-national

Figure 11.   THE U.S.S.R. AND THE PEOPLE'S REPUBLIC OF CHINA: THE ALIGNMENTS WITHIN THE COMMUNIST WORLD

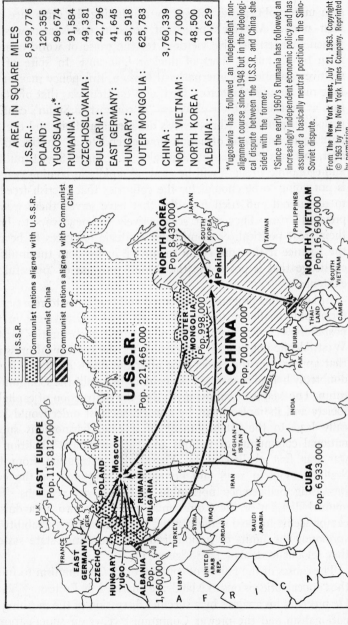

AREA IN SQUARE MILES

U.S.S.R.:	8,599,776
POLAND:	120,355
YUGOSLAVIA:*	98,674
RUMANIA:†	91,584
CZECHOSLOVAKIA:	49,381
BULGARIA:	42,796
EAST GERMANY:	41,645
HUNGARY:	35,918
OUTER MONGOLIA:	625,783
CHINA:	3,760,339
NORTH VIETNAM:	77,000
NORTH KOREA:	48,500
ALBANIA:	10,629

*Yugoslavia has followed an independent non-alignment course since 1948 but in the ideological dispute between the U.S.S.R. and China she sided with the former.

†Since the early 1960's Rumania has followed an increasingly independent economic policy and has assumed a basically neutral position in the Sino-Soviet dispute.

integration. The strains that developed in the Communist bloc after World War II, are traced, *inter alia*, to the central importance which the historical nation-state had for those Communists who were confronted with the practical task of consolidating their position of power and faced with the necessities of constructing their separate totalitarian systems. However, the parallel development of totalitarianism in the countries which succumbed to Communist control gradually led to an outcome other than the one envisaged by the Marxists. Buoyed by a renascent nationalism which was often disguised as "national Communism" or "socialist patriotism," it encouraged the evolution of a polycentric Communist power spectrum whose long-range consequences cannot as yet be accurately prophesied.

The power struggle between East and West, and the one waged within the Communist camp are also reflected in the Soviet views of, and conduct in, the United Nations. But while the former often reached dramatic proportions in the halls of the General Assembly and the Security Council, the intra-Communist dispute, involving both members and non-members, has been kept outside the framework of the United Nations. Viewing this international organization as one of the many arenas in the struggle between the two antagonistic social systems, the Communists do not consider the United Nations as the competent forum for the settling of disputes arising within the "socialist" system. And indeed, as Professor Dallin, Director of the Russian Institute of Columbia University, pointed out in a pioneering study on the subject, "the Soviet Union and its allies have never brought a single dispute among themselves before the United Nations." Nevertheless, the fluctuations in inter-Communist affairs and the nature of the intra-Communist dispute have been periodically reflected in the changing attitudes of the Communist states in the United Nations towards such questions as, for example, the admission of the People's Republic of China into the United Nations organization. Moreover, responding to domestic and foreign pressures (including those brought to bear by Communist China), the Soviet Union has been less than consistent in her evaluation of the importance of the United Nations. These inconsistencies in the assessment of the United Nations have ranged from its "total rejection as an 'imperialist tool' to total support as an imminent Communist 'front.' "

Professor Dallin demonstrates that the U.S.S.R. has participated in the United Nations "for limited purposes and with limited expectations." Membership in the United Nations, according to Professor Dallin, has given the Soviet Union valuable opportunities:

> for the settlement of relatively minor disputes;
>
> for international contacts, both to exchange views and to initiate and pursue negotiations, often informally rather than at official sessions;
>
> for gathering information, political intelligence, technical know-how, and securing economic and other goods and services, as a matter of self-interest;
>
> for gaining prestige and respectability as a major power in the family of nations; and
>
> for engaging in propaganda, in the broadest sense of the term, and attempting to influence the views, attitudes, and political alignments of other states.

In the light of the presently available evidence, it appears that the changing position of the Soviet Union in world affairs as reflected by her actions both within and outside the United Nations system is to a large extent determined by the periodic changes in the Soviet perception of the outer world and the ever recurring shifts in the ideological preconceptions of the regime. The one constant characteristic of the Soviet version of *Realpolitik* has been the Soviet leaders' political pragmatism in interrelating their consideration of "national" interest and doctrinal requirements as defined in terms of power.

THE FOREIGN POLICY OF THE SOVIET UNION

Soviet Foreign Relations

W. W. ROSTOW[*]

1) Introduction

Soviet relations with the external world have, in general, come to be governed by the same empirical criteria for the exercise of power which evolved in Soviet internal policy. One can observe in the immediate postrevolutionary years a similar struggle between inherited ideological notions and the raw limitations which the historical environment imposed on the new Soviet state. From 1917 to 1923 Lenin made a series of foreign policy decisions which were governed by short-run practical power considerations. As in internal policy, these set the format which Stalin more fully elaborated. After an ineffective rear-guard action, those who clung to an ideological basis for Soviet foreign policy were eliminated from effective power by 1929 and, for the most part, were physically eliminated by the end of the Great Purge a decade later.

[*] Formerly Professor of Economic History at the Massachusetts Institute of Technology, Dr. Rostow is Chairman of the Policy Planning Council of the U.S. Department of State (1965). He is the author of *The Stages of Economic Growth. A Non-Communist Manifesto* (1961), *The Prospects for Communist China* (1954), and *An American Policy in Asia* (1955).

On balance, the foreign policy techniques of the Soviet state have been generally conventional and its performance similar to that of other ambitious national states with the following important exceptions:

1. As in internal policy, a residue of what might be called "ideological rationale" for foreign policy has been maintained and applied in those circumstances where it has been judged empirically to be useful or where it has not conflicted with the maintenance and enlargement of Soviet power.

2. In particular, the Soviet state has, with a few recent exceptions, maintained direct control over Communist parties abroad and has manipulated their policies, on an ostensibly ideological basis, to conform to changing judgments concerning the power needs of the Soviet state.

3. An ideological residue has combined with the needs of internal policy to maintain the Soviet state in a posture of almost continuous hostility to the external world; this hostility is aggressive in the particular sense that, within the limits imposed by its prime goal of protecting its control over Soviet domestic society and the perhaps unconscious limits imposed by the techniques it is prepared to use, the regime seeks, as opportunity may offer, to expand indefinitely its external power.

4. The status of direct authority acquired in Eastern Europe by the Soviet regime after World War II has led to a progressive imposition of a system of total control which has reflected fully the patterns of contemporary Soviet internal policy.*

5. The system of internal controls, including information controls, has permitted the Soviet regime, notably since 1929, to alter its foreign policy tactics more sharply than is possible in societies where governments are dependent on the understanding and consent of public opinion.

There is no evidence that before 1939 Soviet foreign policy was governed by a serious long-range plan, as opposed to long-run hopes and ambitions. It appears to have responded to problems, threats, and possibilities thrown up by the course of events outside the Soviet Union which it was, for the most part, incapable of

---

* Ed. note: For information on the institutional and ideological diversity that characterized Eastern European affairs since 1956, see pp. 503–514.

determining or controlling. Its response took the form of such actions as were judged most likely, on a short-range basis, to maintain or expand the national power of the Soviet regime. Further, over this period the Soviet regime chose in general to forego an enlargement of its external power on occasions where such enlargement was judged to involve major risks to the internal stability of its national base. Similarly, in the conduct of its relations with Communist parties abroad the Soviet regime has chosen to maintain absolute control over their policies, and to govern those policies on the basis of the believed short-run interest of the Soviet Union rather than permit the parties abroad those forms of organization and policy which would maximize their effective power in their own areas. Although the post-1945 status of the Soviet regime in Eastern Europe and the development of Communism in Asia and the Middle East have given the Soviet regime a new and more promising environment in which to operate, there is no evidence that the foreign policy criteria of the regime have changed.

2) *The Case of Brest-Litovsk*

The first great issue of foreign policy confronted by the Soviet regime in November 1917 was the issue of war or peace with Germany. It evoked a searching conflict between ideology and the short-run requirements of Soviet internal power, which was decided in favor of the latter. In a sense the decision foreshadowed much of future Soviet policy, internal as well as external.

Failure to carry out either a successful war or an effective peace policy had been largely responsible for the weakness of the Provisional Government, and immediate cessation of hostilities had been a cardinal point in Bolshevik appeals throughout 1917. At the same time, the idea of a world revolutionary struggle was prominent in the minds of many Bolshevik leaders and imbedded at the core of their ideology. Yet Lenin, and gradually more of his followers, insisted at every turn on the priority of attainable interests, first among which was the maintenance of the Soviet position in Petrograd and Moscow. This view could, of course, be argued within the Party as a necessary means to achieve the ultimate purposes of world Communism; but, as generally, the end actually attained was heavily determined by the means, and the priority of the Russian base has conflicted at every turn with the cause of world Communism and given that peculiar movement its present cast.

On November 8, 1917, Lenin read to the Congress of Soviets a "Decree of Peace" proposing immediate negotiations with all belligerent powers for a "just and democratic peace," without annexations and without indemnities. A separate peace, with the conception of a Russian Communist evolution in isolation, was definitely not yet part of the Bolshevik platform, based as that program still was on the anticipation of an international workers' revolt. But when it became clear that the Allies were not favorable to peace talks, the Bolsheviks made formal application (November 26) to the German High Command for an immediate armistice for the purpose of concluding peace. Two days later a cease-fire order went out to all Russian troops, and on December 15 a four-week armistice was concluded with the Central Powers.

The Russian delegates did not come to the conference at Brest-Litovsk as old-style diplomats. They used every opportunity to spread revolutionary propaganda and to ridicule their German antagonists before the outside world. Their two-fold purpose was to advance the cause of world revolution at the same time as they were bargaining for terms for Soviet Russia. But it is significant that Lenin realized as early as January 1918 that his expectation about the rising proletariat of Europe, particularly of Germany, was wrong, and that his principal attainable, though by no means assured, goal was the consolidation of the November Revolution in Russia.

Fortunately for the unity of the Bolshevik Party, plans for the delayed world revolution and for the consolidation of the Soviet regime were not yet in conflict. Both aims called for a "breathing space" at this time, and Trotsky the spellbinder was sent to replace Joffe at Brest-Litovsk, with instructions to prolong the discussion as much as possible.

The details of the peace negotiations need not be rehearsed here. The Allies continued to be unresponsive, Europe's industrial workers did not rise, and the German High Command rejected Trotsky's "no indemnities, no annexations" proposals. In answer to the German counter-proposals Trotsky requested an adjournment and returned to Petrograd for consultation.

In spite of continued accusations of being a German agent, Lenin insisted on immediate peace. In his famous "Twenty-one Theses" he put his position very simply:

> The Russian Socialist Government is confronted with a question which requires an immediate solution: either to accept the annexationist peace or to start at once a revolutionary war. . . . The question whether it is possible to undertake at once a revolutionary war must be answered solely from the point of view of actual conditions and the interest of the Socialist Revolution which has already begun. . . .

Bukharin, however, led an enthusiastic group within the Party in favor of immediate revolutionary war; and Trotsky hit upon the formula "no war no peace" by which the Soviet government would simply declare the war ended without accepting any terms in anticipation that the German Command would not then order its troops to advance—a formula perhaps not forgotten by recent Communist negotiators in Korea.

In the winter of 1918 control of policy was more directly dependent on opinion within and without the Party than it later became, and thus Lenin had to compromise. With great misgivings he yielded to Trotsky's formula, with which the latter returned to Brest-Litovsk. As Lenin had feared, the slogan was no more effective than its predecessors had been; less than a week after the formula had been pronounced, General Hoffmann ordered his troops to advance. Chastened by the failure of its first attempt at revolutionary orthodoxy on the international scene, Soviet policy now had to follow the line urged by Lenin, who had enough of that "very pretty fairy tale"—World Revolution.

German terms had stiffened. In fact, they now proposed what the Bolsheviks regarded as a "shameful peace." But there was no Russian army, and the Revolution in Russia had to be saved. And so, although he was called "traitor," "Judas," and "German spy," Lenin won the fight within the Party. The German peace terms were accepted. The priority of the Soviet Russian Revolution and the priority of actual over potential circumstances were established.

3) *The Elaboration of Practical International Politics, 1918–33*

With few exceptions the primacy of domestic power considerations established in the discussion over Brest-Litovsk has remained paramount in Soviet foreign policy decisions. In terms of the maintenance of power, the principal need in the spring of 1918 was to save Petrograd and to preserve the regime's base. Therefore Brest-Litovsk had to be signed. In the next few years the general aims of the Soviet government were equally obvious and practical: to preserve itself, the regime required termination of foreign intervention, noninterference in Russia's domestic affairs, and lifting of the blockade and the trade restrictions imposed by the victorious Allies.

The Versailles Treaty, though annulling Brest-Litovsk, deliberately isolated Russia and created a *cordon sanitaire* of buffer states. The Soviets, in riposte, initiated a series of bilateral agreements with the Baltic countries (February–August, 1920), recognizing their independence and establishing diplomatic relations. Similar agreements were concluded with Finland, Persia, Afghanistan, China, and Turkey. Eventually, after a seesaw military struggle, Russia also made peace with Poland. By 1921, about the same time that the civil war ended, the Soviet government had attained the primary initial aim of its external policy, that is, freedom from outside disturbance. While the Soviet state was still diplomatically isolated from the major powers, there was no longer a military threat; and all the neighboring states had resumed relations. Principles such as the inevitability of world revolution and self-determination were applied where they were judged useful in terms of the real possibilities and disregarded where not. By the time fighting ended, the Soviet government controlled the Ukraine, Georgia, and most of Northern Asia, but not the other states formerly belonging to the Tsar.

At the same time the Soviet leaders forced the establishment of the Communist International (Comintern), on the assumption that revolutions outside Russia were necessary for preservation of the Soviet Revolution. After the fall of Bela Kun in Hungary and the failure of the various German Communist attempts, this consideration seems to have become ever less important in the minds of those Soviet leaders who dominated the Party. Nevertheless, the Comintern provided a convenient means for keeping in contact with the outside world despite the isolation implicit in the Versailles settlement, and it afforded, as well, a limited instrument for exercising a degree of Soviet power abroad. The Comintern's usefulness in these secondary roles was judged sufficient to justify its maintenance on practical grounds, although its interests have been systematically overridden when they conflicted with those of the Soviet regime.

In the period of the twenties the main concern of the Bolshevik leaders was the consolidation of their domestic political base and the economic reconstruction of the country they now effectively controlled. Although the Revolution was secure in the sense that Russian territory remained more or less intact and no immediate alternative to Soviet rule was in sight, problems of internal economic and political management demanded enormous efforts and presented a primary threat to the regime. The failures of War Communism had revealed the administrative inadequacies of the Soviet state. The building of an efficient bureaucracy occupied a considerable proportion of the energies of the leadership as did, of course, their internecine struggle for the succession to Lenin.

Russia was under further pressure to establish reasonably conventional international arrangements in order to acquire foreign economic assistance. However distasteful this was to the Bolshevik leaders, Lenin's Party was determined not to be bound to "revolutionary phrases." As early as 1919 there had been tentative proposals for Anglo-Russian trade talks; and by 1922 Soviet Russia had already concluded trade agreements with Turkey, the Balkan countries, Norway, Austria, and Italy. When the opportunity came to capitalize on the disunity of the Allies and their hostility to Germany, Soviet diplomacy took full advantage, broke up the Genoa conference, where the powers had been discussing questions of recognition, economic aid, and the repudiated tsarist debts with Soviet representatives. The U.S.S.R. then proceeded to conclude with Germany the Treaty of Rapallo, whereby the two powers ostracized by the European concert agreed to political and economic co-operation. The German and the Russian diplomat skillfully played cat-and-mouse both with each other and with the Versailles powers in a thoroughly traditional manner; and both emerged with highly favorable agreements on reparations, secret military collaboration, and economic assistance. Thereafter one nation after another, except the United States (until 1933), accorded recognition to the Soviet government. The political regime of the foreign country never deterred the Bolshevik leaders—even Fascist Italy signed a pact with the Soviet Union in 1924. The Soviet Union began to frequent international economic and disarmament conferences, though still denouncing the League of Nations in principle.

Within this developing framework of conventional arrangements, the Comintern continued to operate, often to the embarrassment of Russian policy. The fall of the British Labour Government in connection with the Zinoviev affair (1924), continued nonrecognition by the U.S., and the general distrust with which Europe viewed Russia are doubtless traceable to fear of Comintern activity. But certainly after the abortive rising in Germany in 1923, the Soviet regime accorded a low priority to the encouragement of European Communism. The debacle in China in 1927 completed the practical isolation of Communism and confirmed the primacy of Stalin's already enunciated doctrine of "socialism in one country." It is significant that the Comintern held only one World Congress between 1924 and 1935, and held that one (1928) to give its blessing to what was in effect an act of Russian isolationism—the decision to proceed with accelerated industrialization on a strictly national basis.

So long as no power seemed to be a direct threat to Russia's development, it was in the interest of the Soviet Union to support generalized antiwar and disarmament proposals, given the dominant concern of the regime with internal problems. Major allies were neither needed nor available, and disarmament could have no disadvantage for the least armed and economically weakest power. Moreover the more Chicherin or Litvinov talked peace and took pains to dissociate themselves from the Comintern, the more likely the Soviet Union was to receive favorable treatment from the West.

Thus Litvinov announced Russia's adherence to the Kellogg Pact in 1926 and proposed total disarmament to the League's disarmament commission in 1927. Early in 1927 he proclaimed the

Litvinov Protocol whereby Russia, Poland, Estonia, Latvia, and Rumania accepted the Kellogg Pact and renounced war. Finland, France, Persia, and Italy were added in the years 1930–33 to the Russian system of nonaggression pacts.

The extent of the regime's concentration on domestic affairs was shown during the world economic crisis of 1929–33. What would seem to have been a partial vindication of the Marxist prophecy of increasingly severe capitalist crises, and a first-rate opportunity for Communist agitation, found Communist parties the world over futilely engaged in obstinate struggles with other parties which showed, in part at least, socialist aspirations. Principal Soviet diplomatic efforts were directed, not to helping these parties or furnishing them with positions which would maximize their possibilities for developing effective local leadership, but rather to taking advantage of the crisis to secure economic agreements to tide over the First Five-Year Plan.

4) *Maneuver and Bankruptcy, 1933–39*

The German Communist Party constituted the most flagrant example of energy dissipated in contest with other parties of the Left, although its activity can hardly be called without consequence in view of its substantial contribution to Hitler's rise to power. What the motivations were for the Kremlin leaders who gave orders to the German Communists is not clear. This is one of the few major instances in the history of Soviet foreign policy for which no obvious rational explanation in terms of Soviet power interests can be supplied. To the extent that Soviet leaders believed that German Communists could attain power alone, or that Fascism was merely a transitory precursor to Communism, they can be said to have been prisoners of some version of Marxism. But the realism that Lenin and Stalin had demonstrated since Brest-Litovsk and the peculiarly ambivalent relationship of the Soviet government to the German Communist Party indicate that this is an insufficient, if not completely incorrect, answer. Apparently the Politburo, with its attention centered on the Five-Year Plan, collectivization, and other internal problems, simply misunderstood the German situation and underestimated the danger of Nazism, a mistake not uncommon at that time in the council chambers of Europe.

The accession of Hitler and the earlier attack by Japan on Manchuria induced the Soviet Union to make changes in its foreign policy, or, perhaps more accurately, to invent a new foreign policy. The principal aim remained, that is, the safeguarding of the security and integrity of the Soviet state. But the period of idyllic, utopian foreign relations in which one dealt in nonaggression pacts, outlawing of war, and disarmament, and in which the principal immediate concerns were foreign trade and loans, was clearly past.

Under these circumstances the regime judged that it now required positive alliances to protect its security. Since the buffer states set up at Versailles to protect Europe from Bolshevism could serve as a buffer to a potential German advance, Russia could now wholeheartedly support the League, collective security, and maintenance of the *status quo*.

Formerly the League had been denounced as an "international organization of the capitalists for the systematic exploitation of all the working peoples of the earth," and as "the holy alliance of the bourgeoisie for the suppression of proletarian revolution." But the overriding priority of security interest and the complete control of public expression enabled the Soviet regime to accomplish its change of position with comparative ease. Soviet Russia entered the League as a permanent Council member in September 1934.

By 1935 Soviet declarations such as those on the "advisability of peace," and the rising power of Nazi Germany had overcome Western suspicions sufficiently to bring about mutual-assistance pacts between the Soviet Union and France, and the Soviet Union and Czechoslovakia. England, led by a conservative government, refused to join in a defense pact with Russia despite considerable popular support, including that of the then-dissident Winston Churchill.

The continuing growth of Fascism confronted the Soviet leaders with a dilemma. They could either suppress the internal revolutionary tradition and try to work with conservative governments within and without the League in order to build defenses against Hitler, or they could try to use their still extensive Communist network as a skeleton around which to build a united anti-Fascist front. They tried to follow both policies.

The Seventh Congress of the Communist International in the

summer of 1935 proposed "the establishment of a united front for the purpose of combating the capitalist offensive, capitalism, and war." Comintern activity took on new life, and all talk of "social fascism" was given up in favor of the new policy of co-operation with the bourgeois governments and Social-Democratic parties. Again it was the requirements of Russian security that determined Soviet policy, and again the change in the Party line was made with comparative ease at home and with Communists abroad, to whom the new dispensation gave enlarged scope for action and maneuver.

For a time the new anti-Fascist allies appeared to be quite successful, and both France and Spain elected "Popular Front" majorities. But the stronger and more vocal Popular Front movements became, the more distrust was aroused by both local and Moscow Communist activity. In the eyes of the conservative West, Communists could not wholly live down their character as revolutionaries and Russian agents. The rise of Popular Front governments in some ways inhibited the possibilities of cementing more formal security links between Russia and the West.

The first test of anti-Hitler strength came in March 1935 when Hitler occupied the Rhineland. Russia's pleas for countermeasures went unheeded. The Spanish Civil War brought out even more fully the disunity of Europe. Stalin's initial hesitancy, followed by his policy of intervention and exploitation, did not enhance the confidence of the Western powers. The British policy of vacillation and nonintervention, French dependence on Britain, and the bad impression made on the West by the purges of 1936–38 served to complete the defeat of Russia's collective-security policy, and may have strengthened that element in the Kremlin's thought which led toward an alternative and simpler means of assuring Soviet security.

In November 1936, Germany and Japan signed the anti-Comintern Pact, which Italy soon joined. Then the Popular Front government fell in France. The spread of the Great Purge to the army made Russia appear to be an even more uncertain factor on the international scene. The rebel forces in Spain had increasing success. By the time Hitler was ready to begin his expansionist campaigns in 1938 it was evident that the Soviet Union had failed to gain the confidence of the Western powers. At the same time, the Kremlin had lost such confidence as it may have had in the strength of the Western powers as a result of their performance over the Rhineland and Spain. If there was any united front by the autumn of 1938, it was the Fascist and not the anti-Fascist front.

Stalin's motivations in the matter of the Spanish Civil War are not wholly clear. Conceivably he thought the protection of France's southern frontier and the prevention of another Fascist government justified intervention. The prospect of gaining influence over the Spanish government, of furthering a possible revolution, and of testing the tactics and weapons of the new Red Army may all have appealed to him. But the half-hearted way in which the intervention was conducted and the obvious fact that Soviet policy in Spain only antagonized those countries on whose support Russia would have to depend in case of German aggression, make these explanations somehow deficient. On balance, it seems most likely that the tying down of Italian and German energies in Spain, far distant from the Soviet frontiers, had sufficient appeal to justify an intervention of limited resources and limited liabilities. Whatever Stalin's purposes, it is evident that the gambit failed and he cut his losses.

The crisis of 1938 exhibited the utter collapse of the Soviet anti-Hitler policy. On March 17, less than a week after the *Anschluss*, Litvinov called for joint action among the European states to insure against further German aggression; but the British Cabinet rejected the proposal as "premature." By the time of the Czech crisis in September, Russia had definitely been excluded as a partner by the Western countries and was pointedly not invited to Munich, though she had been a guarantor of the Czech frontier. There is no doubt that the Chamberlain government wanted to keep Russia out of any European settlement; and that, if a war had to come, the Western nations would have preferred a German-Russian struggle.

After Munich, which had shown France and Britain to be incapable of making an effective front against Germany, Russia was left in a position of relative diplomatic isolation, with no firm allies, no assurance of co-operation in case of attack, and facing a growing menace in Germany. Perhaps the traditional Communist fear of a bourgeois coalition led to a disproportionate emphasis in the Soviet leaders' minds of the possibility of a German-English-French alliance. Yet it was a fact that the Western nations had treated directly with Hitler, without Russia's participation. The Soviet reaction was to seek to protect itself as well as possible. This aim was furthered by European developments in the next few months.

Hitler, ignoring his Munich promises, occupied Czechoslovakia and the Memel Territory in March 1939. Thereupon Britain and France hastily pledged aid to Poland, and both the Western Allies and Germany began negotiating for Russian support. It is not certain whether it was Germany or the Soviet Union which took the initiative in the talks between the two powers. Apparently both nations had been extending feelers since the summer of 1938, and a German-Russian trade agreement was promptly renewed (for a year) in December 1938. In the latter half of the year the domestic propaganda of each country began to ease off its attacks on the other. In the spring of 1939 these preliminary overtures began to be taken seriously in Berlin, notably after Stalin's speech of March 10 to the Eighteenth Party Congress. In any case, Russia suddenly became no longer the outcast of Munich but rather the balancing element in the European power structure, for whose support both sides in the coming struggle were prepared to bid.

The dismissal of Litvinov in May was an overt sign that Russia was prepared to change her policy of the past five years, to jettison, if necessary, her anti-Fascist ideological framework and to accept that offer which promised the best short-run chance of security. Negotiations for both possible combinations were conducted simultaneously in the spring and summer of 1939, and Stalin, in the historical manner of European diplomats, took full advantage of this situation. Particularly in the latter stages of the negotiations, Stalin was able to bargain hard, although clearly he needed an agreement as much as anyone.

Britain and France had pledged aid to Poland; but Poland was not prepared to offer the Russian Army passage through its territory. Furthermore, though the Western powers desired Russian support, they were not willing (in contrast to the Germans) to compromise third parties such as Poland and Rumania. Therefore an understanding between the Western powers and the Soviet Union was difficult to attain. What the Allies demanded of Russia, it appeared, was active collaboration, that is, an agreement to fight against Germany in any war that might develop with Hitler. Hitler, on the other hand, required merely a promise of neutrality, to which end he was willing to concede large pieces of Europe and Asia to Russian influence.

Since the immediate danger of an unopposed frontal attack upon Russia had been averted by the precipitate guarantee to Poland, and since the Allies had shown themselves by no means eager to accept Soviet terms, Hitler's seemed to be the better short-run offer. As Stalin trusted neither party, he prolonged the negotiations up to the last possible moment before the weather-set deadline for the German invasion of Poland, September 1. But when the time came for decision, Soviet policy disregarded world opinion, disregarded the ideological battle with Fascism, even disregarded, perhaps, long-range considerations of power politics as they were in fact revealed by the course of World War II. On August 23, 1939, Molotov and Ribbentrop signed their Non-Aggression Pact. Ten days later there was war.

Just what Stalin expected after the Pact and after the outbreak of war is not certain. Apparently what he anticipated, or at least wished for, was a long-drawn-out struggle in which Germany and the Allies would slowly exhaust each other, leaving to Russia the role of arbiter at some later date. Certainly Stalin expected neither the quick collapse of the Poles nor the even more surprising collapse of France. What he would have done had he known of the overwhelming initial German superiority cannot be told.

While the Soviet Union was living in the precarious security of 1939–41, it continued the dual policy of strengthening its own forces while appeasing Hitler. Russian trade enabled Germany largely to overcome the effects of the British blockade, and Communist movements throughout the world, with less relation to their own national needs than ever, condemned the Allies for starting the war, undertook sabotage, and campaigned against lend-lease and military-preparedness legislation wherever possible. At the same time, Russia's own mobilization was given top priority, and its foreign policy was clearly designed to secure all possible strategic advantages. Thus the Soviet Union initiated new mutual-assistance pacts with the Baltic states almost immediately after the partition of Poland (October 29), and tried unsuccessfully to reach an agreement with Turkey. When Finland balked at a similar offer of a defense pact, Russian troops marched in (November 30). Once again, though probably with less success than ever, revolutionary jargon about "liberation of the workers," "crushing the Mannerheim clique," and so on, was used to explain a maneuver of a primitive strategic character.

German and Russian interests began to clash in the Balkans in the summer of 1940, and relations between the two countries gradually cooled after that point, although economic relations were continued to the outbreak of war in June 1941. On the eve of Hitler's invasion of Yugoslavia in April 1941 Stalin signed a treaty of friendship with Yugoslavia in an ineffective gesture to avoid the impending German move, or, perhaps, to impress Hitler with Russia's intent to draw a line at some point in Germany's movement to the East. At the same time the Soviet Union signed a treaty with Japan ensuring, so far as diplomacy could, the security of its Far Eastern position. When Germany attacked Russia in June the very event whose prevention had been the chief aim of Soviet policy for eight years apparently found the Russian forces tactically unprepared, though specific warning—including the time and place of the German invasion—had repeatedly been offered to the Soviet government by Britain and the United States. There is some evidence that Stalin found it difficult to believe that the strong short-run power interests which were shared by Germany and Russia would not sustain the pact of 1939 and override Hitler's impulse to pursue his ambitions in the East. To his cost Stalin discovered that Hitler gave to *Mein Kampf* more serious status, as a plan for action, then he himself accorded to Communism's sacred texts.

5) *Some General Observations on the Postwar Position*

The course of Soviet foreign policy since 1945 is so close upon us that it is difficult to view it in a firm historical perspective. In general it would appear that Stalin saw in the aftermath of World War II unique opportunities for extending the power and influence of the Soviet regime. The ground-force positions attained or negotiated in the course of the war, the temporary elimination of Germany and Japan as independent elements of power in the world political arena, the weakness of Western Europe, the rise of powerful nationalist movements in Asia and the Middle East, and especially the success of the Chinese Communists have all presented possibilities of some attraction to the Politburo. These possibilities have been exploited within a framework set by the Soviet appreciation of American military strength and weakness. Stalin avoided the risk of U.S. strategic air attack; but he exploited to the full U.S. postwar demobilization and the inhibitions on the use of U.S. military force imposed by American and Western coalition politics.

In their determination to make the most of the practical possibilities available, the ideological background and, perhaps more important, the historical experience of the Russian Communist leaders have probably played a part. The theories of Marx and Lenin place a peculiar importance on war as a historical instrument for creating the conditions for revolutionary advance. More particularly, it has not been forgotten in the Kremlin that the Bolshevik opportunity to seize power in 1917 arose directly from a situation of weakness created by a protracted war. In addition it has probably not been forgotten that anti-Communist forces proved capable of rallying and re-establishing themselves to a degree which proved disappointing to the Bolsheviks in the years after World War I. It seems likely that these elements of ideology and remembered history joined with the long institutionalized posture of Soviet hostility to the external world to produce a policy of aggressive exploitation of opportunities after World War II.

In keeping with previous performance, the Soviet regime has pursued what it has believed to be its power interests in various parts of the world on an *ad hoc* basis, adjusting to potentialities and limitations as they have emerged. The fundamental facts about the postwar world, as opposed to the position before 1939, would appear to be:

1. The potentialities for the extension of Soviet power were vastly increased.

2. The increase in Soviet (as in U.S.) power has placed the Soviet Union in a position where its own actions are of such influence on the world environment that they help significantly to determine the environment and the issues which confront the Soviet Union.

It is no longer rational for the Soviet Union (or the U.S.) to behave as if the world environment it confronts is independently determined, and to construct its foreign policy on a series of specific reactions to events as they arise. There is, however, no conclusive evidence that the criteria for Soviet foreign policy have altered or that a systematic plan is serving as the touchstone for day-to-day Soviet foreign policy decisions.

Nevertheless, the shifting from the essentially defensive pursuit of power from a relatively weak base, which characterized the Soviet position from 1918 to 1941, to its offensive posture after 1945 in a world arena in which the Soviet Union is a major power base constitutes an enormous historical transition. It has raised, in particular, the following fundamental issues:

1. The degree to which major war should be risked by the Soviet regime in pursuit of its objective of enlarged external power.

2. The extent to which reliance should be placed on conventional diplomacy in expanding Soviet power, as opposed to the use of Communist parties and other instruments of subversion and internal interference abroad.

3. The manner in which relations should be conducted with Communist regimes abroad, whether indigenously generated or installed in power by the Soviet Union.

4. The shielding of the internal Soviet control system from the impact of enlarged relations with the non-Soviet world.

A full view of postwar Soviet foreign policy in the light of these central issues lies outside the scope of this essay, involving, as it would, Soviet actions throughout the world. In general it may be said that, under Stalin's direction, the Politburo has:

—firmly disciplined its pursuit of external power within the limitation that major war be avoided;

—attempted, as in the inter-war years, to use both diplomatic and subversive techniques simultaneously, shifting the relative weight attached to each in different areas at different periods of time, and accepting the political costs of this evident ambivalence;

—accepted, with the possible exception of China (up to the present), the political losses consequent upon the continued exercise from Moscow of direct absolute power in Communist areas abroad, rather than permit the development of partially independent Communist regimes;

—taken extraordinary measures to limit the direct knowledge

and experience of its citizens concerning the outside world, and heightened its effort (begun before 1939) to associate the regime with historic xenophobic Russian nationalism.

It is a theme of this essay that, while the external expansion of Soviet power holds a priority second to the maintenance of the regime's internal control, the maximization of external power over time is a persistent goal of the Soviet rulers. What, then, are the roots of this posture of aggression?

First, it is doubtful that the Soviet regime is operating by a schedule or timetable of world domination or has so operated from the moment it abandoned its hopes of detonating world revolution through the catalytic agency of Russia's November Revolution. However, Marx's and Lenin's analysis of the course of future world history still exerts, after a fashion, a hold on the minds of Soviet leaders. It will be recalled that, while Lenin made his peace with Germany at Brest-Litovsk, and while the new regime was unprepared to take major risks to aid the later revolutionary efforts of German Communists, still the notion of world revolution was not wholly or cleanly abandoned for the long run. More important, perhaps, than its persistence as an ideological residue, this conception became institutionalized in the ties of the Soviet regime to the Communist parties of the world by means of the Comintern. These ties have been used in the interests of the Soviet national state—often at the expense of the progress of Communism abroad. Nevertheless, the ingrained habits of thought of the regime have steadily looked to an expansion of its world power, even though this expansion is not an overriding priority nor governed by a fixed plan; and these habits of thought have their origins in the original ideological conception of Communism's world triumph. This conception constitutes in its present modified form, like government ownership and operation of industry, one of those ideological elements which converged with the pursuit of Soviet power, and thus it has survived.

Second, and more important, the internal stability of the regime has come to be judged dependent on the maintenance within the Soviet Union of the view that the external world is hostile, which, in turn, justifies Soviet hostility. Even if this Soviet hostility were a pure position of propaganda disassociated from aggressive Soviet moves abroad (which it has never been), it would tend to set in motion reactions which would, in turn, give an element of substance to the propaganda. Chronic hostility and the insecurity that goes with it lead to actions of aggression. Psychologically, in part, it may be that Soviet aggression is defensive rather than offensive, based on fear as well as hope. In the end, for practical purposes, and notably in the context of the residuum of ideological aggression discussed above, Soviet hostility is to be judged positively aggressive, even if partially based on an insecurity which in the end stems from overriding concern with the maintenance of the regime's domestic base. For there is no evidence that any action of assurance or appeasement by the external world is likely to give that sense of security to the regime which would lead its present leaders to settle down; and there is considerable evidence that weakened positions in the external world will be fully exploited by the Soviet regime. If this analysis is correct, the ultimate source of the regime's insecurity lies in its relation to its own peoples, and this relationship is not easily susceptible to reconciliation by initiatives from the outside world.

Third, the habits, now firmly bureaucratized, for handling power within the Soviet Union condition the external behavior of the regime. The exercise of domestic power is based on attitudes and methods of as nearly total control as modern techniques permit. These attitudes and methods make it difficult if not impossible for the present regime to operate comfortably in the situations of diffused or shared authority which a firm stucture of world order demands. In Germany and Eastern Europe, notably, as well as in disarmament negotiations in the United Nations, the somewhat musclebound stage of Soviet internal evolution has certainly contributed in recent years to behavior which, by any objective test, is to be judged aggressive.

The picture which thus far emerges, then, is of a regime which is prepared to exploit fully such possibilities for expanding its power as the world scene may offer but which is limited consciously in its pursuit of power by the desire to avoid major war and limited unconsciously by the institutionalized methods to which it is attached both in conducting its foreign relations and in controlling its own society.

THE POLICY OF "PEACEFUL COEXISTENCE"

The Meanings of Coexistence

PHILIP E. MOSELY[*]

I

In the deeply divided world of today, one main obstacle to achieving a genuine state of peaceful coexistence is the gap in the meanings attached to these two words in different societies and political systems. The gap is, of course, just one additional example of the estrangement of vocabularies that besets every effort at direct and sincere exchanges of ideas across or through the ideological and psychological barriers. Words like "democracy," "freedom," "progress" are, as we know only too well, employed in very different and even opposite senses in the two worlds.

Another obstacle lies in the confrontation of absolutes, the insistence on the total good of one ideal and the total evil of the way of life that it seeks to displace and destroy. This sense of serving as a mere instrument of History justifies, in the minds of its champions and supporters, a vast arrogance of self-righteousness. To them, the adversary is not only doomed but is morally wrong in his every act and thought.

[*] Former Director of Studies of the Council on Foreign Relations and former Director of the Russian Institute at Columbia University, Professor Mosely is Director of the European Institute at Columbia University. He is the author of The Kremlin and World Politics (1960) and editor of The Soviet Union, 1922–1962. A Foreign Affairs Reader (1963).

From "The Meanings of Coexistence" by Philip E. Mosely, Foreign Affairs, New York, Vol. XLI, No. 1, October 1962, selections from pp. 36–46. Copyright 1962, by the Council on Foreign Relations, Inc., New York. Reprinted by permission. For footnote references, see original source.

Finally, the ideological armor that encases the Communist leaders is wrought of that contradiction in terms, "scientific revelation." Its theoretical bases, which were laid down over one hundred years ago at the beginning of the industrial era, must be proven to be uniquely correct and infallible today; and therefore those who dare re-examine or question any part of its fundamentalist dogmas must be silenced or destroyed.

The most recent and most authoritative statement of Communist dogma is, of course, the new Program of the Communist Party of the Soviet Union, unanimously adopted by the Twenty-second Party Congress on October 31, 1961. Despite its repetitious length and its many internal contradictions, it was carefully designed to serve as the main guide to Soviet thought, policy and action over "the next historic epoch." In the ten weeks between the publication of the draft program and the convening of the Congress, it was "discussed" in tens of thousands of meetings; since the Congress, it has been distributed in millions of copies printed in scores of languages. Hence, its statements on the nature and purpose of coexistence must be studied seriously. First:

> Peaceful coexistence of the socialist and capitalist countries is an objective necessity for the development of human society. War cannot and must not serve as a means of settling international disputes.

Excellent! All reasonable people can welcome this position as a basis for a lively and earnest give-and-take discussion on how best to guarantee mankind against the danger of a new and terrible war and especially on how, in practical terms, we can concert our actions so as to diminish, contain or eliminate some or all of the conflicts that threaten to escape our control and balloon into a total struggle.

Here, however, the Program brings its non-Communist partners-in-dialogue up sharp against a flinty dogma of Communist fundamentalism:

> Imperialism is the only source of the war danger. The imperialist camp is making preparations for the most terrible crime against mankind—a world thermonuclear war that can bring unprecedented destruction to entire countries and wipe out entire nations.

Here dogma, as so often, takes precedence over reality. After all, the Soviet Union has also been hard at work constructing horrendous weapons systems. Its leaders have, indeed, addressed blackmail notes to more than 30 governments, in which it has threatened their peoples specifically with nuclear destruction unless they abandon certain policies and postures of which Moscow disapproves. Semantically, the Kremlin, like its opponents, argues that it is not preparing for "aggression" but "to deter aggression." The distinction rests in the degree of faith or confidence in the government that makes the threat. Today any nuclear threat raises the level of international tension. This is all the more its effect when the Kremlin stretches the concept of "self-defense" to include the demand for Communist control over West Berlin and for the breaking up of alliances that Moscow views as obstacles to the extension of its own power.

The completely one-sided nature of the Communist interpretation of world politics appears in one small but interesting correction that was inserted in the final version of the Party Program. The draft of August 5 referred with approval to ". . . a growing number of countries that adhere to a policy of neutrality and strive to safeguard themselves against the hazards of participation in military blocs." This wording apparently gave too strong praise to non-alignment. At bottom, Communists are bound by dogma to view non-alignment as a way-station to joining their own power bloc. The words of the draft program might even imply an endorsement of Tito's posture, were it not for his heresy of claiming to be both Communist and uncommitted. And some Communists might have wondered why Khrushchev had used his tanks and artillery, in October 1956, to put down the attempt of the Imre Nagy government to declare Hungary neutral.

The drafters of the final version caught this awkward ideological ambiguity and changed "participation in military blocs" to "participation in aggressive military blocs." Since "aggressive" is an adjective that is applied only to "imperialists" and never to "the countries of socialism," the revised wording modifies the Kremlin's praise of non-alignment and leaves the gate open for presently uncommitted countries to commit themselves later to the "good" military bloc of "socialism."

The pursuit of "peaceful coexistence," in Moscow's view, must not lead to any slackening in the effort to reshape the rest of the world to the Communist pattern. On the contrary, the struggle for the triumph of Communism must be pressed even more vigorously and with the wider and more varied arsenal of instruments that is now available:

> Peaceful coexistence serves as a basis for the peaceful competition between socialism and capitalism on an international scale and constitutes a specific form of class struggle between them. As they consistently pursue the policy of peaceful coexistence, the socialist countries are steadily strengthening the positions of the world socialist system in its competition with capitalism. Peaceful coexistence affords more favorable opportunities for the struggle of the working class in the capitalist countries and facilitates the struggle of the peoples of the colonial and dependent countries for their liberation.

The Program specifically warns Communists everywhere against pinning to a new world war their hopes for their worldwide triumph. Indeed, the expectation of victory through cataclysm might lead them to relax their efforts and to slacken their discipline. However, in accord with a long Leninist tradition, the Soviet leadership is not against all types of wars:

> The C.P.S.U. and the Soviet people as a whole will continue to oppose all wars of conquest, including wars between capitalist countries, and local wars aimed at strangling peoples' emancipation movements, and consider it their duty to support the sacred struggle of the oppressed peoples and their just anti-imperialist wars of liberation.

This reservation leaves a wide range of military actions open to Soviet arms, for the Kremlin reserves to itself the right to decide what peoples are "oppressed" and which wars are "wars of liberation." Despite the great risks that may accompany its participation, direct or indirect, in a variety of wars, the Program affirms the self-confident belief of the Soviet leadership that it can achieve complete victory without becoming involved in a nuclear war:

> The growing superiority of the socialist forces over the forces of imperialism, of the forces of peace over those of war, will make it actually possible to banish world war from the life of society even before the complete victory of socialism on earth, with capitalism surviving in a part of the world. The victory of socialism throughout the world will do away completely with the social and national causes of all wars. To abolish war and establish everlasting peace on earth is the historic mission of Communism.

In the Soviet view, "peaceful coexistence" is the correct policy in "an epoch," more or less prolonged, during which "capitalism" (the label the Kremlin attaches to those who resist its embrace) is to be compelled to retreat from one position to another until it finally gives up the ghost. The means for enforcing each such retreat are to be varied according to the local and international balance of power.

In some countries the transition to socialism (*i.e.* to rule by the Communist Party) may take place by peaceful, in others by "non-peaceful," means. Of course, even if "the working class" (those who obey and support the Communist Party) manages to ". . . win a solid majority in parliament. . . ," it must also ". . . launch a broad mass struggle outside parliament, smash the resistance of the reactionary forces, and provide the necessary conditions for a peaceful socialist revolution." Since the Communists would then hold the monopoly of force, they would also be able to define "the reactionary forces" to suit their own interests. In any case they would have no further interest in providing conditions of "peaceful coexistence" with any groups or individuals that they considered hostile or recalcitrant to that monopoly of power.

The Program emphasizes that the struggle must be waged untiringly and relentlessly, with a rapid succession of tactics, in order to keep the various opposing forces off balance and disunited:

> The success of the struggle which the working class wages for the victory of the revolution will depend on how well the working class and its party master the use of all forms of struggle—peaceful and non-peaceful, parliamentary and extra-parliamentary—and how well they are prepared to replace one form of struggle by another as quickly and unexpectedly as possible.

In the end, of course, all roads lead to Rome, to the dictatorship of the proletariat, *i.e.* of the Communist Party:

> . . . whatever the form in which the transition from capitalism to socialism is effected, that transition can come about only through revolution. However varied the forms of a new people's state power in the period of socialist construction, their essence will be the same—dictatorship of the proletariat, which represents genuine democracy, democracy for the working people.

It is essential, of course, for the main center of the Communist movement to assure the unquestioning unity of "the working class," in order to lead a well-orchestrated offensive against "capitalism." In recent years this has not proved easy or simple even within those countries and Parties that acknowledge Moscow's hegemony. In fact,

> Revisionism, Right opportunism, which is a reflection of bourgeois influence, is the chief danger within the Communist movement today. The revisionists, who mask their renunciation of Marxism with talk about the necessity of taking account of the latest developments in society and the class struggle, in effect play the role of peddlers of bourgeois-reformist ideology within the Communist movement.

However, "dogmatism and sectarianism, unless steadfastly combated, can also become the chief danger at particular stages in the development of individual parties."

Finally, who is to define "revisionism" and "dogmatism?" Obviously Khrushchev is determined to keep this "lever of power" in his own hands. He demonstrated this most dramatically at the Twenty-second Party Congress where he made his famous attack on the Albanian Party leaders, only to be rebuffed by Chou En-lai, who protested the bringing into the open of this bitter inter-party quarrel, and then departed for Peking. The Chinese leadership could, had it been so minded, have cited the very words of the Soviet Party Program on this crucial point:

> The Communist Parties are independent and they shape their policies with due regard to the specific conditions prevailing in their own countries. . . . The Communist Party of the Soviet Union . . . regards it as its internationalist duty to abide by the appraisals and conclusions which the fraternal parties have reached jointly concerning their common tasks in the struggle against imperialism, for peace, democracy and socialism. . . .

Apparently the Soviet leadership has been unusually sensitive to the accusation that it dictates its policies unilaterally to other Parties, for it inserted a significant rewording in the final version of the Program. The draft of August 5 stated:

> The C.P.S.U. will continue to strengthen the unity and cohesion of the ranks of the great army of Communists of all countries.

This could be read to mean that the C.P.S.U. will, by its direct action within or upon those Parties, strengthen their "unity and cohesion" and assure their obedience to Moscow. In the final draft this slip of the drafters was softened:

The C.P.S.U. will continue to direct its efforts to the unity and cohesion of the ranks of the great army of Communists of all countries.

Indeed, it is becoming increasingly difficult for Khrushchev to exercise over a wide diversity of régimes and Parties Stalin's "internationalist discipline." As the Program states in another context: ". . . not only the big states, but also the small ones . . . are in a position, irrespective of their strength, to pursue an independent foreign policy." The forces of division seem to be working within "the camp of socialism" as well as beyond its bounds. The impact of fissiparous trends may be all the more serious for Khrushchev's policy just because these tendencies run directly counter to Communist dogma as well as to Soviet ambition.

II

It is important to know the new Party Program. It is not mere rhetoric or a pious affirmation of hopes or aspirations. Lenin and his successors have prided themselves on "the unity of theory and practice," and since the new Program, despite Peking's carpings, is genuinely Leninist, it lays down not a theory but a set of comprehensive and coherent guidelines for action.

Modern practices of scientific analysis also affirm "the unity of theory and practice," but this means something quite different to the West. Under conditions of free inquiry it means that theories are formed on the basis of carefully examined facts for the purpose of giving order to larger and more complex bodies of facts. Then, when new or previously unexamined facts can no longer be explained or contained within existing theories, these comprehensive concepts must be revised, sometimes radically. Thus, the generalizing role of theory in a system of free inquiry means that all theories have a utility value rather than a moral value, that many theories are competing to establish their validity as scientific tools, and that they are basically tentative rather than absolute in character.

Despite the recent and modest enlargements of the sphere of inquiry in Soviet scientific thought, the fundamental duty of the political leadership to define the limits of inquiry and to state in advance the conclusions it must reach has been strongly reaffirmed in the 1961 Program:

The investigation of the problems of world history and contemporary world development must disclose the law-governed process of mankind's advance toward communism, the change in the balance of forces in favor of socialism, the aggravation of the general crisis of capitalism, the break-up of the colonial system of imperialism and its consequences, and the upsurge of the national-liberation movement of peoples.

In Soviet theory and practice, what is desired is stated as already proved "scientifically." The only purpose of inquiry is to prove again what has already been affirmed by political authority to be "true." The Soviet insistence that new data, or facts that cannot be fitted to the only valid theory, are "non-facts" is a continuing obstacle to any genuine freedom of discourse. The habit of raising each disagreement to a quarrel between "sin" and "virtue" also remains strong. This means that the examination of new or unwelcome facts is regarded, not as an interesting exercise in scientific skill, but as another form of political combat.

The rigidities of Communist thought make it very difficult (outside the natural sciences and technology) for the shapers of policy to have available the findings of objective research. Nevertheless, the range of useful investigation is definitely wider today in domestic policy than it is in the analysis of world affairs. The Soviet leaders have made numerous adjustments in their domestic economic policy: breaking up the machine-tractor stations, cutting back long-range investment in hydroelectric power plants in favor of more numerous and less costly thermal plants, and so forth.

The quality of rational inquiry has been improved substantially in those fields where its validity is of direct advantage to the decision-makers. Unfortunately, even in this area of policy many of the major decisions seem still to be based primarily on deeply rooted prejudice. What will the Soviet people do with all the steel that has been promised by 1980? What can it do with a vast flow of petroleum if the output of private cars remains as low as is planned? Can agriculture possibly meet the growing and more varied needs of the Soviet people without a far larger investment of resources?

In the study of foreign countries and world politics, on the other hand, there has been almost no relaxation of political rigidities. Everything is painted in black and white. On one side, angels; on the other, devils. If dialectical materialism can provide a scientific basis for analysis, it should make it possible for Soviet experts to examine more objectively than they now do the causes of the high rate of growth in several of the free-world economies. It should actually encourage them to state calmly and without indignation why other systems operate differently from the Soviet one. A strong and powerful country needs objective information and, conscientious analysis, and its rulers should not be afraid to permit the full use of scholarly inquiry if they want to be well served.

Because "science" had become a magic word in his time, Karl Marx baptized his theory of economic history with the name of "scientific socialism," and the same honorific adjective has been claimed by Lenin, Stalin and Khrushchev for their political programs. In practice, however, many of the judgments made by Soviet leaders have chiefly reflected ingrained ideological prejudices and strong political ambitions. As often as not, Soviet appraisals have fallen wide of the mark.

By the late 1920s the Comintern, along with some "bourgeois" economists, was predicting the onset of an economic crisis in Western Europe and North America. On the other hand, the first Five Year Plan was drawn up on the assumption that world prices of foodstuffs and raw materials, Russia's main exports, would remain stable. Moscow's oracles insisted, in the face of obvious facts, that the depression of 1929 was driving the United States down the path of fascism. In 1941 Stalin assumed that, if Hitler attacked the Soviet Union, Britain would make a compromise peace with him because of common "class interests." Fortunately for the people of the Soviet Union, Churchill and Roosevelt had already concerted a policy of alliance with Russia against the common enemy. In 1948 Stalin thought he could take West Berlin by a cruel blockade, and since 1958 Khrushchev has made several misjudgments of the Berlin question. Until recent months Soviet spokesmen have had little or nothing to say about the rapid steps that Western Europe has been taking toward economic unification; the "law" of capitalist competition made this historic process, in Moscow's eyes, an absurdity. The record of Soviet predictions suggests that it is more faith or habit than practical performance that supports the Kremlin's claim to possess the sole "scientific" and "infallible" instrument for predicting the future course of events.

III

Since 1953 many things have changed for the better in Soviet life. The improvements in food, housing, clothing and household conveniences have been widespread and substantial. In literature new themes of individual love and suffering, together with a cautious criticism of recent Stalinist "excesses," have become almost fashionable. More than at any time since the early 1930s the Party and the press seem to be trying to remedy some of the most callous features of Soviet administration and to improve the workings of Soviet justice.

All this is extremely welcome. The people of the Soviet Union, as they approach the forty-fifth anniversary of the October Revolution, have earned over and over the right to a modest return for their vast sacrifices and patience. Through this long travail they have preserved many fine qualities of friendliness, hospitality and patriotism. The modest comforts many of them have now attained, the pride in the scientific and material achievements of their country, and a burning memory of the Second World War combine to make them deeply and genuinely eager for peace and coexistence. They are now confident of the good intentions of their new rulers toward themselves, and therefore they accept more readily the Kremlin's protestations that only Soviet policy is "peace-loving" and that the sole risks of war now arise from the "imperialists" and their conspiracies.

"Making a peace treaty" with East Germany, "putting an end to the occupation régime in West Berlin"—all this sounds very reasonable to Soviet people. They are not aware that the people of West Berlin regard the token garrison as their protector and that they resent profoundly Ulbricht's insistence on "liberating" them from their hard-won freedom and prosperity. If people in the Soviet Union did know this, with whom could they discuss it? All they can do is hope that Khrushchev, who seems to them a human sort of man, knows what he is about and will, as he promises, safeguard peace.

The same old attempt to maintain a low level of strain at home and a high level of tension abroad has again been standard Soviet tactics in recent years. For many months Soviet readers heard all about the 400 or so American military advisers in Laos and the supply of American military matériel and economic support. It was many months before one relatively obscure Soviet newspaper gave one solitary hint that Soviet supplies and planes were engaged on the Communist side. Even now Soviet readers have no inkling that in Laos a major part of the fighting has been conducted by North Vietnamese units. Similarly, after the Soviet Government had announced on August 31, 1961, the forthcoming renewal of hydrogen bomb tests, it gave no further information to Soviet readers for some six weeks. Even so, the news apparently spread rather widely, at least in the major cities, and gave rise to a good deal of muted anxiety.

A fierce patriotism, a defensive resentment of any condescension on the part of foreigners, a strong pride in Soviet strength and achievements—these emotions are widely shared. They make it easy for many Soviet people to accept a messianic ideology of Russia's unique mission, without thinking very much about the historic foundations of this notion or about its intellectual inconsistencies. The extreme self-righteousness of the Kremlin's boasts and demands is more troubling to many thoughtful Soviet people. Sometime they wonder whether there is not a contradiction between Russia's being "the strongest power" in the world, as Khrushchev often claims, and the strenuous effort to protect its people against all but carefully screened and denatured information about the "imperialist" world.

Coexisting on the same globe with a one-eyed and angry giant is dangerous rather than exhilarating. In one breath he demands "friendship" and describes the many achievements, mainly material, that he admires in American life. In the next, he explains with "scientific" certainty why Communism will inevitably "bury" this much envied America. Even without benefit of Freud, it is not hard to see the power lust bursting out from behind the appeals for "peace and friendship."

We must, nevertheless, deal with the world as it is, and two of the facts of the world are the Soviet messianic fantasy and the power the Soviet leaders wield. It is, of course, a sign of good judgment that the Soviet leadership recognizes the mutually suicidal character of a nuclear war, and we must welcome its stated intention to contain the conflict within a rather elastic definition of "peaceful coexistence." As the Soviet spokesmen have made clear at Geneva, however, the Kremlin is not actively interested in bringing nuclear arms under control, and it believes it can gain more political advantages by continuing the arms race at a high pitch.

Moscow regards the present period of "peaceful coexistence" as a prolonged contest in which it must exert its full strength and will in order to make decisive gains by all means short of nuclear war. By the leverage of its strategic, political and economic power it hopes, within a few years, to bring about a great shift of political power in its favor, In contrast to Stalin's cautious peripheral probings, Khrushchev's declared ambitions, and the current Soviet programs of action, now extend to all continents except, perhaps temporarily, Australia. Since Soviet military and economic strength will be growing rapidly in coming years, it is not going to be enough for the countries that cherish freedom to repeat old and tried formulas that have served them well in previous crises. They must seek actively for new ways to bring their great political, economic and strategic resources to bear in the balance if they are going to survive in freedom the multiple challenge that is posed by Khrushchev's program of "peaceful coexistence."

INTER-COMMUNIST AFFAIRS

─────────────

Communism, Nationalism and the Growth of the Communist Community of Nations after World War II

PAUL SHOUP[*]

─────────────

In the apocalyptic visions of Marx, the world revolution which was to destroy capitalist society was also to sweep away the entire system of nation-states, and in its place to substitute a world proletarian society, a new supra-national community ruled over by the victorious working class.

Of all the prophecies of early Marxism, none proved more ill-founded than this belief in an international socialist order. The revolution, when it came, was confined to Russia. Only after the victories of the Soviet armies in World War II did it become possible to extend Communist rule beyond the borders of the Soviet Union. After less than two decades, this new international Communist community of nations has become divided into blocs of quarrelling states, and the goal of international Communism seems still distant. The Communists, like other universalistic movements of the past, have apparently proved incapable of

[*] Formerly on the faculty of Kenyon College, Professor Shoup is with the Foreign Affairs Department of the University of Virginia.

From "Communism, Nationalism and the Growth of the Communist Community of Nations after World War II" by Paul Shoup, *The American Political Science Review*, Washington, D.C., Vol. LVI, No. 4, December 1962, selections from pp. 886–898. By permission of the publisher and the author. For footnote references, see original source.

surmounting the limits of the nation-state system they set out to destroy. Why?

It seems immediately obvious that the Communists were themselves divided by the forces of nationalism. But this observation, while not necessarily incorrect, needs more precise formulation and further analysis. In the pages to follow, the formation and the growth of the Communist community of nations after World War II will be re-examined, to reveal more clearly the dynamics of the process. The central point, which will emerge as the discussion proceeds, is that nationalism did not lie at the root of the centrifugal pressures which appeared within the Communist bloc. Nationalism came later, and when it did, developed a variety of forms which reflected the unique conditions under which each Communist state evolved. Before we get into the details of this process, however, it will be necessary to comment briefly on two points: the meaning of nationalism, and Communist views prior to World War II on the subject of supra-national integration.

I) *The Meaning of Nationalism*

Definitions pose one of the most exasperating problems in all the literature dealing with nationalism. Those who have wrestled with them seem to agree on one point only: nationalism is an elusive phenomenon that defies exact description. Nevertheless, definitions cannot be avoided. This is especially true when dealing with the emergence of nationalism in Communist nations. The confusion which this problem has engendered can often be traced to the lack of common agreement on the meaning of the terms employed. Rather than formulate one comprehensive definition of nationalism, we shall attempt to deal with the difficulty by suggesting several complementary situations, each of which can be said to reflect the presence of nationalism. These distinctions will be useful in analyzing the character which nationalism has assumed in Communist states.

National Pride. Many writers have suggested that nationalism is a state of mind in which the individual ascribes special virtues to the national way of life (language, culture, or national history), and so demands that the supreme loyalty of each citizen be given to the individual nation-state. This approach is legitimate if not construed too narrowly. The idea of nationalism may develop in a revolutionary context, in which it can be inspired by ideals which transcend the framework of the nation-state. "Supreme" loyalty to the state is never unconditional: it rests on underlying assumptions of what the desirable state is. For our purposes it is sufficient to allow that *nationalism, is, in one sense, the product of a fundamental attachment to the values embodied in the national culture and history of a people.*

National Independence. Nationalism may also refer to the process, so often noted in discussions of international politics, by which states, unsure of each other's motives and seeking the fullest possible security, attempt to maximize their power and maintain their independence of action. Here again, there is no absolute standard for determining what is and what is not a "national" position. Cooperation between nations may be in the national interest even to the point of giving up considerable freedom of action. On the other hand, nations which are linked through mutual understanding and compatibility of interests may still deem it wise to pursue independent paths which lead to clashes of national interest. Taking these factors into consideration, we suggest that *a second form of nationalism manifests itself in the belief that there exists a fundamental need—arising from fear, lack of understanding, or the unpredictable nature of international politics—for the maintenance of a considerable degree of national independence and for giving priority, in most cases, to one's own immediate national interests.*

The Nation-State as a Vehicle of Progress. In the course of the vast social and economic revolutions of the past several centuries, the nation-state has emerged as the most effective socio-political mechanism by which change can be stimulated or channelled by a ruling elite or dominant class. There is no need to interpret this process—as the Marxists have done—in terms of narrow class interest. On the contrary, the mechanisms of the state, acting through a national culture or economy, may be used for an infinite variety of purposes, and today these channels of action are more and more becoming associated with the pursuit of economic progress through industrialization.

We therefore suggest that in this day and age *nationalism also reveals itself in the belief that progress toward whatever new goals men aspire to comes about through the creation of the nation-state and the stimulation of its growth, strength and effectiveness, regardless of whether the final end may be narrower than the state (a class or group interest) or universal in scope.*

National communism may be interpreted in a number of ways. It may mean the adoption, by a national party, of certain ideas or methods not generally approved by the rest of the Communist bloc. A recent work on the Communist bloc follows this approach in defining national communism as "the explicit assignment of priority to internal considerations even if openly challenged by those who consider themselves to be the central spokesmen of international communism." Such a situation could of course arise even if nationalism never entered into the picture. Our own interpretation of national communism, to be given later, will suggest that the term is most appropriately used in association with the third type of nationalism just described.

II) Views on Supra-National Integration Prior to World War II

Before the Second World War the Communists gave surprisingly little attention to the subject of the integration of states into a supra-national community. Early Marxist writings seldom bothered with the issue, for it was assumed that the victory of the proletariat would bring the final destruction of the nation-state system. After the victory of communism in the Soviet Union, reference was made to a World Federation of Soviet Socialist Republics, but discussion even of this goal vanished in the 1930s.

At the same time, the Soviet party prior to World War II developed positions on the question of nationalism and relations among Communist parties that were of central importance for any future Communist community of nations. Although these developments were complex, we can only deal briefly with them here.

First, communism came to be identified with suppressed national aspirations, a position we shall refer to as "revolutionary nationalism." Revolutionary nationalism differed from the original Marxist views insofar as it recognized the importance of national feelings and encouraged the notion that every nationality exhibits

its own particular virtues (language, culture, history) and there-fore enjoys the right to its own existence. The practice of appeal-ing to revolutionary nationalism first arose during the Russian revolution and was later extended to the colonial countries. The doctrine was fully articulated in the theory of Soviet federalism, according to which each Soviet Republic was "sovereign" and free to develop national cultural forms with a socialist content.

Second, the victory of the Bolsheviks in Russia established the doctrine as well as the fact that the world Communist movement would operate on the basis of monolithic unity under the control of the Soviet party. The dogmatic insistence on the need for monolithic unity, and the ruthless fashion in which the Soviet party applied this Leninist precept, are too well known to require further elucidation.

Third, the consolidation of Stalin's power in the Soviet Union was paralleled by the growth of Soviet nationalism. The necessity of building socialism in one country encouraged a fusion of Rus-sian nationalism and Soviet patriotism; Soviet totalitarianism, when it matured in the 1930s, proved to be a blend of both revolutionary and traditional Russian elements. The international Communist movement, under Soviet leadership, was forced to subordinate the aim of world revolution to the national interests of the Soviet Union—often to the discomfiture of communist parties in other countries.

At first glance it might seem difficult to reconcile the doctrines of revolutionary nationalism, monolithic unity and the supremacy of Soviet national interests. For some, of course, it was more than difficult; it became impossible. But for the hard-core Communists who were later to come to power in Eastern Europe, the Com-munist interpretation of these problems was consistent and be-yond criticism. Revolutionary nationalism, although it tolerated a certain degree of national feeling, made a sharp distinction be-tween "Socialist patriotism" (which was acceptable) and "na-tionalism" (always a pejorative term). Nationalism was associated with attachment to a pre-revolutionary way of life and a refusal to give supreme loyalty to the goal of world communism. Ultimately, the toleration of national cultures would lead to their fusion in a world socialist culture; when this point was reached, concessions to revolutionary nationalism would no longer be necessary. Dedicated

Communists saw no contradiction in subordinating themselves to an international movement whose primary aim was to advance the interests of the Soviet Union; after all, the Soviet Union stood alone, encircled by capitalist foes, and the first duty of Communists everywhere was to come to her defense. Revolutionary unity, under the leadership of the Soviet party, was accepted as an absolutely necessary pre-condition for the success of the revolution in other parts of the world.

In general, the Communist approach to the problem of establishing an international socialist system was conditioned by the importance of the current struggle to defend the Soviet Union and strengthen the revolutionary movement in capitalist countries. No concrete plans seem to have been made to meet the problems which would arise if Communist states were formed outside the Soviet Union, in particular in Eastern Europe.

Nevertheless there were some hints, long prior to the war, of the eventual Soviet view on the form of a Communist community of nations. There is evidence that Stalin himself did not fully accept the position that Soviet federalism could be applied at the international level. Another fact of importance was the introduction in the mid-1930s of the idea of "Proletarian United Front Governments." These were to be transitional, between bourgeois democracy and socialism, Communist-dominated, and apparently free from any machinery of supra-national control or coordination. In fact, they were the original concept from which the "Peoples' Democracies" of Eastern Europe developed after the war.

III) The Method of Consolidating Communist Power in Eastern Europe

On the basis of this ill-digested body of doctrines concerning the world Communist state, the construction of a new Communist community of nations began after World War II. The power of the Soviet Union was such that she might conceivably have absorbed these nations directly into the Soviet federation. But a host of practical considerations weighed against this course of action. It would have needlessly antagonized the West, weakened the international Communist movement, and, at the very least, complicated enormously the tasks of occupation, if it did not, indeed, provoke the peoples of Eastern Europe to revolt against the newly established Communist regimes. National differences in Eastern Europe were simply too great to be ignored. On similar grounds Hitler in 1940 had chosen to establish the Vichy regime rather than occupy all France; and a century earlier, *mutatis mutandis,* the British had preferred a system of indirect rule in India and elsewhere. Purely tactical considerations were therefore sufficient to dictate a policy of Soviet caution in integrating the new states within some supra-national framework.

These differences among the peoples of Eastern Europe did not, however, exist within the national Communist parties. The party leaders in Eastern Europe were a group apart, trained and selected by Moscow in the years prior to the war. They came to power convinced of the need for monolithic unity, contemptuous of the bourgeois nationalism of the people, and eager to begin the process which would eventually lead to a new supranational Communist order. The strong national feelings of the people were not, therefore, automatically transferred to the Communists who assumed power in Eastern Europe. Nor did the obvious obstacles to immediate integration of the newly formed Communist nations imposed by the attitude of their masses rule out the formulation of a policy by which this goal might sooner or later be achieved.

A different sort of difficulty arose from the fact that Moscow now had to deal with established parties and official governments rather than with the revolutionary movements which had struggled so desperately to survive between the two world wars. Indeed, it was unwise in the altered circumstances to formalize the power of the Soviet party over the new officials in Eastern Europe in a set of rules analogous to those which existed within each party. And it would seem only natural that the national party leaders, under the influence of their lately acquired power and prestige, might interpret a too direct Soviet supervision of their actions as unwarranted control over the "domestic" affairs of the nation.

It would be wrong, however, to consider this new-found legality a decisive factor for the development of the Communist system in Eastern Europe after the war. In all likelihood the majority of national party leaders did feel that their new formal authority should be acknowledged by the Soviet Union. But the proper limits of interference by Moscow were never clearly defined, and practical necessities kept reminding them of their dependence on the Russians. More important, the Communist leaders of Eastern Europe continued to acknowledge the primacy of Moscow in all matters touching on the monolithic unity of the bloc, a position which, in the last analysis, recognized the right of the Soviet party to play a decisive role in the concerns of the national parties.

Finally, it could be argued that the Communist parties of Eastern Europe had, in coming to power, assumed the burden of protecting the national interests of their peoples, and that this was bound to create special problems which did not exist before the war by revealing the contradictions involved in equating the interests of each Communist party with the national interests of the Soviet Union.

While there is much to be said for this interpretation of the situation created by the formation of Communist governments outside the Soviet Union, it leaves too much unexplained. Although not couched exactly in these terms, the discussion in the pages to follow will be aimed at analyzing more closely just what "national interest" meant in the context of the Communists' views on the method to be pursued in constructing a totalitarian system in Eastern Europe. For the postwar developments in Eastern Europe cannot be fully understood without reference to a broader issue closely connected with the ultimate aim of supranational integration: the method by which Communist power was to be consolidated throughout the bloc as a whole. Although means, not ultimate ends, may originally have been at stake, this was not the first occasion in the Communist experience when means became ends in themselves and profoundly influenced the course of Communist evolution.

Theoretical analyses of totalitarianism agree on its built-in bias toward unlimited expansion. But there is also agreement that a totalitarian system may, through its own methods of operation, put obstacles in its path to world domination. The Nazi method of empire building was an obvious case in point. The Stalinist type of totalitarianism, we think, must also be analyzed from this point of view.

To understand how Soviet totalitarianism developed in ways detrimental to its own universalistic aspirations, we must re-examine the concept of building socialism in one country alone.

The idea was a natural one, since world revolution did not seem imminent. But the decision to pursue such a policy was arbitrary in so far as it implied that circumstances unfavorable to the creation of a Communist utopia (the existing obstacles to the creation of an advanced economy or socialist society, such as lack of a working class) could be overcome by sheer determination and will on the part of the revolutionary party and its leadership. This underlying assumption became a mystique in the Soviet Union with the emergence of Stalinist totalitarianism in the 1930s. To its disciples, Soviet development seemed to prove that by mobilizing political power through a disciplined party one might destroy the existing society, build up an industrial base, and attain socialism through one's own efforts. The size of the country, and other material factors relevant to its potential industrial capacity, were largely overlooked.

We think these assumptions, so different from the original precepts of world revolution, were in fact a decisive influence on the development of the international Communist community. After World War II a strong bias arose toward transforming the principle of building totalitarianism ("socialism") in one country alone into a more general principle which, for want of a more appropriate term, we may call the building of a Communist totalitarianism in each country separately.

Did the Soviet Union actively inculcate this notion among national party leaders in Eastern Europe after World War II? The answer to this question is by no means clear-cut, for the Soviet position was shifting and ambiguous. First let us deal with its ideological aspects, and then turn to the practical policies guiding Soviet actions in the satellite nations.

In Soviet writings after the war the Communist states of Eastern Europe were referred to as "Peoples' Democracies," a transitional form of Communist rule less advanced than the Soviet Union's. The significance of the Peoples' Democracies was first said to lie in the fact that they were pioneers in the development of a new path to socialism. After 1948 (the year of the Soviet-Yugoslav break) the line changed, and Soviet writers insisted that Peoples' Democracies were following the laws of development first applied in the Soviet Union. "National" roads to communism—

such as Tito's—were made the object of a vicious, uncompromising attack.

The earlier interpretation of the meaning of People's Democracy seemed a linear descendent of the pre-war notion of the "Proletarian United Front Government." This view suggested that conditions in Eastern Europe precluded simple imitations of Soviet development. For this reason, it might be expected to find favor among those satellite leaders who wished to build socialism in one country by adapting Soviet practices to local conditions. By comparison, the post-1948, "narrow" interpretation of People's Democracy left the satellites with little room for independent development. But it is important to note—and this is often overlooked—that after 1948 it was clearly spelled out for the first time that each Eastern European nation, since it must follow the Soviet path, *could* do so. Soviet socialism could be duplicated in each Communist state. Communist totalitarianism could be built in each country separately.

In one sense, at least, this suggested more, not less power for the new Communist states: if the East European nations could duplicate the Soviet performance, they might one day become her equals. Imitation of the Soviet Union, after all, did not necessarily imply subordination and dependence. It could also mean power and independence for each Communist nation separately. But the Soviets were at pains to deny just this set of conclusions after 1948. It was claimed instead that the formation and development of the Peoples' Democracies rested on the decisive role played by the Soviet Union in Eastern Europe after World War II. Indeed, the aim of Soviet policy after 1948 was to bind the satellites even more tightly to the Soviet Union, and the new version of Peoples' Democracy was rightly interpreted as one means to this end.

The ideological issue was even more complex than this brief summary suggests. But enough has been said to indicate that national party leaders, especially those *most* imbued with Stalinist concepts of building totalitarianism in each country separately, might accept the premise of Soviet theory—the necessity of following Soviet laws of development—and reject the important *caveat* that the process would result in greater, not less, dependence on the Soviet Union.

The policy of the Soviet Union in regard to economic and political matters also suggested that the methods of building totalitarianism in each country separately were being applied, in a somewhat contradictory fashion, to build communism and to favor the narrow interests of the Soviet Union.

As noted earlier, Stalin had on occasion made a distinction between the federal form of government, suitable for the Soviet Union, and a looser confederation, suitable for a number of Communist states. In the years 1945–1948, Soviet policy went to considerable lengths to adjust to the special problems facing the formation of an intergrated Communist community among formerly independent nation-states. During this time satellite leaders were permitted a degree of flexibility which allowed them to consolidate their power in accordance with local conditions. In 1948 a reversal of policy took place. The national parties were then forced to apply Soviet cultural standards as well as Soviet political methods without regard for local conditions or the national feelings of the population.

Even after 1948, however, there was ample evidence that the Soviets continued to develop their policies within the framework of the existing pattern of nation-states in Eastern Europe. One striking example of this was the manner in which treaties between the Soviet Union and the states of Eastern Europe adhered to traditional concepts of territorial integrity and diplomatic rights. More important was the increasing emphasis on autarchic economic development within each Eastern European state after 1948. The exact reasons for the adoption of such a policy have remained a source of debate. Both the Soviets and the satellites seem to have had complete faith in the methods of economic development which had worked so well in the Soviet Union, even when the arguments for economic autarchy would seem difficult to justify under East European conditions. On the other hand, Stalin's support for this policy can be interpreted as consistent with his desire to isolate the satellite nations from one another in order to assure their control by the Soviet Union. Stalin may also have calculated that self-contained autarchic development would permit the maximum exploitation of the East European economies.

In our opinion, Stalin accepted the principle of building totalitarianism in each country separately as the basic method of consolidating Communist rule. Within, and sometimes contrary to this principle, he attempted to exploit and control the satellite nations. Certainly the frame of reference for the international Communist community as a whole, even before 1948, was the duplication, through a series of stages, of Soviet development within the existing nation-state system, rather than political and economic integration throughout the bloc as a whole. The pattern of development which was to lead to a world Communist state was therefore unique. It was not integrative so much as it was reproductive. One could say that each nation was going along parallel tracks, guided by Moscow. More concretely, each was engaged in an effort to duplicate, *in toto*, the structure of Soviet totalitarianism.

IV) *Strains in the Communist Bloc after World War II*

As a result of the Communist approach to the problem of consolidating power, the historical nation-state came to have a central importance for those Communists faced with the postwar task of constructing a totalitarian system in Eastern Europe. The ultimate goal was still to create a uniform pattern of totalitarian rule that would destroy all differences among nations. But it is clear from the discussion of People's Democracy above that considerable confusion prevailed concerning the immediate consequences of the development of totalitarianism in each country separately.

Broadly speaking, three possible alternatives were envisaged: (i) the nation in question might develop a form of Communist rule somewhat different from that in the Soviet Union but adapted to her own conditions (a pattern hereinafter referred to as "domesticism"); (ii) the nation might adopt Soviet institutions and practices in their entirety but remain so dependent on the Soviet Union that any form of integration would only make permanent the inferior status of the satellite nation and its party; (iii) the nation might pattern herself after the Soviet Union in the belief that the successful construction of a totalitarian state required (and would lead to) the duplication not only of Soviet institutions, but also of Soviet power. In this case integration, if and when it took place, would have to be among equals.

The kinds of problems that arose in relations between members of the Communist bloc after World War II can be associated, for the most part, with attempts to pursue one or another of these courses of development. It might be supposed that the choice among these alternatives, since it revolved around means rather than ultimate ends, would not necessarily have been of importance for the new Communist nations. Yet the dynamics of the process did indeed create strains between the national parties and Moscow, and ultimately prejudiced the end of supranational integration itself.

The manner in which Eastern Europe developed these distinctive patterns is well known. In the countries where the national parties were weak (such as Poland), there was a tendency to accept the first alternative suggested above—domesticism. In Yugoslavia, on the other hand, the third alternative—the duplication of Soviet institutions *and* Soviet power—came to be accepted as the only proper method of building communism in each country separately. After 1948, the nations within the Soviet orbit were forced to accept the second course—duplication of Soviet institutions artificially and with extreme reliance on Soviet power.

The trend toward domesticism has sometimes seemed to be potentially the most divisive force. It is closely associated with nationalism and the desire to question the infallibility of Soviet methods. But such an interpretation makes too mechanical a connection between the lingering effects of nationalism and the dynamics of Communist development—at least in the years immediately after the war. If our analysis is correct, the trend toward domesticism in the immediate postwar period was not a preferred choice but essentially a sign of weakness among parties that were not yet *able* to duplicate the Soviet pattern of development. Poland is a case in point. Here, opposition to the Soviet demands for conformity from the satellites in 1948 was inspired not by a wish to pioneer in the development of new institutions, but by a desire to move slowly in the introduction of Soviet methods, especially in the field of agriculture.

It was the Yugoslav path to Communism which, as events proved, posed the greatest threat to the unity of the Communist bloc. The Yugoslav case is extremely instructive, for the party leaders, working in a multi-national state to begin with, had no strong national loyalties and were the most eager, among the Communists of Eastern Europe, to follow the Soviet path of development. On the other hand the Yugoslav Communists had, since the time of the Partisan campaigns in World War II, developed the habit of independent thinking and an overbearing confidence in their own abilities. This arrogance has been well described as "Partisan chauvinism." It led the Yugoslav Communist Party to believe that it was the dominant party in the Balkans and not unnaturally produced friction with the Soviet leadership. Many of the difficulties that then arose, far from being peculiarly national in origin, can be traced back to differences over the tactics to be pursued in the world revolutionary struggle for the consolidation and spread of Communist power.

The dispute between the Yugoslav and Soviet parties might be described in this context alone. But to do so would overlook another essential element in the struggle. The Yugoslav Communists had been led, by their very success in building communism, to believe that they had become indispensable for the task of socialist construction in Yugoslavia. Within the broad and ambiguous bounds of the prevailing mystique of building totalitarianism in each country separately, this position of duplicating Soviet institutions *and* power seemed absolutely orthodox to the Yugoslav Communists, although it immediately precipitated them into conflict with the Soviet party. Matters were only made worse when the Soviets accused the Yugoslavs of moving *too fast* down the road to socialism. Correctly or not, their own Stalinist outlook led Tito and his associates to the conclusion that Moscow, by questioning the means pursued by the Yugoslav Communist party, had renounced the end of socialism itself—at least as far as Yugoslavia was concerned. Thus fortified by the belief that the very fate of the revolution was at stake in Yugoslavia, the Yugoslav Communists were able to take the momentous step of openly defying the military, political and ideological pressures brought to bear by the Soviet Union.

The Chinese party also adhered to the method of building communism followed by the Yugoslavs. Stalin learned from his experience in 1948 that strong-arm tactics could not reverse this trend, while the Chinese, for their part, were careful not to provoke a split with the Soviet Union. The outward unity between these two great Communist powers could nevertheless not disguise the fact that the Chinese party had decided upon an autarchic path of economic development resting on an independent power base. Thus it came to pass that historical national boundaries, which should only have been incidental factors in Communist plans for the future world society, came instead to represent crucial dividing lines between separate, and often clashing, concentrations of power.

V) *The Growth of Nationalism*

We can now return to the problem of nationalism and inquire more closely into its role in the development of the Communist bloc after World War II. Nationalism, as already noted, should be considered in its several meanings: first, as a positive commitment to the values embodied in the national culture and history; second, as a belief in the fundamental need to maintain independence in the international sphere; and third, as a belief that progress comes about through the vehicle of the nation-state. "National communism" was tentatively associated with this third type of nationalism.

Following one line of argument, the failure of the Communists to establish a supra-national state after World War II could be interpreted as the last of a series of concessions on the part of communism to one or another of these forms of nationalism. In support of this theory one could point to the acceptance of the idea of revolutionary nationalism; the rise of aggressive Soviet chauvinism; and, finally, the application of the concept of building totalitarianism in each country separately. The logical conclusion, after such an enumeration, might be that nationalism had swallowed communism.

Yet this view oversimplifies the situation. Our analysis has not indicated that the first type of nationalism listed above was of crucial importance after the war: *i.e.*, that the Communist leaders of Eastern Europe were infected with the nationalistic prejudices of the former ruling groups in their countries, or that Soviet chauvinism came into immediate conflict with the principles associated with revolutionary nationalism. Nor would it be correct to say that Tito's national communism, although it gave priority to the interests of the Yugoslav state, was originally motivated by a belief in the desirability of establishing independence for Yugoslavia in the international sphere (the second type above).

Might we say that the pattern of development in the Communist bloc after World War II reflected the acceptance of nationalism in the third sense—the belief that progress is accomplished through development of the nation-state? Here we meet a curious paradox. As we have described it, the process of building Stalinist totalitarianism took place within the boundaries of existing historical states for precisely the opposite reason, not out of a desire to strengthen the nation-state, but in order to carry out more swiftly the "de-nationalization" of the states concerned and the "atomization" of their populations.

On the other hand, those who most faithfully followed the Soviet method of building totalitarianism—the Yugoslavs and the Chinese—came almost immediately to champion the need and desirability of an independent power base, built within the existing pattern of nation-states, in order to carry out the construction of a Communist totalitarian state in the most ruthless and effective manner. The result was, at least in the short run, to reinforce rather than to destroy the role of the nation-state as a vehicle of change.

Some of the reasons why this was so have already been suggested: the difficulty of insisting on uniform practices throughout the Communist bloc at an early stage of its development before national differences had been levelled; the feelings of the Yugoslavs and Chinese that the rapid progress of communism in their states was the result of their own efforts; and, finally, the suspicion that Moscow did not actually wish communism to develop as rapidly in these countries as the national leaders felt was possible.

The most important point remains, however, the context in which these problems arose: the doctrine of building totalitarianism in each country separately. This perspective, by assuming that industrialism and socialism were the product of political factors, completely divorced the concept of progress through economic betterment from its original class determinants (the international proletariat) or environmental factors (resources, population, the location of markets) and gave the concept of the nation-state a new significance which, although the product of the totalitarian mentality, was akin to the third type of nationalism we have distinguished.

As long as this mystique held sway it would seem impossible to envisage any real integration of the Communist bloc under the conditions prevailing after World War II. Upon reflection it seems clear that none of the three alternative modes of building communism in each country separately (domesticism; the duplication of Soviet institutions on a weak power base; the duplication of Soviet institutions and Soviet power) could really create the preconditions for integration. The most likely path in the short run, the duplication of Soviet institutions on a weak power base, was thoroughly compromised by the Stalinist excesses between 1948 and 1953. Domesticism was either the result of weakness (the situation in most European nations between 1945 and 1948) or was transformed into a reaction against Stalinist exploitation. In the former case it was largely a temporary phenomenon; in the latter, an explosive force that stimulated a national reaction against the whole idea of duplicating Soviet institutions—of which more presently.

Building Soviet institutions and power might seem the most realistic path to eventual integration if all the parties in question were willing to accept each other as equals. Militating against this solution, however, was a dogma equally as strong as that of building totalitarianism in each country separately—that of monolithic solidarity based on the dominance of one party. This latter principle, usually considered a cohesive force in the Communist bloc, was ultimately responsible for the collapse of the Communist international order, for it made integration between equals an impossibility and forced the more radical and powerful parties of Yugoslavia and China to abandon the goal of integration entirely.

In general, the articulation of nationalism in its more concrete forms begins in each Communist country *after* these alternative paths to integration have been foreclosed, and the doctrine of building socialism in each country separately is no longer viewed as a means to an end but as an end in itself. In its least complicated aspect, such nationalism should most closely resemble the third type of nationalism we have mentioned (the belief that progress is made possible through developing the nation-state). And its identification would be most sure when a Communist country has incorporated this idea into its ideological view of the national question.

Yugoslavia has, indeed, made such an ideological re-evaluation, criticizing the canons of Marxism-Leninism in this field—in particular, Stalin's *Marxism and the National Question.* The present Yugoslav view is strongly internationalistic. But it departs significantly from earlier Marxist-Leninist views by stressing the essential role of the nation-state in the building of socialism, even after the revolution.

Whether articulated in the ideology or not, the primary role of this third type of nationalism has been to facilitate a re-interpretation of the *goals* of communism in the light of national capabilities. The process should be distinguished from the domesticism of the period immediately following World War II and in our view is the only case where the term national communism is correctly applicable. The development of Titoism in Yugoslavia illustrates this type of change. The introduction of the communes in China is a similar, although less clear-cut, example.

The Soviet Union, after several years of hesitation in the mid 1950s, has now launched a counter-attack within her own orbit against this form of nationalism. Khrushchev, while avoiding the excesses of the Stalinist period, has pressed the nations of Eastern Europe to adopt Soviet practices, especially the collectivization of agriculture. These nations are now to work for the elimination of differences in levels of economic development within their own ranks. Eventually, they are to reach the same stage of development as the Soviet Union, and all will enter the stage of "communism" more or less simultaneously. The emphasis on eliminating differences within the bloc has been paralleled by a cautious modification of the principle of economic autarchy, and forms of economic cooperation unknown in the Stalinist era have now developed within the Soviet sphere.

By re-examining the practice of economic autarchy, the nations of the Soviet bloc have initiated a trend away from the dogma of building totalitarianism in each country separately. Conceivably, this could lead to new forms of integration impossible in the Stalinist period. In practice, however, each satellite state has resisted proposals which would work to its own economic disadvantage. These disagreements have operated to strengthen the feeling that each country must protect its own interests in building social- ism, thus encouraging the type of nationalism about which we are speaking. Poland has even refused to collectivize agriculture, and sustains a form of national communism in which the goals of socialism are reinterpreted in accordance with local Polish condi- tions. The Communist world as a whole seems to have reached a stage where competing modes of socialism encourage, to an ever greater degree, the identification of national institutions with universally desired ends.

It would still be premature, however, to predict the ultimate victory of nationalism over communism in this way. No fixed pattern has yet emerged. Much will depend on the future com- mitment of each nation to autarchic economic development. It would also be misleading, in our opinion, to identify centrifugal forces within the Communist bloc solely, or even primarily, with this form of nationalism. In Yugoslavia, for example, the trend toward nationalism must also be measured by the degree to which the regime has stressed nonalignment in foreign affairs and the protection of immediate national interests (the second type of nationalism described earlier). Yugoslavia interprets many of her most vital interests from the perspective of a neutral power in the East-West struggle, and this stand, far more than her domestic innovations, has led to Yugoslavia's isolation from the rest of the Communist world.

The crystallization of the second type of nationalism takes place, we would suggest, *after* a Communist nation is isolated from the bloc by a concerted attack against its leadership. Such a country is then obliged to consider its former partners as enemies and poten- tial aggressors. This situation—and therefore the nationalism it breeds—seems most likely to arise in the case of small Communist states whose powers of resistance to attack by the rest of the bloc have been underestimated by Moscow (Yugoslavia, and now, perhaps, Albania). Unfortunately for the West, this second form of nationalism, while it is of decisive importance for the balance of power in the cold war, is therefore apt to develop in the least important of the Communist states.

The failure of post-war plans to consolidate the Communist bloc have also created conditions for the appearance of the first type of nationalism (a positive commitment to the values embodied in the national culture and history). Here again the pattern is a complex one, and generalizations are dangerous. Some brief comments may nevertheless serve to clarify the problem. First, if nationalism was to appear in this form a necessary preliminary was to re-interpret the doctrine of revolutionary nationalism in such a way that it could provide a link with the bourgeois nationalism of the masses and the pre-revolutionary ruling elites. In Yugoslavia and China, the ground was laid for such a step by the attempt to build socialism on an independent power base. Under such conditions, a gradual infusion of nationalistic values into the system would enable the leadership to strengthen its power and thus actually facilitate a rapid transformation of the society and the economy. In this case, a parallel can be drawn with the growth of Soviet nationalism in the 1930s. In the East European satellites of the Soviet Union, on the other hand, revolutionary nationalism came to be associated with bourgeois national values as a result of the reaction against Soviet cultural chauvinism in the period 1948–1953. The situation at that time encouraged the Communists of these nations to identify their plight with that of the oppressed peoples of the non-Communist world for whom the doctrine of revolutionary nationalism had originally been formulated. In its origins, therefore, this reaction did not imply a re-interpretation of the doctrine of revolutionary nationalism, but only a demand that the doctrine be faithfully observed. When the satellite leaders realized the necessity of re-establishing links with the masses after the campaign to duplicate Soviet institutions on a weak power base was abandoned in the post-Stalin period, the doctrine of revolutionary nationalism became infused with nationalistic elements, above all in Poland and Hungary.

Local conditions must be taken into account from this point on. The decisive stage in the development of this type of nationalism comes when the nation in question admits to an historical continuity between past and present, between the pre- and post-revolutionary systems. If the nation has an imperial tradition, such an identification will be easier, as in the case of China. The existence of large national minorities in neighboring states may also encourage appeals to this type of national feeling, as in the case of Albania's quarrel with Yugoslavia. On the other hand, nationalism of this sort may be curbed in a multi-national state. Thus ethno-centrism has never developed in Yugoslavia because of the delicate nationalities question within that country.

The growth of this sentimental form of nationalism, and its association with the national forms of communism discussed earlier, would indeed mean the triumph of nationalism over communism. But here again a word of caution is in order. No Communist nation, not even the Soviet Union, has gone so far as to claim that its own form of communism is the product of the unique genius of its people, thus transforming communism from a universalistic to a particularistic philosophy. To do so would be to undercut the revolutionary appeal of the doctrine, and this no Communist nation is at present prepared to do. Nor should the divisive effects of this form of nationalism be overestimated. Relations between Poland and the Soviet Union in recent years have demonstrated how mutual interest and sheer necessity can overcome national antipathies. The postwar history of the Communist bloc suggests that disputes over minorities or boundaries have become acute only when the countries in question were already at odds for other reasons.

These observations all must be viewed in the light of current transitions within the Communist bloc; predictions concerning its future evolution are hazardous. Nationalism, in its various forms, seems on the increase. This should not, however, lead us to forget that some of the strongest centrifugal forces within the bloc originated in the "pre-national" period after World War II, and that the conditions of that time were in many ways unique. Communist doctrine was committed to the construction of a supra-national community on the basis of a universalistic model of so-cialism—the Soviet Union—and the monolithic solidarity of na-tional parties under Soviet leadership. However sound a basis this might at first glance seem to provide for beginning the construc-tion of a supra-national community, the facts were otherwise. Soviet totalitarianism, by its fascination with what could be achieved through political power and organizational skills—to the almost total disregard of other factors—encouraged the consolida-tion of power separately within existing nation-states. This delayed the obvious first step to integration, the development of a supra-national economic bloc, and meant that integration could only be achieved through sharing power at the top—something the Soviet Union would not agree to and something which, even if it had been achieved, would probably have destroyed the monolithic unity on which the whole structure of the supra-national community supposedly rested.

National boundaries thus became crucial dividing lines between separate and often clashing centers of power. But could not a new start now be made toward integrating the Communist nations, when the shortcomings of economic autarchy are slowly becoming appreciated, and when the Soviet leadership is increasingly willing to tolerate diversity within the Communist bloc? The possibility should be considered, even in the face of the current drift toward nationalism and the importance of Sino-Soviet tensions. For paradoxical as it may appear, only through the consolidation of nationalism may the conditions ultimately be created for the integration of the Communist nations. First, the principle of monolithic unity under the direction of one party must give way to a flexible form of cooperation which will permit the internationalization of the leadership of the world Communist movement. Only then can the national parties be assured of equal treatment in a supra-national union. Second, the drive for world domination must spend its force. As long as this dynamic goal is urging on the nations of the Communist bloc, quarrels such as that presently going on between China and the Soviet Union over the proper tactics of the revolutionary struggle seem inevitable. Third, the powerful nations of the Communist bloc must exhaust the possibilities inherent in development within national boundaries in order to re-focus their energies on the construction of supra-national institutions. National consolidation would favor such a process; the growth of virulent nationalism would, of course, have an opposite effect, destroying any hope of integration. Situations conducive to the second type of nationalism would have to be avoided.

We believe, on reflection, that the West may take comfort at what lies ahead. It seems difficult to imagine that the Communist states will be able to meet the conditions just laid down for effective integration across national boundaries. But this is not all; for while the powerful supra-national community of Communist dreams may not be entirely a chimera, its realization may well entail a prior national development which would emasculate those elements of the Communist system most dangerous to our survival. The nation-state system will then have performed its function of stemming the Communist drive for world conquest. While the victory of the Bolsheviks in 1917 was indeed a setback for those who believe in national self-determination and democracy, we may also be thankful that Communism appeared when it did, before integration of the nations of the world had progressed to the point—as it someday may—when the groundwork for an international totalitarian state would already have been laid.

· 4 ·

THE U.S.S.R. AND THE UNITED NATIONS

The Soviet View of the United Nations

ALEXANDER DALLIN[*]

The United Nations has patently not fulfilled the high hopes which some of its sponsors had for it. A major share of responsibility for this failure has commonly been assigned to the Soviet Union, and not without reason. Yet the Soviet view and Soviet conduct have not been products of perversity or malice. They follow logically, first, from the world view held by the communist

* Director of the Russian Institute of Columbia University, Professor Dallin is the author of *German Rule in Russia* (1957), *The Soviet Union at the United Nations* (1962), and editor of *Soviet Conduct in World Affairs* (1960), and *Diversity in International Communism. A Documentary Record: 1961–1963* (1963).

From "The Soviet View of the United Nations" by Alexander Dallin, *International Organization*, New York, Vol. XVI, No. 1, Winter 1962, selections from pp. 20–36. By permission of the World Peace Foundation, Boston, Mass. For footnote references, see original source.

leadership, which sees the United Nations as another arena in the struggle between the two "world systems" of our age, and, second, from the Soviet experience as a minority power seeking to frustrate the efforts of the hostile majority "in control" of the UN.

One World, Two Camps, Three Blocs

The Soviet leadership sees world affairs as a secular conflict between irreconcilable opposites. "Forces" and therefore attitudes have an organic tendency to polarize around the two antagonistic camps. Deviations from this law tend to be viewed as temporary aberrations which cannot alter or affect the basic dichotomy.

The presence of a super-power with a deeply engrained "two-camp" view in a "one-world" Organization presents a challenging problem, for how can that agency function if one of its principal Members fails to subscribe to its assumptions and rules? One must inquire then whether Soviet participation in, and praise for the principles of, the United Nations heralds the acceptance of a "one-world" view. A further element in this picture has been the emergence of the new nations as a result of the collapse of colonial empires. Does Soviet recognition of the "emerging states" as objects of particular attention and as presumptive allies—indeed, under the proposals for tripartite reorganization, their inflation into a coequal third bloc in the UN—mark a retreat from the Soviet commitment to dichotomic perception?

The evidence points overwhelmingly to the continued acceptance of the "two-camp" view. Whatever its appeals to universal goals and values, Moscow does not see the world as one international community. And, however vigorous its assertions of solidarity with the Afro-Asian world, the U.S.S.R. does not in fact recognize the permanent fissure of the globe into three mutually antagonistic segments. As the 1961 Program of the Communist Party of the Soviet Union declares, "The basic contradiction of the contemporary world [is] the contradiction between socialism and imperialism." Events of recent years have no doubt reinforced Soviet belief in the correctness of its bifocal vision and in the inevitability of the shift in the balance of power in favor of the "socialist camp."

Premier Khrushchev's frequent and facile comments bear this

out. They abound in such images as the balance, the see-saw, and communicating vessels where the emptying of one (the capitalist) is tantamount to the filling of the other (the communist). The United Nations itself, he reasserted upon his return home from New York in October 1960, was the stage for "a struggle of the new and progressive against the old and the moribund." Identifying the Soviet Union, as usual, with the fight for "peace," he continued: "Lining up the forces for peace and war is a process that will quicken and develop, and will augment the forces that stand for peace. The peoples of the neutral countries face a historic choice." Neutrality, in other words, must ultimately yield to alignment. As Khrushchev told the World Federation of Trade Unions congress in Moscow on December 9, 1961, "If today you are against communism, tomorrow you will have nowhere else to go, tomorrow you will come to communism."

It has become standard practice for Soviet writers on foreign affairs—and particularly on the UN—to juxtapose "the two lines" or "two opposite approaches" to world affairs, not three. Bracketing the "objective" interests of the communist and unaligned states, the Communist Party's official organ, *Kommunist*, commented on the fifteenth Assembly session:

> The historic struggle taking place on the world stage in our days finds expression within the walls of that Organization [the UN], where the world is represented in all its manifold and of course contradictory complexity. Here a polarization is taking place in the course of which the forces of peace, freedom and social progress unite, while the advocates of aggression and colonial slavery doom themselves to isolation.

Allowing for the contrived optimism of the prognosis, the approach is clear: it permits of no lasting neutrality. Leading communists have from time to time spelled out the purely tactical and manipulative nature of their present support of the neutral states. Indeed, in the Soviet definition neutrality no longer means what it did: an active struggle against "imperialism" is a "necessary condition" of Soviet recognition of a state's neutrality.

The typical Soviet policy in the United Nations has been to keep the UN alive but weak. While it has sometimes advocated UN action in defiance of other nations' claims to domestic jurisdiction or of regional doctrines elsewhere in the world, Moscow's normal aim has been to safeguard its own freedom of action, to keep the United Nations out of the communist bloc, and generally to minimize the Organization's power. The Soviet Union and its allies have never brought a single dispute among themselves before the United Nations. When other states have raised issues relating to the "socialist camp," Moscow has labeled them illegitimate interference. Khrushchev in April 1958 reiterated Stalin's old warning to the "imperialists" "not to try to put their pig snouts into our socialist garden." Undiplomatic in form, the attitude itself follows inexorably from the hypothesis that the rest of the world—including the United Nations—is controlled by the enemy camp.

The Soviet efforts to restrict the UN's jurisdiction go back to the days prior to the adoption of the Charter. Ever since then, the U.S.S.R. has favored a strict and literal construction of its terms and has invariably objected to attempts to broaden the prerogatives of the Assembly and the Secretariat. Subsumed under the obsessive emphasis on "sovereignty," the Soviet attitude springs from a determination not to be bound by the desires or decisions of others.

This has led Moscow to minimize the achievements of the United Nations. It has denied the UN's role even where it is manifest. The Soviet press insists that the Iran affair of 1946 was settled, not thanks to the United Nations but by direct negotiation. The UN had nothing to do with the easing of international tensions after Stalin's death: the Geneva spirit of 1955 was a product of the Great Powers' own pursuits. The Suez crisis of 1956, Khrushchev asserted, was settled not by the UN but by the Soviet Union's threat of intervention. More often than not, the United Nations has in the past acted either "under pressure from the USA" (as in Korea) or as "nothing more than a passive registrar of world events."

The special interpretation given to the term, status quo, has been peculiarly well suited to take advantage of the Soviet approach. It gives the Soviet Union sanction to ignore the outside world when it comes to relations within its own bloc, and it permits the Soviet Union also to make the problems of other nations, in and out of the UN, its own concern. For, as Khrushchev has repeatedly suggested, the essence of the status quo is revolution itself. Ultimately, this means acquiescence in the process of change whose culmination is the world-wide drift to communism.

What to the outsider might appear to be a double standard turns out to be natural and consequent, once Soviet assumptions are spelled out. The seeming ambiguity or conceptual contradiction in such cases, for instance, the Soviet view of just and unjust wars, stems from the clash of two distinct categories of analysis— of iron "laws of history," as Moscow sees them, with man-made "international law in the epoch of coexistence." In its internal analysis of the world scene, Moscow is bound to opt for the organic, fundamental laws which inform the historical process rather than the "formal, technical" and transient "bourgeois" rules.

It remains true that the Soviet approach is by no means free of unreconciled ambiguities and unresolved problems of analysis. As can be shown with numerous examples, there have been conflicting priorities of revolution and diplomacy, of exclusiveness and universality, of sovereignty and "proletarian solidarity," of esoteric class analysis and tactics of compromise. Any of these may at times confront the Soviet leadership with genuine dilemmas. Thus, to accept the world as it is means to betray its long-range goals and visions; but to oppose it frankly and explicitly is to sacrifice all the advantages of propaganda, negotiations, and alliances—and, in this case, effective participation in international organizations.

Despite the fundamental constancy of the Soviet view of the world—and of the United Nations—Moscow has had its share of disagreements over strategy and tactics at home and abroad. Communist assessments of the United Nations have ranged from total rejection as an "imperialist tool" to total support as an imminent communist "front." While in the minds of some Soviet leaders such expectations regarding the UN have vacillated with changing conditions abroad, others have adhered to the same positions more or less rigidly impervious to new experiences and opportunities.

As recently as October 1961, at the 22nd Congress of the Soviet Communist Party, the major protagonists of the current "moderate" line went out of their way to deny that they had "excessive faith in personal contacts and conversations" abroad; no doubt the

United Nations was part of this skein of relations. Viacheslav Molotov was identified as "opposed to contacts between our statesmen and party leaders with foreign politicians, to visits abroad. . . . He warns us: look out and beware of contacts!" The problem of disarmament was now added to the issues over which spokesmen for different communist policies ostensibly disagreed. Undoubtedly we do not know the full range of disagreements relating to the UN. Yet the experience of recent years is likely to have reduced the differences in the Soviet assessment of the United Nations: neither total withdrawal nor total reliance on the UN is likely to find many advocates among the leaders of the Soviet camp.

International organizations are after all expected to be but a passing stage. Both the strategy of the "zone of peace" and pursuit of "peaceful coexistence" are deemed appropriate for the "given historical epoch"—the transitional era in which "capitalist" and "socialist" states exist side by side. Moscow has been frank in stating not only that the principle of "proletarian international-ism" among communists is a law superior to "bourgeois" codes and mores, but also that it is intended "for a longer period of time" than "peaceful coexistence." Unlike the more "pragmatic" responses of other states, in the Soviet case such a long-range perspective is by no means irrelevant to the conduct of actual policy.

UN—For What?

It is commonplace to argue that Soviet "conflict strategy" encompasses a practical, if somewhat condescending, willingness to use any individual or group, institution or symbol to advance its aims. In Moscow's estimation the United Nations is—or can be—one such tool. Until about 1954, it was considered an instrument of subordinate importance; since then, its potential in Soviet eyes has substantially increased.

This statement is not in conflict with the underlying skepticism about what the United Nations can do and what the Soviet Union can expect to gain from it. Fundamentally, Moscow continues to hold, an international body of diverse and antagonistic sovereign states cannot solve the problems of our days.

The Soviet Union has participated in the United Nations for limited purposes and with limited expectations. If, some observers have found, there is in the United States an acute contrast between hopes and results in the UN, no such hiatus exists on the Soviet side—simply because Moscow had no such naive expectations to begin with. It sees membership as a contract based on the mutuality of certain interests. The United Nations, it maintains, has no rights or powers of its own—only those derived from its Member States. It is at all times an organ subordinate to these states, not the independent voice of a world conscience or of a common will.

Many Western observers found it hard to predict in what direction the United Nations would evolve. On a number of points, the Charter is inevitably and perhaps intentionally vague. If, in a widespread view, the UN may be considered either a locus for the exercise of national policy or else a nucleus of international government, for Moscow there has been no such choice: the UN must serve only the former, never the latter goal. Soviet writings continue to assail all projects giving the United Nations greater power and to "expose" all advocates of "the reactionary idea of 'world law.'"

By the same token, the Soviet Union has not indulged in any optimism with regard to "functionalism" or "welfare internationalism" through the UN. Neither the faith that international "togetherness" will overcome basic rifts, nor the belief that the UN could or should attempt to resolve the economic and social ills of the modern world has characterized the Soviet view. This is not at all surprising. Indeed, in its predominantly political approach to the International Organization, the Soviet Union has differed fundamentally from the spokesmen of underdeveloped countries whom it has sought to court—countries for whom the health, education, and welfare activities often loom as among the most constructive tasks of the UN.

Internal Soviet estimates of the United Nations' utility appear to have changed in the course of time. The initial Soviet commitment to participate in the League of Nations and then in the United Nations was due in large measure to a desire to buttress Russian security. Since 1950 this has been a receding consideration. Experience showed that both the League and the UN were at best dubious guarantors of peace. And with the growth of Soviet military and economic power, with crucial breakthroughs in weapons technology, and with a deep reluctance to trust the mechanics of a "non-power" club, the Soviet Union has not relied and need not rely on the United Nations for its defense. One of the most bothersome of Khrushchev's arguments since 1959 has been that of Soviet reliance on its own forces—without the UN and even against the UN. In case of crisis, Soviet resort to the UN is of course considered infinitely less promising than its own armed might, its alliance system, and other instruments which it controls.

The subordinate place of the United Nations in the Soviet scheme is also reflected in Moscow's disinclination to have the UN handle issues requiring sensitive dosage or urgent action. For such purposes, it prefers "summits" and bilateral negotiations.

A similar power-conscious realism is revealed in the omission of the United Nations from the most authoritative and detailed communist analyses of contemporary affairs. The official handbook of the Communist Party of the Soviet Union, used for political training throughout the U.S.S.R. and translated into various languages, in its 890 pages (including a lengthy section on world affairs, the Korean war, and the Suez crisis) does not contain a single reference to the United Nations! Likewise, the Declaration of 81 Communist Parties meeting in Moscow in November–December 1960, perhaps the most significant theoretical and strategic document produced by the communist universe in recent years, fails to make a single reference to the United Nations, as does the Program of the CPSU adopted in October 1961.

This does not mean that Moscow lacks theoretical criteria by which to judge the UN:

> Under conditions when there are in the world states with differing social systems, international political organizations—constituting phenomena which belong to the superstructure—have the right to exist only so long as they correspond to the actual relationship of forces which constitute their base.

If the Organization fails to change in accordance with these "basic" forces, it tends to become "essentially a separate bloc, hardly distinguishable from aggressive military alliances." This is the rationale of the Soviet proposals of 1960–61: the demand that the

Organization be brought in line with the "realities" of international power.

What then does Moscow expect to gain from its efforts in the United Nations? Membership, even at times of considerable adversity, has given the Soviet Union valuable opportunities:

> for the settlement of relatively minor disputes;
>
> for international contacts, both to exchange views and to initiate and pursue negotiations, often informally rather than at official sessions;
>
> for gathering information, political intelligence, technical know-how, scientific data, and securing economic and other goods and services, as a matter of self-interest;
>
> for gaining prestige and respectability as a major power in the family of nations; and
>
> for engaging in propaganda, in the broadest sense of the term, and attempting to influence the views, attitudes, and political alignments of other states.

Soviet analysts have frequently stressed the value of the United Nations as a "broad forum"; as a gathering point for the different blocs, including the young nations of Africa and Asia; and as a vehicle for the dissemination of Soviet declarative proposals (such as the draft declarations on peaceful coexistence, stopping nuclear tests, and pledges not to employ nuclear weapons; the total disarmament scheme; and the anticolonialist declaration). Upon returning from the UN in the fall of 1960 Khrushchev declared that his trip had been "useful in that we had many meetings and exchanged views with the statesmen of various countries on a whole range of important international issues." With all its vagueness, this comment no doubt corresponded to his view.

In the pursuit of these objectives, Soviet policy-makers have had the choice between several models of behavior in international organizations:

(1) *Non-participation.* This course commended itself until 1934 with regard to the League and has been consistently rejected for the UN.

(2) *Minimum participation.* Basically an isolationist strategy, it is restrictive in its interpretation of UN authority, stressing Soviet prerogatives of sovereignty and strict interpretation of agreements, and minimizing outside jurisdiction in communist affairs. Adopted

at a time when the Soviet bloc was in the position of a perennial minority, it has been the predominant policy ever since 1945, though in the 1950's Moscow began to shed some of its features as it felt a distinct improvement in its "position of strength" and opportunities abroad.

(3) *Selective cooperation* against a specific foe. This strategy—seeing the UN as the equivalent of a military ally—is practiced when the Soviet Union needs international support in some form of collective action or assurance against a third power. In this fashion it sought to strengthen its position vis-à-vis Germany and Japan in the 1930's. An analogous situation has not occurred since the Second World War. While no one will admit it, Communist China may theoretically present such a problem at some future date.

(4) A broad, expansive strategy of *maximizing United Nations authority*. This is the normal Soviet policy for a communist-controlled organization. No doubt, Moscow would welcome a situation in which its "camp"—together with assorted camp followers—would emerge in control of the UN. But, after a brief interlude of extravagant hope, Khrushchev seems to have convinced himself that the day is not at hand. This policy therefore has seen and in the foreseeable future will see no systematic application.

Perplexingly Soviet policy in 1960–62 fits none of the above prescriptions precisely. The Soviet role is no longer minimal in many fields: it has increased in economic and social work; there has been greater Soviet use of the Assembly; in Soviet propaganda, the UN "principle"—but not its practice—has unmistakably become a positive symbol. Yet precisely the threats and demands voiced by the Soviet Union underscore the continuing gap between the "United Nations mentality" and that of the U.S.S.R.

Beyond the immediate opportunities that Moscow sees available for itself, is there a longer-range objective of Soviet policy in the UN? At one time it was conceivable that Moscow would merely maintain nominal membership, seeking neither to win control nor to withdraw. No longer is this a reasonable prospect; given the growth of Soviet might, activity, and ambition, such a retreat to silent partnership is difficult to conceive. Nor is the Soviet bloc likely to pull out, in spite of all its threats. If it stuck it out during the isolation of the Korean War, it is sure to feel that the present advantages of membership are infinitely greater and the prospects more encouraging still. Its threats of withdrawal, moreover, would obviously lose their bargaining value—without netting the Soviet Union any commensurate gain—were it indeed to leave the Organization.

The question remains whether (in President Eisenhower's words) the Soviet leaders "in alternating moods look upon the United Nations as an instrument for use or abuse," whether (as others have put it) Moscow seeks "the power to manipulate the United Nations for its own designs," or whether Khrushchev strives to render the Organization impotent. One may suggest that the two objectives—to neutralize and to control—can coexist in Soviet minds: they may be most usefully thought of as maximum and minimum aims. The simultaneous identification of such divergent goals has a long history in Bolshevik experience and has often been characteristic of Soviet foreign affairs.

No doubt the most extreme and optimistic Soviet vision is the transformation of the United Nations into a communist "front" organization, in the manner of world peace congresses, "solidarity" meetings, and labor federations which, behind a non-Soviet façade, communists seek to control (but not overtly to direct, so as not to drive noncommunists out). But obviously Moscow cannot bank on the UN's conforming to this scheme. In practice, the Soviet bloc has never even been close to controlling a majority of votes. Moreover, the Western Big Three still possess their veto power. Thus, of necessity, the Soviet Union has had to turn to more immediate and more modest goals—especially since, by 1960, Khrushchev saw it as a matter of considerable urgency to stop the Organization from being "used" by the enemy camp.

Even if Moscow prefers to have two strings to its United Nations bow, choices must sometimes be made which preclude a return to an alternative policy. In general Moscow has sought to avoid such irreversible commitments, and from the Soviet point of view a major shortcoming of the tripartite proposals is precisely the fact that their adoption would make it difficult at some future point to return to a veto-free pursuit of majority control of the General Assembly and the Secretariat. As it now stands, the Soviet plan would guarantee the veto to both the West and the collective voice of the unaligned. At present Moscow would not seriously expect to "sell" its proposal without giving such "equality" to the American-led "imperialist camp."

Thus Moscow finds itself prepared for the time being to freeze the tripartite relationship and accept a far more limited goal than its control of the UN. The most immediate Soviet task is to make sure that the United Nations will not be used against it and its friends.

But this does not exhaust what Moscow expects to achieve in or through the UN. The Soviet bloc can hope to use it in a variety of ways until such a time as, hopefully, the Charter may again be altered to bring it in conformity with what Moscow expects will then be the reality of even greater Soviet might.

Continuity and Change

A substantially constant ideological framework has permitted significant variations in Soviet strategy and tactics at the United Nations. The contrast between Moscow's policy in Stalin's days and in the Khrushchev era measures both the extent and the limits of variation.

But what has determined shifts in Moscow's policy? The primary determinant is to be found outside the UN system: this has been the Soviet perception of changes in the "real world"—above all, changes of power and of opportunity. It was precisely the contrast between the glorious sense of growing Soviet world power and the lack of commensurate success or influence in the United Nations that permitted Moscow to argue for "realistic" adjustments in the Organization's system of staffing and representation.

Another determinant is the structure of ideological preconceptions. True, certain fundamental axioms—conflict, dichotomy, optimism—have shown remarkable tenacity; and certain generalities in the Soviet world view—the call for "realism," the approach to "sovereignty," the verdict that the United Nations is "useful" but not "important"—have remained virtually unchanged. Yet the doctrinal revisions of the Khrushchev era have been important in rationalizing the Soviet policy of nonviolent competition and widening the framework of permissible techniques.

This is not to suggest that the doctrinal reformulations preceded the new perception of a changing world. It should be clear, moreover, that the specifics of Soviet policy, in or out of the United Nations, are not explicable in ideological terms alone. Like the demand for parity, the troika proposition exemplifies a Soviet effort to gain as much as the other powers might concede—a demand fully consistent with, but not predictable in terms of, its world view alone. Political realism, as Moscow sees it, is thus superimposed on ideological commitments. Only the combination of the two can explain the nature and the timing of the Soviet reorganization proposals.

Soviet policy has been capable of crude and unprincipled practicality when the rewards have seemed to warrant it. The traditional commitment to the tenet of *pacta sunt servanda* is not allowed to stand in the way of demands for greater rights due to greater power. The most "principled" insistence on the reality of three power blocs easily yields to a plethora of Soviet formulae for four, five, six, or seven Under-Secretaries when Hammarskjöld's successors are being discussed. Soviet opposition to the existing order in the United Nations, Moscow admits at times, is due not to the belief that a *single* group of powers controls the UN but that the *wrong* group does—"reactionaries" and "monopolists." Soviet insistence on unanimity as a *sine qua non* in the United Nations, which Moscow does not control, contrasts dramatically with its efforts to promote majority rule within the conclave of international communism, where it does have most member parties on its side against Chinese Communist advocacy of unanimity. Even the sacred principle of sovereignty can be suspended when political utility demands it. "Principles," too, in other words, can be weapons in the struggle of systems, in and out of the UN.

Among the strands of Soviet experience which contribute to the reassessment of strategy is the record of the United Nations itself. The UN action in the Congo is a case in point. While on the whole events inside the UN have played a subordinate part in the crystallization of Soviet policies, the Soviet Union's own experience of being a "loser" for over a decade has surely reinforced Moscow's inclination to keep the United Nations' power at a low level. The minority position of the Soviet bloc during the early years intensified its members' resentment and sense of isolation. Then their collective nonparticipation for a time set them apart even more. While some of this gap was bridged in the post-Stalin era, the suspicion that the United Nations was part of the hostile camp remained.

It was of course true that the majority of the United Nations—and of the Great Powers—was anticommunist. With some exertion, the Western powers could usually command a majority of votes, something the U.S.S.R. could not do. At every step, from San Francisco to Korea and Suez, it must have seemed to Moscow that the United States had won out. And in 1960–61 the UN was perhaps more indulgent toward the United States, over the U-2 flight and the attempted landing in Cuba, than it might have been toward other nations. All this of course did not make the UN a "tool of the State Department," as Moscow alleged, but it provided an objective basis for the Soviet claims.

Finally, the Soviet world view contains a strong self-fulfilling element. George F. Kennan, among others, has suggested that Soviet expectation and behavior are bound to engender precisely the sort of response abroad and create just such a dichotomy as Moscow professes to see. In practice, too, many United Nations agencies became "Western" during the formative years when the U.S.S.R. refused to take an active part in their work. The realization that this was the case was probably among the reasons for the later change in Soviet tactics—from absence to participation in many, though not all, activities of the UN.

Nothing would be further from the truth than to suggest that the Soviet Union has been the only culprit at the UN. In fact, most powers have violated the spirit of the Charter, and many have ignored its letter time and again. Most Members have failed to rely on the United Nations as a primary instrument of national policy. Most states have valued it for what they can get out of it. All have loyalties higher than those to the UN. All the Great Powers would refuse to surrender the veto. Others, too, have insisted on keeping the domestic jurisdiction clause. Rather than entrusting their security to the United Nations, most states have bolstered their defenses or moved to regional alliance systems. Other countries, too, have resisted UN regulation of their commerce and tariffs, and have preferred to put their own label on economic aid and exercise direct control over its destination.

Moscow is right in arguing that, if universality is an objective, the absence from the UN of Communist China and Germany is difficult to defend. It is correct in stressing that "Great Power unanimity" *was* the original presupposition of the United Nations; it if implies the essentiality of agreement, it also spells the impotence of the UN when such consensus is not achieved. Many, outside the Soviet bloc, have also found the formula of "one state, one vote" in the Assembly highly unrealistic. Many new nations have felt their interests inadequately reflected on the United Nations staff and in the Security Council. Just as the Soviet Union came to look askance at a plain majority principle after its experience in the Assembly, so the United States appears to have lost some of its enthusiasm for that body since the accretion of Afro-Asian votes and the loosening of the Latin American bloc has made the Western powers a minority group too. The United Kingdom has been frankly pessimistic about the future of the UN. In its insistence on the imperative of change, the Soviet Union finds a considerable echo among other states, for there are many who, in H. G. Nicholas' words,

> have joined the UN less to preserve, by mechanisms of law and order, an existing state of affairs, than to effect, by the pressure of their votes and their voices, a change not only in their own circumstances but often in their relation with the rest of the world.

Even in its refusal to think and act in terms of a world community the Soviet Union is by no means alone. Indeed, a series of studies of national attitudes toward the UN prompted the conclusion that the idea of universal solidarity of man has not yet penetrated deeply. To use Maurice Bourquin's expression, the world over "People don't *feel* the unity of humankind."

And yet, when all is said and done, the Soviet outlook on the United Nations remains unique in some essential ways. This unique feature is not even Soviet defiance of the UN, including its asserted willingness to use force to resist it, as illustrated by the Hungarian episode in 1956, when it ignored the body's verdict—at the same time that other violators of the Charter's spirit obeyed the UN's call to stop action at Suez. Other states—notably France—have been known likewise to challenge and ignore the UN.

The area of uniqueness lies above all in the Soviet view of the historical process and its translation into action. The profound conviction that in the long run neutrality and impartiality are impossible or nonexistent vitiates the fundamental assumption on which international organizations such as the United Nations are built. The communist image of the United Nations as an arena of struggle is not a reluctant recognition of a tragic fact but an exhilarating ride on the wave of the future.

The Soviet view, in sum, combines a revolutionary outlook with a conservative pursuit of its security and a pragmatic effort to make the most of the complex and shifting United Nations scene.

The hardheadedness of the Soviet approach contrasts strikingly with the fuzzy thinking about the UN that has often characterized others abroad. Yet—on this point the record should be convincing—Moscow has made its full share of errors and miscalculations. Soviet policy, Stalin told Anthony Eden in 1945, was "neither as simple as some thought nor as skillful as others believed." Indeed, we have too often mistaken absence of information for absence of conflict or doubt on the Soviet side. We have been too much inclined to endow the masters of the Kremlin with infallible cleverness—and they to an even greater extent have seen a pattern, a design, a purpose, a conspiracy in every move and gesture of the outside world: "There are no accidents."

Soviet analysis and expectations have, in the Khrushchev era, tended to be fairly realistic about power relations, capabilities and vulnerabilities of states. They have permitted Moscow to ignore the United Nations as a decisive obstacle on its path. Indeed, what *could* the UN do in the face of overt Soviet hostility? But a substantial lack of realism intervenes when Soviet analysis concerns a pluralistic world. As bipolarity is the natural shape to which, Moscow imagines, the universe tends, the standard Soviet image of the United Nations, too, has been one of two opposites. So long as the facts can be made to fit such formulae, Soviet analysis is simple and often shrewd even if its view of capitalism and democracy remains hopelessly out of date. But they don't always fit.

It is precisely with regard to neutralism and nonalignment that the Soviet view is apt to go awry. Which way the uncommitted will go when forced by the logic of international strife and Soviet (and American) prodding remains in doubt. But it is clear that the assumption that the ultimate interest of the neutral bloc is on the Soviet side is unwarranted and naive. Moscow has ignored the fact that the United Nations occupied a far more important place in the thinking and expectations of the developing nations than in those of the U.S.S.R., with regard to their own security and progress; their view of the UN's welfare and economic activities is far more positive; and their perspective on UN finances differs drastically from that of the Soviet Union. While on issues such as anticolonialism the Soviet bloc has naturally identified itself with the new nations, Moscow may in fact have begun to realize that the "third" bloc is not necessarily—and surely not yet—to be counted on the communist side. And it is no doubt at least a subsidiary purpose of the Soviet reorganization plan to deprive the United Nations of its ability to compete with the communists for leadership of the "national liberation" movement. In the last analysis, the Soviet assumption that the nonaligned world—any more than the Western grouping—constitutes a cohesive, homogeneous, lasting bloc is plainly wrong. Whether or not the communist orbit is any more cohesive or lasting only the future will tell.

The Limits of Logic

The Soviet stand, enunciated in the fall of 1960 and reiterated since, is logical within the framework of Soviet assumptions and objectives. It is, to be sure, more extreme than the view Moscow had previously propounded about the United Nations. Allowing for some improvisations in the actual proposals, it has the virtue that the assumptions in back of the troika plan remove an area of suppressed ambiguity which has inhered in the Soviet compromise between inward communist hostility toward and outward identification with the UN. The view that there exists no just arbiter or administrator above the two major camps revives, almost verbatim, positions voiced in days of greater Soviet candor.

The Soviet formula made little constitutional sense: it would have frozen the balance of three blocs by institutionalizing a haphazard and transient political alignment from which the sovereign Member States might choose to withdraw at some future time. Many borderline states could not easily be put into any of the three categories. The assumption that each of the blocs had unity and permanence was obviously open to serious challenge. Indeed, Soviet insistence on sovereign equality of states seemed to be violated by its plan to give equal weight to nine communist states, some fifty neutrals, and the forty-odd Western powers and their allies.

Administratively, objections no less weighty were voiced by the United Nations staff itself. The troika would have stymied the Secretariat's work and made the use of the UN in another Korean or Congolese crisis impossible. But this was at least part of Moscow's purpose.

No elaborate evidence is required to show that Khrushchev has not been willing to tolerate an analogous *ménage à trois* either within the leadership in the Kremlin, or in Soviet industrial management, or in relations among communist parties. Soviet insistence on tripartite equality and veto in the executive organs conflicts directly with the time-honored Bolshevik administrative principle of *edinonachalie*—unity of authority—which has been reaffirmed on innumerable occasions as "the basic method of operating the Soviet economy and the Soviet state." Since the objective of *edinonachalie* is above all maximum efficiency, one may conclude that the Soviet purpose in opposing it in the United Nations is its reverse.

The political incongruity of the troika is well illustrated by Adlai Stevenson's remark that the application of the Soviet plan in the sixteenth century would have produced an organization "in which the administration of international affairs was entrusted to a triumvirate consisting of the Pope, the Sultan, and Martin Luther."

If adopted, the proposals would reduce the United Nations to the highest common denominator of its Members' views. Moscow has gone so far as to insist that "the main goal of this organization consists in finding solutions acceptable to *all* its members." That this is no slip of the pen is shown by the recurrence of the theme on a number of occasions since Khrushchev, in his UN speech of September 19, 1959, declared that "only such decisions should be taken in the United Nations which everyone would vote for." When asked, the following year, whether he would let a two-thirds majority of the Member States decide whether or not Hammarskjöld should stay, Khrushchev replied: "This is not a parliament. It is a forum in which the questions should be resolved in

such a way as not to endanger the interests of even a single state.
. . ."

There is ground to question whether Moscow means quite what
it says. While the extension of the unanimity rule to all Members
of the United Nations is consonant with that strain of Soviet
thinking which emphasizes sovereign prerogatives, the *liberum
veto* would permit a single Member—say, the Union of South
Africa—to prevent the adoption of a decision favored by all other
states. This clearly would not be welcome to the U.S.S.R. It would
be impossible, under the circumstances, to "isolate" any state or
bloc of states; yet this is precisely what Soviet spokesmen have
time and again called for at the UN.

What Moscow means, one may surmise, is that its own con-
currence—as the leading power of the world, or so it likes to
think—should be required at all times and in all organs of the
United Nations. But this it cannot say openly, any more than it
can afford to ask for a selective extension of the veto to a few
favored nations, at a time when it courts precisely those countries
of whom virtually none would be the beneficiaries of such a move.

That the operation of a United Nations in which all of its
hundred-odd Members would possess a *liberum veto* would be
destructive not only of the United Nations but of Soviet interests
as well, is nowhere better put than in a Soviet critique of the
League of Nations. As Grigorii Morozov writes in his volume on
the UN, a recent and authoritative Soviet account,

> This impotence of the League flowed, in particular, from the fact
> that the Covenant required unanimity of all its members for the
> adoption of all political decisions taken by its Council and Assembly.
> This harmful pseudo-democratism vitiated the role and responsibility
> of the several states in the cause of supporting international peace
> and practically rendered impossible the effective operation of an
> organization for the maintenance of peace and the prevention of
> aggression.

An extreme expression of the Soviet view is the contention that
the sovereign Member States need not be bound by what the
United Nations says and does. This has been implicit in the series
of Khrushchev's references, since mid-1960, to the use of force.
Speaking initially about the failure of the Security Council to
support the Soviet demands stemming from the U-2 incident, he

remarked (on June 3, 1960) that under such circumstances in the future "we have no other way out but to rely on our own strength." At the UN that fall, he went further: the Soviet Union would ignore United Nations decisions which it deemed incompatible with its own interests. If it did not get its way, it would "uphold our interests outside this international body, outside the United Nations, by relying on our own strength." The final step in this progression came in Khrushchev's speech welcoming President Nkrumah of Ghana to Moscow in July 1961:

> Even if all the countries of the world adopted a decision which did not accord with the interests of the Soviet Union and threatened its security, the Soviet Union would not recognize such a decision and would uphold its rights, relying on force. And we have what [it takes] to rely on.

What constitutes a threat to its security is, of course, at all times up to Moscow to decide.

Such strident formulations reveal the extent of Soviet determination to maintain its full freedom of action. Once again Soviet insistence on "unanimity" and "sovereignty" turns the clock backwards. The unanimity rule, Nicolas Politis said in 1928, amounts to an admission that "among nations no real organization is possible, for the rule of unanimity may lead to paralysis and anarchy. . . ."

Moscow watched with unmitigated enmity the tragic—or pathetic—search for an international authority to deal effectively with forces greater than itself. The United Nations had not been expected to cope with disagreements among the Great Powers, and Moscow vigorously protested Western attempts to shape the UN into a serviceable tool in the conflicts between the "two camps." To its mind, what has taken place amounts to an illegal "triple play" from Security Council to General Assembly to Secretariat, as the United States and its allies tried to use one organ after another for their ends. The Council, stymied by the veto, declined in importance and use, and was widely recognized to be unable to do its job. The General Assembly, even under the Uniting for Peace Resolution could not compel compliance with its recommendations; and there were political and constitutional limits to what it could do. Even prior to its recent inflation, disappointment was widespread—in the Soviet judgment as well as in that of the West. Both its inherent weakness and the growth of numbers in the General Assembly finally encouraged an expansion of executive power in the UN Secretariat—a process likewise promoted by the delegation of authority by the Security Council, as in the Laotian and Congolese crises.

Experience suggests that there are inherent flaws in the way the Secretariat was conceived. The Charter granted its Secretary-General explicitly far more authority than his inconspicuous predecessor in the League had possessed. His office has been not merely administrative but also political, both in intent and in practice. As a consequence both Trygve Lie and Dag Hammarskjöld were bound to antagonize the Soviet bloc. To have avoided acting so as to clash with it would have meant failing in the fulfillment of their duties.

Yet the necessity to perform political tasks does not make "disinterested" or "objective" service impossible, as Dag Hammarskjöld argued trenchantly in his Oxford speech in May 1961. It has been a matter of honorable tradition and established policy, reiterated over many years, that an international staff, to be fair and effective, must not be imbued with the values and special interests of any one state. Yet this is precisely what Moscow has challenged. As Walter Lippmann reported on the basis of his interview with Khrushchev,

> the Soviet government has now come to the conclusion that there can be no such thing as an impartial civil servant in this deeply divided world, and that the kind of political celibacy which the British theory of the civil servant calls for is in international affairs a fiction.

Beyond a doubt, the troika does radical violence to the entire UN approach, seeking to substitute for a distinguished civil service the crude arithmetic of political patronage.

It may well be that, from the Soviet viewpoint, the Secretary-General had gone beyond the original purview of his tasks. Once more, Moscow stuck to the minimal construction of the UN's role, while the Secretary-General found support for his initiatives in the broad view (expressed, for instance, in the Report of the Preparatory Commission for the United Nations) that he, more than anyone else, "must embody the principles and ideals of the Charter."

Moscow objected not only to his arrogation of authority (at the behest of the "imperialists," it would maintain) but also to his philosophy under which the United Nations must be interposed between the major camps and fill the power vacuums wherever it can. In Moscow's reading this is a pernicious doctrine incompatible with its view of the inevitable course of history. It is this attempt, more than anything else, which identified the Secretary-General, for the communists, with reaction, and which prompted the vigorous expression of Soviet determination not to tolerate efforts which would frustrate potential communist gains in fluid areas around the globe.

The Road Ahead

The Soviet Union may at times keep silent its belief that ultimately "one or the other must prevail." It has never abandoned the either-or approach.

The choice of when to mute and when to trumpet the extreme formulation of incompatibility is up to Moscow. Even if the outside world can help fortify or provoke a given Soviet response, it can never expect to control it. The Soviet Union may alter at will its readiness to compromise on the organization of the United Nations or its resolve to cooperate on a given task. It cannot be compelled or effectively induced to do so. With some oversimplification, one may then conclude that the United Nations is only as much as its least cooperative Members want it to be.

The question was raised earlier whether a state committed to objectives at variance with those of the United Nations can and should operate in international bodies such as the UN. Sheer logic might well lead one to answer in the negative. In the long run the contending forces as now defined and inspired may well be unable to coexist. Theoretically, or ultimately, one may indeed maintain that "international organization is hardly compatible with rampant imperialism by one state which seeks hegemony over the world." Yet in the short run the essence of power politics—even on the brink of the thermonuclear precipice—remains restraint from recourse to extremes and retreat from the logical to the political, from incompatibility to coexistence, and from the inexorable to the possible. So long as this is true, there is continuing and important room for the United Nations in the duel of our age, and for the Soviet Union in the World Organization.

This would be true even if the Soviet long-range objective of controlling the UN had greater chances of success than now seems likely. Once its efforts succeeded, of course, the need for the UN would promptly disappear, for in a future commonwealth of communist nations, the United Nations with its present complexion and philosophy can have no place.

The Soviet Union can be expected to pursue its own ends with all the vigor and determination which its "active, aggressive struggle demands." Soviet policymakers realize no doubt that their reorganization proposals are not likely to be adopted in their present form. On at least one occasion—the crisis enduced by Dag Hammarskjöld's death—Moscow has demonstrated that its demands need not always amount to ultimata. In March 1961 no one would have dared predict that within six months agreement on a successor to the Secretary-General was possible—even as an "interim" solution—without fundamentally modifying the structure and operation of the UN. The deadlock likely to obtain when U Thant's term expires in April 1963 may be fraught with even graver dangers, at a time when the Soviet position promises to be considerably less flexible—unless, once more, broader considerations of policy produce a propitious climate for Soviet moderation unforeseeable today. While various compromise formulae have been suggested in response to the troika plan, Moscow has actually allowed itself little room for negotiation or retreat without sacrificing the heart of its proposals—a veto over the activities of the Secretariat. It remains to be seen whether anything short of this will satisfy the U.S.S.R.; nothing like it will be acceptable to the major noncommunist states.*

To this extent, the future of the United Nations is in Soviet hands. Moscow can wreck it or build it up: in the UN's present state, Moscow is unlikely to do either. It is, however, certain to

* Ed. note: Secretary-General U Thant was re-elected for a full term on November 30, 1962.

keep the United Nations from taking that giant step which Dag Hammarskjöld, in his final months, spoke of as the transition from "institutional systems of international coexistence" to "constitutional systems of international cooperation." That bridge between standing international conference and organized international community, which he saw envisaged in the UN Charter, is certain to remain unspanned (among other reasons) so long as Moscow has the right and the might to interpose its veto.

The Soviet bloc cannot be expected to adopt the philosophy of the UN and pursue the objectives of the UN. As Adlai Stevenson put it to the Senate Foreign Relations Committee on January 18, 1961,

> the United Nations—as an idea and as an institution—is an extension of Western ideas; of Western belief in the worth and dignity of the individual; of Western ideology. It is based on a Western parliamentary tradition. Its roots are in the Western idea of representative government. In short, it is thoroughly anti-totalitarian.

Indeed, the United Nations is founded on the belief in at least some perfectability, gradualism, and consensus. In many respects its outlook is analogous in international affairs to that of liberal democracy at home. We have been reminded that

> international organization rests upon the belief that man is at liberty, not only to surrender to the operation of the iron laws of the system, or to attempt an apocalyptic leap from an era of determinism into an era of freedom, but to shape his collective destiny in the here and now.

The non-Western nations may and perhaps will overwhelmingly come to share these assumptions. The communist states, as we know them, cannot.

But too much must not be anticipated or asked of the United Nations. It was never intended to clash with a Great Power or to resolve conflicts among them. The UN can be expected to alter neither the fundamental power relations among states nor the motives of their rulers. This is not an argument against the United Nations: with all its inherent limitations, its uses and values for all mankind are many. Moscow, on its part, does not expect any major impact on its world policy to come from or through the UN. The roots of conflict lie outside the Organization and extend far beyond it. In this regard, "their" and "our" view is likely to coincide, for, in the words of George F. Kennan,

> it is not fair to the Organization today to ask it to resolve the predicaments of the past as well as of the present. No international organization can be stronger than the structure of relationships among the Great Powers that underlies it; and to look to such an organization to resolve deep-seated conflicts of interest among the Great Powers is to ignore its limitations and to jeopardize its usefulness in other fields.

Whither U.S.S.R.?

The changes that have taken place in the domestic and international policies of the Soviet Union since the death of Stalin in 1953 have engendered a serious academic controversy among Western experts about the future development of the U.S.S.R.

On the one hand there are those who believe that the current Western mood of optimism elicited by the de-Stalinization program in the Soviet Union and the development of polycentrism within the Communist camp is unfounded and illusory. They also believe that the assumption that the Soviet Union is experiencing a fundamental change is ultimately dangerous, for it instills in the peoples of the West an attitude of complacency which with its attendant relaxation of vigilance is bound to aid Communist aspirations. The changes in Soviet policy, impressive as they are, are construed as merely temporary changes in tactics induced by the firm though flexible stand of the West, and the ultimate goal of the Soviet leaders is still considered to be the Communization of the world, to be brought about, if possible, without the risk of a general thermonuclear war.

On the other hand there are those who believe that the fundamental changes in Soviet domestic policies, coupled with the ever exacerbating rift between the two Communist colossi and the gradual triumph of "national Communism" in Eastern Europe, will inevitably lead to a further "liberalization" of Soviet life. These commentators claim that the increasing affluence of the Russian people and the emergence of an intellectual elite well aware of the great discrepancies between Soviet promise and performance will further the "thaw" which set in in the late 1950's. They are convinced that a thaw affecting any aspect of culture in a totalitarian system has the inherent tendency to extend to all of its aspects and eventually to engulf the political sphere as well. The process is expected to gain momentum with the gradual extension of the "liberalization" movement. While there may be temporary relapses due to changing domestic and international conditions, the trend cannot be reversed. Each concession wrested from the regime will logically whet the appetite of the Soviet people for further concessions. The taste of freedom in the arts and sciences is bound to generate a thirst for freedom in all other spheres of human activity as well.

The industrialization and technological development of Russia and the concomitant increase in the living standards of the Soviet people have undoubtedly affected both the political and social structure of the U.S.S.R. and the revolutionary *élan* of Communism. In the following essay on "Soviet Society in Transition," Raymond Aron, a French sociologist and political scientist, is concerned with answering the following fundamental questions: (1) "To what extent, if any, will the development of industrial civilization bring about an evolution of the Soviet totalitarian regime and of the social forms inherited from the past? (2) What direction will this evolution take?"

Soviet Society in Transition

RAYMOND ARON[*]

The future development of Soviet society is manifestly one of the most crucial issues under investigation by social scientists today. Studies in this field are necessarily speculative not only for the obvious reason that they deal with future unknowns but because there has been so little opportunity for outsiders to familiarize themselves with the Soviet-Russian reality. Social scientists face a further difficulty in that there are several possible—and somewhat incompatible—approaches, or bases, for an interpretation of Soviet society.

Studies to date have proceeded along three principal avenues of approach, investigating Soviet society, first, as an industrial civilization; second, as a totalitarian system (dealt with as a unique phenomenon without historical precedent); third, as the successor to Tsarist Russia (with stress laid on aspects of cultural continuity between past and present). Any of these conceptual approaches can lead to confusion in attempts to predict the Soviet future. In the first instance, little is known as yet about the laws of economic development in a system of the Soviet type. Analyses stressing the totalitarian aspect often suffer for lack of a clear definition of totalitarianism itself (*e.g.*, does it date back to Lenin or just to Stalin?). As for the continuity approach, stress on the constant

---

[*] A distinguished French journalist and scholar, Dr. Aron is Professor of Sociology at the Sorbonne. He is the author of many books, among them *The Opium of the Intellectuals* (1957), *A Century of Total War* (1954), *France, the New Republic* (1960), and *The Dawn of Universal History* (1961).

From "Soviet Society in Transition" by Raymond Aron, *Problems of Communism*, Washington, D.C., Vol. VI, No. 6, November–December 1957, selections from pp. 5–10. Reprinted by permission.

factors in Russian culture as a key to the future can too easily lead to underestimation or disregard of the impact of economic and political changes.

Synthesizing the issues implied by these three approaches, the basic question to be answered may be phrased: To what extent, if any, will the development of industrial civilization bring about an evolution of the Soviet totalitarian regime and of the social forms inherited from the past? What direction will this evolution take? Some observers, in attempting to answer this question, have put forward theses based on one or another of the above schemes of interpretation in virtual disregard of the issues raised by the others.

Two such theses are worth mention as categorical and contradictory extremes of opinion; both, in this writer's view, are invalid. One asserts that the stupendous development of productive forces in the Soviet Union will pave the way to democracy; the other, that the totalitarian regime is invulnerable to economic forces.

Extremist Theories

The first of these has been expounded in particularly crude terms by Mr. Isaac Deutscher. His formulation lends itself to numerous objections, raised so often already that they can be dealt with briefly here. The explanation that terrorism and ideological orthodoxy are determined solely by the needs of primary accumulation or of the Five-Year Plans runs up against the incontrovertible fact that the great purge of 1936–38 took place after the first Plan had already been carried out and the collectivization of agriculture completed. The terror that accompanied the latter may, at a stretch, be attributed to economic "necessities," but this explanation cannot apply to the great purge, during which millions of real and imagined opponents, faithful Bolsheviks and even Stalinists were thrown into prison.

The tremendous development of Soviet productive forces, on which neo-Marxists always dwell as a portent of the better life to come, is of course no fiction. By and large, however, it applies only to heavy industry. The lot of the Soviet citizenry has remained relatively unaffected, since the living standard is determined not by *per capita* production but by the value of goods intended for consumption by individuals. Considering additionally the lag in agricultural output, it is unlikely that the Soviet planners can greatly increase the purchasing power of the population in the foreseeable future.

In any thesis on the Soviet future, the meaning of the word "democracy" is crucial. If by democracy is meant the organized competition of parties—as it seems to in Deutscher's formulation—and there is no obvious connection between democracy and economic progress. But it is absurd to insist on rigid and unalterable concepts of democracy in its Western form (characterized by multi-party systems, legislative representation, intellectual liberties, *etc.*) as opposed to totalitarianism (characterized by the single party, ideological terrorism, police controls, *etc.*). Neither Western democracy nor Stalinist totalitarianism can be considered as fixed entities, as "historic atoms" which cannot be transmuted. Thus, if it is illogical to assert that totalitarianism will develop into full-fledged democracy with the development of productive forces, it is just as illogical to exclude dogmatically a softening up of totalitarianism.

This is the weakness of the second theory, opposite to Mr. Deutscher's, which asserts that totalitarianism is invulnerable to outside forces. It is usually posited as part of a political and almost metaphysical interpretation of totalitarianism, conceived of as a disease which is liable to infect any modern society—even though, so far, only Russia and Germany have experienced it in "pure" form. Its proponents argue that although totalitarianism is favored by certain economic and social circumstances, it is essentially something political and ideological. It is supposed to be the outcome of an obsessive drive of a group of people bent on shaping society according to their own ideology. The power of a single party, ideological orthodoxy, police terror, the creation of a world of superimposed conventional meanings, with no reference to the real world and yet forced on the masses as something truer than reality—all these features, we are told, are linked together and constitute the characteristics of a global, or self-contained, phenomenon—a phenomenon which has emerged and will eventually disappear, but which it would be idle to expect to return to normality by gradual stages.

In this definition of totalitarianism, three of the above features are essential: ideological orthodoxy, police terror, and world-wide victory or else apocalyptic collapse. These three elements are said to be closely linked. The will to set up an arbitrary and often absurd ideology as The Truth necessitates the recourse to police inquisition, which is used for hunting not only enemies, but also heretics. The truth of the ideology can triumph only when it is no longer rejected by anybody. So long as there is opposition anywhere, communism will not be entirely true, because its truth will still clash with reality, and its complete truth depends on its universal application. Thus communism is in a constant state of war with unbelievers both inside and outside its borders. The greater the progress, the more it is impelled to struggle, for nothing has been achieved so long as something still remains to be done. This line of analysis affords an explanation for the great purge having descended upon Soviet society after the completion of rural collectivization; the latter is viewed not as an economic and rational—however ruthless—measure, but as the expression of a policy which is *alien* to economic rationalism, and is intelligible only in terms of an ideological and emotional logic.

This kind of interpretation, which Hannah Arendt has developed with great skills, seems to me to be dangerous. It amounts to creating a certain ideal type, a kind of essence of totalitarianism—and to assuming, thereupon, that the regime, both in the present and in the future, must conform to this type or this essence. If the Soviets behaved as "perfect" totalitarians, as Miss Arendt understands the word, then it is quite true that we could expect no normalization or evolution of the Soviet regime. The real question is, however, whether the regime has even been completely totalitarian, whether the "essense" has not simply been created by theorists like Miss Arendt on the strength of certain historically-observed and historically-explicable phenomena. The Soviet regime *became* totalitarian by degrees, under the influence of certain circumstances. Why, then, could it not cease to be totalitarian, or become less totalitarian, under the influence of other circumstances?

The Impact of Economic Development

Once the extremes of the neo-Marxist and the totalitarian theory have been rejected, it must be decided what either of them can contribute to a logical assessment of the Soviet future. What transformations, social and economic, are brought about by the development of productive forces? What is the likely effect of these transformations on the political regime? To what extent is totalitarianism (or certain totalitarian elements) inseparable from the regime, regardless of economic progress?

There are at least three important social and economic consequences of the development of productive forces. The first is a rise in the general level of culture and the creation and development of an intelligentsia, whose broad base—in addition to traditional cultural and professional elements—is the swelling ranks of technical and managerial specialists who man the economy. It is as true for the Soviet Union as for the West that modern industry requires a higher proportion of technicians and specialized "cadres" than in the past, and Soviet statistics show a steady increase in the proportion of intelligentsia to the whole working population.

Even outside this intelligentsia with its higher-level specialization, the priority given to production and to productivity is bound to encourage the spread of specialized training and of technical education. More than half the Soviet labor force is at present employed in industry or its auxiliary services, and more than half the population is urban. This urban population can read and write, and it is no longer as cowed—or as malleable—as it was in the early years of Stalin's reign.

The second consequence of industrial development, closely related to the first, is an increase in the economic wants and demands of the population. In the Soviet Union, the development of productive forces has not been accompanied by a corresponding rise in the standard of living of the masses. The concentration of capital investments in heavy industry, the failures in agriculture, and the housing shortage have meant that the average citizen is worse housed, worse fed and less well-dressed than the average citizen of the West, even in some of the less prosperous countries. In recent years, however, there has been some improvement in material conditions, and various pressures have led the regime to pay some limited deference to consumer needs. The indications are that this limited satisfaction of certain wants has whetted the population's appetite for more goods. In particular, the intelligentsia has shown increasing eagerness to acquire commodities typical of the way of life of the Western bourgeois (durable consumer goods, automobiles, refrigerators, *etc.*).

The third consequence of developing productive forces is a trend toward a more rational economy. Over the last thirty years, the Soviet economy has become not only more powerful but technologically far more complex. To what extent and how long the crude planning methods of the first Five-Year Plans can continue to be applied is a highly complicated and controversial issue. Yet the general direction of evolution seems fairly clear to this writer. As shortages become less severe, the consumers' choice will tend to be of growing importance to the market. Technological complexity will strengthen the managerial class at the expense of the ideologists and the militants, at any rate on the enterprise level, if not on the state level. The decentralization of industrial administration, in reinforcing the managerial elements, should reduce the part played by fear and coercion in the Soviet management of an industrial society.

Stabilizing Forces in Soviet Society

While the rate at which any of these social and economic trends will develop is hard to foresee, certain political implications seem clear. Briefly, it is the writer's view that none of these trends—toward a higher cultural level, toward increasing popular demands, or toward a more rational economy—constitutes a threat to the basic organization of the Soviet state or society.

Apart from its peculiarly totalitarian features, Soviet society is essentially bureaucratic and hierarchical, just as was prerevolutionary Russian society. The reliance of an industrial society on a state bureaucracy with vested interests—under a system which prevents the formation of organized opinion or pressure through professional groups, genuine trade unions, or political parties—obviously creates a certain tendency toward stability. A further stabilizing factor is class mobility; since the intelligentsia is expanding with each generation, it can absorb the ablest children of the masses without the regime's having to resort to purge or to demotion of the children of the already privileged.

As noted above, there is bound to be some tension between the economic desires of the masses and the intelligentsia, on one hand,

and the exigencies of regime policy on the other (requiring the continued priority of heavy industry). There is probably also a latent conflict between the desire for rationality and security on the part of the managerial and technocratic elements, and the desire for power and prestige on the part of the party men. But such conflicts do not imply any explosions or fundamental changes in the society.

In short, there is nothing to indicate that economic progress will force the ruling class, composed of party men and higher-level bureaucrats, to authorize the creation of rival forces—in the form of either parties or workers' trade unions. And there is nothing to indicate that such a challenge can come from below; neither the masses nor the intelligentsia have the means of overriding the ban on organized pressure groups. The leadership seems quite capable of maintaining the principle of the single hierarchy, of the single party, and of the legal *status quo* of the ruling bureaucracy. If any basic change is to take place, it will have to occur *within* the ruling elite—*i.e.*, inside the Communist Party.

Evolution and the Regime

What can be said, then, of the effects of progressing industrialization on the Communist regime itself, and specifically on those aspects of the regime which have come to be identified as "totalitarian." The question may be discussed under several heads: 1) Will the internal structure of the party undergo basic changes as a result of the spontaneous evolution of the economy and the society? 2) Will ideology continue, in the long run, to play the same role as it has in the past? 3) Is the movement still inspired by the same boundless ambition, by the same violence, or may it be expected eventually to rest content with what it is—that is, something less than universal?

The most crucial change in the party structure of recent years—the substitution of collective leadership for one-man dictatorship—is attributable to an historical event, to the death of an individual, rather than to the evolution of either the society or the regime. Nevertheless, the change was, in a way, logical. For the very nature of Stalin's power—or his misuse of it—dictated against the rise of a single successor. None of the members of the Presidium could face without anxiety the prospect of a repetition of the process whereby Stalin, little by little, had liquidated virtually all of the men who had once been his allies in the party leadership.

Some observers have held that Khrushchev's increasing domination of the ruling clique has already put an end to collective leadership. But Khrushchev has had to lean heavily on the support of allies to push through his policies, and in this sense group rule certainly continues. Acting as a group of leaders, the Presidium has appeared to be less indifferent to public demands, less able or less determined to carry out programs regardless of cost, than was Stalin with his unlimited personal power.

Whether further fundamental changes will take place in the structure and balance of power within the party is a matter of conjecture at this stage. However, it is worth noting that Khrushchev effected his purge of the so-called "anti-party" leaders [in June 1957] through appeal to the Central Committee, over the objections of a majority of the Presidium. Before that time the Presidium appeared to be just as independent of the Central Committee as Stalin had been. Since the authority of the proletariat originally passed from the party to the Politiburo (*i.e.*, Stalin) *through* the Central Committee, it is interesting to speculate on whether the reverse could take place. So far, there is no sign that any such basic shift in power is in the offing; if it were to occur, however, it would be directly attributable to the struggle for power rather than to broader forces of evolution.

The changeover from personal to collective leadership has been accompanied by the mitigation or abandonment of certain aspects of totalitarian rule. Perhaps the epitome of totalitarianism, certainly the feature most frequently mentioned, is the instrument of the purge, characterized by a combination of arbitrary police action (pragmatically unjustifiable), ideological terrorism and pure fantasy, defined by the inquisitor-theologians as more real than reality itself. The confession trials were the symbolic expression of this aspect of totalitarianism.

The collective leadership has renounced such excesses, and in doing so has revealed that it was never taken in by the mad logic of Stalinist ideological terrorism. At the same time, it may reasonably be objected that Khrushchev has not hesitated, on occasion, to employ it himself, as for instance when he has called Beria an "imperialist agent" or the Hungarian revolution a "counter-revolution." This leads us to perhaps the most crucial issue under consideration in this paper: that is the future role of ideology in the evolving Soviet society.

A Trend Toward Skepticism?

Communist ideology is based on a few simple ideas: the party *is* the proletariat; the seizure of power by the party is the *sine qua non* for the establishment of socialism. In places where the party has not taken over power, capitalism reigns and the masses are exploited. The inevitable culmination will be the extension throughout the world of regimes similar to the Soviet regime.

As is frequently pointed out, this orthodoxy has little connection with either Marx *or* reality. A society which has developed a great industrial complex side by side with a relentlessly low standard of living resembles what Marx called capitalism: a welfare state, albeit "capitalist," in which the additional resources accruing from technical progress are used for the benefit of the masses, does not. The dialecticians have been obliged to place an arbitrary interpretation on facts, often at variance with the most obvious reality. The element of fantasy in the great trials is merely the supreme expression of this logic.

It is the writer's belief that Soviet society, with the improvement in its standard of living, its culture and its technology, not only is becoming economically more rational, but must in the long run lose its ideological fervor. As it makes further progress and becomes more stable, as its technical level draws closer to that of industrialized Western societies, so both its militants and the people at large are bound to incline to some degree of skepticism. They will come to admit certain incontestable facts, such as the plurality of methods of industrialization, the raising of the standard of living in the West, *etc.* As soon as Polish writers and educators were able to talk freely, they proceeded to admit these facts and to escape from the absurd logic of Communist ideology.

Orthodoxy vs. Rationality

Does this mean that the dialecticians and Soviet leaders will cease to profess their belief in the universal mission, in the coming, through socialism, of a classless society? Certainly they have shown no such tendency thus far, leading to still another question: is it possible for Soviet society, under its present organization and ideological restrictions, to go very far in the direction of *either* economic rationalism *or* the return to common sense? In both respects, regime attitudes are the source of basic contradictions in the society, in conflict with evolutionary trends.

In the matter of ideology, the Soviet leadership is faced with a profound dilemma: it is hard to maintain a faith, but it is harder still to do without one. The leadership could, without too much difficulty, abandon the absurd excesses of Stalinist orthodoxy. Stalin had not only made a nightmare farce out of the system of trials and concessions. He had set himself up as the supreme arbiter in matters of biology and linguistics. He had decreed what, in literature, painting or music, conformed or failed to conform to socialist doctrine. But this kind of madness was not inherent in the system. It was simple for his successors to restore to biologists the right to accept the laws of genetics or to grant novelists or composers a greater measure of freedom in their work.

The leaders cannot, however, permit freedom of discussion to extend to the dogma itself, since its premises, as we have seen, are patently absurd and at variance with the facts. They do not want to return to Stalinist excesses, but they cannot permit any challenge of the dogma, which legitimizes their rule and provides the justification for the perpetuation of communism. The compromise is an uneasy one. The leaders are constantly threatening to deprive the intellectuals of some of the freedom they have been granted, while the intellectuals, on their side, are continuously straining to transcend the limits which have been set for them.

In Poland and Hungary, where the desire for intellectual freedom was reinforced by the desire for national freedom, the conflict was resolved by explosion. In Hungary, order has been restored— but it is a foreign order, a police and military order. In Poland, a large measure of intellectual freedom still exists, but the dogma *as such* has vanished. The regime still pursues a socialist path of development, but the people are aware that it is simply one of many systems, that it offers no mystical guarantee of the welfare of the masses.

In the Soviet Union, on the other hand, the dogma is still

intact; even though it is no longer as comprehensive or imperative as in the past, it continues to permeate the society. Certainly the leaders, judging by their pronouncements, still believe in the perpetuation of communism. They have not ceased to see themselves as engaged in a relentless struggle with the capitalist camp. Their outlook on the world is a long-term one, dominated by an over-simplified conception of good and evil.

This leads us to the second major contradiction in Soviet society—the obstacles which stand in the way of economic rationalization. From the inception of the Five-Year Plans, the objectives and methods of Soviet economic planning have been keyed to the concept of world struggle and to a desperate effort to catch up and surpass the level of industrialization in the capitalist countries. The system has the characteristics of what, in the West, would be a war economy: a rigid system of priorities has been established to ensure that the goals of heavy industry are achieved at all costs, the rest, if necessary, being sacrificed. When these goals have not been reached quickly enough, additional labor has been brought in from the countryside, and out-of-date industrial equipment has remained in operation.

Gradually however, transferable labor reserves have dwindled, with the result that increases have to come, in ever greater measure, from increased productivity. The problems of depreciation, renewal of equipment and economic planning are becoming more and more acute. Light industry and agriculture can no longer be sacrificed indiscriminately. The situation obviously demands an increasingly rational economy; but what kind of rationality is there in a planning system which concentrates not on satisfying demands but on the expansion of heavy industry, which refuses to grant enterprises more than a bare minimum of independence, which continues to allocate the country's resources on the basis of decisions taken at the top, and which still aims at authoritarian administration in so large a sector of the system? The recent highly-touted reform of industrial administration, while transferring various executive functions to newly-created regional authorities, does not basically change these governing principles of the Soviet economic system.

As long as the Soviet leaders adhere to Stalinist principles, insist on the priority of heavy industry, and maintain disproportionate ratios between investment as *vs.* consumption and heavy industry as *vs.* agriculture and light industry, the Soviet economy will continue to bear the marks of an authoritarian, police regime. The return to a normal peacetime economy depends, in the final analysis, on the modification of the objectives fixed by the leaders—in short on their outlook.

All of the foregoing suggests two conclusions. It is not true to say that the Soviet regime is becoming increasingly totalitarian as the society comes to need totalitarianism less and less. Many of the worst aberrations of the regime appear to have stemmed from the abnormality of Stalin himself; and they have disappeared with him. But neither is it true to maintain that the main features of the economic system and of the political regime are attributable to Stalin exclusively; they are rooted as firmly in the views and methods of the men who helped build the U.S.S.R. and who now rule it.

These conclusions, however, still do not answer the basic issues of the future; namely, *could* the regime change fundamentally without crumbling? And what freedoms is it capable of tolerating?

The Prospects for a Freer Society

When making a simplified analysis, a distinction can be drawn between three different kinds of freedom: firstly, what Montesquieu called security; secondly, the freedom the Hungarian intellectuals claimed, namely, the right to tell the truth about everything; and finally, Rousseau's freedom, participation in sovereignty, represented in the twentieth century by free elections and the multiparty political system.

Individual security is, as a rule, most favored by a parliamentary type of government. But many nondemocratic regimes give a fairly broad measure of security to those who do not engage in politics. The Tsarist regime, during its final period, interfered little with the life and liberty of citizens who minded their own business. In the Soviet Union, the insecurity of the Stalin era appears to have been greatly lessened by Stalin's successors. But as long as the Soviet regime continues to apply political sanctions in order to make the economy work, as long as it demands unquestioning respect for the dogma, the Soviet citizen will not be able to enjoy a true or stable measure of security.

To what extent could intellectuals and ordinary Soviet citizens be allowed to enjoy the second kind of freedom—to tell the truth about things, to exchange ideas, to visit the capitalist West, *etc.?* In the writer's view, the regime could, without endangering its own safety, grant musicians, painters and writers, more freedoms than it does at present. But the word "could" here has a double application; the question is whether the leaders of the regime and the party could bring themselves to grant such freedoms. Again, as long as they believe in their dogma, they will not allow it to be discussed, and there will be a harness on truth. Yet even if they themselves become skeptical, would they admit it publicly? For the future this is a matter of speculation; for the present, they certainly would not dare to do so. For even though there may be a tendency in Russia to evolve into a semi-ideological technocracy, the dogma is still a vital factor in less-advanced Communist countries and is crucial in justifying the unity of the socialist camp. To hope that the dogma will fade out in the near future would be over-optimistic.

In the long run, however, this writer holds to his view that increasing ideological skepticism is inevitable among both the leaders and the masses. Already the problems of Soviet planning are completely out of touch with the official economic textbooks, which are simplified versions of *Das Kapital*. Though tribute may still be paid to Marx, the day may come when an industrial society, concerned more with efficiency than with orthodoxy, will cease to follow the Lenin-Stalin ideology. Revolutionary fervor—though revived by the successes of communism in Asia and the Middle East—is nevertheless bound, in the end, to die down, and probably to die out.

Will the Soviet citizen eventually obtain Rousseau's freedom—participation in sovereignty—through either the development of factions within the party, or perhaps even the emergence of a multiparty system? The prospect of any move toward full-fledged political freedom in the Western style is so far beyond the scope of present or even predictable evolutionary trends that speculation would be foolish. Only time and the forces already at work in Soviet society will provide the clues to Russia's political future.

APPENDIX A

Constitution (Fundamental Law) of the Union of Soviet Socialist Republics*

CHAPTER I

The Social Structure

ARTICLE I

The Union of Soviet Socialist Republics is a socialist state of workers and peasants.

ARTICLE II

The political foundation of the U.S.S.R. is the Soviets of Working People's Deputies, which grew and became strong as a result of the overthrow of the power of the landlords and capitalists and the attainment of the dictatorship of the proletariat.

ARTICLE III

All power in the U.S.S.R. is vested in the working people of town and country as represented by the Soviets of Working People's Deputies.

ARTICLE IV

The economic foundation of the U.S.S.R. is the socialist system of economy and the socialist ownership of the instruments and means of production, firmly established as a result of the abolition of the capitalist system of economy, private ownership of the instruments and means of production, and the exploitation of man by man.

ARTICLE V

Socialist property in the U.S.S.R. exists either in the form of state property (belonging to the whole people) or in the form of co-operative and collective-farm property (the prop-

* As amended by the Seventh Session of the Fifth Supreme Soviet of the U.S.S.R.

From *Constitution (Fundamental Law) of the Union of Soviet Socialist Republics.* Moscow: Foreign Languages Publishing House, 1962.

erty of collective farms or co-operative societies).

ARTICLE VI

The land, its mineral wealth, waters, forests, the factories and mines, rail, water and air transport facilities, the banks, means of communication, large state-organised agricultural enterprises (state farms, machine and tractor stations, etc.), as well as municipal enterprises and the bulk of the dwelling-houses in the cities and industrial localities, are state property, that is, belong to the whole people.

ARTICLE VII

The enterprises of the collective farms and co-operative organisations, with their live-stock, buildings, implements, and output, are the common, socialist property of the collective farms and co-operative organisations.

Every collective-farm household, in addition to its basic income from the collective farm, has for its own use a small plot of land attached to the house and, as its own property, a dwelling-house, livestock, poultry, and minor agricultural implements —in conformity with the Rules of the Agricultural Artel.

ARTICLE VIII

The land occupied by the collective farms is made over to them for their free use for an unlimited time, that is, in perpetuity.

ARTICLE IX

In addition to the socialist system of economy, which is the predominant form of economy in the U.S.S.R., the law permits the small private undertakings of individual peasants and handicraftsmen based on their own labour and precluding the exploitation of the labour of others.

ARTICLE X

The right of citizens to own, as their personal property, income and savings derived from work, to own a dwelling-house and a supplementary husbandry, articles of household and articles of personal use and convenience, is protected by law, as is also the right of citizens to inherit personal property.

ARTICLE XI

The economic life of the U.S.S.R. is determined and guided by the state economic plan for the purpose of increasing the wealth of society as a whole, steadily raising the material and cultural standards of the working people and strengthening the independence of the U.S.S.R. and its capacity for defence.

ARTICLE XII

Work in the U.S.S.R. is a duty and a matter of honour for every able-bodied citizen, in accordance with the principle: "He who does not work, neither shall he eat."

The principle applied in the U.S.S.R. is that of socialism: "From each according to his ability, to each according to his work."

CHAPTER II

The State Structure

ARTICLE XIII

The Union of Soviet Socialist Republics is a federal state, formed on the basis of a voluntary union of equal Soviet Socialist Republics, namely:

The Russian Soviet Federative Socialist Republic,

The Ukrainian Soviet Socialist Republic,

The Byelorussian Soviet Socialist Republic,

The Uzbek Soviet Socialist Republic,

The Kazakh Soviet Socialist Republic,

The Georgian Soviet Socialist Republic,

The Azerbaijan Soviet Socialist Republic,

The Lithuanian Soviet Socialist Republic,

The Moldavian Soviet Socialist Republic,

The Latvian Soviet Socialist Republic,

The Kirghiz Soviet Socialist Republic,

The Tajik Soviet Socialist Republic,

The Armenian Soviet Socialist Republic,

The Turkmen Soviet Socialist Republic,

The Estonian Soviet Socialist Republic.

ARTICLE XIV

The jurisdiction of the Union of Soviet Socialist Republics, as represented by its higher organs of state power and organs of state administration, covers:

a) Representation of the U.S.S.R. in international relations, conclusion, ratification and denunciation of treaties of the U.S.S.R. with other states, establishment of general procedure governing the relations of the Union Republics with foreign states;

b) Questions of war and peace;

c) Admission of new republics into the U.S.S.R.;

d) Control over the observance of the Constitution of the U.S.S.R., and ensuring conformity of the Constitutions of the Union Republics with the Constitution of the U.S.S.R.;

e) Approval of changes to boundaries between Union Republics;

f) Approval of the formation of new Autonomous Republics

and Autonomous Regions within Union Republics;

g) Organisation of the defence of the U.S.S.R., direction of all the Armed Forces of the U.S.S.R., definition of guiding principles for the organisation of the military formations of the Union Republics;

h) Foreign trade on the basis of state monopoly;

i) Safeguarding the security of the state;

j) Determination of the economic plans of the U.S.S.R.;

k) Approval of the consolidated state budget of the U.S.S.R. and of the report on its implementation; fixing taxes and revenues that go to the Union, Republican and local budgets;

l) Administration of banks, industrial and agricultural institutions and enterprises and trading enterprises under Union jurisdiction; general direction of industry and building under Union-Republican jurisdiction;

m) Administration of transport and communications of all-Union importance;

n) Direction of the monetary and credit system;

o) Organisation of state insurance;

p) Contracting and granting of loans;

q) Definition of the basic principles of land tenure and of the use of mineral wealth, forests and waters;

r) Definition of the basic principles in the spheres of education and public health;

s) Organisation of a uniform system of economic statistics;

t) Definition of the fundamentals of labour legislation;

u) Definition of the fundamentals of legislation on the judicial system and judicial procedure and the fundamentals of criminal and civil legislation;

v) Legislation on Union citizenship; legislation on rights of foreigners;

w) Definition of the fundamentals of legislation on marriage and the family;

x) Promulgation of all-Union acts of amnesty.

ARTICLE XV

The sovereignty of the Union Republics is limited only in the spheres defined in Article XIV of the Constitution of the U.S.S.R. Outside of these spheres each Union Republic exercises state authority independently. The U.S.S.R. protects the sovereign rights of the Union Republics.

ARTICLE XVI

Each Union Republic has its own Constitution, which takes account of the specific features of the Republic and is drawn up in full conformity with the Constitution of the U.S.S.R.

ARTICLE XVII

The right freely to secede from the U.S.S.R. is reserved to every Union Republic.

ARTICLE XVIII

The territory of a Union Republic may not be altered without its consent.

ARTICLE XVIII-a

Each Union Republic has the right to enter into direct relations with foreign states and to conclude agreements and exchange diplomatic and consular representatives with them.

ARTICLE XVIII-b

Each Union Republic has its own Republican military formations.

ARTICLE XIX

The laws of the U.S.S.R. have the same force within the territory of every Union Republic.

ARTICLE XX

In the event of divergence between a law of a Union Republic and a law of the Union, the Union law shall prevail.

ARTICLE XXI

Uniform Union citizenship is established for citizens of the U.S.S.R.

Every citizen of a Union Republic is a citizen of the U.S.S.R.

ARTICLE XXII

The Russian Soviet Federative Socialist Republic includes the Bashkirian, Buryat, Daghestan, Kabardinian-Balkar, Kalmyk, Karelian, Komi, Mari, Mordovian, North Ossetian, Tatar, Tuva, Udmurt, Checheno-Ingush, Chuvash and Yakut Autonomous Soviet Socialist Republics; and the Adygei, Gorny Altai, Jewish, Karachai-Cherkess and Khakass Autonomous Regions.

ARTICLE XXIII

Repealed.

ARTICLE XXIV

The Azerbaijan Soviet Socialist Republic includes the Nakhichevan Autonomous Soviet Socialist Republic and the Nagorny Karabakh Autonomous Region.

ARTICLE XXV

The Georgian Soviet Socialist Republic includes the Abkhazian and Ajarian Autonomous Soviet Socialist Republics and the South Ossetian Autonomous Region.

ARTICLE XXVI

The Uzbek Soviet Socialist Republic includes the Kara-Kalpak Autonomous Soviet Socialist Republic.

ARTICLE XXVII

The Tajik Soviet Socialist Republic includes the Gorny Badakhshan Autonomous Region.

ARTICLE XXVIII

The settlement of questions pertaining to the regional or territorial administrative division of the Union Republics comes within the jurisdiction of the Union Republics.

ARTICLE XXIX

Repealed.

CHAPTER III

The Higher Organs of State Power in the Union of Soviet Socialist Republics

ARTICLE XXX

The highest organ of state power in the U.S.S.R. is the Supreme Soviet of the U.S.S.R.

ARTICLE XXXI

The Supreme Soviet of the U.S.S.R. exercises all rights vested in the Union of Soviet Socialist Republics in accordance with Article XIV of the Constitution, in so far as they do not, by virtue of the Constitution, come within the jurisdiction of organs of the U.S.S.R. that are accountable to the Supreme Soviet of the U.S.S.R., that is, the Presidium of the Supreme Soviet of the U.S.S.R., the Council of Ministers of the U.S.S.R., and the Ministries of the U.S.S.R.

ARTICLE XXXII

The legislative power of the U.S.S.R. is exercised exclusively by the Supreme Soviet of the U.S.S.R.

ARTICLE XXXIII

The Supreme Soviet of the U.S.S.R. consists of two Chambers: the Soviet of the Union and the Soviet of Nationalities.

ARTICLE XXXIV

The Soviet of the Union is elected by the citizens of the U.S.S.R. voting by election districts on the basis of one deputy for every 300,000 of the population.

ARTICLE XXXV

The Soviet of Nationalities is elected by the citizens of the U.S.S.R. voting by Union Republics, Autonomous Republics, Autonomous Regions, and National Areas on the basis of 25 deputies from each Union Republic, 11 deputies from each Autonomous Republic, 5 deputies from each Autonomous Region, and one deputy from each National Area.

ARTICLE XXXVI

The Supreme Soviet of the U.S.S.R. is elected for a term of four years.

ARTICLE XXXVII

The two Chambers of the Supreme Soviet of the U.S.S.R., the Soviet of the Union and the Soviet of Nationalities, have equal rights.

ARTICLE XXXVIII

The Soviet of the Union and the Soviet of Nationalities have equal powers to initiate legislation.

ARTICLE XXXIX

A law is considered adopted if passed by both Chambers of the Supreme Soviet of the U.S.S.R. by a simple majority vote in each.

ARTICLE XL

Laws passed by the Supreme Soviet of the U.S.S.R. are published in the languages of the Union Republics over the signatures of the President and Secretary of the Presidium of the Supreme Soviet of the U.S.S.R.

ARTICLE XLI

Sessions of the Soviet of the Union and of the Soviet of Nationalities begin and terminate simultaneously.

ARTICLE XLII

The Soviet of the Union elects a Chairman of the Soviet of the Union and four Vice-Chairmen.

ARTICLE XLIII

The Soviet of Nationalities elects a Chairman of the Soviet of Nationalities and four Vice-Chairmen.

ARTICLE XLIV

The Chairmen of the Soviet of the Union and the Soviet of Nationalities preside at the sittings of the respective Chambers and have charge of the conduct of their business and proceedings.

ARTICLE XLV

Joint sittings of the two Chambers of the Supreme Soviet of the U.S.S.R. are presided over alternately by the Chairman of the Soviet of the Union and the Chairman of the Soviet of Nationalities.

ARTICLE XLVI

Sessions of the Supreme Soviet of the U.S.S.R. are convened by the Presidium of the Supreme Soviet of the U.S.S.R. twice a year.

Extraordinary sessions are convened by the Presidium of the Supreme Soviet of the U.S.S.R. at its discretion or on the demand of one of the Union Republics.

ARTICLE XLVII

In the event of disagreement between the Soviet of the Union and the Soviet of Nationalities, the question is referred for settlement to a conciliation commission formed by the Chambers on a parity basis. If the conciliation commission fails to arrive at an agreement or if its decision fails to satisfy one of the Chambers, the question is considered for a second time by the Chambers. Failing agreement between the two Chambers, the Presidium of the Supreme Soviet of the U.S.S.R. dissolves the Supreme Soviet of the U.S.S.R. and orders new elections.

ARTICLE XLVIII

The Supreme Soviet of the U.S.S.R. at a joint sitting of the two Chambers elects the Presidium of the Supreme Soviet of the U.S.S.R., consisting of a President of the Presidium of the Supreme Soviet of the U.S.S.R., fifteen Vice-Presidents —one from each Union Republic, a Secretary of the Presidium and sixteen members of the Presidium of the Supreme Soviet of the U.S.S.R.

The Presidium of the Supreme Soviet of the U.S.S.R. is accountable to the Supreme Soviet of the U.S.S.R. for all its activities.

ARTICLE XLIX

The Presidium of the Supreme Soviet of the U.S.S.R.:

a) Convenes the sessions of the Supreme Soviet of the U.S.S.R.;

b) Issues decrees;

c) Interprets the laws of the U.S.S.R. in operation;

d) Dissolves the Supreme Soviet of the U.S.S.R. in conformity with Article XLVII of the Constitution of the U.S.S.R. and orders new elections;

e) Conducts nation-wide polls (referendums) on its own initiative or on the demand of one of the Union Republics;

f) Annuls decisions and orders of the Council of Ministers of the U.S.S.R. and of the Councils of Ministers of the Union Republics if they do not conform to law;

g) In the intervals between sessions of the Supreme Soviet of the U.S.S.R., releases and appoints Ministers of the U.S.S.R. on the recommendation of the Chairman of the Council of Ministers of the U.S.S.R., subject to subsequent confirmation by the Supreme Soviet of the U.S.S.R.;

h) Institutes decorations (Orders and Medals) and titles of honour of the U.S.S.R.;

i) Awards Orders and Medals and confers titles of honour of the U.S.S.R.;

j) Exercises the right of pardon;

k) Institutes military titles, diplomatic ranks and other special titles;

l) Appoints and removes the

high command of the Armed Forces of the U.S.S.R.;

m) In the intervals between sessions of the Supreme Soviet of the U.S.S.R., proclaims a state of war in the event of military attack on the U.S.S.R., or when necessary to fulfil international treaty obligations concerning mutual defence against aggression;

n) Orders general or partial mobilisation;

o) Ratifies and denounces international treaties of the U.S.S.R.;

p) Appoints and recalls plenipotentiary representatives of the U.S.S.R. to foreign states;

q) Receives the letters of credence and recall of diplomatic representatives accredited to it by foreign states;

r) Proclaims martial law in the U.S.S.R. in the interests of separate localities or throughout the defence of the U.S.S.R. or of the maintenance of law and order and the security of the state.

ARTICLE L

The Soviet of the Union and the Soviet of Nationalities elect Credentials Committees to verify the credentials of the members of the respective Chambers.

On the report of the Credentials Committees, the Chambers decide whether to recognise the credentials of deputies or to annul their election.

ARTICLE LI

The Supreme Soviet of the U.S.S.R., when it deems necessary, appoints commissions of investigation and audit on any matter.

It is the duty of all institutions and officials to comply with the demands of such commissions and to submit to them all necessary materials and documents.

ARTICLE LII

A member of the Supreme Soviet of the U.S.S.R. may not be prosecuted or arrested without the consent of the Supreme Soviet of the U.S.S.R., or, when the Supreme Soviet of the U.S.S.R. is not in session, without the consent of the Presidium of the Supreme Soviet of the U.S.S.R.

ARTICLE LIII

On the expiration of the term of office of the Supreme Soviet of the U.S.S.R., or on its dissolution prior to the expiration of its term of office, the Presidium of the Supreme Soviet of the U.S.S.R. retains its powers until the newly-elected Supreme Soviet of the U.S.S.R. shall have formed a new Presidium of the Supreme Soviet of the U.S.S.R.

ARTICLE LIV

On the expiration of the term of office of the Supreme Soviet of the U.S.S.R., or in the event of its dissolution prior to the expiration of its term of office, the Presidium of the Supreme Soviet of the U.S.S.R. orders new elections to be held within a period not exceeding two months from the date of expiration of the term of office or dissolution of the Supreme Soviet of the U.S.S.R.

ARTICLE LV

The newly-elected Supreme Soviet of the U.S.S.R. is convened by the outgoing Presidium of the Supreme Soviet of the U.S.S.R. not later than three months after the elections.

ARTICLE LVI

The Supreme Soviet of the U.S.S.R., at a joint sitting of the two Chambers, appoints the Government of the U.S.S.R., namely, the Council of Ministers of the U.S.S.R.

CHAPTER IV

The Higher Organs of State Power in the Union Republics

ARTICLE LVII

The highest organ of state power in a Union Republic is the Supreme Soviet of the Union Republic.

ARTICLE LVIII

The Supreme Soviet of a Union Republic is elected by the citizens of the Republic for a term of four years.

The basis of representation is established by the Constitution of the Union Republic.

ARTICLE LIX

The Supreme Soviet of a Union Republic is the sole legislative organ of the Republic.

ARTICLE LX

The Supreme Soviet of a Union Republic:

a) Adopts the Constitution of the Republic and amends it in conformity with Article XVI of the Constitution of the U.S.S.R.;

b) Confirms the Constitutions of the Autonomous Republics forming part of it and defines the boundaries of their territories;

c) Approves the economic plan and the budget of the Republic and forms economic administration areas;

d) Exercises the right of amnesty and pardon of citizens sentenced by the judicial organs of the Union Republic;

e) Decides questions of representation of the Union Republic in its international relations;

f) Determines the manner of organising the Republic's military formations.

ARTICLE LXI

The Supreme Soviet of a Union Republic elects the Presidium of the Supreme Soviet of the Union Republic, consisting of a President of the Presidium of the Supreme Soviet of the Union Republic, Vice-Presidents, a Secretary of the Presidium and members of the Presidium of the Supreme Soviet of the Union Republic.

The powers of the Presidium of the Supreme Soviet of a Union Republic are defined by the Constitution of the Union Republic.

ARTICLE LXII

The Supreme Soviet of a Union Republic elects a Chairman and Vice-Chairmen to conduct its sittings.

ARTICLE LXIII

The Supreme Soviet of a Union Republic appoints the Government of the Union Republic, namely, the Council of Ministers of the Union Republic.

CHAPTER V

The Organs of State Administration of the Union of Soviet Socialist Republics

ARTICLE LXIV

The highest executive and administrative organ of the state power of the Union of Soviet Socialist Republics is the Council of Ministers of the U.S.S.R.

ARTICLE LXV

The Council of Ministers of the U.S.S.R. is responsible and accountable to the Supreme Soviet of the U.S.S.R., or, in the intervals between sessions of the Supreme Soviet, to the Presidium of the Supreme Soviet of the U.S.S.R.

ARTICLE LXVI

The Council of Ministers of the U.S.S.R. issues decisions and orders on the basis and in pursuance of the laws in operation, and verifies their execution.

ARTICLE LXVII

Decisions and orders of the Council of Ministers of the U.S.S.R. are binding throughout the territory of the U.S.S.R.

ARTICLE LXVIII

The Council of Ministers of the U.S.S.R.:

a) Co-ordinates and directs the work of the all-Union and Union-Republican Ministries of the U.S.S.R. and of other institutions under its jurisdiction, exercises guidance of the Economic Councils of the Union Republics and those of economic administration areas through the Councils of Ministers of the Union Republics;

b) Adopts measures to carry out the economic plan and the state budget, and to strengthen the credit and monetary system;

c) Adopts measures for the maintenance of law and order, for the protection of the interests of the state, and for the safeguarding of the rights of citizens;

d) Exercises general guidance in the sphere of relations with foreign states;

e) Fixes the annual contingent of citizens to be called up for military service and directs the general organisation of the Armed Forces of the country;

f) Sets up, whenever necessary, special Committees and Central Boards under the Council of Ministers of the U.S.S.R. for economic and cultural affairs and defence.

ARTICLE LXIX

The Council of Ministers of the U.S.S.R. has the right, in respect of those branches of administration and economy which come within the jurisdiction of the U.S.S.R., to suspend decisions and orders of the Councils of Ministers of the Union Republics and of the Economic Councils of the Republics and those of the economic administration areas, and to annul orders and instructions of Ministers of the U.S.S.R.

ARTICLE LXX

The Council of Ministers of the U.S.S.R. is appointed by the Supreme Soviet of the U.S.S.R. and consists of:

The Chairman of the Council of Ministers of the U.S.S.R.;

The First Vice-Chairmen of the Council of Ministers of the U.S.S.R.;

The Vice-Chairmen of the Council of Ministers of the U.S.S.R.;

The Ministers of the U.S.S.R.;

The Chairman of the State Planning Committee of the Council of Ministers of the U.S.S.R.;

The Chairman of the Commission of State Control of the Council of Ministers of the U.S.S.R.;

The Chairman of the State Labour and Wages Committee of the Council of Ministers of the U.S.S.R.;

The Chairman of the State Research Co-ordination Committee of the Council of Ministers of the U.S.S.R.;

The Chairman of the State Committee on Vocational and Technical Education of the Council of Ministers of the U.S.S.R.;

The Chairman of the State Automation and Machine-Building Committee of the Council of Ministers of the U.S.S.R.;

The Chairman of the State Committee of the Council of Ministers of the U.S.S.R. on Aircraft Technology;

The Chairman of the State Committee of the Council of Ministers of the U.S.S.R. on Defence Technology;

The Chairman of the State Committee of the Council of Ministers of the U.S.S.R. on Radio-Electronics;

The Chairman of the State Committee of the Council of Ministers of the U.S.S.R. on Electronic Technology;

The Chairman of the State Committee on Shipbuilding of the Council of Ministers of the U.S.S.R.;

The Chairman of the State Committee on Chemistry of the Council of Ministers of the U.S.S.R.;

The Chairman of the State Committee of the Council of Ministers of the U.S.S.R. on Ferrous and Non-Ferrous Metallurgy;

The Chairman of the State Committee of the Council of Ministers of the U.S.S.R. on Fuel Industry;

The Chairman of the Atomic Energy State Committee of the Council of Ministers of the U.S.S.R.;

The Chairman of the State Building Committee of the Council of Ministers of the U.S.S.R.;

The Chairman of the State Committee of the Council of Ministers of the U.S.S.R. for Farm Produce Purchases;

The Chairman of the State Foreign Economic Relations Committee of the Council of Ministers of the U.S.S.R.;

The Chairman of the State Foreign Cultural Relations Committee of the Council of Ministers of the U.S.S.R.;

The Chairman of the State Security Committee under the Council of Ministers of the U.S.S.R.;

The Chairman of the All-Union Board for the Sale of Agricultural Machinery, Spare Parts, Mineral Fertiliser and Other Production and Technical Supplies, Organisation of Machinery Maintenance and Service on State and Collective Farms;

The Chairman of the Administrative Board of the State Bank of the U.S.S.R.;

The Chief of the Central Statistical Board under the Council of Ministers of the U.S.S.R.;

The Chairman of the State Council on Economic Research of the Council of Ministers of the U.S.S.R.

The Council of Ministers of the U.S.S.R. includes the Chairmen of the Councils of Ministers of the Union Republics by virtue of their office.

ARTICLE LXXI

The Government of the U.S.S.R. or a Minister of the U.S.S.R. to whom a question of a member of the Supreme Soviet of the U.S.S.R. is addressed must give a verbal or written reply in the respective Chamber within a period not exceeding three days.

ARTICLE LXXII

The Ministers of the U.S.S.R. direct the branches of state administration which come within the jurisdiction of the U.S.S.R.

ARTICLE LXXIII

The Ministers of the U.S.S.R., within the limits of the jurisdiction of their respective Ministries, issue orders and instructions on the basis and in pursuance of the laws in operation, and also of decisions and orders of the Council of Ministers of the U.S.S.R., and verify their execution.

ARTICLE LXXIV

The Ministries of the U.S.S.R. are either all-Union or Union-Republican Ministries.

ARTICLE LXXV

Each all-Union Ministry directs the branch of state administration entrusted to it throughout the territory of the U.S.S.R. either directly or through bodies appointed by it.

ARTICLE LXXVI

The Union-Republican Ministries, as a rule, direct the branches of state administration entrusted to them through corresponding Ministries of the Union Republics; they administer directly only a definite and limited number of enterprises according to a list confirmed by the Presidium of the Supreme Soviet of the U.S.S.R.

ARTICLE LXXVII

The following Ministries are all-Union Ministries:

The Ministry of Foreign Trade;

The Ministry of Merchant Marine;

The Ministry of Railways;

The Ministry of the Medium Machine-Building Industry;

The Ministry of Power Station Construction;

The Ministry of Transport Construction.

ARTICLE LXXVIII

The following Ministries are Union-Republican Ministries:

The Ministry of Higher and Secondary Special Education;

The Ministry of Geological Survey and Conservation of Mineral Resources;

The Ministry of Public Health;

The Ministry of Foreign Affairs;

The Ministry of Culture;

The Ministry of Defence;

The Ministry of Communications;

The Ministry of Agriculture;

The Ministry of Finance.

CHAPTER VI

The Organs of State Administration of the Union Republics

ARTICLE LXXIX

The highest executive and administrative organ of the state power of a Union Republic is the Council of Ministers of the Union Republic.

ARTICLE LXXX

The Council of Ministers of a Union Republic is responsible and accountable to the Supreme Soviet of the Union Republic, or, in the intervals between sessions of the Supreme Soviet of the Union Republic, to the Presidium of the Supreme Soviet of the Union Republic.

ARTICLE LXXXI

The Council of Ministers of a Union Republic issues decisions and orders on the basis and in pursuance of the laws in operation of the U.S.S.R. and of the Union Republic, and of the decisions and orders of the Council of Ministers of the U.S.S.R., and verifies their execution.

ARTICLE LXXXII

The Council of Ministers of a Union Republic has the right to suspend decisions and orders of the Councils of Ministers of its Autonomous Republics, and to annul decisions and orders of the Executive Committees of the Soviets of Working People's Deputies of its Territories, Regions and Autonomous Regions, as well as decisions and orders of the Economic Council of the Union Republic and of those of the economic administration areas.

ARTICLE LXXXIII

The Council of Ministers of a Union Republic is appointed by the Supreme Soviet of the Union Republic and consists of:

The Chairman of the Council of Ministers of the Union Republic;

The Vice-Chairmen of the Council of Ministers;

The Ministers;

The Chairmen of State Committees, Commissions, and the heads of other departments of the Council of Ministers set up by the Supreme Soviet of the Union Republic in conformity with the Constitution of the Union Republic.

ARTICLE LXXXIV

The Ministers of a Union Republic direct the branches of state administration which come within the jurisdiction of the Union Republic.

ARTICLE LXXXV

The Ministers of a Union Republic, within the limits of the

jurisdiction of their respective Ministries, issue orders and instructions on the basis and in pursuance of the laws of the U.S.S.R. and of the Union Republic, of the decisions and orders of the Council of Ministers of the U.S.S.R. and the Council of Ministers of the Union Republic, and of the orders and instructions of the Union-Republican Ministries of the U.S.S.R.

ARTICLE LXXXVI

The Ministries of a Union Republic are either Union-Republican or Republican Ministries.

ARTICLE LXXXVII

Each Union-Republican Ministry directs the branch of state administration entrusted to it, and is subordinate both to the Council of Ministers of the Union Republic and to the corresponding Union-Republican Ministry of the U.S.S.R.

ARTICLE LXXXVIII

Each Republican Ministry directs the branch of state administration entrusted to it, and is directly subordinate to the Council of Ministers of the Union Republic.

ARTICLE LXXXVIII-a

The Economic Councils of the economic administration areas direct the branches of economic activity entrusted to them, and are directly subordinate to the Council of Ministers of the Union Republic.

Economic Councils of economic administration areas in Union Republics where Republican Economic Councils exist, are subordinate in their activities to both the Council of Ministers and the Economic Council of the Union Republic.

The Economic Councils of the economic administration areas issue within their jurisdiction decisions and orders on the basis and in pursuance of the laws of the U.S.S.R. and the Union Republic and decisions and orders of the Council of Ministers of the U.S.S.R. and the Council of Ministers of the Union Republic.

ARTICLE LXXXVIII-b

The Republican Economic Council co-ordinates the economic activities of the Economic Councils of economic administration areas and is subordinate directly to the Council of Ministers of the Union Republic.

The Republican Economic Council, within the limits of its jurisdiction, issues decisions and orders on the basis and in pursuance of the laws of the U.S.S.R. and the Union Republic, orders and instructions of the Council of Ministers of the

U.S.S.R. and the Council of Ministers of the Union Republic.

The Republican Economic Council has the right to suspend decisions and orders of the Economic Councils of the economic administration areas.

CHAPTER VII

The Higher Organs of State Power in the Autonomous Soviet Socialist Republics

ARTICLE LXXXIX

The highest organ of state power in an Autonomous Republic is the Supreme Soviet of the Autonomous Republic.

ARTICLE XC

The Supreme Soviet of an Autonomous Republic is elected by the citizens of the Republic for a term of four years on a basis of representation established by the Constitution of the Autonomous Republic.

ARTICLE XCI

The Supreme Soviet of an Autonomous Republic is the sole legislative organ of the Autonomous Republic.

ARTICLE XCII

Each Autonomous Republic has its own Constitution, which takes account of the specific features of the Autonomous Republic and is drawn up in full conformity with the Constitution of the Union Republic.

ARTICLE XCIII

The Supreme Soviet of an Autonomous Republic elects the Presidium of the Supreme Soviet of the Autonomous Republic and appoints the Council of Ministers of the Autonomous Republic, in accordance with its Constitution.

CHAPTER VIII

The Local Organs of State Power

ARTICLE XCIV

The organs of state power in Territories, Regions, Autonomous Regions, Areas, Districts, cities and rural localities (stanitsas, villages, hamlets, kishlaks, auls) are the Soviets of Working People's Deputies.

ARTICLE XCV

The Soviets of Working People's Deputies of Territories, Regions, Autonomous Regions, Areas, Districts, cities and rural localities (stanitsas, villages, hamlets, kishlaks, auls) are elected by the working people of the respective Territories, Regions, Autonomous Regions, Areas, Districts, cities and rural localities for a term of two years.

ARTICLE XCVI

The basis of representation for Soviets of Working People's Deputies is determined by the Constitutions of the Union Republics.

ARTICLE XCVII

The Soviets of Working People's Deputies direct the work of the organs of administration subordinate to them, ensure the maintenance of law and order, the observance of the laws and the protection of the rights of citizens, direct local economic and cultural affairs and determine and approve local budgets.

ARTICLE XCVIII

The Soviets of Working People's Deputies adopt decisions and issue orders within the limits of the powers vested in them by the laws of the U.S.S.R. and of the Union Republic.

ARTICLE XCIX

The executive and administrative organ of the Soviet of Working People's Deputies of a Territory, Region, Autonomous Region, Area, District, city or rural locality is the Executive Committee elected by it, consisting of a Chairman, Vice-Chairmen, a Secretary and members.

ARTICLE C

The executive and administrative organ of the Soviet of Working People's Deputies in a small locality, in accordance with the Constitution of the Union Republic, is the Chairman, the Vice-Chairman and the Secretary elected by the Soviet of Working People's Deputies.

ARTICLE CI

The executive organs of the Soviets of Working People's Deputies are directly accountable both to the Soviets of Working People's Deputies which elected them and to the executive organ of the superior Soviet of Working People's Deputies.

CHAPTER IX

The Courts and the Procurator's Office

ARTICLE CII

In the U.S.S.R. justice is administered by the Supreme Court of the U.S.S.R., the Supreme Courts of the Union Republics, the Courts of the Territories, Regions, Autonomous Republics, Autonomous Regions and Areas, the Special Courts of the U.S.S.R. established by decision of the Supreme Soviet of the U.S.S.R., and the People's Courts.

ARTICLE CIII

In all Courts cases are tried with the participation of people's assessors, except in cases specially provided for by law.

ARTICLE CIV

The Supreme Court of the U.S.S.R. is the highest judicial organ. The Supreme Court of the U.S.S.R. is charged with the supervision of the judicial activities of all the judicial organs of the U.S.S.R. and of the Union Republics within the limits established by law.

ARTICLE CV

The Supreme Court of the U.S.S.R. is elected by the Supreme Soviet of the U.S.S.R. for a term of five years.

The Supreme Court of the U.S.S.R. includes the Chairmen of the Supreme Courts of the Union Republics by virtue of their office.

ARTICLE CVI

The Supreme Courts of the Union Republics are elected by the Supreme Soviets of the Union Republics for a term of five years.

ARTICLE CVII

The Supreme Courts of the Autonomous Republics are elected by the Supreme Soviets of the Autonomous Republics for a term of five years.

ARTICLE CVIII

The Courts of Territories, Regions, Autonomous Regions and Areas are elected by the Soviets of Working People's Deputies of the respective Territories, Regions, Autonomous Regions or Areas for a term of five years.

ARTICLE CIX

People's judges of District (City) People's Courts are elected by the citizens of the districts (cities) on the basis of universal, direct and equal suffrage by secret ballot for a term of five years.

People's Assessors of District (City) People's Courts are elected at general meetings of industrial, office and professional workers, and peasants in the place of their work or residence, and of servicemen in military units, for a term of two years.

ARTICLE CX

Judicial proceedings are conducted in the language of the Union Republic, Autonomous Republic or Autonomous Region, persons not knowing this language being guaranteed the opportunity of fully acquainting themselves with the material of the case through an interpreter and likewise the right to use their own language in court.

ARTICLE CXI

In all Courts of the U.S.S.R. cases are heard in public, unless otherwise provided for by law, and the accused is guaranteed the right to defence.

ARTICLE CXII

Judges are independent and subject only to the law.

ARTICLE CXIII

Supreme supervisory power to ensure the strict observance of the law by all Ministries and institutions subordinated to them, as well as by people in office and citizens of the U.S.S.R. generally, is vested in the Procurator-General of the U.S.S.R.

ARTICLE CXIV

The Procurator-General of the U.S.S.R. is appointed by the Supreme Soviet of the U.S.S.R. for a term of seven years.

ARTICLE CXV

Procurators of Republics, Territories, Regions, Autonomous Republics and Autonomous Regions are appointed by the Procurator-General of the U.S.S.R. for a term of five years.

ARTICLE CXVI

Area, district and city procurators are appointed by the Procurators of the Union Republics, subject to the approval of the Procurator-General of the U.S.S.R., for a term of five years.

ARTICLE CXVII

The organs of the Procurator's Office perform their functions independently of any local organs whatsoever, being subordinate solely to the Procurator-General of the U.S.S.R.

CHAPTER X

Fundamental Rights and Duties of Citizens

ARTICLE CXVIII

Citizens of the U.S.S.R. have the right to work, that is, the right to guaranteed employment and payment for their work in accordance with its quantity and quality.

The right to work is ensured by the socialist organisation of the national economy, the steady growth of the productive forces of Soviet society, the elimination of the possibility of economic crises, and the abolition of unemployment.

ARTICLE CXIX

Citizens of the U.S.S.R. have the right to rest and leisure.

The right to rest and leisure is ensured by the establishment of a seven-hour day for industrial, office, and professional workers, the reduction of the working day to six hours for arduous trades and to four hours in shops where conditions of work are particularly arduous; by the institution of annual vacations with full pay for industrial, office, and professional workers, and by the provision of a wide network of sanatoriums, holiday homes and clubs for the accommodation of the working people.

ARTICLE CXX

Citizens of the U.S.S.R. have the right to maintenance in old age and also in case of sickness or disability.

This right is ensured by the extensive development of social insurance of industrial, office, and professional workers at state expense, free medical service for the working people, and the provision of a wide network of health resorts for the use of the working people.

ARTICLE CXXI

Citizens of the U.S.S.R. have the right to education.

This right is ensured by universal compulsory eight-year education; by extensive development of secondary polytechnical education, vocational-technical education, and secondary special and higher education based on close ties between the school, real life and production activities; by the utmost devel-opment of evening and extramural education; by free education in all schools; by a system of state grants; by instruction in schools in the native language, and by the organisation of free vocational, technical and agronomic training for the working people in the factories, state farms, and collective farms.

ARTICLE CXXII

Women in the U.S.S.R. are accorded all rights on an equal footing with men in all spheres of economic, government, cultural, political, and other social activity.

The possibility of exercising these rights is ensured by women being accorded the same rights as men to work, payment for work, rest and leisure, social insurance and education, and also by state protection of the interests of mother and child, state aid to mothers of large families and to unmarried mothers, maternity leave with full pay, and the provision of a wide network of maternity homes, nurseries and kindergartens.

ARTICLE CXXIII

Equality of rights of citizens of the U.S.S.R., irrespective of their nationality or race, in all spheres of economic, government, cultural, political and other social activity, is an indefeasible law.

Any direct or indirect restriction of the rights of, or, conversely, the establishment of any direct or indirect privileges for, citizens on account of their race or nationality, as well as any advocacy of racial or national exclusiveness or hatred and contempt, are punishable by law.

ARTICLE CXXIV

In order to ensure to citizens freedom of conscience, the church in the U.S.S.R. is separated from the state, and the school from the church. Freedom of religious worship and freedom of anti-religious propaganda is recognised for all citizens.

ARTICLE CXXV

In conformity with the interests of the working people, and in order to strengthen the socialist system, the citizens of the U.S.S.R. are guaranteed by law:

a) freedom of speech;

b) freedom of the press;

c) freedom of assembly, including the holding of mass meetings;

d) freedom of street processions and demonstrations.

These civil rights are ensured by placing at the disposal of the working people and their organisations printing presses, stocks of paper, public buildings, the streets, communications facilities and other material requisites for the exercise of these rights.

ARTICLE CXXVI

In conformity with the interests of the working people, and in order to develop the organisational initiative and political activity of the masses of the people, citizens of the U.S.S.R. are guaranteed the right to unite in public organisations: trade unions, co-operative societies, youth organisations, sport and defence organisations, cultural, technical and scientific societies; and the most active and politically-conscious citizens in the ranks of the working class, working peasants and working intelligentsia voluntarily unite in the Communist Party of the Soviet Union, which is the vanguard of the working people in their struggle to build communist society and is the leading core of all organisations of the working people, both public and state.

ARTICLE CXXVII

Citizens of the U.S.S.R. are guaranteed inviolability of the person. No person may be placed under arrest except by decision of a court or with the sanction of a procurator.

ARTICLE CXXVIII

The inviolability of the homes of citizens and privacy of correspondence are protected by law.

The U.S.S.R. affords the right of asylum to foreign citizens persecuted for defending the interests of the working people, or for scientific activities, or for struggling for national liberation.

It is the duty of every citizen of the U.S.S.R. to abide by the Constitution of the Union of Soviet Socialist Republics, to observe the laws, to maintain labour discipline, honestly to perform public duties, and to respect the rules of socialist society.

It is the duty of every citizen of the U.S.S.R. to safeguard and fortify public, socialist property as the sacred and inviolable foundation of the Soviet system, as the source of the wealth and might of the country, as the source of the prosperity and culture of all the working people.

Persons committing offences against public, socialist property are enemies of the people.

Universal military service is law.

Military service in the Armed Forces of the U.S.S.R. is the honourable duty of citizens of the U.S.S.R.

To defend the country is the sacred duty of every citizen of the U.S.S.R. Treason to the Motherland—violation of the oath of allegiance, desertion to the enemy, impairing the military power of the state, espionage—is punishable with all the severity of the law as the most heinous of crimes.

CHAPTER XI

The Electoral System

Members of all Soviets of Working People's Deputies—of the Supreme Soviet of the U.S.S.R., the Supreme Soviets of the Union Republics, the Soviets of Working People's Deputies of the Territories and Regions, the Supreme Soviets of the Autonomous Republics, the Soviets of Working People's Deputies of the Autonomous Regions, and the Area, District, city and rural (stanitsa, village, hamlet, kishlak, aul) Soviets of Working People's Deputies—are chosen by the electors on the basis of universal, equal and direct suffrage by secret ballot.

ARTICLE CXXXV

Elections of deputies are universal: all citizens of the U.S.S.R. who have reached the age of eighteen, irrespective of race or nationality, sex, religion, education, domicile, social origin, property status or past activities, have the right to vote in the election of deputies, with the exception of persons who have been legally certified insane.

Every citizen of the U.S.S.R. who has reached the age of twenty-three is eligible for election to the Supreme Soviet of the U.S.S.R., irrespective of race or nationality, sex, religion, education, domicile, social origin, property status or past activities.

ARTICLE CXXXVI

Elections of deputies are equal: each citizen has one vote; all citizens participate in elections on an equal footing.

ARTICLE CXXXVII

Women have the right to elect and be elected on equal terms with men.

ARTICLE CXXXVIII

Citizens serving in the Armed Forces of the U.S.S.R. have the right to elect and be elected on equal terms with all other citizens.

ARTICLE CXXXIX

Elections of deputies are direct: all Soviets of Working People's Deputies, from rural and city Soviets of Working People's Deputies to the Supreme Soviet of the U.S.S.R., are elected by the citizens by direct vote.

ARTICLE CXL

Voting at elections of deputies is secret.

ARTICLE CXLI

Candidates are nominated for each constituency.

The right to nominate candidates is secured to public organisations and societies of the working people: Communist Party organisations, trade unions, co-operatives, youth organisations and cultural societies.

ARTICLE CXLII

It is the duty of every deputy to report to his electors on his work and on the work of his Soviet of Working People's Deputies, and he may be recalled at any time upon decision of a majority of the electors in the manner established by law.

CHAPTER XII

Arms, Flag, Capital

ARTICLE CXLIII

The arms of the Union of Soviet Socialist Republics are a sickle and hammer against a globe depicted in the rays of the sun and surrounded by ears of grain, with the inscription "Workers of All Countries, Unite!" in the languages of the Union Republics. At the top of the arms is a five-pointed star.

ARTICLE CXLIV

The state flag of the Union of Soviet Socialist Republics is of red cloth with the sickle and hammer depicted in gold in the upper corner near the staff and above them a five-pointed red star bordered in gold. The ratio of the width to the length is 1:2.

ARTICLE CXLV

The capital of the Union of Soviet Socialist Republics is the City of Moscow.

CHAPTER XIII

Procedure for Amending the Constitution

ARTICLE CXLVI

The Constitution of the U.S.S.R. may be amended only by decision of the Supreme Soviet of the U.S.S.R. adopted by a majority of not less than two-thirds of the votes in each of its Chambers.

APPENDIX B

Rules of the Communist Party of the

Soviet Union

Adopted by the 22nd Congress of the CPSU

October 31, 1961

The Communist Party of the Soviet Union is the tried and tested militant vanguard of the Soviet people, which unites, on a voluntary basis, the more advanced, politically more conscious section of the working class, collective-farm peasantry and intelligentsia of the U.S.S.R.

Founded by V. I. Lenin as the vanguard of the working class, the Communist Party has travelled a glorious road of struggle, and brought the working class and the working peasantry to the victory of the Great October Socialist Revolution and to the establishment of the dictatorship of the proletariat in the U.S.S.R. Under the leadership of the Communist Party, the exploiting classes were abolished in the Soviet Union, and the moral and political unity of Soviet society has taken shape and grown in strength. Socialism has triumphed completely and finally. The Communist Party, the party of the working class, has today become the party of the Soviet people as a whole.

The Party exists for, and serves, the people. It is the highest form of socio-political organisation, and is the leading and guiding force of Soviet society. It directs the great creative activity of the Soviet people, and imparts an organised, planned, and scientifically-based character to their struggle to achieve the ultimate goal, the victory of communism.

The C.P.S.U. bases its work on unswerving adherence to the Lenin-

From *Rules of the Communist Party of the Soviet Union*, pp. 5–31. Moscow: Foreign Languages Publishing House, 1961.

ist standards of Party life—the principle of collective leadership, the promotion, in every possible way, of inner-Party democracy, the activity and initiative of the Communists, criticism and self-criticism.

Ideological and organisational unity, monolithic cohesion of its ranks, and a high degree of conscious discipline on the part of all Communists are an inviolable law of the C.P.S.U. All manifestations of factionalism and group activity are incompatible with Marxist-Leninist Party principles, and with Party membership.

In all its activities, the C.P.S.U. takes guidance from Marxist-Leninist theory and the Programme based on it, which defines the fundamental tasks of the Party for the period of the construction of communist society.

In creatively developing Marxism-Leninism, the C.P.S.U. vigorously combats all manifestations of revisionism and dogmatism, which are utterly alien to revolutionary theory.

The Communist Party of the Soviet Union is an integral part of the international Communist and working-class movement. It firmly adheres to the tried and tested Marxist-Leninist principles of proletarian internationalism; it actively promotes the unity of the international Communist and working-class movement as a whole, and fraternal ties with the great army of the Communists of all countries.

I

Party Members, Their Duties and Rights

1. Membership of the C.P.S.U. is open to any citizen of the Soviet Union who accepts the Programme and the Rules of the Party, takes an active part in communist construction, works in one of the Party organisations, carries out all Party decisions, and pays membership dues.

2. It is the duty of a Party member:

(a) to work for the creation of the material and technical basis of communism; to serve as an example of the communist attitude towards labour; to raise labour productivity; to display the initiative in all that is new and progressive; to support and propagate advanced methods; to master techniques, to improve his skill; to protect and increase public socialist property, the mainstay of the might and prosperity of the Soviet country;

(b) to put Party decisions firmly and steadfastly into effect; to explain the policy of the Party to the masses; to help strengthen and multiply the Party's bonds with the people; to be considerate and attentive to people; to respond promptly to the needs and requirements of the working people;

(c) to take an active part in the political life of the country, in the administration of state affairs, and in economic and cultural development; to set an example in the fulfilment of his public duty; to assist in developing and strengthening communist social relations;

(d) to master Marxist-Leninist theory, to improve his ideological knowledge, and to contribute to the moulding and education of the man of communist society. To combat vigorously all manifestations of bourgeois ideology, remnants of a private-property psychology, religious prejudices, and other survivals of the past; to observe the principles of communist morality, and place public interests above his own;

(e) to be an active proponent of the ideas of socialist internationalism and Soviet patriotism among the masses of the working people; to combat survivals of nationalism and chauvinism; to contribute by word and by deed to the consolidation of the friendship of the peoples of the U.S.S.R. and the fraternal bonds linking the Soviet people with the peoples of the countries of the socialist camp, with the proletarians and other working people in all countries;

(f) to strengthen to the utmost the ideological and organisational unity of the Party; to safeguard the Party against the infiltration of people unworthy of the lofty name of Communist; to be truthful and honest with the Party and the people; to display vigilance, to guard Party and state secrets;

(g) to develop criticism and self-criticism, boldly lay bare shortcomings and strive for their removal; to combat ostentation, conceit, complacency, and parochial tendencies; to rebuff firmly all attempts at suppressing criticism; to resist all actions injurious to the Party and the state, and to give information of them to Party bodies, up to and including the C.C. C.P.S.U.;

(h) to implement undeviatingly the Party's policy with regard to the proper selection of personnel according to their political qualifications and personal qualities. To be uncompromising whenever the Leninist principles of the selection and education of personnel are infringed;

(i) to observe Party and state discipline, which is equally binding on all Party members. The Party has one discipline, one law, for all Communists, irrespective of their past services or the positions they occupy;

(j) to help, in every possible way, to strengthen the defence potential of the U.S.S.R.; to wage an unflagging struggle for peace and friendship among nations;

3. A Party member has the right:

(a) to elect and be elected to Party bodies;

(b) to discuss freely questions of the Party's policies and practical activities at Party meetings, conferences and congresses, at the meetings of Party committees and in the Party press; to table motions; openly to express and uphold his opinion as long as the Party organisation concerned has not adopted a decision;

(c) to criticise any Communist, irrespective of the position he holds, at Party meetings, conferences and congresses, and at the plenary meetings of Party committees. Those who commit the offence of suppressing criticism or victimising anyone for criticism are responsible to and will be penalised by the Party, to the point of expulsion from the C.P.S.U.;

(d) to attend in person all Party meetings and all bureau and committee meetings that discuss his activities or conduct;

(e) to address any question, statement or proposal to any Party body, up to and including the C.C. C.P.S.U., and to demand an answer on the substance of his address.

4. Applicants are admitted to Party membership only individually. Membership of the Party is open to politically conscious and active workers, peasants and representatives of the intelligentsia, devoted to the communist cause. New members are admitted from among the candidate members who have passed through the established probationary period.

Persons may join the Party on attaining the age of eighteen. Young people up to the age of twenty may join the Party only through the Leninist Young Communist League of the Soviet Union (Y.C.L.).

The procedure for the admission of candidate members to full Party membership is as follows:

(a) Applicants for Party membership must submit recommendations from three members of the C.P.S.U. who have a Party standing of not less than three years and who know the applicants from having worked with them, professionally and socially, for not less than one year.

Note 1. In the case of members of the Y.C.L. applying for membership of the Party, the recommendation of a district or city committee of the Y.C.L. is equivalent to the recommendation of one Party member.

Note 2. Members and alternate members of the C.C. C.P.S.U. shall refrain from giving recommendations.

(b) Applications for Party membership are discussed and a decision is taken by the general meeting of the primary Party organisation; the decision of the latter takes effect after endorsement by the district Party committee, or by the city Party committee in cities with no district divisions.

The presence of those who have recommended an applicant for Party membership at the discussion of the application concerned is optional;

(c) citizens of the U.S.S.R. who formerly belonged to the Communist or Workers' Party of another country are admitted to membership of the Communist Party of the Soviet Union in conformity with the rules established by the C.C. C.P.S.U.

Former members of other parties are admitted to membership of the C.P.S.U. in conformity with the regular procedure, except that their admission must be endorsed by a regional or territorial committee or the C.C. of the Communist Party of a Union Republic.

5. Communists recommending applicants for Party membership are responsible to Party organisations for the impartiality of their description of the moral qualities and professional and political qualifications of those they recommend.

6. The Party standing of those admitted to membership dates from the day when the general meeting of the primary Party organisation decides to accept them as full members.

7. The procedure of registering members and candidate members of the Party, and their transfer from one organisation to another is determined by the appropriate instructions of the C.C. C.P.S.U.

8. If a Party member or candidate member fails to pay membership dues for three months in succession without sufficient reason, the matter shall be discussed by the primary Party organisation. If it is revealed as a result that the Party member or candidate member in question has virtually lost contact with the Party organisation, he shall be regarded as having ceased to be a member of the Party; the primary Party organisation shall pass a decision thereon and submit it to the district or city committee of the Party for endorsement.

9. A Party member or candidate member who fails to fulfil his duties as laid down in the Rules, or commits other offences, shall be called to account, and may be subjected to the penalty of admonition, reprimand (severe reprimand), or reprimand (severe reprimand) with entry in the registration card. The highest Party penalty is expulsion from the Party.

Should the necessity arise, a Party organisation may, as a Party penalty, reduce a Party member to the status of candidate member for a period of up to one year. The decision of the primary Party organisation reducing a Party member to candidate membership is subject to endorsement by the district or city Party committee. On the expiration of his period of reduction to candidate membership his re-admission to full membership of the Party will follow regular procedure, with retention of his former Party standing.

In the case of insignificant offences, measures of Party education and influence should be applied—in the form of comradely criticism, Party censure, warning, or reproof.

When the question of expelling a member from the Party is discussed, the maximum attention must be shown, and the grounds for the charges preferred against him must be thoroughly investigated.

10. The decision to expel a Communist from the Party is made by the general meeting of a primary Party organisation. The decision of the primary Party organisation expelling a member is regarded as adopted if not less than two-thirds of the Party members attending the meeting have voted for it, and is subject to endorsement by the district or city Party committee. The decision of the district or city committee expelling a member takes effect after endorsement by a regional or territorial committee or the C.C. of the Communist Party of a Union Republic.

Until such time as the decision to expel him is endorsed by a regional or territorial Party committee or the C.C. of the Communist Party of a Union Republic, the Party member or candidate member retains his membership card and is entitled to attend closed Party meetings.

An expelled Party member retains the right to appeal, within the period of two months, to the higher Party bodies, up to and including the C.C. C.P.S.U.

11. The question of calling a member or alternate member of the C.C. of the Communist Party of a Union Republic, of a territorial, regional, area, city or district Party committee, as well as a member of an auditing commission, to account before the Party is discussed by primary Party organisations.

Party organisations pass decisions imposing penalties on members or alternate members of the said Party committees, or on members of auditing commissions, in conformity with the regular procedure.

A Party organisation which proposes expelling a Communist from the C.P.S.U. communicates its proposal to the Party committee of which he is a member. A decision expelling from the Party a member or alternate member of the C.C. of the Communist Party of a Union Republic or a territorial, regional, area, city or district Party committee, or a member of an auditing commission, is taken at the plenary meeting of the committee concerned by a majority of two-thirds of the membership.

The decision to expel from the Party a member or alternate member of the Central Committee of the C.P.S.U., or a member of the Central Auditing Commission, is made by the Party congress, and in the interval between two congresses, by a plenary meeting of the Central Committee, by a majority of two-thirds of its members.

12. Should a Party member commit an indictable offence, he shall be expelled from the Party and prosecuted in conformity with the law.

13. Appeals against expulsion from the Party or against the imposition of a penalty, as well as the decisions of Party organisations on expulsion from the Party shall be examined by the appropriate Party bodies within not more than one month from the date of their receipt.

II

Candidate Members

14. All persons joining the Party must pass through a probationary period as candidate members in order to more thoroughly familiarise themselves with the Programme and the Rules of the C.P.S.U. and prepare for admission to full membership of the Party. Party organisations must assist candidates to prepare for admission to full membership of the Party, and test their personal qualities.

The period of probationary membership shall be one year.

15. The procedure for the admission of candidate members (individual admission, submission of recommendations, decision of the primary organisation as to admission, and its endorsement) is identical with the procedure for the admission of Party members.

16. On the expiration of a candidate member's probationary period the primary Party organisation discusses and passes a decision on his admission to full membership. Should a candidate member fail, in the course of his probationary period, to prove his worthiness, and should his personal traits make it evident that he cannot be admitted to membership of the C.P.S.U., the Party organisation shall pass a decision rejecting his admission to membership of the Party; after endorsement of that decision by the district or city Party committee, he shall cease to be considered a candidate member of the C.P.S.U.

17. Candidate members of the Party participate in all the activities of their Party organisations; they shall have a consultative voice at Party meetings. They may not be elected to any leading Party body, nor may they be elected delegates to a Party conference or congress.

18. Candidate members of the C.P.S.U. pay membership dues at the same rate as full members.

III

Organisational Structure of the Party.
Inner-Party Democracy

19. The guiding principle of the organisational structure of the Party is democratic centralism, which signifies:

(a) election of all leading Party bodies, from the lowest to the highest;

(b) periodical reports of Party bodies to their Party organisations and to higher bodies;

(c) strict Party discipline and subordination of the minority to the majority;

(d) the decisions of higher bodies are obligatory for lower bodies.

20. The Party is built on the territorial-and-production principle: primary organisations are established wherever Communists are employed, and are associated territorially in district, city, etc., organisations. An organisation serving a given area is higher than any Party organisation serving part of that area.

21. All Party organisations are autonomous in the decision of local questions, unless their decisions conflict with Party policy.

22. The highest leading body of a Party organisation is the general meeting (in the case of primary organisations), conference (in the case of district, city, area, regional or territorial organisations), or congress (in the case of the Communist Parties of the Union Republics and the Communist Party of the Soviet Union).

23. The general meeting, conference or congress, elects a bureau or committee which acts as its executive body and directs all the current work of the Party organisation.

24. The election of Party bodies shall be effected by secret ballot. In an election, all Party members have the unlimited right to challenge candidates and to criticise them. Each candidate shall be voted upon separately. A candidate is considered elected if more than one half of those attending the meeting, conference or congress have voted for him.

25. The principle of systematic renewal of the composition of Party bodies and of continuity of leadership shall be observed in the election of those bodies.

At each regular election, not less than one quarter of the composition of the Central Committee of the C.P.S.U. and its Presidium shall be renewed. Members of the Presidium shall not, as a rule, be elected for more than three successive terms. Particular Party officials may, by virtue of their generally recognised prestige and high political, organisational and other qualities, be successively elected to leading bodies for a longer period. In that case, a candidate is considered elected if not less than three quarters of the votes are cast for him by secret ballot.

The composition of the Central Committees of the Communist Parties of the Union Republics, and of the territorial and regional Party committees shall be renewed by not less than one-third at each regular election; the composition of the area, city and district Party committees and of the committees or bureaus of primary Party organisations, by one half. Furthermore, members of these leading Party bodies may be elected successively for not more than three terms, and the secretaries of primary Party organisations, for not more than two terms.

A Party meeting, conference or congress may, in consideration of the political and professional qualities of an individual, elect him to a leading body for a longer period. In such cases a candidate is considered elected if not less than three quarters of the Communists attending vote for him.

Party members not re-elected to a leading Party body due to the expiration of their term may be re-elected at subsequent elections.

26. A member or alternate member of the C.C. C.P.S.U. must by his entire activity justify the great trust placed in him by the Party. A member or alternate member of the C.C. C.P.S.U. who degrades his honour and dignity may not remain on the Central Committee. The question of the removal of a member or alternate member of the C.C. C.P.S.U. from that body shall be decided by a plenary meeting of the Central Committee by secret ballot. The decision is regarded as adopted if not less than two-thirds of the membership of the C.C. C.P.S.U. vote for it.

The question of the removal of a member or alternate member of the C.C. of the Communist Party of a Union Republic, or of a territorial, regional, area, city or district Party committee from the Party body concerned is decided by a plenary meeting of that body. The decision is regarded as adopted if not less than two-thirds of the membership of the committee in question vote for it by secret ballot.

A member of the Central Auditing Commission who does not justify the great trust placed in him by the Party shall be removed from that body. This question shall be decided by a meeting of the Central Auditing Commission. The decision is regarded as adopted if not less than two-thirds of the membership of the Central Auditing Commission vote by secret ballot for the removal of the member concerned from that body.

The question of the removal of a member from the auditing commission of a republican, territorial, regional, area, city or district Party organisation shall be decided by a meeting of the appropriate commission according to the procedure established for members and alternate members of Party committees.

27. The free and business-like discussion of questions of Party policy in individual Party organisations or in the Party as a whole is the inalienable right of every Party member and an important principle of inner-Party democracy. Only on the basis of inner-Party democracy is it possible to develop criticism and self-criticism and to strengthen Party discipline, which must be conscious and not mechanical.

Discussion of controversial or insufficiently clear issues may be held within the framework of individual organisations or the Party as a whole.

Party-wide discussion is necessary:

(a) if the necessity is recognised by several Party organisations at regional or republican level;

(b) if there is not a sufficiently solid majority in the Central Committee on major questions of Party policy;

(c) if the C.C. C.P.S.U. considers it necessary to consult the Party as a whole on any particular question of policy.

Wide discussion, especially discussion on a country-wide scale, of questions of Party policy must be so held as to ensure for Party members the free expression of their views and preclude attempts to form factional groupings destroying Party unity, attempts to split the Party.

28. The supreme principle of Party leadership is collective leadership, which is an absolute requisite for the normal functioning of Party organisations, the proper education of cadres, and the promotion of the activity and initiative of Communists. The cult of the individual and the violations of inner-Party democracy resulting from it must not be tolerated in the Party; they are incompatible with the Leninist principles of Party life.

Collective leadership does not exempt individuals in office from personal responsibility for the job entrusted to them.

29. The Central Committees of the Communist Parties of the Union Republics, and territorial, regional, area, city and district Party committees shall systematically inform Party organisations of their work in the interim between congresses and conferences.

30. Meetings of the active of district, city, area, regional and territorial Party organisations and of the Communist Parties of the Union Republics shall be held to discuss major decisions of the Party

and to work out measures for their execution, as well as to examine questions of local significance.

IV

Higher Party Organs

31. The supreme organ of the Communist Party of the Soviet Union is the Party Congress. Congresses are convened by the Central Committee at least once in four years. The convocation of a Party Congress and its agenda shall be announced at least six weeks before the Congress. Extraordinary congresses are convened by the Central Committee of the Party on its own initiative or on the demand of not less than one-third of the total membership represented at the preceding Party Congress. Extraordinary congresses shall be convened within two months. A congress is considered properly constituted if not less than one half of the total Party membership is represented at it.

The rates of representation at a Party Congress are determined by the Central Committee.

32. Should the Central Committee of the Party fail to convene an extraordinary congress within the period specified in Article 31, the organisations which demanded it have the right to form an Organising Committee which shall enjoy the powers of the Central Committee of the Party in respect of the convocation of the extraordinary congress.

33. The Congress:

(a) hears and approves the reports of the Central Committee, of the Central Auditing Commission, and of the other central organisations;

(b) reviews, amends and endorses the Programme and the Rules of the Party;

(c) determines the line of the Party in matters of home and foreign policy, and examines and decides the most important questions of communist construction;

(d) elects the Central Committee and the Central Auditing Commission.

34. The number of members to be elected to the Central Committee and to the Central Auditing Commission is determined by the Congress. In the event of vacancies occurring in the Central Committee, they are filled from among the alternate members of the C.C. C.P.S.U. elected by the Congress.

35. Between congresses, the Central Committee of the Communist Party of the Soviet Union directs the activities of the Party, the local Party bodies, selects and appoints leading functionaries, directs the

work of central government bodies and public organisations of working people through the Party groups in them, sets up various Party organs, institutions and enterprises and directs their activities, appoints the editors of the central newspapers and journals operating under its control, and distributes the funds of the Party budget and controls its execution.

The Central Committee represents the C.P.S.U. in its relations with other parties.

36. The C.C. C.P.SU shall keep the Party organisations regularly informed of its work.

37. The Central Auditing Commission of the C.P.S.U supervises the expeditious and proper handling of affairs by the central bodies of the Party, and audits the accounts of the treasury and the enterprises of the Central Committee of the C.P.S.U.

38. The C.C. C.P.S.U. shall hold not less than one plenary meeting every six months. Alternate members of the Central Committee shall attend its plenary meetings with consultative voice.

39. The Central Committee of the Communist Party of the Soviet Union elects a Presidium to direct the work of the C.C. between plenary meetings and a Secretariat to direct current work, chiefly the selection of cadres and the verification of the fulfilment of Party decisions, and sets up a Bureau of the C.C. C.P.S.U. for the R.S.F.S.R.

40. The Central Committee of the Communist Party of the Soviet Union organises the Party Control Committee of the C.C.

The Party Control Committee of the C.C. C.P.S.U.:

(a) verifies the observance of Party discipline by members and candidate members of the C.P.S.U., and takes action against Communists who violate the Programme and the Rules of the Party and Party or state discipline, and against violators of Party ethics;

(b) considers appeals against decisions of Central Committees of the Communist Parties of the Union Republics or of territorial and regional Party committees to expel members from the Party or impose Party penalties upon them.

v

*Republican, Territorial, Regional, Area, City
and District Organisations of the Party*

41. The republican, territorial, regional, area, city and district Party organisations and their committees take guidance in their activities from the Programme and the Rules of the C.P.S.U., conduct all work for the implementation of Party policy and organise the fulfil-

ment of the directives of the C.C. C.P.S.U. within the republics, territories, regions, areas, cities and districts concerned.

42. The basic duties of republican, territorial, regional, area, city and district Party organisations, and of their leading bodies, are:

(a) political and organisational work among the masses, mobilisation of the masses for the fulfilment of the tasks of communist construction, for the maximum development of industrial and agricultural production, for the fulfilment and over-fulfilment of state plans; solicitude for the steady improvement of the material and cultural standards of the working people;

(b) organisation of ideological work, propaganda of Marxism-Leninism, promotion of the communist awareness of the working people, guidance of the local press, radio and television, and control over the activities of cultural and educational institutions;

(c) guidance of Soviets, trade unions, the Y.C.L., the co-operatives and other public organisations through the Party groups in them, and increasingly broader enlistment of working people in the activities of these organisations, development of the initiative and activity of the masses as an essential condition for the gradual transition from socialist statehood to public self-government under communism.

Party organisations must not act in place of government, trade union, co-operative or other public organisations of the working people; they must not allow either the merging of the functions of Party and other bodies or undue parallelism in work;

(d) selection and appointment of leading personnel, their education in the spirit of communist ideas, honesty and truthfulness, and a high sense of responsibility to the Party and the people for the work entrusted to them;

(e) large-scale enlistment of Communists in the conduct of Party activities as non-staff workers, as a form of social work;

(f) organisation of various institutions and enterprises of the Party within the bounds of their republic, territory, region, area, city or district, and guidance of their activities; distribution of Party funds within the given organisation; systematic information of the higher Party body and accountability to it for their work.

LEADING BODIES OF REPUBLICAN, TERRITORIAL AND REGIONAL PARTY ORGANISATIONS

43. The highest body of regional, territorial and republican Party organisations is the respective regional or territorial Party conference or the congress of the Communist Party of the Union Republic, and in the interim between them the regional committee, territorial com-

mittee or the Central Committee of the Communist Party of the Union Republic.

44. Regular regional and territorial Party conferences, and congresses of the Communist Parties of the Union Republic, are convened by the respective regional or territorial committees or the C.C. of the Communist Parties of the Union Republics once every two years, and extraordinary conferences and congresses are convened by decision of regional or territorial committees, or the C.C. of the Communist Parties of the Union Republics, or on the demand of one-third of the total membership of the organisations belonging to the regional, territorial or republican Party organisation. Congresses of Communist Parties of the Union Republics divided into regions (the Ukraine, Byelorussia, Kazakhstan and Uzbekistan) may be convened once in four years.

The rates of representation at regional and territorial conferences and at congresses of the Communist Parties of the Union Republics are determined by the respective Party committees.

Regional and territorial conferences, and congresses of the Communist Parties of the Union Republics, hear the reports of the respective regional or territorial committees, or the Central Committee of the Communist Party of the Union Republic, and of the auditing commission; discuss at their own discretion other matters of Party, economic and cultural development, and elect the regional or territorial committee, the Central Committtee of the Union Republic, the auditing commission and the delegates to the Congress of the C.P.S.U.

45. The regional and territorial committees and the Central Committees of the Communist Parties of the Union Republics elect bureaus, which also include secretaries of the committees. The secretaries must have a Party standing of not less than five years. The plenary meetings of the committees also confirm the chairmen of Party commissions, heads of departments of these committees, editors of Party newspapers and journals.

Regional and territorial committees and the Central Committees of the Communist Parties of the Union Republics may set up secretariats to examine current business and verify the execution of decisions.

46. The plenary meetings of regional and territorial committees and the Central Committees of the Communist Parties of the Union Republics shall be convened at least once every four months.

47. The regional and territorial committees and the Central Committees of the Communist Parties of the Union Republics direct the

area, city and district Party organisations, inspect their work and regularly hear reports of area, city and district Party committees.

Party organisations in Autonomous Republics, and in autonomous and other regions forming part of a territory or a Union Republic, function under the guidance of the respective territorial committees or Central Committees of the Communist Parties of the Union Republics.

LEADING BODIES OF AREA, CITY AND DISTRICT (URBAN AND RURAL) PARTY ORGANISATIONS

48. The highest body of an area, city or district Party organisation is the area, city and district Party conference or the general meeting of Communists convened by the area, city or district committee at least once in two years, and the extraordinary conference convened by decision of the respective committee or on the demand of one-third of the total membership of the Party organisation concerned.

The area, city or district conference (general meeting) hears reports of the committee and auditing commission, discusses at its own discretion other questions of Party, economic and cultural development, and elects the area, city and district committee, the auditing commission and delegates to the regional and territorial conference or the congress of the Communist Party of the Union Republic.

The quota of representation to the area, city or district conference are established by the respective Party committee.

49. The area, city or district committee elects a bureau, including the committee secretaries, and confirms the appointment of heads of committee departments and newspaper editors. The secretaries of the area, city and district committees must have a Party standing of at least three years. The committee secretaries are confirmed by the respective regional or territorial committee, or the Central Committee of the Communist Party of the Union Republic.

50. The area, city and district committee organises and confirms the primary Party organisations, directs their work, regularly hears reports concerning the work of Party organisations, and keeps a register of Communists.

51. The plenary meeting of the area, city and district committee is convened at least once in three months.

52. The area, city and district committee has non-staff functionaries, sets up standing or ad hoc commissions on various aspects of Party work and uses other ways to draw Communists into the activities of the Party committee on social lines.

VI

Primary Party Organisations

53. The primary Party organisations are the basis of the Party.

Primary Party organisations are formed at the places of work of Party members—in factories, state farms and other enterprises, collective farms, units of the Soviet Army, offices, educational establishments, etc., wherever there are not less than three Party members. Primary Party organisations may also be organised on the residential principle in villages and at house administrations.

54. At enterprises, collective farms and institutions with over 50 Party members and candidate members, shop, sectional, farm, team, departmental, etc., Party organisations may be formed as units of the general primary Party organisation with the sanction of the district, city or area committee.

Within shop, sectional, etc., organisations, and also within primary Party organisations having less than 50 members and candidate members, Party groups may be formed in the teams and other production units.

55. The highest organ of the primary Party organisation is the Party meeting, which is convened at least once a month.

In large Party organisations with a membership of more than 300 Communists, a general Party meeting is convened when necessary at times fixed by the Party committee or on the demand of a number of shop or departmental Party organisations.

56. For the conduct of current business the primary, shop or departmental Party organisation elects a bureau for the term of one year. The number of its members is fixed by the Party meeting. Primary, shop and departmental Party organisations with less than 15 Party members do not elect a bureau. Instead, they elect a secretary and deputy secretary of the Party organisation.

Secretaries of primary, shop and departmental Party organisations must have a Party standing of at least one year.

Primary Party organisations with less than 150 Party members shall have, as a rule, no salaried functionaries released from their regular work.

57. In large factories and offices with more than 300 members and candidate members of the Party, and in exceptional cases in factories and offices with over 100 Communists by virtue of special production conditions and territorial dispersion, subject to the approval of the regional committee, territorial committee or Central Committee of the Communist Party of the Union Republic, Party committees may

be formed, the shop and departmental Party organisations at these factories and offices being granted the status of primary Party organisations.

The Party organisations of collective farms may set up Party committees if they have a minimum of 50 Communists.

The Party committees are elected for the term of one year. Their numerical composition is fixed by the general Party meeting or conference.

58. In its activities the primary Party organisation takes guidance from the Programme and the Rules of the C.P.S.U. It conducts its work directly among the working people, rallies them round the Communist Party of the Soviet Union, organises the masses to carry out the Party policy and to work for the building of communism.

The primary Party organisation:

(a) admits new members to the C.P.S.U.;

(b) educates Communists in a spirit of loyalty to the Party cause, ideological staunchness and communist ethics;

(c) organises the study by Communists of Marxist-Leninist theory in close connection with the practice of communist construction and opposes all attempts at revisionist distortions of Marxism-Leninism and its dogmatic interpretation;

(d) ensures the vanguard role of Communists in the sphere of labour and in the socio-political and economic activities of enterprises, collective farms, institutions, educational establishments, etc.;

(e) acts as the organiser of the working people for the performance of the current tasks of communist construction, heads the socialist emulation movement for the fulfilment of state plans and undertakings of the working people, rallies the masses to disclose and make the best use of untapped resources at enterprises and collective farms, and to apply in production on a broad scale the achievements of science, engineering and the experience of front-rankers; works for the strengthening of labour discipline, the steady increase of labour productivity and improvement of the quality of production, and shows concern for the protection and increase of social wealth at enterprises, state farms and collective farms;

(f) conducts agitational and propaganda work among the masses, educates them in the communist spirit, helps the working people to acquire proficiency in administering state and social affairs;

(g) on the basis of extensive criticism and self-criticism, combats cases of bureaucracy, parochialism, and violations of state discipline, thwarts attempts to deceive the state, acts against negligence, waste and extravagance at enterprises, collective farms and offices;

(h) assists the area, city and district committees in their activities and is accountable to them for its work.

The Party organisation must see to it that every Communist should observe in his own life and cultivate among working people the moral principles set forth in the Programme of the C.P.S.U., in the moral code of the builder of communism:

loyalty to the communist cause, love of his own socialist country, and of other socialist countries;

conscientious labour for the benefit of society, for he who does not work, neither shall he eat;

concern on everyone's part for the protection and increase of social wealth;

lofty sense of public duty, intolerance of violations of public interests;

collectivism and comradely mutual assistance: one for all, and all for one;

humane relations and mutual respect among people: man is to man a friend, comrade and brother;

honesty and truthfulness, moral purity, unpretentiousness and modesty in public and personal life;

mutual respect in the family circle and concern for the upbringing of children;

intolerance of injustice, parasitism, dishonesty, careerism and money-grubbing;

friendship and fraternity among all peoples of the U.S.S.R., intolerance of national and racial hostility;

intolerance of the enemies of communism, the enemies of peace and those who oppose the freedom of the peoples;

fraternal solidarity with the working people of all countries, with all peoples.

59. Primary Party organisations of industrial enterprises and trading establishments, state farms, collective farms and designing organisations, drafting offices and research institutes directly related to production, enjoy the right to control the work of the administration.

The Party organisations at Ministries, State Committees, economic councils and other central and local government or economic agencies and departments which do not have the function of controlling the administration, must actively promote improvement of the apparatus, cultivate among the personnel a high sense of responsibility for work entrusted to them, promote state discipline and the better servicing of the population, firmly combat bureaucracy and red tape, inform the appropriate Party bodies in good time on shortcomings in the work of the respective offices and individuals, regardless of what posts the latter may occupy.

The Party and the Y.C.L.

60. The Leninist Young Communist League of the Soviet Union is an independently acting social organisation of young people, an active helper and reserve of the Party. The Y.C.L. helps the Party educate the youth in the communist spirit, draw it into the work of building a new society, train a rising generation of harmoniously developed people who will live and work and administer public affairs under communism.

61. Y.C.L. organisations enjoy the right of broad initiative in discussing and submitting to the appropriate Party organisations questions related to the work of enterprises, collective farms and offices. They must be active levers in the implementation of Party directives in all spheres of communist construction, especially where there are no primary Party organisations.

62. The Y.C.L. conducts its activities under the guidance of the Communist Party of the Soviet Union. The work of the local Y.C.L. organisations is directed and controlled by the appropriate republican, territorial, regional, area, city and district Party organisations.

In their communist educational work among the youth, local Party bodies and primary Party organisations rely on the support of the Y.C.L. organisations, and uphold and promote their useful undertakings.

63. Members of the Y.C.L. who have been admitted into the C.P.S.U. cease to belong to the Y.C.L. the moment they join the Party, provided they do not hold leading posts in Y.C.L. organisations.

Party Organisations in the Soviet Army

64. Party organisations in the Soviet Army take guidance in their work from the Programme and the Rules of the C.P.S.U. and operate on the basis of instructions issued by the Central Committee.

The Party organisations of the Soviet Army carry through the policy of the Party in the Armed Forces, rally servicemen round the Communist Party, educate them in the spirit of Marxism-Leninism and boundless loyalty to the socialist homeland, actively further the unity of the army and the people, work for the strengthening of military discipline, rally servicemen to carry out the tasks of military and political training and acquire skill in the use of new technique and weapons, and to irreproachably perform their military duty and the orders and instructions of the command.

65. The guidance of Party work in the Armed Forces is exercised by the Central Committee of the C.P.S.U. through the Chief Political Administration of the Soviet Army and Navy, which functions as a department of the C.C. C.P.S.U.

The chiefs of the political administrations of military areas and fleets, and chiefs of the political administrations of armies must be Party members of five years' standing, and the chiefs of political departments of military formations must be Party members of three years' standing.

66. The Party organisations and political bodies of the Soviet Army maintain close contact with local Party committees, and keep them informed about political work in the military units. The secretaries of military Party organisations and chiefs of political bodies participate in the work of local Party committees.

IX

Party Groups in Non-Party Organisations

67. At congresses, conferences and meetings and in the elective bodies of Soviets, trade unions, co-operatives and other mass organisations of the working people, having at least three Party members, Party groups are formed for the purpose of strengthening the influence of the Party in every way and carrying out Party policy among non-Party people, strengthening Party and state discipline, combating bureaucracy, and verifying the fulfilment of Party and government directives.

68. The Party groups are subordinate to the appropriate Party bodies: the Central Committee of the Communist Party of the Soviet Union, the Central Committees of the Communist Parties of the Union Republics, territorial, regional, area, city or district Party committees.

In all matters the groups must strictly and unswervingly abide by decisions of the leading Party bodies.

X

Party Funds

69. The funds of the Party and its organisations are derived from membership dues, incomes from Party enterprises and other revenue.

70. The monthly membership dues for Party members and candidate members are as follows:

MONTHLY EARNINGS	DUES	
up to 50 rubles	10 kopeks	
from 51 to 100 rubles	0.5 per cent	⎫
from 101 to 150 rubles	1.0 per cent	⎪ of the
from 151 to 200 rubles	1.5 per cent	⎬ monthly
from 201 to 250 rubles	2.0 per cent	⎪ earnings
from 251 to 300 rubles	2.5 per cent	⎪
over 300 rubles	3.0 per cent	⎭

71. An entrance fee of 2 per cent of monthly earnings is paid on admission to the Party as a candidate member.

Selected Bibliography

A. Bibliographies

Braham, Randolph L. *Jews in the Communist World. A Bibliography [of English Sources], 1945–1960*. New York: Twayne Publishers, 1961.

————, and Hauer, Mordecai M. *Jews in the Communist World. A Bibliography [of non-English Sources], 1945–1962*. New York: Pro Arte, 1963.

Grierson, Philip. *Books on Soviet Russia, 1917–1942: A Bibliography and a Guide to Reading*. London: Methuen, 1943.

Hammond, Thomas T. *Soviet Foreign Relations and World Communism. A Selected and Annotated Bibliography of 7,000 Books in 30 Languages*. Princeton: Princeton University Press, 1965.

Hunt, R. N. C. *Books on Communism*. London: Ampersand, 1959.

Langer, William L. *Foreign Affairs Bibliography. A Selected and Annotated List of Books on International Relations, 1919–1932*. New York: Council on Foreign Relations, 1933, pp. 357–399.

Pundeff, Marin. *Recent Publications on Communism. A Bibliography of Non-Periodical Literature, 1957–1962*. Los Angeles: University of Southern California, Research Institute on Communist Strategy and Propaganda, 1962.

Roberts, Henry L. *Foreign Affairs Bibliography, 1942–1952*. New York: Council on Foreign Relations, 1955, pp. 534–566.

Schwartz, Harry. *The Soviet Economy: A Selected Bibliography of Materials in English*. Syracuse, N.Y.: Syracuse University Press, 1949.

U.S. Senate. *World Communism. A Selected Annotated Bibliography*. Washington, D.C.: Government Printing Office, 1964 (Senate. 88th Congress, 2d Session. Document No. 69).

Woolbert, Robert Gale. *Foreign Affairs Bibliography: A Selected and Annotated List of Books on International Relations, 1932–1942*. New York: Council on Foreign Relations, 1945, pp. 486–516.

B. General References

Armstrong, John A. *Ideology, Politics, and Government in the Soviet Union.* New York: Frederick A. Praeger, 1962.

Bauer, Raymond A., Inkeles, Alex *and* Kluckhohn, Clyde. *How the Soviet System Works. Cultural, Psychological and Social Themes.* New York: Vintage Books, 1961.

Brumberg, Abraham, *ed. Russia Under Khrushchev.* New York: Frederick A. Praeger, 1962.

Conquest, Robert. *Power and Policy in the USSR. The Study of Soviet Dynastics.* New York: St. Martin's Press, 1961.

Daniels, Robert V. *The Conscience of the Revolution: Communist Opposition in Soviet Russia.* Cambridge, Mass.: Harvard University Press, 1960.

Fainsod, Merle. *How Russia Is Ruled.* Cambridge, Mass.: Harvard University Press, 1963.

Fitzsimmons, Thomas, *et al. USSR: Its People, Its Society, Its Culture.* New Haven: Human Relations Area Files Press, 1960 (Survey of World Cultures, 7).

Gripp, Richard C. *Patterns of Soviet Politics.* Homewood, Ill.: The Dorsey Press, 1963.

Gruliow, Leo, *ed. Current Soviet Policies: The Documentary Record of the Nineteenth Communist Party Congress and the Reorganization after Stalin's Death.* New York: Frederick A. Praeger, 1953.

————, *ed. Current Soviet Policies. II. The Documentary Record of the Twentieth Communist Party Congress and Repercussions of De-Stalinization.* New York: Frederick A. Praeger, 1957.

————, *ed. Current Soviet Policies. III. The Documentary Record of the Extraordinary 21st Congress of the Communist Party of the Soviet Union.* New York: Columbia University Press, 1960.

———— *and* Saikowski, Charlotte, *eds. Current Soviet Policies. IV. The Documentary Record of the 22nd Party Congress.* New York: Columbia University Press, 1962.

Hazard, John N. *The Soviet System of Government* (rev. ed.). Chicago: The University of Chicago Press, 1960.

Hendel, Samuel, *ed. The Soviet Crucible. The Soviet System in Theory and Practice* (2d ed.). Princeton, N.J.: D. Van Nostrand Company, 1963.

Holt, Robert T. *and* Turner, John E., *eds. Soviet Union: Paradox and Change.* New York: Holt, Rinehart and Winston, 1963.

Inkeles, Alex *and* Geiger, Kent, *eds. Soviet Society. A Book of Readings.* Boston: Houghton Mifflin Company, 1961.

Kennan, George F. *Russia and the West Under Lenin and Stalin.* Boston: Little, Brown, 1961.

Kulski, W. W. *The Soviet Regime. Communism in Practice.* Syracuse, N.Y.: Syracuse University Press, 1959.

Leonhard, Wolfgang. *The Kremlin Since Stalin.* New York: Frederick A. Praeger, 1962.

Maynard, John. *Russia in Flux.* New York: Macmillan, 1955.

McClosky, Herbert and Turner, John E. *The Soviet Dictatorship.* New York: McGraw-Hill, 1960.

Mead, Margaret. *Soviet Attitudes Toward Authority. An Interdisciplinary Approach to Problems of Soviet Character.* New York: McGraw-Hill, 1951.

Mosely, Philip E., ed. *The Soviet Union, 1922–1962. A Foreign Affairs Reader.* New York: Council on Foreign Relations, 1963.

Rostow, W. W. *The Dynamics of Soviet Society.* New York: W. W. Norton, 1953.

Schapiro, Leonard. *The Origin of the Communist Autocracy.* Cambridge, Mass.: Harvard University Press, 1956.

Schuman, Frederick L. *Government in the Soviet Union.* New York: Thomas Y. Crowell Company, 1962.

———. *Russia Since 1917. Four Decades of Soviet Politics.* New York: Alfred A. Knopf, 1962.

———. *Soviet Politics at Home and Abroad.* New York: Alfred A. Knopf, 1946.

Scott, Derek J. R. *Russian Political Institutions.* New York: Frederick A. Praeger, 1962.

Seton-Watson, Hugh. *From Lenin to Khrushchev. The History of World Communism.* New York: Frederick A. Praeger, 1960.

Swearer, Howard R. and Longaker, Richard P., eds. *Contemporary Communism: Theory and Practice.* Belmont, Cal.: Wadsworth Publishing Co., 1963.

Towster, Julian. *Political Power in the U.S.S.R., 1917–1947.* New York: Oxford University Press, 1948.

Treadgold, Donald W. *Lenin and His Rivals: The Struggle for Russia's Future, 1898–1906.* New York: Frederick A. Praeger, 1955.

Tucker, Robert C. *The Soviet Political Mind: Studies in Stalinism and Post-Stalin Change.* New York: Frederick A. Praeger, 1963.

Ulam, Adam B. *The New Face of Soviet Totalitarianism.* Cambridge, Mass.: Harvard University Press, 1963.

Whiting, Kenneth R. *The Soviet Union Today. A Concise Handbook.* New York: Frederick A. Praeger, 1962.

Wolfe, Bertram D. *Communist Totalitarianism. Keys to the Soviet System.* Boston: Beacon Press, 1961.

————. *Three Who Made a Revolution. A Biographical History.* New York: The Dial Press, 1948.

C. *Wordmanship: A Key to Soviet Semantics*

Dekoster, Lester. *Vocabulary of Communism.* Grand Rapids, Mich.: Wm. B. Eerdmans, 1964.

Hodgkinson, Harry. *Doubletalk. The Language of Communism.* London: George Allen & Unwin, 1955.

Hunt, R. N. C. *A Guide to Communist Jargon.* New York: Macmillan, 1957.

SECTION I. *The Geographical and Historical Setting*

1. THE GEOGRAPHICAL AND DEMOGRAPHIC SETTING

Balzak, S. S., Vasyutin, V. F., *and* Feigin, Ya. G. *Economic Geography of the U.S.S.R.* New York: Macmillan, 1949.

Cressey, George B. *The Basis of Soviet Strength.* New York: McGraw-Hill, 1945.

————. *How Strong Is Russia? A Geographic Appraisal.* Syracuse, N.Y.: Syracuse University Press, 1954.

Shabad, Theodore. *Geography of the U.S.S.R.* New York: Columbia University Press, 1951.

Shimkin, Dimitri Boris. *Minerals. A Key to Soviet Power.* Cambridge, Mass.: Harvard University Press, 1953.

2. THE HISTORICAL SETTING

Black, Cyril E., *ed. Rewriting Russian History. Soviet Interpretations of Russia's Past.* New York: Frederick A. Praeger, 1956.

————, *ed. The Transformation of Russian Society: Aspects of Social Change Since 1861.* Cambridge, Mass.: Harvard University Press, 1960.

Carr, E. H. *A History of Soviet Russia.* New York: Macmillan, 1950–1958, 6 vols.

Clarkson, Jesse D. *A History of Russia.* New York: Random House, 1961.

Harcave, Sidney. *Russia: A History.* Philadelphia: J. B. Lippincott, 1952.

Kornilov, Alexander. *Modern Russian History.* New York: Alfred A. Knopf, 1943.

Pares, Bernard. A *History of Russia*. New York: Alfred A. Knopf, 1944.

Rauch, Georg von. A *History of Soviet Russia*. New York: Frederick A. Praeger, 1957.

Treadgold, Donald W. *Twentieth Century Russia*. Chicago: Rand McNally, 1959.

Vernadsky, George. A *History of Russia*. New Haven: Yale University Press, 1945.

SECTION II. *The Philosophical and Ideological Framework*

1. THE PHILOSOPHY OF COMMUNISM

Acton, H. B. *The Illusion of the Epoch: Marxism-Leninism as a Philosophical Creed*. London: Cohen, 1955.

Berdyaev, Nicholas. *The Origin of Russian Communism*. London: Geoffrey Bles, 1948.

Hook, Sidney. *Marx and the Marxists. The Ambiguous Legacy*. Princeton, N.J.: D. Van Nostrand Company, 1955.

———. *From Hegel to Marx*. New York: Reynal and Hitchcock, 1936.

———. "Studies in Communism," *Political Power and Personal Freedom*. New York: Collier Books, 1962, pp. 137–269.

Joravsky, David. *Soviet Marxism and Natural Science, 1917–1932*. New York: Columbia University Press, 1961.

Marcuse, Herbert. *Soviet Marxism. A Critical Analysis*. New York: Vintage Books, 1961.

Meyer, Alfred G. *Communism*. New York: Random House, 1962.

Tucker, Robert C. *Philosophy and Myth in Karl Marx*. Cambridge, England: Cambridge University Press, 1961.

Wetter, Gustav A. *Dialectical Materialism: A Historical and Systematic Survey of Philosophy in the Soviet Union*. London: Routledge and Kegan Paul, 1960.

2. THE IDEOLOGY OF COMMUNISM

Anderson, Thornton, *ed. Masters of Russian Marxism*. New York: Appleton-Century-Crofts, 1963.

Bochenski, J. M. *and* Niemeyer, Gerhard, *eds. Handbook on Communism*. New York: Frederick A. Praeger, 1962.

Brzezinski, Zbigniew K. *Ideology and Power in Soviet Politics*. New York: Frederick A. Praeger, 1962.

Cohen, Carl, *ed. Communism, Fascism, and Democracy. The Theoretical Foundations.* New York: Random House, 1962.

Daniels, Robert V., *ed. A Documentary History of Communism.* New York: Vintage Books, 1962, 2 vols.

――――. *The Nature of Communism.* New York: Random House, 1962.

Haimson, Leopold H. *The Russian Marxists and the Origins of Bolshevism.* Cambridge, Mass.: Harvard University Press, 1956.

Hook, Sidney, *ed. World Communism. Key Documentary Material.* Princeton, N.J.: D. Van Nostrand Company, 1962.

Hunt, R. N. C. *Marxism: Past and Present.* London: Geoffrey Bles, 1954.

――――. *The Theory and Practice of Communism* (rev. ed.). New York: Macmillan, 1957.

Labedz, Leopold, *ed. Revisionism. Essays on the History of Marxist Ideas.* New York: Frederick A. Praeger, 1962.

Leites, Nathan. *A Study of Bolshevism.* Glencoe, Ill.: The Free Press, 1953.

McKenzie, Kermit E. *Comintern and World Revolution, 1928–1943. The Shaping of Doctrine.* New York: Columbia University Press, 1963.

Meyer, Alfred G. *Leninism.* Cambridge, Mass.: Harvard University Press, 1957.

Moore, Barrington, Jr. *Soviet Politics. The Dilemma of Power. The Role of Ideas in Social Change.* Cambridge, Mass.: Harvard University Press, 1950.

Schlesinger, Rudolf. *Marx, His Time and Ours.* London: Routledge and Kegan Paul, 1950, 440 p.

――――. *The Spirit of Post-War Russia. Soviet Ideology, 1917–1946.* London: D. Dobson, 1947.

Ulam, Adam B. *The Unfinished Revolution. An Essay on the Sources of Influence of Marxism and Communism.* New York: Random House, 1960.

3. THE PROGRAM OF THE COMMUNIST
PARTY OF THE SOVIET UNION

Laqueur, Walter *and* Labedz, Leopold. *The Future of Communist Society.* New York: Frederick A. Praeger, 1962.

Ritvo, Herbert, *ed. The New Soviet Society.* New York: The New Leader, 1962.

Schapiro, Leonard, *ed. The U.S.S.R. and the Future. An Analysis of the New Program of the CPSU.* New York: Frederick A. Praeger, 1962.

SECTION III. *The Communist Concept of the State*

Lenin, V. I. *The State and Revolution.* Moscow: Foreign Languages Publishing House, n.d.
Moore, Stanley W. *The Critique of Capitalist Democracy: An Introduction to the Theory of the State in Marx, Engels and Lenin.* New York: Paine-Whitman, 1957.
Zlatopolsky, D. *State System of the U.S.S.R.* Moscow: Foreign Languages Publishing House, n.d.

SECTION IV. *The Ultimate Source of Power: The Party*

Armstrong, John A. *The Politics of Totalitarianism. The Communist Party of the Soviet Union from 1934 to the Present.* New York: Random House, 1961.
Djilas, Milovan. *The New Class. An Analysis of the Communist System.* New York: Frederick A. Praeger, 1957.
History of the Communist Party of the Soviet Union. Moscow: Foreign Languages Publishing House, 1960.
Lenin, V. I. *What Is to Be Done?* Moscow: Foreign Languages Publishing House, 1952.
Meissner, Boris *and* Reshetar, John S. *The Communist Party of the Soviet Union: The Party Leadership, Organization, and Ideology.* New York: Frederick A. Praeger, 1956.
Reshetar, John S. *A Concise History of the Communist Party of the Soviet Union.* New York: Frederick A. Praeger, 1960.
Schapiro, Leonard. *The Communist Party of the Soviet Union.* New York: Random House, 1960.

SECTION V. *The Rationalization of Terror*

The Anti-Stalin Campaign and International Communism. New York: Columbia University Press *for* The Russian Institute, 1956.
Avtorkhanov, Abdurakhman. *Stalin and the Soviet Communist Party. A Study in the Technology of Power.* New York: Frederick A. Praeger, 1959.

Beck, F. *and* Godin, W. *Russian Purge and the Extraction of Confession.* London: Hurt and Blackett, 1951.

Brzezinski, Zbigniew. *The Permanent Purge. Politics in Soviet Totalitarianism.* Cambridge, Mass.: Harvard Univerity Press, 1956.

Heilbrunn, Otto. *The Soviet Secret Services.* London: George Allen and Unwin, 1956.

Leites, Nathan *and* Bernaut, Elsa. *Ritual of Liquidation: The Case of the Moscow Trials.* Glencoe, Ill.: The Free Press, 1954.

Moore, Barrington, Jr. *Terror and Progress U.S.S.R. Some Sources of Change and Stability in the Soviet Dictatorship.* Cambridge, Mass.: Harvard University Press, 1954.

Wolfe, Bertram D. *Khrushchev and Stalin's Ghost.* New York: Frederick A. Praeger, 1957.

Wolin, Simon *and* Slusser, M. Robert, *eds. The Soviet Secret Police.* New York: Frederick A. Praeger, 1957.

SECTION VI. *Soviet Constitutionalism*

Denisov, A. *and* M. Kirichenko. *Soviet State Law.* Moscow: Foreign Languages Publishing House, 1960.

Meisel, James H. *and* Kozera, Edward S., *eds. Materials for the Study of the Soviet System: State and Party Constitutions, Laws, Decrees, Decisions and Official Statements of the Leaders in Translation* (2d ed.). Ann Arbor, Mich.: George Wahr, 1953.

Vishinsky, Andrei Y. *The Law of the Soviet State.* New York: Macmillan, 1948.

SECTION VII. *Structure and Functions of Government**

1. THE STATUS OF NATIONALITIES AND THE FEDERAL SYSTEM

Barghoorn, Frederick C. *Soviet Russian Nationalism.* New York: Oxford University Press, 1956.

Kolarz, Walter. *Russia and Her Colonies.* London: G. Philip and Son, 1952.

———. *Russia and Her Colonies. The Peoples of the Soviet Far East.* New York: Frederick A. Praeger, 1954.

Pipes, Richard. *The Formation of the Soviet Union: Communism*

---

* For bibliographical references on the organs of state power and administration, and the local soviets, see entries listed under B. *General References.*

and Nationalism, 1917 to 1923. Cambridge, Mass.: Harvard University Press, 1954.

Schlesinger, Rudolf, *ed. Changing Attitudes in Soviet Russia. The Nationalities Problem and Soviet Administration.* London: Routledge and Kegan Paul, 1956.

Schwarz, Solomon M. *The Jews in the Soviet Union.* Syracuse, N.Y.: Syracuse University Press, 1951.

2. LAW AND JUSTICE IN THE U.S.S.R.

Berman, Harold J. *Justice in the U.S.S.R.* (rev. ed., enl.). New York: Vintage Books, 1963.

Gsovski, Vladimir *and* Grzybowski, Kazimierz, *eds. Government, Law and Courts in the Soviet Union and Eastern Europe.* New York: Frederick A. Praeger, 1959, 2 vols. (XXXII).

Guins, George C. *Soviet Law and Soviet Society.* The Hague: Martinus Nijhoff, 1954.

Hazard, John N. *Law and Social Change in the U.S.S.R.* London: Stevens and Sons, 1953.

———. *Settling Disputes in Soviet Society. The Formative Years of Legal Institutions.* New York: Columbia University Press, 1960.

Kelsen, Hans. *The Communist Theory of Law.* New York: Frederick A. Praeger, 1955.

Romashkin, P. S., *ed. Fundamentals of Soviet Law.* Moscow: Foreign Languages Publishing House, n.d.

Schlesinger, Rudolf. *Soviet Legal Theory: Its Social Background and Development.* New York: Oxford University Press, 1945.

SECTION VIII. *Civil Rights and Liberties and the State*

Anderson, Paul B. *People, Church, and State in Modern Russia.* New York: Macmillan, 1944.

Bach, Marcus. *God and the Soviets.* New York: Thomas Y. Crowell, 1958.

Bauer, Raymond A. *and* Inkeles, Alex. *The Soviet Citizen: Daily Life in a Totalitarian Society.* Cambridge, Mass.: Harvard University Press, 1959.

Bereday, George Z. F. *and* Pennar, Jaan, *eds. The Politics of Soviet Education.* New York: Frederick A. Praeger, 1960.

Inkeles, Alex. *Public Opinion in Soviet Russia: A Study in Mass Persuasion.* Cambridge, Mass.: Harvard University Press, 1950.

Kolarz, Walter. *Religion in the Soviet Union*. New York: St. Martin's Press, 1961.

Mehnert, Klaus. *Soviet Man and His World*. New York: Frederick A. Praeger, 1962.

Schlesinger, Rudolf, ed. *Changing Attitudes in Soviet Russia. The Family in the U.S.S.R. Documents and Readings*. London: Routledge and Kegan Paul, 1949.

SECTION IX. *The Electoral Process*

Carson, George Barr. *Electoral Practice in the U.S.S.R.* New York: Frederick A. Praeger, 1955.

SECTION X. *Government and the Planned Economy*

1. GENERAL

Baykov, Alexander. *The Development of the Soviet Economic System: An Essay on the Experience of Planning in the U.S.S.R.* Cambridge, England: University Press, 1946.

Bergson, Abram. *The Real National Income of Soviet Russia Since 1928*. Cambridge, Mass.: Harvard University Press, 1961.

———. *Soviet Economic Growth: Conditions and Perspectives*. Evanston, Ill.: Row, Peterson and Company, 1953.

Campbell, Robert Wellington. *Soviet Economic Power: Its Organization, Growth, and Challenge*. Boston: Houghton Mifflin Co., 1960.

Deutscher, Isaac. *Soviet Trade Unions*. London: Royal Institute of International Affairs, 1950.

Holzman, Franklyn D. ed. *Readings on the Soviet Economy*. Chicago: Rand McNally, 1962.

———. *Soviet Taxation: The Fiscal and Monetary Problems of Planned Economy*. Cambridge, Mass.: Harvard University Press, 1955.

Jasny, Naum. *Soviet Industrialization, 1928–1952*. Chicago: University of Chicago Press, 1961.

———. *The Soviet Price System*. Stanford, Cal.: Stanford University Press, 1951.

Schwartz, Harry. *Russia's Soviet Economy* (2d ed.). Englewood Cliffs, N.J.: Prentice-Hall, 1954.

Schwarz, Solomon M. *Labor in the Soviet Union*. New York: Frederick A. Praeger, 1951.

Shaffer, Harry G., ed. *The Soviet Economy: A Collection of Western and Soviet Views.* New York: Appleton-Century-Crofts, 1963.

Spulber, Nicholas. *The Soviet Economy.* New York: W. W. Norton, 1962.

Vucinich, Alexander. *Soviet Economic Institutions: The Social Structure of Production Units.* Stanford, Cal.: Stanford University Press, 1952.

Yevenko, I. *Planning in the U.S.S.R.* Moscow: Foreign Languages Publishing House, n.d.

2. THE INDUSTRIAL SECTOR

Berliner, Joseph S. *Factory and Manager in the U.S.S.R.* Cambridge, Mass.: Harvard University Press, 1957.

Nutter, Warren G. *Growth of Industrial Production in the Soviet Union.* Princeton, N.J.: Princeton University Press, 1962.

3. THE AGRICULTURAL SECTOR

Jasny, Naum. *The Socialized Agriculture of the U.S.S.R.: Plans and Performance.* Stanford, Cal.: Stanford University Press, 1949.

Laird, Roy D. *Collective Farming in Russia: A Political Study of the Soviet Kolkhozy.* Lawrence, Kan.: University of Kansas Publications, Social Science Studies, 1958.

Volin, Lazar. *A Survey of Soviet Russian Agriculture.* Washington, D.C.: U.S. Department of Agriculture, 1951 (Agriculture Monograph, No. 5).

SECTION XI. *The Soviet Union in World Affairs*

1. THE FOREIGN POLICY OF THE SOVIET UNION

Bouscaren, Anthony T. *Soviet Foreign Policy. A Pattern of Persistence.* New York: Fordham University Press, 1963.

Dallin, Alexander, ed. *Soviet Conduct in World Affairs. A Selection of Readings.* New York: Columbia University Press, 1960.

Dinerstein, H. S. *War and the Soviet Union: Nuclear Weapons and the Revolution in Soviet Military and Political Thinking.* New York: Frederick A. Praeger, 1959.

Fischer, Louis. *The Soviets in World Affairs.* New York: Vintage Books, 1960.

Goldwin, Robert A., *et al.*, eds. *Readings in Russian Foreign Policy.* New York: Oxford University Press, 1959.

Lederer, Ivo J., ed. *Russian Foreign Policy. Essays in Historical Perspective*. New Haven: Yale University Press, 1962.

Mackintosh, J. M. *Strategy and Tactics of Soviet Foreign Policy*. New York: Oxford University Press, 1962.

Mosely, Philip E. *The Kremlin and World Politics. Studies in Soviet Policy and Action*. New York: Vintage Books, 1960.

Roberts, Henry L. *Russia and America. Dangers and Prospects*. New York: Council on Foreign Relations, 1956.

Rubinstein, Alvin Z., ed. *The Foreign Policy of the Soviet Union*. New York: Random House, 1960.

Shulman, Marshall D. *Stalin's Foreign Policy Reappraised*. Cambridge, Mass.: Harvard University Press, 1963.

2. THE POLICY OF "PEACEFUL COEXISTENCE"

Khrushchev, Nikita S. *On Peaceful Coexistence*. Moscow: Foreign Languages Publishing House, 1961.

Mager, N. H. *and* Katel, Jacques, eds. *Conquest Without War*. New York: Simon and Schuster, 1961.

3. INTER-COMMUNIST AFFAIRS

Chinese Communist World Outlook. A Handbook of Chinese Communist Statements. The Public Record of a Militant Ideology. Washington, D.C.: Bureau of Intelligence and Research, June 1962.

Crankshaw, Edward. *The New Cold War: Moscow vs. Peking*. New York: Penguin Books, 1963.

Dallin, Alexander, Harris, Jonathan *and* Hodnett, Grey, eds. *Diversity in International Communism. A Documentary Record: 1961–1963*. New York: Columbia University Press, 1963.

Hudson, G. F., Lowenthal, Richard *and* MacFarquhar, Roderick. *The Sino-Soviet Dispute*. New York: Frederick A. Praeger, 1961.

Laqueur, Walter *and* Labedz, Leopold, eds. *Polycentrism. The New Factor in International Communism*. New York: Frederick A. Praeger, 1962.

London, Kurt, ed. *Unity and Contradiction: Major Aspect of Sino-Soviet Relations*. New York: Frederick A. Praeger, 1962.

Mehnert, Klaus. *Peking and Moscow*. New York: G. P. Putnam's Sons, 1963.

4. THE U.S.S.R. AND THE UNITED NATIONS

Dallin, Alexander. *The Soviet Union at the United Nations. An Inquiry into Soviet Motives and Objectives*. New York: Frederick A. Praeger, 1962.

SECTION XII. *Whither U.S.S.R.?*

Deutscher, Isaac. *The Great Contest: Russia and the West.* New York: Oxford University Press, 1960.

————. *Russia in Transition* (rev. ed.). New York: Grove Press, 1960.

————. *Russia: What Next?* New York: Oxford University Press, 1953.

Wolfe, Bertram D. "The Durability of Despotism in the Soviet System." *The Russian Review,* Hanover, N.H., Vol. 17, No. 2, April 1958, pp. 83–103; No. 3, July 1958, pp. 163–175.

Index